TUDOR PURITANISM

TUDOR PURITANISM

A CHAPTER IN
THE HISTORY OF IDEALISM

BY

M. M. KNAPPEN

THE UNIVERSITY OF CHICAGO PRESS
CHICAGO & LONDON

Standard Book Number: 226–44627–1

THE UNIVERSITY OF CHICAGO PRESS, CHICAGO 60637
The University of Chicago Press, Ltd., London

PREFACE TO THE PHOENIX EDITION

THE writing of a new preface normally affords an opportunity to bring the original work up to date. I cannot, however, make full use of this privilege. My professional interests have shifted from the Tudor-Stuart period, and I have not kept up with the scholarly literature of the field. In the circumstances I must content myself with a short review of my current thinking about the general theses and interpretations set forth in the book.

There may have been too much of an effort in the original publication to highlight idealism and single it out as a powerful social force entitled to a distinctive place in the story of the development of human, or at least Western, civilization. Certainly, one reviewer seemed to think this effort a belaboring of the obvious and an attempt to make too much out of what is a universal human and social phenomenon. It may well be that in this instance I did, by scholarly standards, show a bit too much of that zeal which Queen Elizabeth I found such an objectionable Puritan trait. When challenged on a similar issue, however, my former professor, Carl Becker, once observed that he was a man of few illusions and wished to keep those he had. In my case I like trying to show at least a little zeal now and then. In my later years I am as anxious to see what I have called idealism respected as I was in the 1930's.

I am even less repentant about the other major themes of the work—the desirability of having religious and intellectual leaders occupy positions of political influence and my feeling that historical Puritanism was fundamentally a religious rather than a liberal or academic movement. During the years since the first publication of the book my various experiences with the functioning of our plutocratic society—in the occupation of Germany, in Washington, and in the control and administration of several different academic institutions—has, if anything, strengthened rather than weakened my conviction that the closer we could approach the Puritan ideal of the distribution of power in our society and its government the better off we should be. Although I do not subscribe to all the opinions of the late C. Wright Mills, I believe his strictures on the current American social order come closer to the truth than many of us are willing to admit. Philosophers may not always make wise rulers, but neither do those of other backgrounds. In my opinion the abilities and records of individuals with professional experience in the fields of religion or scholarship will very easily bear comparison with those of the men and women of the current American power elite.

As for the religious nature of Puritanism, I readily concede that without the support of powerful lay adherents—and of many others more powerful in the aggregate than in individual influence—the movement would have had little effect. As I still see it, however, these laymen—like those today who on economic issues continue to follow some forgotten scribbler, as, I think, Keynes put it—derived practically all their ideas and much of their inspiration from their professional clerical leaders. However far some of us may have moved from orthodox religious beliefs and however prominent in the modern world of liberal scholarship institutions founded by Puritans may have become, I still cannot believe that these founding fathers and their Puritan friends and associates were not primarily otherworldly, religious men. Their religion was, in general, that current in the Reformed churches of western Europe during the sixteenth and early seventeenth centuries. For the historical background of the Enlightenment and of modern liberal scholarship, I feel one should look to the Renaissance, a movement which I consider to have been something quite different from Puritanism.

In the present reprinting of *Tudor Puritanism*, a number of minor errors have been corrected. I am much obliged and most grateful to the reviewers and other readers whose comments and observations are reflected in these corrections.

NEWARK, DELAWARE
March 23, 1965

PREFACE TO THE FIRST EDITION

MORE than twenty-five years have now passed since the publication of Henry W. Clark's *History of English Nonconformity*. Continued research in the Puritan field during this interval has made another tentative synthesis desirable. But this activity has made it impractical to cover the pre-Restoration period in a single volume. This work is accordingly restricted to the Tudor era.

Aside from considerations of space, there are logical reasons for breaking off the story with the Stuart settlement. Such a division of the narrative serves to focus attention on a neglected side of Puritan history. Puritanism was a transitional movement linking the medieval with the modern. Only recently have students begun to notice the strength and importance of its medieval ties. Puritan asceticism is seen to be directly related to Roman Catholic asceticism; Puritan economic doctrine, to the social teachings of the scholastics. The same is true, in some degree, of most of the other aspects of the movement. It seems desirable, therefore, to devote to this early, semimedieval phase of Puritanism a separate volume, in which its medieval characteristics may be the more clearly brought out. Such a presentation also stresses the contrast between Puritanism in its early and later phases. Whereas seventeenth-century Puritanism was, for all practical purposes, sectarian, largely dependent on lay support, and rarely more than national in its outlook, in the earlier century it was an international, clerical movement which championed a state church. Most important of all, the Puritan under the Stuarts was willing to take the sword against his rulers while his ancestor was not. This early loyalty to the doctrine of passive resistance, which only began to break down with the parliamentary rumblings in the reign of James, is sufficiently important in itself to justify the termination of our narrative at the beginning of its decline. For that was an event which had great consequences not only for the history of Puritanism but for the whole Anglo-Saxon world.

The developing interest in the intellectual, social, and cultural phases of the Puritan movement has necessitated a more extended treatment of these subjects than has hitherto been usual. In fact, so much material has been found on these topics that, to avoid disrupting the main narrative by the insertion of these data in their proper chronological positions, it has seemed best to put them in a separate part of the work where topical arrangement is possible.

Though this study is primarily an analysis of early Puritanism, it is related to the author's interest in idealism as a whole and his view of its place in a well-ordered society. He believes that idealism is a powerful social force, comparable to race, nationalism, and class, and as worthy of serious study. He also believes that a generous admixture of this element is essential to the health of any social organism. One factor which should contribute to securing this proper balance, in his opinion, is a study of the history of past idealistic movements with particular attention paid to the causes of their successes and failures.

In choosing to study Puritanism during the dawn of the modern era, the author is not unmindful that there were rival idealisms in the Anglo-Saxon world of that day. Roman Catholicism, Anglicanism, and the cult of English nationalism were all idealisms. Even the mercantile and industrial activity of the time was not without its idealistic implications. Any of these systems might be analyzed with profit, and no doubt their adherents often were personally more idealistic than the Puritans. But Puritanism as a system seems to the author, on balance, the best of the rivals in its day and the most worthy of study at present. Though its attitude of petty asceticism is unattractive, its theological dress no longer serviceable, and much of its early political theory quite inadequate, there are other features which more than compensate for these deficiencies. Puritanism was anxious to retain the basic values of the old religion while progressive enough to make a serious effort to adapt them to the changing times. It championed the ideal of internationalism as against nationalism and tried to preserve the unity and political power of the intelligentsia. While the author has not consciously allowed these opinions to influence his statements of fact, they have doubtless affected the interpretation of the material treated. It is hoped that this statement of the writer's biases, designed to put readers on their guard from the first, will contribute more to the usefulness of the work than would any effort by him, however successful, to suppress his personal convictions.

Idealism, like race, nationalism, and class, is a great historical force which is easier to discuss than to define. As here used the term applies only to ethical idealism, not to theories of ontology or epistemology. It designates the outlook which is now contrasted with realism in the language of politics and everyday activity. Yet, when we have described it as devotion to an ethical ideal, we have not clearly defined it. For it is at least as hard to say what is ethical or moral as to say what is true. Ethical idealism cannot be absolutely contrasted with materialism or with selfishness. Many men have pursued ethical ends while believing that matter is the ultimate reality, and it is also possible to seek material goods as part of an ultimate idealistic end. On the other hand, careful analysis will convict the most self-sacrificing person of an egoism involved in all his acts. If it is not the desire for heaven or social approval, it is the desire for the feeling of self-satisfaction which comes from following the dictates of conscience or from retaining one's self-respect by being true to one's ideals. Still, when destructive criticism has done its best, idealism remains real in many senses of the term, a definite state of mind in the individual and a positive social force. These facts should give pause to those who glibly contrast this attitude with realism. Yet, fallible as the descriptive guides may be, they are the best we have, and we must use them. Actions done without hope of immediate tangible reward, attitudes in which the interests of others bulk large, are idealistic. Keeping the previous reservations in mind, we must employ "altruistic" and "spiritual" as synonyms, "selfish" and "material" as antonyms. The exact usage should become clearer as we proceed.

The term "Puritan" is used in this book to designate the outlook of those English Protestants who actively favored a reformation beyond that which the crown was willing to countenance and who yet stopped short of Anabaptism. It therefore includes both Presbyterians and Independents, Separatists and Non-Separatists. It also includes a number of Anglicans who accepted the episcopal system, but who nevertheless desired to model it and English church life in general on the Continental Reformed pattern. A more detailed explanation of the terminology employed to designate the different sects of the time is to be found in Appendix II.

In all quotations from the sources spelling, capitalization, and punctuation have been modernized and abbreviations expanded, except where the first version seems necessary to the sense—or obscurity—of the original. In the titles of books capitalization and punctuation have been similarly altered, and the *i*'s, *j*'s, *u*'s, and *v*'s changed to conform to present-day usage. Dates are given according to the Julian calendar, but those between January 1 and March 25 have been changed to conform to the present calendar year except in certain special cases, such as those of parliamentary sessions, where the double dating is employed. The *Dictionary of National Biography* spelling of proper names has commonly been followed. In the case of Tyndale, I have accepted J. F. Mozley's recent argument for the conventional spelling.

The topic of acknowledgments calls up pleasant memories of hunting and consultations on both sides of the Atlantic, of patiently courteous custodians, of discussions on country walks when the repositories were closed. From the mass of accumulated obligations I must select for special mention those to the staffs of the British Museum and the Dr. Williams' Library, London, where the bulk of the work was done. With unfailing cheerfulness and proverbial efficiency these friends have welcomed the American student with the swallows and sent him home with bulging files in the autumn. I have also profited

greatly from the works of my predecessors in the field, notably
Dr. A. F. Scott Pearson, Dr. Albert Peel, and Professor R. G.
Usher among living scholars. I am also obliged to the younger
men and women who have permitted me to use their unpublished theses, though I believe that I have made no extensive
borrowings from them. From my former professors at Cornell
University, under whom this work was begun, Wallace Note-
stein, now of Yale University, Preserved Smith, and Carl
Becker, I am still drawing inspiration and not infrequently more
tangible assistance. Professor F. G. Marcham, of Cornell University, and my colleagues, Louis Gottschalk and John T.
McNeill, have read the work in manuscript and have made
many valuable suggestions. My students, too, have contributed
not a little to the undertaking. The expense of publishing this
volume has been kindly assumed by the University of Chicago
Press, whose highly efficient staff has given most generously of
its technical and artistic skill. To all, my most hearty thanks.

2 BEDFORD PLACE, LONDON

TABLE OF CONTENTS

BOOK I. PARTY HISTORY AND POLITICAL THEORY

TABLE OF CONTENTS

APPENDIXES

SELECT BIBLIOGRAPHY

INDEX

BOOK I
Party History and Political Theory

CHAPTER I

Tyndale and the Continental Background

THE story of English Puritanism is best begun in 1524. In the spring of that year a young Gloucestershire man named William Tyndale decided to leave London for Germany in order to prepare an English translation of the Bible. He was not the first to think of printing an edition of the Scriptures in the vernacular, but the means which he chose to attain his end were epoch-making. For this one decision involved many elements which were to be characteristic of the Puritan movement throughout the Tudor period. True, other features had to be added later to complete the pattern, but a real beginning was made at this time.

Tyndale was violating the law in order to bring about a reformation of the church. The ecclesiastical regulations of the day prohibited anyone from issuing a translation of the Bible without the indorsement of his bishop. Furthermore, a statute of the realm[1] forbade ordinary subjects to leave the country without the royal consent. The *émigré* was therefore defying spiritual and temporal authority alike, a move which foreshadowed years of Puritan insubordination and "reformation without tarrying for any."

Yet he was keeping within the limits of passive resistance. He proposed to flood his homeland with unsanctioned and even prohibited books, but he did not intend to use force against his sovereign. He was taking every precaution to avoid detection

[1] 5 Ric. II, st. I, c. 2. Article Forty-two of the Magna Charta provided that anyone might leave the kingdom and return at will, except in time of war, but this was among the clauses reserved for future consideration in Henry III's first reissue of the Charter, and it was never restored. The 1381 statute was not repealed until 1606 (4 James I, c. 1. iv). In addition, as an ecclesiastic, Tyndale was bound by Article Four of the Constitutions of Clarendon not to leave the realm without the king's consent.

and capture, but, should he be apprehended, he was prepared
to submit to whatever punishment the authorities might ordain.
With one or two notable exceptions this doctrine of passive resistance was the burden of Puritan sermon, petition, and
pamphlet throughout the century. It is essential that this be
clearly understood at the beginning of our story, as it is fundamental to nearly everything that follows.

In making his momentous decision, Tyndale was greatly influenced by his contacts with certain London merchants. They
not only helped to provide the necessary financial assistance but
also formed a community in which advanced ideas and illegal
methods of propaganda might be freely discussed and advocated. They typified the importance of laymen, and especially
the mercantile element, in the Puritan movement—an importance which was to be more marked in the seventeenth century but which even in the Tudor period distinguishes Puritanism from its medieval predecessor.

Tyndale's object in going to Germany was not only to escape
the attentions of the law-enforcement agencies at home but to
consult Martin Luther,[2] the model from whom he was drawing
his chief inspiration. Tyndale was not a great, original thinker,
but a translator; one who was, for the most part, content to
render works in foreign tongues into English. Both in his biblical work and in his other writing he drew heavily on Luther.[3]
Tudor Puritanism generally conformed to this pattern of dependence on the ideas of foreigners, though it later shifted its
allegiance to other individual leaders beyond the channel. It
was not an indigenous, English movement, but the Anglo-
Saxon branch of a Continental one, dependent on foreign theo-

[2] Preserved Smith, "Englishmen at Wittenberg in the Sixteenth Century," *English
Historical Review* (hereafter cited as *EHR*), XXXVI (1921), 422–33. J. F. Mozley, in his
William Tyndale (London and New York, 1937), which has now supplanted Robert
Demaus' life as the standard biography, works over the evidence on this moot point
without being aware of Smith's article, but comes to the same conclusion—that Tyndale
did go to Wittenberg.

[3] H. E. Jacobs, *A Study in Comparative Symbolics: The Lutheran Movement in Eng-
land during the Reigns of Henry VIII and Edward VI and Its Literary Monuments*
(Philadelphia, 1908), pp. 14–38; L. F. Gruber, *The First English New Testament and
Luther* (Burlington, Iowa, 1928); A. H. Gerberich, *Luther and the English Bible* (Johns
Hopkins University dissertation [Lancaster, Pa., 1933]).

logians both for its theory and for its direction in practical matters.

Finally, Tyndale's important resolve reflected his devotion to the Bible. It showed how much he respected its authority and indicated that to place it in the hands of the people was, in his judgment, the greatest good he could do them. In the circumstances of that day this marked him as a follower of the new religion which was to be known as Protestantism. But it also marked him as one who accepted the major outlines of the medieval system of otherworldly, supernatural Christianity. He might object to such peripheral doctrines as those of the mass, penance, and the celibacy of the clergy, but in his thinking on the Trinity, the atonement, and the future life he was a thoroughgoing medievalist. His economic and social outlook was indistinguishable from that of the Middle Ages, and he also retained many of the political ideas of his predecessors. Though he had tasted the new learning, he was not affected by the cynical, skeptical attitude of so many of the Renaissance leaders. Nor was he capable of appreciating the more refined outlook of such a thinker as Pietro Pomponazzi, who in Italy was teaching that, while death ends all, altruistic virtue is the chief end of man and its own all-sufficient reward, far preferable, cost what it might, to long life with dishonor.[4] He believed in a future life and in the authority of the revealed Scriptures, not in framing a program for this world alone or in finding ultimate truth by experiment. To this type the Puritan remained true, hating the Catholic, to be sure, but also the atheist, and both with a perfect hatred.

Tyndale was led to take his decisive step rather by force of circumstances than by a deliberate desire to be the English pioneer in an illegal type of reforming activity. For Tyndale was an Oxford man,[5] and the first master of all the university-

---

[4] A. H. Douglas, *The Philosophy and Psychology of Pietro Pomponazzi*, ed. Douglas and Hardie (Cambridge, 1910), pp. 248–69.

[5] It is very unlikely that Tyndale was ever a student at Cambridge. The tradition that he was rests on the information supplied to John Foxe by an anonymous west-country friend, who knew that Tyndale had been a member of one university and

trained reformers of his generation in England was the cautious, law-abiding Erasmus. At Cambridge the original reforming leader was Thomas Bilney, fellow of Trinity Hall, who received his initial impetus from reading the Latin translation and notes which the great Dutchman supplied to his edition of the Greek New Testament published at Basel in 1516.[6] Not until several years after Tyndale went to Germany did Bilney or any of his followers, who included Hugh Latimer, fellow of Clare Hall, and Robert Barnes, prior of the local monastery of the Augustinian friars, do anything of which Erasmus would not have approved.[7] They did not take any advanced stand on doctrinal matters; and, when their mild reforming discourses were called in question, they recanted, quite after the manner of the great humanist who preferred to dissemble on ten doctrines rather than drench the world in blood, and who privately confessed that he lacked a martyr's courage.

Tyndale spent his Oxford years at Magdalen Hall, where he seems to have encountered the moderate reforming doctrines of Erasmus and his friend John Colet,[8] then Dean of St. Paul's but

---

thought it was Cambridge. As a Magdalen man, Foxe knew that Tyndale had been at Oxford, and in his later narrative inserted the correct identification, but allowed the story of a stay at Cambridge to stand also (see the two versions of Foxe's narrative printed in parallel columns in E. Arber's *First Printed English New Testament* [London, 1871], pp. 8–9). Tyndale's first biographer, John Bale, who was a Cambridge man, and nearly contemporaneous with the time of Tyndale's supposed study there, states that he was trained at Oxford ("Oxonii ab adolescente studiis incumbens," *Illustrium Maioris Britanniae scriptorum .... summarium* [Wesel, 1548], fol. 220[v]).

[6] The possibility that Bilney used the second edition which appeared in 1519 is rendered improbable by a comparison of the excerpts quoted in his letter to Tunstall (n.d., John Foxe, *Acts and Monuments of the Christian Church*, ed. Townsend [7 vols.; London, 1837–41], IV, 633) with the texts of the two editions. The excerpts agree much more closely with the earlier version.

[7] It is true that Bilney's group read and approved of Lutheran works in the early 1520's (R. Demaus, *Latimer* [London, 1869], pp. 1–59). But before the famous quarrel over predestination it is impossible to detect any doctrinal difference between Erasmus and Luther. The contrast is rather one of emphasis and temperament, which manifested itself in the Lutheran willingness to take definitely illegal steps to spread the new ideas (see my "William Tindale—First English Puritan," *Church History*, V [1936], 210–11).

[8] There is some dispute as to whether Colet rather than Erasmus should be given credit for first directing English humanist thinking into moral and religious channels, but I have labeled the party with the name of the Continental leader since he was the one who propagated this attitude most widely.

a former lecturer in the university. After taking his M.A. in 1515, he spent several years in his native county acting as tutor and chaplain in the family of one of the local country gentry, Sir John Walsh. From this base he endeavored to disseminate Erasmian principles in the countryside, and to that end translated his master's *Enchiridion*[9] into English. He managed to ward off a charge of heresy, but he found his work handicapped by the lack of an English Bible to which he could refer laymen. In the summer of 1523 he therefore resolved to abandon his position, go to London, and there produce a Bible which even the plowboy could understand.

At this point Tyndale was still no more than a good Erasmian, for the Dutch scholar was a strong advocate of the translation of the Scriptures into the vernacular,[10] and Tyndale proposed to do nothing illegal. Arming himself with proof of his learning in the form of a translation which he had made of one of Isocrates' orations and with letters of introduction from his Gloucestershire patron, who had family connections in the capital, he set out to secure a position as chaplain in the household of Cuthbert Tunstall, the Bishop of London. Tunstall was an old friend of Erasmus and, as a bishop, would have power to approve any biblical translation that might be made. As yet the young reformer's plans were quite open and aboveboard.

But he had reckoned without recent developments in the field of religion and politics. The preceding two years had witnessed a heated exchange between the King and Luther, and the more conservative of the humanist group were rallying to the support of church and crown. Reaction was in the air. A few months before Tyndale's arrival, Tunstall had written an urgent letter to Erasmus imploring him to trounce the Wittenberg upstart.[11]

[9] John A. Gee has suggested ("Tindale and the 1533 English *Enchiridion* of Erasmus," *Publications of the Modern Language Association*, XLIX [1934], 460–71) that this translation was the one published by Wynken de Worde in London in 1533 (reprinted, London, 1905), but no satisfactory proof is available. The abridgment published by Coverdale in 1545 (*Writings and Translations*, ed. Pearson [Cambridge: Parker Society, 1844]), is extracted from the 1533 version.

[10] Erasmus, "Paraclesis," in his 1519 edition of the New Testament (Basel), pp. 7–8.

[11] *Opus epistolarum Des. Erasmi Roterdami*, ed. P. S. and H. M. Allen (Oxford, 1905 ff.), V, 290 (No. 1367).

In such circumstances Tyndale's design would receive slight sympathy in the Bishop's palace. Now that the whirlwind had been reaped, the translation project which had appeared mildly liberal as set forth by Erasmus some years earlier would seem to be a barefaced proposal to give aid and comfort to the enemy. When the interview with the Bishop was at length arranged, Tyndale soon discovered that he could expect no help from that quarter.[12]

The disappointed reformer had now to decide on his future course. If he continued to be loyal to the principles of Erasmus, he must forego his plan rather than do anything illegal. But in London he met men who were familiar with other methods. While waiting for his interview with Tunstall, he had secured a few preaching appointments at St. Dunstan's in the West, Fleet Street, the parish church of Thomas Poyntz, a distant relative of Lady Walsh. Poyntz was a merchant engaged in the wool trade, and at St. Dunstan's Tyndale met another merchant, Humphrey Monmouth, who was so attracted by his teaching that eventually he took him into his own household. The London merchants were a spirited and independent lot, unwilling to submit to clerical domination. For years they had carried on a controversy with the ecclesiastics over the financial claims made by the church. Many of them were tainted with Lollardy, as the celebrated case of Richard Hunne had shown ten years before. This Protestant[13] tradition, which derived from the fourteenth-century reformer, John Wyclif, had by no

[12] Demaus (*Tindale*, ed. Lovett [London, 1904], pp. 102–3) and Mozley (*op. cit.*, p. 43) think that Tyndale explained his entire plan to Tunstall, but the documents make clear that Tunstall treated him merely as an ordinary office-seeker. The oration of Isocrates, if presented to Tunstall—Tyndale only says it was given to Guildford (Preface to *The Five Books of Moses* in *Doctrinal Treatises*, ed. Walter [Cambridge: Parker Society, 1848], p. 395)—would be offered as evidence of general learning, and it may be that Tyndale hoped that, once the place had been secured, he would gain the Bishop's further confidence. But, if Tyndale did not raise the translation question, it was doubtless because he had already realized the uselessness of doing so, and it is therefore fair to imply that the English authorities were opposed to the transaction from the beginning.

[13] I feel that Wyclif was essentially a Protestant, though Gotthard Lechler (*John Wiclif and His English Precursors*, tr. Peter Lorimer [London, 1878]) set the fashion of denying him that title because of his failure to preach the full Lutheran doctrine of justification by faith.

means died out in England. Not only did it have a hold in London, but in Kent, the east counties, and Buckinghamshire as well. A fugitive from one section might expect to find shelter in another, and informers were subjected to social and economic boycotts. With the devastating simplicity of the unlearned, the rustic adherents showed their contempt for the doctrine of transubstantiation by jesting, as they took up their flails, about threshing "God Almighty out of the straw."[14]

Since the Lollards, furthermore, had well-established precedents for translating the Bible—two different English versions had been prepared in the early days of the movement—it might have been expected that Tyndale would affiliate with this group and continue his work under their auspices, but he did not. The reasons seem fairly clear. With the exception of the Lollards among the London merchants the supporters of this movement were of the lower classes. The nobility and gentry had fallen away from Wyclif's doctrines after the collapse of the Cobham revolt a century before, while the purging of Oxford had deprived Lollardy of intellectual leadership at an even earlier date. Most of the remaining "known men," as they were sometimes called, were husbandmen, "wheelers," and blacksmiths. Furthermore, years of persecution had broken their spirit. Bold words at home were followed by humble submission in the bishop's palace, a pattern of conduct which belied their favorite title of "justfast men." While we have records of nearly fifty individuals who suffered for their beliefs in the first quarter of the sixteenth century, the overwhelming majority of cases ended in recantations and a penance surprisingly mild. The average Lollard does not seem to have been taken very seriously by the authorities, for a frequent punishment in the Chiltern area was the pleasant one of a pilgrimage to the shrine of Our Lady of Missenden in the splendid vale of the Misbourne. Little was to be expected from such people; and, when absorbed in later English Protestantism, they contributed almost nothing except numbers and the memory of a great past.

[14] Foxe, *op. cit.*, IV, 122–35, 173–246, 557–58, 580–85. W. H. Summers has worked over this material and put it into chronological order in his *Lollards of the Chiltern Hills* (London, 1906), pp. 74–142.

It was not likely, therefore, that a restless Tyndale would be attracted to such circles if a more respectable environment for his chosen activity were available. And it was. The London merchants were not only familiar with Lollardy but with the new Lutheran religion coming from Germany. Some had encountered it abroad, but doubtless many more were affected by their contacts with the local community of German merchants gathered in the Steelyard, just above the great bridge. These traders brought in quantities of Lutheran literature, and some probably did a certain amount of missionary work among their susceptible English associates. Consequently, the disappointed Gloucestershire man would soon learn of the possibilities of carrying out his project abroad. Germany could provide both a friendly intellectual atmosphere and printing facilities, and foreign residence held no great terrors for the mercantile community. Even the illegal and quasi-revolutionary aspects of the project could be viewed with equanimity in such circles. In that age, as in all others, rulers made a practice of encouraging men who were plotting rebellions in the territories of their rivals. In this fashion France had supported the expedition of the first Tudor Henry against Richard III, and in the following years the Low Countries were a center of Yorkist plots. Traders going back and forth across the channel would be accustomed to meeting in foreign parts fellow-countrymen who were out of sympathy with the prevailing regime at home. To Germany, therefore, Tyndale went, with Monmouth supplying most of the funds.

On the Continent the English *émigré* found himself in the midst of a revolution—religious, social, and political. For centuries the medieval system had maintained a nice balance between idealism and realism, with the organized intelligentsia, in the form of the church, sharing the control of society with secular rulers. Moral and intellectual prestige combined with the efficiency of a disciplined, international organization had maintained the clerical influence at its high level. But at length the organization became too centralized and bureaucratic, too inflexible to permit of any more of those waves of reforming enthusiasm which had periodically revived the ecclesiastical body in the earlier Middle Ages. The teachings of Wyclif, Huss, and many other critics were contemptuously rejected. As a result, the moral and intellectual credit of the church slumped in many quarters. At the same time the materialistic side of life was suddenly made vastly more attractive by the tapping of new sources of worldly wealth in Africa, America, and the Far East. The result was that in many districts of Central Europe the church was no longer able to maintain its position against the assaults of the reformers, on the one side, and the forces of secularism, on the other.

The exact type of system which the victorious coalition substituted for the old varied from place to place depending on the circumstances and, particularly, on the relative strength of the allied parties concerned. Two things, however, the new codes had in common—the doctrine of justification by faith, which undermined the sacerdotal system, and a belief in the Bible as the sole authority in religious matters. Both were revolutionary weapons, forged in the heat of conflict, and, as time was to show,[15] unbalanced and quite inferior to the more flexible teachings on these matters which their opponents had carefully worked out through the centuries. But for the destructive work of the moment they were the best available and served very well. For however theoretically excellent may be the doctrines of salvation by a combination of faith and works and of the ultimate authority of the church, they break down in practice when the church becomes corrupt and some explosive force is necessary.

On other important issues there were striking differences. In Protestant Germany outside the Rhineland the secular rulers dominated the new regime. Luther had no taste for organization—at first he thought, with the reformer's optimism, that, once the Bible was made accessible to all, none would be needed beyond a simple congregational framework for independent churches voluntarily professing the same creed. But, even had he been of a different mind, the results would doubtless have

[15] See below, pp. 341–42; 394–95; 366.

been the same. For the secular rulers, grown wealthy from the returns of increased trade and highly profitable mining operations and also practically free from the control of Emperor or Diet, were too strong to be successfully opposed. The result was the establishment of state churches with compulsory uniformity enforced by courts whose members were appointed by the princes. It was the kind of relationship between the temporal and spiritual arms of the state which was later to be called Erastian.

In another matter, however, Luther's background and temperament did play a decisive part. Since his outstanding spiritual experience involved a reaction from monastic rules and regulations, it was natural that he should take the liberal side of the controversy over asceticism which had agitated the Christian church from its earliest days. Not only did he sanction the breaking of vows by monks and nuns but he strove to free the laity from the impression that they were obligated to imitate the monastic, or even the clerical, way of life. The right to private property was stated without equivocation. The shoemaker's occupation was a calling as holy as the clergyman's. The joys of domestic happiness, of eating and drinking, were frankly praised and freely practiced. Justification by faith covered everything. Hostile critics have no doubt exaggerated these teachings of Luther, who was neither a glutton nor a libertine, but the fact remains that he appreciated the good things of this life and saw no objection to a reasonable indulgence in them.

In the Protestant portions of Switzerland and adjacent Germany a different system developed. There the leader was a Swiss named Huldreich Zwingli, who in 1518 became the cathedral preacher in German-speaking Zurich. A man of no great spirituality, he possessed a clear head and a humanistic training, as well as courage and a flair for managing things. About 1522 he transferred his allegiance from Erasmus to Luther, but soon set himself up as an independent and rival reformer. The chief theological point of difference was on the sacrament. The former friar of Wittenberg had denied the doctrine of transubstantiation but nevertheless declared for a real physical presence of the body and blood of Christ in the consecrated elements, thus involving himself in difficulties from which the theologians have not yet succeeded in extricating him. The Zurich preacher, on the other hand, adopting a more coherent idea which Luther had rejected, declared that the bread and wine remained unchanged throughout the rite and that Christ was present only "to the contemplation of faith." In his system the sacrament thus became little more than a bit of commemorative symbolism. The result of this disagreement was schism among the reformers which neither political pressure, debate, nor time could heal. Thus there was early made evident the heavy cost of the Reformation and the weakness of the new doctrine of biblical authority. The old unity of Western Christendom was destroyed, and the revolutionary leaders could not even agree among themselves.

Circumstances enabled Zwingli to take a much stronger line than Luther in his dealings with the temporal arm. The Zuricher had a taste for politics, and he found himself in a territory devoid of strong secular rivals. In the Rhineland and Switzerland there were few important princes. In· their place were semi-independent towns with ramshackle governments in which two or more councils and possibly a nonresident bishop or count were involved in various and vague relationships. At the sight of a mob, or even at the suggestion of one, any of these authorities would tremble. In such cities a vigorous reformer who was a good popular preacher and inclined toward political activity might reasonably hope to set up an established Protestant church without forfeiting its position as one of the dominating elements in the state. Especially was this true, if, like Zwingli, he began his reforms even a few years after the first fury of the anticlerical blast had spent itself and if he did not hesitate to champion the doctrine of the right of revolution in the name of religion. In his efforts along this line the Swiss leader was so successful that eventually Zurich became a virtual theocracy, and the preacher did not scruple to move in the direction of merging the powers of church and secular gov-

ernments. Under his influence there were organized local and
district synods or conferences of the clergy which preserved the
unity of the preaching class and decided on principles of theology and ethics. But the councilors were so much in their control
that these secular authorities might safely be left to put these
decisions into effect. The church ceased to practice excommunication in ordinary cases, because the state was Christian-
ized and the magistrates duly attentive to the prophetic utterances. Furthermore, the theocratic state could be, and was,
expected to wage war on less enlightened neighbors, forcing
them to admit the true gospel to their territories.[16] At length,
however, an unsuccessful venture of this sort cost Zwingli his
life and nearly ruined his political system. His arrangement of
clerical pressure groups was not so strong as to survive the loss
of the inventor and leader. The Zurich clergy dropped from a
position of pre-eminence to one of subordination to the secular
magistrate. Heinrich Bullinger, who succeeded the slain reformer as the leading minister of the city, though continuing to
advocate his theological and ethical system, had to be content
with a very limited amount of clerical power. Another of
Zwingli's ministerial followers, Leo Jud, who endeavored to perpetuate the political power of the church by demanding for it
the right to excommunicate members on its own descretion, was
forced to abandon the claim.[17] Nevertheless, on many matters
the council continued to take the advice of the clergy. They
remained important, and the tradition of their greater power in
earlier days lingered on.

On the question of asceticism Zwingli also differed from
Luther. He had not been a monk in early life. It is clear from
the evidence that he had not even led the celibate life required
of the clergy. When we remember his desire to steer a course
independent of his Wittenberg rival and this early background
from which he was reacting, we can understand why, as he came

[16] Zwingli was not always consistent in his statements on these questions, but I
believe the foregoing is a fair summary of the general trend of his teaching (see Alfred
Farner, *Die Lehre von Kirche und Staat bei Zwingli* [Tübingen, 1930], esp. pp. 129-34).

[17] Elsa Dollfuss-Zodel, *Bullingers Einflusz auf das Zürcherische Staatswesen von
1531-1575* (Zurich, 1931), pp. 1-21.

into a position of religious authority, he should seek to enforce the strictest standards of morality on his followers. In the enthusiasm of their reforming activity both leaders revolted against their former way of life. Luther became ultra-liberal and Zwingli a rigorist. At Zurich divorce was permitted in certain circumstances, but never bigamy; adultery and other extra-marital sexual indulgences were severely punished. Private property was allowed, but the possessor was required to use it for the good of his neighbor.[18] The magistrate could not tolerate more than a small rate of interest. Display in clothing was sharply condemned. The contemporary style of slashed costumes was to Zwingli an abomination. Dancing was frowned upon, and even the playing of games such as chess and ninepins.

Gold, silver, jewelry, and both silken and sumptuous clothing are either laid aside or sold and the proceeds distributed to the poor. Evil speaking, perjury, carousing, and gambling are done away with.[19]

Zwingli enunciated the principle that to purify the church it was necessary to remove from its worship all traces of practices associated with Roman Catholicism. Accordingly, though an accomplished musician himself, in 1525 the reformer suspended choir-singing, and two years later insisted that all organs should be removed from the churches. The one in the cathedral was actually broken up in December, 1527. The old clerical robes were abolished. Ministers wore their ordinary dress in the pulpit. The practice of employing written prayers was retained, but they were recast in a Protestant style, and no set form was enjoined. All services were extremely simple, devoid of ceremony of any sort. Church ornaments were removed. Even the gravestones were taken away and used for building purposes unless the relatives requested them. For the music and color of the old service, largely retained in Lutheran churches, preaching was the main substitute. There were three sermons on

[18] Farner, *op. cit.*, pp. 48–49.

[19] Zwingli to Blarer, May 4, 1528, *Corpus reformatorum* (Halle, 1834, etc.), XCVI (1925), 462; Emil Egli, *Achtensammlung zur Geschichte der Zürcher Reformation in den Jahren 1519–1533* (Zurich, 1879), No. 1656; see also Index, topic "Mandate," subhead "Sitte."

Sunday and two every weekday, at five and eight in the morning. On the market day, Friday, there was a special sermon
for the country people.[20] Zurich thus became a drastically reformed town. Visiting clergymen from abroad were much impressed by it. Their desire to emulate their Swiss brethren was
to have far-reaching effects.

A third type of reformed system was the sectarian. Certain
followers of Luther and Zwingli were disposed to carry out the
principles of their leaders to what seemed their logical conclusions. Positions assumed in the first heat of reformation were
exalted by these followers into the main landmarks on their
religious course. Especially was this true of the reformers'
hastily conceived and poorly developed doctrine of the authority of the Bible. If the Scriptures were to be the guide of life,
it were best, thought these enthusiasts, to be conscientious
about this principle and follow the biblical teachings literally.
If this involved the dissolution of current society, it was nothing to them. The duty of a saint was to follow the Master and
to do right though the heavens fell. If the Book of Acts indicated that a communism of goods was characteristic of early
church life, this practice must be adopted by modern believers.
The Bible forbade swearing. Therefore, oaths of allegiance and
all other varieties must go. If only those were saved who could
make their own peace with God, church membership must be
confined to those who were old enough to understand this and
act accordingly. Hence baptism must be administered only to
adults, a principle which involved rebaptizing those already so
treated in infancy. This practice gave the enemies of the movement a most effective talking-point. In the sixteenth century
it was commonly supposed that to prove a similarity between a
contemporary idea and a heresy long since condemned was to
discredit the current movement. That was why Eck labored so
hard to show that Luther's ideas could be found in the writings
of Huss. Now Augustine's opponents, the Donatists, whose
doctrines the church had repudiated in the fifth century, had
practiced this rebaptism or anabaptism, as it was called in

Greek. So the enemies of these new Protestants dubbed them Anabaptists.[21]

Since these enthusiasts were prepared to follow their principles regardless of the effect on contemporary society, they saw no reason to imitate Luther in drawing back when they discovered the incompatibility of the principle of individual freedom to interpret the Bible and an established religion. On the contrary, these earnest students of the Scriptures found in the New Testament neither state church nor organized, privileged clergy. Accordingly, they refused to pay tithes and demanded that congregations should be composed only of true Christians, that they should be independent of outside control and free to elect their own ministers. Sectarianism had no terrors for them. But, while they thus repudiated the doctrine of an authority based on the agreement of the intelligentsia, some of the more eager managed to substitute for it—without altogether abandoning their belief in the authority of the Bible—a primary reliance on personal revelation, by which they meant the inner witness of the Holy Spirit to individuals, usually themselves. On the propriety of resorting to force to establish or maintain their system there was a difference of opinion. Most of the Anabaptists accepted the doctrines of the Sermon on the Mount and denied that a Christian might use violence. But some ten years after the first appearance of the movement a group led by one Melchior Hoffman began to feel the necessity of immediate action. They focused their attention on the apocalyptic sections of the Bible and soon began to preach that the time for nonresistance was at an end, that the millennial kingdom of Christ was at hand, and, finally, that it was the duty of the saints to set it up by force if necessary. The attempt to give practical effect to this belief at Münster in 1534 was violently suppressed by the horrified forces of conservatism. Worse than the loss of the one city was the cloud which, in the opinion of most middle- and upper-class observers, this episode cast upon the entire Anabaptist party.

[21] G. L. Burr, "Liberals and Liberty Three Hundred Years Ago," *Proceedings of the Unitarian Historical Association*, III, Part I (1933), 6–7.

Another offshoot of the sectarian movement was a tendency
among a few of the more educated adherents to follow the
Bible more literally in the matter of Christology. Erasmus, in
his first edition of the Greek New Testament, published in 1516,
had disputed the authenticity of the only real biblical proof
text for the doctrine of the Trinity, I John 5:7. The great
humanist quailed before the storm of opposition raised by his
statements and restored the passage in the later editions of his
work. More determined followers, however, mostly drawn from
the ranks of the Anabaptists, took up his arguments, amplified
them, and ended by denying the essential deity of Christ and
the Anselmic doctrine of the atonement. Instead they maintained that the Nazarene's saving work was only that of
setting a good example. By 1531 such ideas were being publicly preached on the Continent,[22] and a Spanish student named
Servetus had set them forth in book form.

Anabaptists and anti-Trinitarians alike were severely persecuted by their Protestant rivals, the Lutherans and the Zwinglians, but they were never entirely suppressed. Thus, as early
as 1524, when Tyndale arrived on the Continent, there were
several distinct types of Protestantism in Central Europe with
which he might associate himself. Anabaptism was, however,
too extreme to suit one who had been so recently an Erasmian,
and he was not immediately exposed to Zwinglian influence. So
for the time being he remained a Lutheran. Soon after landing
at Hamburg, in the spring, he proceeded to Wittenberg, where
he probably spent most of the following year.

Sometime in 1525 Monmouth sent him additional funds and
an assistant in the person of a Cambridge man, William Roy.
Since his departure from the university, this recruit had been
an Observant friar in the Franciscan monastery at Greenwich,
so close to London as to render unnecessary any speculation as
to the source of his reforming zeal. Having joined Tyndale on
the Continent, he helped him in the concluding stages of his
task. Doubtless for purposes of economy it was decided to print

---

[22] William Barlow, *A Dyaloge Descrybyng the Orygynal Ground of These Lutheran Faccyons* (London, 1531), sig. I, fol. 2 (ed. J. R. Lunn [London, 1897], pp. 63–64).

the volume at some place closer to England than Saxony. Antwerp would have been a natural choice because of its close trade relations with the island kingdom and the presence there of many English merchants. But for some mysterious reason[23] the reformers went to Cologne instead. This was a strongly Catholic town, however; and, when a prominent representative of the old faith discovered the secret, the translators were compelled to flee up the river to Worms. There the work was completed in the winter of 1525–26, and in the spring copies began to find their way across the channel. The alliance between the London merchants and the clergymen who refused to be bound by legal restrictions was bearing fruit.

During the five years immediately following the publication of the New Testament the *émigré* party grew in numbers and influence. As its members took the leadership of the reforming movement, they drew both Erasmian and Lollard into their camp and, in spite of official opposition, successfully propagated their ideas in England. The most important feature of this development was the trade in contraband books supplied by the refugees on the Continent. This was a hazardous and not particularly profitable business, but it was facilitated by the cooperation of many merchants and by the organization of the stationer's trade at that date. Not only was most of the paper used in England imported from the Continent but books were commonly brought in unbound. It was therefore a fairly simple matter to smuggle in a barrelful of printed works with several of blank paper. Once the all-important firkin was deposited in a London warehouse, a word to certain clergymen after a Sunday service was sufficient to insure the distribution of its content by daring stationers and colporteurs.

In vain the ecclesiastical authorities strove to suppress this literature. The anti-Lollard legislation was supplemented by

[23] No drastic measures were taken against the new ideas in Antwerp. The English merchants enjoyed good relations with the local authorities there until August 30 of this year. Heretical books and English works were printed in Antwerp before this time (J. Wegg, *Antwerp 1477–1559* [London, 1916], pp. 159, 170, 153; M. E. Kronenberg, "Notes on English Printing in the Low Countries [Early Sixteenth Century]," *Library*, IX [4th ser., 1929], 139–63).

new measures. In 1520 Leo X had issued his famous bull against Lutheran writings. In the following year Wolsey, anxious to curry favor with the Pope, had presided at a solemn burning of Luther's works and stimulated the bishops to issue proclamations calling for similar treatment of heretical literature in their dioceses in accordance with the famous bull of 1520. In the course of the years 1524 and 1525 Tunstall twice warned London printers and booksellers against dealing in such forbidden books, and on the occasion of Barnes's public recantation more Lutheran volumes were burned. Some of these had been obtained from German merchants whose lodgings in the Steelyard had been raided by the officials. With the appearance of Tyndale's New Testament these repressive efforts were redoubled. On October 23, 1526, the Bishop of London issued a proclamation calling in all copies of the offending work under pain of excommunication and suspicion of heresy. Two days later all bookdealers were informed that they must neither print nor import any books not specifically approved by Wolsey, Archbishop Warham, or Tunstall. Such activities on the part of the authorities are a sure indication of continuous violation of the original law.[24]

When their labors on the Worms New Testament were completed, Tyndale, anxious to see no more of his assistant, bade farewell to Roy, as he said, "for our two lives and a day longer." Tyndale was a great man, but like some other pioneers he was severely critical of his associates. Their suggestions he "filliped forth between his finger and his thumb."[25] Historians who have accepted his verdicts have perhaps done Roy less than justice. If the assistant lacked the learning and the patience of his colleague, he was not behind him in courage and deserves to be remembered as one who early put his hand to the plow and never looked back. The daring former friar went to Strassburg, a city possessing many attractions for one of his temperament. An important trading-center, it lay outside the territories of the

[24] A. W. Reed, *Early Tudor Drama* (London, 1926), pp. 160–86.

[25] George Joye, *An Apology*, ed. Arber (Birmingham, 1882), p. 17. Tyndale's criticism of Roy is in the Preface to his *Wicked Mammon* (*Doctrinal Treatises*, ed. Henry Walter [Cambridge: Parker Society, 1848], p. 37).

great princes of the empire and so in the region of free cities which had proved such a fruitful soil for Zwinglian reformers. The new Swiss movement was well advanced in the Argentine, or Silver City, as it was called. Under the leadership of a popular preacher named Martin Bucer the ideas of the Zurich reformer were being adopted, and the mass was virtually abolished. In its stead Bucer taught something approaching the Swiss doctrine that the bread and wine were little more than symbols and remained unchanged throughout the ceremony.[26] This point of view Roy readily adopted. He translated into English a small catechism with a picturesque title[27] which set it forth along with other elements of the Christian faith as taught in the Alsatian city. The work thus signifies a new and important stage in the development of the *émigré* program. When the advanced English reformers first went beyond Erasmus, they naturally accepted Luther as their leader, since he was the most prominent of the aggressive reformers and his works the best known. But when, on the Continent, they met with the Swiss ideas, most of them were quick to shift their allegiance. Luther's doctrine of the sacrament was difficult and obscure compared with Zwingli's, and the Wittenberger's somewhat easygoing acceptance of the supremacy of the secular government and the pleasures of this world made less appeal to zealous exiles than did the attitude of the more politically minded and semi-ascetic Swiss.

In the spring of 1527, while Roy was engaged in this literary activity, he was joined by another English refugee of similar temperament, William Barlow. The origin of this recruit's

[26] Actually Bucer's doctrine represents an attempt to compromise between the Lutheran and Zwinglian teaching and is sometimes given the special name of "Suvermerianism." But the important thing for our purposes is that it marked an advance over Luther. There was never a sacramental issue between Puritan and Anglican, and I have made no effort in this volume to go into the details of the Continental struggles over this point.

[27] *A Briefe Dialoge bitwene a Christen Father and His Stobborne Sonne.* This work was reissued by Walter Lynne in 1550 with the title *The True Belief in Christ.* It was edited at Vienna in 1874 by Adolf Wolf under the title, *William Roy's Dialogue between a Christian Father and His Stubborn Son* (see Robert Steele, "Notes on English Books Printed Abroad, 1525–48," in *Transactions of the Bibliographical Society,* XI [1909–11], 189–236 [also printed separately, London, 1912], esp. p. 195; see also A. Koszul, "Was Bishop William Barlow Friar Jerome Barlow?" in *Review of English Studies,* IV [1928], 25–34; cf. chap. ii, n. 4, below).

interest in the Reformation is uncertain,[28] but he probably knew the London group, because he was able to locate Tyndale at Worms in the course of his journey. The great translator warned him against associating with Roy. Nevertheless, Barlow went to Strassburg and searched out Tyndale's former colleague, who suggested to him the congenial task of writing attacks on the English clergy, and particularly on Wolsey. The first fruits of this labor was a satire sometimes called for its main theme *The Burial of the Mass*, but better known by the couplet on its title-page

Rede me and be nott wrothe
For I saye no thynge but trothe.

The clergy are represented as mourning the death of the mass, after which two priests' servants discuss the question of where it should be buried. Though they decide on the shrine of St. Thomas of Canterbury as the most suitable last resting-place of the deceased, one of them points out that the English church officials will oppose any such evangelical practice. As the chief authority among them, Wolsey comes in for the hardest knocks. The delicate subjects of his origins and offspring are freely discussed and his political and religious policies attacked.

He standeth in the pope's room,
Having of his bulls a great sum,
    I trow a whole cart load,
Wherewith men's purses to discharge
He extendeth his power more large
Than the power of almighty God.[29]

[28] The suggestion (in C. H. and Thompson Cooper, *Athenae Cantabrigienses* [3 vols.; Cambridge, 1858–1913], I, 276; repeated by T. F. Tout in his life of Barlow in the *Dictionary of National Biography*, ed. Stephen and Lee [London, 1885, etc.], hereafter cited as *DNB*) that his adherence to the new movement is to be accounted for by Wolsey's dissolution of the monastery at Bromehill in Norfolk of which he was head is rendered improbable by the chronology of the events. The dissolution did not take place until September 16, 1528, when the *Rede Me* was already in print (Louis Blomfield, *An Essay towards a Topographic History of the County of Norfolk* [11 vols.; London, 1805–10], II, 165–66). For this and other chronological reasons—Prior William Barlow resigned his position as head of the house of the Augustinian canons at Blackmore, Essex, in 1509 while the author-bishop did not die until 1568—it seems best to adopt the suggestion of A. S. Barnes in his *Bishop Barlow and Anglican Orders* (London, 1922)—an otherwise unreliable work—that the Prior William Barlow was an older relative of the author.

[29] In Arber's *English Reprints* (Westminster, 1895), p. 51.

The friars are ruffian wretches and rascals, lodesmen (guides) of all knavishness, while the bishops "can well skill of wines, ... better than of divinity."[30] Though the Strassburg exiles were so hard pressed for funds that many copies of this work were pledged to Jewish bankers as security for debts, enough of them reached England to cause a considerable stir.

About the time Barlow was completing his cutting lines another English exile found his way to Strassburg. This was George Joye—he must be carefully distinguished from Tyndale's first assistant—a fellow of Peterhouse, Cambridge, who was compelled, in his phrase, "to leese [lose] my college, a perpetual sufficient living, and all that I had for saying that any simple Sir John [priest] had as great power to bind and loose (if he could preach the gospel) as had the Pope himself, that never preached it."[31] When summoned to London to answer for his teachings, he found himself confronted with a problem which was to puzzle reformers for the next century. Was it necessary to obey persecuting authorities to the extent of answering their questions truly at the risk of one's life? Latimer and Bilney had taken refuge in half-truths, mental reservations, and like subterfuges. Joye preferred a forthright policy based on the unacknowledged principle that the end justifies the means. When released on what amounted to his recognizance, being asked merely to give the clerk the location of his lodging-house, he did what Luther once advised in similar circumstances—told a good round falsehood:

Here I was so bold to make the scribe a lie for his asking, telling him that I lay at the Green Dragon toward Bishopsgate, when I lay a mile off, even a contrary way. For I never trusted scribes nor Pharisees. I perceived he asked me not for any good.[32]

[30] *Ibid.*, pp. 72 and 59.

[31] *A Present Consolation for the Sufferers of Persecution for Ryghtwysenes* (s.l., 1544), sig. A, fol. vi(v), and sig. A, fol. vii(r). The date of the arrival is fixed by the date ("the 10 day of June," presumably 1528, since he had fled from England in December, 1527) of his reply to the Prior of Ashwell, *The Letters Which Johan Ashwell . . . . Sente Secretely.* This volume was, however, not printed until 1531 (Steele, *op. cit.*, p. 225).

[32] *Letters*, sig. D, fol. ii(r). See the comments on this incident in S. R. Maitland, *Essays on Subjects Connected with the Reformation in England* (London, 1849), pp. 1–12.

With the head start on his pursuers gained by such tactics, he made good his escape. Once safe in "high Almayne," he indited a long defense of his teaching and conduct which he sent back to the one who had made the first accusations against him, John Ashwell, the prior of Newnham Abbey in his native Bedfordshire.

During this period the English authorities scored some minor successes in their repressive efforts. In the spring of 1528 an Oxford M.A. named Thomas Gerard, or Garret, who was supplying the reformers of his university with forbidden books, was only saved from arrest by the advance warning of a friendly official. Friends provided him with a refuge in Dorsetshire, but, before he had completed the journey, "his heart would no other but that he must needs return again unto Oxford." This time he was seized and locked in the bedroom of the master of Lincoln College. While his learned jailor and the members of his college were at evensong, Gerard succeeded in getting a finger through the door and sliding back the bolt. But he had learned no caution by his experience. He searched out one of his friends and was so careless as to betray his identity in the presence of a college servant who was not of the conspiracy. Though he once more managed to leave the town, and his fellow-conspirator lied manfully on his behalf, he was again apprehended and this time he recanted. Other lesser lights were also abjured, and the ramifications of the movement in the university were uncovered. The leader of the party there was found to be George Clark, one of the canons (fellows) of Wolsey's new Cardinal College who had been brought from Cambridge, a brave and able man who deserves to be better remembered in the annals of the Reformation and his adopted university. He and some of his associates were locked in the fish cellar of the new college. After a few months in this unhealthy prison, he contracted a mortal illness. As a heretic he was refused the communion. "Believe and thou hast eaten," was his rejoinder.[33] At about the same time confessions and abjurations were also extracted from a number of London and Essex Lol-

[33] Foxe, *op. cit.*, V, 421–29.

lards who were now purchasing the foreign books, and from various agents for such literature, including a Dutchman named Hans Ruremond, who had reprinted and improved Tyndale's New Testament.[34]

A few months later Wolsey, roused to action by the personal attack in Barlow's *Rede Me*, tried to check the flood of literature at its source. English envoys abroad were commissioned to hunt out those who were responsible for the appearance of such works and have them sent to England for trial. In spite of much searching, the ringleaders could not be found, though Roy was nearly taken when he returned to England in December to visit his mother. Two minor figures were apprehended— an Antwerp merchant named Richard Harman and a cleric named Akerston. But the authorities in the Low Countries were no longer on the best of terms with Wolsey, and they were slow to consent to extradition. The Cardinal himself soon became engrossed in other matters and, to the great discomfiture of his agents, failed to apply the necessary pressure.[35]

Meanwhile, Tyndale seems to have remained at Worms, with occasional visits to Frankfort to look after the sale of his works in that center of the book trade. Six thousand of his New Testaments had been printed, but the return from them was not sufficient to prevent his running in debt. For a time he appears to have lost touch with his English merchant backers. In the spring of 1528,[36] however, the exile at last moved to Antwerp to join his friends, although trade relations between the Low Countries and England were temporarily disturbed by the English-French alliance of the previous summer.[37] There he

[34] John Strype, *Ecclesiastical Memorials* (3 vols. in 6; Oxford, 1822), I, ii, 50–65; Kronenberg, *op. cit.*, p. 150.

[35] *Letters and Papers . . . . of the Reign of Henry VIII*, ed. J. S. Brewer, James Gairdner, *et al.* (London, 1862, etc.) (hereafter cited as *L and P*), Vol. IV, Nos. 4511, 4569, 4714, 5192, 5402, 5692.

[36] The date is fixed by the commencement of the "Marburg" series, May 8, 1528. In all probability these volumes were printed at Antwerp (Steele, *op. cit.*, p. 197; Kronenberg, *op. cit.*, pp. 156–57). On the identification of Hoochstraten see M. E. Kronenberg, "De geheimzinnige drukkers Adam Anonymus te Bazel en Hans Luft te Marburg ontmaskerd (1526–1535)," in *Het Boek*, VIII (1919), 241–80.

[37] Wegg, *op. cit.*, p. 170.

found a printer named Johann Hoochstraten, who was willing to take the risk of producing reforming books in English. On the eighth of May of this year there appeared the first of a long series of such volumes, bearing the fictitious colophon "By me, Hans Luft of Marburg in the land of Hesse." Hans Luft was the name of Luther's printer in Wittenberg, and this plausible identification of the party responsible confused authorities at the time and later bibliographers as well. The first product of this new arrangement was entitled *The Parable of the Wicked Mammon*. It was an expansion of one of Luther's sermons which undertook to prove that the biblical parable of the unjust steward taught nothing contrary to the doctrine of justification by faith.

Roy himself disappears from the scene after his escape from England in 1529. The available evidence seems to indicate that he was burned by the Inquisition in Portugal, after following the coastal trade route in search of new worlds to conquer.[38] Barlow, however, settled in Antwerp and in 1530 contributed to the "Marburg" series another "railing rhyme" called *The Dialogue of a Gentleman and a Husbandman*. This was an anticlerical piece in the Piers Plowman–Lollard tradition, incorporating two Wycliffite tracts. Following up this effort to connect the new movement with its historical predecessor and the surviving Lollards, he seems to have inspired the publication of two hagiological accounts of those who suffered in the old cause.[39]

Other men of the outspoken Barlow-Roy type were also moving to Antwerp. Among the additions to the Barlow group Simon Fish, a London lawyer, was the most noteworthy. He represented the anticlericalism of the London citizens, and his

[38] Thomas More, *Workes* (London, 1557), p. 342.

[39] Cf. Steele, *op. cit.*, pp. 209–11. Joye's movements between 1528 and 1531 cannot be traced. He was doubtless engaged on his plan to translate the books of the Old Testament into English. His edition of Isaiah was published at Antwerp with the fictitious imprint "Printed in Strassburg by Balthassar Beckenth" (misspelled "Beck-euth" in Steele), in May, 1531. It is probable that he had also completed a version of the Psalter before this date (*ibid.*, p. 225; More, *Confutation* [*op. cit.*, p. 343]; cf. A. W. Pollard and G. R. Redgrave, *Short Title Catalogue* [London, 1926], No. 2370; but see *DNB*, art. "Joye").

reforming sentiments were probably as much political as religious. His case is important as marking the adherence to the reforming cause of lay leadership in addition to financial support. It also typifies the growing hostility of the common lawyers to the old ecclesiastical order. Angered by the efforts of clerical chancellors such as Wolsey to increase the jurisdiction of the courts of equity, they were willing to take drastic measures to protect their livelihood.[40] Fish had acted as a dispenser of Tyndale Testaments in London and had once been in trouble for participating in a Gray's Inn play which satirized Wolsey.[41] In exile he began to write in the same vein. Taking up one of the themes with which Barlow dealt in his *Rede Me*— the idleness, wealth, and worthlessness of the clergy—the lawyer wrote a satirical petition to the English king called *The Supplication of the Beggars*.[42] The gist of it was that able-bodied idle rogues of the cloth were monopolizing the beggar's trade to the exclusion of its lawful practitioners—the halt, blind, and impotent. The argument was backed up with figures purporting to indicate the wealth of the clergy and their exorbitant share of the national income—figures grossly misleading and inaccurate, but nonetheless striking.

Several of those who had begun as humanistic reformers also crossed the channel to join the conspirators. Under pressure Barnes had recanted in February, 1526, and had been committed to prison during Wolsey's pleasure. In his confinement Barnes repented of his weakness; and, when the rigor of his detention was relaxed—he was intrusted to the care of his own order—he made use of this new freedom by going over to the more advanced or Lutheran group of reformers, a company better suited to one of his temperament than the Erasmian group at Cambridge. In the autumn of 1526 some of the Essex

[40] A. F. Pollard, *Wolsey* (London, 1929), pp. 59–98; W. S. Holdsworth, *History of English Law* (9 vols.; Boston, 1923–31), I, 460; V, 266–72.

[41] Arber has shown (*The First Printed English New Testament*, pp. 41–45) that Foxe is mistaken in making this play the immediate occasion of Fish's flight, which did not take place until at least a year and a half afterward.

[42] Arber (*ibid.*, p. 42) gives good reason to suppose that this work was published early in 1529.

Lollards found him in the company of several London merchants and bought one of Tyndale's testaments from him. In 1528 he decided to flee to the Continent. Instead of putting his pursuers off the track by the lie direct, he gained time by a simulated drowning. A suicide note and a heap of his clothing beside the water enabled him to make his escape. He did not linger in Antwerp but went on to sit at the feet of the master at Wittenberg.[43] About the same time one of the Cambridge–Cardinal College group named John Frith, released from imprisonment on condition that he remain within ten miles of Oxford, broke his parole and escaped overseas.[44] Tyndale found him a man after his own heart, studious but modest, an earnest reformer but not given to "railing" or disputing Tyndale's opinions. Frith reciprocated the affection and became Tyndale's firm friend and admirer. Not long after his arrival in Antwerp he translated an antipapal tract, *The Revelation of the Anti-Christ* for the "Marburg" series.

Thus toward the end of the decade English reformers of all stripes were drawing together under the leadership of the Antwerp group and its press. After the one outburst in May, 1528, Tyndale seems to have ended his quarrel with his more violent associates and all committed their writing to the same printer. Wycliffite material was being published, and English Lollards were buying the foreign books; laymen like Fish were taking an active part in the movement. Humanistic reformers such as Barnes and Frith were joining the Continental exiles in their revolutionary activities and their championing of theological innovations. But there was one section of the Erasmian party which remained aloof. Throughout these years Latimer and Bilney stayed quietly at Cambridge, preaching morality and engaging in good works, but doing nothing which the cautious Dutchman would not have sanctioned. Visits to prison and the famous Sermon on the Card occupied their attention while others fought for a vigorous reformation.

[43] Strype, *op. cit.*, I, ii, 54; Foxe, *op. cit.*, V, 419.

[44] Foxe, *op. cit.*, V, 5.

Though Wolsey's attention was now diverted to matters of more immediate concern, the lower ecclesiastical officials continued their law-enforcement efforts. In February, 1530, they exacted the supreme penalty from one of the reformer's couriers. A wandering rogue near Gravesend robbed a hedge of some laundry spread out to dry. The irate losers seized and searched the first suspicious character they could find. He turned out to be a cleric named Thomas Hitton carrying messages to the exiles. Accused of heresy, he went to the stake rather than recant, the first non-Lollard martyr of the English Reformation, unless Clark be so considered.[45]

But, for all the officials could do, the trade in contraband books went on. Already it had become evident that neither prosecutions in England nor diplomatic representations abroad could solve the problem. The church authorities therefore decided to supplement their efforts by returning the fire of controversial literature. For this purpose Bishop Tunstall in March, 1528, enlisted the aid of an ideal supporter, Sir Thomas More. As a layman this defender of the old order could not be accused of protecting the interests of his own class. As a distinguished humanist he could not be dismissed as an obscurantist. More took his task very seriously, and in answer to Tyndale's version of the New Testament and his *Wicked Mammon* he produced, in the summer of 1529, a volume called the *Dialogue*, which purported to be a record of an extended conversation in which the author and a young man inclined toward the new faith had discussed the various points at issue.

The questions of the place of images and pilgrimages in religious worship, the nature and authority of the church, and the justification of inflicting punishments for heresy were all discussed in the work, which also included objections to Tyndale's translation of the New Testament and an attack on Luther's doctrines and motives. A few months afterward More replied to the *Supplication of Beggars* with a small treatise

[45] *Ibid.*, VIII, 712–15; More, *Confutation* (*op. cit.*, pp. 343–45); see above, p. 24, on Clark.

called the *Supplication of Souls*, defending the morals of the clergy and the doctrine of purgatory. The souls of the departed are represented as complaining that, because of the spread of Protestant opinions and the consequent decline in prayers for them, their release from purgatory is delayed. To both of these works the reformers prepared replies; but, before they were published, the positions of the contending parties were greatly altered by a change of front on the part of the English secular government.

CHAPTER II

The Reforming Party and the Divorce
Protestant Clericalism versus
Erastianism

CLERICAL opposition, though responsible for both persecution and counterpropaganda, was not the only factor which retarded the progress of the Reformation in England. The growing power of the monarchy played a very important role in the story. The development of the Tudor absolutism must therefore be briefly described.

Up to the time when the crown of England was picked out of the thornbush on Bosworth field and placed on the head of the victorious Earl of Richmond the country was governed by a co-operative system in which king, church, and nobles shared the control. Henry VII broke with the past by virtually eliminating the nobles from the political pattern of the realm. It is not true that most of them had been killed off in the War of the Roses, but the class had been discredited by their activities in those misnamed brawls. By appealing to public opinion in general—not so negligible a factor in those days as the historians of modern journalism imagine—and to the rising mercantile group in particular, the grim young man was able to crush the lords. A miserly attention to government finance rendered the crown practically independent of parliamentary grants, a most important achievement since it enabled the King to dismiss the assemblage whenever he chose and thus to control most of its activities. Statutes of Livery and Maintenance combined with the revived jurisdiction of the Privy Council, exercised in the Star Chamber and branch councils, destroyed the private armies

which were the curse of the land and freed the administration of
justice from the paralyzing fear of the robber barons. While
these prerogative courts—as they were called from the fact that
they operated not according to the common law of the land but
at the royal discretion—could not administer the death penalty,
they could imprison, fine, or mutilate. There were no jurors to
be intimidated; it was not necessary to disclose the identity of
witnesses; and—though in fact it was rarely necessary to employ it—torture could be used to extract evidence. With such an
engine to punish those who tampered with legal routine the
crown speedily regained control over the ordinary tribunals. A
wise marriage with the Yorkist heiress greatly strengthened the
Tudors' claim to the throne; the few remaining rivals and their
supporters could now be hunted down and tried in open court.
Judicial executions supplanted pillows, starvation, and butts of
wine as means of dealing with the opposition. All this machinery was bequeathed to Henry VIII, and a single demonstration convinced the nobility that he was capable of using it.
The King had a distant kinsman, Edward Stafford, Duke of
Buckingham, who enjoyed some claim to the crown if the reigning sovereign died without male heir. In 1521, Henry decided
to be rid of him. He was suddenly brought to trial, charged
with such things as commenting on the King's health and saying
that when he came to the throne he would cut off the head of
the royal adviser, Cardinal Wolsey. The surprised duke was indicted, imprisoned, tried, and executed in the space of six weeks.
From this time on the nobility was thoroughly cowed. In theory
the church's powers remained unimpaired during this growth of
the royal power; but, in view of the close alliance between the
temporal and the spiritual arms, it was evident that the attitude of the King would be an important factor in any religious
change.

Soon after the beginning of the Lutheran agitation it appeared that the royal influence was to be exerted on the side of
the orthodox party. Not only did Wolsey, the King's chief
minister, take steps to suppress the heretical movement in
England, but Henry himself joined in the general fray. He un-

dertook to publish a rejoinder to Luther's argument against the Catholic doctrine of the sacraments. It eventually appeared in July, 1521, as *Defensio septem sacramentorum* and won for the King that title of *Fidei Defensor* which his successors have borne ever since. Some writers have thought that John Fisher, Bishop of Rochester, was the real author. Undoubtedly, the busy sovereign had some assistance with the routine details, but there seems to be nothing in the argument or general style which was beyond the abilities of the versatile author of "Pastyme with Good Companye." It is a treatise in the official Catholic style, ridiculing the monk who dared to speak against the voice of the universal church, and appealing to the authority of tradition. Luther answered the next year with a burst of satirical comments on the work and its author. Thus the lines were drawn. The crown had taken its stand against the reforming movement.

In part this unusual royal activity on behalf of the Catholic cause was a result of a wish to secure the support of the papacy in some rather tangled diplomatic negotiations, but deeper than this passing motive was the belief on Henry's part, as genuine as any theological attitude could be with him, that the old faith was the proper one. Eventually he came to accept certain Erasmian attitudes. He seems to have been sincere in his later stand that his subjects, at least the male half of them, should have access to the Bible in English and that the meaning of religious ceremonies should be made clear to them. When he at length decided to break the power of the clergy and seize their wealth, he sanctioned attacks on their shrines and relics and even on the doctrine of purgatory—attacks which, in fact, implied a heretical attitude on his part. But he did not accept these implications. At no time did he admit that in creed he was anything but an orthodox Catholic, and in the early 1520's even these practical and administrative concessions were far in the future. Throughout the next seven or eight years he gave no indication of sympathy with the Reformation in any aspect.

Consequently, the more active reformers were compelled to grapple with the problem of their relations to their sovereign and his place in the religious system they wished to establish. One of the most frequent charges against them, especially after the appearance of the Continental Anabaptists, was that they caused insurrection and taught "the people to disobey their heads and governors, and .... to rise against their princes and to make all common, and to make havoc of other men's goods."[1] The exiles were, in fact, rebels against their King. Not only had they gone abroad to find a base from which they might attack his religion but they had definitely violated the law of the land in leaving the country without the royal consent. It would not do, however, to admit these things. In the weak position in which they found themselves, it was much better to try to divide their opposition and win the favor of one of its elements by posing as loyal subjects of a theoretically absolute king who was being foully betrayed by the organized clergy. This effort could best be made by preaching the Lutheran doctrine of the absolute sovereignty of the prince, and that was the theme of Tyndale's *The Obedience of a Christian Man*, which appeared from the "Marburg" press in October, 1528. Kings are responsible to God alone. Evil rulers are God's scourge for our wickedness. We should not resist the rod, but even kiss it. With this ingratiating beginning the author went on to suggest that, since it was the King's duty to punish evil, he should discipline the wicked clergy who had usurped his functions and stolen his subjects' money.[2] Thus Tyndale talked of absolute obedience, but neither he nor his associates practiced what they preached. They did not return to England to kiss the rod. Instead they practiced a semi-active resistance by remaining abroad and flooding their sovereign's land with literature which provoked a prohibitory royal proclamation in the next year. Such was the situation when the King's difficulties in securing an annulment of his marriage to Catherine of Aragon caused him appreciably to modify his attitude toward the reformers. It is beside the purpose of this volume to retell the celebrated

[1] Tyndale, *Obedience of a Christian Man* in his *Doctrinal Treatises*, ed. Walter (Cambridge: Parker Society, 1848), p. 163.

[2] *Ibid.*, pp. 188–231.

story of the so-called "divorce." It is sufficient to point out
that, with the failure to secure the royal objective in the Cam-
peggio trial of 1529, Henry was driven to dismiss Wolsey and
consider other means. Of these, there were two main types:
to bring pressure to bear on the Pope by way of persuasion and
threats until the desired decree was forthcoming or to make an
absolute break with Rome and settle the matter in his own
courts. In either case some courting of the reformers was in
order. To persuade Clement, the milder leaders could be employed to prepare arguments about the "king's matter" for
papal consumption, while gestures toward the more radical
among them were calculated to frighten His Holiness with the
specter of a second Germany. And, if the alternative of complete separation were eventually chosen, Henry would need all
the support of all the reforming element during the crisis.

For this double purpose, the King found an ideal tool in
Thomas Cromwell. This remarkable person, a scion of a middle-
class Wimbledon family, had been trained in government service as a subordinate of Wolsey. Prior to his obtaining this connection, however, he had spent some time in military and mercantile adventures on the Continent and then established himself in London as a very successful wool merchant, an occupation in which he undoubtedly made many Lutheran contacts.
He was therefore well acquainted with the new German faith,
and, while he never displayed any evidence of personal religious
interest, he seems to have considered it quite as respectable a
creed as any, well worthy of being employed if it suited his
diplomatic ends to make use of it. While the somewhat more
conservative royal ministers, such as Gardiner and Fox, busied
themselves with making contacts with the humanistic reformers
at the universities, he undertook to establish friendly relations
with the *émigré* faction.

Yet, as long as negotiations with Rome should continue, it
was also necessary to retain a strong Catholic element among
the King's ministers. For this reason, Sir Thomas More, Tyndale's literary antagonist, was an ideal choice for the office of
Lord Chancellor. He was on good terms with Fisher and the

other Catholic bishops. Jealousy between Wolsey and his fellow-clerics had acted as a check on law-enforcement activities. Once More was in office that factor was eliminated. He gave his moral and occasionally his material support to the diocesan officials, and so the wheels of ecclesiastical justice now turned more rapidly. The result was that, during the four or five years while the royal decision hung in the balance, we find both a more vigorous persecution of the reformers and an attempt to win their favor for the royal cause. While one of the King's ministers was seeking to apprehend a suspect, another was urging him to serve as royal emissary on the divorce business. Very narrow was the margin which divided honor from disgrace, ease and safety from hardship and danger.

The effect of this situation on the reformers was what might be expected. Since the King had as yet made no doctrinal changes in his own position, the humanist group could easily win his favor—or rather be won to his support. Gardiner and Fox recruited a good number of Cambridge men, enough to secure a favorable opinion from the University on the divorce question. Stronger measures were necessary in dealing with Oxford, where the new learning had no such a following. But there also the desired opinion was eventually secured, no doubt with the cheerful support of such reformers as were to be found in that institution. The humanistic group thus became the nucleus of the later Anglican church. The list of those who supported the King at this time reads like the roll of the future Anglican episcopate. Cramner originally suggested the consultation of the universities. Heath, Shaxton, Skip, Goodrich, and Latimer himself, were others who co-operated. Latimer's case is a sample of the tight-rope performance these men went through to win and keep the royal favor in a time of political uncertainties. He was asked to preach before the King, but had to pay for the honor by serving in a commission which in the summer of 1530 condemned the writings of Tyndale and his group as heretical. The next year, through court favor, he received a country benefice, but the next Convocation compelled him to make a forthright recantation of his preaching on the subject of reverence to the saints, pilgrimages, and purgatory. Yet he was soon preaching before the King once more, and, with the triumph of Cromwell's anti-Roman policy, he became Bishop of Worcester in 1535.

The more radical faction of the reformers was also greatly affected by the change in the English political situation. Some of its number, including two distributors of Tyndale's writings in London, Richard Bayfield and James Bainham, lost their lives. Here and there, however, the party gained an adherent, as the fury of the Catholic persecution of 1531–32 drove some humanists to take the bolder course. While Latimer, Crome, and others were recanting, "Little Bilney" resolved to "go to Jerusalem." Arming himself with copies of Tyndale's New Testament, he journeyed through Norfolk, preaching the gospel as he understood it and distributing this literature, until he was seized and executed. The next year a young merchant-tailor's apprentice named Richard Hilles felt called upon to write against the doctrine of justification by works, and was compelled to flee abroad to save his life.[3]

But for the most part the ranks of Tyndale's supporters were rapidly depleted by the prospects of the honor and the power to be gained by abandoning the advanced Protestant theological position which they had assumed. William Barlow, whose brother was already acting as a royal emissary on the divorce matter, quickly made his peace with the crown. He published a *Dialogue against the Lutheran Heresies* in 1531. Shortly thereafter he wrote a letter to the King apologizing for his earlier writings,[4] and returned to embark upon the stormy seas of ecclesiastical politics, a venture which in the end brought him a Anglican bishopric and undying fame as one of the consecrators of Archbishop Parker. Barnes made an almost equally striking

[3] *L and P*, Vol. VI, Nos. 99 and 100; C. M. Clode, *Early History of the Guild of Merchant Taylors* (2 vols.; London, 1888), II, 61–62.

[4] *Letters Relating to the Suppression of the Monasteries*, ed. Wright ("Camden Society: First Series," Vol. XXVI [London, 1843]), pp. 6–7. The indorsement *1533* is not in Barlow's hand. With the addition of the motive for his change of course here noted, I believe Koszul's question (chap. i, n. 27) can be definitely answered in the affirmative.

change of front. In 1531 he issued a *Supplicatyon* to the King,
filled with explanations of his conduct and with attacks on the
Catholic clergy, but saying nothing about his attitude on transubstantiation. This volume had the desired effect, for in the
same year we find him negotiating with Luther on the King's
behalf. Though he was unable to secure from the Wittenberger
the favorable opinion desired, he returned to England[5] and became one of Cromwell's assistants. On several later occasions
he was sent abroad with official commissions, one of which involved another unsuccessful visit to his old teacher. Another
interesting case was that of Miles Coverdale, one of Tyndale's
collaborators on the translation of the Pentateuch in 1529 and
1530. He was a friend of Barnes and a former member of his
friary at Cambridge. After preaching for some time in Essex,
he apparently followed his master's example in fleeing abroad.
He also imitated Barnes in coming to terms with Cromwell.
He returned to England and took a Cambridge degree in 1531.
The next few years he spent, apparently under Cromwell's direction, in preparing a translation of the complete Bible, made
largely from Latin and German versions with a heavy debt to
Tyndale's New Testament. The work appeared in 1535.[6] Joye,[7]
Hilles,[8] and others also made their peace and abandoned the
struggle to introduce into England a religion of which the King
did not approve.

The opposition group among the reformers was thus reduced
to very small proportions, but it did not disappear entirely.
Both Tyndale and Frith were approached by agents of the King,
or at least of Cromwell, but they refused to bargain with the
government except on their own terms. However much he
might teach the doctrines of the absolute power of the crown in
order to attack the Catholics, Tyndale's practice did not differ
materially from the medieval clerical one of claiming virtual
autonomy for his group within the state. He did make the concession of holding up the publication of his reply to More, which

5 *L and P*, Vol. V, No. 593.

6 *DNB* and anonymous, *Memorials of . . . . Myles Coverdale* (London, 1838).

7 *L and P*, Vol. VIII, No. 923.   8 Clode, *op. cit.*, II, 63–64.

dealt with theological topics which might offend Henry, and he did not consider his point of view on the sacrament—now Zwinglian—worth contending for. But he insisted that the King should permit the circulation of the New Testament in the vernacular, though not necessarily in Tyndale's translation. This condition the King would not accept, and the negotiations lapsed.

In taking this stand in the celebrated interview with Stephen Vaughan, Cromwell's agent, Tyndale was defining the Puritan type yet more clearly. Whereas in 1524 he had disobeyed the wishes of loyal Roman Catholic authorities only, he was now refusing to accept orders from a monarch who was well on his way to break with Rome. It was not enough for Tyndale or the later Puritans that the ruler should be Protestant, in the sense of antipapal. He must be devoted to a Protestantism thoroughly reformed according to their lights if Puritan insubordination were not to continue.

Frith was as adamant on this point as his master, even when he was apprehended on a visit to England. He stood his ground on the Zwinglian doctrine of the sacrament without insisting upon it as an essential article of the Christian faith. His advance from his earlier position may also be seen in the fact that, whereas in 1528 he had violated the terms of his release to escape to the Continent, he now refused to flee when an opportunity was presented, though on this occasion he was bound by no promise. Rather he declared himself bound to accept the workings of that Providence which had delivered him into the hands of the authorities.

Before [my recent apprehension] I was indeed desirous to escape, because I was not attached but at liberty, which liberty I would fain have enjoyed for the maintenance of my study beyond the sea, where I was reader in the Greek tongue, according to St. Paul's counsel. Howbeit now being taken by the higher power, and as it were, by Almighty God's permission and providence delivered into the hand of the bishops only for religion and doctrine's sake, namely such as in conscience and under pain of damnation I am bound to maintain and defend, if I should now start aside and run away I should run from my God and from the testimony of his holy Word, worthy, then, of a thousand hells.[9]

[9] John Foxe, *Acts and Monuments of the Christian Church*, ed. Townsend (7 vols.; London, 1837-41), VIII, 698-99.

In that way he interpreted the doctrine of obedience and went to his death on July 4, 1533, six weeks after the coronation of Anne Boleyn.

Encouraged by the elimination of this opponent, the authorities renewed their repressive work at Oxford, where New College had become a center of Protestant propaganda. Some of the accused recanted, but one of the fellows, named Quinby, stood his ground. He "was imprisoned very straightly in the steeple of the New College and died, half-starved with cold and lack of food," though not before he had jestingly expressed a desire to eat a warden pie, made not of the baking pears which went by that name but of his persecuting superior.[10]

Two years later disgruntled English Catholic *émigrés* in the Low Countries took vengeance on the only kind of English Protestant they could reach by causing the arrest of Tyndale. Efforts to save him were made by the merchant with whom he had been staying in Antwerp, none other than Thomas Poyntz, the cousin of Lady Walsh. In August, 1535, this merchant wrote to his brother at the English court describing the situation. The Gloucestershire Walshes and Poyntzes had recently entertained the King during one of his progresses through their soft western vales,[11] and presently we find Cromwell exercising his friendly offices on the translator's behalf. But the law against heretics was clear, the Catholics were insistent, and Tyndale would not recant. On October 6, 1536, after nearly eighteen months in prison, he was executed.

The more aggressive branch of the Reforming party was thus nearly extinct, but at least one man remained to represent its position. John Rogers, an English clergyman in Antwerp, possibly a chaplain to the merchant community there,[12] had fallen

---

[10] *Narratives of the Days of the Reformation*, ed. Nichols ("Camden Society: First Series," Vol. LXXVII [London, 1859]), p. 34.

[11] *L and P*, Vol. VIII, No. 823.

[12] J. L. Chester, *John Rogers* (London, 1861). W. T. Whitley in an interesting series of articles in the *Essex Review* for 1934 and 1935 (XLIII, 1–6, 82–87, 155–62, 227–34; XLIV, 40–44, also published separately, Colchester, 1935) entitled "Thomas Matthew of Colchester and Matthew's Bible of 1537" has stated the case for assigning the work to the Colchester man of that name who is listed among the heretics in that city in

under Tyndale's spell and very probably had assisted him in his later work. On the apprehension of his master, he took his manuscripts and fled to safe Wittenberg. Refusing to return to England, he carried on the reforming work according to his own lights, far from royal restrictions. The chief fruits of his labor was the complete English Bible, published under the pseudonym of Thomas Matthew in 1537. In a simple fashion this completed the work begun by Tyndale. Taking his great predecessor's New Testament, his Pentateuch, and in all probability a manuscript translation which his master had made of the books from Joshua to Second Chronicles, he filled the gap with the Coverdale version of the remainder of the Old Testament and the Apocrypha. This work secured the royal license in England and served as the basis of most of the later versions.

So much for what may be called the external fortunes of the advanced reformers during this period. Something must also be said of their internal growth, their intellectual development, and the crystallization of their attitude on various practical questions—processes which went on simultaneously with the more obvious struggle. In fact, they are so closely connected with the controversy with More that there is no better way of presenting these topics than to describe the last years of that debate in some detail.

In the spring of 1531 there appeared Tyndale's *Answer to Sir Thomas More's Dialogue* in which he first dealt with the main points of More's criticism beginning with the objections to his version of the New Testament, and then answered the whole work chapter by chapter. More replied with a *Confutation of Tyndale's Answer*, a huge treatise, virtually reprinting both the previous ones. On each topic is set forth first the original sentence from the *Dialogue*, then the paragraph of refutation from the *Answer*, and lastly a rejoinder to this rebuttal. The *Con-*

1526–28. But, in the absence of any proof that the Essex burgher with the common name was even literate (though members of his circle were), I think the clear statements of Bale and Foxe must be accepted, especially in view of the trial record showing that Rogers used "Matthew" as an alias (cf. J. F. Mozley, *William Tyndale* [New York, 1937], Appen. E, pp. 354–55).

futation appeared in two parts, one published in 1532 and the second in 1533. The latter half also included a reply to a work which Barnes had written on the nature of the church.[13]

In this manner more and more people were drawn into, or rather admitted to, the controversy, especially since Tyndale found himself too occupied with other matters to answer the lengthy treatise. During the writing of his *Confutacyon*, More interrupted the work to compose and publish a short reply to an unprinted letter by Frith setting forth the Zwinglian view of the sacrament. The young enthusiast replied from prison with *An Answer to Sir Thomas More's Letter* and also continued a supplementary exchange with More's brother-in-law, John Rastell, on the subject of purgatory.[14] Shortly before Frith's death in 1533, Joye, not yet having gone over to the royal side, published a volume further defending the theory that the sacrament was purely symbolic.[15] In the following year he also attacked More on the subject of the validity of ecclesiastical tradition.[16]

Meanwhile, in 1532, a London lawyer named Christopher St. German, who still professed himself orthodox, wrote *A Treatise concerning the Division between the Spiritualty and Temporalty*, reflecting the anticlericalism of the city laity.[17] More replied in his *Apology*, which appeared in the spring of

[13] "What the Church Is" included in his *Supplicatyon*. For a more detailed account of the Tyndale-More controversy and its subsidiaries see the Introduction to A. T. Taft's edition of More's *Apologye* ("Early English Text Society: Original Series," No. 180 [London, 1930]).

[14] More and Fisher were also attacked in Frith's first work on this subject, *A Disputacion of Purgatorye* (1531).

[15] *The Souper of the Lorde* in Tyndale's *Answer to More*, ed. Walter (Cambridge: Parker Society, 1850), pp. 217-68. While Walter here assigns the work tentatively to Tyndale, elsewhere ("The Supper of the Lorde," *Notes and Queries*, I, No. 1 [1850], 362-63) he states that, if he thought Joye capable of writing in such an elevated style, he would grant it was his. The external evidence is all in his favor, and I see no reason why it should not be assigned to him. The expression "Master Mocke" for "Master More," employed in the first edition, seems to fit the Joye hypothesis.

[16] *The Subversion of Moris False Foundacion* (Emden, 1534).

[17] Cf. Franklin Le Van Baumer, "Christopher St. German," *American Historical Review*, XLII (1937), 631-51.

1533, defending the persecution of heretics.[18] German's answer, More's rebuttal, and a final rejoinder from the common lawyer in 1534 concluded More's part in the debate. So the arguments were passed back and forth like a tennis ball in a game, as one of the controversialists remarked. Each was striving so to "toss it that the other take it not" lest his adversary "smite it over again" putting "the game in as great jeopardy as it was before." It was a hard game, for "sometimes a man smiteth over and thinketh all won: and yet an ungracious post standeth in the way and maketh the ball to rebound back again over the cord and so loseth the game; and that will anger a man."[19]

In the matter of literary dress for their arguments there can be little question that Tyndale and his fellow-reformers were definitely inferior to their great adversary. As the little exile admitted, they were a "speechless and rude" lot. Joye confessed that before he was charged with heresy in Wolsey's townhouse he had never heard the phrase "presence chamber" and, being ashamed to ask directions, blundered into the kitchen by mistake when told to go to the Cardinal.[20] The arts of a courtier were not for the reformer. Only occasionally were these men roused by their zeal into something approaching literary style. Their outlines are diffuse and hard to follow; their ideas set down in unvarnished fashion. On the other hand, *The Dialogue* is as well written as any English controversial work of the century. The outline is clear and definite, the conversational device is effectively employed, and the "merry tales" which are interspersed in the work serve to hold the reader's interest. While the practice of replying to his opponent's answers paragraph by paragraph deprives More's later works of unity, and

---

[18] While it is possible in some fashion to harmonize More's later attitude on this matter with his earlier *Utopia* (R. W. Chambers, *The Saga and Myth of Sir Thomas More* [London, n.d.], pp. 14–21), there remains, in my judgment, a considerable difference of emphasis, to say the least. All in all, I am inclined to accept the old theory which makes More, like Tunstall and Erasmus, react from an earlier liberalism when faced with its Lutheran consequences.

[19] Frith's *Subsidy or Bulwork to His First Book* in his *Works*, ed. Russell, *The Works of the English Reformers* (3 vols.; London, 1828–31), I [IV], 212–13.

[20] *The Letters Which Johan Ashwell . . . . Sente Secretely*, sig. D, fol. i(r).

his painstaking earnestness makes them diffuse, there still remain the striking turns of individual phrases and the sly humor with which he drives home a shrewd thrust.

As framers of policies both contestants had their strong and weak points. Each must be given credit for manifesting great sincerity while doing a vast amount of hard work. Beyond that, each was true to his own background and apparently quite incapable of appreciating the other's point of view. Tyndale and his group, like many other leaders of irresponsible oppositions, suffered from never having had the experience of wielding power. Tyndale himself did not even know the responsibility of administering a parish, and so had little experience in the necessary and fine art of compromise. True, he did not suggest reform at the cost of destroying the nationalistic or class system of social organization, but short of that he demanded immediate changes without ever stopping, so far as we know, to count the cost. Those who refused to introduce immediate reforms were limbs of Satan. He had little, if any, conception of the valuable contribution to the cause of idealism which could be made by an organization with historical prestige, stability, and international unity. On the other hand, More wrote as what would now be called a member of the government, and long before, in his *Utopia*, he had expressed the opinion that a statesman who would accomplish anything should tolerate a certain amount of evil and follow the policy of gradualness rather than abandon his official position:

If evil opinions and naughty persuasions cannot be utterly and quite plucked out of their hearts, if you cannot even as you would remedy vices which use and custom hath confirmed; yet for this cause you must not leave and forsake the commonwealth; you must not forsake the ship in a tempest because you cannot rule and keep down the winds. No, nor you must not labor to drive into their heads new and strange informations which you know well shall be nothing regarded with them that be of clean contrary minds. But you must with a crafty wile and subtle train study and endeavor yourself, as much as in you lieth, to handle the matter wittily and handsomely for the purpose, and that which you cannot turn to good so to order it that it be not very bad. For it is not possible for all things to be well unless all men were good, which I think will not be yet these good many years.[21]

---

[21] *Utopia*, Eng. trans. Ralph Robinson; ed. A. W. Reed (Reading, 1929), p. 45.

People who demanded more drastic means for remedying the ills of the commonwealth were irresponsible revolutionaries who might easily bring on England some disastrous social upheaval after the pattern of the Peasants' Revolt.[22] More's fear of such a catastrophe amounted to panic and betrayed him into defending the *status quo* with something of the blind fury of a modern red-baiter. If we keep in mind these facts about the backgrounds of the two chief controversialists, we can understand why the general tone of the debate can scarcely be called elevated. Each antagonist impugned the motives of the others. Tyndale alleged that More wrote for pay and promotion. More charged that Tyndale was actuated by envy, pride, and a desire to violate his vows of celibacy. Strong language and harsh names followed as a matter of course.[23]

As for the theoretical arguments, the Tyndale group had rather the worst of the exchanges. It was not to be expected that a band of fugitives could immediately give their movement an intellectual framework comparable to that which was the product of the experience and reflection of a millennium and a half. They had a burning zeal to correct certain obvious evils in ecclesiastical life and worship, but the intellectual justification for their reforms was a matter of very slow development. After his death sentence, Bilney, having read and distributed Tyndale's works and being a relapsed heretic who could not possibly be saved by a recantation, nevertheless professed himself a good Catholic.[24] Tyndale himself and Frith, while convinced Zwinglians, did not wish to make their sacramental belief binding on all Christians—a sensible attitude, no doubt, but one which shows how little theologically minded they were. The younger man, when in prison, had a discussion with

[22] *Confutacion* in *Workes* (London, 1557), p. 353.

[23] There is a pleasant exception to this statement in Barnes's "Another Declaration of the Church Wherein Hee Answereth to Maister More," written after the Chancellor's fall but before his execution. "Truly, as God shall judge me, I am sorry for his trouble. If I could help him with any lawful means I would do my best" (*The Whole Workes of W. Tyndall, J. Frith, and Doct. Barnes* [2 vols.; London, 1572–73], II, 253*b*).

[24] I agree with the opinion on this disputed point expressed by T. F. Tout in his article on Bilney in the *DNB*.

Stephen Gardiner, who was his former Cambridge tutor, and the royal agent's nephew. According to the circumstantial account left by Germain Gardiner, it was not long before the reformer found himself quite beyond his depth. Beginning with an assertion in the early Lutheran style that, if it could be shown that the Church Fathers taught anything resembling the doctrine of transubstantiation, he would abandon his position, he was soon presented with the necessary evidence and forced to abandon his intellectual argument for the sounder one of the validity of the workings of his own conscience. "He could not think Saint Austin [Augustine] would write so, and yet," said he, "if it were so (and there advised himself a pretty while) a man might (and after another like pause) *tergiversari* [retract] but I will not."[25] Furthermore, the conditions under which the advanced reformers wrote were not conducive to the best presentation of what ideas they did have. Tyndale frequently lacked for food, clothing, and books. Frith complains that he had to play his controversy-tennis like a man tied to a post. Writing from prison, he excuses the defects of his work by the explanation that

I may not have such books as are necessary for me; neither yet pen, ink, nor paper, but only secretly. . . . . Whensoever I hear the keys ring at the doors straight all must be conveyed out of the way, and then if any notable thing had been in my mind it was clean lost.[26]

The crucial question was the one of authority. In general, Tyndale championed the Bible and More the historic church. But many were the natural weaknesses in those arguments, the ungracious posts in their tennis court. Each sifted the other's proof until both were compelled to take refuge in what the modern reader would call the purest subjectivism. Tyndale destroyed More's argument from age and numbers by reference to the superior qualifications possessed by the "churches" of the Jews and Turks, so that his adversary was forced to appeal to God's grace as certifying to the authority of his church.[27]

[25] Germen Gardynare [*sic*], *A Letter of a Yonge Gentylman* (London, 1534), fol. xl(*r*).

[26] *Subsidy*, in *Works*, I [IV], 242. .

[27] More, *Second Parte of the Confutacion*, in *Workes*, p. 705.

More demanded to be informed how the individual knew that the Bible was authoritative, and was told that it was by a feeling faith.[28] Both felt the need of supernatural, infallible authority, however, and would not put their admissions in philosophic terms.[29] Yet on that basis of supernaturalism, More's criticism of his opponent's position was devastating. "Was there not true faith before the days of the Bible?" he asked. Lame indeed was the reply that divinely given signs such as Abel's sacrifice and Noah's rainbow took the place of written scripture in those times.[30]

In the handling of practical topics relating to morals and worship, however, the opposition made the most of its natural advantage in having a record to attack but none to defend. One feels that Tyndale is putting his finger on real abuses in such passages as the following:

[In Catholic churches] now we hear but voices without significations, and buzzing, howlings, and cryings as it were the hallooing of foxes or baiting of bears; and wonder at disguising and toys, whereof we know nothing. . . . .

To kneel before the cross unto the word of God which the cross preacheth, is not evil. Neither to kneel down before an image, in a man's meditations, to call the living of the saint to mind, for to desire God of like grace to follow the ensample, is not evil. But the abuse of the thing is evil, and to have a false faith; as to bear a piece of the cross about a man thinking that so long as it is about him spirits shall not come at him, his enemies shall do him no bodily harm, all causes shall go on his side, even for bearing it about him, ... this is plain idolatry. . . . . In like manner it is that thousands, while the priest pattereth St. John's gospel in Latin over their heads, cross themselves with, I trow, a legion of crosses, behind and before and (as Jack-of-napes [a monkey] when he claweth himself) pluck up their legs and cross so much as their heels and the very soles of their feet and believe that if it be done in the time that he readeth the gospel (and else not) that there shall no mischance happen them that day because only of those crosses. And where

[28] Tyndale, *Answer to Sir Thomas More's Dialogue*, ed. Walter (Cambridge: Parker Society, 1850), p. 55.

[29] Earlier in the argument More stated that reason was not an enemy to faith Given time to argue, he thought he could demonstrate the truth of his religion to an unbelieving Turk (*Dialogue* in *Workes*, pp. 141, 152–54 [ed. Campbell (London, 1927), pp. 64, 84–87]). Tyndale, on the other hand, thought of reason as a deceptive thing, a quality of the natural man, which if trusted turned one from faith. "Except a man cast away his own imagination and reason, he cannot perceive God" (*Doctrinal Treatises*, pp. 16 and 24–26; cf. Frith, *Works*, p. 95, and Barnes, *Workes* [London, 1573], p. 307).

[30] Tyndale, *Answer to More's Dialogue*, pp. 26–27.

he should cross himself to be armed and to make himself strong to bear the cross with Christ, he crosseth himself to drive the cross from him, ... which is also idolatry and not God's word.[31]

Tyndale maintained that the Kingdom of God was not meat or drink but the keeping of the commandments and the loving of one's neighbor, so that "a man may eat and drink at all needs in all degrees so far as it letteth [hinders] him not" to fulfil these obligations.[32] On the other hand, More, after correctly stating in his *Dialogue* the Catholic position that ceremonial observances are generally helpful but unessential to the practice of true religion, in a later work, when heated by the controversy, asked in all seriousness, "What can be a worse belief than to believe that a man may as slightly regard Whitsunday as Hock Monday, and as boldly eat flesh on Good Friday as on Shrove Tuesday?"[33]

Whether the doctrine of justification by faith alone made for a higher morality than its Catholic rival was a matter of dispute then, as now.[34] Tyndale scandalized his contemporaries by his blunt statement of this doctrine in the prologue to the quarto edition of his New Testament. There he maintained that a woman of ill fame, if she repented, should have as high a place in heaven as one who lived in wedlock. Certainly, the breaking of vows, which he defended as a corollary to his main doctrine, was scarcely a practice to be indorsed lightly. But, on the whole, there can be little doubt that at this time, whatever the theological doctrine of justification may have had to do with it, the Protestant leaders were championing the

---

[31] *Ibid.*, pp. 11, 60–61.

[32] *Ibid.*, p. 153. [33] *Confutacion* in *Workes*, p. 340*b*.

[34] Cf. K. Holl, "Der Neubau der Sittlichkeit" (*Gesammelte Aufsätze zur Kirchengeschichte* [3 vols.; Tübingen, 1921], I, 131–244) on the Protestant side, and H. Grisar, *Luther* (3 vols.; Freiburg, 1911–12), III, 1–137 (Eng. trans. [6 vols.; London, 1913–17], V, 1–164) on the Catholic. In this connection, though it is not exactly an indication of inferiority as a stimulus to morality, it is something of a shock to find such a saint as Bishop Fisher, before his execution, expecting to spend time in purgatory because he had not done enough good works in this life and there was not sufficient time available in which to atone for that delinquency (Fisher's *English Works*, ed. Mayor ["Early English Text Society: Extra Series," No. 27 (London, 1876)], pp. 349–63, esp. p. 357).

higher type of conduct. The most striking proof of this may be seen in the works of More himself. Many of his "merry tales" depend for their point on the assumption that monks were to be considered adulterers and cheats as a matter of course. The author gives no indication that he is particularly alarmed by such a situation. It is all part of the good old system which must be defended. This complacence is all the more surprising because More's ultimate argument against the reformers—to which he recurs again and again, especially when others failed— was that in their system monks and nuns married. Public and legalized repudiation of vows by Protestants was an unspeakably vile thing, but the *sub rosa* violation of them by clerics of the Catholic persuasion was merely a theme for pleasantries. Hitton was to More a "beggarly knave" whose martyrdom was a good joke, but that the greatest ecclesiastic in England should use his position to seek benefices for his illegitimate son was merely a vice which use and custom had confirmed.

One other detail of Tyndale's position must be explained. On the subject of the proper organization of the church, the translator, as a man without practical experience, was stronger as a destructive critic than as a creator of a workable substitute for the old system. He believed that the New Testament documents made no distinction between bishops and presbyters (elders), and that deacons to look after the needy were the only other order of clergy they mentioned. He therefore advocated an essentially Zwinglian system of church rule, but he was not very clear as to how the clergy were to be chosen. Probably he had in mind appointment by their fellow-clergy, after the apostolic practice in the passage which he cites—that containing Paul's instructions to Timothy—but he took no definite stand against the current advowson system, by which wealthy laymen named the clergy. He does not appear to have considered congregational election a possible method. The principle with which he was mainly concerned was that the clergy should be conscientious and able preachers rather than worldly potentates or performers of unintelligible rites.[35]

[35] *Doctrinal Treatises*, pp. 229–31.

But, although the Tyndale group were more advanced than their Catholic and humanist contemporaries in their moral attitude and in some aspects of their thinking, it should be remembered that the Continental Anabaptists were much farther to the left than they. As we have seen, one of the reasons for Tyndale's composing *The Obedience* was to refute the charge that the reformers accepted Anabaptist principles. There,[36] in addition to his political teaching, he expressed his belief in the doctrine of infant baptism, and also by his economic teaching[37] sought to make clear that he was not of the extremist school. The dreaded doctrines of this group were maintained in England during this period, but only by foreigners. In June, 1535, fourteen Dutch Anabaptists were executed, and others were deported at about the same time. Similar measures in the succeeding years indicate that the movement was not killed out, but so far as we know it remained, as yet, an alien thing.

[36] *Ibid.*, p. 253.
[37] See p. 402 below.

CHAPTER III

The Second Henrician Exile: The Doctrine of Ceremonies

THE reformers who had allied themselves with the royal policy in the early 1530's—and, as we have seen, this group included nearly all those who were not Anabaptists—had done so with the hope and expectation that under the leadership of the King the Anglican church would gradually advance to a position which would approximate that of the German and Swiss Protestantism. The full realization that there were to be permanent divisions among the forces revolting against Rome did not come until the seventeenth century. In the heat of the conflict the leaders of the new movement, with the incurable optimism of all reformers, viewed their undertaking as a great rediscovery of the true faith, which, with discussion and Bible study, would soon be clear to all. Time was on their side. A little patience, and all would be well.

For some years it seemed that their confidence was to be justified. As the King pushed through his "divorce" and severed more and more of the ties that bound the country to Rome, he not only took over the political control of the church but he approved and even urged certain changes in its worship and theology. The Ten Articles of 1536 and the injunctions issued in the same year by Cromwell as Henry's Vicar-General introduced a great number of reforms. The doctrines of purgatory and worship of the saints were greatly modified in the direction of Protestantism. The cults of relics, images, and pilgrimages were discouraged. Most of the old religious ceremonies were retained, but the people were to be taught their meaning. They were also to have access to the Bible in their own language. Taking advantage of such concessions, students at the Inns of Court, who had adopted the new faith, began to mix theological persuasion with their requests for money when writing home. New Testaments were carefully selected with a view to securing type sizes suitable to elderly eyes and were sent along with the assurance that they would not bring their readers into any heresy but into the true light of the gospel.[1] At about the same time the government began the huge task of destroying monasticism. Times were good for the Protestants. True, there were some contradictions in the orders which issued from the court during these turbulent years. One month the clergy were forbidden to preach; the next, exhorted to use their pulpits to the utmost for the advance of the great work in hand. Nor was even the general purport of the orders very logical or consistent. Believers were told to pray for the dead, but the authorities frowned on talk of purgatory. It was fairly evident, furthermore, that the royal policy on religion was largely determined by the exigencies of foreign affairs, and so subject to change without notice. But, in spite of all these unfavorable elements in the situation, the fact remained that Catholics were treated as rebels, and the whole drift of the royal policy was toward Protestantism. High officials of the Anglican church were on friendly terms with the Continental reformers. Cranmer kept up the friendships formed in Germany when negotiating about the royal divorce in 1532, and both he and Latimer entered into correspondence with the Zurich divines.[2] English travelers, well-to-do merchants, students, and noble tourists were the medium of communication. With one accord the English writers expressed the opinion that the complete abolition of Catholicism in their country was only a matter of time.

Then there came a change. A variety of factors combined to cause it. Perhaps the most fundamental was the natural tendency of political movements to run their course and produce a

---

[1] *Plumpton Correspondence*, ed. Stapleton ("Camden Society: First Series," Vol. IV [London, 1839]), pp. 232–33.

[2] Partridge to Bullinger, September 7, [1538]; Cox to Bullinger, November 1, 1550, *Original Letters Relative to the English Reformation*, ed. Robinson (2 vols., single pagination; Cambridge: Parker Society, 1846–47), pp. 611–12 and 121.

reaction in a few years' time—that phenomenon of human fatigue which causes mankind to be bored with its lot at periodic intervals. The popular sentiment which blames all its ills on the government in power was now directed against the Protestant advisers of the King. The reform movement had not yet won the support of the populace to any great extent, except among the old Lollards. Under Wolsey and More there had always been some sympathy for those Protestants persecuted for their religion. Now this sentiment was transferred to the Catholic cause. The Tudors were quick to adapt themselves to changes in public opinion, and Henry was quite ready to cease his reforming activities. Although he sponsored alterations in church government and worship, he always considered himself an orthodox Catholic. The doctrine of transubstantiation was a resistance point on the road to Protestantism beyond which he would not go. In November, 1538, he ordered the execution of John Lambert, a former Cambridge man, who like Frith had advocated the Zwinglian doctrine of the sacrament. "I will not be a patron of heretics," stormed the King in passing sentence on this representative of the "sacramentaries," as these advanced reformers were now called. Assisting at the trial was Cromwell's rival, the conservative Stephen Gardiner, Bishop of Winchester, who had recently been recalled from France, where he had spent three years as the royal ambassador.[3] He was not high in the King's favor at this time; in fact, he was charged with having mismanaged his work abroad. But he now devoted himself to regaining the King's confidence and to the destruction of Cromwell and all his works. In the events of the succeeding years his hand may be clearly seen. Lastly, the ever changing situation on the Continent played a large role in bringing about the English reaction. Fear of an invasion by the Emperor, either alone or in conjunction with France, had kept Henry negotiating with the German Lutheran princes for some years. In the spring of 1539, however, a new French ambassador succeeded in persuading the King that his country held no such de-

[3] For the career of Gardiner see J. A. Muller, *Stephen Gardiner and the Tudor Reaction* (New York, 1926).

sign.[4] Thus relieved of the necessity of placating the Germans, Henry pushed through Parliament the Act of the Six Articles, "the whip with six strings," as the Protestants called it. That statute declared the denial of transubstantiation a heresy punishable by the stake and made hanging the penalty for such offenses as broken vows of chastity, the denial of the necessity of auricular confession, and advocating the distribution to the laity of both elements in the mass. The Continental Protestants were scandalized and insulted.

But in the autumn a new threat of foreign invasion frightened Henry into an alliance with Cleves, supposedly cemented by his marriage with the Duke's sister. The German prince was not a Lutheran. He was rather an Erastian after the manner of Henry himself, but he was a brother-in-law of the Elector of Saxony and closely allied with the members of the Protestant Schmalkaldic League. The English agreement with Cleves therefore checked the Catholic movement for the time. In the following spring, however, Henry lost interest in his German bride, and the Anglican counterreformation was resumed in earnest. The marriage with Anne was dissolved. Cromwell was attainted and executed, July 28, 1540. Gardiner thereupon became the King's chief minister. While he remained in England, the Six Articles Act was enforced with some rigor, though not consistently. During much of 1544 and 1545, when he was absent on diplomatic errands, the stringency of the law was considerably modified and the persecution was relaxed. But on his return in 1546 it blazed out afresh, and the anxieties of the Protestants were not entirely relieved until Henry's death in January of the following year.[5]

By a useful anachronism, the government policy during the period of Gardiner's influence may be called Anglo-Catholic. The authority of the Pope was not recognized, and monasticism was abolished. But with the exception of these and a few minor

---

[4] R. B. Merriman, *The Life and Letters of Thomas Cromwell* (2 vols.; Oxford, 1902), I, 252. For the full story of the negotiations with the German Protestants see F. Prüser, *England und die Schmalkaldener, 1535–1540* (Leipzig, 1929).

[5] John Foxe, *Acts and Monuments*, ed. Townsend (London, 1837–41), V, 262–696.

elements which survived from the era of Thomas Cromwell, the attempt was made to retain all the doctrines and ceremonies of the old church. Transubstantiation, the mass in one kind, auricular confession, an unmarried clergy, Latin services, images, and the traditional ecclesiastical costume—all these familiar features of the medieval religion were still considered essential parts of the Anglican worship.

This new royal policy and the succeeding years of persecution split the reforming party into several different elements. A considerable number of men who had begun as moderate reformers followed the example of More and Tunstall and went over to the conservative camp, affording further examples of the "tired radical" attitude of which we shall see a great deal in the course of this work. Bonner and Heath, newly appointed bishops of London and Rochester, respectively, were the most prominent of this group. Thomas Wriothesley, one of Cromwell's protégés, made a similar change and throve to the dignities of Lord Chancellor and Earl of Southampton. Nicholas Shaxton, Bishop of Salisbury, who resigned on the passing of the Act of the Six Articles, stood his ground for some years; but, when threatened with the stake in 1546, recanted and thereafter followed Heath's example.

Other reformers compromised only so far as was necessary to save their positions or their lives, quietly retained their old ideas, and waited for the storm to blow over. They may be called, by another convenient anachronism, the low church or evangelical party in the Anglican body. Cranmer himself was of this type and remained as Archbishop of Canterbury, striving—with some success in the King's later years—to moderate the tempest. Latimer belonged to the same group, but he was forced[6] to resign his bishopric and was for a time imprisoned. Released in July, 1540, he spent the next years in retirement, but in 1546 he was on trial before the Council, though there is no record of the outcome. More unfortunate still were three prominent Protestant preachers, William Jerome, vicar of Stepney, and two whom we have met before, Robert Barnes and

[6] R. Demaus, *Hugh Latimer* (London, 1869), p. 335.

Thomas Gerard, the former Oxford colporteur, now vicar of a London parish. These men all promised to recant when summoned before the King in 1540, and later did so. But they were too closely identified with Cromwell's policy, since at least Barnes and Gerard had been his protégés. Without a hearing, the three were accordingly attainted by Parliament. On July 30, 1540, two days after the beheading of their patron, they were used to give the world a horrible but striking illustration of Henry's Anglo-Catholic orthodoxy. Along with three Roman Catholics who had denied the King's supremacy they were executed; the Protestants for heresy, the Romanists for treason. Others recanted with more success. Edward Crome, an influential Protestant preacher, saved his life in that manner in both 1541 and 1546. His curate, Robert Wisdom, and a friend, Thomas Becon, followed his example on the first occasion but then retired to the country. In Staffordshire they found a friend, John Old, who was fortunate enough to have retained his ecclesiastical position. He entertained them for some time, and, when he later moved to Warwickshire, Becon accompanied him. Latimer was also seeking seclusion in the same neighborhood, and the refugees spent much time together. During this period of enforced retirement Becon put out several popular religious tracts under the name of Theodore Basil. Though sufficiently Protestant in tone to justify the use of a pseudonym, they dealt with such comparatively harmless topics as justification and the Christian virtues, and the author was not further molested in this reign.[7] Many prominent laymen similarly retained their reforming beliefs but did not publish them abroad too boldly while they waited for a change in public policy. The most distinguished of these was Charles Brandon, Duke of Suffolk, whose first wife was the sister of Henry VIII. He was not troubled for his faith during this period, though his chaplain, a Scotch reformer named Alexander Seton, was compelled to recant in 1541.[8] Thomas Wentworth, Baron of Nettlestead, a veteran soldier and courtier, was another nobleman of similar

[7] The Early Works of Thomas Becon, ed. Ayre (Cambridge: Parker Society, 1843).

[8] Foxe, op. cit., V, 449–51.

opinion and practice. Lesser men followed their example. Many of Cromwell's protégés left the court and found employment in more obscure locations. In London five hundred people were charged with heresy before the commissioners appointed under the 1539 act. All received the royal pardon, but the experience was apparently not lost upon them, for we hear little more of heretical activities in the city during this period. Thus most of the reforming party was effectively terrorized by the royal hostility to their opinions.

There was a bolder group, however, who refused to keep silent. Some adherents of this party remained in England and stood their ground in time of trial. During nearly every year of this period there were executions of Protestants.[9] In the year 1546 four were burned, including a prominent woman named Anne Askew. She championed the Zwinglian doctrine of the sacrament with such vehemence that her husband turned her out of his house. Coming to London in 1545, she was arrested the next year but refused to recant or to name her accomplices, though racked until she could not stand. While bishops and Doctors of Divinity were fearfully repudiating their earlier teachings, she went to the stake without flinching.

But most of the determined opponents of the royal policy preferred to flee abroad. There they found a warm welcome both in Switzerland and in Germany, "High Almain" as they called it. Luther was still living at Wittenberg, and Bucer remained very influential at Strassburg. Bullinger was a shining light in Zurich, but in the French-speaking part of his country a younger colleague was beginning to rival his fame. John Calvin, the French reformer, had settled there in 1536, shortly after publishing the first edition of his famous theological work, the *Institutes of the Christian Religion*. Expelled in 1538, he found refuge in Strassburg with Bucer but returned in triumph in 1541 to resume the work which was to make Geneva the most celebrated reforming center in western Europe.

[9] S. R. Maitland (*Essays on Subjects Connected with the Reformation in England* [London, 1849], pp. 259–308) undertakes to minimize the extent of the persecution under this act, but an average of more than three executions a year was enough to make for an effective "terror."

Some of the English reformers who sought the company of these leaders were veterans of the first exile. Coverdale, who had been employed by Cromwell on the preparation of the so-called Great Bible, first in Paris and later in London, went abroad on his patron's fall. He spent some time in Denmark but soon settled as a clergyman in Germany, at Bergzabern, between Strassburg and Frankfort in the duchy of Zweibrücken. There he remained until the end of Henry's reign, spending his spare time writing and translating for the benefit of his party. George Joye remained in London until 1541 but then went to the Continent, where he followed a wandering career as a controversial writer. One of his works was printed at Antwerp in 1543 and another at Geneva in 1545, which would suggest that he spent some time in those two places.[10]

Richard Hilles, the merchant tailor, was another who went into exile a second time in order to escape "being a traitor to God and man," as he put it. He settled in Strassburg soon after the passage of the Act of the Six Articles and carried on an extensive cloth trade both in Germany and in Switzerland. He soon made contact with Bullinger, who was a great friend of religious exiles. For the remainder of Henry's reign he kept up a friendly correspondence with the Swiss reformer, whom he occasionally used as an unofficial business agent and credit man. The two exchanged presents—theological books and Swiss cheeses for English cloth and gloves—and less material benefits, news of England for counsel on the godly life.[11]

Hilles was a great patron of his less fortunate fellow-exiles. Many who had no previous experience in such a life found refuge and support with him. To some he even gave regular

[10] Robert Steele, "Notes on English Books Printed Abroad, 1525-48," *Transactions of the Bibliographical Society*, XI (1909-11), 230. Though the evidence is often used in biographies of men of this period, the fact that a volume contains a colophon stating that it was printed in a certain place does not necessarily mean that the author was residing in that town at the time, even though the colophon be correct. Authors might and did send manuscripts to friends in cities with printing facilities requesting that they be seen through the press in the writer's absence (cf. Coverdale to Calvin, March 26, 1548, *Original Letters*, pp. 31-32).

[11] Hilles to Bullinger, [August, 1540], to July 9, 1553, *Original Letters*, pp. 196-275.

annuities.[12] The most prominent of these friends of Hilles was John Hooper. He was a scion of a prominent Somersetshire family, an Oxford B.A. with some experiences at the royal court. Reading the works of Zwingli and Bullinger, he was converted to the Protestant point of view. With the change of royal policy in 1539, he retired, first to the country and later to France. He returned to London for a short time but was forced to flee once more, this time to Strassburg, where Hilles' family tended him through a nearly fatal illness. On his recovery he joined the ranks of those who have married one of their nurses. His choice was a daughter of a noble Flemish family, a girl who was being educated in Hilles' household.[13] In 1546 he returned to England once more, this time merely to secure funds for a sojourn at Zurich. After three months of peril, including imprisonment and storms at sea, he accomplished his purpose. In March, 1547, he arrived in the Swiss city and remained two years.

Even more important, at the time, were two other reformers who do not appear to have had dealings with Hilles—William Turner and John Bale. Both were Cambridge men who had been influenced by Lord Wentworth. Turner, something of a genius and too much neglected in the history of early Puritanism, had been sent to Pembroke Hall, Cambridge, at the Baron's expense, and remained there as a fellow for some ten years after taking his B.A. Having translated several works of Continental reformers during the Cromwellian era, he found it advisable to go abroad soon after the government's change of policy. He traveled in Germany and Italy, studying medicine and botany, as well as theology. In 1543, under the name of William Wraghton, he published at Basel a small and witty volume dedicated to Henry and directed against the Catholic elements remaining in Anglican worship. It was entitled *The Huntyng and Fyndyng Out of the Romish Foxe*. Ignoring the

[12] Hilles to Bullinger, December 18, 1542, *ibid.*, p. 238.

[13] Hilles to Bullinger, January 28, 1546, *ibid.*, pp. 251–52; Hooper to Bullinger, January 27, [1546], *ibid.*, p. 38.

King's own Catholic attitude and beginning with the thesis that
the King had ordered the Pope driven out of his realm like a
predatory beast, he undertakes to show his sovereign how the
treacherous clergy were concealing the royal enemy and his
works in such practices as the mass, the requirement of unmarried clergy, the use of Latin services, vestments, organs,
etc. Gardiner, who was already engaged in controversy with
Bucer on the subject of clerical celibacy,[14] replied with *The Examination of a Proud Praesumptuous Hunter* and was answered
by Turner in *The Seconde Course of the Hunter at the Romish
Fox and Hys Advocate*,[15] published in 1545. On the back of the
title-page was the colored woodcut of a vested, crop-eared fox
standing on his hind legs and carrying a bishop's crosier. Under
it were these semiprophetic lines:

> The Banished Fox of Rome speaketh:
> My son Steven Gardiner with weeping tears
> Hath cut away the tops of mine ears,
> But the rest of my body abideth whole still
> With all my ceremonies even at my will.
> I trust mine ears shall grow again
> When all the gospellers are once slain,
> Which Steven my son, both stark and stout,
> Doth now right earnestly go about.
> If he can bring this matter to pass
> He shall be Cardinal as Fisher was.

The colophon declares in the facetious style of which Bale was
also fond that the work was "Imprinted have [*sic*] at Winchester
Anno Domini 1545　4 nonas martii　By me Hanse hit prik."
Geneva was the probable place of publication, though by this
time Turner had settled as a physician in Emden, where he remained until it was safe to return to England.

Bale was a man of great vigor and asperity, characteristics
which a conventionally minded artist has masked behind a

[14] P. Janelle, "La Controverse entre Etienne Gardiner et Martin Bucer sur la
discipline ecclésiastique (1541–1548)," *Revue des sciences religieuses* (Strassburg), VII
(1927), 452–66.

[15] Since this work reprints Gardiner's answer, it bore first on its title-page Turner's
version of the title of that work, *The Rescuynge of the Romishe Fox, Otherwyse Called
the Examination of the Hunter*, and is therefore often listed under that title.

calm, kindly face and a great beard in the prints which have survived. Educated at Jesus College, he had been led to adopt his
reforming ideas, through the agency of Lord Wentworth, at
least as early as the period of the divorce agitation.[16] Later he
became a protégé of Cromwell and distinguished himself by
writing satirical plays against the Roman Catholic clergy. On
the fall of the great Secretary he went to Germany, where he
continued to publish works in support of his party's program.
One, ostensibly printed at Geneva in 1545,[17] was an answer to
an apparently unprinted "Genealogy of Heretics" compiled
in verse by John Huntington, a protégé of Gardiner. Much
more important for our purposes is his *Yet a Course at the Romyshe Fox*, published under the name of John Harryson, allegedly
at Zurich in December, 1543. As the title indicates, there was a
very close relationship between this work and Turner's volume
published at Basel in the preceding September. Later Bale appears to have settled at Wesel. At any rate, several of his works,
including accounts of Anne Askew's trials, were printed on a
press in that city in the years 1546–48.[18]

In the writings of these refugees may be found the principles
with which the works of the first exiles have made us familiar.
There is the same uncritical appeal to the Bible as the ultimate
authority. There is the same assertion of the doctrine of justi-

[16] Bale was tried before Edward Lee, Archbishop of York, for his Reformed beliefs
in 1534. His conversion must therefore be dated somewhat earlier than this year.
Jesse W. Harris' careful study, "The Life and Works of John Bale" (University of
Illinois dissertation [Urbana, 1935]), p. 28, gives good evidence for dating it 1533.

[17] *A Mysterye of Inyquyte Contayned within the Heretycall Genealogye of Ponce Panto-
labus Is Here Both Dysclosed and Confuted*. Theodore Vetter in his *Literarische Beziehungen zwischen England und der Schweiz in Reformationszeitalter* (Zurich, 1901), pp.
12–13, points out that the printer, Michael Wood, to whom the work is assigned by
the colophon, was not in Geneva at that time, though he may still have had a branch
office in the city. He was also unable to locate any printer by the name of Oliver Jacob-
son (to whom the *Yet a Course* is attributed) in the Zurich records of 1543. There is,
however, clear evidence that Bale was in Switzerland at about this time (cf. the Preface
to his *Acta Romanorum pontificum* [Basel, 1558], reprinted in Vetter, *op. cit.*, pp. 33–37;
see also Vetter's *Relations between England and Zurich during the Reformation* [London,
1904], pp. 23–24). Harris (*op. cit.*, pp. 42–44) establishes the probability that Bale was
in Antwerp during part of the period 1543–45.

[18] Steele, *op. cit.*, pp. 232–35.

fication by faith alone, much of it growing out of certain articles which Barnes set forth at his execution.[19] There is also the same repudiation of all connection with the Anabaptists. When Bale comes to comment on a passage in Huntington's poem in which the author includes an Anabaptist martyr, Peter Frank, among the Protestant heretics, he retorts with vehemence.

Now couple ye these good men with the Anabaptists, the more to blemish their names though they never agreed to that superstitious sect. Rather should the Anabaptists seem to be of your sort rather than theirs. For they have in a manner the same opinion of free will, and of justification by works that you have. They will obey no temporal magistrates and no more will you, but by compulsion. They force not to break their oath of allegiance and no more do you. They would have all men's goods in common and so would you also, your owne always excepted, and this foredele [advantage] of them ye have in that article, ye are sure in every man's goods to have a portion by title of tithes, offerings, confessions, testaments, masses, and so forth, doing little or nothing for it and so are not they. And therefore I cannot see but ye are a member of theirs as dangerous, coyeshe [coyish?] and diverse as ye make it. Marry, indeed a zeal they have unto the gospel, though nothing to knowledge; which you never had, but a most bitter hate instead thereof.[20]

Along with this repudiation of the Anabaptist name and principles the exiles sought to maintain their old stand on obedience to secular authorities. They asserted that they were loyal subjects of the King, whose right it was to regulate matters of religion. They prayed that his eyes would be opened to complete the reformation, or that a Jehu would be sent to finish what this Jehoshophat had begun.[21] But the fact was that they were rebelling against their sovereign's laws and doing all in their power, short of employing physical force, to change them. To rationalize this situation, they reiterated the old contention that the clergy were deceiving the King and therefore were to blame for all the oppressive legislation. But they added a justi-

---

[19] E.g., Coverdale's *A Confutacion of That Treatise Which One John Standish Made against the Protestacion of D. Barnes in the Yeare MDXL* in his *Remains*, ed. Pearson (Cambridge: Parker Society, 1846), pp. 320–449.

[20] *Mysterye of Inyquyte*, fols. 52–53. Elsewhere (*Yet a Course*, fol. 91) Bale says on this subject: "Only is this opinion [to have all things common] holden and maintained of the Anabaptists which had it first of their [Catholic] monkish sects, whose custom was sometimes for themselves to have all in common, but for no man else."

[21] *Yet a Course*, fol. 11; cf. I Kings 22:43 and II Kings 10:15–28.

fication of the practice of flight, or, failing that, passive resistance.

> If the king forbid the New Testament or any of Christ's sacraments or the preaching of the word of God or any other thing that is against Christ, [his subjects should beg him to rescind the order. But] if he will not do it, they shall keep their Testament, with all other ordinance of Christ, and let the king exercise his tyranny if they cannot flee, and in no wise, under pain of damnation, shall they withstand him with violence.[22]

Rather the "vengeance of it" should be left "unto their Heavenly Father."

There are other passages which savor vaguely of an even stronger attitude. Bale emphasizes the point that no secular power can really produce a religious attitude and, in another passage, speaks briefly of being willing to die to bring in a reformation.[23] Foreshadowing the protests at the time of Elizabeth's accession, Turner would not style Henry "Supreme Head" of the Church of England, though he maintained that "Supreme Governor" was even more honorable. Before his return from exile, Hooper went so far in talking of the duty of rulers as to quote with approval a story of Trajan saying to one of his captains as he gave him a sword, "Use this sword for me, if I command the things that be right; if not, use it against me."[24] But as yet these ideas were quite undeveloped.

The period of the persecution was, however, productive of fundamental changes along other lines. To the basic pattern of Puritanism already described there was added another characteristic attitude which was to be important throughout its history—opposition to religious ceremonialism. The new conditions in which the writers found themselves stimulated this new idea. The earlier exiles had confined their attacks on the old regime to major issues, such as the Catholic doctrines of authority and salvation. As we have seen,[25] Tyndale was willing

---

[22] Robert Barnes, *The Whole Workes of W. Tyndall, J. Frith, and Doct. Barnes* (2 vols.; London, 1572–73), II, 294; see also Bale, *Yet a Course*, fol. 81.

[23] *Yet a Course*, fols. 7(v) and 97.

[24] *Seconde Course*, sig. C, fol. ii; John Hooper, *Declaration of the Ten Holy Commandments*, in his *Early Writings*, ed. Carr (Cambridge: Parker Society, 1843), p. 363.

[25] P. 47.

enough to tolerate ceremonial forms of worship as long as their meanings were explained. But, as the attack on the old religion developed, the front widened. Party spirits rose, and the advanced reformers now began to urge more drastic purgings. The second exile greatly strengthened this attitude, not only because it further exacerbated partisan feelings but because it brought the English reformers in direct contact with Swiss practices which were much simpler than those to which they were accustomed.

Barnes had all unwittingly laid the intellectual foundations for this anticeremonial drive. Amid his diplomatic and preaching activities he had found time to prepare a collection of the lives of the popes. In it much emphasis was placed on the innovations which they introduced into ecclesiastical worship and conduct, and the contrast between the ideal of the early church and its medieval successor was repeatedly brought out. Peter was married and so was Luke. This pope forbade laymen to sue clergy at law. That one thought of having archbishops.

The rites of the mass were multiplied in the course of time. Celestine added the introit, Gregory the *Kyrie eleison*. Telesphorus the *Gloria in excelsis Deo*, Gelasius the collects, Jerome the Epistle and Gospel. The Alleluia was taken from the Church of Jerusalem. The Nicene Council added the creed, Pelagius the commemoration of the dead, Leo III incense, Innocent the kiss of peace, Sergius the *Agnus Dei*. What the other pontiffs added will be told for each in his own place.[26]

This, of course, was by no means full-blown Puritanism. To prove that rites were not original with the church was not necessarily to argue that they should be abandoned. Barnes's friend and master, Luther, who was far from Zwinglian in his ceremonial ideas, contributed an indorsement to the work. But, whatever the author may have thought, his historical data could be used as Zwinglian ammunition as far as ceremonies were concerned. If these were of post-apostolic invention, they were

[26] *Vitae Romanorum pontificum* (Basel, 1555; dedication to Henry VIII signed "Wittmebergai: X September Anno Domini MDXXXV"), pp. 1–2. I have been unable to locate a copy of the first edition. The work ended with the biography of the twelfth-century Pope Alexander III. Bale's *Acta Romanorum pontificum usque ad tempora Paul IV*, of 1558, is an independent work and much more critical of historical evidence.

human additions to the gospel, and so might be abolished—
must be abolished, said the Zwinglian. Turner's initial blast
shows clearly that he had made a close study of Barnes's work
and had drawn this conclusion. The proof of the Romishness
of the fox was in the origin of the hated ceremonies, which went
back to Gelasius, Gregory, Alexander, and the rest. As he tells
us:

> About seven years ago, when men preached earnestly against the Pope
> and he with all his ordinances was like to be driven out of England, a certain
> man to set him forward gathered together out of Platina[27] and such other
> writers what popes had made all the ceremonies that are now in the church,
> and to every ceremony he assigned one pope or other, which thing made, the
> ceremonies began to be less regarded than they were before.[28]

From this beginning a new theory of reformation was developed—a theory which was to be standard equipment for the
Puritan party throughout its history. The assault was no longer
directed at the Catholic religion as a separate and established
institution—a strategy which had meant a concentration on its
essential doctrines of justification, sacerdotalism, and sacraments—but against the remnants of Catholicism in a church already partially reformed. Once the objectives were stated in
such terms, the field for possible change was enormous.

Like the German Anabaptists, the exiled reformers appealed
to the authorities with the argument that the steps already
taken were an acknowledgment of the necessity for a change
which must therefore be completed. "None that setteth handle
to the plow (sayeth Christ) and looketh again back is fit for
the kingdom of God. Ye know Lot's wife for doing such a feat
was turned into a salt stone."[29] All true Christians were urged
to work for the elimination of traditional ecclesiastical practices, which were "nothing . . . . but doctrines of men, beggarly
traditions, and dirty dregs of the pope."[30] Even if some parts
were harmless, or even true, yet because the remainder would

[27] Bartolomeo de Sacchi di Piadena (1421–81), *De vita et moribus summorum pontificum historia* (Paris, 1530).

[28] Turner, *Huntyng*, sig. C, fol. i(v). There are two editions of this work bearing
identical dates. I have used the one without pagination.

[29] *Yet a Course*, fol. 78; cf. Gen. 19:26, Luke 17:32.   [30] *Yet a Course*, fol. 3.

corrupt innocent believers who were unable to discriminate, the whole Roman Catholic system should be abolished, as the Catholics themselves destroyed the writings of those like Frith, whom they alleged to be a false teacher, though they admitted that the books contained some truth mixed with the error.[31] This was the root idea in the attack on ceremonies—that they were popish and so to be abolished with their chief patron.

As a corollary to this teaching, the principle was laid down that instead of the papal standards true Christians should accept the biblical one of the teaching of Christ and the early church. In the New Testament there was no approval of complicated rituals such as were required in the Catholic system. If one was to be declared a heretic for attacking current usage, Bale suggests that Jesus should also be so classified.

> For He never allowed their ceremonies. He never went procession [sic] with cope, cross, and candlestick. He never [in]censed images nor sang Latin service. He never gave orders nor sat in confession. He never preached of purgatory or pardons. He never honored saints nor prayed for the dead. He never said mass, matins nor evensong. He never fasted Friday nor vigil, Lent nor Advent. He never hallowed church nor chalice, ashes nor palms, candles nor bells. He never made holy water nor holy bread, with such like. But such dumb ceremonies not having express commandment of God he called the leaven of the Pharisees and damnable hypocrisy, admonishing his disciples to beware of them. He curseth all them that addeth unto his word such beggarly shadows, wiping their names clean out of the book of life.[32]

> These mitres, tippets, furred amises, and shaven crowns. These crosses, copes, censers and candlesticks. These matinses, masses, ceremonies, sorceries shall not he know for his. For he commanded no such things to be done. He told them he would require mercy at their hands and no sacrifice, and thereof have they [the Catholics] now nothing at all.[33]

It was freely granted that the Old Testament required the observance of certain ceremonies, but, according to a medieval principle of exegesis, the ordinances of that part of the Bible were to be divided into three classes: moral, which were still binding on the Christian; judicial, which applied only to the peculiar government of the Jews; and ceremonial, which pertained to the signs in the Hebrew worship typifying the coming

---

[31] Turner, *Huntyng*, sig. C, fol. ii(*v*).   [32] *Yet a Course*, fol. 18.   [33] *Ibid.*, fols. 8(*v*)–9.

Messiah. These last ceased to be of any force with the coming
of the Savior whom they foreshadowed. To retain such practices after the substance was come, or to employ devices taken
over from pagan worship, was to offer insult to the great sacrifice already made.

> Will [Bonner] make us Jews again? Will he make us bond servants and
> Christ hath made us free children? St. Paul saith, If we clog ourselves again
> with that yoke we fall from grace, we go quite from Christ and his death
> shall profit us nothing. Therefore there ye offer us wrong. Your own laws
> and doctrines, besides the scripture, granteth abrogation of the laws cere-
> monial. If ye bring us in any rites, therefore, taken of the heathen customs
> as are your saints' holy days, your processions, your litanies, your diriges
> [dirges], your [in]censing of altars, your kneeling to images, your calling upon
> dead men, your kissing of relics, your conjuring of spirits, your consecrations,
> vows, and sacrifices for sin, with such other, ye do us great injury also.
> . . . . Christ hath said also in John that the true worshippers should worship
> God only in spirit and in verity. Then are they the false worshippers which
> worship in outward things, specially the outward thing [it]self.[34]

Of course, this last principle literally applied would abolish all
public and outward worship. Bale and his followers modified
this extreme position by granting that certain rites had been
definitely commanded in the New Testament and so were still
to be observed. Baptism and the Lord's Supper were Christ's
holy instructions, not popish ceremonies. But "those not having express command of God" were to be removed altogether—
a principle which was to be the cornerstone of Puritan teaching
on the subject for years to come.[35]

To these arguments Gardiner made the reply which was also
to do service for several generations: "The King's majesty
. . . . hath rejected the Bishop of Rome so far as he swerveth
from the truth, and so far as the truth will bear, his Majesty
agreeth with all the world." No sensible man, he said, ever

---

[34] *Ibid.*, fols. 77(*v*)–78.

[35] In addition to the items of worship and costume already mentioned, Bale took
exception to some of the formalities of the marriage ceremony in which "negligent
priests or ignorant hob lurches doth join [the parties] together with 'who shall have
this woman' and a few babblings more, giving them no manner of godly instructions
how thay should in the fear of God behave themselves to one to the other in that
comely estate of living" (*Yet a Course*, fol. 79). His friend Turner followed the example
of the Zurich church still farther by adding organs and descant (counterpoint) to the
list of proscribed means of worship (*Huntyng*, sig. B, fol. v(*v*); *Seconde Course*, sig. K,
fol. v(*v*).

thought that "all that which was taught either by the Bishop of Rome, or under his authority, was his own doctrine and to be cast away." The good was "to be retained and kept, not because it was his, but because it was good. Shall we not confess Christ the Son of God because the devil said the same?" Richard III was a usurper, but his Statute of Uses was a good one and still rightly observed, and the Bishop makes this plea for the aesthetic element in religion:

These men speak much of preaching, but note well this, they would we should see nothing in remembrance of Christ, and therefore can they not abide images. They would we should smell nothing in memory of Christ and therefore speak they against anointing and holy water. They would we should taste nothing in memory of Christ, and therefore they cannot away with salt and holy bread. . . . . Finally they would have all in talking, they speak so much of preaching, so as all the gates of our senses and ways to man's understanding should be shut up, saving the ear alone.[36]

The response was a reiteration of the original theses. Truths taught in papal times were certainly to be preserved, but the scripture was the standard by which truth was to be tested. Usurpers could make satisfactory secular laws but not divine doctrine. The rule for heretics applied to the Pope and his works. The Bible and preaching[37] were better guides to a sound doctrine than stinking oil poured on dead carcasses or unsavory salt used for conjuring.[38] Ceremonies such as the reading of the Six Articles were used as an excuse to avoid sermons being preached.[39] The fox always hated the cock whose crowing betrayed the invader

when he would on the night time come to worry hens, [and] then when all the cocks are dead or else put to silence the fox reckoneth that he hath good peace that he may worry hens and "chikkings" and do what so ever he list, no man speaking one word against him.

[36] *Examination of the Hunter* quoted in Turner's *Seconde Course*, sig. D, fol. vii; sig. C, fols. vi–vii; sig. G, fol. i.

[37] But Turner points out that Gardiner was not really keen about genuine appeals to the eye, since he had forbidden "the players of London, as it was told me, to play any more plays of Christ, but of Robin Hood and Little John and of the Parliament of Birds and such other trifles" (*Seconde Course*, sig. G, fol. ii; cf. Maitland, *op. cit.*, pp. 295–96).

[38] Sig. C, fol. vii; sig. D, fols. i and vii(v); sig. G, fol. v (actually iii).

[39] Sig. A, fol. vi(v).

So the two-footed foxes had killed "three well crowing cocks at a cast" (Barnes, Gerard, and Jerome), and had "pulled all the feathers off two cocks of [the] kind [Latimer and Shaxton] and have put them to silence."[40]

Turner's position may well be summed up by this clear statement which the exchanges drew from him:

Whenas the end of a perfect law of the church, which alone is sufficient by itself to order the church, is to command all thing [sic] that is necessary to salvation; to forbid all thing that is hindrance to salvation; to teach, to reprove, to correct, to instruct, to make a man perfect and ready to every good work and to be salvation unto all them that believe, and the law of the gospel can do all these things, what shall we need to have any other law in the church, seeing that this law containeth all thing in it that is necessary for the church of Christ and hath all the points that belong unto a perfect law which needeth no other law to be added unto it? Almighty God told his son Christ all laws that was necessary for Christ's church, and Christ taught his Apostles all that he heard of his Father, and all that the Apostles learned of Christ necessary for Christ's church they and the Evangelists have written it in the New Testament which is the law of the gospel. But the Evangelists and Apostles have made no mention of the Pope's ceremonies, laws, and traditions; therefore they are not necessary for Christ's church, but the law of the Gospel is necessary alone.[41]

The lines were thus drawn once and for all. Between these two ideas of ecclesiasticism, the theoretically static Protestant, and the theoretically progressive, developing Catholic, there could be no agreement either then or for years to come. A half-century later Travers and Hooker were still chanting the same antiphony. And if one sometimes grows impatient with Puritan intransigeance in matters of costume and ceremony, it must be remembered that all the theory of it was worked out in a time of great stress, when it was death for priests to marry and when the anticeremonial arguments were only part of a general attack on the whole medieval system of sacerdotalism, which was as yet almost unbroken.

The controversies of this decade deserve more attention than they have received. This is not only because we find in them the first clear statement of the Puritan-Anglican issue. The Turner animal cycle had definite literary merit which would repay more careful study. It furnishes not only the background

but some of the figures for the Marprelate satires and is not unworthy to be compared with them. There is vigor of writing
combined with sly humor and a wealth of popular illustration
which should make them the subject of further investigation.

The chief complaint against all this controversial literature
has been its scurrility. Coverdale and Hooper, it is true, wrote
with a moderation which stands comparison with Gardiner's
calm. Hooper dedicated his reply to the Bishop's work on the
sacrament to his adversary himself, as a proof that his animus
was against the doctrine and not the man. But Joye, Turner,
and especially Bale, wrote with a vigor which has made them
notorious. The characterization of Bonner as the two-headed
beast of the Apocalypse which rose out of the earth is a mild
sample of the playwright's work. This splenetic style unfortunately caused the omission of his most important works from the
Parker Society collection, which has made the writings of so
many of the English reformers available to modern readers.
An age which has shed Victorian squeamishness will perhaps be
more tolerant, especially if the issues involved and the circumstances of composition are kept in mind. After speaking of his
exile, Joye remarks: "If this book, therefore, seem too sharp-
toothed, consider in how sharp a time it was written."[42] And it
is well to hear Bale also in his own defense:

All this have I done, good Christian reader, brotherly to admonish thee
to beware of this cruel enemy and such other which seeketh by their daily
crafts to rob thee of that life which thou hast in Christ Jesus. Peradventure
thou wilt be moved, not because the man of sin is thus set forth in his right
colors but for that it is done here with such extremity. Consider for that the
earnest vein in the scriptures against this wicked generation from the beginning. Both did the holy prophets and the apostles evermore fiercely
reprehend the blasphemy of the Lord's name and verity. Full are all their
prophesies and writings of terrible rebukes and threatenings. Yea, Christ, our
most gentle and patient Redeemer, spared not to call them strangers, hirelings,
thieves, wolves, murderers, dogs, swine, adders, liars, devils, hypocrites,
serpents, oppressors, destroyers, tyrants, abomination, an whore's brood and
many other names of great indignation. Much better is it to the Christian
believer that Satan appear Satan and the devil be known for the devil, than
still to lurk under a fair similitude of the angel of light. For when he is once
known he may soon be avoided.[43]

[42] George Joye Confuteth Winchester's False Articles (Wesel, 1543).

[43] Yet a Course, fols. 95(v)–96.

And this bold defiance is also worth quoting:

> I know certainly I shall for this be called a thousand times heretic, but I weigh it nothing at all, for it is the old name of true Christians. I think some of our feeble, faint brethren which are now neither hot nor cold will diversely say their minds and have sentences much like themselves. I know I shall be burned if I may be caught, but I care nothing for it. For I doubt not my portion to be with Christ, which will not suffer one hair to perish, but will restore it me again at the latter day. Yea, if I lose for him here, I know I shall be a winner again there. Rather I had to die many deaths than to obey such mischiefs to my soul's condemnation. Never shall the life of my sinful carcass be so dear unto me, I hope, as is the glory of my eternal Father and Redeemer, Jesus Christ.[44]

There was yet another side of these controversial exiles which deserves mention. Not only was Bale a dramatist of a sort but, during his stay abroad, he was working on his *Illustrium Majoris Britanniae scriptorum . . . . summarium*, the first bibliography of British writers. This and most of his other works give evidence of great energy and a wide knowledge. Bartholomew Traheron, a lesser veteran of the first exile, who spent some time at Geneva during the period of the second peril, was the translator of the works of John Vigon, a leading Italian physician of the time. As we have seen, Turner also had an interest in medicine, but it was in botany that he made his real mark as a scientist. His *Names of Herbes*,[45] published on his return to England in 1548, is the first modern English work on that subject. When we read that goat's beard "groweth much in the middowes of Colon and in many places in Duchland," we are reminded that even the most zealous of reformers sometimes thought of hunting other things than Romish foxes.

[44] *Ibid.*, fol. 9.

[45] Reprinted by James Britton in 1881 for the English Dialect Society.

CHAPTER IV

Coalition: Vestiarianism and Discipline

ENGLAND, by 1546, was ready for a change of government. The Catholic policy was no longer attracting general support. The six- or seven-year political cycle of enthusiastic indorsement, lukewarm indifference, and active dissatisfaction had once more been accomplished. As a good Tudor, Henry appreciated the fact, and after the July day when Anne Askew was burned at Smithfield before the Lord Chancellor Wriothesley, Norfolk, and the Lord Mayor of London the persecution abated. Peace had been made with France in June, and Henry was once more considering an alliance with the Schmalkaldic League against the Emperor. According to one report,[1] he thought of adopting the full-blooded evangelical policy of substituting the communion for the mass, while the fall of the Howards and Gardiner's personal quarrels crippled the Catholic party in the Council. The good fortune of the Tudors, which brought even their deaths at times when they would most profit the fortunes of the house, eliminated the great Harry at this time and substituted one who was better adapted to riding the pendulum on the long Protestant swing.

The son of Jane Seymour, who now came to the throne, was a child of nine. His early policy was therefore necessarily shaped by regents. As a result, the governmental attitudes were extremely susceptible to the force of public opinion, since the temporary magistrates could not command the respect paid to one who ruled in his own right. Edward Seymour, the first to wield the real power in this reign, was, like a majority of the

---

[1] John Foxe, *Acts and Monuments*, ed. Townsend (London, 1837–41), V, 563–64; cf. A. F. Pollard, *Thomas Cranmer and the English Reformation* (London, 1904), p. 181.

new Council, anxious to bring about a more completely Protestant reformation. But under the circumstances, as a good politician, he attempted to give the people what they wanted rather than to force the pace in religious reforms. There is no evidence that the majority of Englishmen were inclined toward doctrinal Protestantism by this time, but they were tired of the enforcement of heresy acts. In suspending the operation of these laws and eventually securing their repeal by the Parliament which met in November, the Protector was undoubtedly reflecting general public sentiment. The result of this move was to open the floodgates of religious controversy. Long-delayed manuscripts were rushed to the printers, and others hastily prepared for publication. This was a situation favorable to the growth of the young and vigorous Protestant movement, which thrived on free discussion. It is true that at the same time Somerset, to call Seymour by his new title, was not unmindful of the conservative interests. By a series of proclamations and acts of Parliament directed against unlicensed preaching and irreverent speech about the sacrament, he made a gesture toward holding the balance between the contending parties. But his heart was not in this compensating move, and he did not do much to make it effective.

The natural result of the new governmental policy was the return of the *émigré* reformers. Coverdale was in England by March, 1548, and Traheron, Turner, and Bale followed before the end of the summer. Even John Rogers, who had refused to trust Henry in his most Protestant mood, left Wittenberg and appeared in London by August of this year. Hooper lingered on at Zurich, studying theology, but in March, 1549, he took an affectionate farewell of Bullinger and also turned his face homeward. Two months later he was in London, already engaged in theological controversy and promising his late benefactor a bargain in a piece of English hose cloth—actions symbolic of the close connection between advanced Protestantism and the cloth trade.[2]

[2] Hooper to Bullinger, May 3, 1549, and May 31, 1549, *Original Letters Relative to the English Reformation*, ed. Robinson (2 vols., single pagination; Cambridge: Parker Society, 1846–47), pp. 62–64.

The Protestant party in England was further reinforced during these years by an influx of Continental reformers. Cranmer's attractive offers were partly responsible for this immigration, but an equally important factor was the defeat of the German Protestant forces at Mühlberg and the consequent imposition of the Interim upon the Imperial dominions after May, 1548. This famous formulary was designed, as the name suggests, to provide a basis of compromise between Catholic and Protestant until a council should make more satisfactory arrangements. While it made some concessions to the Protestants in the matters of clerical marriages, the use of the cup in the sacrament, and certain elements of the doctrine of justification by faith, on the other hand, it retained transubstantiation, all the seven sacraments, the worship of the Virgin and saints, fasts, and other Catholic ceremonies. Conscientious Protestants could not accept such terms, and over four hundred divines are said to have left southern Germany alone. These men found a variety of refuges in parts of Protestant Europe beyond the Emperor's reach. Switzerland and Scandinavia received many of them, but the English contingent is the only one of importance for our story. Strassburg reformers had been especially hospitable to *émigrés* from the island kingdom, and their English friends now returned the favor. Pietro Martire Vermigli, commonly referred to in England as Peter Martyr, the Italian refugee professor of theology in the Silver City, and Valérand Poullain,[3] who had succeeded Calvin as pastor of the French church there, arrived in 1547. Emanuelo Tremellio, a friend of Martyr and a teacher of Hebrew, came early the next year. Jan Utenhove, a prominent lay member of Poullain's group, followed in the summer, and in April, 1549, came Bucer himself and Paul Fagius, a professor and a great preacher as well. Many more arrived from other parts of the Empire. Augsburg sent Bernardino Ochino, another Italian refugee, and Heidelberg lost Peter Alexander, a prominent theologian. Francisco Dryander, a Spanish Lutheran of no fixed abode, found at Cambridge a short respite from his Continental wanderings. The only other

---

[3] For Poullain's career see Karl Bauer, *Valérand Poullain* (Elberfeld, 1927).

who needs special mention was John à Lasco,[4] who was, after Bucer and possibly Martyr, the most important of the Continental immigrants. The son of a Polish nobleman and nephew of the Archbishop of Gnesen, Primate of Poland, he was educated at Bologna. He returned to accept ecclesiastical preferments in his native country, but in 1524 he traveled through Germany and Switzerland in quest of further broadening. At Basel he lodged with Erasmus and studied Hebrew with Conrad Pellican. He also visited Zwingli at Zurich and no doubt became a secret Protestant at this time. He returned to Poland, however, and spent thirteen years as a Catholic ecclesiastic, seven of them as Bishop of Vesprim.[5] In 1538 he at length fled abroad and after some wanderings settled at Emden, where he became superintendent of the churches in the Protestant duchy of East Friesland. In response to Cranmer's invitation, he visited England in the fall and winter of 1548–49, and, after the Interim was finally forced upon the German duchy, he decided to make his permanent residence in Edward's domain. He arrived in May, 1550, and in July was appointed superintendent of the foreigners' church in London.

Another major influence on the development of the English Reformation during this reign was a refugee who was a foreigner but not a Continental, the great Scotchman, John Knox. The northern kingdom had been exposed to the same waves of reform which had lapped the shores of its southern neighbor. Lollard, Erasmian, Lutheran, and Zwinglian followed one another[6] in disseminating their ideas. Scotland offered to the re-

---

[4] Hermann Dalton, *Johannes à Lasco* (Gotha, 1881).

[5] James Gairdner (*The English Church in the Sixteenth Century from the Accession of Henry VIII to the Death of Mary* [London, 1902], p. 283) says that his name does not appear among the bishops of that see, but the statement is made by both Dalton (*op. cit.*) and Valerain Krasinski (*Historical Sketch of the Rise, Progress, and Decline of the Reformation in Poland* [2 vols.; London, 1838], I, 243–44, 249). Furthermore, a translation from the Greek by Joseph Strusius was dedicated to à Lasco as "Bishop of Vesprim" (Alexander Brueckner, *Różnowiercy Polscy*, Ser. I [Warsaw, 1905], p. 34). According to Krasinski (p. 249), à Lasco was also nominated for the bishopric of Cuyavia shortly before his flight from Poland. I am indebted to my friend Professor Matthew Spinka, of the Chicago Theological Seminary, for help on this point.

[6] For the early history of the Scotch Reformation see Peter Lorimer, *Patrick Hamilton, the First Preacher and Martyr of the Scottish Reformation* ("Precursors of Knox," Vol. I [no more published] [Edinburgh, 1857]).

formers a favorable soil not only because it was like Switzerland and the Rhineland in having a weak central government, but also because the Scotch were accustomed to fighting and bloodshed in the cause of political and social change. For generations nobles and churchmen had quarreled with sovereigns. If now and then one of the rulers "hapenit to be slain," it was a matter of no particular surprise. But feeble as the crown was, when its influence was added to that of the clergy it sufficed to render the development of the reforming movement in Scotland much slower than it was in England, where political considerations had early put the monarch on the side of the Protestants. Many pioneers of the new faith in Scotland ended short careers at the stake. Others went into voluntary exile.

Knox belonged to the latter group. He was an ecclesiastical notary converted under the influence of George Wishart, who had visited Zurich and later introduced the Zwinglian influence into Scotland. When the flames put an end to Wishart's activities as preacher and political conspirator and an avenging band of Protestants murdered Cardinal Beaton for his part in the execution, Knox joined the beleaguered assassins in the Castle of St. Andrews. There he soon demonstrated those qualities of inspiring leadership which caused an English ambassador to declare that his voice put more heart into an army than five hundred trumpets. But superior force prevailed for the time. Taken prisoner by the French forces which came to the aid of the Regent Arran in July, 1547, he spent nineteen months as an oarsman in the galleys of his captors. Fortunately for him the English government, true to the rules of the diplomacy of the time, consistently supported the cause of rebels in the territory of its neighbors. Even at the height of the Six Articles reaction in 1542 an attempt had been made to impose a kind of Protestantism on Scotland by armed force, because the Francophile government was Catholic. The Edwardian authorities now interceded with the French on behalf of the St. Andrews prisoners, and by April, 1549, Knox was safe on English soil.

As previously suggested, the foreign refugees who desired to come to England were met fully halfway by the ecclesiastical

and political leaders who were then in power there. In part
this was due to a general feeling of sympathy for their suffering
coreligionists on the Continent. But there is no doubt that a
majority of the Council wished to see a further reformation in
religion and felt that an influx of distinguished Protestants
would hasten the progress of a movement which they realized
would be at best a slow and gradual one.[7] Cranmer, furthermore, was anxious to introduce some unity into the ranks of
the divided Protestants. All the major reformers paid at least
lip service to the ideal of a visible Catholic church. Diplomatic
considerations had frequently induced the secular authorities
to support negotiations looking toward uniformity of Protestant
belief, and many of the ecclesiastical leaders desired something
approaching a supernational organization of the new church
with a conciliar form of government. Though his Erastianism
seriously handicapped his efforts, Cranmer was one of these.
In 1548 he was planning to convene a Protestant council in
England. It was no doubt with this in mind that he invited
Bucer to cross the channel, though the most explicit and pressing invitations were sent to Melanchthon, the chief representative of the moderate Lutherans, without whose co-operation the
project could be no more than partially successful. The great
weakness of Protestantism, however, was not that the ideal of
unity was lacking or its advantages unrecognized, but that so
many other things seemed more important to its leaders. The
Lutherans were especially susceptible to the spirit of partisanship and political influences nearer home, and on the whole they
do not seem to have taken their Protestantism quite so seriously as did their Swiss brethren. Perhaps it was because they
still cherished more of the laudable desire to heal the breach
with Rome than did the Reformed leaders. In any case, many
of them, including Melanchthon, managed to rationalize an ac-

[7] For the history of the Reformation in this reign see R. W. Dixon, *History of the
Church of England from the Abolition of the Roman Jurisdiction* (3d ed., rev.; 6 vols.;
Oxford, 1895); C. H. Smyth, *Cranmer and the Reformation under Edward VI* (Cam-
bridge, 1926); N. Pocock, "The Condition of Morals and Religious Belief in the Reign
of Edward VI," *EHR*, X (1895), 417–44; "Preparations for the First Prayer Book of
Edward VI," *Church Quarterly Review*, XXXV (1892), 33–68; "Preparations for the
Second Prayer Book of Edward VI," *ibid.*, XXXVII (1893), 137–66.

ceptance of the Interim or a modification of it. Accordingly, there were few Lutheran exiles who came to England, and there was a corresponding waning of Lutheran interest in co-operating with the more outspoken Protestants. Melanchthon never made the English trip, and the scheme for a Protestant general council fell through.[8]

The failure of the Wittenberg theologian to exert himself for Cranmer's scheme completed the ruin of the Lutheran cause in England. Already it was handicapped by the obscurity of its doctrine of the supper, the inaccessability of its German bases, the death of Luther, and recent political reverses. Yet it had the prestige of being the original form of Protestantism, and the potential political strength of its supporters among the German princes was much greater than that of the Swiss and Rhenish city-states. Now that the English government, freed from the repressive conservatism of Henry, was prepared to move forward with a constructive Protestant program, it is not improbable that the presence of the greatest living Lutheran would have turned the balance in favor of his party, or at least have insured it a fair share of influence in the new regime across the channel. As it was, England perforce found its way into the Reformed camp. Vestigial traces of Lutheranism remained here and there, it is true, but for all practical purposes Protestant England, both official and unofficial, is Reformed England for the next generation at least. Its theology is Reformed, its ideal of discipline is Reformed, even its church government can be made to fit the Reformed pattern. Anglican bishops repeatedly assured their Continental friends that they were directing a Reformed system. For there were several kinds of Reformed churches. There is a difference between one in which there still remained some of what Calvin called "tolerable foolish things" and a church "thoroughly" Reformed, but both are Reformed churches. The issue, indeed, on which Anglican and Puritan contended was not whether the church should be Reformed or not, but how far it should be Reformed. It was a struggle between parties within the Reformed circle.

[8] John T. McNeill, *Unitive Protestantism* (New York, 1930), pp. 221–40.

Thus the elimination of Lutheran influences from the sphere of English Protestantism, while unfortunate enough, did not involve as much narrowing of outlook and range of interests as might be expected. Within the bounds of the Reformed territory the spirit of internationalism still flourished and the objective of a general council was still kept in view. Within those bounds there was room for wide differences of opinion on important matters. Zwingli's followers did not see eye to eye with Calvin on the doctrine of the real presence. Bishops or superintendents were retained in some areas and not in others. Ceremonies varied widely from place to place. Most important of all, there was no general agreement on the relation of the secular authorities and the church. At Zurich all power was left in the hands of the Council, at least in theory; at Geneva that body was forced back into its medieval role, ruling the secular sphere while the church officials dominated the spiritual one, and in case of conflict of jurisdictions mutual adjustments were made. On this issue there were many controversies aside from the English one. Leo Jud raised the point at Zurich, as we have seen. Viret was eventually banished from Lausanne for similarly insisting on clerical rights of discipline. The Erastian label for the partisans of the secular ruler is a product of the controversy in the Palatinate in the 1560's.

The fact is that none of the Reformed leaders really thought this problem through, even in the second generation of the movement. In spite of their experiences with Henry VIII and his like, they could not conceive of a purely secular ruler. They could not imagine, in other words, how secularist a secular power could be. On the one side, Cranmer, Erastus himself, and later Hooker believed in an Erastianism quite different from the coldly logical variety later to be upheld by Hobbes and the enlightened despots. All the earlier disciples of this school of thought based their systems on the assumption that the magistrates were thoroughly Christian and would endeavor only to regulate ecclesiastical organization and not doctrine itself. In other words, the magistrate was conceived as an agent of God for the outward affairs of the church and as a Christian ready to listen to the advice of the clergy. In fact, in the Zwinglian form of the doctrine the rulers are so bound by Christian principles that the arrangement is virtually theocratic.[9] On the other hand, Calvin and his followers thought it possible to continue the medieval practice of amicably sharing the sovereignty with the wielders of the temporal sword. He correctly grasped the necessity of the idealist retaining political power, but he did not see that divided sovereignty was a thing of the past and that his Erastian contemporaries had correctly sensed that modern states must be more centralized and unified. Had he asked for clerical representation on the Council, as he had arranged for the Council's election of the elders, he would have made a great contribution toward the ultimate solution of the problem, though the realization of this remedy in a monarchy would be somewhat difficult. But he did not make the request, and things were allowed to drift.

For the time being, these and other differences of opinion did not prevent Englishmen of all shades of Reformed belief from co-operating in the common task. The contrasts at this time between Zwinglian and Bucerian and possibly even Lutheran ideas of the sacrament were not so sharp as later historians have tended to make them. On occasion, Zwingli had granted that there was somewhat more in the bread and wine than bare signs,[10] and by keeping this in mind the reformers avoided quarrels on that point. Positions were found for the more prominent refugees. Knox was sent to Berwick to preach the new gospel and keep an eye on the affairs of his native country.[11] Martyr became Regius Professor of Divinity at Oxford in March, 1548, and Bucer was given the corresponding position at Cambridge the next year. French Protestants were permitted to

[9] Alfred Farner, *Die Lehre von Kirche und Staat bei Zwingli* (Tübingen, 1930), pp. 129–34; W. T. Hobhouse, *The Church and World in Idea and in History* (London, 1916), p. 228.

[10] McNeill, *op. cit.*, pp. 228–29. Hooper is insistent that the sacraments were more than bare signs: "Far be such a belief from the most unlearned Christian" (Hooper to Bucer, June 19, 1548, *Original Letters*, p. 47).

[11] For Knox's career in England see Peter Lorimer, *John Knox and the Church of England* (London, 1875).

have their own churches at Lambeth and in London.[12] The returning English exiles gradually found places commensurate with their talents. Coverdale became chaplain to the King, and Traheron was made royal librarian and tutor to the young Duke of Suffolk. Turner became physician and chaplain to Somerset himself. In 1550 he was given a prebend at York and in December appointed Dean of Wells, though not yet in priests' orders.[13] Bale secured a living in Hampshire, and Rogers was made rector of St. Matthew's, Friday Street, in London. These men fitted quietly into the Edwardian scene, and except for occasional promotions, such as those which made bishops of Bale and Coverdale, they attracted no particular attention during this reign, though we may be sure their influence was on the side of the ardent Protestants.

Among the reformers of all schools there was a fundamental agreement on the necessity of abolishing specifically Roman Catholic institutions, such as the belief in transubstantiation and clerical celibacy. In the first two years of the new reign they succeeded in bringing about a general suppression of Catholic practices. Injunctions and prescribed homilies of a Protestant hue were issued by the government, and these great gains were confirmed in the Prayer Book of 1549 and an accompanying Act of Uniformity. The strenuous efforts necessary to effect this destructive part of the reformer's program so preoccupied them during the early years that not until 1550 did important differences of opinion appear among them. Even then a breach might have been avoided without the sacrifice of principle, had the more advanced thinkers been able to exercise a little moderation. Time and the flood of foreign influence were on their side. Men who had never known the experience of exile were coming to support more and more purging of the old system. Cranmer himself was not unwilling to set up a system of ecclesiastical discipline which would, in fact,

[12] Baron F. de Schickler, *Les Eglises du refuge en Angleterre* (3 vols.; Paris, 1892), I, 8, 26.

[13] The details of Turner's job-hunting maneuvers may be read in the State Papers, Domestic, Edward VI, Vol. VII, No. 32, and Vol. XIII, Nos. 1, 4, and 19 (*Calendar, 1547–80*, pp. 18, 32–33).

have strengthened the hand of the church against the magistrate. One of his favorite projects during this reign was a revision of the canon law by which the rights of the new-old
church would be safeguarded and her powers strengthened.
Had the zealous Protestants been conciliatory in their dealings
with him and his supporters, a powerful ecclesiastical party
might have been built up, and it is not impossible that the
Anglicans might have been won over to the cause of a quasi-
autonomous international Protestant church, as they were to
the Reformed doctrine of the eucharist.

Unfortunately, the leadership of the Continental party was
taken by one who was neither a statesman nor a diplomat but
a violent and erratic partisan. Years of exile do not sweeten
dispositions, and Hooper had spent some of his time abroad
in the stronghold of Zwinglian controversialists. Before he left
the mainland he was referring to the Strassburg group, with their
mediating view on the sacrament, as Lutherans.[14] Arriving in
London, where he joined Turner as a chaplain to Somerset, he
plunged at once into all available frays. He held liberal views
on divorce and defended them with great vigor; he was one
of the accusers of Bonner when that prelate was deprived of
his bishopric; he quarreled with Traheron over predestination.
But he also made a name for himself as a preacher. He lectured
at least once a day, and often the audience overflowed the city
church in which he spoke.[15] As a result, he was ordered to
preach before the court on the Wednesdays during Lent of
1550. For this series he took the Book of Jonah as his theme
because it enabled him "freely to touch upon the duties of individuals."[16] On the appearance of a new ordinal, prepared under
Cranmer's auspices, he was most tactless. He was incensed at
the requirement that the candidates should swear by the saints
when they accepted the royal supremacy, and the regulation
that they should appear in white vestments also smelled of
popery to him.

The institution of distinctive clerical dress in the Christian

---

[14] Hooper to Bullinger, April 26, 1549, *Original Letters*, p. 61.
[15] Hooper to Bullinger, February 5, 1550, *ibid.*, p. 75.   [16] *Ibid.*

church dates from the Middle Ages. Most of the garments were originally part of the ordinary lay attire in the twelfth and thirteenth centuries. But, like many other established institutions, such as the bar, the universities, and the liveried companies, the church tended to be conservative in the matter of costume. It retained the old garb long after styles had changed, until it came to be regarded as a distinctive ecclesiastical dress. A good example of this development is the modern nun's wimple which may be seen in medieval illustration as the headdress of women of all classes. By the sixteenth century it was generally understood in the Catholic church that the clergy should be so clothed on all occasions as to be easily distinguishable from laymen. No rigid rules had as yet been laid down for these clerical costumes, and in practice there was much variation.[17] The authorities were commonly satisfied if the clergy wore "sad" and "becoming" costumes. For appearances outside church this usually meant the wearing of a black gown and pilatus, or four-cornered cap of the modern academic variety, though often without the square stiffening material. When officiating at services other than the mass, the priest or deacon wore a loose white gown called a surplice. When about to administer the sacrament, he exchanged this for a somewhat tighter-fitting garment, called an alb, and an overgown with the outlines of a large cross embroidered on the back, called a chasuble. Bishops wore white linen sleeves on their street gown, called a chimere, and under it a tighter-fitting white garment called a rochet which also served them as a surplice. The system was calculated not only to lend color and dignity to the services of the church but to provide a visual demonstration of the Catholic doctrine that the clergy were a peculiar people, a class set apart from ordinary men.

Following the principle that all things might be tolerated which were not condemned by Scripture, Luther and his follow-

[17] T. A. Lacey, "The Ecclesiastical Habit in England," *Transactions of St. Paul's Ecclesiological Society*, IV (1896–1900), 126–34; N. F. Robinson, "The Black Chimere of Anglican Prelates," *Transactions of St. Paul's Ecclesiological Society*, IV (1896–1900), 180–220; "The Pileus Quadratus," *ibid.*, V (1901–5), 1–16; H. J. Clayton, *Cassock and Gown* ("Alcuin Club Tracts" No. XVIII [Oxford, 1929]).

ers retained most of the traditional clerical costume, along with many other ecclesiastical ceremonies. But to many zealous reformers this seemed incompatible with the Protestant doctrine of the priesthood of all believers. In Switzerland, where the effort was made to purge ecclesiastical worship of all Roman taints, the distinctive dress was generally abandoned, and the clergy preached in the full black gown which was then the common dress of the academic and professional classes, though in the course of time it also became the peculiar church attire of the Protestant clergy. Hooper's protest against the traditional garb was therefore more than a mere quibble about a piece of cloth. It involved the speeding-up of the reformation process, a sharper break with the Roman churches, and an outward recognition of the priesthood of all believers. Most of all, it was an effort, whether conscious or not, to bring the English church more clearly into line with the one Continental Protestant group which gave signs of rising above national limitations to something of the power and grandeur of its medieval predecessor. It was an appeal from the narrowing Erastianism of England to something better. In the long run there was far more promise in this program than in Cranmer's impractical dream of a Protestant council under secular auspices, which to be successful required harmony among rival princes as well as the clergy.

But it was a matter which required careful handling. Cranmer had not been abroad for more than fifteen years, and he had become so accustomed to peculiarly English institutions of worship that he saw little need for international conformity in that regard. Furthermore, there was now arising a new generation of English Protestant bishops who had been brought up in the new national tradition. Like Nicholas Ridley, recently transferred from Rochester to London, who had never been abroad, they duly reflected their insular background. They saw no reason to imitate foreign ways, and they were naturally jealous of their powers, resenting keenly any attempt to modify or limit them. Nevertheless, they were anxious to forward the Protestant cause—"a pious and learned man" was Hooper's estimate of Ridley at this time[18]—and with diplomatic handling might have been brought around to appreciating the weight of the Continental arguments.

Unfortunately, diplomacy was not Hooper's strong point. Though he granted that the vestments required in the ordinal were "tolerable things" and "to be borne with for the weak's sake awhile,"[19] instead of quietly negotiating with Cranmer about them, with a view to the adoption of purer forms in a later edition of the ordinal, he sarcastically denounced them from the court pulpit while commenting on the duties of those in authority, as illustrated by the throwing of Jonah into the sea.

> And how it is suffered, or who is the author of that book I well know not. I am led to think it to be the fault of the corrector in the printing. . . . ? Where and of whom and when have they learned that he that is called to the ministry of God's word should hold the bread and chalice in one hand and the book in the other hand? Why do they not as well give him in his hand the fount and the water? For the one is a sacrament as well as the other.[20]

Naturally incensed, Cranmer complained to the Council, but Somerset was now out of prison, and his fortunes were once more rising. His protégé went unpunished,[21] and at Easter the King and Council offered him the bishopric of the recently created see of Gloucester. Hooper had no objection to the institution of episcopacy, but he refused to serve unless the offensive ceremonies were eliminated from his consecration rites. He would not be made a magpie, as Christopher Hales remarked,[22] referring to the color of the chimere.

On the matter of the oath there was little difficulty. "What wickedness is here, Hooper? Are these offices ordained in the name of the saints or of God?" said the young King, striking

---

[18] Hooper to Bullinger, March 27, 1550, *Original Letters*, p. 79.

[19] *Sermons on Jonas*, in his *Early Writings*, ed. Carr (Cambridge: Parker Society, 1843), p. 479.

[20] *Ibid.*

[21] Hooper to Bullinger, March 27, 1550, *Original Letters*, p. 81.

[22] Hales to Gualter, May 24, 1550, *ibid.*, p. 187.

out the offending words with his own pen.[23] To this the bishops made no objection, for no doubt the retention of the obsolete phraseology had been something of an oversight. But in the matter of the vestments they saw their chance to even the score with the bishop-elect. When the Council sent a letter authorizing them to consecrate without the required ceremonies, they refused, through their spokesman, Ridley, to employ any but the form prescribed by Parliament.[24] This was a mere pretext on their part, for in 1548, Cranmer, Ridley, and Holbeach had consecrated Robert Ferrar, or Farrar, Bishop of St. David's with a form quite different from the one then legally established.[25] Furthermore, at the height of the controversy with Hooper, Ridley ordained as deacons two men who also scrupled at the ceremonies; John Bradford, the Marian Martyr, and Thomas Sampson, who had married Latimer's niece, and who was to be famous as a Puritan under Elizabeth.[26] The whole trend of the Edwardian reformation was toward simplicity, and a further step in that direction would have facilitated Cranmer's conciliar project.

But long-run considerations of statesmanship follow logic and consistency out the window when personal feelings are roused.

[23] John ab Ulmis to Bullinger, August 22, 1550, *ibid.*, p. 416.

[24] Micronius to Bullinger, August 28, 1550, *ibid.*, p. 567.

[25] John Strype, *Memorials of . . . . Thomas Cranmer* (2 vols.; Oxford, 1812), I, 261. W. H. Frere (*The Marian Reaction* [London, 1896], p. 111) states that the only variations were in the mass, not the consecration. But Parker (writing to Cecil, April 28, 1566, *Correspondence*, ed. Bruce [Cambridge: Parker Society, 1853], pp. 280–81) refers to Cranmer's laboring with Ferrar as though about vestments, and certainly he refused to wear the cap after he became bishop, for that was one of the charges made against him by George Constantine in 1552 (Foxe, *op. cit.*, VII, 8). Even if the variation in the ordination ceremonies were only in the language of the mass, however, the principle remains unchanged, in that Ridley was a party to an illegal service, since the Latin mass was still required for the clergy at that time.

[26] Strype, *Memorials* (3 vols. in 6; Oxford, 1822), II, i, 403; *Cranmer*, I, 273; Foxe, *op. cit.*, VII, 143–44. The dating of Sampson's ordination as 1549 in Strype's *Cranmer* is an obvious error, confuted by the accurate date in the *Memorials* and by the fact that in 1549 Ridley was still Bishop of Rochester.

In the summer of 1551 Ridley boasted of his good fortune in securing as a prebendary of St. Paul's John Rogers, who, according to Foxe, never wore any cap but a round one all through the period of the Edwardian vestment controversy (Foxe, *op. cit.*, VI, 610–11; J. L. Chester, *John Rogers* [London, 1861], pp. 79–80; cf. *Puritan Manifestoes*, ed. Frere and Douglas [London, 1907], p. 112).

As autumn followed summer there were stormy scenes at the
Council board and wrathful exchanges of controversial treatises. The rationalizations adopted by both sides were a sufficiently sorry lot. Ridley maintained that the ceremonies were
adiaphora, things indifferent, that is not essential to salvation
one way or another.[27] But instead of granting, therefore, that
they need not be exacted, he maintained that this fact merely
took the force out of Hooper's objections, because the magistrate might rule in such matters. The Puritan, who had so recently asserted that these ceremonies might be borne for the
time, now felt constrained to declare that they were not things
indifferent, and submitted a confused and ill-tempered brief to
prove his point.[28] Ridley responded with a masterpiece of destructive criticism and then gave his case away at the end by
offering to do the very thing at which he had first balked.
Denying the charge that he regarded the vestments as necessary, he made this surprising offer:

> Let him [Hooper] revoke his errors, and agree and subscribe to the doctrine
> and not to condemn [sic] that for sin that God never forbade, ungodly adding
> unto God's word, and I shall not, for any necessity that I put in these vest-
> ments, let to lay my hands upon him and to admit him bishop, although he
> come, as he useth to ride, in a merchant's cloak, having the king's majesty's
> dispensation for the act and my lord archbishop's commission orderly to do
> the thing.[29]

But in a political struggle innuendo and scandalous charges
are much more to the point than logic. At those games Hooper
made a real effort, but still came off a decidedly second best.
He called the Anglican party "masking, dreaming, children of
this world, superstitious and blind, papists" conspiring with
papists to keep England in superstition, and he warned the
Council that the bishops were their enemies. But in the process
he gave his adversary some fatal openings. At one point he
told the royal advisers that the whole matter was beyond their

[27] Micronius to Bullinger, August 28, 1550, *Original Letters*, p. 567.

[28] See Appen. I for a reconstruction of Hooper's theological argument and a summary of Ridley's reply.

[29] John Bradford, *Writings*, ed. Townsend (2 vols.; Cambridge: Parker Society,
1848-53), II, 390.

jurisdiction. He talked vaguely of tyranny in the requirement of the ceremonies, and elsewhere he touched on the rights of individual consciences. Though he ended with an admission that the sovereign might institute ceremonies in the church if they were not derived from Catholicism,[30] Ridley leaped upon the earlier passages and made the welkin ring with cries of Anabaptism, the bolshevism of his time. If the Scripture be the only guide, we must abandon our churches, worship in homes, and baptize in the fields because the Apostles did so. We must follow the Anabaptist model and give up our property, because the early disciples left all to follow the Master. We must practice adult baptism. "Oh wicked folly and blind ignorancy!"[31] To Ridley a demonstration that a thing smacked of Anabaptism was equivalent to a triumphant *reductio ad absurdum*.

If this be received, who shall in the order of the church regard either the commandment of the king or of his council, either parliament, prelate or any other ordinary power, whatsoever they command, not commanded in scripture, though else it be never so good? And the aforesaid sentence—as a thing which is a subversion of good order, wholesome discipline and obedience, and of other many godly ordinances made for the amendment of people's manners, as the case diversely doth require—and as also the very root and well-spring of much stubborness and obstinacy, sedition and disobedience of the younger sort against their elders, contrary unto St. Peter's doctrine—I suppose no good man that is wise will or can allow.[32]

Hooper's cause was now lost. The Council ordered him to keep his house and to refrain from preaching. He appealed to the foreign divines, Bucer and Martyr, for their judgment, but they replied that, while they would like to see the ceremonies abolished, they did not deem it wise to press the matter for the time being.[33] Even Calvin took the same stand.[34] Of the prominent theologians only Bullinger and à Lasco supported

[30] *Ibid.*, pp. 378–79, 392.

[31] *Ibid.*, pp. 382–83.   [32] *Ibid.*, p. 392 and Corrigenda, p. 408.

[33] Martyr to Hooper, November 4, 1550, in George C. Gorham, *Gleanings of a Few Scattered Ears during the Period of the Reformation in England* (London, 1857), pp. 187–96; Strype, *Cranmer*, I, 304–7; Bucer to Hooper, n.d., Gorham, *Gleanings*, pp. 200–209; Strype, *Memorials*, II, ii, 455–65.

[34] Calvin to Bullinger, March 12, 1551, in Gorham's *Gleanings*, pp. 241–43.

their embattled friend. In vain Hooper published a confession
of his faith, designed to refute the charge of Anabaptism.[35] It
went through two editions in a few days, but the Council considered it a breach of their order. Hooper was committed to
custody, first in Cranmer's household, where the Archbishop
reasoned with him, and later in the Fleet prison. During the
heat of the controversy the bishop-elect had promised to maintain his position "unto death," whereupon Ridley shrewdly remarked, "We have seen oftentimes great clouds and small rain,
and heard great cracks of thunder and . . . . small harm done."[36]
He was right. There was very little substance, indeed, behind
the big words. On February 15, 1551, after less than three
weeks in prison Hooper professed himself converted to the belief that the vestments were things indifferent, of which only
the abuse and not the proper use was impious.[37] On March 8
he was consecrated in Lambeth in the usual fashion, and afterward preached before the King in white rochet and scarlet
chimere. "Upon his head he had a geometrical, that is, a four-
squared cap, albeit his head was round. What cause of shame
the strangeness hereof was that day to that good preacher,"
says Foxe, "every man may easily judge."[38] The thoroughness
of his conversion may be judged by the fact that, though he was
required to wear the prescribed costume at his ordination and
whenever he preached "before the King, or in his cathedral,
or in any other public place," he secured permission to dress
as he chose on other occasions.[39]

Inadequate leadership, a weakness which for some mysterious
reason—possibly the overwhelming strength of the opposing
Tudor monarchy—was to beset the Puritan party in England
throughout its history, had cost the advanced reformers the first

[35] *A Godly Confession and Protestation of the Christian Faith*, in Hooper, *Later
Writings*, ed. Nevinson (Cambridge: Parker Society, 1852), pp. 65–92.

[36] Bradford, *op. cit.*, p. 380.

[37] Hooper to Cranmer, February 15, 1551, in Hooper, *Later Writings*, p. xv.

[38] *Op. cit.*, VI, 641.

[39] Gilbert Burnet, *History of the Reformation*, ed. Pocock (7 vols.; Oxford, 1865), II,
286.

round in this long struggle. But in a subsidiary encounter some
slight progress was made. As we have seen, a French Protestant congregation had been holding services in London since
1548. The Flemish and Germans were desirous of having a
similar arrangement, and, with the arrival of à Lasco in May,
1550, the matter of the foreign refugees was pressed upon the
attention of the Council, probably by Hooper, who was then in
their good graces. On July 24—after Hooper's nomination as
bishop and before Ridley had won over the Council to his point
of view on the vestments—the church of the Augustinian friars,
abandoned since the dissolution, was made over to them by a
royal letter patent, and the Polish former bishop was appointed
superintendent of the two congregations. By the same document the municipal and ecclesiastical authorities were charged
to

permit the aforesaid, the superintendent, and ministers and their successors,
freely and peacefully to enjoy, use, and exercise their own rites and ceremonies and their own peculiar ecclesiastical discipline, notwithstanding that
they do not agree with the rites and ceremonies customary in our kingdom,
without impeachment, molestation, or disturbance of them, or any one of
them, by any statute, act, proclamation, injunction, restraint, or use to the
contrary previously made.[40]

Ridley and his associates, already alarmed by Hooper's stand
and also, no doubt, by à Lasco's support of him, did all in their
power to block the establishment of the Reformed discipline
within the diocese of London. The governmental restoration
and repair of the Jesus Temple, as the edifice was now called,
was deliberately delayed. Paulet, the Lord Treasurer, to whom
à Lasco complained, reasoned with him on the lawfulness of
the English forms and gave him no help.[41] Another building
was secured, however, and in October a Reformed constitution
was adopted.[42] But the bishops continued to oppose the project, and in the summer of 1551 the right of administering the
sacrament was still withheld.[43] In the fall the King came to à

[40] *Ibid.*, V, 305–8. The English translation of this document is in Smyth, *op. cit.*,
p. 198.

[41] Micronius to Bullinger, August 31, 1550, *Original Letters*, p. 569.

[42] Micronius to Bullinger, October 13, 1550, *ibid.*, p. 570.

[43] Utenhove to Bullinger, April 9, 1551, *ibid.*, p. 586–87.

Lasco's support, and the disputed privilege was conceded. Un-reconciled, the ecclesiastical authorities in 1552 arrested some of the foreigners for not attending their parish churches. But eventually this difficulty was adjusted, and for the few remaining months of Edward's reign the autonomy of à Lasco's church was recognized.[44] During all these troubles the foreigners' church grew and flourished. It was necessary to secure a second building for the use of the Flemish-German congregation, and arrangements were made to obtain the chapel and sacristy of the hospital of St. Anthony in Threadneedle Street, probably the substitute edifice referred to before.[45] An Italian congregation was formed in the spring of 1551 and included in the autonomous church. Thus there were three congregations in one church, not three separate bodies.[46] By 1553 the foreigners' church was so well established that no foreigner could secure the rights of an English citizen without previously having made a satisfactory confession of his faith to the ministers of this body.[47] In 1551 a similar semi-independent arrangement had been perfected for the French and Walloon linen workers whom Somerset had settled at Glastonbury. Poullain became their minister and soon published a service-book for his congregation which shows them to have been a Reformed group after the Strassburg order.[48]

According to à Lasco's account, written at a later date, the purpose of the King and Council in permitting these variations from the official order was to set an example to the country of the further reform which was to be instituted as soon as the ground was prepared for it.[49] The spectacle of German-,

[44] Micronius to Bullinger, August 14, 1551, *ibid.*, p. 575. For the details of the controversy and the later history of the church see Schickler, *op. cit.*, I, 33–35; Smyth, *op. cit.*, pp. 198–201; and Dalton, *op. cit.*, pp. 334–413.

[45] The permanent agreement for its use was dated October 16, 1550, three days after Micronius' letter announcing the securing of the alternative meeting place (Schickler, *op. cit.*, I, 36).

[46] *Ibid.*, p. 37.   [47] Micronius to Bullinger, February 18, 1553, *Original Letters*, p. 581.

[48] V. Poullain, *Ordre des prières ... en l'église de Glastonbury* (London, 1552); Schickler, *op. cit.*, I, 59–67, and Bauer, *op. cit.*, pp. 148–68.

[49] John à Lasco, *Forma ac ratio tota ecclesiastici ministerii, in peregrinorum potissimum vero Germanorum ecclesia* (Frankfort, 1555; Dedication to King Sigismund of Poland); *Opera*, ed. Kuyper (2 vols.; Amsterdam, 1866), II, 10.

French-, and Italian-speaking Christians working together in
harmony under a single constitution should indeed have been
an inspiring sight and an incentive to further efforts in the
cause of that international Protestant unity to which the Puritans were committed.

The internal organization of the church is even more important, for in spite of some minor differences it was typical
of the Reformed ideal which the Puritans were to struggle so
long and hard to make the official English system. It thus reflects the appearance for the first time on English soil of another
fundamental Puritan characteristic.

This organization involved a nice combination of clerical
leadership and lay responsibility, all designed to produce a
people at the same time intelligent and disciplined, a community united in the service of a common principle. In this
scheme the clergy retained most of the powers they had enjoyed in the Catholic church. They could control elections,
decide on excommunications, and determine the attitude of the
church courts as before. But little of this power was due to
any assumption of special status or to a claim of sacrosanct character for their order. Rather it depended on the respect they
commanded for their learning and devotion and on their pulpit
influence. The members of their congregations were made to
feel that the laity were an essential part of the church. Provision was made for carefully instructing and effectively disciplining the rank and file, so that they might be fit to share in
the direction of their organization. They were allowed a voice
in the selection of church officers, and these officials were nearly
always associated with the professional clergy in the performance of the ministers' functions. In the exercise of ecclesiastical
discipline lay officials were theoretically as important as the
preaching clergy. Technically, in fact, the ruling elders were
ordained in precisely the same way as the occupants of the pulpit and had the same standing. It was this attention given to
the layman, and the responsibility put upon him, that made the
Reformed churches such efficient instruments for the inculcation
of religious attitudes. If the Calvinists eventually became more

diligent in business than their fellow-Christians, the historian, in accounting for this fact, might do well to pay more attention to their peculiar system of church government and discipline, and less to their doctrine of predestination, which was held in common by most of their Protestant contemporaries during this period.

To be specific, all foreign refugees were not automatically members of the London church. They must enter, either by infant baptism and catechetical instruction or, if mature, by giving evidence of their knowledge of the elements of the Reformed faith and promising to lead a Christian life. Theological instruction did not end with admission to the group. On the contrary, some time was devoted to it in one of the services each Sunday.[50]

À Lasco's church was provided with only two orders of clergy, deacons and elders, or presbyters, to use the Greek word. The deacons were officers elected annually, charged with the duty of looking after the poor. The elders were the important officials, elected for life. They were divided into two classes: the ruling, or disciplinary; and the preaching, or teaching. Only the latter were paid for their work, and one of them acted as superintendent of all the congregations in the community. He was *primus inter pares*, first only in point of responsibility to guard the welfare of the church, but not in his preaching or disciplinary function. Theoretically, at least, his colleagues might outvote him when excommunications were being considered. When vacancies occurred in these official positions, the congregations nominated several candidates from whom the existing officials made a choice, which was submitted to the congregation for final approval. Pure democratic procedure was avoided as tending to tumult and hence to excessive state interference. According to the terms of the letters patent in this particular case, however, the crown was also to give its approval to the

[50] This description of the organization, discipline, and worship of the foreigners' church in London is summarized from à Lasco's *Forma ac ratio*, in his *Opera*, II, 1–277; a French translation was published by Giles Clematius in 1556 under the title *Toute la forme et manière du ministère ecclésiastique en l'esglise des estrangers dressée à Londres en Angleterre l'an après l'incarnation de Christ 1550.*

preaching elders selected. Once a month the officers of all the congregations gathered in a meeting called a coetus, the forerunner of the later presbytery, though as yet their meetings appear to have been for spiritual edification rather than for the transaction of business routine.

The discipline of the group was taken very seriously and produced corresponding results. Communion was held the first Sunday of the month and was preceded by a service of preparation at which attendance was required. Here the religious life of the community was examined by the elders, and a list of those fit to receive the sacrament was drawn up. Formal excommunication was not used until private interviews and public hearings had failed to produce the desired obedience. It was then pronounced by the elders, with the approval of the congregation, and was a solemn thing, excluding the offender from receiving the sacrament but not from the service where it was administered. Until he repented, he was to be treated as an unbeliever and avoided socially, but so far as the church was concerned he retained civil and commercial rights. Children who refused to confirm their baptismal vows and receive communion were, however, to be reported to the magistrates for punishment. The clergy themselves were subject to discipline. Once every three months there was a meeting at which any member of the church might lodge complaints against any of them. These were carefully considered by the remaining officers of the congregations, and reprimands and even sentences of deposition might result. An iron discipline it was; but, when allowed to operate, it produced men of the same quality, capable of standing up to crowned monarchs without flinching.

The meetings of the church were designed to produce an intelligent worship and an informed congregation. The Sunday morning service consisted of a short prayer, followed by the Lord's Prayer, a psalm sung without organ accompaniment, a sermon, additional prayers interspersed with the recitation of the Ten Commandments, and the Apostles' Creed. Then followed any additional services fixed for that day, such as marriages, baptisms, or communion, in the last of which the participants were seated around the sacred table. The sermons lasted an hour and were purely expository. The plan was to proceed through different books of the Bible in methodical fashion, taking successive passages for treatment on consecutive Sundays. In addition to the morning gathering, there was another in the afternoon for public exposition of the faith. This took the form of a commentary on the catechism, in the case of the Flemish church a composition of à Lasco translated by Utenhove; in the French church, probably one of Calvin's. During the week, in each congregation there were two other gatherings for spiritual edification, called prophesyings. These were devoted to resolving doubts and reviewing the Sunday morning sermons. Ministers added further to their exposition of the Scriptures, and were followed by elders, deacons, or other members of the congregation who might be chosen to add comments. Elsewhere in the discipline provision was also made for visiting the sick and for a simple funeral service.

Few of the hopes that this church would furnish a model for the English establishment were realized, but some progress was made, as the 1552 Prayer Book shows. In that volume, probably drawn up by much the same group of thirty-two churchmen and lawyers who prepared the abortive revision of the canon law, the alb and chasuble were quietly eliminated, and the sacrament took on a Zwinglian form. Some have doubted whether Cranmer was entirely pleased by the result,[51] but in the main he must have been satisfied, since the alteration of conservative passages in the communion service cut the ground from under the imprisoned Gardiner's claim that the book did not exclude the possibility of a Catholic interpretation. But he did not wish to go farther in a Protestant direction, and the fact that the final form of the book did represent still another advance is largely the work of John Knox. The irrepressible Scot had spent two years in Berwick and two more in Newcastle. At the border town he had met his future wife, Marjory Bowes, whose mother's religious melancholia was so sorely to test his patience and pastoral skill. But that was merely a side

51 Smyth, *op. cit.*, pp. 248–50.

issue. In both towns Knox had acquired a great reputation as a Protestant preacher. He had evangelized the whole border, and had boldly employed the Swiss method of administering the sacrament with the recipients seated. In the winter of 1551–52 he became one of the six royal chaplains appointed to preach before the King and to do itinerant work as well. This gave him an opportunity of championing his cause in a wider sphere. In 1550 Hooper and à Lasco had raised a protest against the practice of kneeling at the communion, because the posture was a worshiping one and thus one that suggested an idolatrous attitude toward the elements, that is, belief in the doctrine of transubstantiation.[52] While the 1552 Prayer Book was in the course of preparation, the same points were raised, probably by Hooper once more, but without success. When Knox was asked to preach at court in the autumn, however, he seized his opportunity and denounced the kneeling posture, which was for the first time definitely prescribed by the new book. Knox was a more able man than Hooper, and his sermon produced immediate results. The Council asked Cranmer, Ridley, and Martyr to reconsider this point, although the book was already approved by Parliament. Thereupon, Cranmer, the administrator, temporarily forgot his international conciliar schemes. In considerable heat, he responded with the old cry of Anabaptism and sedition:

I trust ye will not be moved by these glorious and unquiet spirits, which can like nothing but that is after their own fancy, and cease not to make trouble and disquietness when things be most quiet and in good order. If such men should be heard, although the Book were made every year anew, yet should it not lack faults in their opinion.

But, say they, it is not commanded in the Scripture to kneel, and whatsoever is not commanded in the Scripture is against the Scripture and utterly unlawful and ungodly. But this saying is the chief foundation of the error of the Anabaptists and of divers other sects. This saying is a subversion of all order, as well in religion as in common policy.[53]

[52] Hooper, *Sermons on Jonas*, in *Early Writings*, p. 635; à Lasco to Cranmer, n.d., *Opera*, pp. 665–62.

[53] Cranmer to the Council, October 7, 1552, in Lorimer, *John Knox and the Church of England*, pp. 103–5, esp. p. 104.

Knox and his supporters avoided the force of this argument, once so effective, perhaps because they were not so extreme in their attitude as Hooper had been. But they were persistent. When a few days later the royal chaplains were asked to comment on the proposed creed of Forty-two Articles, one of which declared that the ceremonies of the established church were not repugnant "to the wholesome liberty of the Gospel," the Puritans made the best use of this opening and rammed home another charge. Knox and one or more associates submitted a memorandum, largely embodying à Lasco's ideas on the subject, once more attacking the kneeling rubric.[54] This had the desired result, and Knox secured most of his objective. Though the practice of kneeling was retained, the Archbishop was ordered by the Council to insert an explanatory declaration in the completed volume. This was what High Churchmen later dubbed the "Black Rubric," an express statement that the action in question did not imply any belief in the doctrine of transubstantiation. A natural accompaniment of this victory was the elimination from the Articles of the offending phrase about the ceremonies.

The difference between Hooper and Knox is well illustrated by the Scotchman's attitude toward the objectionable requirements which remained. Writing to his old congregation at Berwick shortly after the decision in the matter of the Prayer Book, he reiterates his conviction that the sitting posture is the better, but recommends and justifies conformity to the new regulation as a ceremonial matter expressly divorced from any superstitious belief.

Because I am but one, having in my contrair magistrates, common order, and judgments of many learned, I am not minded, for maintenance of that one thing, to gainstand the magistrates, in all other and chief points of religion agreeing with Christ and his true doctrine; nor yet to break nor trouble common order thought meet to be kept for unity and peace in the congregation for a time; and least of all intend I to damn or lightly regard the grave judgments of such men as unfeignedly I fear, love, and will obey in all things by them judged expedient to promote God's glory. . . . .

It is not fear of corporal punishment, but the only fear that Christian

[54] *Ibid.*, pp. 107–18 and 267–89.

charity be violated and broken, that suadeth and moves me to give place in this behalf. Albeit I could, with all soberness and obedience, shew causes reasonable why sitting at the Lord's Table is to be preferred unto kneeling, yet if the upper powers, not admitting the same, would execute upon me the penalty of their law (because they may not suffer a common order to be violated), assuredly Christian charity was broken and dissolved upon the one part, either by me, that, for so small a matter, obstinately would gain-stand such magistrates as profess themselves earnest promoters of Christ's Gospel; or else by them, that, persuaded by some manlye [human] reasons of certain danger to follow if common order should not universally be kept in the realm, should trouble the body or stop the mouth of him that, to his knowledge, hath spoken nothing but Christ's plain verity.[55]

So, in spite of all the heat and commotion, the Puritan group remained as yet no more than the left wing of the reforming party. They created a good deal of excitement and some unpleasantness, but for this long period they continued to side with their stronger allies on major questions. Together they fought the conservatives on the right. If Cranmer wrote a book against Gardiner on the mass, so did Hooper. If Cranmer was president of the commission which deprived Bonner, Hooper was one of the denouncers of the defendant. While Ridley was changing altars into tables in his diocese, Knox was explaining to the Council of the North that the mass was idolatry. Together the two factions also fought the extremists on the left. Cranmer and Ridley might hold up pious hands in holy horror at the mere thought of Anabaptist doctrines; Hooper not only attacked them in his London sermons but also made a tour through Kent and Essex preaching against them, and in his published confession refuted their principles at length.[56] The foreigners' church in London, Puritan to all intents and purposes, did all it could, with its discipline and its careful instruction of its members, to check the sectarians.[57] Like modern communists baiting social democrats before the days of the United Front movement, the Anabaptists and Arians fought back, tormenting their less radical brethren with theological puzzles about pedobaptism and the Trinity. But so long as the

[55] Knox to the congregation of Berwick, n.d., *ibid.*, pp. 261–62.

[56] Hooper to Bullinger, June 25, 1549, and June 29, 1550, *Original Letters*, pp. 65 and 87.

[57] Micronius to Bullinger, August 14, 1551, *ibid.*, p. 574.

Puritan leaders could preach and write, they did not cease to testify against them.

The advanced reformers were also one with the Anglicans in their attitude toward powerful individuals guilty of misconduct. Hooper was abused in open court and struck in the face by a local dignitary whom he dared to summon to answer a charge of adultery. Knox in a daring court sermon compared the royal ministers to such shady biblical characters as Judas and Shebna.[58] It is true that it was Cranmer who so enraged Northumberland by his attempt to gain parliamentary sanction and enforcement for his revised code of church law that the Duke told him and his clerical supporters to mind their own business and threatened them with dire consequences unless they restrained those who dared to criticize their superiors. But Knox must have been one of those whom the irate politician had in mind on this occasion, because in the above-mentioned court sermon the Scotch reformer had suggested a similarity of character between Northumberland and David's treacherous councilor Ahithophel, and he had also refused Dudley's profferred ecclesiastical promotion to the bishopric of Rochester. Hooper indeed accepted a second, or at least an enlarged, bishopric at the hand of this disreputable character, and the church must have suffered thereby. But even if all the charges against Hooper on the Northumberland count were true, he would not lack for good Anglican company in the person of Ridley, whose see was also despoiled and who was far more closely connected with Dudley's abortive plot to alter the succession to the throne.

But if their objectives were substantially the same, the Puritans surpassed their rivals in the ardor with which they pursued these ends and the efficiency of the means adopted to attain them. In his visitation articles and in the revised canon law[59] Cranmer made provision for securing a learned and preaching clergy, but the most vigorous efforts in this direction seem to

[58] Knox, *A Faythfull Admonition unto the Professors of God's Truth in England*, in *Works*, ed. Laing (6 vols.; Edinburgh, 1895), III, 280–84.

[59] *Documentary Annals of the Reformed Church of England*, ed. E. Cardwell (2 vols.; Oxford, 1844), I, 49–59, esp. p. 53.

have been Hooper's. He has left on record accounts of actual inquisitions which extracted from the clergy of his diocese astounding confessions of ignorance.[60] Out of three hundred and eleven clergy, one hundred and seventy-one were unable to repeat the Ten Commandments, and thirty-three of these did not know where they were to be found. Thirty could not tell where the Lord's Prayer was written, and twenty-seven of them could not name its author. Ten could not even say it. Hooper took definite steps to remedy this deficiency. The clergy were required to study one book of the Bible each quarter and stand an examination upon it. They were also to be gathered together every three months for public discussion of current theological controversies.[61] Superintendents were appointed in each section of his diocese to supervise the rank and file of the clergy,[62] and an earnest appeal was made to Cecil to correct the prevailing abuse of pluralism (the holding of two or more livings by one man)[63]—a practice which naturally diminished the efficiency of the church.

The Puritans were similarly more thorough in their efforts to produce an intelligent and disciplined laity. In their visitation articles Cranmer and Ridley, repeating the words of the royal injunctions, required that the communicants should be examined as to their ability to say the Creed, the Lord's Prayer, and the Ten Commandments. Cranmer also provided for effective church courts in his canon law project, and as a kind of afterthought he allowed—possibly by way of concession to Hooper and à Lasco, who were also in the commission which drew up the document—for lay participation in the diocesan synods which were to be revived. Hooper copied some of Ridley's articles verbatim, but he added others. He not only required quarterly instruction on the elements of the Christian

[60] *Later Writings*, pp. 117–56, esp. p. 151; James Gairdner, "Bishop Hooper's Visitation of Gloucester, 1551," *EHR*, XIX (1904), 98–121, esp. pp. 98–99.

[61] *Later Writings*, pp. 131–32.   [62] Strype, *Cranmer*, I, 313.

[63] Hooper to Cecil, April 17, 1551, in P. F. Tytler, *England under the Reigns of Edward VI and Mary* (2 vols.; London, 1839), I, 365. Knox also objected to this practice ([William Whittingham], *A Brief Discourse of the Troubles at Frankfort, 1554–1558 A.D.*, ed. Arber [London, 1908], pp. 55 and 65).

faith but even saw to it that the poor who were fed daily at his charitable table should first be examined on their knowledge of these matters.[64] He also ordained that the laity should be specifically taught that "the church of God is not by God's word taken for the multitude or company of men, as of bishops, priests and such other, but that it is the company of all men hearing God's word and obeying unto the same."[65] We have noticed the emphasis which the foreigners' church in London put on congregational discipline. To Hooper and to Knox also this right of discipline, up to and including the power of excommunication, was an essential mark of the true church, without which little of profit might be accomplished. Knox told the Council that

many things were worthy of reformation in the ministry of England, without the reformation whereof no minister did discharge or could discharge his conscience before God: for no minister in England had authority to divide and separate the lepers from the heal [whole or sound] which was a chief point of his office.[66]

John Foxe, later to be famous as the martyrologist, showed his Puritan sympathies at this early date by a treatise advocating more and better church discipline, independent of the secular authorities.[67] In the administration of his dioceses, Hooper strove mightily to enforce this discipline on high and low, so far as the necessary means were available.[68] In education and congregational discipline lay the Puritans' chief hope of converting the adherents of the old religion and repressing the sectaries. They co-operated with the Anglicans in executing such Anabaptists as Joan Bocher and George van Parris—Coverdale served on the commission in the latter case[69]—but in the effort to suppress the divisive forces in their earlier stages they exerted themselves more.

[64] *Later Writings*, p. 132; Foxe, *op. cit.*, VI, 644.

[65] *Later Writings*, p. 121.   [66] *Ibid.*, pp. 125, 126–27; Knox, *Works*, III, 86.

[67] *De censura, sive excommunicatione ecclesiastica* (London, 1551).

[68] John ab Ulmis to Bullinger, December 4, 1551, *Original Letters*, p. 442.

[69] *Concilia magnae Britanniae et Hiberniae 446–1718*, ed. David Wilkins (4 vols ; London, 1737), IV, 44–45.

Finally, and most important, the Puritans were more independent of the secular government in shaping their policy. The
Bible and the example of the "best reformed churches" on the
Continent—to which they often appealed—provided them with
standards unaffected by the changing political scene about
them. If the Council or the sovereign chose to help them, so
much the better. They recognized the right of godly magistrates to regulate church order to a certain limited extent, and
did not reject such assistance. On occasion, they might compromise a bit with the secular authorities rather than stir up too
much dissension in the commonwealth. But they were by no
means dependent on them for guidance. Behind the Puritans
was the force of a rising international Protestantism.

To all outward appearances in the spring of 1553 the Puritan
party needed only time. Though multitudes, especially in the
north and west, remained loyal to the old faith and were even
willing to take the field for it, the packed audiences of the vigorous preachers of advanced reformation were producing a steady
drift to the left in the more populous areas. Name after name
of those nobles and gentry who were to be prominent Puritan
patrons in Elizabeth's time first appear on the Protestant side
in the records of this reign. Merchants, their wives, and appren-
tices, in London and the outports, cloth workers and yeomen in
obscure east-county villages—all were receiving the instruction
and catching the enthusiasm which made them such strong supporters of the new faith in later years. It is true that as yet
most of these, so far as they had an opinion on the disputed
points, were doubtless Anglican rather than Puritan in their
point of view, but the "Black Rubric" and the vestiarian changes
recorded in the 1552 Prayer Book showed the trend of the
times. Already there were rumors of a third and thoroughly
reformed prayer book to follow at a convenient interval. Still
more important was the fact that the young King had twice
supported the cause of the advanced reformers against their
more moderate rivals. When the Puritan Josiah grew up, all
would no doubt be well.

CHAPTER V

The Conservative Terror

THE reformer's hope for a progressively more thorough reformation was doomed to disappointment. Edward's frail physique proved incapable of supporting the burden put upon it by a crowded program of studies, and in the spring of 1553 it became evident that he was dying of tuberculosis. Northumberland's effort to divert the crown from the Catholic heiress was a ludicrous failure. In July, Mary took the throne. The most devoted and conscientious of the Tudors, she aimed to restore the old religion as soon as possible. The normal reaction from the policies of a party in power for several years, the pronounced recoil from Dudley's abortive plot, and the initial popularity of a new administration during its political honeymoon all combined to facilitate the carrying-out of her program. For the moment, Protestantism was identified with treason and Catholicism was loyalty. The two parties exchanged prison accommodations and offices. Cranmer and Ridley were arrested and confined as traitors. Three other bishops, Hooper, Coverdale, and Ferrar, and such prominent preachers as Bradford, John Rogers, John Philpot, Rowland Taylor, and Edward Crome were incarcerated on less specific accusations. Gardiner, Bonner, Heath, and Day, the prelates deprived and imprisoned in Edward's time, were restored to their sees along with Tunstall and Veysey, who had been only deprived.

But much remained to be done, and, in spite of all the political advantages she enjoyed, Mary's progress toward her religious goal was slow. Protestantism had taken deeper roots in the last twenty years than was originally suspected. The first Catholic to speak at Paul's Cross, the outdoor preaching-center for the city, had a dagger flung at him and, but for Bradford's intervention, might have been killed by the enraged audience. The fact that one out of every six clergymen in the country was deprived for being married[1] is a further indication of the widespread departure from orthodox Catholicism. No doubt, doctrinal Protestantism was mostly confined to the southeast, but Henrician precedents were strong, and the lay holdings of monastic lands constituted a strong argument against a thoroughgoing counterrevolution. Fingering his sword, Henry's great friend, John Russell, the Earl of Bedford, who had lost an eye at the sack of Morlaix and gained the great monasteries at Tavistock and Woburn, vowed he would never part with abbey lands.[2] Even Mary found it convenient for the time to make use of her Erastian Protestant heritage and exercise her powers as supreme head of the church. Though Parliament repealed in October the Edwardian legislation on the sacraments, uniformity, and priests' marriages, the acts against the Roman supremacy remained the law of the land for another year. Not until the last months of 1554 was the country legally reconciled to Rome, the medieval heresy acts restored, and the way cleared for a thoroughgoing effort to reduce the land to Catholic uniformity.

The resulting governmental measures were severe. But, before considering their effect on the Puritan party, it will be well to secure some perspective. It is true that the martyrdoms, like the presence of the Spanish retinue of Mary's husband Philip, aroused considerable opposition to the government in certain quarters. But it is a mistake to suppose that the majority of Englishmen were seriously disturbed by the executions for heresy during these years. At a time when the persecution was hottest a Protestant leader testified that his fellow-countrymen, "for the most part," were "never more careless nor maliciously merry than they are now."[3] Even among the serious-

---

[1] W. H. Frere, *The Marian Reaction* (London, 1896), p. 54.

[2] Morrice I ("A Chronological Account of Eminent Persons," Dr. Williams Library), fol. 373 (22).

[3] Bentham to Lever, July 17, 1558, in John Strype, *Ecclesiastical Memorials* (3 vols. in 6; Oxford, 1822), III, ii, 134.

minded the religious struggle was not the only one to receive attention during this period. While Protestants risked their lives in the quest of the heavenly city, London and outport traders braved the terrors of storm and pestilence in their search for earthly El Dorados. The risk run by the faithful adherents of the banned religion was slight compared to the dangers of a West African voyage from which less than a third of the crew might return. Yet boat after boat put off for the Gold Coast, defying government regulations, Portuguese men-of-war, and tropical fevers alike. Richard Chancellor, on a northeastern voyage in 1553, lost his leader and two of the expedition's three boats. Scotch traders familiar with the Arctic urged him to turn back. But

persuading himself that a man of valor could not commit a more dishonorable part than, for fear of danger, to avoid and shun great attempts, [he] was nothing at all changed or discouraged with the speeches and words of the Scots, remaining steadfast and immutable in his first resolution, determining either to bring that to pass which was intended, or else to die the death.[4]

The discovery of the Archangel route to Russia and the consequent establishment of the Muscovy Company, the first English joint-stock overseas trading enterprise, were the results of this bravery. The North Cape and the Bight of Benin tried men's souls as severely as Newgate and Smithfield.

We must also try to remember that in Tudor times, as in the Middle Ages, heresy stood on much the same level as any other crime. It was considered not only an offense against the law of the land but a menace to society. In trying to stamp out this evil, the sovereign was merely doing his or her duty by protecting susceptible subjects from endangering their souls' salvation, and also by perhaps terrifying the heretics themselves into repentance. The overwhelming majority on both sides accepted this principle. Whatever protest there may have been was not so much against the principle of religious persecution as against the direction in which the government chose to exercise this acknowledged power.[5]

[4] Richard Hakluyt, *Principal Navigations* (8 vols.; London, 1927), I, 273–74.
[5] See below, p. 150 (Trew).

But when all these qualifying remarks have been made, the fact remains that, for the conscientious Protestant minority, the repressive measures were obviously of great importance. They tested not only the sincerity and courage but also the political strength and tactical wisdom of the opposition group.

To face the storm, Anglican and Puritan naturally drew closer together. Hooper had long since been reconciled to Cranmer, in whose house he stayed while attending the late Edwardian parliaments,[6] and it is probable that Ridley did not long cherish the grudge of 1550–51.[7] Now the imprisoned bishops took pains to complete an explicit reconciliation. After two letters from Hooper, Ridley found opportunity to send a written response containing the following significant passage:

Forasmuch as I understand by your works, which I have yet but superficially seen, that we thoroughly agree and wholly consent together in those things which are the grounds and substantial points of our religion, against the which the world so furiously rageth in these our days, howsoever in time past in certain bye-matters and circumstances of religion your wisdom and my simplicity (I grant) have a little jarred, each of us following the abundance of his own sense and judgment; now, I say, be you assured that even with my whole heart, God is my witness, in the bowels of Christ I love you in the truth, and for the truth's sake which abideth in us, and, as I am persuaded, shall by the grace of God abide in us for evermore.[8]

And he went on to exhort his one-time opponent to join him in standing by their common profession to the day of dissolution.

But though martyrs of both factions died for substantially the same beliefs, the Puritan element—as befitted the more advanced reformers and the group not hampered by accusations

---

[6] Cranmer to Bullinger, March 20, 1552, *Original Letters Relative to the English Reformation*, ed. Robinson (2 vols.; Cambridge: Parker Society, 1846–47), p. 24.

[7] R. W. Dixon, *History of the Church of England from the Abolition of the Roman Jurisdiction* (6 vols.; 3d rev. ed.; Oxford, 1895), III, 256, though the evidence there cited is not conclusive. But the 1552 Prayer Book, with its simplified clerical costume, had eliminated some of the chief causes of contention. Before his death, Ridley had certainly come to accept Hooper's position on the vestments, if Foxe is to be believed. At his degradation prior to execution he is reported to have denounced the surplice and the other parts of the priest's costume as foolish and abominable, "yea, too fond for a vice in a play" (John Foxe, *Acts and Monuments*, ed. Townsend [London, 1837–41], VII, 544).

[8] Ridley to Hooper, n.d., in Foxe, *op. cit.*, VI, 642–43.

of treason growing out of the Northumberland-Grey plot—took the bolder course in the face of persecution. The conclusion of Ridley's letter to Hooper contained a rather timid request to refrain from publishing anything under his own name, lest further opportunities for writing be denied the prisoners. But the Puritans made their voice heard, regardless of Anglican advice. The one man who dared attack the mass in the convocation debate in the autumn of 1553 was John Philpot, whose lack of long gown and tippet on that occasion is sufficient evidence of his party affiliation.[9] In their examination before the new authorities the Anglicans now found their Erastianism a broken reed. But the Puritan had a more sure foundation in his allegiance to biblical authority. The case of John Rogers illustrates this point. He had never worn the offending clerical attire in Edward's day, and he looked forward to a Puritan restoration, with superintendents after the Continental manner,[10] so that his essential Puritanism cannot be doubted. In the course of his examination Rogers not only opposed scripture to the authority of the church but also, while professing to be a loyal Englishman, came out squarely against the authority of the secular government in ecclesiastical affairs.[11] This position he stated at some length in the statement which he prepared to make in court but was not permitted to deliver. Foxe naturally chose to suppress those passages when he edited the matter for publication in the early years of Elizabeth's reign, but the manuscript has fortunately been preserved.

I or any other man, having the word of God on our sides, may speak against such an act [viz., the statute restoring the papal supremacy] and ought to be heard and the parliaments to give place to the word of the ever living God and not God to the act of parliament. Of God's word there shall not one tittle perish, but it shall all be fulfilled and performed that is therein contained, and unto it must all men, king and queen, emperor, parliaments and general councils obey—and the word obeyeth no man—it cannot be changed nor altered, neither may we add or put anything thereto, nor take no thing therefrom. But the parliament or general council may be altered and changed and a con-

[9] John Philpot, *Examination and Writings*, ed. Eden (Cambridge: Parker Society, 1842), p. 213.

[10] Foxe, *op. cit.*, VI, 610–11.   [11] *Ibid.*, pp. 593–94, 600.

trary thing determined, as also there be diverse and enough examples already shewed. . . . .

If there came in twenty years ten kings of diverse religion and made ten changes in the twenty years, that is in every two year [*sic*] a change, adding I say force thereunto, they [the laity] would care for no god but turn about with the kings and every king's god should be a true god and his religion the true religion—I mean the living and reigning king should be set forth to the uttermost and his god and religion to be the true god and true religion and the dead king should have the false god and the false religion; so that these bishops and the clergy would live twenty years and still say that they had the true god and true religion and yet every two year preach a contrary religion. How can this be?[12]

Most important of all the Puritan contributions to the Protestant cause at this time, however, was their firmness in the ultimate test. Rogers it was who bravely "broke the ice," as the contemporary phrase had it, and set the example which nearly three hundred others followed. The medieval theory of religious persecution was that, at the most, a few executions would bring a heretical people to their senses and that perhaps the mere threat of death would produce recantation and humble obedience. The experience of the Henrician government with the Erasmian group tended to confirm this theory. Had the first prospective victim of the Marian persecution recanted in the face of death, as did some of those tried later in this reign, the remaining prisoners might easily have done the same, and the reforming movement would have suffered a serious, if not irreparable, injury. But Rogers belonged to the Continental school, and so began the long line of Marian martyrs which was in time to sicken English stomachs and damn the cause of Roman Catholicism on the island for centuries. Thinking that he was to die with Hooper, he sent word to him that "there was never little fellow better would stick to a man than he would stick to him."[13] When it developed that he must die alone, he went through the ordeal without wavering. Awakened on February 4, 1555, with the news that his last hour had come, he remarked coolly, "If it be so, I need not tie my points." Neither the sight of his family nor the proffer of the Queen's pardon in

[12] Printed in J. L. Chester, *John Rogers* (London, 1861), pp. 322, 324–25, from Lansdowne 389, fols. 190(*v*)–202 (new numeration, fols. 187[*v*]–199).

[13] Foxe, *op. cit.*, VI, 611.

return for a recantation could shake his courage, and so Smith-field claimed the first of its many victims. Bradford and Ridley both recorded their determination to follow the example thus set,[14] and the former, the second Puritan prebendary of St. Paul's who had been ordained "without any abuse,"[15] followed his predecessor on the first of July. Hooper gave a similar example to the bishops. Shortly before Rogers' execution it was reported that he was about to recant. His response was a general denial: "I have taught this truth with my tongue and pen heretofore, and hereafter shortly will confirm, by God's grace, the same with my blood."[16] Taken to Gloucester to be executed in his former diocese, the veteran of many hazardous channel crossings wrote with charcoal on the wall of his room in the New Inn:

> Let nothing cause thy heart to fail;
> Launch out thy boat, hoist up thy sail,
>   Put from the shore;
> And be sure thou shalt attain
> Unto the port that shall remain
>   For evermore.[17]

The next day, February 8, he steadfastly endured the agonies of a lingering death.

Both Rogers and Hooper had ample warning of their peril and might have fled the country without difficulty. But Rogers, like Frith, once summoned before the Council, felt obligated to defend his cause there,[18] and Hooper refused to desert his official post. "Once I did flee and take me to my feet, but now, because I am called to this place and vocation, I am thoroughly persuaded to tarry, and to live and die with my sheep."[19] Long before, Luther had discussed this problem and given his verdict that flight in the face of danger was the act of a hireling and not of a true shepherd, and many thus followed his precept.

[14] *Ibid.*, VII, 217.   [15] *Ibid.*, p. 144.

[16] *Later Writings*, ed. Nevinson (Cambridge: Parker Society, 1852), p. 622.

[17] *Ibid.*, p. xxx. It should be noted, however, that Foxe (*op. cit.*, VII, 369) attributes these lines to another martyr named Robert Smith; but since he died after Hooper, he may have been merely quoting him in copying out the stanza.

[18] Foxe, *op. cit.*, VI, 592.   [19] *Ibid.*, p. 645.

To the foreign refugees in England such considerations did not apply.[20] They had no official position in the English church, and the government, which felt responsible only for Englishmen, was anxious to be rid of their influence. Gardiner, indeed, took special pains to frighten them into leaving the country.[21] On September 19, 1553, five days after Cranmer was sent to the Tower, Peter Martyr was given a passport with the Queen's sign manual. In the same month à Lasco and most of his congregation sailed for Denmark. The Lutherans of that country could not stomach their sacramental doctrine, and they wandred across northern Germany in search of a refuge, finally arriving in Emden in April, 1554. Poullain and his Glastonbury flock of Frenchmen made their way to Frankfort during the winter and obtained a church there, with permission to worship in it after their own manner. The next spring the remnant of à Lasco's London group went to Hamburg.

Many English Protestants, including those in prominent ecclesiastical positions, found reasons for saving their lives also. They alleged the necessity of preserving a nucleus of leaders until better times should come, an excuse which sounds sensible enough to modern ears.[22] The Book of Matthew comes before John, and these Protestants, leafing through their Testaments, stopped short of the description of the good shepherd and concentrated on the injunction to flee from one city to the next in times of persecution. Some, like Matthew Parker, the future Archbishop, then Dean of Lincoln, went into hiding in England. Others fled the country, in defiance of the law and their avowed principles. As we have seen, it was illegal for any subject to leave the realm without the royal consent, and the Protestants were loud in their affirmations of loyalty to the Queen. Nevertheless, some eight hundred[23] made their way to the Continent

---

[20] Cranmer specifically approved of flight from persecution in the case of foreigners and laymen (Strype, *op. cit.*, III, i, 226; Terentianus to ab Ulmis, November 20, 1553, *Original Letters*, p. 372).

[21] *Calendar of State Papers, Spanish* (hereafter cited as *Spanish Calendar*), XI, 217.

[22] Strype, III, i, 404.

[23] Miss Christina H. Garrett's recent work, *The Marian Exiles* (Cambridge, 1938), p. 32, has confirmed the original estimate of Foxe on this point. Unfortunately,

through a maze of intrigue, blackmail, and deception. Many of these were of the Puritan group. Bale, en route from his Irish bishopric by ship, hovered between hope and despair as his identity was discovered, and the sailors bled him for hush money. Coverdale was delivered from prison at the request of the King of Denmark, at whose court the translator's Scotch brother-in-law, John McAlpine, or Maccabeus, was a favorite preacher. A young refugee named William Whittingham, of whom we shall shortly hear more, threatened with exposure by a Dover innkeeper, saved himself by quick thinking:

> Whilst they were in this anxiety, there being a fair greyhound waiting on the table for relief [food]; Master Whittingham chanced to say, "Mine host, you have here a very fair greyhound."
>
> "Aye," said the host, "this greyhound is a fair greyhound indeed; and is of the Queen's kind."
>
> "Queen's kind!" said Master Whittingham, "what mean you by that? This is a strange speech. What good subject can endure to hear such words of his Sovereign, to have her Majesty to be compared in kind with the kind of a dog?" and said that the words were very treasonable, and that he could not see how they could be excused if they should not go and acquaint the Magistrate with it; and did further so aggravate the matter, even of purpose, as they did drive the host into such a fear as he durst not once mention the carrying of *them* before the Magistrate any more; but was glad to be so freed from their encumbrance. By this means all the company escaping this interruption, they proceeded on their journey.[24]

Others had less difficulty in making their escape. William Turner, the scientist Dean of Wells, declared that in a time of slaughter the only feasible courses were to join the wolves or to flee where no wolves were, and announced his intention of choosing the second alternative.[25] His plan succeeded, and he was shortly back at the congenial avocation of cultivating botanical gardens in Germany. John Knox, though not an Englishman, held a position in the English church and felt some scruples about abandoning his adopted country. But in Jan-

Miss Garrett's work appeared too late for me to make full use of it. Though I am unable to follow the author's reasoning at all points, the volume contains much useful information and should be consulted on the subject of this and the following chapters.

[24] Anonymous "Life of Whittingham" in *A Brief Discourse of the Troubles at Frankfort, 1554–1558 A.D.*, ed. Arber (London, 1908), pp. 2–3.

[25] *The Huntyng of the Romyshe Wolfe* (London, 1554), sig. F, fol. 4.

uary, 1554, "somewhat contrary to his own mind," as he alleged, he yielded to the advice of friends in the north and fled
to Dieppe.

To reach the Continent did not end the troubles of the refugees. Many of the *émigrés* experienced the greatest difficulty
in sustaining life. They begged for the smallest positions as
proofreaders and editorial assistants. John Rough, the Scotch
preacher who had first induced Knox to minister to the congregation in the castle of St. Andrews, earned a meager living
knitting stockings with his wife in Friesland. Men who had
been fellows of colleges at home were reduced to eating mice.[26]

But it is a mistake to think of the Protestant party as completely shattered during Mary's reign. Leaders of the Reformed
churches on the Continent lent what support they could to
refugees who had to compete economically with their own citizens. Even the Lutherans in many sections were not unchari-
table, in spite of the differences over the sacrament. English
merchants, both at home and abroad, kept up a steady stream
of contributions to the exiles. Some of them ransomed Bale on
his landing in Antwerp. Knox was in constant communication
with London citizens, who undoubtedly assisted him financially,
and, though Richard Hilles could not find the courage to face
a third exile, another merchant, Richard Chambers, took his
place as a traveling Maecenas to the refugees. Even the imprisoned Ridley managed to smuggle donations across the channel to his impoverished though more fortunate friends.

Most important of all, the Protestants were able to continue
their propaganda. In spite of the vigilance of governmental authorities, a secret press poured out opposition literature. The
printer was a Londoner, one Hugh Singleton, who deserves to
be better known. At the beginning of Mary's reign he was
printing "in Tem street, over against the Hiliardes, at the sign
of the double hood." It has been conjectured that he transferred his base of operations to Dublin during the period of

---

[26] Anthony Wood, *Annals*, ed. Gutch (London, 1796), II, 166. I am indebted to Mr.
A. B. Emden, Principal of my old Oxford society, St. Edmund Hall, for generous assistance with this note.

danger,[27] but the rapidity with which manuscripts originating abroad reached his press and the speed with which all his products found their market make a London location seem more probable. While some works of Cranmer and Ridley were published by Singleton, the Anglican faction—as we have seen—was generally opposed to publication as tending to incite further persecution, and most of the books sent out from this press were by the more advanced reformers. With Singleton's help Bale published before Christmas of 1553 an account of his escape, and also heaped coals of fire on Gardiner's head by issuing an English translation of the Bishop's *De vera obedientia*,[28] written in the time of Henry VIII to justify the royal supremacy.

More important for our purposes was the further contribution to Turner's animal allegory series, made sometime in 1554 by the Wells botanist. It also came from the Singleton press and was entitled *The Huntyng of the Romyshe Wolfe*. Dedicated to the young gentlemen of England, with a passage in praise of hunting as a pastime when used in moderation, it took for its theme the suggestion that the fox of a decade previous had now become a wolf—in other words, that secret propaganda had now been transformed into open popery as exemplified in the case of Gardiner and the other clerical supporters of the crown. After a curious scientific discussion of the transmutation of species and spontaneous generation, Turner launched into some anti-Catholic theological arguments of the conventional sort. But at the end of the volume he came out with a demand for a sweeping reorganization of the church on the Reformed model, the first of a long line of proposed Puritan disciplines for the English church. Ecclesiastical lands were to

[27] Henry R. Plomer, "The Protestant Press in the Reign of Mary," *Library*, I (3d ser., 1910), 54–72. This is a very useful article, but the suggestion of a move to Ireland is based on very slight evidence. See also Garrett, *op. cit.*, pp. 288–89.

[28] P. Janelle, *Obedience in Church and State* (Cambridge, 1930), pp. xxxiv–xxxvii. Unfortunately, Janelle overlooks the contributions of Mr. Plomer on this subject, and he thinks the time factor makes difficult the otherwise probable attribution of this translation to Bale. Since Turner professes to write the *Huntyng of the Romyshe Wolfe* before his flight, I see no reason to think that Bale might not have done a similar piece of literary work before his journey if the Singleton press were still in England or Ireland, as we have reason to suppose. Harris ("The Life and Works of John Bale" [University of Illinois dissertation (1935)], pp. 75–77) accepts the attribution to Bale, though he does not offer any assistance with the time difficulty.

be restored to provide a learned ministry, though it was easier "to pull out the mace out of Hercules' hand than to get the fat parsonages out of their hands that have them now." Pastors were to be chosen by the congregation, not by the popish system of advowsons. To the usual objection that the common people were like a wild beast, not to be trusted with political power, he replied that baptism tamed them. But to be safe, lest any be found fleshly, he suggested that seven elders be chosen in each parish to choose the pastor and aid in excommunication. Four overseers or superintendents, annually elected by the clergy of each shire, were to take the place of the old bishops. They were to have the right to veto the election of both ministers and elders. One-quarter of the value of episcopal lands should be used for their support, and the remainder was to be divided equally among schools, poor livings, and the repair of churches and highways. Cathedral lands were to be used to supply a few preachers in the diocesan center, and the surplus was to go for additional schools. For the time being this modest proposal of eight or ten pages—apparently an afterthought—fell upon ears deafened by the immediate uproar of the Catholic-Protestant struggle. It raised great questions, but it was a blast blown out of season.[29]

More timely and penetrating were the contributions of John Knox. He saw that to call royal ministers wolves, without admitting that the sovereign herself was primarily responsible for the havoc among the Protestant flock, was merely to act the ostrich. Before leaving England, he was grappling with the old problem of the Christian's obligations to his temporal rulers. At Dieppe he finished a treatise on the subject, which Singleton published in July. Called *A Godly Letter Sent to the Faythfull in London, Newcastle, and Barwicke*, it was primarily an exhortation to believers to stand fast in their faith for fear of God's wrath. But, in developing this theme, Knox was also seeking to extract as much comfort as possible from an expansion of the traditional reformers' doctrine of passive obedience, as set forth by Luther and Tyndale twenty-five years before. That theory, while condemning the subject's use of violence

[29] Turner, *op. cit.*, sig. E, fol. vi and sig. F, fol. iii.

against tyrannical rulers, had not left the evil rulers unpunished. Their case was merely referred to a higher court. The all-seeing God was to punish them in due time, after the Old Testament manner. To the sixteenth-century thinker this was a very real vengeance, which might, and usually did, strike both in this life and in the one to come. Critical modern reflections on the apparently spineless character of early Protestant political theory should take more account of this fact. While threatening fearful Christians with punishment in case of apostasy, Knox found occasion, therefore, to explain the present time of trial and offer hope for the future. People and nations who despised the preaching of the gospel were punished. England was now reaping the harvest of her indifference to the godly preachers of Edward VI's time. The remedy was to repent and stand fast in the true profession. Then God would shorten the time of trouble and punish his agents in the present chastisement. For wicked rulers were not to be excused merely because their evil actions were serving God's purpose. Their triumph would be short-lived.

And thus leave I them (as of whose repentance there is small hope) to the hands of Him that shall not forget their horrible blasphemies spoken in despite of Christ's truth and of his true messengers. . . . .
Shall we then believe that England shall avoid the vengeance that is threatened? No, dear brethren, if idolatry continue as it has begun, no more may England escape God's vengeance nor [than] God himself may lose his justice. . . . .
For the Lord himself shall come in our defence with his mighty power. He shall give us the victory when the battle is most strong, and He shall turn our tears into everlasting joy. He shall consume our enemies with the breath of his mouth, and he shall let us see the destruction of them that now are most proud and that most pretendeth to molest us. From God alone we abide redemption.[30]

But, when all this was said, the author confessed that it came from "ane sore trubillit heart." The traditional doctrine was inadequate to meet current needs, and the Scotchman's active mind was beginning to think along other lines.[31] In a contemporary manuscript copy of this letter there is a comment

[30] John Knox, *Works*, ed. Laing (6 vols.; Edinburgh, 1895), III, 165, 189, 215.

[31] The Magdeburg *Bekenntnis* had been published four years perviously, and Knox doubtless knew about it (see below, p. 145).

on the work of an Old Testament prophet, which is lacking in
the versions printed at the time. "Let a thing be here noted,
that the prophets of God sometimes may teach treason against
kings and yet neither he, nor such as obeys the word spoken in
the Lord's name by him, offends God."[32] With this dangerous
thought in his mind, the middle-aged exile set off on a flying
trip to Switzerland to consult the leading Reformed theologians
on the subject. With Calvin he had a general discussion. To
Bullinger he submitted four specific questions.

Whether the son of a king, upon his father's death, though unable by reason
of his tender age to conduct the government of the kingdom, is nevertheless by
right of inheritance to be regarded as a lawful magistrate, and as such to be
obeyed as of divine right?

Whether a female can preside over, and rule, a kingdom by divine right, and
so transfer the right of sovereignty to her husband?

Whether obedience is to be rendered to a magistrate who enforces idolatry
and condemns true religion; and whether those authorities who are still in
military occupation of towns and fortresses are permitted to repel this ungodly violence from themselves and their friends?

To which party must godly persons attach themselves, in the case of a religious nobility resisting an idolatrous sovereign?[33]

To the first of these, obviously designed to justify the reforms
of Edward VI, the Swiss reformer gave an affirmative answer.
He was equally explicit about the first part of the second, but
for the rest he took the equivocal position that the answer depended on the particular circumstances. Knox was not yet
ready to give a final interpretation of the particular circumstances in England, but the direction of his thought may be
seen in his *Faythful Admonition . . . . unto the Professours of
God's Truthe in England*, which he composed on his return to
Dieppe in the late spring and published in July. Much of this
manifesto was taken up with a further explanation of God's
purpose in allowing troubles to come upon the righteous, and
how they were to be accepted. But it also included a direct
attack upon the Queen, as more bloodthirsty than Jezebel or

[32] *Works*, III, 184.

[33] *Ibid.*, pp. 221–25. I have here followed P. Hume Brown (*John Knox* [2 vols.;
London, 1895], I, 156–57) in attributing these questions to Knox rather than Goodman.
Garrett (*op. cit.*, p. 164) ascribes them to Goodman, but yet she places him in England
the day before Bullinger's letter about the interview.

Herodias' daughter, though the burnings of Protestants had not yet begun and the executions resulting from Northumberland's plot and the Wyatt revolt were the only grounds for the charge. At one point the author even prayed for a Jehu to remedy the situation, but this suggestion of revolution implied divine leadership of an unusual and extraordinary type. He did not yet think in terms of a popular or national uprising without such assistance.[34]

Much more important was Knox's effort to summon patriotism to the support of his cause. Mary's match with Philip was brewing, and the Scotchman sought to appeal to English nationalism to ward it off. Spain surpassed all other nations "in pride and whoredom, so, for idolatry and vain papistical and devilish ceremonies, they may rightly be called the very sons of superstition."[35] The Emperor (Charles V) was, he said—allegedly quoting one of his sermons preached in Buckinghamshire the year previous—"no less enemy unto Christ than ever was Nero." Declaring that "the ancient laws and acts of Parliament pronounceth it treason to transfer the crown of England into the hands of a foreign nation," he thundered:

And now doth [Mary] not manifestly show herself to be an open traitress to the imperial crown of England, contrary to the just laws of the realm, to bring in a stranger and make a proud Spaniard king, to the shame, dishonor, and destruction of the nobility; to the spoil from them and theirs of their honors, lands, possessions, chief offices and promotions; to the utter decay of the treasures, commodities, navy, and fortifications of the realm; to the abasing of the yeomanry, to the slavery of the commonalty, to the overthrow of Christianity and God's true religion and, finally, to the utter subversion of the whole public estate and commonwealth of England?[36]

As time was to show, to consider the possibility of a revolution was to approach the only sound solution of the problem. But to raise the banner of patriotism was a serious error. In the long run, English nationalism would drive out Catholicism, it is true, but it would not champion the Reformed religion as Knox understood it. Events at Frankfort the next spring demonstrated the flaw in this strategy.

[34] *Works*, III, 309.

[35] *Ibid.*, p. 297.   [36] *Ibid.*, p. 295.

CHAPTER VI

Frankfort: Nationalism versus Internationalism

S THE number of English *émigrés* on the Continent increased, many of them began to desire some sort of communal life and to look for the most favorable location for such an experiment. Calvin had not yet won his desperate struggle with the Libertines at Geneva, but Berne and Zurich were hospitable, and there were some possibilities in Germany. The triumph of Prince Maurice over the Emperor Charles, resulting in the Peace of Passau, had restored to German Protestants the liberty of worship of which they had been deprived by the Interim. In the Rhineland there were several Reformed strongholds, and where Lutheran opinions on the sacrament were not too strongly held the *émigrés* could find a refuge in other parts of "Dutchland." By the fall of 1554 there were groups of English scholars gathered around Martyr at Strassburg and Bullinger at Zurich. There was an organized church at Emden, and one was permitted for a time at Wesel, in Westphalia,[1] though it was soon compelled to move to Aarau in Bernese territory.

But with the help of the tolerant Melanchthon, the most generous concessions were secured from the magistrates of Frankfort on the Main, and there in 1554 the greatest number of the English refugees settled. The advanced guard was a group led by William Whittingham, the hero of the Dover dog story, and our chief source of information concerning subsequent events at

---

[1] [William Whittingham], *A Brief Discourse of the Troubles at Frankfort*, ed. Arber (London, 1908), p. 26. On the subject of this and the succeeding chapters see Christina H. Garrett, *The Marian Exiles* (Cambridge, 1938). See above, p. 110, n. 23.

Frankfort.[2] He was both a gentleman and a scholar, a product
of a good Lancashire family and a former student of Christ
Church, Oxford. He had spent the last years of Edward's reign
on a Continental grand tour. He was on good terms with the
English Ambassador in Paris, Sir William Pickering, later suitor
to Elizabeth, and frequently went to the French court with him.
But he also visited the universities and spent some time at
Geneva. There he apparently acquired the religious convictions
which had such a marked effect on the history of the English
church in Frankfort. Arriving in the German city on June 27,
1554, he and his party were promptly visited in their lodgings
by Poullain, the pastor of the French congregation recently
come from Glastonbury, who, like Martyr at Strassburg, did
all in his power to repay the hospitality he had received in
England. With his indorsement, the Englishmen first received
permission for themselves and all religious refugees from their
country to settle in the city and, on July 14, the right to share
in the use of the Church of the White Ladies (*Weissfrauen-
kirche*) already assigned to the French congregation. This
grant was made conditional upon their accepting the French
Confession of Faith and using an order of service which, if not
identical with that of Poullain's congregation, should at least
meet with its approval, lest the English "should thereby minister occasion of offense."

Accordingly, Whittingham's group drew up a form of service
which differed greatly from the Second Prayer Book. The litany, surplice, and many other details of the old service were
dropped. A revised general confession, a psalm in meter sung
by the congregation "in a plain tune," and a prayer for assistance by the Holy Spirit preceded the sermon. Afterward there
was a general prayer for all estates, and a special one for England. Then came the Lord's Prayer, the Creed, another psalm,

---

[2] The common attribution of the *Troubles at Frankfort* to Whittingham seems to me
altogether probable, especially in view of his known attitude and interest in propaganda.
The objection raised by P. Hume Brown (*John Knox* [2 vols.; London, 1895], I, 167)
that the author of Whittingham's biography seems ignorant of his authorship does not
appear to me of great force. While the writer was obviously well acquainted with the
details of Whittingham's later career at Durham, he may easily have been ignorant of
his connection with the 1574 work.

and the benediction. Scripture-reading was omitted as a use-
less formality. In addition to the creed and form of service
which the town council had required, the English also made
provision for that discipline which all the Reformed group
deemed so necessary to the well-being and effectiveness of the
church.[3] In this discipline, or constitution, rules were made for
the congregation as a whole and also for the church officials. No
one was to be admitted as a member unless he made a declaration of his faith before the pastor and the elders, showing that
he agreed with the doctrine of the church and promising to
submit to its discipline. No one whose beliefs or morals were
tainted was to be accepted without due repentance. Members
must attend the meetings of the church for prayer, preaching,
or the administration of the sacraments. Provision was made
for catechizing the youth of the congregation and for the excommunication of offenders. The church officials were to be a
pastor, or superintendent, preachers, elders, and deacons, after
the Reformed pattern as described for à Lasco's London church.
They were to be subject to the same discipline as other offenders, except that it was to be used "towards them rather with
more severity." John MacBray, or Makebray, a Scotch refugee,[4]
was elected minister; deacons were promptly chosen; and organized worship was first held on July 29.

[3] *Troubles at Frankfort*, pp. 143–49. I have here followed Arber in accepting the Old
Discipline as containing the substance of the original constitution of the Frankfort
church. But it is to be noted that the document as we now have it does not include the
declarations of the "necessity" and "causes" (*ibid.*, p. 26) mentioned as being in the
original. It also contains references to earlier elections (p. 147), and suggestions of the
strife in the congregation (p. 146) and the Jewel case (p. 144). There is a copy in Egerton 2836 (fols. 1–13), which was formerly the property of Thomas Sampson. It is
printed in H. J. Wotherspoon and G. W. Sprott (eds.), *The Second Prayer Book of King
Edward the Sixth and the Liturgy of the Compromise* (London, 1905), pp. 232–56. Along
with the discipline in this version are a form of service, a catechism, and prayers, including one for Philip and Mary which requests that their hearts be changed or that
their devices be confounded and their power weakened. This version is very difficult
to date as a whole. In the prayers there is a reference to the burning of bishops in
England which would seem to place that section after the triumph of the Cox party.
Yet the introductory paragraph contains rather disparaging comments on the Edwardian Prayer Book. It seems necessary to conclude that, like the version in the *Troubles
at Frankfort*, it is a composite document. Miss Garrett (*op. cit.*, p. 135) believes, however, that the liturgical portion, at least, is entirely Cox's.

[4] For his career see Thomas McCrie, *Life of Knox* (2 vols.; Edinburgh, 1814), I, 359.

No other community of English exiles had as yet obtained such concessions as the use of a church building and virtual autonomy in their government. On August 2 the Frankfort group accordingly sent out a form letter to the other *émigré* congregations, inviting them to share in their good fortune. In fact, it was more than an invitation; rather, a peremptory summons, couched in the hortatory and holier-than-thou language of a call to repentance. On first reading it has a strange ring for a message from one set of exiles to others who have also left their country rather than betray their faith. After the good news of the Frankfort concessions comes the demand that their fellow-exiles leave their present locations and join the writers. They are not to be swayed by opportunities of pursuing learning or making a living elsewhere. They would be able to sustain existence in Frankfort and fulfil their primary obligation to carry on the worship of an organized church:

> What thing then ought we to have in greater recommendation than order and policy [polity] which God hath established in his Church? that we may be taught by His word, that we may worship him and call upon his name with one accord, that we may have the true use of the Sacraments to help us to the same. For these be the means whereby we must be confirmed in the faith, in the fear of God, in holiness of conversation, in the contempt of the world, and in the love of life everlasting. . . . .
>
> Let us all mark that [Paul] saith not that God hath left the Scriptures only, that every one should read it; but also that he hath erected a policy, and order that there should be some to teach and not for one day; but for all the time of our life, even to the death, for that is the time of our perfection.
>
> Wherefore, brethren, let us submit ourselves and leave off farther to tempt God, seeing that if we will be the body of Christ we must obey to this general rule.[5]

As a last argument there was added the suggestion that the lack of coherence and organization among the exiles made the Catholics rejoice, and that waverers at home thought they might "dissemble until a church be confirmed." When we remember the importance which the Reformed party attached to organization and discipline, the main point of the letter becomes intelligible and the reason for the hortatory tone may be understood, though the wisdom of employing it remains doubtful. It is also

[5] *Troubles at Frankfort*, p. 29; cf. Eph. 4:11-13.

clear that the authors had in mind the establishment of a pattern of worship to guide the Protestant church of England whenever it should be restored to its home country.

An answer was soon received from Strassburg. Edmund Grindal, one of Ridley's prebendaries and the later Archbishop of Canterbury, was the most prominent among the group in the Alsatian city, and the exiles there could not be expected to respond too warmly to the Puritan project. Either by design or by accident, they misinterpreted the Frankfort letter as a call for the supply of a minister. Though well educated, Whittingham was not ordained, and none of the other signers of the letter was a man of any prominence. Accordingly, the Strassburg group suggested the names of John Ponet, the Edwardian Bishop of Winchester, John Scory, recently Bishop of Rochester, John Bale, and Richard Cox. Grindal promptly supplemented this with a letter to Scory, then superintendent of the church at Emden, requesting him to take the position at Frankfort. The most the Strassburgers offered to their fellow-countrymen at Frankfort was, in default of the acceptance of the office by any of these, to send a minister to alternate with one from Zurich. This was far from satisfying the Frankfort group, which felt fully competent to choose its own ministers, and though John Bale had joined them since the August letter, on September 24 they elected Knox, who had by then returned from Dieppe to Geneva, and two other prominent Edwardian preachers, Thomas Lever, then at Zurich, and James Haddon of the Strassburg group.

The Zurich exiles, who included in their number Lever, Chambers, and Robert Horne, later Bishop of Winchester, understood the original letter perfectly, in fact—with the aid of private communications from Frankfort—all too well. In a letter dated October 13, they recognized the force of the arguments for coming to Frankfort but suggested that their "unfeignedly travailing in the necessary knowlege of Christ, to the profit of his church hereafter" was an effective counterbalance. But, if the Frankfort group insisted that their need was such as to justify interrupting the Zurichers' studies, they would come by the next Easter, provided they might be assured that they might worship God "as freely and as uprightly . . . . as the order last taken [the Second Prayer Book of Edward VI] in the Church of England permitteth and prescribeth—for we are fully determined to admit and use no other." Before the Frankfort group received this response, they had sent a reminder of their first communication, with a request for an answer. In reply to this follow-up letter the Zurich group sent their patron, Richard Chambers, with a commission to negotiate on their behalf.

By this time Haddon had declined the proffered position at Frankfort, but Knox had arrived from Geneva to strengthen the hand of Whittingham and the other Puritans. On November 15 the Frankforters told Chambers that under the terms of the original concession they could not use the Edwardian Prayer Book without endangering their standing with the local magistrates, and justified their position to the Zurichers in this fashion:

> As touching the effect of the Book, we desire the execution thereof as much as you, so far as God's Word doth commend it: but as for the unprofitable ceremonies, as well by His consent as by ours [they] are not to be used. And although they were tolerable, as some are not; yet, being in a strange commonwealth, we could not be suffered to put them in ure [use]: and better it were they should never be practiced than they should be the subversion of our church, which should fall in great hazard by using them. . . . .
>
> If any think that the not using of the Book in all points should increase our godly fathers' and brethren's bands, or else in anything deface the worthy ordinances and laws of our Sovereign Lord of most famous memory, King Edward VI, he seemeth either little to weigh the matter or else, letted [hindered] through ignorance, knoweth not that even they themselves [the compilers of the Book of Common Prayer] have, upon considerations of circumstances, altered heretofore many things as touching the same. And if God had not, in these wicked days, otherwise determined, they would hereafter have changed more: yea, and in our case we doubt not but that they would have done the like.[6]

Chambers thereupon made a flying trip to Strassburg, and two weeks later returned with Grindal, bearing a letter from the Alsatian group offering to join the Frankforters by February 1 if satisfactory arrangements could be made. They re-

---

[6] *Troubles at Frankfort*, p. 37.

quested that the magistrates be asked to permit the use of the
English order. They repeated the argument that to alter the
form of service would "seem to condemn the chief authors thereof
[Cranmer and his fellow-bishops still in prison]." They also
asserted that changes would cause the Catholics to accuse "our
doctrine of imperfection and us of mutability," and declared
that such alterations would cause the "godly to doubt in that
truth wherein before they were persuaded, and to hinder their
coming hither which before they had purposed."[7] At the same
time Grindal glossed the letter and gave away most of his case
by granting that such ceremonies as their Protestant hosts
could not tolerate might well be omitted, and that his group
would be satisfied if the Frankforters had the "substance and
effect" of the Prayer Book. When Knox and Whittingham
asked the visitors to explain what they meant by the substance
of the Book, they said that this was beyond their commission.
They in turn inquired what parts of it the Frankfort group
would accept and were told that, subject to the approval of
the Germans, all that could be proved "to stand with God's
word" was to be received. There followed a general discussion of the merits of the Prayer Book in which Knox made
specific charges of superstition in connection with such practices
as private baptism, the churching of women, and the use in the
litany of the phrase "by Thine agony and bloody sweat."[8] At
length it was evident that the clash between nationalism and
the desire for a thorough reformation made agreement impossible, and a polite pretext for breaking off the negotiations was
sought and found. The visitors requested a separate church
building, and were told that this could not be granted by the
magistrates while the Diet of Augsburg was in session. Grindal
and Chambers thereupon returned to Strassburg with a letter
from the Frankforters refuting the arguments in the letter of
commission which they had brought. The Prayer Book itself
had granted that ceremonies might be altered, said the Whit-

---

[7] *Ibid.*, p. 38.

[8] Knox, *Works*, ed. Laing (6 vols.; Edinburgh, 1895), IV, 61. This is evidently the
time when the questions there mentioned were discussed.

tingham group, and their changes had not been sufficiently great to warrant a charge of imperfection or mutability. Any Christians who were so offended by these slight changes as to refuse to come and share in the Frankfort benefits—if indeed such reports were correct—were inadequately grounded in the truth. With a polite acknowledgment of this communication, the effort to induce all the English exiles to move to Frankfort came to an end on December 13, 1554.

There still remained the problem of the order to be observed in the Frankfort church itself. The leaders of the congregation were not planning merely for themselves. They were not sectarians nor schismatics. They had in mind a national church, and wished to set up a system which would be acceptable to their fellow-countrymen. As the only fully organized church, with the possible exception of Emden, they might have claimed the right to legislate for the entire body of exiles, but to take advantage of such a legal quibble would be politically inexpedient and could only defeat their own ends. Knox, Whittingham, John Foxe, the recently arrived martyrologist, and two other newcomers, Thomas Cole and Anthony Gilby, were appointed a committee to draw up an order of worship, and they recommended the Genevan order, of which an English translation had been published in 1550. But, though the congregation accepted their report, Knox refused to use the service without the consent of the learned of the other English communities, a further indication of his interest in unity and discipline as opposed to sectarianism. At the same time he declined to use the Edwardian book, and requested permission to preach only, and to have someone else administer the sacraments. This solution was unacceptable to the congregation, and yet the church refused to accept Knox's proffered resignation.

The opposition to their pastor's proposal is doubtless to be explained by the appearance of an Anglican minority among the Frankfort exiles as the refugee tide swelled.[9] This group soon

[9] *Troubles at Frankfort*, p. 52. R. W. Dixon (*History of the Church of England from the Abolition of the Roman Jurisdiction* [6 vols.; 3d rev. ed.; Oxford, 1895], IV, 692 n.) suggests that Sampson's letter to Calvin of February 23, 1555 (*Original Letters Relative to the English Reformation*, ed. Hastings Robinson [2 vols.; Cambridge: Parker Society,

found a voice when Thomas Lever, Knox's elected colleague, arrived from Zurich. He suggested the adoption of an order independent of both Swiss and English models, but evidently it included the "substance and effect" of the Anglican form, for on inspection it was found "not altogether such as was fit for a right reformed church." Charges of newfangledness and singularity were answered with taunts of popery and narrow-mindedness.

During the controversy the Puritan party resolved to seek assistance from outside the English communities. An abstract of the Edwardian book was accordingly drawn up and sent to Calvin for his criticism.[10] Knox also wrote to Calvin's fellow-ministers in Geneva, soliciting their aid in securing a favorable reply from Calvin. He concluded with the request that they would ask their great colleague whether the writer might not leave Frankfort in good conscience, since his presence made rather for dissension than unity in the congregation.[11] On January 20 the oracle replied, deprecating the contention on ceremonial matters in such serious times, but supporting the Puritan party. In the English liturgy he saw many foolish things which could be tolerated for a time, but should be put away with ripening judgment. To love popish dregs because they are things to which one is accustomed was "both trifling and childish."[12]

This answer proved a "club of Hercules"[13] to the Puritan party, and with it the opposition was persuaded, on February 6, 1555, to accept a compromise liturgy prepared by Knox and Whittingham, on the one side, and Lever and Thomas Parry, from the other. It was drawn partly from the English Prayer Book, and it was agreed in writing that the order was to be observed until the last of April. Any differences of opinion

---

1846–47], p. 170), is our only source of information concerning a division of opinion at Frankfort prior to Cox's coming. But this is clear from the *Troubles* and not clear from Sampson's letter, which does not mention Frankfort at all.

[10] See *Corpus reformatorum* (Halle, 1834, etc.), XLIII (1876), 337–44, for the full letter.

[11] *Ibid.*, pp. 370–71; cf. Brown, *op. cit.*, p. 175, n. 3.

[12] *Troubles at Frankfort*, pp. 50–51.   [13] *Ibid.*, p. 87.

meanwhile were to be arbitrated by five prominent Reformed divines, Calvin, Bullinger, Martyr, Musculus of Augsburg, and Viret of Lausanne. A joyful reconciliation followed. For six weeks peace reigned, but on March 13 there came to Frankfort a new group of English exiles headed by Richard Cox, who in happier times had been Headmaster of Eton, tutor to Edward VI, Vice-Chancellor of Oxford University, and Dean of Westminster. In his Eton days he had acquired the reputation of being a good teacher but also the greatest beater in the school,[14] and his later career gives us little ground to doubt the justice of this characterization. It is unfortunate that the Anglican cause at this time could not have found a better tempered leader, who would have reflected more credit upon it. During the Hooper-Ridley controversy Cox had written to Bullinger:

I embrace your sound and wholesome counsel respecting the reformation of the church of God with the greater readiness, inasmuch as you so entirely coincide with me in that belief which a merciful God has given me in these things. For I am of the opinion that all things in the church should be pure, simple, and removed as far as possible from the elements and pomps of this world. But in our church what can I do, who am so deficient both in learning and authority? I can only endeavor to persuade our bishops to be of the same mind and opinion with myself, and in the mean time commit to God the care and conduct of his own work.[15]

As the most distinguished figure in the Frankfort group, Cox was now in a position of influence, but he seems to have forgotten his earlier words. Time and trouble were on the side of the Anglicans, for nationalism thrives on tradition, and the English service was already securing the respectability which persecution and the passage of years could bestow. Cox proceeded at once to flout the compromise, by "answering aloud after the minister, contrary to the church's determination." When the elders remonstrated with him, he and his followers replied that "they would do as they had done in England, and that they would have the face of an English church." An English church! Here was the whole issue in a phrase. "The Lord

[14] *Victoria County History, Buckinghamshire*, ed. William Page (4 vols. and Index; London, 1905–26), II, 181.

[15] *Original Letters*, p. 122.

grant it to have the face of Christ's church," said Knox.[16] To him and his followers a truly Reformed church was an international affair, in which Scythian and Parthian were all equal. But many of the post-Reformation generation, who had never been out of England before, were already beginning to regard the peculiar forms of the royal church with affection, if not reverence.

On the following Sunday morning, Lever, whose turn it was to preach, intrusted the service to one of the newcomers, John Jewel, later Bishop of Salisbury, who had escaped from England only after signing Catholic articles. He proceeded to read the English litany.[17] That afternoon it was Knox's innings. He reiterated his stand against the Edwardian Prayer Book and asserted that the imperfect state of the English Reformation was shown by pluralism, the want of discipline, and Hooper's troubles about the rochet. Cox reproved him as he came from the pulpit, and the following Tuesday a meeting was held to discuss the controversy further. As yet Cox and his supporters were not members of the congregation, and so not eligible to vote. When he requested the franchise for his group, the congregation refused on the ground that there was still a controversy between them, that the newcomers had not signed the discipline, and that some had attended mass and subscribed Catholic articles in England. But Knox was still true to his principle of taking no steps without the consent of the whole *émigré* body; moreover, he had the reformer's optimistic conviction that the justice of his case was so manifest—especially in the matter of the broken agreement—that even his adversaries could not deny it. He interceded for the Cox party. The request was granted, and the Anglican group was accordingly in the majority. But Knox's confidence was misplaced. Cox and his faction promptly forbade the Scotchman to preach again or otherwise to meddle in the affairs of the congregation.

At this turn in events Whittingham complained to the chief German patron of the exiles, Johann von Glauberg, a Frankfort magistrate, who had been influential in securing for them

---

[16] *Troubles at Frankfort*, pp. 54 and 62.   [17] *Ibid.*, p. 63.

the original concessions. The Councilor forbade anyone to preach on the ensuing Sunday and requested Poullain to settle the quarrel, in consultation with two of the leaders from each side. Knox and Whittingham with Cox and Lever made up the committee, but no agreement was possible. The Puritan party now petitioned the entire Frankfort Council, citing the broken agreement of February 6, and requesting that the matter be referred to the five Continental divines originally chosen as arbitrators. On March 22 von Glauberg brought them the answer—that they must conform rigidly to the terms of the first grant and adopt the French order or lose their church and leave the city. This dictum was accepted perforce, but the Cox party had one trump card yet to play. A certain Edward Isaac of Kent seems first to have thought out the plan, but he was supported in it by Cox, Jewel, Parry, and the former Puritan, John Bale, who was growing more conservative with age. Taking a copy of Knox's *Faythful Admonition*, they marked the passage in which the Emperor was compared to Nero, and several others which reflected on Mary. The damaging document was then presented to the harassed magistrates. At first they merely forbade Knox to preach further. But Charles was then at Augsburg with his Council, too close for comfort, and Knox's accusers were insistent, refusing to remain in church while Knox was in the audience and otherwise creating a disturbance which threatened to reach the Emperor's ears. Reluctantly, the magistrates sent word, through Whittingham and a colleague named William Williams, that Knox should leave the city. This he did, departing for Geneva on Tuesday, March 26, less than two weeks after the arrival of Cox and his party.

With Knox thus removed from the scene, his opponents had a comparatively smooth path. An Anglican delegation, which included three Doctors and thirteen Bachelors of Divinity, persuaded the magistrates that, with the exception of certain ceremonies which they agreed to drop, the Edwardian Prayer Book measured up to Reformed standards and might therefore be used by the English congregation. Adolphus von Glauberg, a Doctor of Laws and nephew to John, took Cox's side in the controversy and notified Whittingham of this decision. At Cox's suggestions he even refused Whittingham's request that he and his party might be permitted to join themselves to some other church, presumably the French, and commanded him to agitate the matter no more. With the second in command thus silenced, Gilby succeeded to the leadership of the Puritan group. He and a delegation interviewed Johann von Glauberg, but that worthy supported his nephew's decision, and the Puritan cause was lost so far as Frankfort was concerned.

It only remained for the victorious Anglicans to consolidate and defend their gains. Without troubling to secure resignations from the previous incumbents, or even formally removing them from office, Cox and his friends proceeded to hold a new election. According to their original plan only those who had been priests and ministers in England were to vote. Against this procedure a protest was made by Christopher Goodman, formerly Lady Margaret Professor of Theology at Oxford. He had been a member of the Strassburg congregation and had signed the Anglican letter sent by that group in the preceding November, but he was now moving toward the left.[18] His objection was overruled, however, and the franchise would have been confined to the clergy had not the Frankfort magistrates intervened to require lay balloting after the Reformed pattern.[19] By their edict, also, each voting member of the congregation was required to subscribe to the Edwardian Forty-two Articles. Some of the Puritans refused to sign this creed, and the Anglicans had no difficulty in sweeping the election. David Whitehead, now of the Anglican faction, who had temporarily filled the office of pastor, or superintendent, before the advent of Knox,[20] was given that office once more. Two ministers, four elders, and two deacons were also elected.

The new party in power also interested itself in the important work of propaganda. Letters were sent off to Calvin and the

---

[18] The details of Goodman's life and his political theory have been well worked out by Althea Cherry, "The Life and Political Theories of Christopher Goodman" (University of Chicago thesis [1935]).

[19] *Troubles at Frankfort*, pp. 72, 77, and 89.   [20] *Ibid.*, p. 33.

imprisoned Ridley, explaining and defending the changes which had taken place. From the Oxford gatehouse the doomed Bishop smuggled a reply, approving of the Anglican actions and rebutting several of Knox's charges against the Prayer Book.[21] Naturally Calvin was more critical, but he recognized the *fait accompli*, and, although he felt bound to protest against the treatment of Knox, he did not try to reopen the controversy, especially since his Anglican informants gave him to understand that nearly everyone had accepted the change and that even the few recalcitrants might be expected to do so shortly.[22]

Nevertheless, in response to the Genevan's letter, the Anglican group went over the entire ground once more,[23] charging the opposition with factional partisanship, and putting the best face possible on the wretched business of Knox's expulsion. It was stated that the safety of the entire congregation was at stake, and it was hinted that graver charges might have been leveled.[24] Appropriately enough, the writers included in this closing statement a paragraph on the basic issue of national Protestantism as opposed to the international variety. After pointing out that some ceremonies had been dropped in order to placate the Puritan party, they went on to defend their formalism:

We make this concession to the love of our country, to which, forsooth, we are too much inclined. These, your friends, however, are altogether a disgrace to their country. For whatever has been bestowed from above upon our country in this respect, with exceeding arrogance, not to say impudence, they are treading under foot. You must know that we do not entertain any regard for our country which is not agreeable to God's holy Word. Neither, in the meanwhile, are we so ungrateful to our country, nor have we so cast off every feeling of humanity, as rashly to despise the benefits which God has bestowed upon it. Nor have we such a mean opinion of the judgments of our countrymen, who resisted ungodliness even unto blood, as that, by reason of the clamors of individuals possessing no weight whatever, we should brand them with the foulest marks of papistical impiety.[25]

Meanwhile, the defeated Puritan faction at Frankfort had to solve the problem of avoiding superstitious worship without

[21] Knox, *op. cit.*, pp. 61–62.

[22] *Troubles at Frankfort*, p. 79.

[23] *Ibid.*, pp. 87–93.

[24] *Ibid.*, p. 91.

[25] *Ibid.*, p. 88.

falling into the equally damnable error of schism. All the pious hopes that they would shortly conquer the Anglicans with reason were dashed. At the same time they continued to cherish the ideal of a nation-wide, established Protestant church for which the exiles were laying the foundations. To separate from the Anglican body was to separate from what they admitted to be a part of the true church. In their dilemma they apparently developed the idea of forming their own church, one with ceremonies differing from those of the Anglican body, but still in communion with that group, somewhat after the manner of different Reformed churches on the Continent which did not always agree precisely with one another in matter of ceremonies. At first they considered organizing another church in Frankfort, probably in loose affiliation with the French band,[26] but Cox's influence with the magistrates blocked that project. The possibility of securing a haven elsewhere was then considered. Calvin was apprised of the situation, and he favored such a move, advising the Anglicans to let the dissenting brethren depart in peace. Whittingham was accordingly dispatched by his followers to the upper Rhineland and Switzerland to negotiate for another refuge. During the early summer he made a successful trip. At Zurich the increasingly cautious Bullinger diplomatically expressed his disapproval of certain of the Anglican ceremonies, at least two of which the Coxian group at Frankfort had consented to abandon.[27] But he did not offer the Puritans a church. Both Basel and Geneva—where Calvin had now completed the conquest of his secularly minded opponents, the Libertines[28]—proved more hospitable, however, and promised the

[26] This would seem to be the explanation of the phrase "join themselves to some other church" (*ibid.*, p. 70). To merge completely with the French would be impossible because of the language difficulty; and, if emigration had been contemplated at that time, Cox's appeal to the magistrates to frustrate their plan would have been pointless. Doubtless the Puritans were considering some such arrangement as that by which German- and French-speaking Protestants had been affiliated under one superintendent in London some years previously.

[27] *Ibid.*, pp. 75 and 77.

[28] The Geneva negotiations took place about June 10 (Charles Martin, *Les Protestants anglais réfugiés à Genève au temps de Calvin* [Geneva, 1915], p. 37).

desired building. This good news Whittingham carried down the Rhine in triumph.

It remained to evacuate Frankfort with the honors of war, absolution from the charge of schism for their withdrawal. This the rival faction refused to concede, maintaining that the projected action of the Puritan minority proved the accusation. On August 27 the Puritans demanded the appointment of two arbitrators on each side to settle the question of the lawfulness of their departure. Whitehead and Cox demurred, and at length refused, declaring that whatever reasons might be given, or however the arbitrators might decide, "yet can you not let [hinder] men to think." The Puritans defended their favorite principle, that the ecclesiastical matters in dispute "might be decided by the authority of God's word and the arbitrament of godly learned men." But all was in vain. "Certain warm words passed to and fro from one to the other, and so," toward the end of September, 1555, "in some heat they departed."[29]

[29] *Troubles at Frankfort*, pp. 81–83, 85.

CHAPTER VII

The Genevan Model and Its Anglican Propagandists

THE doubly exiled group was now confronted with a choice between Basel and Geneva. Whittingham, still clinging to the remnants of his plan for one big, ideal church, hoped to induce the entire party to go to Geneva, where, in addition to the free use of a place of worship, they might enjoy the company of both Calvin and their former pastor Knox. But Basel had the advantage of being a great publishing center, and so attracted some of the wanderers, including Foxe, already planning his great work. Furthermore, the martyrologist, though a signer of the Puritan request for arbitrators on the matter of schism, was much milder in his Puritanism than Whittingham and Gilby. Throughout the Frankfort struggle he deprecated the tumult and had, for the most part, essayed the difficult role of a neutral.[1] He was not unwilling, therefore, to keep clear of the partisan activity into which he realized the Geneva group would be plunged. In due time a church was set up at Basel, but fond is the idea that geographical change suffices to evade issues. Soon afterward Bale came to the town of the printing presses, and presently we hear him complaining that the disputes which had turned the English world at Frankfort upside down had come there also.[2]

For our purposes, the history of the church at Geneva is much more important. For though, as we have seen, there were many varieties of Reformed belief, and many different Reformed

[1] See his letter to Martyr, n.d., in John Strype, *Ecclesiastical Memorials* (3 vols. in 6; Oxford, 1822), III, ii, 310–11.

[2] Bale to Ashley, n.d., *ibid.*, pp. 313–15.

leaders who influenced the development of English Puritanism, none was nearly so important from this time on as the Genevan. It is, accordingly, worth pausing a moment for a closer look at that city's leader and his system.

John Calvin had a mind that was good, but not too good, and thorough training for his work. He had studied the classics, law, and theology. But it was his determined self-assurance which made him what he was. Without it a clear head and a broad training would have counted for little. Never cursed with any doubts as to the correctness of his ideas, he had the salesman's gifts of absolute confidence in his product and the strength of will to compel the acceptance of his point of view. To these all-important qualities he added some sense of political realities. As a young man this deterred him from accepting Anabaptist doctrines, and in his mature years it kept him from attempting the impossible and also enabled him to stoop now and then to a necessary compromise. With this equipment he succeeded in making both his theology and his city-state models for the Protestants of northwestern Europe.

Orderliness was his chief mental quality, not originality. He developed few, if any, new doctrines. But he arranged and stated the now familiar Protestant theories in admirable fashion. He was calm, confident, and clear. He could blandly state the most contradictory doctrines of divine predestination and human responsibility with such persuasiveness as to make them seem both harmonious and palatable to all but the most recalcitrant. Although more than Zwinglian in his doctrine of the spiritual presence in the sacrament, he managed to phrase it in a form which the Zurichers could accept, and thus he nicely combined mystery and sense in his teaching on this vital point.

Calvin was a second-generation reformer, and so could make use of several highly serviceable Catholic doctrines which were unavailable to his predecessors. The shine was off the doctrines of the liberty of a Christian man and the supremacy of the secular state. The Protestant world was willing to submit to discipline and an up-to-date clericalism. Calvin provided both. He accepted the Catholic doctrine of a visible church wielding

the spiritual sword. He believed that the organized body of believers could and should share in the responsibilities of governing a Christian commonwealth. He associated the laity with
the professional clergy in the work, and he preached a division
of powers, but in reality his minister was the old priest, reformed
indeed, but nonetheless "writ large." Taking the rudimentary
disciplinary ideas of Oecolampadius, the reformer of Basel, and
Bucer, he worked them into a drastically effective system. The
stigma of antinomianism or lawlessness was forever removed
from his followers. At long last medieval ideals began to be
realized once more.

As learning and discipline took the place of strife, Geneva
became the wonder of the Protestant world, and life there a
blissful experience long enshrined in the memories of those
foreigners who were privileged to share it. One refugee called
Geneva the holy city.[3] Knox considered it "the most perfect
school of Christ that ever was in the earth since the days of the
apostles."[4] Even Bale, though his Puritan zeal was cooling,
thought it a miracle that men of so many nationalities "dis-
agreeing in manners, speech, and apparel, sheep and wolves,
bulls and bears, being coupled with the only yoke of Christ,
should live so lovingly and friendly" there.[5]

Furthermore, Calvin did more than any of his fellow Reformed leaders to advance the cause of international Protestantism. He was not satisfied to reform one town. He was setting up a system which he hoped would in time become universal. His theology knew no national bounds, and his church
organization began to ignore borders also. Germans, French,
Poles, Hungarians, Dutch, English, and Scotch took it up. He
too looked forward to a general council which would smooth out
all remaining difficulties, unite all Protestants. His advice was
sought from far and wide. In many lands men turned to him for
inspiration, consolation, definitive judgments. He sent out mis-

---

[3] *Narratives of the Days of the Reformation*, ed. Nichols ("Camden Society: First
Series," Vol. LXXVII [London, 1859]), p. 84.

[4] John Knox, *Works*, ed. Laing (6 vols.; Edinburgh, 1895), IV, 240.

[5] *Pageant of Popes* (London, 1574), prefatory letter to Sulcer, Bullinger, Calvin, and
Melanchthon. The Latin original was published in 1558.

sionary pastors and circular letters which were received as ency-
clicals. Like Washington, another great childless man, he became the father of a mighty people. His enemies called him the
Pope of Geneva, and there was much to justify the epithet.
Indeed, it seemed for a time that a new Catholicism, like the
old, might be born on a lake shore.[6]

Yet we must guard against confusing the ideal with the
reality. Tempting as it is to think of Calvinism as fighting the
old ecclesiasticism with its own weapons, opposing serried rank
to serried rank and curse to curse, the facts do not justify such
a picture. Calvin's power has been greatly exaggerated. He
was, after all, only one of the ministers in one of the towns in
one of the smallest Protestant countries of Europe. Not until
1555 did he gain anything like a free hand in Geneva, so that his
real power lasted only some ten years. Even then it was by no
means absolute. He was frequently forced to compromise with
the Council, and might even be outvoted by his fellow-ministers.
His international influence, though greater than that of any
other Protestant clergyman, was by no means undisputed. Bullinger did not always see eye to eye with him, nor did the
Zuricher's contrary judgments always fall on deaf ears. Musculus at Berne and Martyr at Strassburg were others who were
by no means entirely overshadowed by the Genevan. Looking
back on the scene, Calvin's figure may appear to tower over the
others, but perspectives are sometimes deceiving, because history tends to concentrate on a few great names. The plan for
general council went the way of Cranmer's, and, outside of
Geneva, Calvin never enjoyed any real power except that of
personal and literary influence. Great as this was in many countries, it had little effect on central and eastern Germany. The
Lutherans went their own way with small regard for Geneva.

Doubtless the nationalistic and individualistic forces evoked

---

[6] See the splendid summary of Calvin's achievement in Imbart de la Tour's *Calvin et
l'institution chrétienne* ("Les Origines de la Réforme," Vol. IV, ed. Jacques Chevalier
[Paris, 1935]); cf. also H. D. Foster, "Liberal Calvinism: The Remonstrants at the
Synod of Dort in 1618," *Harvard Theological Review*, XVI (1923), 1–37; "International
Calvinism through Locke and the Revolution of 1688," *American Historical Review*,
XXXII (1927), 475–99; both articles reprinted in his *Collected Papers* (privately print-
ed, 1929).

by the Reformation were largely responsible for this failure, but Calvin's own personality was a contributory factor. Though he spent three years in Strassburg, he never learned German. Even in that Latin-speaking age this is an evidence of an unstatesman-like indifference to a full understanding of the thought and culture of his eastern neighbors and to the necessity of coming to an understanding with them.[7] Of his Roman Catholic fellow-Christians he was even more contemptuous. When reform was under way in the older church and the hand of fellowship was tentatively extended at Ratisbon in 1540, he did his best to thwart the plan of reunion and was exultant when the project failed. His statesmanship, therefore, though genuine and able within limits, was not such as to make possible the establishment of any lasting international Christian unity.

Time has hallowed his memory in most countries with strong Reformed churches, but in the generation immediately following his death his sway was by no means unquestioned. Beza remained loyal to his tradition at Geneva, but elsewhere each national church went its own way. Zurich and Heidelberg were often appealed to as equal in authority with Calvin's city. The French flouted the clear purport of his teaching in the matter of civil war, and the Scotch had their own ideas about observing church festivals. We must not be surprised, therefore, if in England we find not only the Anglicans but also the Puritans adding to and taking away from the words written in the Genevan book of life. For though ideally Calvinism was a vision glorious, in all too many of its aspects it became no more. And of no aspect is this statement more true than of the international one. Beyond the borders of Geneva, Reformed unity was a matter of a gentleman's agreement, and not all the Reformed leaders co-operated by any means.

Yet, when all necessary allowances are made, the original statement concerning the Genevan's importance still stands. Though not a superman, Calvin was easily the greatest Reformed leader of his time, and the welcome he extended to the

[7] Martyr found himself handicapped in his dealings with the English during the vestment controversy by his ignorance of the vernacular (C. H. Smyth, *Cranmer and the Reformation under Edward VI* [Cambridge, 1926], pp. 243 and 246).

English refugees was to have far-reaching influence. Arriving at their destination, October 13, 1555—three days before Latimer and Ridley "lit the candle" at their execution in the Balliol ditch—the Whittingham group soon obtained the promised church. It was arranged that they should share the Temple de Notre Dame la Neuve with the congregation of Italian exiles already established in the city, as they had shared the Frankfort church with the French congregation. The English were to have the use of the building Mondays, Tuesdays, and Fridays and at nine o'clock on Sunday. Church furniture and even a bell were provided. No time was lost in setting up the long-desired model system. On November 1[8] the church was organized, with Goodman and Gilby as ministers in the absence of Knox, who was in Scotland canvassing the religio-political situation and accomplishing the long-deferred marriage with the daughter of the querulous Mrs. Bowes. By February of the following year an order of worship and government had been agreed upon and published.[9] Though in its major outlines it resembled the Frankfort order already described, it constituted the first detailed platform of the Puritan party, and so is worth describing at some length.

At the beginning of the work stands an address "To our Brethren in England, and elsewhere, which love Jesus Christ unfeignedly." Couched in scriptural language and plentifully supplied with proof texts, it opens with the familiar declaration that the cause of the Marian persecution which had driven the English Protestants abroad was the incompleteness of the reformation under Edward, which justly drew the wrath of God upon his disobedient children. Since the best form of repentance is to conform to God's will, the authors thought best to make this possible by presenting

[8] Final arrangements about the church were not made until November 21, and the Council confirmed the elected ministers in their office eight days later.

[9] *The Forme of Prayers and Ministration of the Sacraments, etc., Used in the English Congregation at Geneva and Approved by the Famous and Godly Learned Man, John Calvin.* Reprinted in Knox's *Works*, Vol. IV. For the history and sources of the *Forme of Prayers* see William D. Maxwell, *John Knox's Genevan Service Book* (Edinburgh, 1931).

a form and order of a reformed church limited within the compass of God's Word, which our Saviour hath left unto us as only sufficient to govern all our actions by; so that what so ever is added to this Word by man's device, seem it never so good, holy, or beautiful, yet before our God, which is jealous and can not admit any companion or counsellor, it is evil, wicked, and abominable.[10]

The address continues with a statement concerning ceremonies. Hezekiah's destruction of the brazen serpent is cited as evidence of the fact that old forms may breed superstition, and then with a curious, but not uncommon, lack of logic the writer,[11] who has just appealed to the Scriptures as the only guide, further illustrates this point by showing that the church in the time of Augustine dropped the practice of feet-washing which was instituted by Christ himself. Psalm-singing is then defended, and the address closes with a justification of the adoption of the Genevan catechism. Part of this passage illustrates so well the international outlook which was part of the clericalism for which this party stood that it is worth quoting. After indicating the general merits of the work as a medium of instruction, the writer adds:

Moreover the dangers which hang over Christ's church in these days moved us very much: for as men may see present signs of certain barbarousness, and puddles of errors which are like to chance in the church of God, so there is no better preservation against the same, than if all godly churches would agree in one kind of doctrine and confession of faith, which in all points were agreeable to God's holy Word, that our posterity might be confirmed, by the universal example of Christ's church against all heresies, persecutions, and other dangers; perceiving that it is not only the doctrine of one man, but the consent of the whole Christian church, and that wherein all youth hath been brought up and trained in. The which thing, seeing none hath so far performed, nor yet is in such towardness to the same as this catechism is, being for the worthiness thereof already translated into Hebrew, Greek, Latin, French, Italian, Spanish, Dutch, and English, we could do no less but willingly and gladly embrace the same.[12]

Then follows "The Confession of our Faith, which are assembled in the English Congregation at Geneva." It is an expansion of the Apostles' Creed, and chiefly remarkable for its

[10] Pp. 160–61.

[11] Probably Whittingham.   [12] Pp. 167–68.

Calvinistic teaching in the matter of the church. God ordains some men to be lost and some to be saved. The latter make up the true church, which is invisible. But there is also a visible church, which may be known by the three signs of a proper preaching of the Word, correct ministration of the sacraments, and ecclesiastical discipline. The political magistrate also belongs to this church and is to be obeyed in "all things which are not contrary to the Word of God." He is charged with the responsibility of rooting out all "idolators and heretics, as Papists, Anabaptists, with such like limbs of Antichrist."

Next is given a description of the duties of the church officers and the manner of their election. Under Calvin's influence the Reformed institution of the pastor, in the sense of overseer or chief minister, is dropped, though no Protestant minister was ever more the dominant leader of his colleagues than the Pope of Geneva. There are to be ministers, apparently an indefinite number in each congregation, charged with preaching and administering the sacraments, elders to assist them in ruling the church, and deacons to care for the poor. All are to be examined as to their fitness by other church officers, presumably including those from neighboring congregations if they are available, though, when once certified in that regard, the candidates are to be elected by the congregation. Once a week all the church officers of a given area gather to correct their own faults and those of their congregations. A few pages farther on the need of this discipline is explained, and mention is made of the type of fault to be corrected:

In public discipline, it is to be observed that the ministry pretermit [pass over] nothing at any time unchastised with one kind of punishment or other. If they perceive any thing in the congregation, either evil in example, slanderous in manners, or not beseeming their profession: as if there be any covetous person, any adulterer, or fornicator, forsworn, thief, briber, false witness-bearer, blasphemer, drunkard, slanderer, usurer; any person disobedient, seditious, or dissolute; any heresy or sect, as Papistical, Anabaptistical, and such like: briefly, what so ever it be that might spot the Christian congregation, yea, rather what so ever is not to edification, ought not to escape either admonition or punishment.[13]

[13] P. 205.

There followed the forms for the different services of the church. Provision was made for a weekday meeting for the interpretation of the Scriptures, in which any member of the congregation might participate. The weekly service of public worship consisted of a confession of sins, the singing of a psalm, a sermon, a prayer for the church universal, a recitation of the creed, the singing of another psalm, and finally the benediction. Baptism was to be administered to infants, but with no other ceremonies than prayer, exhortation, and application of water. The Lord's Supper was to be a memorial meal, taken apparently in a sitting posture. Marriage was performed without the use of the ring. Ministers were to visit the sick and pray with them, but no provision was made for anointing them. The dead were to be given reverent burial, but there were to be no ceremonies except a sermon in the church, which was to follow the interment.

With the congregation thus organized to their liking, the Puritan group faced the old problem of persuading their fellow-English exiles that this order ought to supplant its Edwardian rival. One method of approaching this goal was the original Frankfort one of persuading as many of their fellow-countrymen as possible to join them on their terms. From the testimony of their church register[14] and similar documents, they enjoyed considerable success in this undertaking. Though there were only forty-seven persons in the new church at its founding—twenty-seven of the original Frankfort party and twenty other English already resident in Geneva—one hundred and thirty-nine others were added later, and there is reason to believe[15] that at least twenty-six more were members at one time or another. Something like a quarter of the total number of English religious exiles, therefore, came under Genevan influence. Among these additions to the Frankfort group, either earlier settlers in Geneva or later arrivals, there were included

---

[14] *Livre des Anglois*, printed with notes by J. Southerden Burn (London, 1831), and reprinted in his *History of Parish Registers in England* (London, 1862), pp. 271–88. Also reprinted with notes by A. Ferrier Mitchell (*s.l.*, n.d.).

[15] Charles Martin, *Les Protestants anglais réfugiés à Genève au temps de Calvin* (Geneva, 1915), p. 47.

such prominent laymen as Sir William Stafford, Mrs. Locke, Knox's London correspondent, and John Bodley, whose thirteen-year-old son and fellow-exile was later to become famous as the founder of the Oxford library. Prominent clerical members of the congregation were Thomas Lever, whom we have already met at Frankfort; James Pilkington, President of St. John's College, Cambridge, and later Bishop of Durham; John Scory, the former Bishop of Chichester; Thomas Sampson, former Dean of the cathedral chapter in the same see; William Kethe, whose version of "Old Hundred" is not yet forgotten; Thomas Bentham, an Oxford Hebraist; William Cole, fellow of Corpus Christi College, Oxford; Laurence Humphrey, fellow of Magdalen College, Oxford; and Miles Coverdale. Some indication of the success of the Geneva undertaking may be seen in the fact that two of these men, Lever and Sampson, had opposed the Puritan party at Frankfort. Many of the clergy whose names appear on the Geneva lists did not stay long in Calvin's town; either, like Coverdale, coming late in the period of the exile, or, like Pilkington, departing shortly for other refugee centers. Yet, however short their stay, few, if any, were unaffected by the example of the thoroughly reformed church which they found in the Swiss city. Though somewhat battered by the blows of an unfriendly government, the Geneva stamp was still discernible years later in many an English character.

To strengthen the new movement, it was also necessary to furnish it with devotional and theological literature. Bound up with the copies of the *Forme and Order* were several items designed to deepen and enrich the spiritual life of the new church. There were prayers for private householders, a reprint of an English translation of Calvin's catechism, published at London in 1550, and an English psalter. This last was largely a reprint of the famous work of Sternhold and Hopkins which had appeared in 1549, but seven additional paraphrases were added by Whittingham. To make clear to Continental Protestants the purity of the doctrine for which the English suffered, a Latin translation of Ridley's treatise on the sacrament was issued.[16] To buttress the

---

[16] *D. Nicolai Ridleii episcopi londenensis de coena dominica assertio* (Geneva, 1556); Martin, *op. cit.*, p. 304.

theological foundations of the model church against Anabaptist attacks, Whittingham translated a work of Beza on predestination,[17] and Gilby and Knox also produced works on the same subject.[18]

But the most important contribution of this church to the intellectual armory of the Puritan faction was the Geneva translation of the Bible. New editions of the Scriptures in Latin and French were pouring from Swiss presses during the middle of the century, and it was only natural that the English exiles should be drawn into the work of providing an accurate vernacular text. Taking a Latin translation by Beza as his model, an English scholar, probably Whittingham, revised the Tyndale text of the New Testament as found in the Great Bible, and published the new work, June 13, 1557. This version is notable as being the first English one to copy the recent innovation of the French printer, Robert Estienne, the division of the chapters into verses. But, as in the earlier translations, the marginal comments were not the least important part of the volume. When it was stated that the locusts of the Apocalypse were not only heretics and monks but "Archbishops, and Bishops, Doctors, Bachelors, and Masters which forsake Christ to maintain false doctrine," a handle was provided for future attacks on the episcopacy. Not content with this achievement, the English community pushed ahead with a project for a complete new translation of the English Bible. The men of wealth bore the expense, and a number of scholars, including Whittingham, Gilby, Cole, Kethe, and John Baron did the work. Knox, Goodman, and Coverdale doubtless rendered occasional assistance.[19] Here again, though the Hebrew text was consulted, much help was derived from current Latin and French translations.

More vigorous kinds of literary propaganda were also em-

[17] *Beza: His Briefe Declaraccion of the Chiefe Poyntes of Christian Religion, Set Forth in a Table of Predestination* (Geneva, 1556); Martin, *op. cit.*, pp. 125 and 303.

[18] Anthony Gilby, *A Briefe Treatice of Election and Reprobation with Certain Answers to the Objections of the Adversaries to This Doctrine* (Geneva, 1556); Knox, *An Answer to a Great Number of Blasphemous Cavillations* (Geneva, 1560) (reprinted in *Works*, Vol. V).

[19] Martin, *op. cit.*, pp. 241–42.

ployed. Before the work of biblical translation was completed, Knox had resumed the issuing of political tracts, an activity interrupted, as we have seen, by the Frankfort episode and also by his daring visit to Scotland. Summoned once more to his native land in the spring of 1557, he set out on the journey in September, but at Dieppe discretion prevailed over courage, and he remained there awaiting developments, unable to return to Geneva with good grace. In the French town he relieved the tedium by composing a tract for the times. Much had happened since Knox had last concerned himself with the subject of political revolution. The troubles of the French Huguenots had caused him to meditate somewhat bitterly on the character of princes.[20] The Queen Regent of Scotland had scorned a mild exhortation from Knox to push forward the Reformation in that country, and her daughter was about to marry the Catholic Dauphin of France. No help was therefore to be expected from the Scotch royal house. The English government had begun to execute its subjects for heresy, at the rate of one hundred a year, and the persecution gave no sign of slackening. The Queen of England was now a married woman, expecting to have issue which would perpetuate the Catholic control of the state. So far as the exiles knew, her health was good, and only in the realm of wishful thinking was there any prospect of Elizabeth's succeeding to the throne. At Strassburg, Grindal, the leading Anglican, had practically abandoned hope and was learning German, preparing for an indefinite stay abroad. But Knox was made of sterner stuff, and, though for the moment he quailed at the dangers attendant upon personal revolutionary activity in Scotland, he did attempt to secure the same end by spreading appropriate propaganda. There was no lack of models. The Magdeburg *Bekenntnis*, which advocated the eventually triumphant doctrines of the social compact and the right of subjects to resist their rulers, had been in print since 1550, and Knox had

[20] It is not certain, however, as J. W. Allen suggests (*A History of Political Thought in the Sixteenth Century* [London, 1928], pp. 108–9) that Knox intended to suggest by the phrase "that Princes . . . . be compelled also to reform their wicked laws" that subjects should do the compelling. Divine or external compulsion may have been intended.

probably seen a copy while in Germany.[21] Furthermore, in 1556, the exiled Bishop of Winchester, John Ponet, trained under that master of political theory, Sir Thomas Smith, had already developed these theories in English. From his Strassburg exile the Anglican Bishop had composed a reasonable justification of the right of revolution and even tyrannicide.[22] With a wealth of biblical and classical illustrations Ponet maintained the social compact idea, the right to private property, and the principle that the king should rule according to laws which it was the duty of Parliament, the clergy, and the people to enforce. What was now needed was some sharper and more specific application of these principles to the particular problem in hand. Under the circumstances, with his mind steeped in biblical teachings, Knox quickly came to the conclusion that it was his duty to add to the general revolutionary theory of Ponet a denial of the right of women to rule, which would meet the current situation by attacking the authority of both the English and the Scotch sovereigns. The result was the celebrated *First Blast of the Trumpet against the Monstruous Regiment of Women,* published anonymously a few months later at Geneva. In it were presented scriptural and classical arguments to show that woman was taken from man, was naturally subordinate to him, and could not, therefore, without special divine authorization, be a magistrate. The nobles and people of the two island realms were consequently called on to depose their sovereigns.[23]

In the *First Blast* Knox promised to discuss the social compact theory and its various implications more at length, in a second blast to follow. But the whole community of exiles at Geneva, which had been under his ministry, was feeling the

---

[21] *Ibid.,* pp. 103–6.

[22] *A Short Treatise of Politike Power* (s.l., 1556). Reprinted in 1639 and 1642.
On stylistic grounds, Miss Christina H. Garrett (*The Marian Exiles* [Cambridge, 1938], pp. 28–29, 84, 254–55, 280) assigns to Ponet the major share in the composition of *The Humble and Unfained Confession of the Belefe of Certain Poore Banished Men* (Wittenberg [?], 1554), which she regards as having been of considerable importance, both political and theoretical. I am unable to see in it, however, any clear indication of authorship, or more than a conventional anti-Catholic tract of the time—with possibly a slight variation in the usual teaching on the plan of salvation, which served as a background for the later Covenant theology (p. 395).

[23] *Works,* IV, 416.

same sharpening of their political outlook, and at about the time Knox was composing his attack on female rule its other pastor, Christopher Goodman, published a work which rendered the supplementary volume largely unnecessary.[24] It developed Knox's arguments on the elective nature of monarchy and also declared the enjoyment of that office a male prerogative. Later in the same year Knox published two appeals to his Scotch countrymen, which set forth the same principles in a somewhat milder form.[25] But as far as England was concerned all these propaganda efforts were in vain. No revolution took place in the southern kingdom. Instead, these publications raised a storm of protest and created an impression of Puritan rashness which the party never quite succeeded in living down.[26] In the next century Cromwell's Ironsides were to demonstrate the soundness of the social compact theory. But for the time being the greatest diplomacy was necessary in setting it forth. When all allowances are made for the extreme provocation to which Knox was subjected, to couple this teaching with an attack on women rulers was to invite disaster. It must be admitted that Knox was most shortsighted in not considering the alternatives to the rule of Mary Tudor in England. If the Queen were deposed, who was next in the line of succession? Was Elizabeth also to be passed over on the ground of sex? If Knox had stopped to ask such questions, as any realistic politician should have done, he must have been led to question his interpretation of the Scriptures. Deborah's case would not have seemed such an anomaly, and the future path of the English Puritan might have been far smoother.

But while the fortunes of the Puritan movement during the

[24] *How Superior Powers Oght To Be Obeyed of Their Subjects* (Geneva, 1558). Reprinted in facsimile by the Facsimile Text Society (New York, 1931).

[25] *The Appellation of John Knoxe from the Cruell and Most Unjust Sentence Pronounced against Him by the False Bishoppes and Clergie of Scotland* (Geneva, 1558); *To His Beloved Brethren, the Communaltie of Scotland* (included in the same volume with the above). Reprinted in *Works*, Vol. IV. *An Admonition to England and Scotland To Call Them to Repentance* (Geneva, 1558), by Anthony Gilby, was also included in the same volume.

[26] Knox, *Works*, IV, 539; Goodman to Martyr, August 20, 1558, *Original Letters Relative to the English Reformation*, ed. Robinson (2 vols.; Cambridge: Parker Society, 1846–47), pp. 768–71.

Marian period were chiefly bound up with the Genevan experiment, there were some developments elsewhere which are worth noticing. *Toujours à la gauche* ("Always to the left"), says the modern French politician, and so it was with the early English Protestants. Just as the conservative Protestants under Edward VI soon found themselves carried beyond the position they assumed in opposition to Hooper in 1550, so the Anglican majority among the exiles found the pressure of the Continental Reformed communities difficult to resist. At Zurich and at Strassburg, Sandys, Jewel, and other Anglicans were growing accustomed to a simple Reformed worship, which by 1558 they considered "most godly." Even at Frankfort great concessions were made by the victorious Coxians. At the height of the controversy there the nationalist group had only demanded the substance and effect of the English Prayer Book and had granted that such ceremonies as their hosts "could not bear" might be omitted.[27] In the final settlement they "gave up private baptisms, confirmation of children, saints' days, kneeling at the holy communion, the linen surplices of the ministers, crosses, and other things of like character."[28] Perhaps Cox's group thus still retained "the face of an English church," but not many Anglicans of the next century would have been willing to admit it. In the later controversies in the troubled community on the Main, Calvin was quoted with the greatest respect by all concerned, and his catechism was adopted as the best medium for exilic Christian instruction.[29] Time moderated the feelings roused by earlier strife, and, toward the end of the exile,[30] at least some of the participants were exchanging visits, salutations, and apologies. So among the *émigrés* outside Geneva the Puritan tide was steadily rising, silently but nonetheless effectively.

[27] *A Brief Discourse of the Troubles at Frankfort*, ed. Arber (London, 1908), p. 39.

[28] *Ibid.*, p. 77.   [29] *Ibid.*, pp. 154–55, 158, 164–65.

[30] Goodman to Martyr, August 20, 1558, *Original Letters*, p. 768; John Jewel to Whittingham and Goodman, n.d., *Works*, ed. Ayre (4 vols.; Cambridge: Parker Society, 1845–50), IV, 1192–93. The date of this letter may be 1558, instead of 1557 as the editor suggests. Jewel's opinion of Goodman and his actions may easily have undergone considerable change after Elizabeth's accession. Certainly the two men seem to have been on friendly enough terms in August, 1558, judging by the letter to Martyr.

CHAPTER VIII

Another Revolutionary Technique
Congregationalism

FROM Tyndale to Knox, the spokesmen for the Protestant opposition consistently repudiated any suggestion of Anabaptism. In spite of occasional lapses by men like Barnes, they were, on the whole, correct in their claim to be considered a distinct group. For between the middle-class moderation of the one and the proletarian radicalism of the other there was a great gulf fixed. The Reformed group advocated a national church, a generally predestinarian theology, the right to private property, the lawfulness of secular government, and of all the means to that end, such as the use of violence, law suits, and civil oaths. The Anabaptists, moved primarily by an extreme literalism in their interpretation of the Bible, seldom, if ever, troubled themselves with the needs of society as a whole. Let the faithful adhere to the true religion though the heavens should fall. They were content with small, gathered churches, free-will theology, and whatever solutions of social problems individual leaders might choose. Constantly persecuted as they were, able to exist only in small, secret bands, handicapped by ignorant and inexperienced leadership, anything like a program suitable to the needs of an entire commonwealth was beyond the range of their thought. Accordingly, it has not hitherto been difficult to distinguish between these two idealistic forces.

The problem is somewhat complicated, however, by the appearance in the reigns of Edward and Mary of a group of English sectaries who may be called halfway Anabaptists. They held conventicles in Essex and Kent, denounced the doctrine

of predestination, and refused to have their children baptized
by Roman Catholic clergy, though they did not object to infant
baptism as such, or hold many of the other Anabaptist principles of which they were accused.[1] Their Protestant contemporaries, chiefly alarmed by their stand on election, called them
free-willers, but their attitudes toward amusements and religious
persecution are of more permanent interest. When confined in
the King's Bench Prison along with Bradford, Philpot, and another irreconcilable Protestant of Puritan leanings, a Coventry
weaver named John Careless, the zealous sectaries were scandalized that these men who looked "every day to suffer for the
truth" should indulge in "vain play" at cards, dice, and bowls.
The Puritan had not yet become the ascetic, and the appropriately named Careless retorted that Christ made all things clean
for the elect, citing the story of Peter's vision. He asserted,
furthermore, that those once called cannot be lost, no matter
what games they played, and that any who thought otherwise
believed in salvation by works. As his opponent, John Trew,
complained, he "also threatened us that we were like to die for
it if the gospel should reign again, affirming that the true
church might shed blood for belief's sake." To disprove this
remarkable indorsement of the principle under which the Puritan was himself suffering, the free-willers quoted the Sermon on
the Mount and many other scriptural passages. "But it would
not serve."[2]

So there was a schism among the schismatics, much to the
glee of the Roman Catholics.[3] Excommunications and recrimi-

---

[1] John Strype, *Ecclesiastical Memorials* (3 vols. in 6; Oxford, 1822), II, i, 369–71;
Champlin Burrage, *The Early English Dissenters* (2 vols.; Cambridge, 1912), I, 50–53;
II, 1–6. For the history of the movement under Mary see John Bradford, *Writings*, ed.
Townsend (2 vols.; Cambridge: Parker Society, 1848–53), I, 306, and the references
there cited.

[2] John Trew, "The Cause of Contention in the King's Bench," Bodleian MS 53,
fols. 116–24. Inaccurately printed in Richard Laurence (ed.), *Authentic Documents Relative to the Predestinarian Controversy* (Oxford, 1819), pp. 37–70, esp. pp. 56–57.

[3] John Foxe, *Acts and Monuments*, ed. Townsend (London, 1837–41), VIII, 164–66.
They also made much of the Frankfort strife. When these points were brought up by
his Roman Catholic interrogator, Careless blithely records, "I lied falsely," and later
adds, "This I spake to make the best of the matter: for I was sorry that the papists
should hear of our variance."

nations flew back and forth within the prison walls, until the creed that did reign silenced some of the leaders on both sides with the ultimate argument of the stake. Many of these primitive Arminians, however, survived at least the first fury of the blast,[4] and it is tempting to see in their activities some of the preliminary stirrings of the later English separatist movements. But since no continuity of names can be traced, and since none of these liberals was of the "learned" class, it seems more likely that this semi-Anabaptist movement was overwhelmed by the waves of predestinarian orthodoxy which rolled in from the Continent in the early years of Elizabeth's reign.

Nevertheless, similar circumstances produce similar institutions. If no direct connection can be traced between Puritanism and Anabaptism, some of the Reformed group felt driven by extreme necessity to adopt devices very similar to those of their despised leftist rivals. It is, however, a mistake to imagine that, either during the exile or later in the century, congregationalism was ever considered by any of the Puritans as anything but a means to an end. Always the ultimate objective was an all-embracing Reformed religion. To reach that goal, many felt it wise to proceed by way of gathered churches which should set a model to be followed by the entire commonwealth. Since this was commonly illegal, congregationalism became a revolutionary technique, a tool for those who wished to push the reform "without tarrying for any." But no sixteenth-century Puritan ever thought that the church should permanently remain a thing of scattered, independent bands.

The circumstances of the *émigrés* made the organization of a national church difficult, and eventually, as we have seen, the effort was abandoned. Unless they settled under the aegis of some vigorous Continental leader, such as Calvin, who amalgamated their organization into the local Reformed body, they assumed an independent pattern. Though advice was occasionally solicited from other refugee communities, it was not regularly followed, and the different groups became virtually gathered churches. The Frankfort practice, already noted, of ac-

[4] *Ibid.*, p. 384.

cepting no members who would not subscribe to the doctrine and discipline of the church, was characteristic of later Independent practice. For all practical purposes the Frankfort discipline constituted a church covenant, after the definition of the leading student of this topic.[5] On the departure of the Genevan element, the requirement of subscription continued to be the rule of the body.[6] The fact that there were Englishmen in Frankfort who were not considered members of the church[7] is a further indication of how far the *émigré* community had declined from the ideal of a national church.

In its internal organization the Frankfort congregation showed a similar trend toward congregational practice. Here again circumstance rather than principle dictated this policy. The desire to change an administration, rather than devotion to democracy as such, was the chief motive. To modern ears even such an attitude on the part of the group so recently victorious in the struggle for the Edwardian Prayer Book sounds very strange. But at that time the ceremonial party recognized no essential relationship between ecclesiastical rites and church polity, and thus saw nothing amiss in using arguments which later became the sole property of the anticeremonial faction. To understand this situation, we must glance briefly at the story of previous relations between the Frankfort congregation and its clergy.

The ministerial office of this church suffered both from an uncertain constitutional position and from the poor quality of its incumbents, except during the Knox-Lever period. Originally a single minister, John MacBray, had been elected,[8] but the discipline which was drawn up shortly afterward had provided for a chief pastor or superintendent and assistant preachers, on the à Lasco model.[9] Nevertheless, a few months later the congregation decided to have the "church governed by two or three

[5] Champlin Burrage, *The Covenant Idea* (Philadelphia, 1904), p. 14.

[6] *A Brief Discourse of the Troubles at Frankfort,* ed. Arber (London, 1908), pp. 96 and 190.

[7] *Ibid.,* p. 134.　　　　[8] *Ibid.,* p. 25. *Liturgia sacra* (Frankfort, 1554), p. 92.

[9] *Troubles at Frankfort,* pp. 147–48.

grave, godly, and learned ministers of like [equal] authority, as
is accustomed in the best reformed churches."[10] It was then
that invitations were dispatched to Knox, Lever, and Haddon.
Haddon declined, and, before replies were received from the
others, David Whitehead, formerly tutor in the Duke of Suffolk's family and more recently one of à Lasco's company of
refugees at Emden, arrived (October 24, 1554) and was asked
to assume the responsibility temporarily.[11] No fixed term of
office had been provided for in the discipline, and MacBray was
apparently displaced without difficulty. On the arrival of Knox
in the following month, Whitehead seems to have retired, leaving the Scotchman the sole minister. On February 6, 1555, Lever,
who had come some weeks previously, became cominister, each
leader taking one service a Sunday.[12] Following the triumph of
Cox, an effort was made to return to the pattern of the discipline, in the matter of ministerial offices at least. Lever disappears from the picture, and without bothering formally to
depose the previous incumbents or to secure resignations from
them, the faction in control once more elected David Whitehead
as a single "Bishop, Superintendent, or Pastor."[13] Two assistant preachers were also said to have been chosen,[14] though their
names are unknown, and they do not appear further in the
story.

Had Cox taken the office to which his dominating personality and his service to his party entitled him, he might have
ruled the congregation successfully in spite of its independent
constitution and the lack of control from neighboring churches.
But he preferred to move to Strassburg, and the Frankfort
group, whose chosen leaders he had driven out, was left to get
on with Whitehead as best it might. Brandon's former tutor
disliked responsibility. In the preceding reign he had declined
the archbishopric of Armagh, and under Elizabeth he is said
to have refused the see of Canterbury. At Frankfort he soon

[10] *Ibid.*, p. 31.

[11] *Ibid.*, p. 33.   [13] *Ibid.*, p. 72.

[12] *Ibid.*, pp. 53 and 63.   [14] *Ibid.*, p. 77.

showed himself quite unsuited to the pastoral office. When an
effort was made to organize a school, he resigned his position
rather than give the divinity lecture, and "great hold [conten-
tion] there was about this matter." But, when steps were taken
to elect a new pastor, he withdrew the resignation. Finally, on
January 6, 1556, he was persuaded once more to abdicate.[15]
Robert Horne, the former Dean of Durham, was elected in his
place; but, while he was clearing himself of certain slanders,
MacBray filled the office, and it was not until March 1 that
Horne began his pastorate.

For almost a year we hear of no commotion in the Church of
the White Ladies. In September, in fact, Horne felt sufficiently
secure to be planning to assemble a Protestant council after
Cranmer's pattern, including Bullinger and Calvin in the gathering.[16] But in January there was another furious outbreak of
that contentiousness which explains something of the sixteenth-
century distrust of democracy. This time the issue was the
manner of administering the community poor relief system.[17]
Since most of the church were living on or below the poverty
line, this was a very important matter. In theory the deacons
were charged with this responsibility, but, because some of them
were recipients of alms themselves, it was considered improper
for them to raise and distribute the funds, and the work was
actually done by the wealthy merchant, Richard Chambers.
He was the delegate from the Zurich group who, with Grindal,
had tried to compose the original disorders at Frankfort. Staying on after the Geneva schism, he became an elder in the continuing body, and took over the charitable work of the church.[18]
He was doubtless chosen for this work because of his connection
with other merchants in the homeland, from whom most of the

---

[15] *Ibid.*, p. 95.

[16] Horne and Chambers to Bullinger, September 19, 1556, *Original Letters Relative
to the English Reformation*, ed. Robinson (2 vols.; Cambridge: Parker Society, 1846–47),
p. 134.

[17] A minor, related issue was a demand for registration of wills and publicity in their
probating, so as to eliminate fraud in such matters (*Troubles at Frankfort*, pp. 200, 208,
213).

[18] *Ibid.*, pp. 118–20.

funds were gathered.[19] This had to be done with the greatest secrecy[20] in order to protect the donors from the wrath of the government, which was not minded to leave the exiles in peace.[21] As might be expected in this clandestine business, Chambers' exact status as a welfare worker was not clear. The Frankfort group asserted that he was acting as their agent, under their commission,[22] but he maintained[23] that he acted solely on his own responsibility, with the approval but not the appointment of the church.

In such a situation dissatisfaction inevitably developed. Beneficiaries declared the donations inadequate and accused the pastor and collector of using the veil of secrecy to cover up the withholding of funds meant for them. To the officials the clamorous poor often seemed unworthy, given to fraudulent concealing of assets or unwilling to help themselves.[24] But some of the men who had been clergymen at home scorned to work as printers or serving men, and maintained that, while Chambers collected money elsewhere, he distributed in Frankfort no more than the local donors contributed.[25] Frayed tempers at length gave way in January, 1557, and for nine months the Frankfort church was torn with controversy. A two-thirds majority, mostly composed of the poorer members,[26] attempted to remove Horne and the elders—who generally supported Chambers—to gain control of the church machinery, and to re-organize the relief system. Fortunately, the details of the strife do not concern us. It is enough to say that it revealed refugee temperament at its worst. Resignations were submitted and retracted, and services omitted for lack of a minister willing to serve. Secret caucuses were held in the church building with

[19] Horne and Chambers to Bullinger, February 3, 1556, *Original Letters*, p. 130.

[20] *Troubles at Frankfort*, pp. 129, 171–73, 179–82, 206–15, esp. pp. 180 and 207.

[21] Cf. the kidnaping of Cheke and the efforts to force the return of Bertie and the Duchess of Suffolk (I. S. Leadam, "Narrative of the Pursuit of the English Refugees in Germany under Queen Mary," *Transactions of the Royal Historical Society*, XI [2d ser., 1897], 113–31).

[22] *Troubles at Frankfort*, pp. 118 and 122.

[23] *Ibid.*, pp. 216–17.   [25] *Ibid.*, p. 212.

[24] *Ibid.*, pp. 119, 174–75, 214.   [26] *Ibid.*, p. 162.

the rival party barred, and slanders were spread in the market place, with insult answering insult and taunt matching taunt. At the church the minority made stormy exits, and, on one occasion, an equally stormy entrance, properly timed by a signal from spies.[27] Papers full of argument were "sticked" upon the pulpit.[28] All attempts by magistrates, the French pastor, and English exiles elsewhere to arrange a compromise were rejected by both sides with equal zest.

The economic issue was soon obscured by the constitutional one of the rights of the congregation as against its officers. "The church was above the pastor and not the pastor above the church,"[29] said the majority, led by Whitehead and John Hales, the hero of the attempt to enforce the anti-inclosure acts under Somerset. Anglican and Puritan tradition alike were on the side of the church officials in this quarrel. The discipline of the body made no provision for overriding the elected officials of the congregation during their term of office. Though it was rather a teapot tempest, the irregular action of the congregation in demanding a new discipline incorporating their view of the issue may be called revolutionary.

At length the magistrates intervened, deposed all the church officials, and authorized the amendment of the discipline and the election of new officers. Amid much recrimination most of the committee which was appointed to revise the disputed document accepted a new constitution which embodied the wishes of the majority faction. Forty-two of the sixty-two members of the congregation subscribed it, and new officers, headed by two equal ministers, were elected. Horne and Chambers protested vehemently and one spring morning quietly departed for Strassburg. This trip apparently produced one last attempt at arbitration, but the congregation's blood was up, and, though the suggested settlement bore the names of such personages as Thomas Wroth, Francis and Henry Knollys, and Edwin Sandys, it was summarily rejected, and the congregational party held the field in the name of its new discipline.

[27] *Ibid.*, p. 134. [28] *Ibid.*, p. 115. [29] *Ibid.*, p. 113.

This document was an explicit statement of the majority view of the points at issue, and together with the arguments offered in its defense constitutes a remarkably clear enunciation of independent polity. After a preliminary declaration concerning the utility of assemblies for worship, the second article continues:

The congregation thus assembled is a particular [distinct] visible church, such as may be in divers places of the world very many. And all these particular churches joined together, not in place (for that is not possible) but by the conjunction of true doctrine and faith in the same, do make one church in this world.[30]

No mention is made of presbytery or synod. Theoretically, the congregation is the only ecclesiastical unit. Robert Browne made this point no more clearly. A doctrinal statement follows, and then the vexed question of the authority of the ministers is considered. In order to render impossible a repetition of such claims of pastoral power as Horne's, it was provided that in the future there should be two ministers or teachers, "of like authority, and neither of them superior or inferior to the other."[31] Scripture, Jerome, and Calvin were quoted to support that decision, and then follows an appeal to history:

Where they speak so much of the mischief of contention in the church [caused by equal ministers] we confess it a great evil, but that tyranny is a more pestiferous destruction to the church and that tyranny crept into the church by one, the Bishop of Rome may teach us at large.[32]

This was a body blow at the whole episcopal notion, repudiating even the à Lascan modification held by Horne's group, that, though the pastor ought not to "be above the rest [of the ministers] by lordship, so yet ought he to be above others in charge and in burden, inasmuch as he must needs give a greater account than the rest for the flock committed unto him and to his charge."[33] Thus was the cry of "No prelacy" raised for the first time in English controversy.

After a statement providing that deacons able to live of their

[30] *Ibid.*, p. 150.
[31] *Ibid.*, p. 153.
[32] *Ibid.*, p. 164.
[33] *Ibid.*, pp. 163–64.

own should collect and distribute alms with somewhat more publicity than hitherto,[34] the discipline of the church is described. Here the rights of the congregation are much more carefully safeguarded than in the previous document. Though there are to be six elders to assist the two ministers, in that activity none of them is "to make any manner of decrees or ordinances to bind the congregation or any member thereof, but shall execute such ordinances and decrees as shall be made by the congregation and to them delivered."[35] Though they were to continue to perform their official duties, both elders and deacons were to quit their offices and become "private persons" from the first of each March until the date of the new election.[36] While the ministers and elders had authority to assemble the congregation, if they refused to do so the body of the church might legally assemble itself—do we feel here a preliminary breath of the Triennial breeze?—and the majority of such a meeting might bind the entire organization.[37] Provision is made for trying the church officials as a body, or any part of them, by means of a congregational committee. This was to act by itself in case all those in power are suspect, but otherwise to supplement the officials not accused.[38] Any disagreement among the ministers and elders about the interpretation of the discipline was to be referred to the entire congregation.[39]

For all this independent doctrine there was no intention of separating church and state. The magistrate was charged with the responsibility of protecting the true religion, and in case of congregational action against the officials as a body an appeal might lie to the magistrates.[40] There was obvious reluctance to take church affairs to such a tribunal, and only the most important were to be handled in that fashion; but, once the magistrates intervened, there was no disposition to question their authority or to dispute their decision.[41] On the other hand, the

[34] Ibid., pp. 167–69.
[35] Ibid., p. 185.
[36] Ibid., p. 186.
[37] Ibid., pp. 187–88.
[38] Ibid., pp. 196–99.
[39] Ibid., p. 199.
[40] Ibid., p. 198.
[41] Ibid., pp. 102–4, 116, 122.

secular Council in deposing the officials and authorizing the amendment of the discipline by a majority of the congregation, all being private persons, obviously backed the congregational party. They had scant respect for ordination and clericalism. In this attitude they foreshadowed the seventeenth-century Cromwells and Iretons, who found Independency a more pliable tool for secular interests than Presbyterianism.

In the homeland the exigencies of the terror also compelled the Reformed[42] party to have recourse to congregationalism for the time being. There were gathered churches in London, in the north,[43] and in Colchester.[44] Though mention is made of preachers and pastors, nothing further is known of the organization of any one of these groups except the one in the metropolis, which at times had more than two hundred members.[45] There an effort was made to approximate the à Lascan model, with a chief pastor, at the head of a central congregation, directing the others.[46] By means of daring messengers communication was maintained with the Reformed churches on the Continent, whence books were imported and advice was secured on matters of ecclesiastical discipline.[47] But in practice each congregation seems to have been a law unto itself. There is no evidence of any group being compelled by outside forces to do anything against its will, and these units are therefore to be considered as virtually independent churches. In fact, since under the circumstances they acknowledged no secular control, they were more purely separatist in their polity than their Frankfort contemporary.

In their brief life-span the question of the relative powers of

[42] That these were not Anabaptist groups may be concluded from the facts that one of the London adherents was accused of reading a book against that sect (Foxe, *op. cit.*, VIII, 384, 478), that members of the Colchester group had formerly received the sacrament after the Edwardian manner (*ibid.*, p. 388), and that the Stoke group desired such a communion (*ibid.*, p. 557).

[43] Strype, *op. cit.*, III, ii, 149.

[44] Foxe, *op. cit.*, VIII, 383–88.   [45] *Ibid.*, p. 559.

[46] Strype, *op. cit.*, III, ii, 132; cf. Foxe, *op. cit.*, VIII, 450.

[47] Strype, *op. cit.*, III, ii, 133–35; Foxe, *op. cit.*, VIII, 384.

congregation and clergy apparently did not present itself, so
they made no contribution to this aspect of congregational
theory. They did, however, have the officers and powers of an
independent church. In addition to their pastors, they had
deacons[48] and, in view of their conformity to the Reformed
type, probably elders. When ordained men were not available,
laymen took their place as exhorters, but otherwise there is
no evidence of anything like congregational ordination of new
ministers. The deacons kept lists of the membership of the congregation, gathered and distributed relief, and served as executors for the estates of those who died.[49] Offenders were excommunicated by the pastor, with the consent of the congregation.[50]
As in the Frankfort instance, the Edwardian service was used,[51]
since the Anglican ceremonies were not considered incompatible
with congregational polity.

While the London congregations were far behind the Frankfort one in the development of their constitutional theory, they
made a much more important contribution to the cause of
future independency. By the dangers they braved to hold their
secret meetings, and the sufferings of those who were apprehended, they inspired imitators in later years. There was little
or nothing to be proud of in the history of Frankfort congregationalism, born as it was of indigent *émigrés* squabbling over
the division of relief funds. Its influence was not entirely lost,
as we shall see,[52] but it was the London example which later
zealots chose to cite as a precedent for their actions.

To avoid suspicion, these devoted worshipers were compelled
to change their place of meeting very frequently. Many were
the hairbreadth escapes which enlivened the chronicle of this
movement. Spies and false brethren were counterbalanced by
eternal vigilance and clever ruses. Maying parties, plays, and
feasts served as camouflage for their meetings. Once, when sur-
rounded in a house on Thames Street, a seaman in their number

---

[48] Foxe, *op. cit.*, VIII, 454, 459.

[49] Strype, *op. cit.*, III, i, 586–87.	[51] *Ibid.*, pp. 445 and 458.

[50] Foxe, *op. cit.*, VIII, 451.	[52] See below, p. 212.

swam out from the back, procured a boat, used his shoes for oars, and slowly ferried the company away.[53] Those who were apprehended, in spite of all precautions, showed the greatest fortitude. Though racked for what he judged to be three hours, and otherwise tortured, a captured deacon, Cuthbert Symson, refused to betray his associates. An excommunicated woman showed her mettle by aiding the imprisoned pastor who had pronounced sentence upon her, and ultimately dying with him.[54] Though one of their ministers, John Rose, recanted under pressure,[55] the others set a fine example of courage. Edmund Scambler, later Bishop of Peterborough and Norwich; Thomas Fowle, formerly fellow of St. John's, Cambridge; John Rough; Augustine Bernher, Latimer's faithful Swiss servant; and Thomas Bentham successively held the dangerous honor of chief minister to the London groups. Rough, a Scotch Protestant who had settled in England under Somerset, fled to the Continent in Mary's time. In Freisland he supported himself by knitting stockings.[56] Returning to London for yarn in the fall of 1557, he was persuaded to remain as preacher to the secret congregation. A month later he was betrayed. He went to his death without flinching, having taken care to learn the way by witnessing the end of another martyr some time before. Bravest of the brave was Bentham, whose sense of ministerial duty led him to leave his comfortable Swiss refuge to take Rough's place. When royal proclamations forbade spectators to encourage or comfort victims at the stake, he took the lead in violating the order at the next group execution, toward the end of June, 1558.

Turning his eyes to the people . . . . [he] said, "We know that they are the people of God, and therefore we cannot choose but wish well to them and say,

[53] Foxe, *op. cit.*, VIII, 444, 558–60.   [54] *Ibid.*, pp. 455 and 451.

[55] Foxe describes his case as an example of providential deliverance, but from the account it is evident that under examination he virtually repudiated his Protestantism (*ibid.*, pp. 581–90).

[56] See above, p. 112. With his customary carelessness on chronological details Foxe states in one place (*ibid.*, p. 444) that he returned on November 10, but later (p. 448) has him present at the burning of Austoo, which took place "about the 17th day of September" (p. 405).

'God strengthen them.' " . . . . With that all the people with a whole consent and one voice followed and said, "Amen, Amen."[57]

The resulting tumult, doubtless used as a pretext by officers reluctant to enforce the royal order, enabled him to escape detection.[58] Such exploits, preserved in Foxe's familiar pages, endeared the London congregation to Protestant memory. In future times of stress neither the precedent nor the technique was forgotten.

[57] *Ibid.*, p. 559; cf. Bentham's own account in a letter to Lever, July 17, 1558, in Strype, *op. cit.*, III, ii, 133–34.

[58] It is equally pleasant to be able to record that he survived the Marian persecution and under Elizabeth was rewarded with the bishopric of Coventry and Lichfield.

CHAPTER IX

The Elizabethan Settlement

> Though thus the fort was almost gone
>   By cruel assault of enemies bold,
> Yet some within the fort alone
>   To God did cry, "Lord keep thy hold."
>
> The God did send his slave Death down
>   Into the Papists' hosts among,
> Which slew the chiefest in all the town
>   And greatest captains in the throng.
>
> By this great stroke of mighty Jove
>   The vehement force of Papists fell,
> And sent this fort (which is his love)
>   A godly captain to keep it well.[1]

O SANG the contemporary ballad-writer, celebrating the events of mid-November, 1558. London Protestants exchanged nightmares for bonfires. Prison doors swung open at Colchester, Salisbury, Maidstone, and elsewhere. Up the frozen Rhine Valley went the good news. In Frankfort, Worms, Strassburg, and the Swiss cities hearts leaped up at the first report, beat joyfully when it was confirmed. So Pole had been taken along with "the chiefest"! Surely this was the Lord's doing.

Thoughtful observers, surveying the religio-political landscape after the first excitement was over, saw the Protestant forces still confronted by many problems, though on the whole in a favorable position for a forward movement. Much depended on the character of the new Queen, as yet almost an unknown quantity. She might be as hostile as Henry VIII or as benignant as Edward VI. But the circumstances of her birth

[1] From "The Cruel Assault of God's Fort," in *Ballads and Broadsides*, ed. Collman, CLXIII (Oxford: Roxburghe Club, 1912), 8.

almost required her to support the reformers in some degree, and as a political figure she must yield to political pressure. If the Protestant leaders could form a single phalanx, she must join them, whatever part of the field they selected. At the moment the channel divided the important Protestants, but by far the great majority were on the Continent. It is true that nearly all the parish clergy in England accepted the Elizabethan settlement without protest, but they were Vicars of Bray. Bentham and a few like Parker, May, and Bill, who had remained in hiding in the home country, were the only influential reformers who were not abroad. If properly handled, the hundreds deployed along Europe's chief trade artery represented a force capable of dominating the situation. As we have seen, practically all of them had advanced far beyond the standard set by Edward's Second Prayer Book. True, some had gone much farther than others, the degree of advance corresponding almost exactly to the length of the journey from England. But none wished to go back to the earlier position. If they could arrange a common front and waste no time in returning to the scene of action at Westminster, much could be accomplished, whatever the Queen's attitude might be.

Unfortunately, in their enthusiasm over the change of rulers, the *émigrés* did not think it necessary to take precautions against the possibility of finding a reactionary Protestant on the throne. Only Knox, the indefatigable revolutionary, considered laying down terms to Elizabeth, a woman whose title to the throne must depend on an explicit acknowledgment of God's extraordinary providence in her case.[2] On receipt of the good word from England, he and his Geneva associates promptly dispatched William Kethe, the paraphraser of the Psalms, with a plea to their fellow-exiles in other communities for a united front, on the Genevan terms. In the great work of re-establishing their church at home, they suggested, they would meet with much opposition.

Yet if we (whose suffrance and persecutions are certain signs of sound doctrine) hold fast together, it is most certain that the enemies shall have less

[2] Knox to Cecil, April 10, 1559, *Works*, ed. Laing (6 vols.; Edinburgh, 1895), VI, 19.

power; offences shall sooner be taken away; and religion best proceed and flourish.

For what can the Papist wish more than that we should dissent from one another; and instead of preaching Jesus Christ and profitable doctrine, to contend one against another, either for *superfluous* ceremonies, or other like trifles; from the which, God of his mercy hath delivered us.[3]

They accordingly proposed that past offenses be mutually forgiven and forgotten, as "by good experience we have [already] proved, and also have received by your letters," while all strove together to "reach and practice the true knowledge of God's word, which we have learned in this our banishment and by God's merciful providence seen in the best reformed churches." Lever and his associates at Aarau in the Bernese territory, most of whom had formerly been at Zurich, wholeheartedly accepted the Genevan proposals.[4] But at Frankfort, as might be expected, the Puritan emissary was more coolly received, though the congregation there was now led by James Pilkington, former President of St. John's College, Cambridge, who had joined it since the earlier disputes.

For ceremonies to contend [so ran the response], where it shall lie neither in your hands or ours to appoint what they shall be; but in such men's wisdoms as shall be appointed to the devising of the same, and which shall be received by common consent of the Parliament, it shall be to small purpose. But we trust that both true religion shall be restored; and that we shall not be burdened with unprofitable ceremonies. And therefore, as we purpose to submit ourselves to such orders as shall be established by authority, being not of themselves wicked; so we would wish you willingly to do the same.[5]

The Continental churches differed among themselves in ceremonies, but had a unity of doctrine. It was sufficient, Pilkington and his friends suggested, that the English agree with them in the chief points of religion and not concern themselves with exact identity of forms.

On this optimistic basis of leaving all to the secular arm many of the *émigrés* had already acted. Thoughts of home, and possibly the desire to advance personal rather than party interests,

[3] *A Brief Discourse of the Troubles at Frankfort*, ed. Arber (London, 1908), p. 224. (Italics mine.)

[4] *Ibid.*, pp. 226–27.

[5] Pilkington, etc., to the Geneva congregation, January 3, 1559, in *ibid.*, pp. 225–26.

commonly took precedence over strategic plans. Many of the
leaders of the Frankfort group had departed for England before
the arrival of Kethe about the first of January. Similarly, the
absence of replies from Strassburg and Zurich suggests the rapid
exodus from those cities of refuge. The day after the group in
the Alsatian city were assured of Mary's death, Sir Thomas
Wroth and Sir Anthony Cook began the homeward journey.
After working far into the night to complete his preparations,
Sandys followed at dawn the next day with Horne and others.[6]
Jewel left Zurich in the middle of January and endured the
miseries of a two-month journey in the dead of winter. Within
a few weeks of his return he was joined by such other recent
exiles as Scory, Cox, Whitehead, Grindal, and Aylmer.[7] Cursed
by divergent plans, unable to agree among themselves even in
the absence of the Geneva group,[8] they were at the mercy of a
strong-minded Queen. Collective bargaining was abandoned for
a series of private contracts, each man making what terms he
could with the sovereign. The brilliant scheme of the Geneva
congregation thus broke down for lack of co-operation. When
the game resolved itself into a mad, individual scramble at
Westminster for place and preferment, the refugees at Geneva
had their choice between participating, in the hope of salvaging
something from the wreckage of their plans, or continuing their
exile indefinitely. The second alternative was considered, but
Calvin frowned on the proposal and urged the exiles to hurry
home.[9] Most of them took his advice, though Whittingham and
a few associates remained abroad until 1560 to finish their
translation work. After a preliminary volley of propaganda calculated to win the Queen and country to their point of view,
the other leaders set out on the return journey. In January,
Knox rushed off a *Brief Exhortation to England*—calling for the
establishment of the true religion with a preaching ministry,

[6] Sandys to Bullinger, December 20, 1558, *Zurich Letters*, ed. Robinson (2 vols.;
Cambridge: Parker Society, 1842 and 1845), I, 5–6.

[7] Jewel to Martyr, March 20, 1559, *ibid.*, I, 11.

[8] Cf. Jewel's remarks about Sir Anthony Cook, *ibid.*, I, 21.

[9] *The Seconde Parte of a Register*, ed. Peel (2 vols.; Cambridge, 1915), II, 58.

discipline, and schools—and then started for Dieppe, intending to lend a hand with the English religious settlement on his way to Scotland. In the middle of February the remainder of the congregation dispatched a special edition of the English psalter, taking the text from their incomplete version of the Old Testament and adding a dedicatory preface to the Queen. Calvin lent his support with a copy of his recently completed *Commentary on Isaiah*.[10] Goodman followed Knox by April, and Coverdale and Gilby were not far behind. In a few short months the Genevan English were thus reduced from the hope of dictating terms for an alliance with the home government to a rather cheerless choice. Either they could accept whatever conditions for such a coalition the Queen cared to lay down, or they could adopt a policy of passive resistance and refuse to take office at all if her settlement proved unsatisfactory. But if the Queen would only lend an obedient ear, all might yet be well. Fervently they prayed that she might be a Deborah to the Lord's people.

Had they been dealing with another Edward, or even a Jane Grey, such hopes might have been realized. But Elizabeth was made of different stuff. She was no inexperienced adolescent taking advice from relatives and preachers, but a woman of the world who knew how to walk softly in the valley of the shadow of death. Quite as well educated as her unfortunate English cousin, she had none of her feeling for religion. She never appears to have worried about the future life. In fact, she virtually ignored all such considerations. Nor did she ever display the slightest altruism in the affairs of this life. Her treatment of Davison is typical of all her dealings with her agents. Without a qualm she repaid faithful service with slander and disgrace. She was no idealist, but a realist through and through, a most powerful representative of those secular forces to which the church in all its branches had traditionally been opposed. Self-preservation and power were her chief objectives. To obtain them, she subordinated everything else. Princes, ambassadors, fleets, and borders were constantly in her mind. Personal

---

[10] Calvin to Cecil, n.d., *Zurich Letters*, II, 34.

affection and sexual desire were merely pawns in her great game
of politics. Religion was but another. During lulls in the main
contest she might take a passing interest in these minor matters.
Now she dallied with a Leicester or a Hatton, and now she expressed an idea about church affairs. On such occasions, when
she felt free to speak sincerely, her opinions were, as might be
expected, those of a provincial, conservative woman. She had
never been outside of England. She had no sense of internationalism and saw no point in conforming to Swiss or German
customs. She preferred a celibate clergy, on her father's model.
She liked display and ceremony, light and color. But none of
these tastes was more than superficial. Let an opponent stir
as though to make a move on the political board, and she no
longer had eyes for the style of carving on the pieces. Instantly
alert, she sacrificed any or all of these preferences to the demands of security and power.

So her primary religious policy was one of caution. Though
she enjoyed pomp and circumstance, she could not be a Catholic. That was to weaken her claim to legitimacy and the throne.
For practical purposes she was therefore a Protestant of the
variety best calculated to serve her material ends. She avoided
clear-cut theological definitions which might alienate potential
political support. A thorough reformation after the Calvinist
pattern would offend her Catholic subjects. It might also give
a foothold to international religious forces which could challenge
her supremacy. Specifically it was linked up in her mind with
the unthinkable doctrines that a woman had no right to govern,
and that in certain circumstances subjects might justly rebel
against their rulers. Her personal feeling of hostility to Puritanism was thus supported by her political instincts. And this attitude was no passing fancy. Her character was already formed
in the rough school of experience. Nothing ever changed it.
Religiously she was in 1603 what she was in 1558, a huge
boulder in the path of Puritanism, unavoidable, insurmount-
able, immovable.

The long process of disillusioning the hopeful Puritans began
with the religious settlement in the early months of 1559. The

scheme followed was in all probability drawn up by Cecil,[11] who was most skilful in reading the Queen's mind and in devising means to her ends. It provided for a committee composed of Bill, Parker, May, Cox, Whitehead, Grindal, and Pilkington, who were to meet at the home of the great civilian, Sir Thomas Smith, to revise the Edwardian prayer books. The author foresaw that some would wish for a more extensive reformation than the Queen desired and would call his projected alteration "a cloaked papistry or mingle-mangle." Strict conformity laws were accordingly suggested, so to repress them that "it is a great hope it shall touch but few. And better it were that they did suffer than her highness or commonwealth should shake or be in danger." Few sentences could more clearly express the royal attitude toward the religious problem than this last one.

The government authorities suggested to the revisers that they include in the new draft many conservative features of the first Edwardian book, among them prayers for the dead, the use of crosses, processions, and vestments.[12] How far ahead of the Queen's position even the most conservative of the Protestant leaders were may be seen from the cool reception given to these suggestions. The committee was hand picked. Bill, May, Parker, and Guest, who was apparently added later, had remained in England during the preceding reign, and the first two had actually held office under Mary. Cox, Grindal, and Whitehead had all taken the Anglican side in the first Frankfort troubles, and Pilkington had been the first signer of the strong letter of the Frankfort congregation rejecting the Genevan proposals in the preceding January. Nevertheless, the reforming tide was running so strongly that this carefully selected committee not only disregarded all these suggestions but even recommended

[11] John Strype, *Annals of the Reformation under Elizabeth* (4 vols. in 7; Oxford, 1824), I, ii, 392–98; Albert Peel, "From the Elizabethan Settlement to the Emergence of Separatism," in *Essays Congregational and Catholic*, ed. Peel (London, 1931), p. 248, n. 1. The dating must be in the middle of January, not in December, 1558, as Strype (*op. cit.*, I, i, 74) suggests, since the Continental exiles are included in the committee.

[12] This is clear from the communication sent by Guest, who apparently substituted for Parker, to Cecil (Strype, *op. cit.*, I, ii, 459–64). Our sources for these transactions are regrettably scanty. We have no actual proof that the committee as originally named ever met, but some such group must have done the work, judging from Guest's letter.

going beyond the second Edwardian book in several important respects. The communion service was to be divided into two parts, with all excommunicated and unconfirmed persons excluded from the church during the actual distribution. This was a step in the direction of a stricter discipline. Part of the consecration prayer was omitted as contrary to scriptural practice. Lastly, the posture during the reception of the elements, the subject of dispute in 1552, was left as a thing indifferent. Standing or kneeling were to be equally acceptable. Even the most conservative Protestants desired a further reformation.

The Queen, however, rejected all these suggestions, and in the final Act of Uniformity forced the acceptance of a book considerably more conservative than the second Edwardian volume.[13] Not only was kneeling at the sacrament required, but Knox's "Black Rubric" was dropped. The 1549 form of words to be used in distributing the elements was added to the 1552 version, in order to make further room for the doctrine of the Real Presence. The request for deliverance from "the tyranny of the Bishop of Rome and all his detestable enormities" was dropped from the litany. The ornaments rubric required the wearing of such clerical costume as was in use in the second year of Edward VI, and therefore called for a restoration of alb, cope, and chasuble. In addition, it was provided that the Queen might further alter the regulations for church ornaments, through the agency of her ecclesiastical commissioners, if she so desired. Acting under this provision of the law, the authorities who drew up the injunctions for the great visitation of the country during the summer took two more conservative steps. By royal authority a semi-Catholic form of communion wafer was adopted, and the table when not in use was restored to its altar position. Furthermore, clergy were forbidden to marry without the consent of their bishop and the two nearest justices.[14]

[13] R. W. Dixon (*History of the Church of England from the Abolition of the Roman Jurisdiction* [6 vols.; 3d rev. ed.; Oxford, 1895], V, 99) holds Parliament responsible for this reactionary step, but that it was the work of the crown may be gathered from the tone of Guest's letter to Cecil quoted above.

[14] W. H. Frere (ed.), *Visitation Articles and Injunctions of the Period of the Reformation* (3 vols.; "Alcuin Club Collections," Vols. XIV, XV, XVI [Vol. II with W. P. M. Kennedy] [London, 1910]), III, 18–20, 27–28.

Though the Queen permitted her commissions to destroy images found in the churches, they were not ordered to do so. In her own chapel, she retained the cross and candles, to the great scandal of the Protestants of all stripes.[15]

It is thus clear that in matters religious the Queen stood much farther to the right than the most Anglican of her non-Roman clergy. In reality she represented a third Protestant party, a throwback to the days of her father. Only with difficulty could the most conservative of her clergy bring themselves to work with her. Parker threatened passive disobedience in order to forestall measures against married clergy, using the Puritan cry, "We ought to obey God rather than man." Even Cox refused at one time to officiate in her private chapel because of its ornaments. Both Sandys and Jewel opposed her in this matter, to the point of nearly losing their bishoprics.[16] On such occasions possibly some of them regretted their earlier scorning of the Genevan suggestions for a united front.

If their Anglican colleagues suffered considerable embarrassment in serving the Queen, the more advanced reformers could only be stepchildren in such a household. The Geneva group soon felt the rod of her displeasure. Calvin's gift was very coldly received.[17] Knox was refused permission to enter the realm. Goodman returned by April but was forced to remain in hiding,[18] and soon saw fit to join his colleague in the northern kingdom. Coverdale returned before November, 1559, but, though the government used him as a preacher at Paul's Cross and as one of the consecrators of Archbishop Parker in December, he was not restored to his bishopric of Exeter. The reason for this attitude was not far to seek. The political writings of the Geneva leaders had made them odious to the Queen.

[15] Sampson to Martyr, January 6, 1560, *Zurich Letters*, I, 63; Parker, etc., to Elizabeth, 1559, *Parker Correspondence*, ed. Bruce and Perowne (Cambridge: Parker Society, 1853), pp. 79–95; Cox to Elizabeth, n.d., Strype, *op. cit.*, I, ii, 500–502.

[16] Sandys to Martyr, April 1, 1560, *Zurich Letters*, I, 73–74; Jewel to Martyr, February 4, 1560, *Works*, ed. Ayre (4 vols.; Cambridge: Parker Society, 1845–50), IV, 1229.

[17] Calvin to Cecil, n.d., *Zurich Letters*, II, 34. I have been unable to find any record of the Queen's reaction to the gift of the Genevan psalter, if it was ever presented.

[18] Jewel to Martyr, April 26, 1559, *Zurich Letters*, I, 21.

For this reason, the attitude to these unfortunate tracts is
the touchstone by which we may test the degree of Puritanism
among the English Protestants during the early months of
Elizabeth's reign. On their first appearance these tactless expressions of political theory had had a lukewarm reception
among the Continental reformers and the English exiles outside Geneva. Martyr and Foxe had both doubted the wisdom
of such writing.[19] In the absence of any common front the English Protestants now felt themselves under no obligation to defend Knox in their dealings with Elizabeth. Naturally, they
dissociated themselves from his stand, with emphasis varying
according to the degree of their reforming zeal. After the new
Queen's accession, Knox observed that the *First Blast* had blown
from him all his friends in England.[20] In March, 1559, Parker,
writing to Nicholas Bacon, repudiated all such theories:

> If such principles be spread into men's heads, as now they be framed and
> referred to the judgment of the subject, of the tenant, and of the servant to
> discuss what is tyranny and to discern whether his prince, his landlord, his
> master is a tyrant by his own fancy and collection supposed, what lord of the
> council shall ride quietly minded in the streets among desperate beasts?
> What master shall be sure in his bedchamber?[21]

A joint statement of faith presented to the Queen by returning
exiles, who had preached before her, contained such phrases as
these:

> The word of God doth not condemn the government or regiment of a
> woman. . . . .

> A tyrant or evil magistrate . . . . is a power ordained of God and is also
> to be honored and obeyed of the people in all things not contrary to God, as
> their magistrate and governor. It is not lawful for any private person or
> persons to kill, or by any means to procure the death of, a tyrant or evil person,
> being the ordinary magistrate. All conspiracies, seditions, and rebellions of
> private men against the magistrates, men or women, good governors or evil,
> are unlawful and against the will and word of God.[22]

[19] Goodman to Martyr, August 20, 1558, *Original Letters Relative to the English Reformation*, ed. Robinson (2 vols.; Cambridge: Parker Society, 1846–47), p. 768; Knox
to Foxe, May 18, 1558, *Works*, V, 5–6.

[20] Knox to Mrs. Lock, April 6, 1559, *ibid.*, VI, 14.

[21] Parker to Bacon, March 1, 1559, *Parker Correspondence*, p. 61.

[22] Printed in Dixon, *op. cit.*, V, 114–15 n.

Here it is to be noted that the way is left open for parliamentary restrictions on the royal power, or even a revolution, if led not by private individuals but by men in official positions.

An even more gentle though more detailed disavowal of *First Blast* doctrines was that of John Aylmer, who had resided at Strassburg, Zurich, and Basel during the exile and had aided Foxe in the preparation of his great work. With the appropriate title of *An Harborowe for Faithfull and Trewe Subjectes* (against the *First Blast*), it appeared at Strassburg in April, 1559.[23] Though ostensibly intended as a corrective to Knox's theories, in several passages it advocates semi-Genevan principles, and it is quite possible that it was really designed as another, though belated, attempt to draw the reforming forces together. The spirit of this work is therefore rather that of the mediating martyrologist than the animus of the later Bishop of London. It opens with a handsome acknowledgment of Knox's good intentions and of the extreme provocation under which he composed his treatise. Then Aylmer grants that he was, however, in error in discussing the general question of women rulers rather than the particular one of Mary's rule. "If he had kept him in that particular person [Mary of England], he could have said nothing too much, nor in such wise as could have offended any indifferent man."[24] He therefore undertakes to analyze and correct Knox's generalizations, "For I have that opinion of the man's honesty and godliness that he will not disdain to hear better reasons nor be loth to be taught in any thing he misseth." Going over the same ground, he emphasizes the exceptional cases where women have been called to rule by God's special providence. Deborah, Judith, and Anne Boleyn replace Jezebel, Athaliah, and Mary Tudor in the center of the stage. This done, some puritanical passages are interjected. The right of Parliament to share the rule with the sovereign, and so to restrict and regulate the exercise of her power, is expressly stated.[25]

---

[23] Either the place is fictitious or the work was published in Aylmer's absence, for he was appointed to participate in the Westminster disputation in March (Jewel to Martyr, March 20, 1559, *Zurich Letters*, I, 11).

[24] Sig. B, fol. 2.   [25] Sig. H, fol. 3.

Bishops should be content with a lowly station in life, giving up
their thousands for hundreds, that the Queen might use the balance for a better ordering of the kingdom. A superintendent was
to be appointed for each town, and schools were to be established. The whole ends with a peal of patriotism probably designed to enable both sides to forget past differences. All must
give and fight to preserve the best of commonwealths lest "the
pocky Frenchman" and "scurvy Scot" despoil it. Not Italy
but England was the earthly paradise. No other country could
compare to her. The nether stocks of the Italian husbandman's hose are of his own skin. Taxes and soldiery devour the
French peasant. The Germans live on roots "and stinking herbs
which they call kraut." And "they pay till their bones rattle
in their skin, and thou layest up for thy son and heir."[26]

Aylmer's irenicon met the usual fate of such efforts. Without
pausing to read it, Knox, in the heat of the Scotch revolution,
took it as an attack on his work and, in writing to Cecil, made
some unpleasant insinuations about the motives of the author.[27]
South of the Tweed, Elizabeth remained coldly unresponsive to
all the Scotchman's requests for permission to cross the border,
even when the alleged object was to treat with agents of the
English government about their common problems arising from
the tumults in the north.

Prudent men, noting the reception of the *Harborowe*, would
have been convinced of the futility of further efforts along this
line. For all practical purposes, to put out more puritanical
treatises of this sort was certainly a waste of time and effort.
But reformers, like explorers, are not given to prudence. Un-
deterred by the stillbirth at Strassburg, another of Foxe's
friends, this time rather on the Geneva side, undertook to catch
up Knox's dropped stitches and put together a Puritan political
theory which would be acceptable in the homeland. This optimist was Laurence Humphrey, formerly a fellow of Magdalen
College, Oxford. Most of his exile had been spent at Basel and
Zurich, but he joined the Geneva congregation in April, 1558.
This was after the appearance of *Superior Powers* and the *First*

---

[26] Sig. P, fol. 3.   [27] Knox to Cecil, July 18, 1559, *Works*, VI, 45.

Blast, and therefore he could not be denied a hearing on the ground that he was implicated in their publication. He had, however, adopted most of the basic Genevan principles, and is henceforth a champion of the Puritan position, though not quite so radical as were Knox and Goodman. He returned to Basel, probably after the accession of Elizabeth,[28] and during the summer of 1559 composed two tracts for the times which are all too little known to students of political theory.[29] For them he wisely secured a Basel rather than a Geneva imprint, doubtless with Foxe's aid.

The more important of his efforts, *De religionis conservatione et reformatione vera*, appeared in September, with a dedication to Francis Russell and some congratulatory verses to Elizabeth by the Zurich divine, Gualter. In a hundred pages the author discusses the religious and political situation in England. After a general exhortation to his fellow-countrymen to give serious attention to religion, both public and private, including the elimination of personal wrongdoing, he describes the true church which should be established. Taking the Calvinistic model as the ideal, he urges the necessity of an effective discipline. He marvels that in England this is either too lax or even nonexistent. Fear is a very useful thing to restrain people from wrongdoing. "And there should be censure and jurisdiction in the church not less than the sword in the state."[30] The secular arm must not dictate in religious matters, because religion is independent of the occasion and rule of man.[31] In turn the church must not interfere with secular affairs. Christ's kingdom is not of this world. The pope's political demands make men traitors.

Turning in the last twenty pages to the sore points in the

[28] Humphrey to Bullinger, June 23, 1559, *Zurich Letters*, II, 20–21.

[29] S. R. Maitland (*Essays on Subjects Connected with the Reformation* [London, 1849], p. 224) considers Aylmer's *Harborowe* "the only public apology of those who had written or countenanced the most ferocious libels on the late queen and her government." J. W. Allen deals with Ponet, Knox, Goodman, but ignores both Humphrey and Aylmer in his *Political Thought in the Sixteenth Century* (London, 1926).

[30] "At in Ecclesia manere debet censura et iurisdictio non minus quam gladius in respublica" (p. 23).

[31] "Non enim pendet ab hominum vel ocasu vel regno divina religio" (p. 27).

current discussion, Humphrey repeated Aylmer's argument that women, though naturally the weaker vessels, were occasionally called by God to rule in special cases. Unlike Knox, he does not demand that Elizabeth make a formal acknowledgment of this special providence in her case. He is, however, much more explicit and "constitutional" than Aylmer in emphasizing the rights of Parliament over the ruler. Votes and reason were to be used rather than arms, but they were to be nonetheless effective. If a tyrant refuses to call a Parliament, that body should assemble to restrain him of its own volition.[32] Though every commonwealth needed a single head to guide it, that head was an elective one and could be deposed if it proved that an unwise choice had been made.[33] The question of rebellion or tyrannicide is then discussed. Humphrey denied that private individuals had such rights in ordinary cases. Using Parker's argument, he pointed out that, if this were conceded, the servant might rise against his master or the child against his father.[34] Christians are to be sheep not wolves. The actions of Jehu and the son of Eleazar in the Old Testament are explained as those of officially annointed persons, lesser magistrates rising against higher, or kings against kings, steps which are quite proper. Ehud's actions are to be justified as those of a private individual whom God has especially called to execute judgment.[35]

This frank justification of a system of limited monarchy and properly sponsored rebellion was unlikely to win Elizabeth's favorable attention. But Humphrey complacently concluded his work with a statement implying that he had taken the curse off the works of Knox and Goodman by this reasonable interpretation of their position.

And therefore even if I knew no one who thought otherwise [on the matter of private rebellion]; nevertheless, since I have understood that a few works

[32] P. 83.

[33] "Vetus est eum qui legem rogavit posse abrogare, et qui conjunctim aliquem magistratum renunciarunt eum eodum consensu, si minus aptus sit aut patriam prodat, poterunt abdicare" (p. 85).

[34] P. 85.

[35] "Non nego tamen licere interdum inferioribus magistratibus adversari superioribus et uni etiam privato; si tamen privatus ille habendus sit quem Deus excitat" (p. 99).

of certain good men, not of ordinary piety and doctrine, have been taken by some in this sense, I have tried in this section rather to explain than confute their opinion; for, although some rather harsh words may seem to tend in that direction, nevertheless, I think that the authors would agree with me if they were called to interpret their mind.[36]

Interesting as this forerunner of Triennial acts and the doctrine of parliamentary supremacy should be to students of political theory, it apparently passed unnoticed at the time of its publication. But Humphrey's second effort, *Optimates*, finished in July, 1559, two months before the appearance of *De religione*, was at least deemed worthy of an English translation in 1563.[37] As the title indicates, it was a discourse on the nature and duties of the nobility. At first glance it appears to be a rather ordinary treatment of the subject, in the manner of contemporary social theory. After justifying the existence of the nobility as a necessary check on the monstrous many-headed beast of the populace—a Horatian metaphor which the sixteenth-century theorists frequently quoted—the author gives in a rather routine fashion his theories of their origin and his prescriptions for their religion, morality, and education. But, when considered in its political setting, coming close on the heels of Knox's appeals to the nobility of Scotland and England to establish the true religion, and at a time when the Puritans were feeling the need of support against the new English Queen, the volume takes on a more particular significance. In effect it was a gesture in the direction of the rising class of Protestant landlords, soliciting their co-operation in the great work of reformation which yet lay ahead. The appeals for unity among the nobility[38] and the repetition of the teaching that the better elements in society might take the lead in bridling tyranny[39] were doubtless intended to have an immediate application to the contempo-

[36] "Itaque etsi nullum esse sciam qui contra sentiat: cum tamen quorundam bonorum virorum pietate et doctrina non vulgari, libellos aliquot a nonnullis in eum sensum rapi intellixerim: volui in hac parte illorum magis explicare quam confutare sententiam: quod licet verba duriuscula eo tendere videantur, tamen eos consentire mecum existimo si qui auctores sunt, iidem etiam mentis suae interpretes adhibeantur" (p. 100).

[37] *The Nobles* (London).   [38] Pp. 231–32; English translation, sig. O, fol. 4.

[39] P. 79; English translation, sig. D, fol. i(v).

rary situation.[40] Incidentally, such works should also serve to
remind us how little there was of the genuine democrat about
the Puritan. As a political opportunist he might occasionally
make use of congregational, equalitarian terminology. But, as
in the days of Lilburne, his real sympathies were with the upper
classes or even with the monarch, should the sovereign prove
pliable.

Nothing came of such efforts, however. The nobles did not
unite. Parliament did not adopt the practice of assembling on
its own responsibility, and the Queen retained a firm hold on
the government. The Geneva leaders were never permitted a
voice in English affairs. Knox stayed in Scotland. Goodman
only returned years later, and then after a humiliating recantation, to the temporary security of a minor parish living. The
lesser lights who were at Geneva when the offending tracts appeared were either neglected or kept far from court. Gilby
found a refuge as minister in the Huntingdon pocket borough
of Ashby-de-la-Zouche. In 1563 Whittingham was permitted
to become Dean of Durham under Pilkington. Only in the same
year did Coverdale secure a London living. Great man-power
was thus wasted on petty tasks, because the Queen feared its
leftist inclinations. She preferred to see the English Protestant
church sink into a state of mildly scandalous torpor than to give
it capable leadership which might in time disturb her political
equilibrium.

The Elizabethan settlement thus resulted in the virtual elimination of the Geneva group as a religious and political force.
As far as the cause of a thorough reformation after the Continental manner was represented in England during the next few
years, it was by men who had spent all or most of their exile
in other places. Lever from Aarau, Parkhurst and Jewel from
Zurich, Foxe from Basel, Grindal and Sandys from Strassburg,
Coverdale, Humphrey, and Sampson who had been in several
places besides Geneva—all these were disposed to go beyond
Parker in opposing the reactionary tendencies of the Queen.

[40] That the English translation should appear in the year of the defeat in Convocation is probably not without further significance (see p. 184).

Lever succeeded in persuading Elizabeth to substitute "Supreme Governor of the Church" for "Supreme Head." Parkhurst and Jewel both opposed the requirement of the old-fashioned vestments, and in April, 1559, Sandys wrote Parker that he did not intend to use them.[41]

The appointive power of the Queen brought matters to an issue. When a bishopric or other important office was to be filled, she made conditions which sorely tried the consciences of all who had the interests of the Reformed church at heart. She demanded that ancient landed endowments be surrendered to the crown in exchange for less valuable tithes and impropriate rectories. The prominence of the places also implied the obligation to wear the official costume and enforce its use upon subordinates. Against this royal attitude the reformers of all stripes protested vigorously. But when their protests were almost if not completely ignored, there rose the question of the next step. Should the Queen be subjected to a general boycott, with most of the advanced Protestants refusing to accept her appointments except under compulsion? Or should they register their protest and then take the offices lest the church suffer the even worse fate of having them filled by more objectionable types, such as the Catholic or the indifferent? It was a difficult decision of the sort which has troubled idealistic leaders in all ages, and the argument was heated. Good taste and political considerations necessitated its being kept under cover, but enough traces have survived to indicate its importance.

It divided the returning Puritan group and cost the party many of the remaining leaders, who decided, after consultation, "not to desert our churches for the sake of a few ceremonies, and those not unlawful in themselves, especially since the pure doctrine of the gospel remained in all its integrity and freedom."[42] Not only Parker and Cox took office in the new government but Sandys, Grindal, Jewel, and even Parkhurst eventually did the same. Once installed, they tended to lose their

[41] Sandys to Parker, April 30, 1559, *Parker Correspondence*, pp. 65–66.

[42] Grindal to Bullinger, August 27, 1566, *Zurich Letters*, I, 169; cf. Sampson to Martyr, May 13, 1560, *ibid.*, pp. 75–76.

Puritan attitude, though occasionally they might dispute with their more conservative colleagues about such things as the Queen's cross or be charged with having too "Germanical" [advanced Protestant] opinions.[43] The responsibilities of office tended to make them conservative. As administrators they felt constrained to enforce regulations with which originally they had no sympathy. Continued opposition in time exasperated them to the point of denouncing their former friends and becoming less reluctant supporters of the royal policy. Like her father in the early days of Cromwell's influence, Elizabeth thus managed to sap the strength of the Protestant opposition by the simple process of exercising her appointive power.

Sampson, Coverdale, Lever, Foxe, and Humphrey took the other course. Sampson was offered the bishopric of Norwich. Months previously on the Continent, a few days after learning of Mary's death, he had anticipated such an offer and had disclosed his scruples to Martyr. He objected to vestments, the title "Supreme Head," the lack of church discipline and of popular or clerical voice in the election of bishops,[44] and also to the financial exactions levied upon these officials. Although the stumbling block of the royal title was removed after his return to England, he continued to protest about the other points. From Zurich, Martyr returned his usual timid and uncertain answers to such inquiries.[45] Bolder than his distant adviser, Sampson stood his ground, and the appointment went to Parkhurst. Lever accepted no official position in the new establishment. Wandering away from the court, he found employment as a supernumerary preacher at Coventry, the first of a long line of Puritan "lecturers" who expounded the word without

<hr>

[43] Cox to Cassander, March 4, 1560, *ibid.*, II, 42; Sandys to Parker, October 24, 1560, *Parker Correspondence*, p. 125.

[44] Sampson to Martyr, December 17, 1558, *Zurich Letters*, I, 1–2.

[45] At first he approved of the use of the required vestments under the circumstances, lest the offices be bestowed on unworthy men. Then, on consulting Bullinger, he approved the use of those demanded for preaching and daily life, but not the sacramental garments. Finally he resumed his original position (Martyr to Sampson, July 15, 1559, November 4, 1559, February 1, 1560, *ibid.*, II, 25–27, 32–33, 38–41). The reference to his original advice is in the second letter.

enjoying a regular living.[46] Coverdale, Foxe, and Humphrey remained almost completely unprovided for, preaching now and then in London when occasion offered. Too few in numbers to be a major political factor, but sufficiently distinguished to make their unemployment a scandal to conscientious Protestants, they endeavored to preserve the purity of their principles while they waited for better times.[47]

Meanwhile the advanced reformers made what propaganda they could for their position. In 1560 Whittingham and his associates at Geneva brought to a successful conclusion their labors on the new translation of the Bible with its puritanical comments in the margin. At the same place, in the following year, the Geneva *Forme of Prayers* was reprinted in English. In 1562 there was another edition put out from Edinburgh, where the Calvinistic reformation was taking root. Equally important was the work of Rowland Hall, one of the lay members of the Geneva colony, who returned to London and set up a printing press. At his plant he not only turned out English translations of Calvin's tracts but also an English edition of the laws of Geneva, setting forth in detail the blueprints of the Continental utopia.[48]

The Puritans also made bold to defy the Queen's orders in

[46] In the following year, like Sampson and Humphrey, he accepted a minor post, that of Archdeacon of Coventry in his case. But for a year, at least, he was dependent on the charity of his listeners (Lever to Bullinger, July 10, 1560, *ibid.*, I, 86–87).

[47] It is barely possible that there is another explanation for some of this unemployment. There was a curious reluctance among the Protestants of all sorts to assume office, which would seem to go beyond the conventional *nolo episcopari*. In addition to the well-known case of Parker, Young of St. David's was reluctant to accept a greater see (Young to Parker, May 3, 1560, *Parker Correspondence*, p. 114). Parkhurst and Jewel both make similar professions of unwillingness to accept bishoprics (Jewel to Martyr, August 1, 1559; Parkhurst to Simler, December 20, 1559, *Zurich Letters*, I, 40, 61). Whitehead's case has been already noted (see above, p. 153).

But from the statement of Sampson to Martyr (May 13, 1560, *Zurich Letters*, I, 75–76) that he had lost friends and received injury in the struggle and his request that Martyr should suspend judgment until he had heard both sides of the story, as well as from the preceding letters, it seems clear that his unemployment was not caused by unwillingness to assume responsibility but by the conditions attached to the appointment.

[48] Charles Martin, *Les Protestants anglais réfugiés à Genève au temps de Calvin* (Geneva, 1915), pp. 276–79.

many instances, nullifying her edicts and going their own way, anticipating, as in the days of Edward, what they confidently expected would be the further course of the reformation.[49] Lever had taken the lead shortly after his return, by holding forth in the parish churches in defiance of the Queen's proclamation silencing all preachers.[50] Even the Anglican leaders used these tactics. During the visitation of 1559 the legal requirement of alb and chasuble for priests during the communion service was quietly ignored by the Queen's commissioners, and in the interpretation of the next year the bishops formally required only cope and surplice. The regulations for clerical marriages speedily became a dead letter, though the Marian statute prohibiting such unions was not repealed and the children of the clergy remained technically illegitimate until the time of James. The practice of congregational singing, which was regarded as a Protestant innovation, was introduced in one London church and spread to others. It was soon so popular that thousands remained to sing after the service at Paul's Cross.[51] Visitors from London introduced the custom into the services of Exeter Cathedral, though not without some opposition from the authorities of the chapter,[52] and the ecclesiastical commissioners supported them. To supply the need of Protestant ministers, the authorities winked at Puritan violations of the law. Besides dropping the sacramental vestments, many of the clergy abandoned even the use of the surplice, and preached in their black Geneva gowns. At Parker's ordination Coverdale, though one of the consecrators, appeared in a plain black gown. Bishops promised their zealous clergy a free hand in eliminating such Romish abuses in their individual churches, and full advantage was taken of these concessions.[53] So far, indeed, did this move-

[49] W. H. Frere and C. E. Douglas, *Puritan Manifestoes* (London, 1907), p. ix.

[50] Lever to Bullinger, August 8, 1559, *Zurich Letters*, II, 30.

[51] Jewel to Martyr, March 5, 1560, *ibid.*, I, 71.

[52] David Wilkins (ed.), *Concilia magnae Britanniae et Hiberniae* (4 vols.; London, 1737), IV, 201; Parker, etc., to the President and Chapter of Exeter, December 23, 1559, *Parker Correspondence*, p. 107.

[53] Withers to the Prince Elector of the Palatinate, n.d., *Zurich Letters*, II, 161.

ment spread, that an archdeacon in the London diocese actually forbade his clergy to use the surplice, and took steps against those who did.[54]

More satisfying changes in the legal structure of the establishment itself depended on a change of rulers, or on devising some means to bring effective pressure to bear upon the present one. In the early years of Elizabeth, since both her brother and sister had ruled but a short time, many thought in terms of another brief reign. Because Elizabeth herself constituted the conservative wing of the Protestant party, any change of rulers was almost sure to produce a leftward movement in that body. The claims of the Catholic Mary Queen of Scots were, at this time, scarcely considered. Under the terms of Henry VIII's will, the crown would pass to Catherine Grey, who, as far as can be determined, represented the advanced Edwardian viewpoint in religion. In the autumn of 1560 Parker accused Sandys of "Germanical" actions designed to curry favor "against another day." When, in the next year, the unfortunate Lady Catherine incurred the Queen's displeasure and damaged her chances by her questionably legal marriage to Edward Seymour, Somerset's son, a new Protestant heir presumptive to the crown was found in the person of Henry Hastings, third Earl of Huntington, a descendant through his mother of Edward IV. He was a great patron of Puritans and had none other than the Geneva pastor, Anthony Gilby, for his minister. More important still, he was apparently not taking this attitude for political reasons but was most sincere in his profession.[55] Should he become king, all would indeed be well. Even were the succession disputed the advanced reformers stood to gain by the consequent weakening of the monarchy which was a hindrance to them. On the evening of October 16, 1562, some such Puritan prospects seemed about to be realized as the Queen sank into unconscious-

[54] Strype, *The Life and Acts of Matthew Parker* (3 vols.; Oxford, 1821), I, 304; Dixon, *op. cit.*, VI, 8. Whether this archdeacon was Cole or Calfhill or John Pulleyne cannot be determined with certainty. If it were Calfhill, as Dixon suggests, Strype has misdated the document, since he did not become archdeacon until 1565 (Le Neve, *Fasti ecclesiae Anglicanae* [3 vols.; Oxford, 1854], II, 342).

[55] See below, p. 411.

ness with a severe attack of smallpox.[56] The character of a nation was in the balance that night at Hampton Court as the anxious Council gathered in the antechamber of the royal bedroom. Two mutually exclusive powers, organized idealism and the strong secular monarchy, were contending for the soul of England. With Elizabeth out of the way, the forces of Calvinism would have had comparatively free play. For better or for worse, a second Scotland might very possibly have developed south of the Tweed. But it was not to be. At midnight the Queen rallied, and the cause of English Puritanism went into a lingering decline.

One last disappointment filled the Puritan cup. They had anticipated some delay in securing the complete adoption of their program and were prepared to wait a few years, if need be, until the ground could be prepared. So they had done under Edward, and they fully expected that time would bring about a gradual, and almost automatic, reformation by legal means. But the result proved otherwise. When Parliament met in January, 1563, the Convocation of the Province of Canterbury convened in St. Paul's. This legislative body for most of the Church of England was flooded with suggestions for improving the ecclesiastical condition of the country. These ranged from the conservative proposals of Bishop Alley of Exeter, who wished to repress Puritan nonconformity, to a sweeping program of reform submitted by the Puritan party, which included the use of the Geneva gown and abolition of such conservative institutions as compulsory kneeling at communion, saints' days, and the cross in baptism. In the inferior branch of the assembly, the farthest removed from the Queen, the advanced reformers were strong. After failing to secure majority support for their full program, they substituted the surplice for the Geneva gown and tried once more. On this occasion they actually had a majority present in the lower house, but the royal party, which numbered among its ranks Parker's three chaplains, had a greater number of proxies and triumphed by the narrow margin of 59 to 58. The Puritan party saw the Queen's hand clearly

[56] De Quadra to the Duchess of Parma, October 16, 17, and 25, 1562, *Spanish Calendar, Elizabeth*, I, 262.

enough, though the bishops took the blame.[57] It was necessary. to seek better lines of attack.

One such was indeed available at the time, had there been a Puritan statesman large-minded and daring enough to grasp the fact. The Council of Trent was holding its final sessions, and once more the Protestants were invited to attend. Had they but known in this day the things which belonged unto peace, they would have strained every nerve to restore the united front which was broken at Worms. The main purpose of the Reformation was now accomplished. A sorely chastened Rome was hastening to mend its ways. The indulgence abuses were checked, clerical education and morals reformed. Papal bastards no longer ruled Italian states. The Catholic church of the Counter Reformation bears no more resemblance to the church of the fifteenth century than modern Germany does to the Holy Roman Empire. To all intents and purposes it was a separate and distinct institution, one of the new religious bodies to rise from the turmoils of the first part of the century. Had the Protestants consented to co-operate, it is quite possible that further doctrinal liberalism might have been introduced into the system of the mother-church. There was certainly much more to be gained by an alliance with the Roman Catholics than by one with hard-swearing Elizabeth. Unfortunately, the heat of the Reformation conflict had caused both sides to lose sight of their main objective. The mirage of party advantage had obscured the vista of concerted moral action to check the rising forces of materialism. At Trent, Cardinal Pole, who represented the best element in the Roman church, had already spoken of the chief objective as the defense of that particular body. In England, as in Geneva, the reformers spoke of the papal nuncio as a messenger of Antichrist. When the Council ended and the reforming decrees and canons were issued, the only response of the English Protestants was a contemptuous commentary[58] of which the main theme was that the "principal-

[57] Withers and Barthelot to Bullinger and Gualter, February, 1567, *Zurich Letters*, II, 150.

[58] *A Godly and Necessarye Admonition of the Decrees and Canons of the Counsel of Trent* (London, 1564).

lest care ought to be for the restoring and preserving of godly, sincere, and uncorrupt doctrine,"[59] and that without that all movements toward a higher moral standard were insincere and worthless. They thus played directly into the hands of the Queen, who was only too anxious to prevent the clergy recovering anything like their medieval power. So the great Catholic reunion plan failed, and for many years we must recount the unedifying details of Puritan efforts to purge the English churches of abuses, such as nonresidence, which the despised Roman Catholics had already overcome. What labor might have been spared by joint action in England need only be suggested. It is perhaps too much to expect of human nature that the Catholics should have treated the revolutionists as equals, or that the Puritans should so speedily forget the recent sufferings of their companions under Mary. But it must be remembered that both parties were drawn from the intelligentsia and professed the religion of which loving one's enemies is a cardinal principle. Many secular political forces have speedily forgotten past battlefields in new alliances, as expediency dictated diplomatic revolutions. It is regrettable that the godly are so seldom wise as serpents.

[59] *Ibid.*, p. 113.

CHAPTER X

The Elizabethan Vestiarian Controversy

ISPIRITED and lacking in leadership, the Puritan faction was slow in developing any new tactics after the proroguing of Convocation in April, 1563. For the most part, in default of any better plan, the nullification policy was continued, though as an individual matter. Each advanced clergyman wore what was right in his own eyes and picked and chose among the forms of service prescribed in the Prayer Book. The more prominent members of the party made only half-hearted attempts to keep the controversy alive. The indefatigable Turner, who, once more installed at Wells, was training his dog to snatch the papistical caps from visiting bishops' heads, wrote a treatise on ecclesiastical costume which was circulated in manuscript but was apparently never printed.[1] In August, Humphrey renewed the requests for Continental support which Sampson had made in 1560. Writing to Bullinger, he solicited an opinion as to whether costumes once connected with superstition could be considered things indifferent, and whether they might be worn if enjoined not by the Pope but by royal authority.[2] If there was any response, it has not survived. The Puritan fortunes were at a low ebb. The time was ripe for a governmental counterattack.

Fortunately for the advanced Protestants, it developed slowly. A severe attack of the plague drove the court to Windsor. Furthermore, the Queen was occupied with negotiations for

---

[1] "The Earl Diary" (Cambridge University MS Mm. I. 29), fol. 1(v); John Strype, *History of the Life and Acts of Edmund Grindal* (Oxford, 1821), p. 145; *The Marprelate Tracts*, ed. Pierce (London, 1911), p. 86.

[2] August 16, 1563, *Zurich Letters*, ed. Robinson (2 vols.; Cambridge: Parker Society, 1842–45), I, 134.

peace with France and, until they were concluded, could not afford to take steps which would alienate the Huguenot party across the channel. Parker had been ignoring most of the vestiarian legislation for years and, in any case, was loath to persecute. He took special pains to see that the drastic anti-Catholic statutes enacted at the last Parliament were not enforced in their full severity, and did nothing about the recalcitrant Puritans. But after the French treaty was concluded in April, 1564, it suited the Queen to play a more Catholic role. In England something like a popular ground swell of reaction from the Protestantism of the last few years could be felt. Mary was gaining strength in Scotland and had to be placated. The interminable Austrian marriage negotiations were reopened. On her return from Cambridge in the autumn, Elizabeth gave the bishops to understand that she wished uniformity of clerical dress enforced.[3] Parker, in characteristic fashion, undertook to persuade Sampson and Humphrey—now Dean of Christ Church and President of Magdalen College, Oxford, respectively—by reason rather than by force. In December he addressed to them ten questions on the subject. He inquired, among other things, whether the surplice was to be considered an indifferent thing, and, if not, why not. The answers show that the logical bulwarks of the Oxford Puritans were much more carefully designed than Hooper's in similar circumstances. They admitted that the vestments were in substance indifferent. But they drew a distinction between theory and practice. Under the circumstances, the surplice, having by long association become a badge of popery and consecrated to idolatry, could no longer be considered an indifferent matter. Decency and reverence for the sacrament were not to be secured by using copes which had been employed to deface the rite. On the question of a distinctive everyday dress of long gown and square cap they quoted the Pauline maxim that all things were lawful but not always expedient. They did not wish to condemn or forcibly correct ministers using such attire, but, on the other hand, they did not believe the bishops had the right to force the surplice on them.

[3] De Silva to Philip, October 9, 1564, *Spanish Calendar*, I, 387.

Even though the vestiarian injunctions were already made and the ordinary merely called upon to enforce them, he should not do so, "neither exact obedience of any minister to it." So far did they carry their nullification theory.[4]

In the rebuttal, of which he sent a copy to Cecil, Parker or one of his chaplains denied that these garments were necessarily superstitious and asserted that, since they were ordained not as essential to Christian worship but as a means of obtaining that good order which the magistrate must secure in the church, he could see no valid objection to them. Distinctive clerical dress was known before the development of the papacy, and the abuse did not destroy the proper use. Even if the robes were heathen or Jewish originally, they could be turned to Christian uses, as Gideon employed the wood of Baal's pillar to sacrifice to the true God.[5] Guest, Bishop of Rochester, though leaning somewhat heavily on the arm of the secular authority, similarly labored to answer Puritan arguments on the subject.[6] Not the Anglicans but the Puritans, with their scrupulous niceties, were the troublers of Israel, in his opinion.

So the issue was joined. We need not stop for a detailed analysis of the Anglican argument, which was a rationalization by reluctant men of a position forced on them from without. The basic elements of the royal strategy and a clear understanding of the importance of the issues at stake are all that concern us. By attacking vestiarian nonconformity first, the Queen very cleverly put the costumary aspect of the Puritan controversy in the foreground, obscured the important disciplinary and governmental differences, and made the entire struggle appear a matter of no great consequence, springing from the stubbornness of petty minds. Because the immediate points at issue were so trivial, many contemporaries were hoodwinked by this strategem, and some later historians have been similarly deceived. But careful consideration of even these preliminary arguments reveals the magnitude of the real conflict. Did the secular ruler have the power to compel the clergy to adopt a

[4] John Strype, *The Life and Acts of Matthew Parker* (3 vols.; Oxford, 1821), I, 329–32.

[5] *Ibid.*, pp. 334–39; cf. Judges, chap. 6.   [6] Strype, *Parker*, III, 98–107.

practice which was, in the opinion of a majority of them, inimical
to the cause of true religion? Was the church to settle its own
affairs and set its own course, or were the intelligentsia of England to be reduced to the level of tutors in the households of the
great?

Reason alone failed to sway the Puritans. Parker soon saw
the necessity of using a bigger stick. Open support from the
Queen would probably suffice. He asked Cecil to draw up a
letter ordering him to enforce uniformity of clerical dress and
get the Queen to sign it. So began the long wooing. Elizabeth
had a keen instinct for avoiding responsibility for unpopular or
dangerous actions. All her servants from Winter to Davison
knew it, and Parker was no exception. They were accordingly
prepared to suffer any necessary consequences of their actions,
but they strove to avoid as many as possible. The Archbishop's
first effort met with a kind of left-handed success. The Queen's
diplomatic barometer was registering a general rise in Catholic
power throughout Europe, and, to meet the new situation, she
gave Parker more than he had asked. As Cecil had feared, she
considerably strengthened the charge. She struck out a paragraph of the original draft, and substituted one of her inimitable
tongue-lashings, this time for the bishops, whom she held responsible for the prevailing disorder.[7] She wished the laws enforced, but she did not want to be publicly involved. It was
the beginning of sorrows for the unhappy Archbishop.

The Puritans, also in uncertain despair, took what steps they
could devise to defend their position. Anticipating Parker by
several months, they began by asking for secular assistance.
Surprisingly enough, one of the disillusioned Anglican bishops
took the initiative here. Sad experience of the workings of the
royal supremacy had taught Pilkington to rue the day at Frankfort when he signed the letter rejecting the Genevan request
for a united front. Safe in his semi-autonomous bishopric of
Durham, in 1563 he had secured Whittingham as his Dean and
was anxious to further the work of reformation at every oppor-

[7] Cecil to Parker, January 15, 1565; Elizabeth to Parker, January 25, 1565, *Parker
Correspondence*, ed. Bruce and Perowne (Cambridge: Parker Society, 1853), pp. 223–
27.

tunity. At the first alarm, in October, 1564, he dispatched an appeal to Robert Dudley, the Queen's favorite, who had recently been created Earl of Leicester. He was the Hapsburg Archduke's chief rival for Elizabeth's hand and so the hope of the Puritan faction, though there is no evidence that he ever had a sincere religious thought. In addressing him on the vestiarian issue, Pilkington maintained that such quarrels about trifles were stirred up by Satan himself. Good men would often yield in such matters, as he did himself, rather than destroy the unity of the church, but it was unchristian to compel those who wished to be more scrupulous, as Paul had demonstrated in the matter of circumcising Titus. In his rude diocese priests wore "sword, dagger and such coarse apparel as they can get, not being curious or scrupulous what color or fashion it be and none is offended at them." For civilized men to dispute about a cap was lamentable. The best reformed churches had cast away popish apparel with the Pope. As lords dressed in such a fashion as to be distinguished from common people, so Protestants should not dress like Catholics. To enforce the traditional costume would drive godly and learned ministers from their livings when there was a dearth of preachers already. Godly courtiers were raised up of God to save his people on occasion, as Esther's example showed and, if they failed in their duty, Mordecai's threat of divine vengeance would be carried out.[8]

Before the end of the year, Whittingham added his voice to his Bishop's. To wear the attire of Roman Catholics was to seem to consent to their "blasphemies." He was willing to wear distinctive ministerial costume if the magistrates thought it necessary, so long as it was not corrupted by idolatrous associations. But, if the proposed steps were taken to enforce the traditional apparel, he implored the newly created Earl to secure for the Puritans the same immunities which the crypto-Catholics were enjoying in the established church.[9] In London another important church official tried to stem the tide, this time by a compromise proposal. Alexander Nowell, the Dean of St. Paul's, proposed that the disputants concede that the magis-

[8] Strype, *Parker*, III, 69–76, esp. p. 70.   [9] *Ibid.*, pp. 76–84.

trate had the right to enforce the wearing of the disputed attire, but petition the authorities to abolish it as a source of misunderstanding and contention.[10]

It was all wasted effort. If Leicester dared to play the role of Esther, he certainly did not care to do more than come into the kingdom. To that end he fished in all waters and was not unwilling to listen to the Puritans when occasion served. But he could read the political weather signs almost as well as Elizabeth, and, for the time, he was busy assuring the Spanish ambassador of his continued loyalty to his former master, Philip. Nor would the Queen hear of compromise. All her energies were directed toward coming to a working agreement with the Catholics, even to the extent of offering Dudley to Mary for a husband. Lent began with the Queen abruptly terminating the astonished Nowell's sermon at Paul's Cross with a shouted order to cease his remarks against images. It ended with a strong discourse on the real presence from the royal almoner, and with Elizabeth performing the traditional Catholic foot-washing rites of Maundy Thursday.

Dutifully, Parker took up his assigned role of ecclesiastical disciplinarian. Soon after the receipt of the Queen's thunderbolt, he communicated the order to Grindal, Bishop of London, through whom the other prelates were customarily notified of provincial orders. With the help of Grindal, Horne, Cox, and Bullingham of Lincoln, he proceeded to draw up formal regulations for clerical costume and certain other matters connected with church worship and discipline. Early in March the rules, which were later known as the Advertisements, were sent to Cecil to secure the Queen's formal approval. The Queen was also asked to write a special letter to stir up the reluctant Grindal, in whose diocese most of the trouble was located. At the same time Humphrey, Sampson, and four of their London clerical supporters were called before the ecclesiastical commissioners. When they proved recalcitrant, they were referred to the royal Council itself.[11]

[10] *Ibid.*, I, 344–45; Parker to Cecil, March 3, 1565, *Parker Correspondence*, pp. 233–34.

[11] Parker to Cecil, March 3 and 8, 1565, *Parker Correspondence*, pp. 233–34; Strype, *Parker*, I, 313–15; III, 89–93.

Now Elizabeth's shifting, responsibility-shirking nature began to assert itself. To Parker's dismay and disgust the Queen refused to sanction the proposed articles, and no letter was sent to Grindal, though in consultation with some of the bishops Cecil cut short their puritanical objections to the surplice and ordered them to enforce conformity or take the consequences.[12] Some lesser offenders were deprived,[13] and one Puritan, George Withers, preacher at Bury in Suffolk, resigned his living under the threat of similar treatment. But Parker complained that the Council used nothing but words on the principal defendants, and soon afterward he was astounded to find that they were actually appointed by Grindal or the Mayor of London to preach at Paul's Cross. At the end of April, however, the commissioners finally decided to deprive the Oxford men.[14] Soon afterward Parker revoked all preaching licenses issued prior to April 1, 1565. No new ones were to be granted to nonconformists. This clipped the wings of the wandering exhorters, who, as the Advertisements indicate, were often effective agitators for the Puritan cause.

Under this pressure from Parker the Puritans continued their former tactics. The intellectual arguments were repeated. Petitions against the enforcement of the law were sent to the bishops, to Leicester, and to the Queen herself.[15] A hardy clergyman named Cole even went to court in hat and short cloak to work for his cause.[16] Even when the commissioners

[12] De Silva to Philip, March 12, 1565, *Spanish Calendar*, I, 406.

[13] In the *The Seconde Parte of a Register* (ed. Peel [2 vols.; Cambridge: Parker Society, 1915], I, 52 and xx) a Mr. Broklesby is described as "the first put out of his living for the surplice," April 3, 1565. But De Silva, writing to Philip on March 12 (*Spanish Calendar*, I, 406), states that one Puritan had already lost his position for this reason. George Withers had resigned for the same cause some time before May 24, when he made his peace with Parker (Strype, *Parker*, I, 375).

[14] Strype, *Parker*, I, 327.

[15] *Ibid.*, pp. 313, 323–26, and Appen. XXX of Vol. III; State Papers, Domestic, Elizabeth, XXXVI, 64 (*Calendar*, I, 253), reprinted in R. W. Dixon, *History of the Church of England from the Abolition of the Roman Jurisdiction* (6 vols.; 3d rev. ed.; Oxford, 1895), VI, 61–63; Strype, *Annals of the Reformation under Elizabeth* (4 vols. in 7; Oxford, 1824), I, ii, 142.

[16] Parker to Cecil, April 7, 1565, *Parker Correspondence*, p. 237. Dixon (*op. cit.*, p. 101) identifies this Cole with Thomas Cole, Archdeacon of Essex, who had been promi-

reached their decision, hope was not abandoned. Humphrey wrote to Foxe, urging him to move his patron, the Duke of Norfolk, to stay the blow.[17] Finally, passive resistance was resorted to. Neither college head would resign at the commission's demand, and it could be argued that neither was subject to its jurisdiction. As Dean of Christ Church, Sampson held a royal donative, a lay office beyond ecclesiastical control. Without the Queen's special intervention it was difficult to remove him.[18] But the common lawyers had not yet undertaken to exhaust the possibilities of legal obstructionism in the Puritans' defense.[19] In June the deprivation was finally accomplished, and for a time the stubborn former Dean was imprisoned.[20] But Parker had no desire to be severe. Now that an example had been made, the Archbishop interceded for Sampson with Cecil. The Puritan Earl of Huntingdon joined in this mediation, and the unfortunate man was soon released.

Humphrey also had a legal defense for his position, but his story had a different ending. As President of Magdalen he was elected by the fellows, and supposedly removable only by the visitor, for violation of the college statutes. Horne, Bishop of Winchester, had the supervisory post, but, though he had taken the Anglican side at Frankfort, he was not inclined to persecute. In fact, at this time, he presented Humphrey with a benefice in the diocese of Salisbury, much to Jewel's disgust.[21] Perhaps one example was considered enough. Possibly Humphrey was thought the less dangerous of the two Puritans. In any case,

---

nent in the Frankfort struggle on the Anglican side, but there is no proof of this. There were several prominent clergymen of this name at the time, including one William, who was a member of the Geneva congregation, and Robert, who was the mannikin at the Lambeth meeting in 1566.

[17] Strype, *Parker*, I, 368–69.

[18] *Ibid.*, pp. 327–28, 371.

[19] See below, p. 273. This accounts for the Puritans' comparatively docile compliance with ecclesiastical decisions at this time, which excites Dixon's surprise (*op. cit.*, pp. 61–63, 99–100).

[20] Dixon denies this (*ibid.*, p. 63), but see Sampson to Parker, June 3, 1565, *Parker Correspondence*, p. 243.

[21] Jewel to Parker, December 22, 1565, *Works*, ed. Ayre (4 vols.; Cambridge: Parker Society, 1845–50), IV, 1265.

after a short period of rustication, he returned to Oxford and resumed his normal activities.

In spite of the Queen's refusal of open support, Parker's program was proceeding smoothly by the summer of 1565. An outstanding example of disciplinary action had been given to the country in Sampson's case. Withers had made his peace with the Archbishop and had promised to wear the required garb at Bury, thus incidentally acting as collection agent for some Puritan merchant friends who in a moment of rash optimism had sold goods to be paid for when he next preached in Bury.[22] Itinerant preachers were under control. Apparently all would be well in time. Then came the Darnley marriage, and for a period in the early fall it seemed that Elizabeth might support Moray and the Scotch Protestants, who were in revolt against their queen. Anti-Puritan activities were promptly suspended. Thus one whiff of Knox's doctrine of rebellion, even though coming from across the border, did more for the Puritan cause in England than bales of petitions and seas of foamy talk of passive resistance.

But as Mary successfully surmounted all obstacles, Elizabeth changed her mind, and the government resumed its repressive operations. Cambridge University first required attention. There, when the Scotch war seemed most probable, Withers had provoked an epidemic of window-smashing by some of his anti-Catholic sermons. Exuberant undergraduates at Trinity College, where the Master, Robert Beaumont, once pro-Puritan, was ceremoniously using a footcloth for his processions and was otherwise suspected of being too conservative, had added to the excitement one night by clipping the tail of Beaumont's horse and also giving it a "popish crown." The following Sunday the shearings were strewn in the path of the Master's procession, as though for a carpet. The outraged authorities offered a reward for information as to the identity of the pranksters, but none was forthcoming. Worse still, St. John's College had turned openly Puritan. Led by the Master and an outspoken fellow, almost the entire body threw off their surplices on Octo-

[22] Strype, *Parker*, I, 375, 395.

ber 12, 1565, Weeks of effort by Parker and Cecil, the Chancellor, were necessary to reduce the university to order. New statutes were drawn up, and the system of university preaching licenses was revised. To one of the Puritan protests against these actions a young fellow of Peterhouse named Thomas Whitgift incautiously set his name. That was to require considerable explanation in later years.[23]

London was next in line. Sampson's experience had not daunted the clergy there. Knowing Grindal's reluctance to enforce the regulations, many of them used what forms they pleased. The Spanish ambassador, between spells of complaining about the doings of that redoubtable slave-trader, Mr. "Achins" (Hawkins) of Plymouth, noted that the disorder and irregularity had done much good to the Catholic cause.[24] Grudgingly, the Bishop yielded to the pressure from above. On February 1, 1566, he proposed to his clergy a compromise measure, requiring the surplice in church and a round cap, "turkey" gown, and falling cape for exterior wear.[25] But Parker continued to press for the full Advertisements program. Once more he sent the document to Cecil, soliciting the Queen's approval. Disappointed again, he finally resolved to publish it in spite of doubts as to the legality of the act.[26] At the same time he moved to reduce the metropolitan area to order. The clergy of the diocese of London, of Southwark, which was under the see of Winchester, and of the Archbishop's London peculiars, the churches directly under his control, were summoned before the ecclesiastical commissioners at Lambeth on March 26. Parker tried in vain to get lay support from the Council on this occasion.[27] Even some of his fellow-ecclesiastics deserted him. But Grindal and Gabriel Goodman, the Dean of Westminster, were there. About one hundred and ten ministers appeared. The authori-

---

[23] *Ibid.*, pp. 381–94; State Papers, Domestic, Elizabeth, XXXVIII, *passim* (*Calendar*, I, 261–63). For the tail-clipping incident see Wood to Gilby, October 4, 1565, Baker MS XXXII (Cambridge University Library MS Mm. I, 43), fol. 430.

[24] De Silva to Philip, April 14, 1565, *Spanish Calendar*, I, 418.

[25] W. H. Frere, *The English Church in the Reigns of Elizabeth and James I* (London, 1904), p. 117.

[26] Dixon, *op. cit.*, pp. 88–92.   [27] *Ibid.*, p. 95 n.

ties exhibited a properly dressed clerical mannikin in the person
of one Robert Cole, a London minister who had submitted after
a period of nonconformity. The ministers were ordered to signify their willingness or unwillingness to use the attire as indicated. Arguments were cut short and the roll called. It was a
difficult decision, conscience pitted against economic security.
"We are killed in our souls for this pollution of ours, for that we
cannot perform in the singleness of our hearts this our ministry,"
wrote one of the harassed Puritans.[28] Thirty-seven refused and
were suspended from their positions. Their incomes were sequestered, that is, impounded, and they were notified that, if
they did not conform in three months, they would be deprived
of their livings completely. The best of the clergy, according to
Parker's own reckoning, were among the nonconformists, and
Coverdale had absented himself from the gathering. Two days
later the Advertisements were published, with a preface which
concealed in much verbiage their lack of royal sanction. Parker
promptly dispatched them to his clerical subordinates with orders to enforce them.

Once more the Puritans scurried about in quest of a not too
violent means of meeting the situation. They would not talk
of rebellion. Emigration was not considered. As yet they did
not even dare take active legal steps to defend themselves. No
one braved the wrath of the court by contesting the legality of
Parker's suspensions and deprivations, though there were ample
grounds.[29] The leaders contented themselves with sending more
petitions to court, a literary warfare, and an appeal for assistance from foreign divines. Lever wrote to Leicester and Cecil,
urging them to prevent the eviction of godly ministers of whom
the church stood in need.[30] Humphrey, writing to Cecil, added
his voice to Lever's, and a short time later urged Foxe to use
his influence where it would do the most good.[31] From the prov-

[28] "The Earl Diary" (Cambridge University MS Mm. I. 29), quoted incorrectly in
Strype, *Grindal*, p. 145.

[29] Dixon, *op. cit.*, pp. 89–93, 99–100.

[30] Strype, *Parker*, I, 421–22, and Appen. XLVII of Vol. III.

[31] *Ibid.*, I, 439; Humphrey to Cecil, April(?), 1566, State Papers, Domestic, Elizabeth, XXXIX, 63 (*Calendar*, I, 271).

inces reforming zealots hurried to London to lend their aid, and
even continued to preach at court without the proper attire, as
the Queen left all the unpopular disciplinary measures to Parker.[32]

All the old arguments were refurbished and brought into
play. A manuscript answer to the Lambeth proceedings was
filed at the time.[33] When Parker's Advertisements appeared in
print, the Puritans also had recourse to the press. A tract now
lost, called *The Voice of God*, was among the first to appear.
The author was a coalman and amateur musician, whose enemies alleged that he would gladly have worn the surplice could
he have secured a position at St. Paul's.[34] More important was
the work of Robert Crowley, the poetic controversialist. This
doughty fighter, who had been an active reformer under Edward VI, had taken the Anglican side at Frankfort, but now,
like Lever and Pilkington, found himself pushed into the Puritan camp by the Queen's policy. As Archdeacon of Hereford
and Prebendary of St. Paul's, he was a man of some consequence
in the church. As Rector of St. Peter le Poor, Vicar of St. Giles,
Cripplegate, and reader (lecturer) at St. Antholin's, he was not
only something of a pluralist but a power among the London
clergy as well. With the assistance of his Puritan friends he
drew up and published *A Briefe Discourse against the Outwarde
Apparell and Ministering Garmentes of the Popishe Church*. Besides rephrasing the old explanation of when a thing indifferent
was not a thing indifferent, it contained an explicit statement of
the Puritan doctrine of passive resistance:

And if the Prince shall take in hand to command us to do any of those
things which God hath not commanded, in such sort that we may not leave
them undone unless we will thereby run into the penalty of the law we (when
we shall see that in doing thereof we cannot edify but destroy) we must then
refuse to do the thing commanded by the Prince and humbly submit ourselves to suffer the penalty, but in any case not consent to infringe the Christian liberty which is to use things indifferent to edification and not to destruction. . . . .

[32] Parker to Cecil, April 12, 1566, *Parker Correspondence*, p. 278.

[33] Printed in Daniel Neal, *History of the Puritans* (3 vols.; London, 1837), I, 141–43.

[34] John Stow, "Memoranda," in *Three Fifteenth Century Chronicles*, ed. Gairdner
("Camden Society: New Series," Vol. XXVIII [London, 1880]), p. 139.

And this is not to give example of disobedience (as it is before objected) but by example to teach true obedience both to God and also to man. First we obey God, in that both in doing and leaving undone we seek the edification of his church. And then we obey man, in that we do humbly submit ourselves to suffer at man's hand whatsoever punishments man's laws do appoint for our doing or refusing to do at man's commandment. . . . .

Our goods, our bodies, and our lives we do with all humble submission yield into the hands of God's officers upon earth: but our consciences we keep unspotted in the sight of Him that shall judge all men.[35]

The authors and printers of both these treatises were discovered. By May, 1566, the printers had spent a fortnight in the Counter, but the writers went unpunished, since "they had friends enough to have set the whole realm together by the ears." Some of the court agitation was bearing fruit. But Parker, or one of his assistants, answered Crowley with *A Brief Examination for the Tyme of a Certaine Declaration Lately Put in Print*. In addition to the old arguments from common sense and scripture, and the need of good order in the church, there was one of a political turn. To demand absolute authority for the individual priest "to admit no orders which may not manifestly appear unto them that they do edify" was to reject the biblical doctrine of the royal supremacy, for "kings shall be thy nurse-fathers and queens thy nurses."[36] Subjects cannot know as much as the king and council, and must obey, even if they do not see why, so long as the order is not directly contrary to God's law. To advocate individual judgment in such cases was tantamount to countenancing rebellion, a worse stumbling block to the weak than any garment:

This smelleth of . . . . either . . . . Donatistry or papistry, which sects think always the true Catholics to give too much to princes and magistrates, when, as by God's word, they acknowledge them to be supreme governors, not only to see laws framed by the clergy put in use but to disannul the naughty and to decree good and godly.[37]

Another type of rejoinder was the action of the commissioners in securing a decree of the Council forbidding the publication of anything directed against the laws of the realm, the Queen's

[35] Sig. B, fols. ii(*v*)–iii; sig. C, fol. v.

[36] Sig. **, fol. 4 (British Museum Press Mark: C. 37, c. 1).   [37] Sig. ****, fol. 4.

injunctions, or the ordinances of the commission.[38] But secret presses were already an old story to the Puritans, and the flood continued.

Safe under the shadow of Huntingdon's wings, Anthony Gilby of Ashby-de-la-Zouche now joined battle. Quickly he composed the outstanding controversial work of the period, *A Pleasaunt Dialogue betweene a Souldior of Barwicke and an English Chaplaine.* Though generally neglected by students of literature, this satire, remarkable for humor and spirit, belongs with the works of Turner, Bale, and Martin Marprelate in the first rank of Puritan controversial productions. In fact, the author shows the direct influence of the animal literature, referring to Turner's exposé almost thirty years back, and calling the royal policy a mere "cropping of that Romish Reynold's [Reynard's] ears, and so to bring in an English popery."[39] The general nature of the work is indicated by the description, in the full title, of the chaplain "who of late soldier was made a parson and hath gotten a plurality of benefices, and yet had but one eye and no learning: but he was priestly apparelled in all points, and stoutly maintained his popish attire by the authority of a book lately written against London ministers." The ignorant pluralist who has obtained place and promotion praised the ease of his life compared to the hardships of his former situation. Since being made a priest he could hawk, hunt, dice, and card with gentlemen. His friend, the soldier, could secure the same status with money, or by fawning upon some gentleman who had a benefice to dispose of. Money would also buy a dispensation to cover any lack of learning or physical disability. There was no need to preach. The bishops disliked the Genevan fashion, with "nothing in the church but naked walls and a poor fellow in a bare gown telling a long tale and brawling and chiding with all this auditory."[40] Sermons pricked consciences too much. In the present establishment one read a hasty service and then went merrily to one's dinner, without any foolishness such as instructing the common people. "It was never good world with

[38] Strype, *Parker*, I, 442–43.

[39] Sig. D, fol. vii; sig. E, fol. ii.   [40] Sig. B, fol. iv.

us since every soldier and every serving man could talk so much of the scripture, and these foolish ministers are the cause thereof, which would make all men as wise as themselves."[41]

But the honest soldier spurned the suggestion:

Rather would I starve under Berwick walls than do as thou doest and hast counselled me to do, either in taking of a benefice by such unlawful means or to enter into the Pope's livery, my sworn enemy because I am an Englishman and to me most detestable of all other earthly creatures because I am a Christian man.[42]

With a theological and political knowledge somewhat out of character, the border fighter then went on to cover the entire field of the controversy. He took up the examiner's arguments and refuted them one by one. To the charge that Puritans used churches once desecrated by popery he boldly answered that edifices such as the one at Walsingham, a famous pilgrim shrine in the old days, should be destroyed as dedicated primarily to superstition. But the others were to be regarded merely as assembly places which belonged of old to God's people.[43] He anticipated a long line of Puritan lawyers by asking his adversary why the alb was abandoned as a precept of man but not the surplice; the stole but not the tippet.[44] The offending garments were once more branded as marks of idols, "worse than lousy, for they are sib [closely related to] the sark of Hercules that made him tear his own bowels asunder."[45] Nor were the garments the real issue, for the Advertisements upheld the whole prayer-book system which contained a hundred points of popery. These were listed, including lord bishops, the proud dean and his office, the chanter, organist and organ-blower, hired mourners, and godfathers. Turning to impersonal abuses, the soldier enumerated absenteeism, the wedding ring, "the grey amice with cat's tails," the want of true discipline, the lack of exercise of learning, etc.[46] If these were considered trifles, so is all popery. A little leaven leavens the whole lump.

With the political points at issue the author dealt vigorously

[41] Sig. C, fol. iii(v).

[42] Sig. C, fol. iv(v).

[43] Sig. G, fol. iii(v).

[44] Sig. K, fol. ii.

[45] Sig. K, fol. iv(v).

[46] Sig. L, fol. vii–sig. N, fol. ii.

if not very penetratingly. The Puritans were no Anabaptists.
They recognized governmental authority. It was an old craft
of Satan to charge God's servants with being factious and seditious. But no one could be expected to do evil at the magistrate's command.[47] Even the sovereign was bound by God's
word.[48] Therefore the use of the surplice could not be required
as a purely civil matter. If the Queen could command one piece
of popery as a matter of policy, she could command all.
Hezekiah and Josiah knew no such authority. Jeroboam and
Nebuchadnezzar are the types of rulers using such methods.
God was an exacting God who prescribed even the loops of
curtains and the buttons and clasps in the Tabernacle. "Better
to have all the world to run in hurly-burly and heaven and earth
to shake than one jot of God's glory should decay."[49] The best
policy was to root out idolatry. It was a pity that Bonner and
the other Catholic bishops were not made to suffer the fate de-
creed for all false prophets. In short, let the state support us
against all others, for we have the true faith.

The whole was topped off with some shrewd personal hits.
The Puritan superiority was to be seen in the conduct of their
London clergymen, who, the author alleged, had remained at
their posts at the risk of their lives

in that late plague of London when you four-horned [square-capped]
gentlemen fled from your ewes and hired journeymen in your places. At
what time [he continued] these men showed themselves the good shepherds
jeoparding their lives for the sheep and you were found hirelings, taking
still the gain, but flying from the perils.[50]

And look at the record once more:

All these [conservative practices] were abhorred as popish, superstitious,
and idolatries among our English gospellers, both bishops and others, when
they were under God's rods in poverty. But they have now learned courtly
divinity, to ground all upon policy. Humble them again, O Lord![51]

This vigorous and detailed statement of the Puritan cause
was not published for seven years. The author explains the
delay on the ground that "there was hope of reformation soon

---

[47] Sig. C, fol. viii(v).   [49] Sig. A, fols. iii–iv.

[48] Sig. E, fol. i(v).   [50] Sig. B, fol. vii(v).   [51] Sig. A, fol. iv(v).

after. Therefore was it of charity by the writer suppressed."
Perhaps discretion was also a contributing factor, for an ex-
purgated edition of the address to the reader, with the omission
of the most telling direct references to the Queen, appeared in
1566, along with Pilkington's letter to Cecil, under the title *To
My Lovinge Brethren That Is Troubled about the Popyshe Apparrell Two Short and Comfortable Epistels*. Many of its arguments were also presented in *An Answere for the Tyme to the Examination Put in Print without the Authours Name Pretending To
Mayntayne the Apparrell Prescribed against the Declaration of the
Mynisters of London*. In addition, the anonymous author of
this last-mentioned tract contributed certain more definite interpretations of the Puritan doctrine. The writer admitted the
charge that the Puritans demanded freedom for the individual
priest to admit no royal orders except what seemed to edify,
but he denied that this was contrary to the biblical theory that
kings were to be ecclesiastical nurse-fathers. Each minister
should be learned enough to judge for himself. As Paul recommended, each was to be persuaded in his own mind. The position of nurse-father obligated the ruler to defend and cherish
the church but not to burden it with superstitious ceremonies.
Such stumbling blocks to the weak were not to be received
though all the princes in the world commanded them. It was
true that a subject must pay an unjust tribute and not dispute
the magistrate's rulings in secular affairs. But this was not so
in the ecclesiastical sphere.[52]

> You think it dangerous for subjects to restrain the prince's authorities
> to bounds and limits. We think it as dangerous to enlarge the prince's
> authority beyond the bounds and limits of holy Scripture. . . . . We neither
> take from the prince's authority with the Donatists and papists nor add unto
> it with the clawbacks and flatterers.[53]

In fact, the Anglicans were more like Donatists in rejecting the
Puritans for such trifles, and like the Catholics in retaining popery. Lastly, in reply to the query whether God's people were so
senseless as to think ill of ministers for wearing the disputed

---

[52] *An Answere for the Tyme*, pp. 27–28, 32–33, 80–81.

[53] *Ibid.*, pp. 82, 85–86.

garments, the champion of the intelligence of the individual minister replied:

We judge God's people to be as by experience we find them, and it is rather like they will believe our doings than our sayings. If we say all marks of idolatry are to be abhorred, many seeing us use them ourselves will think there is no great danger in using them nor truth in our words, whatsoever we say of them. It is the best persuasion if the tongue and the coat talk and teach the same thing.[54]

The Puritan controversialists also endeavored to strengthen their position by an appeal to the authority of great churchmen of the past and to that of the Continental reformers. By a judicious selection of passages, great names from Ambrose and Theophylactus to Musculus and Gualter could be quoted on the insurgent side, and they were accordingly so marshaled.[55]

While the English Puritans were writing their own controversial literature, they were hoping for more effective contributions from abroad. The Scotch brethren were informed of the English situation and eventually sent to the bishops a general request for leniency in their dealings with the Puritans.[56] Greater things were expected of the Swiss divines, especially those of Zurich, who still stood in almost a teacher-pupil relationship to many of the Anglican bishops. Apparently, Humphrey received no reply to his 1563 inquiry. So, when the controversy broke out again in 1566, he and Sampson wrote separate letters to Bullinger, stating their case afresh and asking for answers to a number of specific questions.[57] But the Anglican bishops had anticipated this move. In July, 1565, Horne had written to Gualter, Bullinger's fellow-pastor, that the bishops were themselves opposed to the costume but countenanced it in order to retain offices which might otherwise be filled with Catholics.[58] With the passage of the years Bullinger, never a vigorous con-

[54] *Ibid.*, p. 145.

[55] *The Fortress of Fathers, Earnestlie Defending the Puritie of Religion and Ceremonies* (s.l., 1566); *The Mynd and Exposition of That Excellent Learned Man Martyn Bucer* (Emden, 1566). To this second tract is appended *Objections and Answers concernynge Apparell of Prestes and Ministers*. All the Puritan works here mentioned except *The Voice of God* and the Berwick dialogue are in British Museum Press Mark: c.37, d. 46.

[56] Strype, *Parker*, III, 150–52.

[57] February 9 and 16, 1566, *Zurich Letters*, I, 151–55.   [58] *Ibid.*, p. 142.

troversialist, had grown somewhat at ease in his Swiss Zion, and like Martyr he disliked such difficult puzzles. But when pressed he continued the Martyr tradition by coming out on the side of those in authority. In November he cautiously approved of Horne's stand.[59] In the next February, Jewel strengthened this resolution by a missive similar to Horne's,[60] just as the Puritans were renewing their request for an opinion. So the Puritan letters fell on stony ground. But, rather than offend the writers, Bullinger at first returned a somewhat noncommittal response. Told that this was unsatisfactory, he at length broke the bad news. In a long letter to the Puritans, written May 1, he and Gualter indorsed the bishops' case almost *in toto* and sent copies to Horne and Grindal.[61] Without waiting to secure permission, the prelates had the precious document printed. Its effect was telling. Under its impetus many of the waverers decided to conform.[62] The Puritans, who had been appealing to the example of the Continental churches, quickly published a collection of excerpts from Bullinger's earlier works[63] to show that he could speak in another voice. They also appealed from the Zurich pope badly informed to the same worthy to be better informed, and took steps to see that this further education was immediately effected. In July, Turner, who had gone so far at Wells as to cause an adulterer to do penance in a square cap, wrote a sharp letter to Bullinger, suggesting that the bishops were misinforming him and accusing him of an inconsistency like Melanchthon's, not unmixed with a timorous respect for authority.[64] The Oxford Puritans were more moderate, but tried to point out that more was at stake than dress alone, adding a list of thirteen Roman flaws remaining in the English pearl, including the lack of discipline.[65] This was intrusted to

[59] *Ibid.*, pp. 343–44.   [60] *Ibid.*, pp. 148–49.   [61] *Ibid.*, pp. 345–57.

[62] Grindal to Bullinger, August 27, 1566, *ibid.*, p. 168; Grindal and Horne to Bullinger and Gualter, February 6, 1567, *ibid.*, p. 175. It was shortly reprinted, together with the similar verdicts of Melanchthon, Bucer, and Martyr, in a larger tract entitled *Whether It Be Mortal Sinne To Transgresse Civil Laws Which Be the Commandments of Civil Magistrates* (London, n.d.).

[63] *The Judgement of H. Bullinger in Certeyne Matters of Religion* (s.l., 1566).

[64] *Zurich Letters*, II, 124–26.   [65] *Ibid.*, I, 157–65; cf. *ibid.*, II, 358–62.

one of the suspended London ministers, who was dispatched to Switzerland as a kind of Puritan ambassador. He was Percival Wiburn, or Wyburn, one of the Geneva congregation in Mary's time, later senior fellow of St. John's College, Cambridge, and canon of both Rochester and Westminster. At the same time an appeal was made to a more sympathetic ear. Calvin was dead, but Geneva was still a power, and Beza was now its prophet. Coverdale, Humphrey, and Sampson sent along with Wiburn a letter to Beza and his associates, Farel and Viret.[66] Informed of the situation from some other source, Beza had already written to Grindal expostulating with him on his compliance in what appeared to the Genevan as a semi-Catholic program.[67]

Wiburn arrived in Switzerland early in September and on the whole proved a capable emissary. Beza received him cordially, indorsed his program, and sent him on to Bullinger with a long letter pleading the Puritan cause. Because the *First Blast* literature was published at Geneva, Beza was *persona non grata* with the English government, but he suggested that Gualter visit the island and use his influence to secure a remedy for the Romish evils remaining in the establishment there. If that could not be done, at least strong representations should be made to the English authorities by letters.[68] Bullinger avoided seeing Wiburn for more than a short time, and no Zurich agent was sent to England.[69] But Bullinger and Gualter did busy themselves for several days with vestiarian matters. Without abandoning their previous position, they now put the emphasis on the other side of their program—the need for reform and, pending that, mildness in dealing with the more scrupulous brethren. First, Grindal and Horne were justly rated for publishing the earlier epistle without the authors' consent.[70] An apology for the mis-

[66] *Ibid.*, II, 121–24.

[67] Beza to Grindal, June 27, 1566, Epistle 8, *Tractationum theologicarum* (3 vols.; Geneva, 1582), III, 209–13; Strype, *Grindal*, p. 167.

[68] *Zurich Letters*, II, 127–35.

[69] Wiburn to Bullinger, February 25, 1567, *ibid.*, I, 187–88; Gualter to Beza, September 11, 1566, *ibid.*, II, 143–44.

[70] *Ibid.*, I, 357–58.

use of the May letter was sent to Coverdale.[71] Parkhurst was praised because he and Pilkington had refused to eject any nonconformists.[72] Bedford, as a member of the Council, was exhorted to play the true nursing-father to the church.[73] On September 10, after four days of these literary exertions, the weary Zurichers concluded with a message to Humphrey and Sampson, exhorting them to conform and at the same time refusing to discuss the matter further.[74]

But Bullinger and Gualter were not to be let off so easily. Anglican and Puritan continued to write, justifying their conduct and disputing about the extent of the surviving Roman Catholic practices.[75] Each dealt in half-truths, the exaggerations of the one neatly balancing the understatements of the other. The Puritan slander of the Anglicans as using spittle and oil in baptism was balanced by Grindal's claim that the "Black Rubric" was still in force. The summer of 1567 saw another Puritan delegation sent abroad, this time consisting of Withers and George Barthelot or Bartlett, the suspended preacher at St. Giles, Cripplegate. Aside from another intercessory letter to the bishops, nothing could be extracted from Bullinger, who considered both sides far too quarrelsome.[76] Beza, weary of the dispute, counseled patience.[77] The last Continental hope was for assistance from the Calvinistic Elector of the Palatinate, Frederick III. To that end an interesting historical account of the controversy was drawn up, with the added request that he use his influence with Elizabeth on behalf of the Puritans, preferably for a thorough reformation, but at least for toleration

---

[71] *Ibid.*, II, 136.

[72] *Ibid.*, pp. 140–42. Sandys had been similarly lenient (Withers and Barthelot to Bullinger and Gualter, August, 1567, *ibid.*, II, 151).

[73] *Ibid.*, pp. 137–39.　　　　　　　　[74] September 10, *ibid.*, I, 360–62.

[75] Withers and Barthelot to Bullinger and Gualter, August, 1567, *ibid.*, II, 146–51; Horne to Bullinger, n.d., with appendixes, *ibid.*, pp. 354–62; Grindal and Horne to Bullinger and Gualter, February 6, 1567, *ibid.*, I, 175–82.

[76] Bullinger to Beza, March 15, 1567, *ibid.*, II, 152; Bullinger and Gualter to Beza, August 3, 1567, *ibid.*, pp. 154–55; Bullinger and Gualter to Grindal, Sandys, and Parkhurst, August 26, 1567, *ibid.*, pp. 166–68.

[77] Beza to certain Englishmen, October 24, 1567, Epistle 12, *Tractationum theologicarum*, III, 218–21.

of their nonconformity. In so doing, the authors took pains to suggest that the blame be laid, not on the Queen, where they half-admitted it really belonged, but on the long-suffering bishops, against whom they were growing more and more bitter as the controversy went on.[78] Nothing came of this effort, however, and the second Puritan embassy to the Continent was a complete failure.

In spite of all the defensive measures of the Puritan leaders, Parker's program was carried out with only minor hitches. Though Parkhurst, Sandys, and Pilkington refused to deprive any dissenters in their dioceses, a measure of conformity was secured in the all-important metropolis. The Archbishop had shrewdly calculated that some of the nonconformists—even of the conscientious, but especially those who resisted out of "spiced fancy" while the wound was still green—would yield when the stroke was really felt, toward the close of the quarter's probation.[79] Even so, he overestimated the stiffness of the opposition. The Puritans were taken aback by Parker's firmness. Their attitude at the original interview had been much more mild than the anxious Archbishop had anticipated. Their original manifesto, "The Reasons" for refusing the apparel, had announced a determination to suffer any fate in order to keep their consciences clear. But, if this ever reflected the sentiment of more than the zealous composer,[80] it was not for long. In two days after the Lambeth scene one recalcitrant sued for peace.[81] The nonconformists had counted much on the effect of a popular outcry when pulpits would be vacant for lack of surpliced preachers. But Parker had counted the cost. He had already vetoed the appointment of two nonconformists to deliver the Spital sermons,[82] discourses delivered in the interests of the London hospitals. He now did all in his power to fill the vacan-

[78] Withers to the Prince Elector, n.d., *Zurich Letters*, II, 156-64.

[79] Parker to Cecil, March 26, 1566, *Correspondence*, p. 270.

[80] Probably Crowley, at the conclusion of whose *Briefe Discourse* (sig. C, fol. v) this language is very nearly duplicated.

[81] Parker to Cecil, March 28, 1566, *Correspondence*, p. 272.

[82] Parker to Cecil, March 12, 1566, *Correspondence*, p. 264.

cies, distributing his own chaplains around as far as they would go. No appreciable concessions were made to the opposition, though one of the Easter preachers at Paul's Cross was asked to spread his remarks over two days.[83] When, in spite of all efforts, the mutterings and tumults came, the conscientious administrator grimly rode out the storm according to his plan, meanwhile answering the complaints of the secular arm with the sharp reminder of his previous warnings, which they so richly deserved.[84] Crowley forcibly barred his church to surpliced singers gathering for a funeral, dared Parker to deprive him, and had his challenge accepted. Shifting his ground, he took refuge in legal technicalities. This was rather anticipating the policy of his party, and it caused his adversary some trouble, but in this maze he was finally run to earth and ejected from his living.[85] Some of the Londoners defied the suspensions and continued preaching, but, in June, five of the worst offenders— including Crowley's two associates at St. Antholin's, Philpot and Gough—were called before the Council and parceled out to Winchester, Norwich, and Ely for a mixture of enforced episcopal hospitality and persuasion.[86] This considerably reduced the pressure in London, and the publication of Bullinger's letter at the same time virtually completed the rout of the Puritan clergy. One by one they made their peace.[87] In the autumn Philpot returned from Winchester to London and subscribed.[88] In a formal disputation when the Queen visited Oxford, Humphrey denied the right of the subject to take arms against even a wicked ruler and was told by Her Majesty that his long gown

[83] Parker to Cecil, April 3, 1566, *ibid.*, p. 275.

[84] Parker to Cecil, April 12, 1566, *ibid.*, pp. 277–79; Stow, *op. cit.*, pp. 139–40.

[85] Parker to Cecil, April 3 and 4, 1566, *Correspondence*, pp. 275–77; Withers and Barthelot to Bullinger and Gualter, August, 1567, *Zurich Letters*, II, 147.

[86] Parker to Haddon, June 6, 1566, *Correspondence*, pp. 284–85; Stow, *op. cit.*, pp. 139–40.

[87] Parker to Cecil, April 3 and 12, 1566, *Correspondence*, pp. 275, 278; Grindal to Bullinger, August 27, 1566, *Zurich Letters*, I, 168; Grindal and Horne to Bullinger and Gualter, February 6, 1567, *ibid.*, p. 175.

[88] Stow, *op. cit.*, p. 140.

became him "mighty well."[89] In March, 1567, Whittingham himself yielded, quoting Calvin to the effect that to forsake the ministry for such matters of ceremony would be to tithe mint and neglect greater things.[90] Exactly how many persisted in their stand to the point of being finally deprived is uncertain, but the learned ones were so few as to be negligible, a fact which the Anglican apologists were quick to point out.[91]

Parker proved a generous victor. Even those of the defeated party who persisted in their course did not feel driven to any desperate measures. In 1567, Sampson was provided with the mastership of a Leicester hospital, a position which did not require conformity. Not only did the Archbishop co-operate in securing this post for the leader of the Puritan faction but he secured lenient terms for all the others deprived. For example, those who still owed the Queen for first fruits were discharged from the obligation, so that no one could impute a pecuniary motive to the authorities.[92] With the approach of Parliament in the autumn, Council and bishops alike co-operated to secure the release of such recalcitrants as Crowley from their episcopal custody.[93] Accordingly, there was no general movement toward another Protestant exile. Withers, who took a degree at Heidelberg in 1568 and started the famous Erastian controversy by his doctoral disputation, was the only prominent Puritan to make any such gesture. The rest remained in England, biding their time, making what shift they could, waiting for something to turn up. Passive resistance was proving a rather futile policy.

[89] *The Progresses and Public Processions of Queen Elizabeth*, ed. Nichols (2 vols.; London, 1788), I (*anno* 1566), pp. 3 and 53.

[90] *A Brief Discourse of the Troubles Begun at Frankfort*, ed. Arber (London, 1908), p. 9.

[91] Withers and Barthelot writing to Bullinger and Gualter in August,1567 (*Zurich Letters*, II, 147), list the learned who were deprived as Lever, Penny, Gressop, Crowley, Gough, Philpot, and Wiburn. But Philpot made his peace and held Anglican livings, as we have seen, and Lever lost only a canonry and not his hospital mastership at Sherburn. To these must, however, be added Sampson, Allen, Whitehead, and Brokelsby (Strype, *Grindal*, p. 145).

[92] Strype, *Parker*, I, 458–59.

[93] *Acts of the Privy Council*, ed. Dasent, New Series (32 vols.; London, 1890–1907), VII, 315 (hereafter cited as *APC*).

Help came at last from the practitioners of a sterner creed. Across the border Mary was dissipating her political strength in a blaze of personal passion. After the crime of Kirk o' Field and the Bothwell marriage, the Scotch Protestants dared the displeasure of the Puritan President of Magdalen by taking arms against the ruler whom they considered evil. Quick and sure are the workings of military and diplomatic physics. As Mary's army dribbled away that Sunday afternoon at Carberry Hill, the Catholic pressure in Elizabeth's presence chamber disappeared, and the weight of episcopal displeasure was removed from Puritan backs. The conformity struggle continued, but only in a desultory fashion. The abortive second Puritan embassy to the Continent and several episcopalian rejoinders belong in 1567. But not for more than six years would Elizabeth greatly concern herself about the Puritans. And when the Queen found something else to occupy her attention, the bishops gladly did the same. Deprived Puritans such as Sampson and Lever were allowed to preach unmolested. The bishops only attempted to suppress such extreme Puritan tendencies as the one we are about to discuss.

A by-product of the vestiarian controversy was a recrudescence of separatism or independency. If the learned clergy had been moderate and even timid in the face of authority, the populace had not always followed their example. Blows had been exchanged in churches. Irate parishioners tore surplices and spat in the faces of those who wore them. When Grindal deprived Barthelot, he was plagued by a delegation of sixty women who would know the reason why. Two or three hundred of these feminine saints turned out to hearten Philpot and Gough with a shower of food and money on their departure for Winchester and confinement. When one of the women was forced to mount the cucking-stool the next January for heckling square-capped Grindal in St. Margaret's Church with cries of "horns," her companions turned out to honor her as worthy to suffer persecution for righteousness.[94] In this milieu some action

[94] Grindal to Cecil, May 4, 1566, Grindal, *Remains*, ed. Nicholson (Cambridge: Parker Society, 1843), pp. 288–89; Strype, *Annals*, I, ii, 126; Stow, *op. cit.*, pp. 139–40.

more positive than petitioning and tract-writing might be expected.

So it proved. Zealous Londoners remembered and followed the precedents of Marian days. A veteran of the Frankfort congregational experiment, one John Browne, probably at this time chaplain to the Duchess of Suffolk, supplied Continental examples.[95] In August, 1566, Grindal told his Swiss friends that there was talk of separation and the setting-up of private meetings.[96] In spite of the moderation of the bishops' attitude after the Darnley murder, the agitation continued, and by the following summer two such groups had been uncovered, one a body meeting in Plumbers' Hall. In the next year there are traces of several others, composed of "more women than men" and "citizens of the lowest order, together with four or five ministers remarkable neither for their judgment nor learning," as Grindal described them. They ordained their own officials— ministers, elders, and deacons—disciplined and excommunicated their members, and at least two of the groups[97] had something approximating the later Independent church covenant. Several times in their literature we find this statement repeated:

I have now joined myself to the church of Christ wherein I have yielded myself subject to the discipline of God's word as I promised at my baptism, which if I should now again forsake and join myself with the traditioners I should then forsake the union wherein I am knit with the body of Christ and join myself to the discipline of Antichrist.

In all, there were probably around a thousand who were connected with the movement at one time or another, although the ones capable of enduring persecution would not have been more than a fraction of that number.[98]

[95] Albert Peel has collected the sources for this phase of our story in *The First Congregational Churches* (Cambridge, 1920).

[96] Grindal to Bullinger, August 27, 1566, *Zurich Letters*, I, 168.

[97] From the documents printed in Peel (*op. cit.*, pp. 3, 25; cf. *ibid.*, p. 38) it is evident that the covenant in question was used not only by Fitz's church but by another frequented by the anonymous author of the treatise which Browne is attacking. "You have a church alone by yourselves and Fitz hath another" (*ibid.*, p. 25).

[98] *Ibid.*, pp. 44–45.

Toward the existing authorities their attitude differed only in degree from that of the main body of the Puritan party. To the general denial of the royal right to compel beliefs or actions contrary to the scripture they added a refusal to make the preaching of the gospel subject to a popish license, and so by implication claimed also the right of maintaining separate assemblies. Replying to Grindal, one Pattinson,[99] the first Separatist minister apprehended, declared:

The Archbishop of Archbishops hath not suspended me from preaching, but continueth His commandments to me still: and besides that, I praise Him for it, He hath not decayed in me the gift of preaching, but rather increased it; and hath also given me a congregation that looketh that I should bestow it among them; and therefore I may not disobey Him to obey you.[100]

But there is no evidence that they intended a permanent separation. On the contrary, the Plumbers' Hall group appealed to the Geneva book as their model; and, if they ever thought in terms of the future, they must have regarded their separatist activity as a mere temporary expedient, useful until the magistrate should be enlightened[101] but not an ideal for all time. Nor did they advocate forcible resistance to the government decrees. "Our bodies, goods, and lives be at [the Queen's] commandment, and she shall have them as of true subjects."[102] In dealing with the government, they occupied a little more territory than their more conservative Puritan colleagues, but their resistance was still passive.

This leftward movement put the leaders of the Puritan party in an awkward position, much like that of the post-war Social Democrat in relation to the Communist. They sympathized with the aims of their more extreme brethren, but they could not approve of their tactics. To separate from a church sound in doctrine, however corrupt in ceremonies, in their judgment

---

[99] Peel is unable to identify this man, but it is worthy of note that a minister of that name was a member of the Northampton classis at a later period, though he is said to have taken his B.A. as late as 1568 (*The Presbyterian Movement in the Reign of Queen Elizabeth*, ed. Usher ["Camden Society: Third Series," Vol. VIII (London, 1905)], p. xlv).

[100] Peel, *op. cit.*, p. 8.

[101] *Ibid.*, pp. 7–8.   [102] *The Seconde Parte of a Register*, I, 58.

was to destroy the unity of the Protestant forces and eventually to ruin the cause of clerical idealism altogether. It was quite proper to protest from within the ranks against wearing an improper uniform, to use another, and, if that were not allowed, to abandon one's official position. But to step out of the line altogether, raise a band of *condottieri*, and plan a campaign of one's own—that was unthinkable. In their opinion it not only disgraced but threatened to ruin the whole reform movement. So the unhappy Puritan leaders were forced to fight simultaneously on both right and left. In 1567 we find our sturdy naturalist, Dr. Turner, in the same breath denouncing the mass, as the damnable sacrifice of Antichrist, and the notion that no parishioner should hear the preaching of those who used the Pope's garments.[103] Lever took the same stand,[104] and so did John Knox, though at first only in a private letter.[105]

Meanwhile fumbling, kind-hearted Grindal had been puzzling over the problem. He was too much inclined toward Puritanism himself to be very severe about such conscientious objectors unless subjected to pressure from above, and, besides, the Duchess of Suffolk and other unidentified prominent people of influence—like the London merchants of Tyndale's time—who were more forward than the reforming clergy, used their influence to protect the offenders. On one occasion the weary Bishop, informed of a conventicle in progress almost under his nose, told the too efficient constables to let it proceed undisturbed.[106] Yet he thought something ought to be done. He tried arresting the offenders, reasoning with them, and giving the leaders short terms of imprisonment. It was no use. At forensics the prisoners, unabashed, repaid the uncomfortable prelate with as good as he gave, citing arguments with which he was all too familiar. A taste of prison only gave them a sense of martyrdom and confirmed them in their convictions. Eventually it occurred to him that these stubborn Protestants might fit into the ranks of his Scotch Protestant allies. If they wanted the perfection of the

---

[103] *Ibid.*, pp. 53–54. [104] *Ibid.*, pp. 54–55.

[105] Peter Lorimer, *John Knox and the Church of England* (London, 1875), p. 240.

[106] Stow, *op. cit.*, p. 143.

best reformed churches at once, let them go to a country where it was immediately available. If he already knew of Knox's attitude toward the separatist problem, this would make another argument for sending the recalcitrants north. They would not listen to a horned bishop. Let them be persuaded of their folly by one of whose reforming zeal there was no doubt, and, if they did not choose to remain in Scotland, let them return as obedient citizens. In either case the problem would be solved.[107] So, by offering commendatory letters and possibly by talking of banishment as the only alternative to prison, he arranged for the northern trip.

This did not prove to be a cure-all, but it did weaken the Separatist party. One delegate, disgusted by the sight of the Good Friday creeping to the cross in Dunbar, seems to have become reconciled to the English church.[108] He was promptly excommunicated by his Separatist brethren. The embassy brought back a sealed letter from Knox which, when opened before the congregation in London, proved not at all to their liking.[109] The Scotch leader advised the English zealots to bear with the current abuses for the time rather than divide the Protestant ranks. This was, of course, the equivalent of Bullinger's famous dictum in the case of the more prominent Puritans, and weakened and divided the little band of Separatists. Grindal was disappointed when they did not return to Scotland, but Knox's letter set them to debating the question of how much separation should be practiced. Must one refuse altogether to hear sermons by otherwise godly men who were compelled to wear surplices in the parish churches? If so, was it necessary to have no communion with individuals who thought differently? Soon there were at least three rival schools of thought,

[107] Peel (op. cit., p. 15) expresses surprise that this plan should be adopted, but it is of a piece with the later tactics of the Anglican authorities in sending Puritans like Egerton to reason with the imprisoned Separatists of Barrow's time (see below, p. 311). Compare the modern practice of sending as ambassadors persons who will be as acceptable to the foreign country concerned as is consistent with loyalty to the home government.

[108] Grindal, Remains, pp. 295–96; cf. Peel, op. cit., pp. 16 and 26.

[109] Lorimer, op. cit., pp. 298–300.

each with its own little church.[110] So conscience devoured her children.

Nevertheless, the Separatist movement did not die out. Though it was confined to London and, even there, was not strong either in numbers or in leadership, it survived both schism and imprisonment. When the old leaders died or grew weary, new ones arose to take their place, among them two vigorous preachers named William Bonham and Nicholas Crane. The learned Puritans might scoff. Even Knox might forsake them. Misunderstandings and hot tempers might break the bonds welded by persecution. But the congregations continued, moving from ship, to private house, to shop, as occasion demanded. If some leaders were incarcerated, others carried on. Grindal was not too much concerned, and with the whole north in revolt there were other things for the Court to think about.

[110] Peel, *op. cit.*, pp. 24–25.

CHAPTER XI

Years of Revival: 1568-73

THE half-dozen years following the collapse of Mary's political power in Scotland afforded the Puritan party a much-needed breathing-spell. While Elizabeth's attention was distracted by more pressing matters of state, the advanced Protestants found new adherents, new leaders, and new tactics. Engaged at first in a death struggle with the Catholic faction on the right, the Queen could make only an occasional gesture toward keeping order on the left. And, when the major fight was won, the victory was so complete that for a year or two after the exposure of the Ridolfi plot there was no conservative force left to help resist the liberal pull. Even the partial destruction of the Huguenot allies on St. Bartholomew's Day, 1572, did not stem the Puritan tide in England. For another year the flood of agitation continued, until a false move from the progressive idealists' own ranks restored the balance and enabled Elizabeth to take the middle way once more.

During these years most of the old Puritan leaders disappeared from the scene. Turner died in August, 1568—his widow married Richard Cox, of all people—Coverdale in the next February, Whitehead and Thomas Cole in the summer of 1571. Others wearied of the struggle, or lost sympathy as it entered on a new phase. Goodman returned to his native country in 1565, but was content to spend the rest of the reign in virtual obscurity. In 1570, under Sandys' regime, Sampson became a prebendary in St. Paul's Cathedral. He does not appear to have conformed in the matter of costume, but, though questioned by the bishops as a Puritan suspect in 1571, he was no longer prominent in the movement. Humphrey similarly retired from the struggle. In

1571 he was in such good favor with the authorities that he became Dean of Gloucester, and a few years later actually served
on a commission to enforce the Advertisements of 1566.[1]

The cause was by no means dead, however. If the London
riots were symptomatic of the popular unrest which produced
the Separatist movement in the city, the tumult in St. John's
college, Cambridge, was indicative of a much more important
development on the Cam. As we have seen, Oxford, the home
of lost causes, was slow to accept the Reformation, perhaps as a
result of the Lollard episode in its history. Gualter's son, who
spent some time there in the 1570's, not unfairly reported it to
be a den of papistry,[2] for Allen, Parsons, Campion, Harding,
Harpsfield, and Sander were all Oxford men. There was a slight
strain of Puritanism at Magdalen under Humphrey; at Merton, Parkhurst's old college; and at Corpus under John Rainolds. But the movement was not able to make much headway
in the atmosphere that eventually produced William Laud. At
Cambridge the situation was entirely different. Except for
Hooper, the most prominent of the Marian martyrs, and many
of the exiles, had been from that university. Shortly after Elizabeth's accession three of the *émigrés*, Pilkington, Beaumont,
and Kelke, became heads of colleges, presiding over St. John's,
Trinity, and Magdalene, respectively. Pilkington was soon appointed Bishop of Durham, but his successors, especially Long-
worth, were similarly pro-Puritan in their policy. Matthew
Hutton, Master of Pembroke Hall and later Archbishop of
York, though not an exile, was also sympathetic to advanced
Protestantism.

By the end of the decade the court was keeping a closer
watch on Cambridge. Puritans were not acceptable as heads of
colleges, and Kelke was twice barred by political influence from

---

[1] John Strype, *The Life and Acts of Matthew Parker* (3 vols.; Oxford, 1821), I, 319.
In 1573, Grindal noted with satisfaction that Humphrey and Sampson were not in
sympathy with the new group of younger leaders (Grindal to Bullinger, *Zurich Letters*,
ed. Robinson [2 vols.; Cambridge: Parker Society, 1842–45], I, 292). But it should be
noticed that Sampson continued to petition the authorities for ecclesiastical reform,
accused Grindal of being lordly, and wished Dering to succeed him in his lectureship
(Strype, *op. cit.*, II, 324, 375–79 and Appen. XCIII of Vol. III).

[2] Rudolph Gualter the younger to Josiah Simler, July 20, 1573, *Zurich Letters*, II, 218.

a promotion to the mastership of St. John's. But even where the heads were hostile, the fellows could do much, as the case of Christ's College shows. There, Hawford, the Master, was a conservative; but, in spite of his influence, Edward Dering, scion of a prominent Kentish family, and other fellows began a tradition which for the decades before the foundation of Emmanuel made that college the greatest Puritan seminary of them all. Richard Rogers, Nicholas Crane, Laurence Chaderton, William Perkins, Paul Baynes, William Ames, Arthur Hildersam, and John Milton were all at Christ's, and many of them were fellows.[3] With students living in close contact with such men, often sleeping in trundle beds at their tutor's feet, it is easy to see how they would be influenced by the Reformed ideas. Another factor contributed to making Cambridge a Puritan center. Its proximity to the Continent made it more accessible to Calvinist influence than Oxford. The desire for intellectual respectability and consistency was also important. Outside of court circles no one at this time seems to have thought of Anglicanism as anything but a temporary expedient, an incomplete version of the Reformed system. Aquinas they knew and Calvin they knew, but who was Cranmer or Parker? Even after Jewel's apologetic efforts, the memory of the friction between crown and bishops was too clear to give the established religion any standing as the best product of noble minds, and in the idealistic world of youth none but the best can satisfy. The result was that in the decade after Elizabeth's accession Cambridge began pouring out numbers of keen-minded young enthusiasts, convinced that a further alteration of the ecclesiastical system was necessary, and anxious to be about the business.

Equally important for the future history of the party was the fact that circumstances also gave it the support of the great body of moral reformers. Before the Marian period the Erasmian party had merged into, and supported, the Anglican church. Men like Latimer, whose chief concern was not for creed or form but for honesty of conduct and spirituality of religion, had

[3] Laurence Humphrey and Sir Walter Mildmay were also members of the college, though before Dering's time.

found the Edwardian establishment suitable to their purposes. But that was at a time when reforms were being made rather steadily, and now ten years had passed with almost nothing accomplished. Worse yet, many of the bishops were settling down to live the lordly life to which they were legally entitled. Bands of forty or more liveried retainers were not unusual. There were children to be provided for in a manner befitting the parental station, though in the eyes of the law they were all illegitimate, as we have seen. There was pluralism, absenteeism, and nepotism, racking of rents and severity to tenants. Cox, a strong Anglican, had a bad record in this respect, and Parker's was by no means spotless.[4] The Puritans of this generation, in spite of their outcries on the subject, were often pluralists themselves as far as they could manage it, but they were out of power and unable to get their hands as dirty as those of their Anglican brethren. That Sampson should hold a hospital mastership, a prebend, and a lectureship at the same time was a small matter compared to the spoil of the bishopric which his principles denied him. As a result the opposition attracted to its ranks the moralists as well as the controversialists. Many young Cambridge men, like Richard Rogers and Richard Greenham, cared little for theological or ecclesiastical argument, but they cared much for a New Testament standard of daily conduct.

For the same reasons the Puritan party now began to attract a great deal of lay support. While the forces of secularism were gaining on all fronts throughout this century, there was yet a considerable remnant of all the medieval types of the faithful laity, from the noble who offered the oak timbers for the new church tower to the villein who donated cart service for the new bells. Devout laymen did not build many new churches in this century. Community piety was rarely up to that level, and the old ones were big enough in most cases. But at times they did wish to do something for a good cause. Jealous of the bishops with the fierce anticlericalism of Henry's time, they would not further endow the establishment. But a Puritan

[4] Strype, *Annals of the Reformation under Elizabeth* (4 vols. in 7; Oxford, 1824), II, ii, 570–95; *Parker*, II, 26, 46, 355.

preacher offered a worthy object of charity without any apparent clerical menace. Many of these preachers had won the esteem of the laity by their efficient and devoted service as army chaplains. Whittingham and Kethe had done yeoman service at Newhaven, and Goodman had done the like in Ireland.

The sixteenth century took its preaching seriously. It was considered a most difficult art, which required careful preparation. One could not be expected to preach on the spur of the moment. In fact, it was presumed that those appointed to officiate at Paul's Cross would devote the preceding week wholly to preparation. Accordingly, that age saw nothing incongruous in having an extra clergyman attached to a parish for preaching duties alone. He might be a fellow of one of the colleges at the university, a minister beneficed elsewhere, or one solely charged with this responsibility. Perhaps he preached only on the Sunday, but often a discourse before the opening of the weekly market was added to his program. The surrounding country gentlemen made up his salary among them. If he happened to be regularly beneficed, his supporters gave him this as an additional material token of their esteem. Furthermore, the lay magistrates also made it their business to protect these preachers from being disturbed by the Anglican authorities, or, if they were troubled, maintained their cause in the face of prosecution in the ecclesiastical courts. This device of special preacherships also made it possible, if worst came to worst, to take care of the deprived, as well as those unable to conform sufficiently to secure a regular living. The result was that lectureships sprang up on all sides, salaried posts which did not involve pastoral duties or the use of the Prayer Book. Pious town corporations joined the gentry in the creation of these positions, and many of them had one or more lecturers of their own. The Inns of Court also set up their own lectureships. By 1571, the Temple, in fact, had two preachers, one for the Sunday morning and one for the afternoon.[5] The private chaplains of the nobility

[5] R. J. Fletcher, "The Reformation and the Inns of Court," *St. Paul's Ecclesiological Society Transactions*, V (1905), 149–57, esp. p. 156.

were often no more than lecturers in disguise, since the family chapel was thrown open to the neighborhood when the weekly sermon was preached. In the course of time many of these lectureships became endowed, after the fashion of the pastoral posts before them. Within the memory of living men they survived in the quiet, delightful market towns of the east counties.[6]

The form of the attack on the establishment made by these new Puritans was largely determined by the circumstances already described. There was nothing in the Reformed idea which prohibited the church's being ruled by bishops. Neither Calvin nor Knox was opposed to episcopacy as such,[7] and à Lasco's scheme of superintendents was, in fact, quite compatible with it. But, as Aylmer had pointed out, the power of these men was supposed to be moderate, both in its extent and in the manner of its exercise. The New Testament spoke of bishops, but not of lord bishops. Equally important in explaining the turn now taken by the Puritan party was the part played by the bishops in enforcing vestiarian and ceremonial conformity.

Not without reason had Elizabeth delegated this unpopular activity to the clerical authorities and refused, so far as possible, to have her name connected with it. The anticipated wrath developed, and it was visited upon the bishops, who incidentally were thereby so weakened politically as to prevent their becoming in any way obstreperous or obnoxious to the crown. In most cases the Puritans doubtless realized that the Queen was really to blame. In fact, Dering, now settled in a London lectureship, diagnosed the situation perfectly. In February, 1570, four days after the excommunication of the Queen at Rome— an event, of course, unknown as yet in England—he preached a

---

[6] Harold Smith, *The Ecclesiastical History of Essex under the Long Parliament and Commonwealth* (Colchester [1933]), pp. 21–41.

[7] J. Pannier, "Calvin et l'épiscopat," *Revue d'histoire et de philosophie religieuses*, VI (1926), 305–35; J. G. Simpson, "Scottish Episcopacy: A Precedent for Reunion," *Review of the Churches* (N.S.), V (1928), 330–39.

This point and the general line of argument in these two paragraphs are explained at length in Gordon Donaldson, "The Relations between the English and Scottish Presbyterian Movements to 1604" (London University dissertation [1938]), esp. pp. 1–67. This thesis, which came into my hands too late for more than a mention in this and the footnotes on pp. 285 and 298, is a thorough and substantial contribution which must not be allowed to remain unpublished.

sermon before the Queen vigorously attacking the current abuses in the church. In this sharp passage he described the situation and fixed the responsibility:

> I would first lead you to your benefices, and behold some are defiled with impropriations, some with sequestrations, some loaden with pensions, some robbed of their commodities. . . . . Look . . . . upon your patrons and lo, some are selling their benefices, some farming them, some keep them for their children, some give them to boys, some to servingmen, a very few seek after pastors. . . . . Look upon your ministry, and there are some of one occupation, some of another, some shake bucklers, some ruffians, some hawkers and hunters, some dicers and carders, some blind guides and can not see, some dumb dogs and will not bark. . . . .
> And yet you, in the meanwhile that all these whoredoms are committed, you at whose hands God will require it, you sit still and are careless, let men do as they list. It toucheth not, belike, your commonwealth, and therefore you are so well contented to let all alone.[8]

Magnificent perhaps, but it was not politics, and it did the cause no good. In those days the sovereign could do no wrong. The ministers were considered to be responsible, and any attempt to change a royal policy resolved itself into an attack on the ministers, while preserving the pretext of loyalty to the crown. So the next round in the contest developed into an attack on episcopacy—as a matter of tactics, not as a matter of principles of prime importance. Eventually the symbols came close to being real points of difference, but it was not so at first.

The lead in the anti-episcopal drive was taken by the new generation of Cambridge Puritans, and the zero hour quite properly coincided with the darkest period of the northern revolt. Since Elizabeth was primarily occupied at the time with that crisis, it cannot have been entirely an accident that Dering dared to preach as he did at this particular moment, nor that the newly elected Lady Margaret Professor at Cambridge should have chosen to discuss ecclesiastical polity that spring. The Cambridge leader was Thomas Cartwright.[9] Originally from Hertfordshire, in Edward's time he had been at St. John's under Thomas Lever. Being too young to have distinguished him-

[8] *A Sermon Preached before the Queenes Majestie*, in *Works* (London, 1597), p. 27.

[9] For the facts of Cartwright's career see the very careful biography by A. Scott Pearson, *Thomas Cartwright and Elizabethan Puritanism* (London, 1925).

self yet as a Protestant, he did not need to go into exile during the Catholic interlude. Instead he remained to take his B.A. in 1553–54, and then quietly withdrew to the security of a lawyer's office in his native region. Returning to his college under Pilkington, he became a fellow and took his M.A. in 1560. Two years later he transferred to Trinity, where Beaumont was Master. In the formal disputation held when Elizabeth visited Cambridge in August, 1564, he opposed the proposition that monarchy is the best form of government. During the height of the vestiarian controversy he was in Ireland as chaplain to Adam Loftus, Archbishop of Armagh, but he did not resign his fellowship. When Loftus returned to England in the autumn of 1566, Cartwright followed him and became a Cambridge B.D. in 1567. That same year Whitgift renounced his Puritan leanings and succeeded Beaumont as Master of Trinity. When, toward the end of 1569, the new Master resigned his Regius Professorship of Divinity in favor of William Chaderton, Cartwright was elected to the Lady Margaret Professorship from which Chaderton was promoted.

The times were propitious, and he seized his opportunity at once. Throughout the spring of 1570 he lectured on the Book of Acts. Using as a standard his interpretation of the system of ecclesiastical organization there described, he severely criticized the current state of the Church of England. Bishops with purely spiritual functions should be substituted for the existing prelates. Deacons should care for the poor. Church government should be in the hands of a local presbytery, or congregational session. Each parish should choose its own ministers, and none should be a minister without having a congregation. No one should seek the office, nor receive it at a bishop's hands.[10] The university was soon in an uproar. The cautious heads protested to Cecil as Chancellor. He co-operated to the extent of supporting the authorities in denying Cartwright his D.D. degree, and he ordered the Puritan to refrain from discussing these dangerous topics. But counterpetitions were rained on the Secretary by Cartwright's supporters. Thirty-three members of

[10] Strype, *The Life and Acts of John Whitgift* (3 vols.; Oxford, 1822), III, 19–20.

the university signed their names to one or another of these. The reforming tide was running strong throughout the country. At Norwich the canons themselves destroyed the cathedral organ. Cecil, with his ear to the ground, was not so much inclined to severity as were the heads. But in August the Duke of Norfolk was released from prison, and toward the end of the summer the conservatives reasserted themselves in the political sphere. At about the same time Cecil gave the university authorities a free hand in dealing with Cartwright. Under the new statutes, drawn up by some of the heads, which passed the royal seal September 25, the powers of those dignitaries were greatly enhanced. Among other things they received the right to deprive professors. None of the heads but Kelke showed any disposition to support the Lady Margaret Professor, and in December Cartwright was removed. Still retaining his Trinity fellowship, he shortly betook himself to Geneva to study the Reformed model at firsthand.

In spite of the absence of the new leader, the Puritans seized the next opportunity to renew the struggle. Convocation and Parliament met in the spring of 1571. The church assembly was the natural and proper place to discuss ecclesiastical reform, and Puritan petitions were duly presented on this, as on later occasions. They raised the old cry that preaching ministers were silenced while the observers of ceremonies, though worshipers of images, adulterers, and breakers of other commandments of the living God, went "without punishment and have friends many." But this appeal was only a perfunctory gesture to the clerical body. The experience of 1563 had convinced the Puritans that no salvation was to be expected from that quarter, where the bishops had control and the Queen's word was law. But Parliament was something else again. Here the alliance with the lay idealists bore early fruit. It was a dangerous policy to give the political leadership of the party to laymen, and eventually it resulted in the fatal parliamentary Erastianism of 1646-47, but for the time it seemed to be the only alternative.

To explain the nature of the Puritan activities in the 1571

Parliament, it must be made clear that, while the Puritans took the lead in agitating for the passage of ecclesiastical bills, not all of these proposed measures were of a purely partisan nature. Many were solely anti-Roman Catholic in aim, and as such received the additional support of the Anglican clergy of all stripes. Others were intended to correct current abuses in the church to which the more conscientious of the prelates were also opposed, and so secured the backing of what may be called the moral Puritans in the Anglican camp. Only a few were aimed at making changes in the service and ceremonies of the establishment, and so were supported only by the group which had opposed the government policy in the matter of vestments.

Toward the close of the 1566 session there had been introduced a set of six bills on ecclesiastical questions. The first confirmed the Thirty-nine Articles. The others were intended to secure an honestly appointed, disciplined, zealous, and well-paid clergy. They covered simony, benefit of clergy, nonresidence, leases of benefices, and pensions from them.[11] There was nothing in this program of which the serious-minded Anglican could not approve. In fact, the bishops unanimously petitioned the Queen to permit the passage of the bill for the Articles, which was designed to eliminate Roman Catholic clergy from the establishment, and they were as much put out as the Commons when the request was denied.[12] It does not seem reasonable, therefore, to call this the Puritan program.

In the 1571 session, coming as it did so soon after the northern revolt and the Bull of Deposition, there were many more anti-Catholic proposals. Bills were introduced requiring attendance at church and the taking of communion, prohibiting the importation of papal bulls, confiscating the goods of those going abroad without license, and punishing those guilty of reconciling themselves or others to the Roman see, distributing hallowed crosses, pictures, etc. Both Anglican and Puritan agreed on these and all passed both houses, though the Queen

---

[11] Sir Simonds D'Ewes, *A Compleat Journal of the Votes Speeches and Debates . . . . throughout the Whole Reign of Queen Elizabeth* (London, 1693), p. 185.

[12] State Papers Domestic, Elizabeth, XLI, 43 (*Calendar*, p. 284).

rejected the proposal for required communion. The six bills of the previous session were also introduced, and in themselves excited no particular Anglican opposition. Probably the worldly section of the hierarchy did not dare oppose these moves openly, or did not think it necessary, since their object could be defeated by lax enforcement. Although the Queen sent a special message forbidding Parliament to deal with the Articles, the bill was finally enacted, though in a somewhat altered form, and parts of the remainder of the Protestant program were adopted[13] with both factions in substantial agreement.

But in the manner of pushing this legislation the activity of a distinctively Puritan party becomes apparent. On the opening day, Bacon, the Lord Keeper, speaking for the Queen, had charged the Parliament to supply any want in the discipline of the church.[14] Contrary to the general impression among historians, Elizabeth was not opposed to parliamentary action on religious questions any more than her father was. What she objected to was having the initiative taken by other hands than hers, that is, by the laymen rather than the more subservient bishops. So Bacon had referred the matter particularly to the prelates. But when Sir Thomas Smith, the Principal Secretary, speaking as a Council member, for the Queen, proposed to await the bishops' advice on one anti-Catholic measure, William Fleetwood, who sat for London, roundly declared, "We all have as well learned . . . . that there is a God who is to be served, as have the bishops"[15] and the House followed his lead in continuing the discussion. In the Commons version of the Thirty-nine Articles the sections on the homilies and the consecration of bishops were omitted. In the conference with the Lords, Parker inquired the reason and was euphemistically told by Puritan Peter Wentworth, who sat for Barnstable, that the lower house had not had time to consider how these provisions agreed with the scripture.

[13] The act concerning leases of benefices passed, and a section of the first bill prohibited any one under twenty-three from having a benefice with cure of souls. The Articles were not confirmed, but subscription was required from all Marian priests, all candidates for orders, and all incumbents entering on new cures.

[14] D'Ewes, *op. cit.*, p. 137.   [15] *Ibid.*, p. 157.

"What," said [the Archbishop], "surely you mistook the matter. You will refer yourselves wholly to us therein."

"No, by the faith I bear to God," said I [Wentworth], "we will pass nothing before we understand what it is. For that were but to make you popes. Make you popes who list," said I, "for we will make you none."[16]

Not only did the Puritans show this anti-episcopal tendency in pushing the otherwise moderate part of their program but they introduced additional proposals of a definitely innovating nature. Possibly the Anglicans could have accepted the bill to restrict the commutation of penance by ecclesiastical judges, which would have considerably tightened up the discipline of the laity, but they could not tolerate a direct assault on the Prayer Book. On April 6, early in the session, a member named Strickland, who unfortunately cannot be further identified,[17] called for the production in the house of the *Reformatio legum ecclesiasticarum*, the revised version of the canon law drafted by the committee of thirty-two in Edward's time. This had recently been published with Parker's approval, but, in the course of his remarks, Strickland severely criticized the current state of the church and called for a general reformation along Puritan lines. On April 14 he introduced a bill for revision of the Book of Common Prayer. Knollys, the Treasurer of the Royal Household, who was personally not unsympathetic himself, and Sir James Croft, the Comptroller, tried to shut off the discussion by pointing out that these were matters of ceremony with which Elizabeth was empowered to deal, and suggesting that they be left to the Queen's discretion lest the Protestant cause be ruined by such meddling with great matters of state.

Hereupon one Pystor,[18] with a grave and seemly countenance and good natural eloquence, shewed how conscience enforced him to speak and rather to hazard his credit than to the offense of his conscience be silent, albeit he would acknowledge willing that many hundreds of that honourable and worshipful assembly were well able to teach him and he indeed willing to

[16] *Ibid.*, pp. 239–40.

[17] There were two Stricklands who sat in this house, Walter for Westmoreland and William for Scarborough. Walter is more probably the man here mentioned, since he was a knight of the shire and so the more important ("Chronological Account," Morrice MS I, 417 [15–16]).

[18] Tristram Pystor, who sat for Stockbridge, Hampshire.

learn of them all. The matter of his grief was that matters of importance standing us upon for our souls [*sic*], stretching higher and further to every one of us than the monarchy of the whole world, were either not treated of, or so slenderly that now after more than ten days continual consultation nothing was thereon concluded. The cause he showed to be God's, the rest are all but terrene [terrestrial], yea, trifles in comparison, call you them never so great or pretend you that they import never so much. Subsidies, crowns, kingdoms, he knew not, he said, what they were in comparison of this. This, he said, I know, whereof he most thanked God, *primum quaerite Regnum Dei et caetera omnia adjicientur vobis* [Seek ye first the Kingdom of God and all these other things shall be added unto you]. This rule is the direction and this desire shall bring us to the light, whereupon we may stay, and then proceed unto the rest. For in His word and by Him we learn, as saith St. Paul, to correct, to reform, etc. Our true home certainly is not here. *Non habemus hic permanentem civitatem* [here have we no continuing city], and the justice of God moved terror unto all. Which he seemed to mean concerning the bill before-mentioned of Strickland's propositions, and so did set forth with vehemency, that there lacked no modesty, and with such eloquence that it neither seemed studied nor too much affected, but grave and learned throughout and no whit too long, but well approved of.[19]

So far as we know Pystor escaped unpunished, but for Strickland's defiance of the royal wishes he was called before the Council and forbidden to attend the House. A heated debate followed in which Christoper Yelverton, sitting for the Puritan borough of Northampton, who had been most vigorous in his remarks on the abuses of episcopal dispensations,[20] flatly declared that

to say the Parliament hath no power to determine of [limit] the crown was high treason. . . . . He shewed it was fit for princes to have their prerogatives, but yet the same to be straightened within reasonable limits. The prince, he shewed, could not of herself make laws. Neither might she by the same reason break laws.[21]

All the basic elements of the later struggle on this issue were present, except the temperaments. As yet neither side wished to press the point. Strickland was restored to the House, but the offending bill was heard of no more. The Queen had once more proved too strong for the Puritans.

The bishops, however, deeply resented the attitude of their parliamentary opponents. At Paul's Cross, Cox, Jewel, Horne, and others defended the establishment. The canons adopted by

[19] D'Ewes, *op. cit.*, pp. 166-67.   [20] *Ibid.*, p. 167.   [21] *Ibid.*, pp. 175-76.

Convocation provided for the review of all preaching licenses
and the cancellation of those of men refusing to accept the
Articles in the episcopal version, which included the sections on
the homilies and the consecration of bishops.[22] Soon afterward
orders were sent to all churchwardens in the province of Canterbury to enforce conformity and prohibit unlicensed preaching
in their parishes.[23] At the close of parliament the Ecclesiastical
Commission summoned a number of men who were considered
the Puritan leaders and asked them to sign a threefold statement accepting the Thirty-nine Articles, the Book of Common
Prayer, and the surplice.[24] In all, Sampson, Goodman, Lever,
Wiburn, Dering, Whittingham, John Field, R. Johnson, Walker,
and Gough were interviewed. Most of these we have met before. Walker and Gough were minor figures, but Field will appear again. He was a London clergyman, and one of the few
Oxford men to take an active part in the later phases of the
Tudor Puritan movement. Johnson was chaplain to Sir Nicholas Bacon, the Lord Keeper. Parker and his fellow-commission-
ers also secured the assistance of the Council in reducing the
Inns of Court to conformity.[25]

But little could be accomplished, even after the Queen sent a
special supporting message on August 20.[26] Two other London
ministers, Thomas Wilcox and William White, the latter of
Independent leanings,[27] composed and circulated replies to the
episcopal sermons, shrewdly turning the bishops' words against
them. Jewel had advised men having wheat not to complain
about the chaff which came along with it. He was asked wheth-

---

[22] Strype, *Parker*, II, 58, 61–62.

[23] *Ibid.*, p. 65, and Appen. LXII of Vol. III.

[24] *Ibid.*, II, 64; Parker to Burghley, June 4 and 17, 1571; Parker, etc., to Church-
wardens, June 7, 1571; Council to Parker, etc., June 17, 1571; Elizabeth to Parker,
August 20, 1571, *Parker Correspondence*, ed. Bruce and Perrowne (Cambridge: Parker
Society, 1853), pp. 381–86; Edmund Grindal, *Remains*, ed. Nicholson (Cambridge:
Parker Society, 1843), p. 327; *The Seconde Parte of a Register*, ed. Peel (2 vols.; Cam-
bridge, 1915), I, 82.

[25] Strype, *Parker*, II, 73–74.

[26] Elizabeth to Parker, August 20, 1571, *Parker Correspondence*, p. 386.

[27] *Seconde Parte*, I, 79–82; cf. *ibid.*, p. 64.

er he practiced this principle in his own business dealings. His generous offer to resign his position if he were the Jonah in the tempestuous situation was promptly accepted, while the changes were rung on "pompous livings" and "lordly titles." Horne's statement that he had heard only three sermons since coming to Parliament was played up as a scandal.

The attempt to enforce subscription fared little better. While all the suspects were willing to promise loyalty to the sovereign, only qualified assent to the disputed statements could be secured, an acceptance of them "so far as they made to edification."[28] In Leicestershire, Gilby was not touched, probably because of the Huntingdon influence. In London the Duchess of Suffolk protected her chaplain, Browne, and, though Johnson was finally suspended, he became a Canon of Windsor the next year and for a time enjoyed a total of four prebends.[29] Even where deprivations were carried through, the situation was little improved, if not actually made more scandalous. No preachers could be found to take the place of those deprived in Norfolk. The Bishop was reluctant to accept the lazy, immoral, and ignorant candidates whom the lay patrons put forward for the places. The Puritans offered to serve the charges gratis, and Parkhurst was inclined to accept the offer, but Parker frowned on it, and the miserable situation continued.[30]

By the autumn the Puritan ranks were beginning to re-form. As the Ridolfi plot was unraveled, the eyes of the government were diverted to the Catholics on the right once more, and the Puritans began to search for new offensive tactics. The London leaders kept in close touch with Gilby, secure in his stronghold, discussing proposals for issuing more propaganda and urging

[28] *Ibid.*, p. 82. Grindal to Parker, August 28, 1571, Grindal, *Remains*, p. 327; Strype, *Parker*, II, 62; *Annals*, I, i, 184–85; II, i, 141. Goodman's subscription does not affirm the right of a wicked woman to rule, and leaves room for revolutions led by Parliament and for the people taking the sword against their rulers in extreme cases (cf. Jeremy Collier, *Ecclesiastical History of Great Britain*, ed. Lathbury [9 vols.; London, 1852], VI, 262).

[29] Parker, etc., to the Duchess of Suffolk, January 13, 1572, *Correspondence*, p. 390; Strype, *Parker*, II, 71; cf. *DNB* art., "Robert Johnson."

[30] Strype, *Parker*, II, 84–89.

him to procure Huntingdon's active co-operation.[31] At Cambridge the Puritan group asked embarrassing questions, demanding to know why Whitgift, professedly so strong for law
and order, did not obey the medieval statute of the college requiring daily service in prick song.[32] But the first important
move came from another quarter.

It is a striking commentary on the provincialism of Anglicanism that Protestants with any foreign experience almost always
attached themselves to the Puritan party. As a result, the diplomatic corps, from the days of Cromwell, had been liberal in its
outlook. At Paris, Walsingham was keeping in touch with Cartwright,[33] and in later years he aided him whenever possible.
More important at this time, however, were the efforts of another diplomat. German-born Christopher Mont, who had been
an English agent most of the time since the fall of Wolsey, was
a zealous Puritan, though not well informed on the exact situation in England. When on a trip to that country in the summer
of 1571, he somehow gained the impression that Jewel and some
of the other bishops were about to resign in protest over the
vestments. Though something of the sort was threatened ten
years earlier, nothing now was farther from the truth, as we
have seen. But on his return to the Continent he persuaded the
Calvinistic Elector Frederick III of the Palatinate, whom Withers and Barthelot had been unable to move in 1567, to lend his
assistance. Like her father, Elizabeth frequently employed the
German Protestants in her diplomatic schemes, and those located on the French border were especially important at this
time, when negotiations were under way for a Franco-English
drive on the Spanish forces in the Low Countries. Therefore,
it was now supposed that she might listen to word from this
quarter, and Mont proceeded accordingly. Zanchius, then the
leader of the Reformed party in Heidelberg, acting on his ruler's
orders, wrote a strong letter to Elizabeth informing her of the

[31] Baker MS XXXII (Cambridge University MS Mm. I. 43), 441 ff.

[32] Whitgift to Burghley, April 23, 1572, State Papers Domestic, Elizabeth, LXXXVI,
20 (*Calendar*, p. 441).

[33] "Walsingham's Journal," ed. Martin, *Camden Miscellany*, VI (1871), 9 (entry for
July 3, 1571).

threat to the church, and urging her on to further reform.[34] It was dispatched to Grindal to hand to the Queen. It is exceedingly doubtful whether Elizabeth would have paid any more attention to it, had she received it, than she had to the earlier efforts of Gualter and Calvin, but whatever possibility there may have been originally was ruined by Mont's ill-informed choice of a forwarding agent. After consultation with prominent churchmen and councilors, Grindal decided not to show the letter to the Queen, and an explanation of the true state of affairs was sent to Zanchius.[35]

In the spring of 1572 the summoning of Parliament to settle the fate of Norfolk and his fellow-conspirators gave the Puritans another opportunity. Cartwright was called home to lend his assistance. It proved impossible to secure his restoration to his university professorship, but he appears to have returned before the opening of the session.[36] Again a bill was introduced to legalize Puritan nonconformity. The Prayer Book was described as generally sound in doctrine but blemished by superstitious touches. Puritan ministers who had modified its services with the consent of their bishops were being troubled in the courts. It was therefore proposed that the Act of Uniformity be enforced only against Romanists and that every preacher having charge of a congregation might be permitted, subject to episcopal approval, to abridge the required service or to use any other, such as that employed by the Dutch and French churches in London.[37] This bill passed its second reading on May 19, and its third the next day.[38] In the committee to

---

[34] Zanchius to Elizabeth, September 19, 1571, *Zurich Letters*, II, 339–53.

[35] Grindal to Zanchius, n.d., *Remains*, pp. 333–42. That the course of these events is to be attributed to Mont's ignorance rather than his duplicity is to be seen not only in the choice of Grindal as a medium of communication but in the letter sent at the same time by Zanchius to Jewel, reasoning with him to retain his office if the Queen should prove obdurate (*Zurich Letters*, II, 185–88).

[36] Pearson, *op. cit.*, pp. 50–57.

[37] *Puritan Manifestoes*, ed. Frere and Douglas (London, 1907), pp. 149–51. I am unable to follow the editors' interpretation (p. xii) that the last clause of the first bill applied to all ministers. The qualification "such" must refer to the earlier phrase, "being a preacher allowed and having the charge of any congregation."

[38] D'Ewes, *op. cit.*, pp. 207 and 212.

which it was referred, however, some of the more explicit features of the preamble and the specific mention of the French and Dutch order were removed. The re-written bill had its first reading on the twenty-first and was referred to committee,[39] but the next day the thunderbolt fell. The Speaker had been keeping Cecil, now Lord Burghley, informed of the proceedings, and here the Queen sent word that the bills were to be surrendered to her and that in the future no bill concerning religion should be introduced into the House unless previously approved by the clergy. No one dared resist, and so the Commons yielded.[40]

Baffled once more in their attempt to employ ordinary parliamentary tactics, the Puritans had recourse to another printed appeal to public opinion. According to a report published years later,[41] Gilby, Sampson, Lever, Field, Wilcox, and others held a consultation in London and decided upon this venture. In any case it was a natural outgrowth of the Gilby correspondence of the preceding winter. Field and Wilcox were the actual authors, and the tract, entitled *An Admonition to the Parliament*, appeared before the end of the session in June.[42] It was a shrewd application of the New Testament golden-age standard to the current establishment:

> In the old church a trial was had both of [the ministers'] ability to instruct and of their godly conversation also: now by the letters commendatory of some one man, noble or other, tag and rag, learned and unlearned of the basest sort of the people (to the slander of the Gospel in the mouths of the adversaries) are freely received. . . . .
>
> Then every pastor had his flock, and every flock his [*sic*] shepherd, or else shepherds: now they do not only run fisking [frisking] from place to place (a miserable disorder in God's church) but covetously join living to living, making shipwreck of their own consciences, and being but one shepherd (nay, would to God they were shepherds and not wolves) have many flocks. . . . .

[39] The following names were on the back of the bill when sent by the Speaker to Burghley: Mr. Thro(ckmorton?), Mr. Tho. Scott, Mr. Attorney of the Duchy (Sir Ralph Sadler?), Mr. Popham, Mr. Yelverton, Mr. Dannet, Mr. Dalton, Mr. Audeley, Mr. Nicholas St. Leger, Mr. Randall, Mr. Skynner, and Mr. Pystor (State Papers, Domestic, Elizabeth, LXXXVI, 45 [*Calendar*, p. 443]).

[40] D'Ewes, *op. cit.*, p. 213.

[41] Richard Bancroft, *A Survay of the Pretended Holy Discipline* (London, 1593), pp. 54–55.

[42] Pearson, *op. cit.*, p. 59; *Puritan Manifestoes*, p. xiii.

Then [the ministry] was painful: now gainful. Then poor and ignomini-
ous: now rich and glorious. . . . .

Then excommunication was greatly regarded and feared. Now because it
is a money matter, no whit at all esteemed. Then for great sins severe punishment and for small offenses little censures. Now great sins either not at all
punished, as blasphemy, usury, etc., or else slightly passed over with pricking
in a blanket, or pinning in a sheet, as adultery, whoredom, drunkenness,
etc. Agayne, such as are no sins (as if a man conform not himself to popish
orders and ceremonies, if he come not at the whistle of him who hath by
God's word no authority to call—we mean chancellors, officials, doctors, and
all that rabble) are grievously punished, not only by excommunication, suspension, deprivation, and other (as they term it) spiritual coercion, but also
by banishing, imprisoning, reviling, taunting, and what not.[43]

Let Parliament play the role of Jacob or Jehosaphat and all will
be well. Remember the final reckoning. "Is a reformation good
for France and can it be evil for England? Is discipline meet for
Scotland and is it unprofitable for this realm?" To this appeal
were appended detailed comments on the three articles to which
the High Commission was attempting to compel subscription,
and also the pro-Puritan letters of Gualter and Beza written in
the summer of 1566.

Bishop Cooper of Lincoln promptly answered this admonition in a sermon at Paul's Cross, and Field and Wilcox were
soon apprehended and sent to Newgate. But the controversy
went on. An answer to Cooper was composed and circulated
in manuscript. The secret press was not found when the authors of the *Admonition* were taken, and soon more printed
propaganda was available. A second edition of the original
tract was followed by *An Exhortation to the Bishops To Deale
Brotherly with Theyr Brethren*, *An Exhortation to the Bishops
and Their Clergie To Aunswer a Little Booke That Came Forthe
the Last Parliament*, and, toward the end of the year, *A Second
Admonition to the Parliament*.[44] None of these is comparable
either in point of artistry or in point of logic to the *First Admonition*. Though the *Second Admonition* contains a somewhat
detailed exposition of the Puritan ideal of church government,
it is so rambling and confused as to be almost unintelligible and

[43] *Puritan Manifestoes*, pp. 9–11, 17.

[44] The first two were published in a single volume. All are reprinted in *Puritan
Manifestoes*.

virtually to preclude the possibility of Cartwright's being the author, as is sometimes suggested. But these publications did serve to keep the controversy alive. Though at first there was some thought that the tumult would die of itself,[45] it soon became necessary for some Anglican to compose a formal reply.

This task was assigned to Whitgift, who in September found a technicality on which it was possible to deprive Cartwright of his fellowship. But before this rejoinder could be completed others threw fuel on the fire. In the summer of 1572, Gualter accepted a rebuke from Cox, apologized for his pro-Puritan letter of 1566, and supported the Anglican cause in the prefatory epistle to his commentary on First Corinthians published that autumn.[46] This was reinforced by further pronouncements of Bullinger and Gualter to the same effect in the succeeding years, given in response to requests by the bishops for comment on particular Puritan articles taken from Cartwright's works.[47] But, from Geneva, Beza wrote once more in defense of the opposition party.[48] The St. Bartholomew massacre in August crippled for the time the Huguenot allies, by whose assistance in the Netherlands the Puritans hoped to bind Elizabeth to an active Protestant policy. But the resulting anti-Roman reaction in England partially compensated for this loss, and the agitation went on. In a prison conference with Parker's chaplain in September, Field and Wilcox justified the bitterness of their writing:

Isay called the rulers of his time princes of Sodom. John calleth the scribes and Pharisees generation [sic] of vipers. Christ calleth them adders brood and an adulterous nation, and you know the Scriptures, both of the Old and New Testament, especially the prophets, are full of such vehemency. We have used gentle words too long, and we perceive they have done no good. The wound groweth desperate, and dead flesh hath overgrown all, and therefore the

[45] Strype, *Parker*, II, 143.

[46] *Ibid.*, pp. 112–15; Gualter to Cox, June 9, 1572, *Zurich Letters*, I, 362–65.

[47] Bullinger to Horne, March 12, 1573, in Strype, *Parker*, III, 196; Gualter to Cox, August 26, 1573; Gualter to Sandys, October 8, 1573; Bullinger to Sandys, March 10, 1574; Bullinger to Grindal, March 10, 1574; Gualter to Cox, March 16, 1574, and August 26, 1574, *Zurich Letters*, II, 225–35, 238, 240–43, 244–48, 249–54, 258–59.

[48] Epistle 69, July 7, 1572, *Tractationum theologicarum* (3 vols.; Geneva, 1582), III, 283–84.

wound had need of a sharp corsive [corrosive] and eating plaster. It is no time to blanch, nor to sew cushions under men's elbows, or to flatter them in their sins. But God knoweth we meant to touch no man's person, but their places and abuses, which derogate from the truth, as that any minister should take upon him the name of Archbishop and be called Metropolitan, etc.[49]

In December the prisoners put out a creed, designed to clear themselves of the charge of rebellion and separatism, by showing that they wished only for a moderate reformation of the established church.[50]

Although there was no session of Parliament in 1573, that year saw Puritan agitation reach a high-water mark for the period. Whitgift's *Answere* had appeared in November, 1572, and Cartwright's *Reply* in April provided his followers with a full statement of the Puritan position as he conceived it. He was somewhat more mild than the authors of the *Admonitions*, in his explicit admission that the Church of England was a true church and that ecclesiastical ceremonies might vary with circumstances.[51] But he considered the offending garments wicked by such circumstances, and so not to be accepted, whatever authority might ordain them.[52] Though Calvin was quoted by his opponents to the contrary,[53] Cartwright declared that the great French reformer would support him if he were still living. He asserted the scriptural justification for his system of church government by presbyters and deacons, coolly dismissing other orders mentioned in the New Testament, as being only temporary ranks of the hierarchy. He was strong for the democratic principle in the election of ministers.[54] He thought the many were better judges of a person's qualifications than the one. He noted with approval the principle of the canon law and of parliament, that that which concerns all should be approved by all.

[49] *Seconde Parte*, I, 89–90.

[50] *Ibid.*, pp. 83–87.

[51] John Whitgift, *Works*, ed. Ayre (3 vols.; Cambridge: Parker Society, 1851–53), I, 195, 201. Since Whitgift's *Defense of the Answer* reprints Cartwright's *Reply*, it is most convenient to cite the work in that edition.

[52] *Ibid.*, II, 73.   [53] *Ibid.*, I, 248.   [54] *Ibid.*, pp. 84, 301, 372.

And therefore it draweth much the obedience of the subjects of this realm, that the statutes whereby the realm is governed pass by the consent of the most part of it, whilst they be made by them whom the rest put in trust and choose for that purpose, being, as it were, all their acts. . . . .

So it is also when the question is to choose the magistrate, mayor, or bailiff, or constable of every town, which things if they have grounds in civil affairs, they have much better in ecclesiastical. For it is much more unreasonable that there should be thrust upon me a governor of [sic] whom the everlasting salvation or damnation of my body and soul doth depend, than him of whom my wealth and commodity of this life doth hang; unless those upon whom he were thrust were fools, or madmen, or children, without all discretion of ordering themselves; which as I will show, cannot agree with those that are the church of God and are to have a pastor. For they of the church of God, although they be called sheep in respect of their simplicity and harmlessness, yet are they also, for their circumspection, wise as serpents in the wisdom especially which is to salvation; and how vile account soever you will make of them, they are the people of God and therefore spiritual and forthwith those of whom St. Paul saith, "The spiritual man discerneth all things."[55]

Well might Sandys and Parker charge the Puritans with aiming at a "mere popularity."[56]

On the difficult question of the role of the crown in church affairs Cartwright declared that it was to execute, not to make, law.[57] The latter function pertained to the clergy. When cornered with a charge of popery, he admitted that in his system the prince could intervene in emergencies. "If, when there is a lawful ministry, it shall agree of any unlawful or unmeet order . . . . the prince ought to stay that order and not to suffer it, but to drive them to that which is lawful and meet."[58] Who was to determine what was "unmeet"? Optimistic delusion that magistrate and clergy could get along on such a basis!

Though hard pressed on some of these points, the Puritan champion gave his adversary some bad moments also. If Cartwright was nearly in the Roman camp on one or two issues, so was Whitgift on others. The Anglican interpretation of the scriptural prohibition of a Christian bearing rule over his fellows was indistinguishable from that of the mother-church.[59] In justifying the wealth of the bishops in his later *Defense*, the future

[55] *Ibid.*, pp. 370 and 372.

[56] Strype, *Parker*, II, 323; Sandys to Burghley, July 2, 1573, *Puritan Manifestoes*, p. 154.

[57] Whitgift, *Works*, III, 295.   [58] *Ibid.*, p. 311.   [59] *Ibid.*, I, 157.

Archbishop could think of nothing better than the hollow claim that the ordinary ministry and the poor were well provided for already.[60] In Cartwright's plea for uniformity with the Continental Protestants, Whitgift somehow professed to see a dangerous pride.[61] When reminded of his own pluralism, he could only mumble "Anabaptism," and profess his willingness to defend himself against any properly legal charge.[62]

All this served to keep the controversy at white-hot temperature. Signatures were soon being solicited to a promise to stand by Cartwright's book to the death.[63] Leicester and so many others of the powerful laity supported the zealots that Parker was in despair. "Machiavel governance," he called it, when behind his back the Council aided the opposition.[64] Field and Wilcox kept open house in prison, receiving hosts of friends.[65] Petitions in their behalf eventually secured them the milder confinement of an archdeacon's home. London merchants cheerfully offered them financial assistance. At Cambridge a slanderous attack on Whitgift was found on the doors of the schools. A little later William Charke, a fellow of Peterhouse, declared in a public discourse that bishops were introduced into the church by the devil, and other members of the university took similar positions.[66] Men invited to fill the pulpit at Paul's Cross on the assumption that they were favorable to the establishment preached Puritan sermons and slipped back to their provincial refuges before they could be apprehended.[67] The ministers of the French church in London co-operated by expressing their sympathy for the Puritan cause.[68] Appropriately enough, Gilby chose this time to publish his *Berwick Dialogue*, and so added to the hubbub.

So strong was the opposition movement that Sandys was willing to dignify it by acceding to the Puritan demand for a

---

[60] *Ibid.*, II, 389.
[61] *Ibid.*, II, 454.
[62] *Ibid.*, I, 507, 514.
[63] Strype, *Parker*, II, 268.
[64] *Ibid.*, p. 179; Parker to Burghley, March 12, 1573, *Correspondence*, pp. 418-49.
[65] Strype, *Parker*, II, 240.
[66] *Ibid.*, p. 194. [67] *Ibid.*, p. 268. [68] *Ibid.*, p. 269.

formal public disputation on the points at issue,[69] though
Burghley vetoed the proposal. In June a royal proclamation
was issued, calling on all Her Majesty's subjects to keep the
Prayer Book order and within twenty days to surrender to
their bishops or to the Council all the *Admonition* literature attacking it. After the deadline was passed, Sandys reported
that "the whole city of London, where no doubt is great plenty,
hath not brought one [book] to my hands."[70] Though Cartwright was in England and probably in London during this
summer, the individual storm center for the time was Edward
Dering. He was now holding a lectureship in St. Paul's and was
a very prominent figure in the city. On the appearance of
Cartwright's book, he and several others were examined before
the Council, and he was suspended from his lectureship.[71] But
Sandys, his bishop, was a protégé of Leicester, and he interceded
for Dering. Burghley rebuked him for this activity, but the
Council restored the lecturer to his post in June[72] in spite of the,
protests of Cox and Parker.[73] When Sandys advised him to be
more discreet in the future, Dering suggested that in case of
disciplinary action "some disordered fellows [might] bid you
come off your horse when you shall ride down Cheapside."[74]
The practice of circulating manuscript replies to Anglican sermons continued unabated.[75] In Peterborough diocese, which included Puritan Northampton, the Bishop's Chancellor, who tried
to enforce order, found himself subjected to a counterprosecu-
tion started as a backfire by the zealous party.[76]

The bishops and their adherents were made very uncomfort-

[69] *Ibid.*, p. 239.

[70] Sandys to Burghley, July(?), 1573, *Puritan Manifestoes*, pp. 154-55.

[71] Strype, *Parker*, II, 239-41.

[72] *Ibid.*, p. 265; *APC*, VIII, 120.

[73] Strype, *Parker*, II, 266; Parker and Sandys to one of the Commission, July 6,
1573, *Parker Correspondence*, pp. 434-35. The fact that Sandys signed this letter
doubtless indicates his true state of mind. The intercession with Burghley was probably
forced on him by Leicester.

[74] Strype, *Parker*, II, 270.   [75] *Seconde Parte*, I, 97-98.

[76] Scambler to Burghley, April 13, 1573, *Original Letters*, ed. Ellis (London, 1827
etc.), II, iii, 33-36.

able indeed. Parker was driven to make lengthy exculpations of himself in letters to Burghley, defending his wealth and the title of "Lord." These would make better reading had he not been using his influence at the same time to substitute his nephew for a Puritan named Aldrich as Master of Corpus Christi College, Cambridge.[77] Poor Sandys was in the worst position of all. Like Grindal before him, he had a foot in both camps and the hardest situation to deal with. He was inclined to "Germanical opinions" himself and had secured the bishopric of London largely through Leicester's influence. Yet he had the dignity of his office to maintain, and the slightest disciplinary action aroused instant opposition. Shortly after the lifting of Dering's suspension there was circulated in London a printed attack[78] on the Bishop, which reflects very well the Puritan spirit at the crest of the wave. The last vestiges of Mary's party in Scotland had been destroyed by the capture of Edinburgh Castle in May. The hopes of the Presbyterians were high. Not daring to attack Elizabeth, they made every effort to fasten the blame for the current situation on the bishops. They are the Queen's advisers, and have given her bad advice. Instead of threatening her with God's curses, they have thought only of promotion and their own bellies, and so tell her that all is well. She has asked them if the Bible supports her policy.

> And ye like men pleasing mongrels, perceiving to which part the Queen's Grace was most bent have not answered her it [*sic*] that now we find; yea, I myself heard one maggot-a-pie[79] of your profession openly before the Queen and her Council boldly and stoutly say, and another at Paul's Cross, that there is no church in Europe better reformed than this is, and that all things were so well as were possible to be in the primitive church.[80]

The Queen yields to the common law in the temporal sphere. She would yield to the bishops if they stood their ground in the

[77] Strype, *Parker*, II, 258–63, 272–79, 285–87.

[78] *Ibid.*, pp. 290–91; Sandys to Burghley, July 2, 1573, *Puritan Manifestoes*, p. 155. This must be the document printed in *A Parte of a Register* ([Middelburg?], 1593), pp. 371–81, and there dated 1567. The reference to the bishops' treatment of Field and Wilcox (*ibid.*, p. 372; *Puritan Manifestoes*, p. 153) establishes this fact.

[79] Magpie, "bishop"; cf. p. 85. [80] P. 373.

spiritual one. To illustrate his point, the author cites a forgotten precedent for one of Coke's famous cases:

Now it is time, as I promised you to tell you how the judges of Westminster
will be your condemnation at the last day. The laws of the Realm have given
the judges this privilege, to place whom they think best in certain offices.
The Queen's Grace, thinking she might have dispensed with their law, placed
one of her men in the office, but the judges displaced him and set in their own
man. Upon this displeasure was taken, etc. Enquire the rest yourself. But
to be short, the judges (like true and faithful oath-keepers and fathers of the
land) would not yield to no jot against the laws. Neither would the Queen's
Grace (when she understood the matter better) resist any longer, but yielded
unto her laws and was glad to hear that she had such faithful men in those
rooms.[81]

The suggestion of the bishops that to be so stout would be to
lose their places and have them filled with Romanists is to make
the Queen a papist. But let them mistreat the Puritan prisoners
and enrich themselves. Let them bribe Bullinger and Gualter
with presents of cloth, tin, and silver. Soon the rod will make
their "proud buttocks" to smart. Soon they will be put down
like the Friars. The Puritans have waited patiently for reform
in each parliament, but, if there is none in the next, the author
promises to give the Queen a treatise on the bishops' usurped
titles. When the Swiss divines are properly informed, they will
change their attitude. France, Scotland, and Germany will petition the Queen to support the Puritans. Then all will be well,
and so the optimist ends:

> Fare you well and do no worse;
>   Love the church more than your purse.
> Take in good worth I write no name;
>   You in my case would do the same.

Alas for such high hopes! Doubtless as a result of the circulation of this screed, the Council once more suspended Dering,[82]
who, though stylistic considerations prevent our considering
him the author, was probably a party to its publication. In
August the secret press was uncovered, and the printers ar-

[81] P. 379; cf. *Brownlow* v. *Cox and Michell*, 3 Bulstrode 32; Bacon's *Works*, ed.
Spedding *et al.* (14 vols.; London, 1857–74), VII, 683–86.

[82] *APC*, VIII, 133.

rested.[83] But the Puritans were not easily beaten, and for some months matters remained in a state of suspense. Sandys claimed to know the author of the libel, but he could not persuade the Council to bring him to trial.[84] Dering, on the other hand, was equally desirous and equally incapable of securing a final settlement of his case.[85] This deadlock was suddenly and effectively broken by a bungling application of Ponet's doctrine of tyrannicide. On October 14, the sea dog Sir John Hawkins, walking past the Middle Temple with a friend, was overtaken in the Strand and stabbed by a lawyer named Peter Birchet, or Byrchett. Investigation disclosed that the assailant was a half-mad Puritan who had returned from one of Sampson's lectures at Whittington College resolved to play the Ehud. He had mistaken Hawkins for the Queen's favorite, Sir Christopher Hatton, who was reputed the leader of the Catholic faction in the Council. Instantly the Queen flamed into alarmed action. With difficulty Sussex and Lincoln dissuaded her from having the would-be deliverer of the Lord's people executed by martial law. Before his more legal execution she had him narrowly examined as to the origin of his idea, the names of any like-minded people, and possible fellow-conspirators. The prisoner at first stated the biblical precedents and justification for his act quite rationally; then showed his mental instability by recanting, withdrawing his recantation, and, finally, murdering one of his keepers.[86]

There is nothing more damaging to a political party than an unsuccessful attempt to assassinate a member of the opposite faction. Had Elizabeth herself been put out of the way, the Puritan cause might have prospered in the ensuing turmoil, though, of course, this is uncertain. But, in the circumstances, it was hopelessly discredited for some time to come. Any attempt at exculpation on the grounds of insanity or the singularity of the act was difficult at best, but made impossible by the

[83] Sandys to Burghley, August 28, 1573, *Puritan Manifestoes*, p. 155.

[84] Strype, *Parker*, II, 290–91.   [85] Strype, *Annals*, II, i, 399.

[86] Strype, *Parker*, II, 327–29; *Annals*, II, i, 426–29.

assertion soon afterward of one Asplin, formerly a printer of Cartwright's book, but then employed by the Anglican, Day, that the Spirit moved him to kill his master and mistress.[87] Thus freed from the restraint previously imposed upon them by the strength of the opposition, the government took drastic steps to suppress such dangerous doctrines. On October 20 a royal proclamation was issued, calling upon the bishops and other magistrates to show more diligence in enforcing the Act of Uniformity.[88] Special commissions were set up in all the dioceses to see to this matter. Hypocritical but nonetheless sharp letters were sent by the Council to the hapless prelates, charging them to enforce order on the pain of the Queen's displeasure, though refusing all secular aid. If the bishops would tend to their business and not use their visitations only to secure money, all could be reformed by them alone, said the bland Leicester and his companions in this and earlier sabotaging of ecclesiastical discipline.[89] But some secular assistance was actually provided. Burghley, substituting for Bacon at the Star Chamber session in which the assize justices were instructed at the end of Michaelmas term, ordered them to work for uniformity.

Though Cox complained that some of the physicians were still sick themselves,[90] the pressure was generally applied. Subscription to articles on the 1571 order was demanded of suspected clergy and even laymen.[91] In London, by the Queen's express command, Dering was finally prohibited from preaching altogether.[92] The ecclesiastical commissioners issued a warrant for Cartwright's arrest, and he was compelled to flee to the Continent. Field and Wilcox were kept in confinement after their sentence had expired.[93] In Northampton, Norfolk, and Kent, Puritans were troubled and many lost their livings and schools. In places where there had been two sermons each Sunday— places from which laymen had ridden to the bishop in groups to

[87] Strype, *Parker*, II, 331.

[88] *Ibid.*, pp. 320–22.

[89] *Ibid.*, pp. 345–47.

[90] *Ibid.*, p. 349.

[91] "Chronological Account," Morrice MS H, p. 263/2.

[92] E. Dering to his brother, R. Dering, December 24, 1573, *Works*, sig. A, fol. 4(v).

[93] *Seconde Parte*, I, 91.

try to save their preachers—there was now only one each quarter at the most, and those often given by "outlandish men, such as could scarce be understand [sic], and such as have run away from London."[94] For the next two years rumors of Puritan revolutionary plots filled the capital and were used by clever conspirators, led by one Undertree, to extract money from gullible Anglican clerics.[95]

So Elizabeth divided and ruled the Protestant idealists, causing them to wear themselves out in mutual recriminations while she and her kind took what they liked. As the bishops told their Swiss friends,[96] the Puritan outcry against their wealth was used by courtiers as a justification for plunder. With royal backing they compelled the discredited prelates to deed them manors and townhouses. In the strife over vestments and ecclesiastical offices the discipline of the laity was practically forgotten. A bill to legalize usury was passed by the parliament of 1571, and, while Cartwright was having his tit for tat with Whitgift, Drake was sacking Nombre de Dios, seizing treasure trains, and plundering shipping on the Spanish Main. A new type of Englishman was in the making—the man of the open-world frontier, who would care little for clerics of any stripe. In Scot-

---

[94] *Ibid.*, pp. 91–124, esp. p. 122. A Robert Johnson is mentioned in *A Parte of a Register* (p. 111) as dying in the Westminster Gatehouse prison early in 1574. If this is correct, he cannot have been the chaplain to Nicholas Bacon, as Frere suggests (*The English Church in the Reign of Elizabeth and James I* [London, 1904], p. 172), for this Johnson lived until 1609 (*DNB* art., "Robert Johnson").

The case of William Axton, who was deprived by Thomas Bentham, Bishop of Lichfield, is probably to be referred to this period. It is dated 1570 in *The Seconde Parte of a Register* (I, 68–74), but he did not graduate B.A. until 1571, and he took his M.A. in 1574 (J. and J. A. Venn, *Alumni Cantabrigienses* [4 vols.; Cambridge, 1922–27], I, 58).

[95] Strype, *Parker*, II, 368–72, 419–21. In an unpublished Washington University thesis ("History of the Puritan Discipline, 1554–1593" [St. Louis, 1931]), George A. Andrews reviews the evidence for the Undertree conspiracy at some length (pp. 119–59) and suggests that there may have been some substace to it. The difficulty of accounting for Cartwright's movements in the spring of 1574 and the good English of the printing—as yet unidentified—of the *Full and Plaine Declaration* are the chief arguments for this view, which require the presence of Cartwright in England early in 1574. But Andrews considers that the assassination part of the plot was fantastic, and Pearson's reconstruction of Cartwright's Continental travels makes a journey to England at this time highly improbable.

[96] Cox to Gualter, July 31, 1575, and an undated letter of the next year, *Zurich Letters*, I, 316–17, 319.

land, where the churchmen's front was yet united, lords and
ladies could be compelled to do public penance. But, south of
the Tweed, Cox confessed that "should anyone seek to compel
our great men to submit their necks to [the yoke of moral dis-
cipline] it would be much the same as shaving a lion's beard."[97]
When the effort was made in Guernsey, the offending individual
told the clergy that they would "sooner drag the moon from the
sky with [their] teeth than extort from him a public confession
of his crimes."[98]

[97] Cox to Gualter, July 12, 1574; *ibid.*, I, 307.

[98] Bernius to Horne, December 13, 1575, *ibid.*, II, 267. Since this document was
apparently the best proof Horne could find when he wished to offer evidence that discipline was enforced in the Anglican church (Horne to Gualter, August 10, 1576, *Zurich
Letters*, I, 320–21), it may readily be concluded that there was actually very little in
such cases.

CHAPTER XII

The Episcopalian Experiment: 1574-83

THE governmental wrath aroused by the Birchet incident blew itself out in a few months and subsided with the exposure of the Undertree hoax in the summer of 1574. Shamefacedly, Parker consented to the release of Puritan prisoners.[1] But, when the storm had passed, the Puritan party found itself incapable of pursuing a vigorous policy. Bold Dering died in 1576, and the other leaders found their courage badly shaken by the recent ordeal. Field and Wilcox contented themselves with preaching activities in London. Cartwright remained abroad until 1585. During this period of exile he resumed the literary warfare with Whitgift, who had published *A Defense of the Answere* in 1574. Cartwright's second reply was so lengthy that it had to appear in two instalments, but it added nothing material to his argument.[2] Another former fellow of Trinity College, Cambridge, Walter Travers, joined the party leader on the Continent and there produced a systematic exposition of the Puritan idea of church government, entitled *Ecclesiasticae disciplinae et Anglicanae ecclesiae ab illa aberrationis plena e verbo Dei et dilucida explicatio*, but more frequently known by its running-title, *De disciplina ecclesiastica*. This work was most important, for it was soon generally accepted as representing the party attitude on the topic. It retained the term "bishop" to designate the pastor and doctor or teacher, but to all intents and purposes the system described

[1] Parker to Burghley, July 30, 1574, quoted in George Andrews, "History of the Puritan Discipline, 1554–1593" (Washington University dissertation [St. Louis, 1932]), p. 143.

[2] *The Second Replie agaynst Maister Whitgiftes Second Answer (s.l., 1575)* and *The Rest of the Second Replie (s.l., 1577)*.

was the one with which modern Presbyterians are familiar,
with deacons and ruling elders besides the professional clergy.
The church government was on the limited democratic pattern,
though Travers was somewhat more conservative on this point
than Cartwright. The congregation elected the ruling elders
but had no further control over them, and the officials really
governed the church. In fact, they were the church for excommunication purposes.[3] If the people were fit to try a minister or
other officials, no leaders would be necessary, the author declared, though he thought the rank and file of the laity were fit
to choose their officers originally. But, while he clearly championed the social compact theory of government, he strongly
opposed the idea of the church exercising secular powers, and
thus early represents the trend toward withdrawing from certain
fields of human activity which had always been traditionally ecclesiastical. The Puritans had been so far from the prospect of
exercising power for such a long time that this ennervating experience was already beginning to affect the confidence of the
party and the breadth of its platform. Travers did not object
to punishment for heresy, but left that to the secular arm. For
the Anglican churchmen to have a prison was an insult to the
secular magistrate, who should tend to these disciplinary matters in the King's Bench Court. And while he retained deacons
in his church organization, he desired to leave the care of the
poor primarily to the civil authorities. The probating of wills
was also to be left to the secular side of the government.[4]

Though he made clear that he did not agree with this outline
in every detail, Cartwright contributed the preface to the original volume and also prepared an English translation.[5] But in
1577 he broke with his English associates on the issue of clerical
costume. In his first answer to Whitgift he had expressed him-

[3] This was Travers' interpretation of the all-important New Testament teaching on
the subject, "Tell it unto the church" (Matt. 18:17).

[4] *A Full and Plaine Declaration of Ecclesiastical Discipline* (s.l., 1574), pp. 55, 57, 79,
152–63.

[5] *Ibid.* See A. Scott Pearson, *Thomas Cartwright and Elizabethan Puritanism* (London, 1925), pp. 135–41, and especially his discussion of other possible authors of these
works.

self more moderately on this point than had the *Admonition* writers.[6] Now his experience on the Continent, where the Reformed churches were already moderating their original attitude of severe simplicity in such matters, gave him an even broader point of view on the matter. To the dismay of his friends at home he explicitly declared in *The Rest of the Second Replie* that a minister should not forsake his calling rather than wear the prescribed garb.[7] In the same year he forsook his Heidelberg base and attached himself, like Tyndale, to the English trading community in the Low Countries. He became a factor at Middelburg, and married a sister of John Stubbs, or Stubbe, the secretary of the Bertie family who was soon to be famous for his opposition to the Alençon marriage. Through the connivance of Davison and Killigrew, Puritan diplomats of the Walsingham school, Travers soon afterward was ordained in Presbyterian fashion as minister of the congregation of the English merchants in Antwerp. When he returned to England in 1580 without resigning, Cartwright became his *locum tenens*. Elizabeth forced the exile from this position in July, 1582, though Walsingham simultaneously employed him to write a confutation of the Rhemish New Testament. The chief Puritan leaders were thus scattered, distracted, and divided. For six or seven years organized party activity lapsed. The Puritanism of the period was, of necessity, a mild variety.

For the progress of such a moderate movement the circumstances were favorable enough. After the anti-Puritan outburst of 1573–74, the Queen endeavored to resume the middle way, following her announced intention to diverge neither to the right nor to the left. But the invasion of seminary priests and Jesuits forced her far toward the Genevan side once more. Even the French marriage proposals and the accompanying mutilation of John Stubbs could not balance the politico-ecclesiastical budget so filled with Roman Catholic executions. While the peril, or at least alarm, was at its height, the disciplining of

[6] Whitgift, *Works*, ed. Ayre (3 vols.; Cambridge: Parker Society, 1851–53), I, 290–93.

[7] Pearson, *op. cit.*, pp. 148–53.

Puritans was perforce neglected. As Fuller puts it, "Some lenity, of course, by the very rules of opposition fell to the share of the nonconformists, even on the score of their notorious enmity to the Jesuitical party."

Furthermore, the accidents of politics now put the leadership of the Anglican hierarchy in the hands of one most favorable to mild Puritanism, just as they did a generation later when Abbot was given the see of Canterbury in preference to Andrewes, who was much more in sympathy with the sovereign's long-range ecclesiastical policy. Parker died in 1575, and the logical person to succeed him was Richard Cox, Bishop of Ely. He had fought hard for the establishment, from the time of the Marian exile through the days of the *Admonition* controversy. But he was under the Queen's displeasure, in general because he was married, and in particular because he was just then engaged in resisting the assaults of her favorites on the possessions of his see. Perhaps in those disillusioning days when he struggled in vain to keep his London house he may have regretted that he had insisted so belligerently at Frankfort on having the face of an English church instead of carrying out his earlier resolution to co-operate in a thorough reformation. Grindal, on the other hand, was unmarried, experienced, and, though not too effective in maintaining order, was considered good enough. Burghley recommended him, and he was given the post early in 1576.

When the weary Sandys was made his successor at York, and Aylmer moved from his Lincoln deanery to London, the three most important, if not the most remunerative, ecclesiastical posts in the country were held by Germanical veterans of the Marian exile. Aylmer soon showed that his ideas had changed considerably since the period of the Queen's accession, when he had argued in print for a subdivision of existing bishoprics, but the other two were still interested in reform. Especially was this true of Grindal. Having reached the top, perhaps he felt that the time for compromise was past, that he must show some fruits of the long period of waiting to come into the kingdom. Or possibly the added responsibility sobered him. In any case he soon showed his reforming sympathies in no uncertain manner. It was now possible, therefore, to test the theory of those advanced Protestants who had counseled accepting office in 1558–59. If reform was to come from within the establishment, there would never be a more favorable opportunity, short of a change of sovereign. The results showed how limited were the possibilities of such a program.

When Grindal was translated, Parliament was meeting and the Convocation of the province of Canterbury had held its first session. Grindal promptly took over the presidency of this body, and its legislative output shows the effects of his presence. The 1571 canons had supplemented the paliamentary reforming legislation of that year by abolishing the almuce or fur tippet worn by the higher clergy, requiring further training of uneducated clergy, prohibiting the ordination of ministers who could only read the service and not preach, and putting commutations of penance for money payments in the hands of the bishops alone. In addition, restrictions had been imposed on pluralism, and the officials of ecclesiastical courts had been ordered to enforce church discipline. Unfortunately, however, these regulations had been more honored in the breach than in the observance. Grindal's canons not only repeated the substance of these provisions but took further steps to remedy abuses of which the Puritans complained. Ignorant ministers already ordained were not to be admitted to any new living. The practice of conferring orders on men who had no prospective benefice was prohibited. This was designed to eliminate the wandering, unemployed clergy who connived with greedy patrons in simoniacal presentations. The clergy were required to preach and catechize according to their ability. Most striking of all, two "superstitious" customs were eliminated: baptism by women (midwives)—which smacked of the Catholic belief that baptism was essential to salvation—and the ban on marriages during special periods of the church year, such as Lent.[8] Grindal proceeded at once to show that he was really in

[8] John Strype, *History of the Life and Acts of Edmund Grindal* (Oxford, 1821), pp. 537–41.

earnest. A special mandate was issued to the bishops of his province, ordering them to enforce the observance of these rules.[9] The Archbishop also proceeded to clean his own house. The condition of the ecclesiastical courts had long been a scandal. Corrupt officials used their powers for extortion rather than reformation. The Court of Faculties, which was empowered to grant exemptions from the ordinary legal requirements, made a regular business of selling licenses. The new Archbishop soon secured the approval of the Council to a set of regulations designed to curb these abuses. The new rules completely abolished the worst of the licenses, such as those for holding more than two benefices, for boys to have ecclesiastical preferments, and for taking all orders of the ministry at once.[10]

Had this comprehensive program for instructing and disciplining both clergy and laity been carried out, most of the primary objectives of the Puritan party would have been attained, and there would have been little ground for its continued existence. For the strife about vestments and bishops had been ancillary to these major aims, and there is no doubt that Puritan complaints would have soon been silenced by the spectacle of a busy army of educated and zealous clergy, even though uniformed with surplices and marshaled by lord bishops. Unhappily for that bright prospect, Grindal's project was never completed. The dead weight of custom, corrupt human nature, and vested interests broke down the schemes for reforming the courts.[11] This situation might easily have been remedied with the assistance of Elizabeth, for one with her would have been a majority on this matter. She was, however, not only indifferent but hostile. Sparing Catholic sensibilities as far as possible, she refused her consent to the abolition of female baptism and the closed seasons for matrimony. Most fatal of all was the sovereign's implacable opposition to the program of instructing

---

[9] *Ibid.*, pp. 291–92.

[10] *Ibid.*, pp. 300–302.

[11] The document printed in Strype (*ibid.*, pp. 324–25) shows that licenses supposedly abolished in June of 1576 were afterward granted. The document is undated, but the references to a continued custom indicate that it is to be dated subsequent to Grindal's first months in office.

the clergy and the laity. Without instruction there was no hope that the country would accept any high standard of moral discipline. The Reformed system did not depend for its efficiency on the ability of wonder-working priests to terrify an ignorant populace with threats of damnation. It demanded an intelligent understanding and appreciation of a complicated theological scheme. Without freedom of teaching, the whole structure collapsed. But Elizabeth wanted obedience rather than intelligence in her subjects. Popular education bred fantastical notions of equality. Gatherings of clergy smacked of conspiracy against her throne. In vain the reformers pointed out that under her system the only uniformity was that of dull ignorance.[12] To her, cost what it might, ignorance was a small price to pay for docility. Medieval sovereigns delighted in ruling over powerful nobles, who, in their judgment, adorned the royal court and added luster to the royal honor. It might have been thought that such a daughter of the Renaissance as Elizabeth would have a similar delight in ruling a learned kingdom, but, as the Archbishop soon learned, she was even more a daughter of the absolute monarchy.

The issue on which Grindal's eyes were opened to this unpleasant truth was the matter of prophesyings. The ancestry of this institution, so called from the Pauline use of the term, can be readily traced back to the conferences of the Continental Reformed system as reflected in à Lasco's order for his London church and Hooper's quarterly gatherings in his diocese. The device was now being adopted by the more progressive bishops as a chief means of implementing their program of instruction for clergy and laity. In Elizabeth's time we find these exercises in use at Norwich as early as 1564,[13] but we have more details of the operation of the institution in Northampton. The example of this town shows not only the working of this program of adult education but how much Puritanism could be intro-

---

[12] *The Seconde Parte of a Register*, ed. Peel (2 vols.; Cambridge, 1915), I, 189.

[13] State Papers, Domestic, Elizabeth, Addenda, XII, 27 (*Calendar, 1601–1603*, p. 552).

duced within the legal limits of the Anglican system when the ecclesiastical and secular authorities were willing to co-operate. There, as early as 1571, congregational psalm-singing had replaced choir and organ music in the parish churches. The prescribed Prayer Book service was employed, but said in the body of the church where it could be readily heard. Church bells were rung to call people to services but not at other times—a Protestant rule of the sort frequently found in episcopal injunctions of the period. The use of the hand bell, formerly carried before corpses, and bidding prayers for the dead were also banned. On Sundays and holy days each parish service ended by nine o'clock, after which there was a sermon in the main church which parishioners without sermons of their own were expected to attend. After evening prayer on these days the young people of each church were examined on a portion of Calvin's catechism. Each Tuesday and Thursday from nine to ten in the chief church there was a "lecture of the scripture"—possibly at this time a simple reading for the benefit of the illiterate, but certainly the ancestor of the later expository sermons which went by this name. Once each quarter every parish had a communion service, around which was centered the moral discipline of the town. Two weeks before that event the minister and wardens of each parish made a house-to-house canvass, taking the names of communicants and examining the state of their lives. If discords were found, the parties were brought before a joint session of the town council, some of the local justices of the peace, and the minister, where reconciliations were effected or punishment and excommunication administered, as the case might be. After the communion a similar visitation was made to check on absentees, who might also be dealt with by the disciplinary tribunal. The clergy were not overlooked in this quarterly correction. The ministers of the whole shire were gathered into the town four times a year for this purpose. After a public sermon they withdrew to confer among themselves on their manner of life and conduct. Faulty members were exhorted before their brethren, and after three such admonitions the recalcitrants were committed to the bishop for his correction. Less serious charges against both laity and clergy were dealt with in weekly sessions of the two bodies concerned.

The mainspring of the whole system was the prophesying. This was a combination of public forum and literary society, to which the ministers of the town and countryside devoted each Saturday morning from nine to eleven. Each of the clergy in turn was assigned a passage of scripture. When his day came, he expounded it for three-quarters of an hour, correcting any false interpretations of which he knew, but not digressing beyond the limits of what was considered the true meaning of the passage in question. He was followed by several of his brethren, who criticized his performance and added further thoughts on the same theme. The learned ministers present were allowed a final judgment of the performance, and provision was made for answering questions from the audience. Presiding moderators checked contentious speeches and regulated the general conduct of the exercises. Each participant had first to sign an acceptance of these rules, and also a strongly Protestant creed. Though the clergy were the speakers on these occasions, the public was admitted. Only the weekly sessions for clerical discipline, which followed, were private. It is obvious that such exercises must not only have instructed the laity but also have been a powerful stimulus to the rank and file of the clergy to continue their studies and perfect themselves in the preaching art.[14]

This was Anglicanism at its best, and except for the fact that, "for the dispatch of many," people rose from their knees to receive the communion there was nothing illegal about the system. Though it came under the eye of the central government, nothing seems to have been done to suppress it at the time, and the practice spread to other dioceses.[15] When the Birchet scare

[14] Strype, *Annals of the Reformation under Elizabeth* (4 vols. in 7; Oxford, 1824), II, i, 133–40.

[15] *Ibid.*, II, i, 326 and 472–73; II, ii, 494–95; Freake to Parkhurst, June 13, 1574, George Gorham, *Gleanings of a Few Scattered Ears during the Period of the Reformation in England* (London, 1857), p. 492. See Cambridge University MS Ff. v. 14. fols. 85–87 for the rules for the Buckinghamshire exercises. There any minister refusing to take his proper turn was to be noted to the bishop, the Queen's commissioners, or the archdeacon.

drew the Queen's attention to the Puritan problem, however, she told Parker to suppress this kind of exercise throughout his province. Yet when the Archbishop passed the word along to his bishops, the Council countermanded the order. Eventually the Queen's will prevailed on paper, but with the trumpet giving such an uncertain sound the forward zealots were not too scrupulous about obeying.[16] Grindal had not been a year in his new province before Elizabeth renewed her command, with the supplementary injunction to reduce the number of preachers to three or four in each county. The Archbishop was greatly dismayed, but he now displayed that firmness of character which won him the place in Spenser's allegory as the ideal shepherd. He refused to carry out these orders.

Resolutely he stated his position to the Queen in a long and justly celebrated letter. He set forth the scriptural grounds for frequent and diligent preaching. He argued that it promoted loyalty, because the rebellious portions of the kingdom were those with the fewest preachers. Those who complain about these men were the covetous and dissolute who could not endure correction. The reading of homilies, which the Queen had commended as sufficient for most parishes, was only a stopgap, as the original statute stated. The prophesyings were ordained and approved by bishops, and were subject to strict rules. No one was permitted to glance openly or covertly at persons public or private. Current controversies were not to be touched. Diversity of interpretation was no cause for alarm so long as all conformed to the analogy of faith. Experience showed that these exercises produced a zealous and able ministry and corrected the lay opinion that the clergy were an idle lot. He reminded the Queen that she was only mortal. "And although ye are a mighty Prince, yet remember that He which dwelleth in heaven is mightier." In religious matters she should be guided and limited by her clergy, as in legal matters she was by her judges. He was willing and anxious to reform abuses in the prophesyings, and he did put out a set of injunctions calculated to insure

---

[16] Strype, *The Life and Acts of Matthew Parker* (3 vols.; Oxford, 1821), II, 358; *Annals*, II, i, 476–77.

order on such occasions, prohibiting any speaking by laymen or deprived clergy and any attacks on the established religion or the state.[17] But he could not "with safe conscience and without the offense of the majesty of God" destroy such an edifying institution. He was willing to resign, but he would not stultify his convictions.[18]

For months the struggle went on. In May, 1577, the Queen herself sent out letters to the bishops ordering the prophesyings suppressed, alleging that they promoted idleness and disorder. In June, Grindal was confined to his house and sequestered for six months. Toward the close of that period Burghley tried to bring the Archbishop to compliance, but the old man had had his fill of "policy." There was talk of removing him, but the inevitable scandal and consequent comfort to the Roman Catholics rendered that impracticable, as Sir Francis Knollys remarked:

If the Archbishop of Canterbury shall be deprived, then up starts the pride and practice of the Papists, and down declines the comfort and strength of Her Majesty's safety, and then King Richard the Second's men will flock in court apace, and will show themselves in their colors.[19]

In the end he remained sequestered, and a makeshift collection of subordinates did his work. Convocation petitioned for his restoration in 1580–81, but all was in vain.[20] In 1583 it was decided to accept the resignation he at length formally proffered, but, before the terms could be arranged, he died.

Of those who substituted for the Archbishop during this period, Aylmer was the most important for our purposes. He was made president of the Ecclesiastical Commission, and this, added to his position in London, put upon him much of the responsibility of keeping the Puritans in check. Starting bravely, he and his fellow-bishops made some efforts to fulfil this obligation. A London stationer who sold copies of the *Admonition* was imprisoned.[21] In troublesome East Anglia an occasional

[17] Strype, *Grindal*, pp. 327–29.

[18] Grindal to Elizabeth, December 20, 1576, in *ibid.*, pp. 558–74.

[19] Strype, *Grindal*, p. 354.   [20] *Ibid.*, pp. 381–82.

[21] Strype, *Historical Collections of the Life and Acts of John Aylmer* (Oxford, 1821), p. 37.

Puritan minister was suspended.[22] Aylmer strove manfully to keep his clergy from discussing the Alençon marriage in their sermons, and with Elizabeth's help he succeeded in imprisoning Lord Rich's chaplain, who was spreading Puritan doctrines in the Essex countryside. On his visitations he breathed out threatenings and slaughter, asking shrewdly after lecturers who did not administer the sacraments and so avoided the Prayer Book. He proposed to banish the leading Puritans to Lancashire, Staffordshire, Shropshire, "and such other like barbarous countries," that they might wear out their zeal on the papists, and he also wished to appoint apparitors who would attend London church services in quest of nonconformity.[23] Now and then, the Council was goaded into making similar gestures. They once more issued a general order for the suppression of nonconformity in the Inns of Court, though asking the Ecclesiastical Commission to enforce it.[24] They acted to suppress conventicles in Gloucester, and warned Peter Wentworth against permitting outsiders to attend communion in his Northamptonshire country house.[25] They also ordained that lecturers must administer the sacrament as well as preach.[26]

But the Puritan tide was not to be restrained by such flimsy obstructions. Lay public opinion was now a force to be reckoned with. The seeping-down process, which had so saturated London and Cambridge in Elizabeth's first decade, was now affecting many areas in the eastern and southern counties. It was to be expected that the leading men of the London Stationers Company would busy themselves to secure the offending bookseller's release on bond,[27] and that London ministers should tell their congregations that to communicate with wearers of popish rags was to play the Judas—betraying the Master while dipping

---

[22] Strype, *Annals*, II, ii, 266; III, i, 21; Benjamin Brook, *Lives of the Puritans* (3 vols.; London, 1813), II, 174.

[23] Strype, *Aylmer*, pp. 36 and 61.

[24] Strype, *Annals*, III, i, 44–46.   [25] *APC, 1578–80*, pp. 74, 77, 132.

[26] The Council to Grindal, January, 1580, Strype, *Grindal*, p. 363; *APC 1578–80*, p. 367.

[27] Strype, *Aylmer*, p. 38.

the hand in the dish.[28] But the plague was now spreading. The secular authorities in the provinces were co-operating with the Puritans to set up little English Genevas, districts which would be virtually autonomous for ecclesiastical purposes. In rural Shropshire patrons granted congregations the right to elect their own ministers.[29] At Norwich the parishioners purchased the local advowsons and so were legally empowered to choose their own clergy. There John More played the part of a studiously moderate Calvin, while the town council often had the clergy present at their meetings, and usually consulted them before deciding anything of importance.[30]

At Bury the chief congregation claimed that it had named its clergyman ever since the dissolution of the local abbey. A Genevan form of worship was used, and, when a minister was to be chosen, two prominent neighboring clergymen, Dr. Still[31] and Knewstubs of Cockfield, were called on for assistance, after the Reformed fashion of securing the approval of the classis, or presbytery, of the area. Unsatisfactory curates were dismissed by congregational vote. In all this activity the Puritan faction had the enthusiastic support of the local justices of the peace, of whom Sir Robert Jermyn was the most important. These magistrates undertook to exercise virtually all the jurisdiction which had formerly belonged to the ecclesiastical courts in that area. They imprisoned for bigamy and incest; they dealt with tithe controversies; they even disciplined preachers for teaching "false" doctrine.

When the Bishop of Norwich tried to break down this system by intruding conforming clergymen, the sparks flew. The Puritan claimants refused to recognize the Bishop's authority, and

[28] *Seconde Parte*, I, 157.

[29] *Ibid.*, p. 72.

[30] William Burton, *Seven Dialogues both Pithie and Profitable* (s.l., 1606), Preface, sig. A, fols. 2–4.

[31] This would seem to be John Still, then Archdeacon of Sudbury and Master of Trinity College, Cambridge. The play *Gammer Gurton's Needle* is sometimes attributed to him. He was later Bishop of Bath and Wells. Though not so advanced a Puritan as Cartwright, he had signed petitions in his behalf. He had a brother George, who was beneficed at Whatfield, Suffolk, at this time, but George did not have a Doctor's degree.

in one church there was the unedifying spectacle of the rival ministers trying to drown out each other's voices in competing services. The Puritan magistrates forced one of the Anglicans to leave the town and told another he could not serve if he intended observing the established order. When he proved obstinate, they put him under bonds as a disturber of the peace. Thereupon the Bishop sent a commissary to support his man, only to have this agent subjected to even worse treatment. Besides being bound over to the assizes, he was told that his court had no authority. His legal rivals forbade him to hold an inquiry into the matter at issue, and showered him plentifully with such abusive epithets as "beastly merchant," "knave," and "Jack Tosspot."[32]

There were other instances of the same sort. Sussex justices also joined in the sport of fighting fire with fire.[33] They made so bold as to complain to the Council of their bishop, Curteys, accusing him of all manner of crimes and misdemeanors, not the least of which was that he had summoned such great men as themselves to appear before him in open court to be reformed in religion.[34] To all of this protest the Bishop returned a sufficiently humble answer, of which the chief part was a pleading of the principle of double jeopardy and the statute of limitations. When Aylmer troubled Lord Rich's chaplain, the nobleman "did so shake [him] up," that the bishop said he was never so abused at any man's hands since he was born. Rich was finally imprisoned for this, but the minister was presently discovered to be preaching once more in Essex, thanks to an indulgent gaoler.[35] At Norwich the bishop's Chancellor "durst not for his life" hold court in public when Puritan cases were up for trial.[36] At Bury the spirit ran so high that a stationer ventured to paint athwart the royal arms in the local church

[32] Egerton MS 1693, fols. 85–100, esp. 89–90. For another example of co-operation between Puritan clergy and local magistrates see *The Presbyterian Movement in the Reign of Queen Elizabeth*, ed. Usher ("Camden Society: Third Series," Vol. VIII [London, 1905]), pp. 99–100. Dedham, Essex, is the town concerned.

[33] Strype, *Annals*, III, i, 24–25.

[34] *Ibid.*, II, ii, 117.   [35] Strype, *Aylmer*, pp. 54–57; *Annals*, III, i, 177–78.

[36] Strype, *Annals*, II, ii, 61.

the faint apocalyptic praise which begins, "I know thy works and thy love and service and faith and thy patience and thy works and that they are more at the last than at the first. Notwithstanding, I have a few things against thee."[37] Petitions against enforcing the laws rained on Burghley and the Council,[38] and the Puritans had high hopes in that quarter. When the Ecclesiastical Commission deprived a Puritan in Berkshire, a leading layman in those parts named Welden, who was called up to answer for opposing the entrance of a conforming successor, defied the attachment. If the bishop should send another writ, he said that "he had proceeded so far with his Lordship's betters that he should have had an attachment for him [the Bishop], that none should have bailed him, and that he himself would have been his keeper."[39]

This boast was too optimistic, for Welden did go to prison in the end. But in all except the most flagrant cases the councilors took the Puritan side. Behind the Queen's back they cheerfully reversed their own decrees. The Bishop of Norwich, who tried to carry out the Council order to compel preachers to administer the sacrament, received a rating for his pains and a request to let the godly men alone.[40] With tongue in cheek the Queen's advisers composed grave orders for conformity at the Inns of Court. That duty done, they proceeded with great gusto to force Aylmer to accept, as preacher at Lincoln's Inn, William Charke, one of the ringleaders of the Cambridge Puritans, who had been expelled from his fellowship at Peterhouse for nonconformity.[41] They also put pressure on the Corporation of London and the Bishop to provide for two lectures a week in every "convenient division" of the city.[42] Whatever chances Aylmer had of securing the all-important backing of the Council were ruined by his flagrant leasing of episcopal lands

---

[37] Ibid., III, i, 176–77; cf. Rev. 2:19–20.

[38] Seconde Parte, I, 143–44, 153; Strype, Annals, II, ii, 291–92.

[39] Strype, Aylmer, p. 39.

[40] APC, 1578–80, pp. 437–38.   [41] Strype, Annals, III, i, 78–80.

[42] Analytical Index to the . . . . Remembrancia . . . . of the City of London (London, 1878), pp. 365–67.

for his own benefit, transactions which brought him a sharp rebuke from the disgusted royal advisers.[43] His proposals to purge
London of the Nonconformist leaders and to institute a system of ecclesiastical espionage were lost in the bottomless
depths of Burghley's chests. His exercise of his powers under
the Ecclesiastical Commission brought him a stiff warning
from Burghley to forbear meddling, lest more displeasure come
upon him and his colleagues[44]—a threat to which the unhappy
cleric could only respond with a message of humble submission.
Though he had criticized Freake for his slackness in governing
Norwich, he now began unsuccessfully to apply for a transfer
to Ely and a discharge from the burden of disciplining the
puritanical metropolis which had already worn down better
men than he.

With their repressors thus discomfited, the moderate episcopalian Puritans quietly continued their program. The prophesyings were carried on in spite of the Queen. Bishop Barnes, of
Durham, and Cox both dared to express their approval of the
institution at the time of Grindal's trouble.[45] It was necessary
for Elizabeth herself to send a second letter to the recalcitrant
Bishop of Lincoln, in whose diocese the exercises were going
on as though Elizabeth's prohibition had never been issued.[46]
In 1578, Sandys ordered that they be held in each archdeaconry
of the northern province, though the name was changed to
"quarterly synods."[47] In 1580, Bishop Chaderton established
a system of prophesyings in his diocese of Chester, arranging for
meetings to be held at Easter, Midsummer (June 24), and
Michaelmas.[48] These violations of the royal will doubtless enabled the more advanced Puritans to blackmail further concessions from the bishops, since one ingenious brother was
charged before the Council with threatening to inform the

[43] *APC, 1578–80,* p. 411.   [45] Strype, *Annals,* II, ii, 111–14.

[44] Strype, *Aylmer,* p. 61.   [46] *Ibid.,* p. 114

[47] *Ibid.,* p. 164; Strype, *Grindal,* p. 444.

[48] Gonville and Caius College, Cambridge, MS (Moore) 197, pp. 175–76.

Queen about local prophesyings if the bishop troubled him about the Prayer Book.[49] Even where bishops did not themselves protect the exercises, they found more enjoyable occupations than trying to stop them when the Puritans persisted on their own responsibility. In London, Field, Wilcox, Charke, Travers, and others, including Stephen Egerton, formerly of Peterhouse, Cambridge, met together in what was called a conference. In May, 1582, sixty ministers gathered at Cockfield, Suffolk, where the redoubtable John Knewstubs held the living. Around Dedham, in the Constable country of northern Essex, a group met every month and began keeping minutes in official style.[50]

Besides supporting the movement for adult education, the more forward of the Anglican authorities also made efforts to improve the discipline of the church. At Puritan Norwich, where the cathedral service had already been modified by the canons, the Bishop's Chancellor proposed a thorough reformation of the diocese by means of rural deans or superintendents on the Reformed model, a rearrangement which he thought would permit him and his fellow-officials "to enjoy the true comfort of performing their duty to the uttermost of their power."[51] The Convocation of 1581 approved the reforms of the previous session and asked for parliamentary sanction for the most important.[52] In the Commons it was proposed to revise the system of presenting to ecclesiastical livings, in order to secure more efficient men. No one was to be ordained by the bishop alone. Either the dean and chapter or six learned preachers of the diocese must concur in the act. A vacant parish was allowed twenty days in which to protest against the suggested incumbent. In the diocese of Coventry and Lichfield

[49] APC 1578–80, p. 306.

[50] Richard Bancroft, Dangerous Positions (London, 1593; largely reprinted in The Presbyerian Movement), esp. p. 44.

[51] Historical Manuscripts Commission, Salisbury MSS, II, 195–98, also printed with minor variations by Strype (Annals, II, ii, 695–701) from a copy in the Cotton MSS.

[52] Strype, Grindal, pp. 384–85, 587–88, and Appen. XV.

Bishop Overton went so far as to try to put these reforms in practice when he made his visitation.[53]

While something could thus be accomplished behind the Queen's back, no progress was possible when the route lay across her path of vision. Hence nothing could be gained on the parliamentary front. We have the text of a fiery speech which Peter Wentworth began to deliver to the 1576 Parliament. It had been carefully wrought out during a score of walks on his Buckinghamshire estate. In it he bluntly stated that the Queen had "committed great fault" in refusing religious laws.[54] But he was stopped and sequestered before he could finish. A petition for reform, tactfully submitted through the Council, brought the response that the Queen had her own plans which would be carried out by the bishops or her own means.[55] Five years later the House incurred the royal displeasure merely for voting a weekly fast day, on the motion of Wentworth's brother Paul. When puritanical George Carleton, who sat for Dorchester, tried to protest against the ensuing precipitate retreat, the Speaker would not recognize him.[56] The effort to co-operate with Convocation on a reform bill brought the usual fair words from the Queen, but nothing more. When the bishops pressed her, she declared, as usual, that she would tolerate no parliamentary interference. All that she would permit was an episcopal version of the movement to develop a more learned and preaching clergy, a set of provisions for increasing the amount of individual clerical study. Nearly a generation had passed since she came to the throne, but the middle-aged woman was still holding to her original position, on the alert to check any pronounced Puritan innovations, as the young Queen had been in 1559.

[53] *Seconde Parte*, I, 262–65; W. P. M. Kennedy, *Elizabethan Episcopal Administration* (3 vols.; London: Alcuin Club, 1924), III, 167–69.

[54] Sir Simonds D'Ewes, *A Compleat Journal of the Votes Speeches and Debates. . . . throughout the Whole Reign of Queen Elizabeth* (London, 1693), p. 239.

[55] *Ibid.*, pp. 251 and 257.

[56] *Ibid.*, p. 284.

CHAPTER XIII

The Alliance with the Lawyers: 1583-85

O SHIFT in England's foreign policy brought about the next turn of Puritan fortunes. As France sank into the depths of civil war, the island kingdom continued slowly to gather its strength for the great struggle with Spain. Piratical raids beyond the line and steady pressure on Catholic recusants at home continued as before. Nor did excessive party zeal produce a reaction, as in 1573. It is true that separatist tendencies, which we shall consider more at length in a later chapter, began to reassert themselves in the left wing of the Puritan movement at about this time. They were serious enough to involve two executions, but they did not of themselves have any great effect on the governmental attitude toward the more moderate reformers. The decisive factor was again a change of personnel at the top of the Anglican hierarchy, this time caused by the death of Grindal. Sandys was next in line, but he was married, and was also discredited by being the victim of a blackmailing scheme which coupled his name with that of an innkeeper's wife. In any case, Elizabeth had had her fill of the exilic tradition at Lambeth. Bachelor John Whitgift was much more to her liking than Sandys, and he was given the place. Since 1577 he had been Bishop of Worcester, and so was familiar with administrative problems. Much more important, he was committed to a vigorous defense of the establishment against Puritan attacks. The Council and Tyburn were coping with the menace on the right. He could be the shield on the Queen's left hand. For his early vestiarian liberalism was now buried beneath the two weighty tomes of his answers to the *Admonitions* and Cartwright. It would seem, furthermore, that his Anglicanism was by no means entirely a pose assumed for the sake of gaining office. The passage of time was gradually giving the dignity and prestige of age to the Tudor establishment. Since Whitgift had spent all his adult career in Elizabethan England, he had no clear recollection of any other legal rites at home or familiarity with those abroad. So he developed easily and naturally into a middle-aged tory, a firm supporter of the *status quo* which use and custom had confirmed. It is true that by virtue of this attitude he rose high in the world, but it is possible to see how it may have been done without violence to his conscience. His private life and financial transactions were practically untouched by scandal. The lusty Martin, who found such juicy morsels in the careers of his fellow-prelates, got in very little lip-smacking over the Archbishop's record. He was not absolutely opposed to all reform in the church, and occasionally made mild gestures in that direction. But his chief interest was in suppressing his Puritan rivals. His policy therefore represented a resumption of the episcopal tactics of the *Admonition* period, and the end of the Grindalian coalition with the advanced party.

The new primate lost no time in joining battle. He was confirmed in his new office on September 23, 1583. In the same month he issued a set of orders which combined certain features of the episcopal reform program with a direct assault on the Puritans. Henceforth no juvenile, ignorant, or unplaced person was to be ordained. Special licenses and commutations of penance were regulated. But at the same time preachers were required to wear the apparel and give the sacrament according to the Prayer Book system. Most serious of all, no one was to be permitted to exercise any ecclesiastical function unless he subscribed to the three articles which Parker had devised to test the Puritan leaders in 1571. These acknowledged the royal supremacy, approved the Prayer Book, and accepted the Thirty-nine Articles as agreeing with scripture. The first of these caused the Puritans little difficulty. The last they could subscribe in the statutory form of 1571, which required acceptance only of the substance of the doctrine but not the sections dealing with church government and ceremonies.[1] The second, however, was a rock of offense. It bound the subscriber to the belief that the Prayer Book might lawfully be used and to the promise that in his ministrations he would employ it and none other. It also required the explicit statement that the volume "containeth nothing in it contrary to the Word of God."

Once more the Puritan clergy were "killed in their souls." Wrestling with their consciences, they endured agonies of suspense. The first group to be dealt with were from Sussex. When they were suspended for nonsubscription, a delegation was sent to interview Whitgift on December 5, 1583. For two days they discussed the Prayer Book with him at Lambeth, around a table in "a fair chamber, matted, where was a good fire of coals." Two other bishops and the Dean of Westminister assisted the Archbishop. At the second day's session the Puritans pointed out such Romish difficulties as the Prayer Book statement that "children, being baptized, have all things necessary to their salvation and be undoubtedly saved," and the implied permission of women performing the sacrament, a practice which a Convocation of which Whitgift was procurator had tried unsuccessfully to abolish. In their judgment these required that some qualification be attached to their signature. Whitgift assured them that the rubrics were susceptible of a Protestant interpretation, and that his explanation of the articles to that effect was official and so met the difficulty. The ministers should be content to be guided by the bishops. "You are unlearned, and but boys in comparison of us, who have studied divinity before you for the most were born." The argument from the youth of the Puritans, which is vaguely reminiscent of the line of reasoning used by the Catholics against the early Protestants, incidentally indicates not only that Puritanism was still a novelty in most of the country at this time, but also that the movement was growing rapidly among the younger generation —a fact which can be confirmed by the Puritan responses to

[1] *The Seconde Parte of a Register*, ed. Peel (2 vols.; Cambridge, 1915), I, 184.

this accusation on other occasions about this time.[2] The Anglican also told his visitors that their places would be filled by
others if they were stubborn. To this economic argument Bishop Yong of Rochester added a few double-edged lines, admitting the existence of unemployed learned ministers: "There
were some which lost their livings about sixteen or seventeen
years ago for these causes and the like, that have repented
since and are yet without. And there be many learned men
which lack and look for livings to furnish these [*sic*]." But for
the most part the discussion was conducted in good temper.
Whitgift professed his love for Cartwright and his willingness
to favor him if he would return and conform. He offered his
Puritan guests the use of his garden for peripatetic consultation
among themselves, apart from their Anglican confreres. The
ministers preferred to ferry ride to Westminster, but in the end
both sides yielded somewhat, and all was composed. A protestation was allowed, to the effect that the subscribers approved
only such sense of the Prayer Book as was not contrary to the
Scriptures and was agreeable to the substance of religion then
professed in the Church of England. The suspensions were
lifted, and the wives and children—never forgotten in the petitions of the oppressed—were spared.[3]

Whitgift's concession on this occasion was represented at
Court as a Puritan victory. Angered, he declared that the protestation was merely a declaratory statement. He thereupon refused the subscribers an official copy of it and would not permit
its use in the future. The battle was thus fairly joined. On the
Puritan side a semblance of an organization appeared, with

[2] "If it be so, as they say, that none but young men do hear our doctrine, then this
text is well chosen for the auditory, to teach young men that, which if they learn, they
may say with David, 'I have more understanding than the ancient.'

"The young men follow Christ, the young men hear the Word, the young men sancti-
fy themselves, the young men stand for the church, the young men bear the heat of
this day; old Noah is drunk, old Lot is sleepy, old Samson hath lost his strength. . . . .
'God hath chosen the weak things,' saith Paul . . . . so I may say, 'God hath chosen the
young things to do his works' " (Henry Smith, *Sermons* [London, 1599], pp. 215 and
227; *Works*, ed. Thomas Smith ["Nichols Series of Standard Divines, Puritan Period"
(2 vols.; Edinburgh, 1866–67)], I, 217, 228).

[3] John Strype, *The Life and Acts of John Whitgift* (3 vols.; Oxford, 1822), I, 255–60;
Seconde Parte, I, 209–20, esp. pp. 215 and 217.

Field in the role of corresponding secretary and business agent. He sent out letters to the provinces urging all the faithful to stand together against subscription. "Branded men" was the agitator's epithet for those scabs, or blacklegs, who "made a breach" in the front by signing, and he roundly asserted that their usefulness to the church was ended.[4] Doubtless his busy hand was also behind the shower of petitions which descended throughout the winter on the Archbishop and the Council.[5] They came not only from the clergy but also from the country gentry. Norfolk, Suffolk, Essex, Lincolnshire, Oxfordshire, Cambridgeshire, Kent, Northamptonshire, and Rutland were all represented.

A Cromwell headed one of the list of signers, but the day of the country gentleman had not yet fully dawned. For the time being the attitude of the councilors was much more important. The Puritan majority on that body did not fail its friends in the emergency. Both their wiles and their power were turned on the Archbishop. At the very beginning of the controversy they tried to divert his attention to what they considered more desirable objectives by submitting to him a series of suggestions for church reform. Recusants were to be repressed, unlearned and immoral ministers removed, nonresidence restricted, abuses in the system of excommunication and penance eliminated, and visitation charges reduced.[6] Whitgift went through the motions of complying with these requests, but his eye remained on the Puritan problem. Accordingly, in February, he found himself summoned before the Council to defend his conduct against the complaints of the ministers.[7]

He begged off from submitting to this indignity, probably with success, since we hear none of the exultant cries which the prelate dreaded. But the councilors and their friends had other weapons. Elizabeth insisted on being kept out of the unpleas-

---

[4] Strype, *Annals of the Reformation under Elizabeth* (4 vols. in 7; Oxford, 1824), III, i, 350–51.

[5] *Seconde Parte*, I, 223–45; Strype, *Whitgift*, I, 249–55, 271–76.

[6] Strype, *Whitgift*, I, 238.

[7] Whitgift to the Council, February 4, 1584, in *ibid.*, pp. 250–55.

ant business, and everyone knew it. She might give an express command in private, but her name was not to be mentioned in public as being responsible for the resulting actions.[8] So everything had to be done under the guise of law, without direct appeal to the prerogative. This exposed the bishops to the sniping of the common lawyers. These hairsplitting experts could make disciplinary progress extremely uncomfortable by their ministrations if they cared to do so, and they were now in that mood. As we have seen, they had rendered little or no assistance to the Puritans during the vestiarian controversy. But at that time they were as yet almost untouched by the teachings of the zealous. Now this impregnation had been completed by the installation of a preacher at the last of the Inns of Court. Future judges, like Sir Henry Yelverton, son of Northampton's Christopher, were taking notes on Puritan sermons.[9] Nearly all the common lawyers were jealous of the jurisdiction of the church courts and alarmed by the growth of the prerogative courts, which did not use the traditional English law and thus were a peril to their livelihood. So they were anxious to co-operate with the Puritan clergy. Since the law schools were the training-grounds for the more influential of the justices of the peace, we have already seen some of the fruits of this connection. When the gentlemen of Kent complained that Whitgift's policy deprived them of opportunity to hear preaching, the Archbishop reminded them that many of their number were resident in the Inns, where there was no lack of such fare. But in addition to exerting this general political pressure, the lawyers also contributed more technical assistance. When the bishops began to work the creaking machinery of their courts, they laid themselves open to charges of legal irregularities, and the lawyers promptly went into action.

Within a few weeks of the first appearance of the offending

[8] When Aylmer violated the convention under pressure, on the occasion of Cartwright's arrest in 1585, he was made to smart for it (Strype, *Historical Collections of the Life and Acts of John Aylmer* [Oxford, 1821], pp. 76–77).

[9] In 1605, after the minister's death, he published a volume of these which he had taken from the lips of Edward Philips, *Certaine Godly and Learned Sermons* (London). "Chronological Account," Morrice MS I, p. 615 (10).

orders "A Gentleman in the Country" had begun the assault with a widely circulated "Letter."[10] An unknown colleague added "An Abstracte of Certaine Acts of Parliament." But the most troublesome was the diplomatist and Clerk of the Council, Robert Beale, who wrote two volumes on the subject for private circulation and baited the Archbishop to his face. Since he was a brother-in-law of Walsingham, and Knollys was openly on his side,[11] it is not hard to believe that the Puritan councilors were aiding and abetting. Snatches of statutes and technical quibbles filled the air and filtered into the petitions and conferences of these hectic months. By what right, the lawyers demanded, did the prelates require subscription to a book which was different from the one authorized by statute? The Act of Uniformity established a text which varied from the 1552 edition in only three particulars, the Sunday lessons, the excision from the litany of the reference to the Bishop of Rome and his "detestable enormities," and the addition of the two sentences in the communion service. But now a calendar of saints' days with lessons from the Apocrypha had been added, the "Black Rubric" dropped, and other changes made. The ornaments rubric required the use of the alb and chasuble worn in the second year of Edward VI, and the Advertisements and injunctions made since were all illegal because the Reformation statutes expressly required convocation action and royal sanction for all such canons. In fact, if obedience to the law was the objective, the bishops were the ones to be prosecuted, since they did not use the legal apparel and were trenching on the royal prerogative. And, finally, where was the statute which permitted bishops to deprive ministers of benefices for nonsubscription?

Splutters of confused rage greeted such impudent annoyers, but men like Beale were not to be led by the nose "with any Pythagorall or papal *ipse dixit*." The wrangling in the upper part of the Archbishop's gallery reached the ears of hangers-on below, but the lawyer forced the man who had set himself

---

[10] Printed in *A Parte of a Register* ([Middelburg?], 1593), pp. 132–200.

[11] Strype, *Whitgift*, I, 304.

up to the Sussex clergy as a mature and learned scholar to admit
that he had never seen the basic 1552 volume. In a passionate
apologia the layman justified his loyalty and his learning. In
the process he assured the Archbishop that whether or not he
had ever said that the prelate's sermon at court was a good one
for a bishop he was sure that some of his efforts had been such
as to cause Queen, Council, and the rest of the audience to depart with "very evil satisfaction." As a crowning insult he informed the Primate that in his dealings with the imprisoned
Queen of Scots he had discovered that she, like others of her
fellow-papists, thought very well of His Lordship.[12]

When the archiepiscopal head cleared after the ordeal of this
abuse, which he termed the worst he had ever experienced,
Whitgift took steps to improve his disciplinary technique. He
abandoned the practice of punishing men for nonsubscription
alone.[13] Instead, he furbished up a terrible engine which he
found in his legal arsenal, one designed to prove suspects guilty
of overt acts, the ex officio oath. This was a witness's oath
which ecclesiastical authorities by virtue of their office—hence
the name—might administer to accused persons, who were
thereupon questioned about their supposed misdemeanors. In
current ecclesiastical theory this was a device intended to encourage something like auricular confession. In practice it was
indistinguishable from the Roman law procedure of forcing a
man to incriminate himself—a procedure from which it had,
indeed, been originally borrowed. It had long been in use in
ecclesiastical courts, though not frequently employed. Now the
Archbishop drew up a list of twenty-four detailed articles, in-
quiring about the use of the surplice, the sign of the cross in
baptism, the wedding ring, churching of women, the litany,
and the burial service. These were to be administered to any
whom the Ecclesiastical Commission chose to summon. The
oath was grounded on indubitable precedent, but it was contrary to the common law, and, though it might have been supposed that such a zealous racker of Jesuits would have respected

[12] *Ibid.*, pp. 283–99, 401–3; III, 87–98; *Seconde Parte*, I, 202–3, 211–12.

[13] Strype, *Whitgift*, I, 311, 325.

a claim of special law for special cases, Beale managed to find arguments against it. It was true that church courts supposedly enjoyed a separate jurisdiction, but their prestige had been shaken by the Reformation, and the canon law had, of course, never been properly reformed. The common-law judges claimed the right to prescribe limits to the jurisdiction of the ecclesiastical courts, and so a case could be made out. Once the brief was filed, the lawyers could be trusted to delay an unfavorable decision interminably. As it happened, in this case it was nearly ten years before the last doubt was removed.[14] Even where the law was clear, stubbornness, a long purse, and a clever counsel might cost the enforcing agents dear, since some of the cases developed into semicivil suits. One dog-guilty brother from Preston, in Peterborough diocese, spent thirty-one pounds, kept his case going through three years, made seven trips to his diocesan town and ten to London, and in the end defeated the complaining witnesses' claim for their costs.[15] The Puritans might sometimes lose their cases, but, with the common lawyers in alliance with them, the victorious adversaries generally suffered considerably before an incumbent was finally deprived.

Throughout 1584 the political struggle raged, and the assassination of William of Orange in May, while helping the Puritan cause by increasing the anti-Catholic sentiment of the country,

[14] For a detailed account of the oath, together with several important documents, see Mary Hume (Maguire), "The History of the *Ex Officio* Oath in England" (Radcliffe College dissertation [1923]). There is an abridgment in her "Attack of the Common Lawyers on the Oath Ex Officio as Administered in the Ecclesiastical Courts in England" in *Essays in History and Political Theory in Honor of Charles Howard McIlwain* (Cambridge, Mass., 1936), pp. 199–229.

The essence of the Puritan case (set forth in Robert Beale's "A Collection Shewinge What Jurisdiction the Clergie Hathe Heretofore Lawfully Used"—of which the most important part is transcribed in Mrs. Maguire's thesis, pp. 261–75, from Calthorpe MS 44, fols. 99–202—and in James Morice's treatises cited below, pp. 298, 301) was that the ecclesiastical courts were under the common law and drew all their authority from parliamentary statutes. Since the Act of Uniformity of 1559 made no explicit provision for the ex officio oath, it was therefore illegal. On the Anglican side (p. 300) it was argued that after the Act of Supremacy the church courts drew their authority directly from the royal prerogative and were therefore entitled to use any means authorized by letters patent, as was the oath in 1559. This view was upheld by the common-law judges in Cawdry's case (5 Coke f. 8), decided in 1591.

Whitgift's twenty-four articles are in Strype, *Whitgift*, I, 268–69; III, 81–87.

[15] *Seconde Parte*, I, 291–95.

did not end the strife. Suspects refusing to subscribe were put to the test of the oath and the twenty-four articles, and Whitgift did not always keep his promise to await the results of the second process.[16] Forty-five ministers were suspended in a single day in Suffolk. Field himself was caught in the London net.[17] Overton's plan for semi-presbyterian ordination and installation of clergy in his diocese was scotched.[18] When the mastership, or chief preaching place, fell vacant at the Temple, Whitgift succeeded in blocking Travers' advancement.[19] Part of his objection was on the score of the Puritan's presbyterian ordination at Antwerp, a fault similar to that alleged against Whittingham at Durham in 1578. The internationalism of Cranmer was fast disappearing from the English episcopacy. The successful candidate for the lectureship was Sandys' nominee, Richard Hooker. A fine-spirited controversialist, he also saw no particular virtue in internationalism, and in his splendid English did his magnificent best to justify nearly all Elizabeth's ways to those who would listen or read.

But Hooker's genteel tones had no immediate effect on the situation. Whitgift needed more help than the scholarly preacher could offer, and it was not forthcoming. The Queen would grant him audiences but nothing more,[20] while the Council was remorseless in its pressure. A threatening gesture from the prelates, a Puritan complaint to the Council, and a sharp letter to the ecclesiastics constituted the usual round. In vain Whitgift collected and submitted evidence to show that the great majority of the clergy were willing to conform—evidence which the Puritans maintained was quite distorted.[21] Knollys reasoned with the Primate and sent him literature.[22] Writing to Burghley about the same time the councilor pled for the Puri-

---

[16] *Ibid.*, p. 296; Strype, *Whitgift*, I, 310.

[17] *Seconde Parte*, I, 243, 284.   [18] *Ibid.*, pp. 262–65.

[19] Strype, *Annals*, III, i, 352; *Whitgift*, I, 340–46.

[20] Strype, *Whitgift*, I, 333.

[21] *Ibid.*, p. 308; III, 99–103, "The Unlawfull Practices of Prelates," printed in *Parte of a Register*, pp. 280–304, esp. p. 295.

[22] Strype, *Whitgift*, I, 308–9; III, 103–4.

tans in the name not only of legal right but also of patriotism. The Archbishop maintained that observance of the law was necessary to Her Majesty's safety, but in Knollys' opinion he violated the rules of justice himself.

My good Lord, he continued, I have but a life to lose and would to God I might spend it in the field against her Majesty's enemies, for I must not live without her Majesty's safety and I have some skill of forcible fights in the field. But it grieves my heart to see the course of popish treason to be neglected and to see the zealous preachers of the gospel, sound in doctrine (who are the most diligent barkers against the popish wolf to save the fold and flock of Christ) to be persecuted and put to silence as though there were no enemies to her Majesty and to the state but they, and as though their refusal of an unlawful subscription (to such as are not persuaded therein) were a sufficient cause to exempt them and to exile or to condemn them. And I do fear how so ever her Majesty's safety or service is (*verbo tenus*) pretended that yet the absolute authority of Bishops (specially over their brethren) that hath no foundation in the Word of God nor otherwise but by law positive, specially in England. This absolute authority to be drawn up to a high foundation without controlment of Prince or Council is it, I do feare (I say) that doth make all this stir. Whereat the Pope and his adherents may laugh in their sleeves and hope for a day.

I do know that the bishops do and will mislike much of me for this saying. Nevertheless I would have any Bishop, or all the Bishops, labor to charge me with any favoring of Puritans unlawfully or contrary to her Majesty's signified pleasure, unless that I have said to Councillors or to her Majesty shall be interpreted against me.

For conclusion, your Lordship doth perceive that I do think it to be a dangerous matter to her Majesty's safety that the politic government of matters of state, as well as concerning forms and accidents of and to religion as otherwise, should be taken from all Councillors of her Majesty's estate and only to be given over to the rule of bishops that are not always indifferent in their own cases of sovereignty.[23]

The cautious Lord Treasurer himself, though striving like a good administrator to maintain the appearance of supporting all legally constituted authority, was moved to strong measures. He did not deign to answer Whitgift's complaints about Beale in May.[24] In July he used his influence in behalf of two Cambridgeshire Puritans, and told the Archbishop that his twenty-four articles were "so curiously penned, so full of branches, and circumstances as I think the Inquisitors of

[23] Knollys to Burghley, June 13, 1584, State Papers, Domestic, Elizabeth, CLXXIV, 52 (*Calendar, 1581–90*, p. 181).

[24] Strype, *Whitgift*, I, 297–98.

Spain use not so many questions to comprehend and to trap their preys." In September, Burghley relieved his mind on the subject of episcopal morals in general, telling the chief prelate that "he saw much worldliness in many that were otherwise affected before they came to cathedral churches that he feared the places altered the men."[25] Whitgift was not impressed and in turn tried repeatedly to present a satisfactory justification of his proceedings.[26] It could not be done. Two strong men were face to face, and neither would yield. The Archbishop finally fell back on a plea that they might agree to differ without losing friendship.

In the same month of September the whole Council demanded the Archbishop's answer to a statement drawn up by Essex Puritans listing the suspended godly ministers and charging many unmolested incumbents with ignorance, "drunkenness, filthiness of life, gaming at cards, haunting of alehouses, and such like."[27] The Council also demonstrated its Puritan sympathies by other means, apparently going out of its way to do so. At the height of the controversy with the Archbishop they dispatched a letter to William Chaderton, Bishop of Chester, ordering him to increase the number of prophesyings held in his diocese to one for each deanery, and to hold them more frequently. They were to meet once a month except in the winter. The ministers were to be fined for nonattendance, with the penalties doubling and tripling for successive absences. First on the list of the clergy from whom the Bishop was to take advice on this matter was none other than Christopher Goodman, Archdeacon of Richmond and the author of *Superior Powers*, who was to serve as one of the moderators at the Chester meeting.[28] The Council also chose this time to give Aylmer another taste of its displeasure. After listening to a tale of a Puritan minister's woes extending back to 1579, they ordered the Bishop to indemnify his victim with a sizable money grant, a demand

---

[25] *Ibid.*, p. 338.

[26] *Ibid.*, pp. 309–28; III, 104–15, esp. p. 106.   [27] *Ibid.*, I, 328–30.

[28] The Council to Chaderton, April 2, 1584, Gonville and Caius College, Cambridge, MS (Moore), 197, pp. 179–80; Strype, *Annals*, II, ii, 544–49.

which wrung from the distressed Father in God an anguished plaint in almost the best Puritan style.[29]

With the Protestants thus at odds among themselves Parliament met. The assassination of William the Silent was still fresh in the national mind, and the Parry plot was unraveled during the session. Much of the High Court's energy was therefore devoted to sharper legislation against Roman Catholic recusants and a bill for the Queen's safety. But time was found for further discussion on church reform, and the Archbishop once more locked horns with the Puritans, who were reinforced by an assemblage of their ministers in London in February, 1585.[30] The spirit of co-operation between bishops, Convocation, and Commons which had marked the 1581 session was noticeably absent. The only exception to this rule involved an abortive bill for better Sunday observance, doubtless occasioned by the Sabbath tragedy at a bearbaiting in the Paris Garden on January 13, 1583, when the collapse of a gallery killed eight people and injured many others. This was passed by both houses of Parliament but vetoed by the Queen.

For the rest, all was strife. Puritan petitions were showered on the Commons from the zealous areas of the east, west, and south. Dr. Peter Turner, son of the botanist and a celebrated physician in his own right, sitting as a member for Bridport, Dorset, carried on the family tradition by introducing a bill and book, doubtless a revised prayer-book on the Genevan order. This was too radical a suggestion to make much progress. It was opposed by Knollys, in his capacity as the Queen's mouthpiece in the Commons, and eventually dropped. But a reform program of sixteen articles was drawn up and submitted to the Lords. This included not only items of the Grin-

[29] "My poor estate . . . . the great charges that I have of mine own children, together with the great burden of the Parliament and Convocation, which of all other lieth most heavily upon the poor Bishop of London. The premises considered, together with the great vaunt the man will make of this conquest over a Bishop, my trust is that you will deal favorably with me," etc. He ended with an offer to give the Puritan some small benefice when it was convenient, or else to let him sue for false arrest, which trial of the law "I hope will not be so plain for him as he taketh it" (*Seconde Parte*, I, 248).

[30] *The Presbyterian Movement in the Reign of Queen Elizabeth*, ed. Usher ("Camden Society: Third Series," Vol. VIII [London, 1905]), p. 9.

dal sort but direct hits at the Primate's program for securing uniformity. It requested the abolition of all subscription requirements not specifically enjoined by statute, the restoration of deprived and suspended clergy, permission for ministers to make changes and omissions in the Prayer Book service, and the restriction of the ex officio oath procedure to cases in which the suspect was previously indicted by others.[31] Whitgift served on the Lords' conference committee, and his response rejected not only the definitely Puritan suggestions but much of the Grindal program as well. Prophesyings, ministerial associates at ordination, and a probationary period for new incumbents he could not abide. These smelled of a popularity and bred disorder. Even the proposal to purge the ministry of ignorant men admitted illegally, in defiance of the statute of 1571 and the canons of 1576, was rejected as "against charity."[32] As he told Burghley, he knew that the Queen was opposed to innovations, and he agreed with her.[33]

As a practical politician, however, like Elizabeth, he knew that something could not be beaten with nothing. Accordingly, he proposed a few minor reforms, dealing in a general way with abuses of excommunication, commutation of penance, pluralities, and the ordination of unlearned clergy.[34] The Queen approved these proposals and with minor changes they eventually became canons. Provisions were also made in Convocation for compelling unlearned ministers to study at home, without taint of public prophesyings.[35] But the Puritans had seen too many similar good resolutions go unenforced in the past to be satisfied now.[36] Parliament went ahead with bills against pluralities, closed seasons on marriages, and ordination without preliminary trial by laymen.[37] To block this drive, the Primate fell back on

[31] Strype, *Whitgift*, III, 118–24.

[32] *Ibid.*, I, 354–60; III, 124–30.   [34] *Ibid.*, pp. 364–66; III, 130–33.

[33] *Ibid.*, I, 361.   [35] *Ibid.*, I, 400.

[36] See the response to Whitgift's articles in *Seconde Parte*, I, 174–95. These answers seem to refer to the Archbishop's original twelve articles, but there are some variations, as in the matter of commissaries, which must be later additions.

[37] Strype, *Whitgift*, I, 391.

the Queen's authority. Both in public and in private he had recourse to some exceedingly tory arguments. The marriage bill was opposed as "containing matter which tendeth to the slander of this church, as having hitherto maintained an error."[38]   In defending pluralities and nonresidence he reversed the Bishop of Rochester by pleading that there were not enough educated men to go around. He maintained that the bill against these practices "depriveth learned men of due reward" and "increaseth the number of the factious and wayward sort."[39] Under his leadership Convocation, which was supposedly engaged in restricting pluralities itself, set up a similar chorus. They solemnly alleged that the bill

will breed great discontentment in the younger sort of students and make them fly to other seminaries where they may hope for more encouragement; will give the adversary just cause to rejoice and triumph when they shall see the clergy and learning generally so much disgraced and vilified by the gentry and commons of this land; abridgeth all ability in the ministry, either of keeping hospitality of or contributing to the state in case of necessity; and, that which is most lamentable, maketh way to an anarchy and confusion.[40]

This sad effort of the officially constituted moral leaders of the country may serve to explain some of the Puritan heat against the establishment, but for the moment words meant little. Whatever the rationalization might be, the Queen's will prevailed and the Commons' legislation did not pass. In concluding the session, Elizabeth put the blame of admitted scandals in the church on her whipping-boy bishops, threatened roundly to depose them if they did not mend their ways, and sent the Puritans home empty-handed.[41]

Whitgift thus survived one major effort to check his drive for conformity. But his victory was only apparent. He could not continue his program without more effective support. Even during the parliament[42] he was forced to meet the Puritans on

[38] *Ibid.*, p. 392.

[39] *Ibid.*, pp. 380–81.   [40] *Ibid.*, p. 384.

[41] Sir Simonds D'Ewes, *A Compleat Journal of the Votes Speeches and Debates . . . . throughout the Whole Reign of Queen Elizabeth* (London, 1693), pp. 328–29.

[42] The presence of Sandys at one of the sessions suggests this dating, since otherwise it is unlikely that the Archbishop of York would have been in London.

equal terms at what was, in a sense, a rehearsal for the Hampton Court conference. Travers and Sparke, of Magdalen College, Oxford, were the Puritan delegates; Leicester, Walsingham, Lord Grey, and Burghley, the moderators; while Sandys and Bishop Cooper of Winchester held up Whitgift's arms. For two days the discussion continued, with the honors apparently even.[43] Burghley gave the Archbishop some comfort by expressing the opinion that the Puritan scheme of discipline was impractical, but the presence of Walsingham on this occasion is highly significant. He said little, and the Archbishop yielded nothing at the time. But the wily diplomat finally secured the concessions which the others, including Cecil, had been unable to extract. Not for nothing did James dub him the perfect Machiavel. He covered his tracks so well that we cannot trace out all the route followed, and, in fact, the importance of his role in this drama has escaped the most competent critics. But whatever may have been the underlying causes, such as Whitgift's weariness and the continuing anti-Catholic sentiment connected with the growing antipathy toward Spain, the fact remains that Walsingham was the medium through whom the compromise was achieved. In exchange for a promise from the councilor to assist in preserving order in the church, Whitgift agreed not to "suspend or deprive any man already placed in any cure or charge for not subscribing only, if hereafter he would promise unto him in writing to observe the Book of Common Prayer and the orders of the church by law set down."[44]

The Puritans were thus freed from the dreaded obligation to approve as scriptural all parts of the Prayer Book. To use it without approving it did not necessarily hurt the consciences of the more moderate, for, as one explained, to live in a house it was not necessary to approve all the principles of its architecture.[45] The godly breathed freely once more. Thereafter Whitgift required subscription only from ordinands and new in-

[43] *Seconde Parte*, I, 275–83; Strype, *Whitgift*, I, 335.

[44] Strype, *Whitgift*, I, 430–32.

[45] *Seconde Parte*, I, 235.

cumbents of livings, "wherein he found himself somthing eased
of this former troubles." Suspended ministers were generally
restored, and it was deemed safe for Cartwright to return from
the Continent. Walsingham did not keep his part of the bargain very well, for he continued to intercede for Puritans who
were still cramped by the new rule, but administrative standards once lowered are rarely raised, and Whitgift never resumed
his thorough house-cleaning. For the future he was content to
hold his own, repressing only the most violent of Puritan disturbances.

In many ways it was a wise policy. Every year that passed
added dignity to the establishment and made the Puritan idea
seem more foreign to the English scene. Attempts to institute
a Genevan discipline in isolated parishes, without sufficient authority to enforce it, rapidly developed a positively pro-Angli-
can faction among some of the laity. When a section of the
congregation were sufficiently worked up to bar the church
against their minister, who must preach to his followers in the
churchyard, it was evident that many were not anxious for the
new Jerusalem.[46] While a large proportion of these anti-Puri-
tans were doubtless merely the profane, kicking against the
pricks, people who purposely sat so that they could neither see
nor hear the preacher,[47] some were in all probability reacting
against the bare coldness of the Reformed creed and service.
The butcher who beat the Lord's servant in the street for refusing to church his wife[48] may be taken as a somewhat demon-
strative but otherwise not untypical example of these budding
high churchmen. It is not necessary to posit any moral delinquency to understand why fellow-parishioners should be scandalized by some of the Puritan protests against formalism and
superstition. The practice of sitting with covered heads during the reading of Gospel and Epistle, and taking communion
seated around a table, "one drinking as it were to another like
good fellows," are cases in point.[49] Nor were the Puritans themselves always of a kind to command respect, apart from their

[46] *Ibid.*, II, 249.   [48] *Ibid.*, p. 292.
[47] *Ibid.*, I, 239.   [49] *Ibid.*, II, 44; Harleian (Baker) MS 7033, fol. 98 [85](*v*).

type of service. Less than a third of their ministers had university degrees, in spite of their pleas for learning.[50] Not all the former tailors in the ministry were of the Anglican or neuter stripe.[51] A shocking number of nonconformists were pluralists, for all their talking, and the flesh was not always overcome. The spectacle of a professed Puritan minister doubling as the village drunkard was not unknown,[52] and one prominent leader of the faction was so careless about his table manners and personal cleanliness as to turn the stomachs of even that hardy age.[53]

So Elizabeth's policy was finally bearing fruit. By her implacable hostility to the Puritan movement she weakened its morale and in time built up an ecclesiastical faction of her own, complete with creed, form of service, party loyalty, and the respectability that comes with age. Her treatment of the religious problem is a fine illustration of the principle of dividing and ruling. How skilfully she set idealist against idealist! It may be that the Puritan attitude tended to produce the civil wars of the next century. Elizabeth's made them virtually inevitable.

[50] R. G. Usher, *Reconstruction of the English Church* (2 vols.; New York, 1910), I, 251–56.

[51] *Seconde Parte*, I, 240.

[52] *Ibid.*

[53] *Ibid.*, II, 241, 253.

CHAPTER XIV

Failure Once More: 1585-1603

WITH the administrative pressure removed, it remained to be seen whether the Puritans could make any progress with their program or whether the only alternative was a stalemate, disastrous to both parties alike. New tactics were again in order for the progressive faction. But those employed were little more than modifications of the old. It was an open secret that the Queen was the chief, if not the only, obstacle to their success. So in July, 1585, a direct assault on the royal barrier was once more attempted, in the style of Knox and Dering. This time the agent was a prominent layman, William Fuller, of Hertfordshire. Though a veteran of the Genevan exile, he had a certain entree at court for he had known Elizabeth since King Edward's time, when, as a princess at Hatfield, she had once promised to walk down by the river to visit his ailing mother. Dissatisfied with her religious policy in 1559, he had withdrawn to the country, only reappearing once in the interim to plead the Puritan cause. This time his method was to compose a written exhortation, with an introductory sweetening of suggestions of further raids on the wealth of the church. As one who had enjoyed some power during the suppression of the monasteries "without enriching of myself thereby or any of my kin or friends," he claimed to speak with authority on what the crown might gain by such an undertaking. Along with this acceptable advice he put a homily upon the Ten Commandments, with applications to the current situation in the church, such as the "foul idol, the cross" and the false witnesses who dubbed true Christians "Gehennians, precisians, Puritans and all names of heretics." Humbly but stoutly he threatened his sovereign with God's wrath if she neglected her duty as he saw it. One of the court ladies took care of the ticklish business of getting the document into Elizabeth's hands. The Queen, who five years before had listened to his exposition of his ideas on the more palatable subject but not on ecclesiastical reform, professed interest in the new book. Hope was held out for further negotiations. But the Queen was remarkably consistent where Puritans were concerned. She had not kept her promise to do the gracious thing at Hatfield a generation earlier; she did not do it now.[1]

So the Puritans fell back once more on the idea of reformation without tarrying for official sanction. But now, instead of the negative tactics of discarding surplices and omitting required ceremonies, more positive measures were taken, and in a different field. The attempt was made to set up a presbyterial system of ecclesiastical government within the framework of the established church. As we have seen, individual parishes here and there had been so organized for some time. Churchwardens and justices of the peace were transformed into a session of ruling elders by getting their co-operation in disciplinary matters, as in the Northampton order. Even where the congregations did not secure from the patrons the right of electing their own minister, the Puritan appointees did not assume office until the parishioners had ratified the choice.[2] Now the effort was made to supply these scattered units with a proper hierarchy of district, provincial, and national synods. The existing prophesyings offered a framework for such a system, though in the original Reformed plan they were kept separate from the disciplinary bodies. Under the stimulus of the struggle with Whitgift, the indefatigable Field set himself to work constructing a governmental skeleton for these amorphous bodies. By correspondence they were kept in touch with one another and brought to think of themselves as classes in a national organization, presbyteries in the modern sense of the term, though

---

[1] *The Seconde Parte of a Register*, ed. Peel (2 vols.; Cambridge, 1915), II, 49–64.

[2] Travers pled in vain with Hooker to take this course at the Temple in 1585 (John Strype, *Annals of the Reformation under Elizabeth* [4 vols. in 7; Oxford, 1824], III, i, 493).

meeting once a month or even oftener. Where no prophesyings existed Field commissioned a forward brother to organize a classis *de novo*.[3] Two or three times a year there were meetings of provincial synods to which each classis ordinarily sent two delegates. And when Parliament met, something corresponding to the Scotch General Assembly was held in London.[4] Indeed, this constitutional work doubtless owed much to the advice and encouragement offered by Melville and his fellow Scottish clerical exiles who had recently been forced across the border by the so-called "Black Acts" passed during the reaction following the failure of the ultra-Protestant Gowrie plot of 1584.

The next step was the construction of a formal discipline, a constitution set down in black and white. To this all the brethren could be expected to subscribe and conform without delay. Eventually it would become the law of the land. Various preliminary sketches were already in existence, but they were vague and incomplete.[5] The task of doing a full outline was taken in hand by Walter Travers, and, by 1586, manuscript drafts were being circulated among the party members for discussion and criticism. The work consisted of two parts, one entitled "Disciplina ecclesiae sacra Dei verbo descripta," dealing with the discipline of a particular congregation, and the other "Disciplina synodica," describing the hierarchy of classes, synods, and assembly.[6] An English translation, probably pro-

---

[3] Gellibrand to Field, January 12, 1585, in *The Presbyterian Movement in the Reign of Queen Elizabeth*, ed. Usher ("Camden Society: Third Series," Vol. VIII [London, 1905]), p. 8.

For a more detailed treatment of the classis movement see Edna Bibby, "The Puritan Classical Movement of Elizabeth's Reign" (Manchester University dissertation [1929]).

[4] Richard Bancroft, *Dangerous Positions* (London, 1593), largely reprinted in *The Presbyterian Movement*, pp. 1–21.

[5] For one by T. W. (probably Thomas Wilcox) see *A Parte of a Register* ([Middelburg?], 1593), pp. 68–72.

[6] George Andrews ("History of the Puritan Discipline, 1554-1593" [Washington University dissertation (St. Louis, 1932)], pp. 175-79, 192) has compared this volume with French and Scotch parallels without finding any evidence of detailed copying. His conclusion is that all drew on Geneva, with adaptations suitable to the particular environment. Gordon Donaldson, however, has shown very clearly ("The Relations between the English and Scottish Presbyterian Movements to 1604" [London Uni-

vided by Cartwright, was also sent around.[7] This Discipline must not be confused, as it too often is, with the author's volume on the subject composed a decade earlier, which bears a similar name. That was an argumentative exposition of the Puritan theory of church government, a treatise, in all its different forms, of well over a hundred pages. This was a simple description only, intended to serve as the law of the English Puritan church, and the two parts together fill less than a dozen printed pages.[8] The most interesting difference between the two works for our purposes is the somewhat more democratic tone of the later document. In 1574, Travers, not so liberal on this point as Cartwright, had frankly stated that the government of the church should be an aristocracy, in which "a few of the best do bear the rule." Or it might even be called a theocracy, seeing the officials had no authority to do anything but by the word and commandment of God. Certainly the rights of the congregation were to be practically negligible, once the officers were elected. While the main outlines of the oligarchical scheme remain the same in the 1584 code, it was definitely provided that "in all the greater affairs of the church, as in excommunicating of any and in choosing and deposing of church ministers, nothing may be concluded without the knowledge and consent of the church."[9] The initiative still remained with the officers, but the rank and file now enjoyed at least a theoretical right of veto. The fact that Puritanism was gaining more of a hold on the middle than on the upper class doubtless had something to do with this shift of emphasis in Travers' writing.

Closely related to this constitutional activity was the Puritan

---

versity dissertation (1938)], esp. p. 155) that at this time, as at most other crucial ones in the history of Elizabethan Puritanism, Field and his associates were in close touch with their Scotch friends.

[7] Printed in 1644 under the title *A Directory of Church Government Anciently Contended For.*

[8] Daniel Neal, *History of the Puritans* (3 vols.; London, 1837), III, 491–501. The English version is also reprinted by P. Lorimer in facsimile (London, 1872). Pearson (*Der älteste Englische Presbyterianismus* [Edinburgh, 1912], pp. 80–95) and Paget (*Introduction to the Fifth Book of Hooker's Ecclesiastical Polity* [Oxford, 1899], pp. 238–51) print the Latin.

[9] *A Full and Plaine Declaration of Ecclesiasticall Discipline* (*s.l.*, 1574), p. 177; Neal, *op. cit.*, p. 492.

effort to provide an acceptable substitute for the Elizabethan Prayer Book, and to stimulate spiritual life in individual parishes. As early as 1578 the London printer Barker issued an edition of the Bible with a "Form of Common Prayer" appended, from which the term "priest" and the orders of private baptism, confirmation, and churching of women were omitted.[10] Six years later the Puritan printer issued a modification of the Geneva Prayer Book, or Book of Common Order, sometimes known as Knox's Liturgy.[11] This was the "book" of the "bill and the book," which was presented to Parliament in 1585 and again in 1587 and 1589. Though many have confused it with the Book of Discipline, it was a distinct work. But since it also provides directions for the appointment of pastors and doctors, elders and deacons, and implies the existence of lesser and greater conferences, the confusion is pardonable. This book went so far as to permit laymen to join in the prophesyings if the elders consented, though in a second edition published two years later at Middelburg[12] this privilege was explained as a means of training men for the ministry, perhaps to meet Anglican criticism. But whatever democratic trends might appear in the movement, the disciplinary ideal was retained. Provision was made for regular examination and correction, not only of ordinary laity but of the elders and clergy as well.

While the shadow Prayer Book was being circulated, an attempt was made to quicken the religious interests of the laity by means which supplemented the ordinary services. Puritan ministers developed the habit of ordaining public fasts. These were times of abstinence, but this physical privation was not esteemed an end in itself. Rather it served to call people to serious thinking and attendance upon an extra sermon or lecture. Neighboring clergy frequently joined in the public exercises on such an occasion. Less obtrusive but equally effective was the custom of small groups of earnest believers meeting in

[10] *Short Title Catalogue*, No. 2123; Thomas Lathbury, *History of Convocation* (London, 1853), pp. 188–89.

[11] Reprinted in *Fragmenta liturgica*, ed. Hall (7 vols.; Bath, 1848), Vol. I.

[12] Reprinted in *Reliquiae liturgicae*, ed. Hall (5 vols.; Bath, 1847), Vol. I; Andrews, *op. cit.*, pp. 216–20.

private homes for prayer, conference, and mutual "whetting on," after the manner of the ministerial prophesyings. There was nothing separatist about most of these gatherings, for the clergy of the established church were frequently present at them, and the adherents also attended the public services of the official body. This kind of group was simply an ecclesiola, or inner church, the forerunner of the modern prayer-meeting.[13]

In the Puritans' opinion none of these undertakings involved any illegal actions. They realized the danger of misinterpretation, and acted secretly, even to the extent of emasculating their classes and higher assemblies by excluding what should have been an important element, the lay elders. But they made a studious effort to keep within the letter of the law. Legal counsel was frequently taken and carefully followed. Their associations were free and voluntary, and members were not bound to accept decisions made by the various bodies. In fact, there were no definite rulings, only advisory statements; no appeals to higher tribunals, only requests for opinions. Subscription to the Discipline was only an expression of a desire that it be established, a promise to work to that end by all lawful means, and a declaration of intent to be guided by it so far as the laws of the land and the peace of the church would allow.[14] Nothing violent was undertaken or contemplated.

Such quiet, informal activities advanced the cause considerably. Tattered diary pages tell the real story much better than the stilted phrases of the official minutes of Puritan conferences. In the formal record the attendants often appear as perennially resolving, advising, and discussing. In the personal records they are exhorting, praying, and conferring, supplying the isolated country minister with the inspiration to carry him through the next few weeks. Going and coming, and in the intervals between, the Puritan minister was instant, in season and out of season. Firm reasoning with a flat atheist at the inn; a word of exhortation to the chance traveler on the way; yes, a friendly greeting to a known "enemy of the truth"—all these propaganda devices were employed, and not without some success.

[13] See my *Two Elizabethan Puritan Diaries* (Chicago, 1933), esp. pp. 26–27, 67.
[14] *The Presbyterian Movement*, pp. xxi–xxiii; Neal, *op. cit.*, p. 501.

But the objective remained a national one, and to reach it some activities of a more public sort were needed. The persuasive powers of the printed page were tried again. In London, Robert Waldegrave was willing to print for the party, with or without the sanction of the licensing authorities. A Star Chamber decree of June 23, 1586, greatly tightened the regulations and made his task more difficult. But at Middelburg in Zealand an English-speaking printer named Richard Schilders was now established, and he afforded a convenient means of production for volumes which could not be legally produced at home.[15] In 1584, Waldegrave had issued an anonymous *Dialogue concerning the Strife of Our Church*, which contained some hundred and fifty pages of Puritan indictment of the establishment.[16] In the same year Dr. Richard Cosin, dean of the Arches, published *An Answer* to "The Abstracte" in which he pointed out, among other things, that many laws became obsolete and that not all could be observed to the letter. Therefore, the bishops should not be attacked on narrow legal grounds. For this work a *Counter-Poyson* was immediately prepared by a brilliant young Cambridge Puritan named Dudley Fenner, now beneficed at Cranbrook in Kent. While reaffirming the Puritan conviction that the substance of their system of church government was laid down in the Bible, he admitted that there was a vagueness about the details:

Although every particular rite and order which are variable according to circumstance be not so particularly mentioned, yet are they by certain general rules so limited and prescribed that no church can use them at their pleasure, but ought to frame them within the bounds set unto them of God.

The popular election of church ministers he defended by the old device of pointing out that the Anglican system was practically the same as the Roman Catholic.[17]

[15] J. Dover Wilson, "Richard Schilders and the English Puritans," *Transactions of he Bibliographical Society*, London, XI (1909–11), 65–134.

[16] *Short Title Catalogue*, No. 6801, where the volumes in the Harmsworth and Huntington libraries are the only ones noted. There are three copies at Lambeth Palace.

[17] Pp. 8–9 and 26–28. There was a reply to this work in a sermon at Paul's Cross, and a Puritan *Defence of the Reasons of the Counter-Poyson* was published in 1586. It was probably not by Fenner, as generally stated. See its epistle, "To the Christian Reader."

A still more important exchange was brought about by John Field. He had in his possession a treatise which William Fulke, the anti-Catholic writer, had composed eleven years before during the *Admonition* controversy, but which had been withheld from publication as too dangerous for that time.[18] In 1584 he had put it to press under the title of *A Briefe and Plain Declaration*, though it is more commonly known by its running headline, *A Learned Discourse of Ecclesiastical Government*. The writer, like many another tiring radical, was now a conforming Anglican, but respect for the author's rights in such cases was as yet undeveloped. John Bridges, Dean of Salisbury, answered this work in 1587 with an effort of fourteen hundred pages entitled *A Defence of the Government Established*, which was better tempered and more fair-minded than is commonly suggested. The author had a sense of humor, and he admitted that there was some good in the opposition party. Since the Puritans were now ready to grant that some variation from the New Testament standards of church government was necessary, the whole dispute became one as to the degree of difference permissible, and Bridges preferred to leave that to the prince, his lawful sovereign, whose duty it was to supervise in such matters. While a more crushing reply was in the making, Travers and Fenner put out rejoinders.[19] Fenner had fallen a victim to Whitgift's articles and removed to Middelburg as successor to Cartwright in the English church of that town, where for the few months before his untimely death he was fortunate enough to have Schilder's press at his elbow.

As always, Parliament was the chief hope, though gestures were still made in Convocation,[20] and for the 1586–87 session the Puritans made the most elaborate preparations. Draft bills were drawn up for presentation to Parliament and Convoca-

[18] Tomson to Gilby, May 1, 1572, Baker XXXII (Cambridge University MS Mm. i. 43), fol. 444, printed in A. F. Scott Pearson, *Thomas Cartwright and Elizabethan Puritanism* (London, 1925), p. 83; cf. *ibid.*, p. 273.

[19] Walter Travers, *A Defence of the Ecclesiastical Discipline (s.l.,* 1588); Dudley Fenner, *A Defence of the Godlie Ministers* ([Middelburg], 1587); reprinted in *A Parte of a Register*, pp. 387–93.

[20] *Seconde Parte*, I, 296–303; II, 85.

tion,[21] and the number of petitions sent in far exceeded all previous records. The burden of the complaint was that reform should now be undertaken because the realm was no longer in great danger. In any case, reform would make possible a united front against the Catholics. Let a free disputation be held so the truth might appear, or at least make the bishops agree on an interpretation of the Prayer Book so that subscribers may know what their signature involves. London and the east counties were represented among the petitioners, as usual, but Cornishmen are also found lamenting that the "silly sheep" were starving in their county. Members of Cambridge University protested against the pluralists and ignorant who kept them unemployed.[22] These general grievances had been aired often enough before, but now they were reinforced by something more than the mere weight of numerous signatures. Encouraged by the conciliar indorsement of the Essex survey of 1585, the Puritans enlarged their statistical service to cover a large part of southern England.[23] By characterizing the incumbent and describing the services performed in each parish, they hoped to impress the High Court with the desperate condition of the church. Nonpreachers, nonresidents, pluralists, and ignorant were identified by name. According to the Puritans, bankrupts, idiots, and adulterers were holding positions as the official moral leaders of the people. This incumbent is "scarce able to read," that one suspected of conjuring, another a drunkard laden with three benefices. Of the livings in some twenty-five hundred parishes less than a fifth are held by "painful preachers." In spite of the obvious bias of the work, it was an impressive indictment, as well as a valuable mine for the social historian. As a further means of influencing Parliament, it was arranged that a general conference, or national synod, should meet in London during the session, to press for reform.

These extensive preparations testify to the strength of the Puritan movement in the latter half of the 1580's, when the

---

[21] *Ibid.*, I, 304–11; II, 1–4, 196–98, 212–18.

[22] *Ibid.*, II, 70–87, 174–92, esp. pp. 175 and 186.

[23] Eleven counties and the city of London are represented (*ibid.*, pp. 88–184).

assassination of William of Orange and the approach of war with Spain made everyone acutely conscious of the Catholic menace. The mass of data accumulated in the ecclesiastical census, which covered more than a quarter of the parishes in the country at a time when fact-gathering was not easy, is in itself a testimony to the widespread interest in the cause of advanced Protestantism. A rough survey of the London clergy, made about this time[24] by a hostile observer, confirms the Puritan claim that nearly half the clergy in the metropolis were of their persuasion. While among them were numbered such dubious assets as "the blindman in Ironmonger Lane," a one-eyed lecturer, and "the reader at St. Mary Ovaries with the wooden leg," there were others such as "Mr. [Henry] Smith without Temple Bar" and Mr. Egerton, who were to be powers in the land for a few years at least.

But in spite of the widespread interest in the Puritan cause the results did not justify the effort involved in these extensive preparations. The first weeks of the session were taken up with the case of the Queen of Scots, and after her execution nothing constructive could be accomplished. On February 27, Sir Anthony Cope, who sat for Banbury—in which delightful district he was collecting a fine assortment of Puritan ministers, including John Dod—reintroduced the bill and the book, the bill in this draft calling for the abolition of lord bishops and the substitution of a synodical form of government for the church. He was supported by other members, from Sussex, Yorkshire, and Derbyshire. But the Anglicans were on guard. One of Whitgift's chaplains, Richard Bancroft, had been writing speeches on the matter for Sir Christopher Hatton to deliver in the lower house. Dalton as usual added his voice in the negative, and the Speaker managed to block progress until the Queen could send her customary demand for the offending documents. Peter Wentworth made his protest against this infringement of

---

[24] State Papers, Domestic, Elizabeth, XCIII, 8 (*Calendar, 1547–1580*, p. 470, where it is placed under the year 1573). This document can be dated at approximately the end of 1587. Barrow, who was first arrested in that year, is mentioned as being in the Fleet. Smith became lecturer at St. Clement Danes in 1587, and Field, who is mentioned, died in March, 1588.

the liberties of the House in due form and duly went to the Tower, along with Cope and his three vocal supporters. On March 4 there was a chirp of protest from Sir John Higham, who represented Suffolk, but Hatton silenced it with a reference to the Queen, and the inglorious transition from high hopes to bitter disappointment had been made once more.[25]

To add to the Puritans' difficulties, Field and Leicester died the following year, in March and September, respectively. Vacillating Leicester's value to the party probably has been exaggerated by the historians, but Field was the organizer, propagandist, and party secretary all in one. His papers long served his associates as a quarry for further literary efforts, but he could not bequeath his executive ability. Even had he lived, however, it is questionable whether he would have been able to hold his followers together, for the internal divisions in the party were already threatening the collapse of the whole movement. As early as August, 1584, Chapman, the leader of the Dedham classis, had begun to advocate a moderate course. He moved, "Whether it were....good that a reconcilation should be offered to the bishops: that since we profess one God and preach one doctrine we may join together with better consent to built up the church." Though he was outvoted, he again expressed his disapproval of both sides "for their hot and violent manner of proceeding," this time in a letter to Cartwright a few months later.[26] In 1587, when Travers' draft of the Discipline began to be circulated among the classes for adoption and subscription, it soon became evident that there was a difference of opinion on two vital points: the harmony of the Discipline and scripture, and whether it might be used without danger to the peace of the church.[27] General synods were held at Cambridge in September, 1587, in Warwickshire, probably at Cov-

[25] *Seconde Parte*, II, 212–18; Sir Simonds D'Ewes, *A Compleat Journal of Votes Speeches and Debates . . . . throughout the Whole Reign of Queen Elizabeth* (London, 1693), p. 410; Strype, *The Life and Acts of John Whitgift* (3 vols.; Oxford, 1822), I, 490; III, 186–94; State Papers, Domestic, Elizabeth, CXCIX, 1–2 (*Calendar, 1581–90*, p. 392).

[26] *The Presbyterian Movement*, pp. 37 and 81.

[27] Strype, *Whitgift*, I, 502–3; *Annals*, III, i, 692, ii, 477–79.

entry in April, 1588, and again at Cambridge during the Stour-bridge Fair, September, 1589. In these the only unanimity that seems to have been reached was on the soundness of the general scheme.[28] But there was no agreement on the tactics to be employed in securing its establishment. Some were for securing adherents as rapidly as possible, until the system could be in-stalled in certain areas in all its binding force, law or no law. But Cartwright and his group insisted on waiting for the magis-trate. To them the whole scheme represented merely a clarifi-cation of aims, a goal to be sought by legal means. Without their support it was impossible to carry out the more vigorous program, and the effort was not made. The whole movement collapsed for lack of internal agreement, and the majority of classis members never signed the Discipline.[29] The hopelessness of securing power had once more destroyed party unity.

With Field's controlling hand removed, the party organiza-tion rapidly went to pieces. As in 1573, the extremist element, left to its own devices, soon ruined all remaining chances by the violence of their tactics. John Udall, the lecturer at King-ston; Giles Wigginton, Vicar of Sedbergh, Yorkshire; and John Penry,[30] a young Welshman of good family, recently down from Oxford, had all suffered at the hands of the ecclesiastical au-thorities for their religious zeal. Impatient of delay, they pub-lished fiery tracts with Waldegrave's assistance.[31] The authori-

[28] Bancroft, *A Survay of the Pretended Holy Discipline* (London, 1593), p. 68. In the subscriptions published by Neal and Usher (*Presbyterian Movement*, pp. 92–93) the "few points excepted" of the first form have disappeared, which indicates more of an agreement on basic principles than has generally been believed.

[29] Strype, *Whitgift*, II, 83; Pearson, *Cartwright*, p. 333.

[30] For the career of Penry see William Pierce, *John Penry: His Life, Times, and Writings* (London, 1923). One of Penry's notebooks, containing a diary for December and January 1592/3 and some letters, is Ellesmere MS 483 in the Huntington Library. A photostatic reproduction is in the National Library of Wales, Aberystwyth. It de-serves editing. Especially noteworthy is Penry's explicit denial (fol. 47) that either he or Throckmorton was "Martin Marprelate," and the assertion that both disapproved of the tracts.

[31] Udall, *The State of the Church of Englande Laide Open in a Conference betweene Dio-trephes, a Byshop, Tertullus, a Papist, etc.* (1588); *A Demonstration of the Trueth of That Discipline* (1588); Penry, *An Exhortation unto the Governours and People of Wales* (1588). His *Treatise Containing the Aequity of an Humble Supplication* (1587), and his *Defence* (1588) were from other presses.

ties succeeded in destroying the London press, but a wealthy widow[32] provided and sheltered a new one. For nearly a year this evaded detection, largely by frequent moves. Starting from Udall's town of Kingston, near London, it soon reached North-hamptonshire, and there a new author was secured, probably by Penry who had married the daughter of a prominent citizen of the county town. The available evidence as to the identity of this recruit is more than a little confusing and contradictory, but in the main it points to Job Throckmorton, a wealthy country gentleman of the neighborhood, and one of the parliamentary champions of the Puritan bill of 1572. The identity of the author, however, is not of primary importance for us. All that matters is that from the press there now poured forth the bitter, taunting jests of "Martin Marprelate, Gent." When the peripatetic months of mysterious men in green and manuscripts providentially found in pathways were ended, and the printers were at length in custody, Dr. Bridges of the fourteen hundred pages had been demolished and several bishops badly singed. But Whitgift was virtually untouched, the Queen was only angered, and the Puritan party more divided than ever. Cartwright, who was well splattered by the hacks Bancroft hired to answer the Puritan fusilade, repudiated the whole proceedings. Halfway through the series it was necessary to change printers because Waldegrave learned of this stand taken by the party leaders and refused to continue. At Cambridge, Greenham expressed the sober judgment of the great majority of the party when he said that Martin was to be censured because he made sin ridiculous when it ought to be made odious.[33]

The political situation also boded ill for the Puritan chances. With the defeat of the Armada in the summer of 1588, the gravest stage of the Catholic crisis passed, and attention could

---

[32] Elizabeth Crane. Not the relict of the preacher, Nicholas Crane, as often said, but the widow of a prominent courtier (see Julia Norton McCorkle, "A Note concerning Mistress Crane and the Martin Marprelate Controversy," *Library*, XII [4th ser.,1931–32], 276–83).

[33] Samuel Clarke, *General Martyrologie to Which Is Attached Lives of Sundry Modern English Divines* (London, 1677), p. 13 of *Lives*. For the entire controversy see William Pierce, *An Historical Introduction to the Marprelate Tracts* (London, 1908), and his collected edition of the literature, *The Marprelate Tracts* (London, 1911).

once more be given to the thunder on the left. More serious still, with the collapse of the Catholic bogeyman there was no longer any reason for pampering the Puritans as a supposed counterpoise. In Bancroft, who was rising to prominence as chaplain to both Whitgift and Hatton, the Archbishop found the ideal agent of repression. What Walsingham was to Catholic plotters the busy cleric was to the Puritans. In some way he obtained many of Field's important papers, including those dealing with the classis movement and the Discipline. In a sermon delivered at Paul's Cross, February 9, 1589, during Parliament and at the height of the Marprelate excitement, he exposed the whole disciplinarian scheme and attacked it as both unscriptural and treasonable.[34] At the end of the year Udall, who with the help of the Earl of Huntingdon had recently secured a preaching post in Newcastle, was arrested and charged with the publication of the "seditious" *Conference* and *Demonstration*. He was convicted and sentenced to death, but the execution was deferred, and after two years in prison he was pardoned on condition that he go to Syria as minister to the Turkey Company merchants there. His health had been undermined by his ordeal, however, and he died shortly afterward, before taking ship. During 1590, Cartwright and the leaders of the classis movement, except Travers and Gellibrand, were also taken into custody. Some kept their previous agreement not to "appeach" one another in case of arrest, but Johnson, one of the members of the Northampton group, talked freely, and ample evidence was easily secured. Nevertheless, convictions could not be obtained because of the carefulness of the Puritans in keeping within the letter of the law.[35] By refusing to take the ex officio oath,[36] Cartwright blocked the proceedings before the ecclesiastical commissioners for some months. Eventually he and eight others, including Fenn, Wright, and Snape, were tried

---

[34] *A Sermon Preached at Paules Crosse* (London, 1589); reprinted in George Hickes, *Bibliotheca scriptorum ecclesiae Anglicanae* (London, 1709), pp. 247-315.

[35] Strype, *Whitgift*, II, 84.

[36] There is a justification of this stand, possibly drawn up by Cartwright in Historical Manuscripts Commission, *Hastings*, I (1928), 432-46.

before the Star Chamber. Again the trial was indecisive, and in the spring of 1592 the defendants were released.

The collapse of the classis movement and the silencing of Marprelate's jeers marked the end of vigorous activity by the bulk of the Puritan party in Elizabeth's time. Only sporadic efforts were made after these disasters. The reaction to the Marprelate thrusts paralyzed nearly all parliamentary movements during the session of 1588-89, though bills against pluralism and nonresidency were introduced. In July, 1591, the party was further discredited by the conspiracy of three semi-insane extremists, Copinger, Arthington, and Hacket, which had for its object the overthrow of the existing church government, the reform of the Queen and Council, and the release of the Puritan prisoners. In Cheapside, Hacket was publicly proclaimed the Messiah by his two supporters and, as a result, was shortly hanged for treason. While not directly involved, Cartwright and other prominent Puritans were acquainted with one or more of the conspirators and were accordingly put under a cloud by the preposterous debacle.[37]

Only here and there were signs of life apparent. Just as their world began to collapse around them in February, 1589, some of the London ministers ventured on the bold step of sending advice to Drake and Norris on the conduct of their expedition to Lisbon in behalf of Don Antonio, the Portuguese pretender. They strongly expressed their disapproval of giving aid to Catholics, who were rather to be subdued and converted than supported. Because the sea dogs were under orders and the bishops, who, in the opinion of the writers, should have expressed the Protestant view, had not done so, the Puritans consented to the departure of the expedition, but only on stringent conditions. Antonio was to be forced to accept the true religion or else give liberty to the gospel in his land. The admirals were to keep in mind the main end of English operations in that quarter which should be to secure a base for a future attack on the Pope, "for the refreshing of your navy and people when you should pass into the Levant seas to rouse out that Romish Antichrist."

[37] Richard Cosin, *Conspiracie for Pretended Reformation* (London, 1592).

They must also remember on their return to urge the Queen to press forward with the reform of the church.[38] In 1589, Sir Francis Knollys, back to the wars and fortified with a little expert advice from John Rainolds, or Reynolds, a Puritan fellow of Corpus Christi College, Oxford, undertook in a speech in Parliament to convict Bancroft of treasonable utterance in his recent sermon at the Cross, as he had charged Whitgift with a similar offense five years before. Twisting some of the Anglican champion's words with rather more than reasonable force, he fathered on him the doctrine of *iure divino* episcopacy, the assertion that the Bible prescribed ecclesiastical government by bishops as an absolute requirement in the church and therefore those officials held their office independent of the Queen's will.[39] In private correspondence with Burghley and Whitgift he pressed home this point and also an attack on the lordliness of bishops in general, until the Queen's displeasure forced him to desist.[40] Penry, safe for the time being in Edinburgh, where Waldegrave was now the king's printer, also joined in the assault on Bancroft and defended the good name of the Puritans in three works published in 1590.[41] Anonymous authors on the same side contributed *An Humble Motion* and *A Petition Directed to Her Most Excellent Majestie* at about the same time. Somewhat more important was the work of James Morice, attorney of the Court of Wards and a civil servant of the Beale type, who drew up a *Briefe Treatise of Oaths*, which stated

[38] Cambridge University MS Hh. VI. 10, esp. fols. 56–58.

[39] Printed in *Informations . . . . Seconded with D. Reynolds His Letter to F. Knollys and Sir F. Knollys His Speech in Parliament* (s.l., 1608).

[40] Strype, *Whitgift*, I, 597–601; II, 52–55. For a more detailed account of this incident see R. G. Usher, "The Supposed Origin of the Doctrine of the Divine Right of Bishops," *Mélanges d'histoire offerts à M. Charles Bémont* (Paris, 1913), pp. 539–47. Gordon Donaldson (*op. cit.*, pp. 201–41) gives the Scotch side of this story, together with a document (Appen. H of his work, transcribed from National Library of Scotland MS 6. 1. 13, fols. 46–53) containing an apology extorted from Bancroft.

[41] *A Briefe Discovery of the Untruthes . . . . Contained in a Sermon . . . . by D. Bancroft* (1590); *The State of the Church of England* (1590); *A Treatise Wherein Is Manifestlie Proved That Reformation and Those That Favor the Same Are Unjustly Charged To Be Enemies unto Hir Majestie* (1590).

the common-law case against the ex officio procedure.[42] In the Parliament of 1592–93 he introduced bills against the ex officio oath and against enforced subscriptions, but the effort again came to nothing. For Elizabeth intervened once more, and the bold attorney suffered a two-month term of imprisonment.[43]

This session of Parliament was in fact, marked by the passage of a strong bill against separatist Puritans which signalized a general rout of the party all along the line. Francis Bacon's mother believed that God would certainly punish those who stayed the hands of such able laborers in the Lord's vineyard,[44] but many of these workers perforce laid down their tools at this time. The Chester prophesyings, which had enjoyed the conciliar blessing and had outlasted Bancroft's exposure by four years and the Dedham classis by two, came to an end in 1593.[45] In London the visitors at Christ's Hospital were ordered to replace the preachers there with the singing priests which the statutes of the foundation required.[46]

Meanwhile the apologists for the establishment were pouring out an overwhelming torrent of anti-Puritan literature. In 1590 a courtier named Anthony Marten published *A Reconciliation of All the Pastors and Cleurgy of the Church of England*. After the anonymous *Remonstrance* "to the Factious and Turbulent T.C., W.T., J.P. and to the Rest of That Anarchicall, Disordered Alphabet" in the same year, Matthew Sutcliffe, Dean

---

[42] *S.l.*, n.d. British Museum Press Mark C. 30. 517. Mary Hume (Maguire) ("The History of the *Ex Officio* Oath in England" [Radcliffe College dissertation (1923)], p. 97 n.) gives good reasons for dating this either 1591 or 1592.

[43] It should be noted, however, that the royal severity in this case is partly to be explained by the fact that Morice was involved in Peter Wentworth's contemporary effort to raise the succession question in Parliament. Mary Hume (Maguire), *ibid.*, pp. 276–318, transcribes from Baker MS XL (Cambridge University MS Mm. I. 51), pp. 105–34, Morice's own account of these events, with the texts of the original bills. Cf. D'Ewes, *op. cit.*, p. 474.

[44] Lady Bacon to Ambrose Bacon, May 17, 1592, Bacon Papers, Lambeth Palace MS 648, fol. 103.

[45] Gonville and Caius College, Cambridge MS (Moore) 197, fol. 184.

[46] *Analytical Index to the . . . . Remembrancia . . . . of the City of London* (London, 1878), p. 131.

of Exeter, entered the lists with a solid tome, *De presbyterio*, and a more popular and satirical *Treatise of Ecclesiastical Displine*, which came out the next year. In 1592 he replied to the *Petition* in *An Answere to a Certaine Libel Supplicatorie*. In his works he had a keen eye for Puritan disagreements over the terms of the Discipline, and inconsistency in the matter of their own nonresidence. He defended the Queen's prerogative and heaped scorn on his adversaries who "abase the prince under the becks of a pack of clowns and clouters [patchers, cobblers] called church aldermen." Well might they go in russet cloaks, for their religion was a russet religion.[47] Richard Cosin defended the ecclesiastical courts and the use of the ex officio oath.[48] In 1593 there were two contributions by Thomas Bilson,[49] who in 1585 had ingeniously managed to prove that it was right for the English, who might not rebel at home, to aid the Dutch in their revolt.[50] He demonstrated to his own satisfaction, at least, that the New Testament church government ripened naturally into episcopacy, that the head should be preferred to the feet in an election, that advowsons went back to hoary antiquity when freemen were scarce, and that it was preposterous for a "few curious heads" to seek to overthrow an ancient law.[51] In the same year Bancroft himself put forth two damaging works, *A Survay of the Pretended Holy Discipline* and his *Dangerous Positions*, in which he made public the results of his detective work and some other less exciting research, of which the drift was that Puritanism meant anarchy. Finally, in 1594 and 1597, Hooker published his great *Laws of Ecclesiastical Polity*. Here the refrain was one of sweet reasonableness.

[47] *Answere*, pp. 97 and 130 (108).

[48] *An Apologie of and for Sundrie Proceedings by Jurisdiction Ecclesiasticall* (London, 1591).

[49] *The Perpetual Government of Christes Church*, ed. Eden (reprinted; Oxford, 1842); *A Compendious Discourse Proving Episcopacy To Be of Divine Institution.* I have not seen the second work, which is noted in the *Short Title Catalogue* as existing in the Harmsworth Library only. It is possible that it is another version or edition of the *Perpetual Government*.

[50] *The True Difference between Christian Subjection and Unchristian Rebellion* (Oxford, 1585).

[51] *Perpetual Government* (1842), pp. 448 and 472.

Granted that there were some abuses in the establishment, there were also great possibilities. Reason must be used to supplement scripture as an authority, and by its light one could perceive the utility of bishops, ceremonies, the royal control of the church, and many other things to which the Puritans objected. While he tended rather indulgently to gloss over serious shortcomings in the current establishment, the soundness of his logic on the particular theological points at issue has never been successfully challenged.

To all these works the Puritans could only make a half-hearted response. Most of the copies of the first part of the great *Register*, which was to be the Puritans' Book of Martyrs, were seized as they came into England from Middelburg in 1593, and the other half was never printed.[52] Throckmorton and Cartwright put out defenses[53] of their own personal conduct; but, in spite of Sutcliffe's taunts, they would not join issue on the theoretical principles involved. Morice drew up a long reply to Cosin's treatise on the ex officio oath, but it was never printed.[54] The only reply to Hooker was *A Christian Letter of Certaine English Protestants* published in 1599, charging the Anglican champion with the high crimes and misdemeanors of attacking Calvin, teaching the doctrine of free will, allowing the light of nature, and not writing in as simple a style as the fathers of the church such as Ridley and Cranmer. So the last word in the battle begun by Field and Wilcox and carried on by Whitgift and Cartwright, Bridges, and "Marprelate" went to the Anglicans. In 1595 the great "T. C." retired to Guernsey and, after the publication of his *Apologie* in the following year, wrote no more. The Puritans' guns were silenced, and their triumphant adversaries were everywhere on the alert to repress any further disorders. Even the Archbishop of York could not

---

[52] *Seconde Parte*, I, 11–12; Wilson, *op. cit.*, pp. 85–88.

[53] *The Defence of Job Throckmorton* (*s.l.*, 1594); *A Briefe Apologie of Thomas Cartwright* ([Middelburg], 1596). Sutcliffe replied in *An Answere to a Certain Calumnious Letter Published by M. Job Throckmorton* (London, 1595), and *The Examination of M. Thomas Cartwright's Late Apologie* (London, 1596).

[54] "A Just and Necessarie Defence of a Brief Treatise Made against General Oaths Exacted by Ordinaries and Judges Ecclesiastical," Lambeth Palace MS 234.

use a phrase with a hint of Puritanism about it without drawing a rebuke.[55] One of Field's sons was now gaining fame as an actor, and, if the father's mantle had fallen on any of his former associates, it was not apparent as the 1590's waned and England took up the long death watch on her Queen.

[55] "In one of the letters [to the Council] there was put Christ's-tide for Christmas, which because of the novelty thereof (being lately only used by some nice persons more curious in terms than in deeds) was by some of your best friends misliked, and I marvel how it escaped you, being so far from following such novelties" (Whitgift to Hutton, May 2, 1597, Lambeth MS 1138, No. 3).

CHAPTER XV

Separatism

THE Elizabethan Puritan political program, as we have seen, was to agitate for further reform in the church without overstepping the limits of passive resistance. Most of the party further restricted their activities to the bounds set by the constitution of the established church, refusing to set up any rival organization. But passive resistance was compatible with a somewhat more vigorous policy, and from the time of the first serious break with the Queen there were seldom lacking a few ardent radicals who were willing to form conventicles with a separate and distinct ecclesiastical machinery. The lingering medieval horror of sects and the ill repute of the Continental Anabaptists, who had adopted this form of church government, hindered such activities. But a kind of specious logic favored them. If it was sound policy to withdraw from the corrupt Roman communion, why not from the corrupt Anglican one? If it was pointed out that the established church was orthodox in doctrine and possessed of valid sacraments, it could be answered that the Roman Catholic's baptism and much of his creed were also accepted by the Puritans. It took considerable skill to explain how the moderates could refuse to wear the required surplice because it was the uniform of Antichrist and yet insist on being considered a member of the established army whose badge it was. It is not surprising that some enthusiasts considered these defenses mere cowardly hairsplitting, and were too impatient to hear them to the end.

The London conventicles survived the persecutions and internal dissensions of Grindal's episcopate and lingered on to trouble Sandys after 1570. Under the leadership of a minister named Richard Fitz, the Separatists set up an organization with a covenant, an elder, and a deacon. Part of the covenant was identical with passages used by the earlier London congregation and already quoted.[1] The elder was John Bolton, a veteran of the Geneva congregation during the Marian exile. But he was shortly convinced of the error of his new ways. He recanted at Paul's Cross and presently hanged himself in remorse for "judging and condemning a part of Christ's church," thus furnishing the opponents of the movement with a horrible example of the evils of independency which they did not soon forget. But others carried on, and went to prison for their beliefs. Two of them, named Sparrow and King, along with John Browne appeared before the Council during the investigation which followed the Birchet incident in 1573. They were threatened with banishment if they persisted in their opinions, but the threat was not carried out, and the congregation, of which they were joint leaders, maintained its existence.[2]

There were also other groups. In 1572, Bonham and Crane, who had worried Grindal, were active in setting up the separatist church south of the Thames which has come down in history as the Wandsworth presbytery.[3] This was a moderate group, for its leaders were frequently associated later on with Cartwrightian Puritans. There were evidently many divisions within divisions and many degrees of separatism, as evidenced by the many differences of opinion on the perennial question of attending services in the established church. Fitz is unmentioned after the 1570's, and Browne disappears from the story after 1574, when an attempt was made to implicate him in the Undertree plot. But the movement persisted, for in January, 1581, a member named John Nashe, who was in prison, sent a petition to Convocation listing nine comrades whom the bishops had persecuted "to the death." Furthermore, in the next month a similar petition from one William Drewett quotes

[1] P. 212.

[2] Albert Peel, *The First Congregational Churches* (Cambridge, 1920), pp. 31–44.

[3] *Ibid.*, pp. 12, 35, 46; A. F. Scott Pearson, *Thomas Cartwright and Elizabethan Puritanism* (London, 1925), pp. 75–80; Richard Bancroft, *Dangerous Positions* (London, 1593), p. 67 (43).

again the now familiar covenant.[4] There were also conventicles in Gloucester and Northampton.[5] But throughout this period all separatist activities are of a fugitive and temporary character. Though an occasional congregation is equipped with a fully developed constitution, on the whole the movement was merely a fleeting release for reforming zeal, designed, if there was any plan at all, to give way to the thoroughly purged state church when the long-awaited day of victory should come.

Much the same observation can even be made about the attitude of the next leader to appear, the well-known Robert Browne,[6] not to be confused with the John Browne already mentioned. It is true that Robert Browne dignified his separation with rather more theoretical rationalization than his predecessors employed, but he too looked forward to the day when the magistrate should support and defend his system against all adversaries. Browne added to his flair for pamphleteering the further advantages of good birth and a university education. He hailed from Rutlandshire and, like most scions of county families in that tiny domain of the Cecils, was related to Burghley. After taking a B.A. from Cambridge, where he was a member of Corpus Christi College, he spent some time as a schoolmaster. While so engaged, he developed ideas of extreme Puritanism and eventually lost his school as a result. After a short stay at home he returned to Cambridge in January, 1579, and attached himself as a divinity student to the household of Richard Greenham in near-by Dry Drayton. At Benet Church, Cambridge, he preached without license, having decided that the bishops, as false teachers, had no right to approve the true ones. To save trouble, his brother procured him the necessary permission, but he threw the document in the fire and continued his work with-

---

[4] Peel, *op. cit.*, pp. 36 and 43.

[5] See p. 258.

[6] For Browne's career see Champlain Burrage, *The True Story of Robert Browne* (Oxford, 1906), and his own *A True and Short Declaration (s.l.* [1584]), reprinted in *The Congregationalist* [London, 1888]). The most recent survey (Dwight C. Smith, "Robert Browne, Independent," *Church History*, VI [1937], 289–349) is mostly valuable for its summary of the events of Browne's later years.

out benefit of episcopal sanction. After a year of this activity he was forbidden by the Council to preach further. The bearer of these unwelcome tidings was none other than Richard Bancroft, the future archbishop.

Browne promised to deliver no more sermons in Cambridge, but soon found a new field for his labors. In the university town he met a kindred spirit, one Robert Harrison[7] of his own college, who had taken his M.A. the year Browne proceeded B.A. He had then gone to teach school at Aylsham, Norfolk. Losing that position for his Puritanism, he had next been located in Norwich as master of a hospital there and, like Browne, then returned to his university to qualify for a church living. But, "either changing his mind or disappointed of his purpose," he returned to Norwich and took Browne with him. In that forward community the two proceeded to organize a separatist church, in spite of considerable opposition from the more moderate Puritans.[8] By 1581 they had reached the stage of having a formal covenant. Browne also visited Bury St. Edmunds and there helped to provoke the Puritan tumults which we have mentioned in a previous chapter. He was imprisoned at least twice, but his relationship to the Lord Treasurer helped him out of these troubles.

At the end of the year, after considering Scotland and the Channel Islands, the Norwich congregation decided to emigrate to Middelburg. There, in 1582, at the Schilders press Browne published a volume containing three treatises. The most significant title was that of the *Treatise of Reformation without Tarying for Anie*,[9] but the most important document was the *Booke Which Sheweth the Life and Manners of All True Christians*.[10] In the two works Browne denounced the estab-

---

[7] For Harrison's career see Albert Peel, *The Brownists in Norwich and Norfolk about 1580* (Cambridge, 1920).

[8] See Harrison's *Treatise of the Church and the Kingdome of Christ*, printed by Peel in *ibid.*

[9] Reprinted by T. G. Crippen (London, 1903), and also in "Old South Leaflets General Series," Vol. IV, No. 100 (Boston, n.d.).

[10] Largely reprinted in Williston Walker's *Creeds and Platforms of Congregationalism* (New York, 1893), pp. 18–27.

lished Church of England as so corrupt and superstitious that it was unchristian to attend its services. On the other hand, he pictured the true church as composed of believers gathered together of their own volition and bound by a covenant which they had subscribed. This system should be boldly set up at once, without waiting for the magistrate to co-operate. Indeed, Browne said some harsh things about the futility of persecution and even went so far as to declare that the secular rulers had no ecclesiastical authority at all. Yet he did not teach the doctrine of the separation of church and state. With the reformer's optimism he thought that, once the proper ideas were broadcast, everyone would freely accept them. After that the magistrate might compel the converts to keep their original bargain, as the children of Israel used force against the backsliding tribes of Reuben and Gad "because they seemed to forsake the covenant." Nor did Browne in any way approach the Knoxian doctrine of violent revolution. He flatly stated that the Queen "may put to death all that deserve it by law, either of the church or commonwealth, and none may resist her or the magistrates under her by force or wicked speeches when they execute the laws." His entire teaching was well within the bounds of the principle of passive resistance.[11]

After these blasts Browne did not remain long in the Low Countries. The usual contentiousness of such extremists soon manifested itself. Harrison led the opposition, which was partially based on accusations of slander and similar petty personalities, which mostly centered around the wives of the rival leaders. When the quarrel rose above this level, the issue was the propriety of returning to England and attending the services of the established church, to both of which policies Browne was opposed. Harrison complained that "Cain dealt not so ill with his brother Abel" as Browne dealt with him and his supporters.[12] The result was that Browne presently found himself excommunicated by the church, which, ironically enough, used

[11] *Reformation without Tarrying* ("Old South Leaflets" reprint), esp. pp. 2, 10–11.

[12] S. Bredwell, *The Rasing of the Foundations of Brownisme* (London, 1588), sig. A, fol. 2(v).

his own private rooms for its meeting place. After much futile wrangling, he left for Scotland in the autumn of 1583, where he shortly found himself in prison once more for his separatist notions. But, like the English politicians of the middle of the next century, James found the Independents a useful foil to the Presbyterians, and the English agitator was once more liberated. Toward the close of 1584 he returned to England. After his departure from Middelburg, Harrison negotiated with Cartwright on the subject of a union of the English congregations. The moderate Puritan wrote a long letter against the Separatist position. Copies were widely distributed, and one reached Browne, who possibly returned to Middelburg for a short visit at about this time. He promptly composed *An Answere to Master Cartwright*, which appeared in London early in 1585. For this he was once more imprisoned. But the cycle of his radicalism was nearing completion. Some of the expressions in this volume speak more kindly of the established order than had been his custom. While still condemning the dumb unpreaching ministers, he now granted that the magistrates might properly compel church attendance.

It is evident that Browne had not carefully thought through the implications of his original stand, and he now entered upon a period of vacillation. Before Whitgift he signed some very submissive articles, including promises to communicate with the Church of England and not to preach without a legal call, though he afterward endeavored to explain away the full force of these statements. Burghley reasoned with him in person, and once more he seemed to promise conformity. But once at home in Rutlandshire he was soon in trouble with the ecclesiastical courts for refusing to come to church. Then he again signed submissive articles—this time quite explicit—to obtain a position as a Southwark schoolmaster, which he held from 1586 to 1589. During this period he was occasionally active in the Separatist movement, and defended himself against attacks on this system made by one Stephen Bredwell,[13] "a student in Phisicke," who contended that "discipline is not of the essence or being of a church" and that "open notorious offenders not separated from the congregation of Christ do not unsanctifie the same so as to make it no Church of Christ."[14] But at the same time Browne opposed those who held his original attitude about hearing the ministers of the establishment.[15]

By June, 1589, the former agitator was ready to take a living in the Church of England. Two years later his family found him a place in his native county, which he shortly exchanged for one at Achurch in Northamptonshire. On September 30, 1591, he was ordained both deacon and priest, and passed into the relative obscurity of forty years as a conforming country cleric. Not until his old age did he again show, and then only by one choleric outburst, the fiery temperament which had distinguished him in his youth.

Browne has been variously judged as a renegade, a martyr, whose spirit was broken by prolonged persecution, and as a man possessed. The truth doubtless lies somewhwere between these various extremes. To his dying day he was hot-tempered and contentious, and his educational ideas were sweepingly radical. But there was a method in his apparently maddest theories,[16] and no proof is forthcoming that mentally he was ever more than a young men in a great hurry. With increasing years and family responsibilities he moderated his zeal, as many others have done before and since. But the germ of his later conformity was in his early profession of a desire to obey the

[13] Some allusions to Browne in Bredwell's *The Detection of Ed. Glover's Hereticall Confection* (London, [1586]) were answered by the schoolmaster in a work now lost but quoted in Bredwell's *The Rasing of the Foundations of Brownisme*. In the latter work are also included two of Bredwell's exchanges with Browne which were occasioned by advice given to a young man on the matter of attending the established church.

[14] *Rasing*, sig. ¶, fol. 1(v).

[15] *A Reproofe of Certaine Schismatical Persons*, first printed by Champlain Burrage (Oxford, 1907), with the added title, *The Retractation of Robert Browne; A New Years Guift*, ed. Burrage (London, 1904); Burrage, *True Story of Robert Browne*, pp. 48–62.

[16] See below, p. 474; John Strype, *The Life and Acts of John Whitgift* (3 vols.; Oxford, 1822), III, 229–30.

laws of the land, and he seems to have been persuaded to recognize the conservative implications of this principle rather by reason than by fear or suffering. He can thus scarcely qualify either as a coward or as a hero, but merely as another weary zealot tamed by time.

The influence of Browne's early opinions did not end, however, with their author's recantation. His works circulated widely, in spite of a royal proclamation put out against such "seditious" literature in 1583. In June of that year two men, John Copping and Elias Thacker, were convicted at the Bury assizes and hanged for spreading this propaganda, and another, William Denys, was executed at Thetford. In the eyes of the authorities an attempt to set up a rival to the established church was an effort to overthrow the government. In spite of this severity, and the death of Harrison about 1585, a Separatist congregation continued to exist at Norwich. The Middleburg exiles doubtless returned, and the East Anglican congregation outlived Elizabeth.

In London, Browne's influence was also felt. Added to the earlier metropolitan Separatist tradition, it served to keep alive a congregational movement which apparently numbered several hundred adherents. When the former leader wavered, others appeared to take his place, notably two other Cambridge men, John Greenwood, who followed Wright as chaplain to Lord Rich of Rochford, and Henry Barrow,[17] a gentleman of independent means who had spent some time at Gray's Inn and who was also a relative by marriage of the Bacons. In October, 1587,[18] Greenwood was caught by the Bishop's pursuivants in the act of holding a conventicle and rushed to the Clink. There Barrow visited him and was promptly taken in custody himself. For the next seven years the men remained nominal prisoners, though Greenwood and possibly Barrow enjoyed occasional periods of liberty on bail. In accordance with the free and easy

---

[17] For the details of the careers of Greenwood and Barrow and a complete description of their controversial works see F. J. Powicke's *Henry Barrow . . . . and the Exiled Church of Amsterdam* (London, 1900).

[18] Cf. Burrage, *The Early English Dissenters* (2 vols.; Cambridge, 1912), I, 128–29 for the dating of this incident.

customs of those days, even when they were in prison they were allowed a considerable measure of freedom to write and to entertain visitors. It was thus possible to keep up the connection with the London Separatist body and to compose for publication various defenses of their ecclesiastical position.[19]

In these works Barrow, who was the more important of the two men, maintained the familiar doctrine that magistrates were responsible for suppressing false worship, establishing the true, and compelling people to resort to it. But he denied the right of the prince to make laws on matters indifferent or to change the judicial law of Moses.[20] Not all of this Separatist propaganda was directed against the bishops, for like Browne himself the prisoners also had to deal with the more moderate Puritans. Delegations of these—Egerton, Hutchinson, and Lancelot Andrewes, later famous as the Bishop of Winchester but at this time only beginning his conservative metamorphosis—visited and reasoned with the Separatists. At the same time George Gifford, a Puritan minister at Maldon, Essex, kept up a steady fire of printed attacks, of which the burden was that the congregationalists were Donatists who would ruin ecclesiastical discipline at a time when the ship needed wise men in the stern. "Now when the common artificer, the apprentice, and the brewer intrude themselves and they will guide the same, being ignorant, rash and headie, what worldlie wise man will not take it that discipline herself is but a bedlam."[21]

At length the two prisoners fell victims to a bit of political terrorism. In the Parliament of 1592–93 the government introduced an anti-Brownist bill, punishing obstinate refusal to attend parish church services by banishment, with the death penalty for any who returned. During the session, to strengthen

[19] Of these, the most important were *A True Description of the Visible Congregation of the Saints under the Gospel* (Dort, 1589); *A Brief Discoverie of the False Church* (Dort, 1590); and *The Examinations of H. Barrow, J. Grenewood, and J. Penrie* (s.l., 1593).

[20] Powicke, *op. cit.*, pp. 128–29, quoting *A Brief Discoverie*, pp. 218–20.

[21] *A Short Treatise against the Donatists of England* (London, 1590), especially sig. A, fol. 2(v); *Plaine Declaration That Our Brownists Be Full Donatists* (London, 1590); *Short Reply to the Last Printed Books of Henry Barrow and John Greenwood* (London, 1591).

the government's case, Barrow and Greenwood were tried and convicted of the Copping-Thacker variety of sedition. Execution was deferred, but, when the lower house showed signs of opposing the bill, they were both hanged.

A few weeks later John Penry of Marprelate fame met a similar end. During his earlier controversial period and the stay in Scotland, though an outspoken and extreme writer, he had stopped short of the Separatist position. Barrow had criticized his stand, and apparently the arguments were effective. In the summer of 1592, Penry returned from the security of Edinburgh where the Presbyterian clergy were enjoying a period of political success, to the dangers of London conventicle life. He affiliated with the persecuted metropolitan congregation and wrote in their defense, though the works had to circulate in manuscript for the time. In the spring of 1593, after various escapes, he was finally apprehended. He was tried for felony in violating the Act of Uniformity, a procedure of somewhat dubious legality.[22] In his defense, as in his last tract, he maintained that the Queen was bound to rule in accordance with the law, both divine and human. Ordinances contrary to either were of no validity: "Her Majesty [he declared] hath granted in establishing and confirming the Great Charter of England that the church of God under her should have all her rights and liberties inviolate for ever." Asked by the judge whether a subject has the right to scan what oaths princes take and charge the rulers to keep covenant with the ruled, Penry replied in the affirmative, repeating that the prince must rule by law. "Hence it is that the judges of this land are bound by law to administer justice and equity unto the poor subjects, notwithstanding that the prince's letters be directed to them to the contrary."[23] This anticipated Coke's dicta on the subject by more than a decade, but it had no immediate effect. The stormy agitator was convicted and

[22] Burrage (*John Penry the So-called Martyr of Congregationalism* [Oxford, 1913]) has argued for the legality of the prosecution, but it is clear from the opinion of Professor Holdsworth which he quotes (pp. 13–14) that there was an irregularity, since the Act of Uniformity did not create a felony.

[23] *The Examinations of H. Barrow, J. Grenewood and J. Penrie*, sig. D, fols. 1–2; William Pierce, *John Penry: His Life, Times and Writing* (London, 1923), p. 388.

executed on May 28, 1593. He had come closer than any other Puritan of the reign to enunciating a doctrine which would go to the heart of the problem in political theory which was defying the best efforts of the party. But even he proposed no sanction to compel the observance of his principle that rulers are bound by the law, and he remained passive in his resistance to the Queen. He rejected the use of force in securing his ends and in his death exemplified his willingness to suffer whatever fate the magistrate might decree for him.

Another Cambridge man, Francis Johnson, now stepped into the breach. In 1589 he had been expelled from his fellowship at Christ's College, Cambridge, and imprisoned for his strong expression of Puritan sentiments. Released, he followed Fenner as pastor of the Merchant Adventurers at Middelburg. There he encountered some opposition to his demands that all the congregation sign a covenant to accept strict moral discipline. Yet up to this time he had been a moderate Puritan, and, when he discovered that a reply to Gifford by Barrow and Greenwood was being printed in his town, he helped the authorities to seize and destroy the edition. But, saving a copy for himself, he was convinced by its reasoning, resigned his pastorate, and returned to London, where in 1592 he became pastor of Greenwood's church. Eventually he was also imprisoned, along with his brother George and some seventy other Separatists.[24] This figure gives some indication of the growing strength of the movement and explains the anxiety of the authorities to suppress it, as evidenced by the severe statute passed in the 1593 Parliament. Sir Walter Raleigh, speaking in support of that measure, alleged that there were twenty thousand Brownists in England. While this was doubtless an exaggeration, and while those who did take the extreme attitude were mostly from the humble walks of life, the Separatists were nevertheless considered a serious menace. But the statute proved equal to the immediate emergency. The London congregation duly decided

[24] Burrage, *Early English Dissenters*, I, 149. This includes only those in London prisons. There were also some in "other gaols throughout the land." The originals of the records of the trials of these suspects, which Burrage (*ibid.*, II, 45–61) copied from Harleian MSS 6848–49, are in the Egerton MSS (2101–17) in the Huntington Library.

to obey the law and emigrate, and most of the prisoners were released to join in the venture. After stops in Campin and Naar-
den, the exiles finally settled in Amsterdam. Still they continued to hold the doctrine of passive resistance. A *Confession
of Faith* published in 1596 acknowledged once more the right
and duty of the secular arm to root out false ministers and maintain the true. They declared:

> That if God incline the magistrates' hearts to the allowance and protection
> of them they account it a happy blessing of God. . . . . That if God withhold
> the magistrates' allowance and furtherance herein that they yet proceed
> together in Christian covenant. . . . . That they do also willingly and orderly
> pay and perform all manner of lawful and accustomed duties unto all men,
> submitting in the Lord themselves, their bodies, lands, goods, and lives to the
> magistrates' pleasure.[25]

It is small wonder that by 1597 the English government felt
sufficiently in control of the situation to release the Johnson
brothers on condition that they join an expedition to found a
settlement in Canada. The liberated leaders made the outward
voyage, but after a shipwreck the colonizing venture was not
seriously pushed, and they returned with one of the original
boats. After remaining in hiding for a time, they made their
way to Holland, where they joined the bulk of the London
flock.

There a legacy left by Barrow helped to solve the financial
problem,[26] and a promising recruit was obtained in the person
of Henry Ainsworth, another Cambridge man who shortly became the elder of the congregation. But the separatist curse of
contentiousness soon settled on them. While in prison Francis
Johnson had married a wealthy London widow. At that time
her fashionable attire had shocked the little band of ship-
wrights, joiners, and shoemakers. Now the clothes controversy
burst out anew. Stays became literally great bones of contention. Breastpieces were discussed in bated breath, while the
husband solemnly offered to produce the offending gown for in-

[25] *True Confession of the Faith and Humble Acknowledgment of the Allegeance Which
Wee Hir Majesties Subjects Falsely Called Brownists Doo Hould* ([Amsterdam?], 1596),
secs. 41–43, sig. C, fol. iii.

[26] Burrage, *Early English Dissenters*, I, 159.

spection at a formal meeting of the congregational officers. Eventually the pastor excommunicated his brother and also his father, who had come across the channel in a vain effort to settle the controversy. Such were the sad extremes to which the separatist principles carried their followers.

Throughout all these years the English Separatists carefully stopped short of Anabaptist principles. There were a few Dutch Anabaptists in England during Elizabeth's time. In 1575 nine were banished and two were executed "in great horror, crying and roaring," though Foxe appealed to the Queen to spare them and actually secured a month's reprieve. At Norwich some went so far as to deny the doctrine of the Trinity, for which four were burned between 1579 and 1589. But just as the available facts concerning the origin of the English Separatists have defied the best efforts of modern scholars to connect them with the Continental sectaries,[27] so the Separatists of that day indignantly repudiated all relationship. Over and over again they denied that they taught economic communism, resistance to the magistrate, or that the magistrate had no right to regulate the church.[28] Barrow refused to take an oath on the Bible, but he did not logically follow out his declaration that the Roman and Anglican churches were false churches and their sacraments false. He would not require rebaptism for his followers, lest he seem to be an Anabaptist. This inbred horror of the Münster doctrines accounts in no small measure for the refusal of the Separatist Puritans, as well as their less radical brethren, to consider seriously the advisability of abandoning the doctrine of passive resistance.

In spite of their caution on this point, or possibly because of it, the moral progress achieved by the Separatist movement was slight. The Reformation undoubtedly raised the moral tone of all western Europe, Catholic and Protestant alike. Similarly, the Puritan cudgelings of the dilatory Anglican blessed both him that gave and him that took. But it is an interesting ques-

---

[27] Mr. S. S. Slaughter tells me that in a year's work on this point in the Norwich archives he has been unable to find any substantial evidence of a connection.

[28] Pierce, *op. cit.*, pp. 367–72; Powicke, *op. cit.*, pp. 201–18.

tion whether the Separatist movement was productive of comparable moral improvement, or whether the law of diminishing returns had not begun to operate on the process of continuous schism for the sake of reform. There was doubtless an increasing emphasis on a personal religious experience and individual spiritual life as a prerequisite for church membership in the sectarian circle. There was also a tendency toward an even stricter discipline where immediate responsibility was no longer felt for the mass of society. When, in any case, the members of the congregation were in the vast minority, it was relatively easy to deliver one more brother to Satan. The last known effort to enforce the medieval doctrine of the just price was in a Separatist communion.[29] But between Presbyterian Puritan and Separatist Puritan there was really not that great difference in objective which in part justified the earlier subdivisions of the universal church. Both had much the same ideals of Christian life and discipline, as well as doctrine, so that, had the Independents completely eliminated the Presbyterians, no great moral advance could have been registered. On the other hand, the Separatist movement has large debits to account for. There was, in the first place, the obvious weakening of the reforming front by this division of forces, which was a serious handicap to the cause of idealism. Furthermore, the interminable bickering over petty, personal issues discredited the entire Puritan cause, fastening on it the incubus of a reputation for irresponsible individualism which was hard to remove. Both these features made more remote than ever the chances of the Puritans gaining and holding power. And, while power has its dangers for an idealistic movement, it also has its possibilities. Corruption and stultification are not the inevitable results. It may also unify, clarify, invigorate.

[29] See below, pp. 410–11.

CHAPTER XVI

The Stuart Settlement: Bankruptcy

NO HISTORY of Tudor Puritanism would be complete without some account of the Stuart settlement. For the pragmatic test of the Tudor Puritan theory is not how it worked under Elizabeth but how it fared under her successor. All the Reformed thinkers built their political system on the foundation of a Christian magistracy. They occasionally admitted some uncertainty about the Christian attitude toward the temporal power when it was controlled by Roman emperors or Turks. But starting with the natural optimism of reformers, at times reinforced by their experiences with docile councils of mercantile city-states, they arrived at the definite conviction that in a Christian society the ecclesiastical and temporal power might exist side by side as co-operating equals, each supreme in its own sphere, assisting but not dominating the other. Of this theory it could easily be argued that previous English experience was not a fair test. Henry had been only a nominal Protestant. Edward had not really ruled at all. Mary was a Roman Catholic. During her formative years Elizabeth had had comparatively little opportunity to see Reformed Protestantism at its best. Thus cheated and warped by the circumstances of her early life, the Queen scarcely developed any religious feelings whatever. It could even be maintained—in private, to be sure—that she was not a Christian at all.

But James's case was altogether different. Here was a man without father and without mother, who had been educated from childhood in the most favorable Presbyterian environment, a Christian magistrate, trained as such from the beginning. Nor could it be maintained that he was poor material for such polishing. James I of England may not have been a successful ruler, but James VI of Scotland was a great man. Before reaching middle age he mastered his turbulent subjects, introducing into the northern kingdom in two decades the changes that occupied the great Tudor Henries for more than half a century. Furthermore, at times James had shown himself to be at least amenable to clerical influence. Though he had been annoyed by the ministers' response to Bancroft's fiery attack upon their system in his 1589 sermon, he had not suppressed that protest and had expressed a wish that the Anglican would publicly retract. When Elizabeth warned him against the political dangers inherent in Presbyterianism, he responded by making Waldegrave his official printer. In 1591 he consented to sign a letter drawn up by his clergy requesting the English Queen to deal leniently with Udall, Cartwright, and their fellow-prisoners. The following year he had agreed to the establishment of virtually complete Presbyterianism in his country, and had described the resulting establishment as "the sincerest kirk in the world."[1] As late as 1598 he was seriously considering the advisability of including a large number of elected representatives of the clergy in Parliament, a device which would have gone far toward giving the ministers a good share in the control of the realm while eliminating the troublesome division of sovereignty inherent in the Calvinistic-Melvillian theory of the two kingdoms. Certainly, his reign offered as good a proving-ground for Puritanism as any reasonable man could request.

Yet in the spring of 1603 the reasonable man would perforce have admitted that the Puritan prospects could not be considered very bright. For, in spite of his careful training, James had reacted against his Puritan upbringing, and, when the danger of Spanish invasion was past, he had subjected the ministers to the same treatment which he meted out to his nobles. Possibly it was only an expression of that natural antipathy which youth feels toward the standards of the preceding generation. More

[1] David Calderwood, *The History of the Kirk of Scotland*, ed. Thomson (8 vols.; Edinburgh, 1842-49), V, 106. For the reply of the Scotch Presbyterians to Bancroft see John Davidson, *D. Bancroft's Rashnes in Rayling against the Church of Scotland* (Edinburgh, 1590).

probably it was a demonstration of the fundamental antago-
nism between the monarch who wished to be absolute and the
autonomous clericalism of the Calvinistic system. In any case,
when it came to a final decision on the matter of clergy in
Parliament, he had accepted the suggestion of the self-seeking
nobles instead of carrying out the full-blown clerical project.
He had forced bishops on the reluctant church and driven the
protesting ministers from the field. After the "failure" of the
Gowrie "plot" in 1601, he was almost as much master of the religious situation in his country as was the supreme governor of
the Anglican church in hers. Worst of all, he had been looking
forward so long to adding the southern kingdom to his poor
inheritance that his neighboring domain had come in his mind
to assume the aspect of a lush utopia, not needing reform but
only to be enjoyed to the full.[2]

Still there was some hope. James could be a good politician
when he chose, and in the last years of Elizabeth's life he conducted on all fronts a quiet campaign for the English crown.
Anxious not to antagonize any influential sector of English public opinion, he generously made the usual campaign promises in
all quarters. Fortunately for him, they did not have to be made
in public, and so the Puritan could be kept in blissful ignorance
of the honeyed words to the Roman Catholics and Anglicans,
while the word was quietly passed along that the Scotch king
was reaching an understanding with Essex, who was, like the
equally ambitious Leicester a generation earlier, posing as the
Puritan champion. Even after the fall of that rash young man,
there were secret assurances from north of the Tweed that
James would maintain "the Gospel" when he came to the English throne.[3] It was also known that James had not sloughed
off all the effects of his early training. He was well posted on
matters of theology and political theory and dearly loved the

[2] F. G. Marcham ("James I and the 'Little Beagle' Letters," in *Persecution and
Liberty: Essays in Honor of George Lincoln Burr* [New York, 1931], pp. 311–34) brings
out this point very well.

[3] R. G. Usher, *Reconstruction of the English Church* (2 vols.; New York, 1910), I, 289.
This work is easily the best treatment of the events before, during, and after the Hampton Court Conference.

disputations which were the customary intellectual exercises of
those days. Surely the Puritans could gain his ear and might
hope to sway him if their requests seemed moderate and reasonable.

Efforts were accordingly made by the milder Puritans to prepare an acceptable statement of their principles and to heal the
breach with the sincerely religious Anglicans. In 1602, Josias
Nichols, rector of Eastwell, Kent, ventured to reopen the old,
old discussion with a volume entitled *The Plea of the Innocent,
Wherein Is Averred That the Ministers and People Falsely
Termed Puritans Are Injuriously Slaundered for Enemies or
Troublers of the State.* The title-page further assures the reader
that the work is "Published for the common good of the church
and commonwealth of this realm of England, as a countermure
against all sycophantising Papists, statising [meddling] priests,
neutralising atheists, and satanising scorners of all godliness,
truth, and honesty," a long-delayed reminder that Protestant
churchmen had something better to do than to wear themselves
out attacking one another. Though one of those who were deprived in the 1584 troubles, Nichols had not been active in the
succeeding classis and Marprelate period and therefore could
speak as one who disapproved of such dubious measures. In
fact, he fathered both Martin and the Brownists on the devil.
He repudiated the name "Puritan" on the ground that his associates did not claim to be sinless[4] and, in a short history of his
party, undertook to prove that rebellion was not one of its
tenets. On the contrary, that was a papistical practice. The
Puritans loved the Queen and had produced the men of 1588.
After thus calmly appropriating the credit for the Armada victory, he proceeded to elaborate upon a general irenicon. The
Queen was plentifully flattered. The bishops are good men who
oppose atheists and papists, and who can work with Puritans if
they try. He implies that his party may have offended in the
past also, but now asserts that it seeks only for a learned, resident ministry which will not be compelled to subscribe to superstitious or false doctrine. He and his friends do not oppose the

[4] See below, p. 489.

institution of bishops, as such, but only their lordship and civil jurisdiction.[5]

Then at length Elizabeth died, and among those who rode furiously northward was a Northampton gentleman named Lewis Pickering, who proffered his congratulations and attached himself to the royal suite. Together with a Scotch Presbyterian minister named Patrick Galloway, who was also following the court, he kept his English Puritan friends advised as to the proper tactics to pursue. In April, 1603, James started south. Before he reached the border, he had told the Scotch ministers who came to plead the Puritan cause that "he was not minded at the first to urge any alteration."[6] All the circumstances indicated the advisability of giving the party leadership to men of the Nichols type, or at least framing its requests on his model. This plan was followed, and as James leisurely made his way southward through the Promised Land he was somewhere presented with a studiously moderate petiton which professed to represent the wishes of "more than a thousand of your Majesty's subjects and ministers," though there were no signatures attached—the so-called Millenary Petition. On the whole, it represented a return to the Grindal program, requesting the reform of the ecclesiastical courts and the abolition of such abuses as nonresidence, pluralism, and ignorant, nonpreaching, and underpaid ministers. There was no protest against the established form of church government as such. The most puritanical requests included were for the elimination of such objectionable features of the prescribed services as the cap and surplice, the sign of the cross in baptism, and the reading of the Apocrypha. An offer was made to produce proof for all the charges, and a conference was requested in which details of the remedies might be discussed.

The reception of this document was, on the whole, favorable. Feeling himself well qualified to argue down any opposition, James had none of Elizabeth's scruples against a learned minis-

[5] *Plea of the Innocent*, pp. 3, 5–13, 91, 149, 158–60, 195, 212, 216, 224–28. There were two different editions in 1602. I have used the one with 229 pages.

[6] David Calderwood, *op. cit.*, VI, 222.

try, and he soon let it be known that he was prepared to assist the movement toward that objective. This encouragement brought the more radical veterans of the classis struggle into action. Stephen Egerton, the Puritan minister at Blackfriars, London, played the Elisha to Field's Elijah, and sent out instructions to the provinces once more. He was ably supported by Henry Jacob, a Kentish man, formerly of St. Mary Hall, Oxford. In May a secret panel of suggestions was issued under the title "Advice Tending to Reformation," which proposed the revival of the technique of 1585–86.' Petitions were to be sent in, complaining of the identical corruptions but in different words, to give the appearance of spontaneity. Ministers were to prepare arguments on the moot points in anticipation of the projected disputation. By preaching and prayer the laity was to be roused to the necessity of reform. Lawyers were to draw statutes and to pen learned treatises. Lastly, another census of the ignorant, double-beneficed, and nonresident clergy was to be undertaken.[7] Once more Puritans rode, consulted, drafted, and signed, as in the pre-Armada days, and it was soon possible for the party to make rather a formidable showing.

Unfortunately for the success of the Puritan cause, its leaders had not been quite moderate enough in their original petition, and the radical element in their own party would not down. In order to provide for a properly paid ministry, they had proposed that the impropriate livings belonging to bishops and colleges, and a sixth or seventh of those in lay hands, be restored to their original purpose. This naturally alarmed the university authorities and brought them into the field in defense of the *status quo*. Oxford published a formal *Answer*[8] to the Millenary Petition, in which some of the subsequent correspondence of Jacob was exposed. Since he had succeeded in having an ex-

---

[7] Additional MS 28571, fol. 199. This volume and Sloane MS 271 contain most of the important materials relating to the Puritan plans at this time. "The Lamentable Estate of the Ministry in Staffordshire," a document reporting the results of the Puritan survey of that county, is printed by A. Peel in *EHR*, XXVI (1911), 338–52.

[8] *Answere of the Vice Chancellour, the Doctors, Both the Proctors and Other the Heads of Houses in the Universitie of Oxford . . . . to the Humble Petition of the Ministers . . . . Desiring Reformation* (Oxford, 1603).

plicit request for the Reformed discipline inserted in the pattern for future Puritan petitions, the radical implications of the original movement were accordingly disclosed. At the same time Whitgift and Bancroft rallied the Anglican forces. They too sent out requests for information from the various dioceses as to the exact condition of the clergy. When, in July, Galloway persuaded James to notify the vice-chancellors of the universities that he intended to contribute his own impropriations to the improvement of ecclesiastical livings and wished them to follow his example, the Archbishop sent in a strong protest, on the ground that impropriations were being used "to provide for the general necessities of the whole church." On the twenty-second of that month Bancroft entertained the King and Queen at Fulham Palace and apparently poured into the royal ear the bishops' side of the story, for after that date the Puritans found progress more difficult. In October, James was persuaded to order the seizure of the Puritans who were circulating petitions in Sussex, where nearly thirteen hundred signatures had been obtained, and to issue a proclamation expressing his general approval of the established order. Since the government in December took the measure of Raleigh himself in the famous trial, all that could be accomplished by the proposed conference, to which the King had already consented, would be the reformation of some minor abuses in that order.

Nevertheless, the Puritans struggled on. It was something that James had dignified their party by agreeing to a conference, and they were resolved to make the most of this advantage. The Oxford volume was answered by a manuscript work which endeavored to shame the university men who were championing the cause of ignorance. While laymen should contribute the most part, "clergymen for so much as lyeth in their power should show themselves ready by their example."[9] The fact-gathering proceeded apace, and many of the laity were co-opted into the Puritan organization. In Northampton, Cartwright was persuaded to approach Justice Yelverton, who as the mem-

[9] "A True Modest and Just Defense of the Petition for Reformation" (Additional MS 8978), p. 110.

ber for the county town had introduced reforming bills in Parliament thirty years before. The old slogans had not lost their
appeal, and soon Sir Christopher was doing his bit for the cause.
Originally the conference had been set for the first of November, but the appearance of the plague and the pressure of governmental business caused it to be deferred to January, 1604.
In the meantime the moderates among the Puritans regained the
party leadership. It had been intended that Cartwright should
be one of the Puritan representatives, but he died in December,
and the reaction from the discovery of the activity and drastic
proposals of Egerton and Jacob gave the leadership once more
to the university men, Rainolds and Chaderton. As delegates,
they, along with Knewstubs and Thomas Sparke of Bletchley,
Buckinghamshire,[10] were instructed to contend mainly for a
learned ministry and the amelioration of ecclesiastical incomes,
though other objectives such as the reform of ceremonies and
the restoration of prophesyings were also mentioned.

At last the time came, and the Puritans had their eagerly
awaited day in court. The bishops were greatly concerned at
this countenancing of the opposition, but they need not have
worried. James kept to the policy enunciated in the autumn
proclamation, and the forward element fared very badly indeed. Their representatives were not even admitted to the
royal presence at Hampton Court on the opening day, January
14, when the King discussed with the Anglicans some minor reforms in the Book of Common Prayer. When, on the sixteenth,
they were ushered into the audience chamber and permitted to
kneel and speak, Bancroft and the other Anglicans interrupted
their arguments, and the King did not conceal his antipathy.
Rather, he severely browbeat the unfortunate spokesmen. He
aired his own learning and made sport of the Puritan reasoning.
Finally, at the mention of prophesyings with their hint of presbyteries he girded up, gave vent to his wrath against such a
system, threw out his dictum of "No bishop, no King," and told
his hapless guests that they must conform or be harried out of

---

[10] Dr. John King and Richard Feilde or Field, who are mentioned by Usher (*op. cit.*,
p. 319 n.) as possible Puritan representatives, were on the Anglican side.

the land. Only to their requests for a new catechism and a new translation of the Bible would he accede. No wonder the Archbishop assured him that he spoke "by the special assistance of God's spirit." And so, with a cloying burst of Anglican flattery and renewed threats to the Puritans, the long-anticipated hearings ended.

The King had spoken, and the ecclesiastical situation resumed its Elizabethan aspect, with the monarchy definitely committed against the Puritan program. It only remained to be seen whether, within the old limits, conditions would approximate those under Grindal or the situation under Whitgift—in other words, whether James could and would enforce his declared will. There was a year of propaganda and agitation, of hopes and fears, before this question was finally answered. The King began resolutely enough with a royal proclamation on March 5, in which he ridiculed the "weak and slender proofs" adduced by the Puritans at Hampton Court, called on his subjects to conform by Midsummer Day, June 24, and warned them not to "expect nor attempt any further alteration in the common and public form of God's service, from this which is now established." But in response to Chaderton's request on the last day of the conference he had granted certain Lancashire ministers a stay of execution. A Parliament, puritanically inclined as usual, was about to meet. Once more the Puritan political machinery was put in operation. Books were written,[11] petitions drawn up, members of Parliament exhorted, and delegations of ministers sent to London. Hope was not yet dead.

When the excitement over Goodwin's case died down, the Puritan ministers blandly presented the bishops with a request for reformation of the very abuses discussed at Hampton Court. In the Commons, Sir Francis Hastings, brother of the Elizabethan Earl of Huntingdon, moved for a committee on religious matters, and the lower house was soon engaged in another of its

[11] William Stoughton, *An Assertion for True and Christian Church-Policie* ([Middelburg], 1604); Henry Jacob, *Reasons Taken out of God's Word Proving a Necessitie of Reforming Our Churches in England* ([Middelburg], 1604); W. Bradshaw, *A Shorte Treatise of the Crosse in Baptisme* (Amsterdam, 1604); *A Treatise of Divine Worship* ([Amsterdam?], 1604).

struggles with the espiscopate. When Convocation rejected a Puritan petition, this time for reform of the Thirty-nine Articles, the Commons indorsed the request. Vain efforts were made to discredit Bancroft by revealing his negotiations with the Roman Catholic seculars under Elizabeth, and to hold up the Anglican program in Convocation by the arrest of its prolocutor for debt. In a long-delayed conference with the bishops (May 18) the Commons put forward a complete Puritan program, calling for the elimination from the Articles of those concerning episcopacy and the ecclesiastical power of the crown, the institution of a presbyterian type of ordination, the limitation of episcopal authority, the abolition of pluralism, and more to the same effect. But Bancroft was doing all in his power to delay proceedings—even scheduling conferences for Sunday, a day, of course, unacceptable to the Puritans[12]—while he pushed through Convocation a set of canons which would make inescapably definite the Anglican structure of the established church. At length, without tarrying for the bishops, Sir Edward Montagu introduced a bill in the Commons against pluralities and non-residence, and another for a learned ministry. Bancroft had Convocation pass a resolution denying the power of the Commons to consider religious subjects except under episcopal direction. Once more the drama of Wentworth and Parker was played. The Commons wrathfully repudiated this doctrine and pushed through a swarm of Puritan bills which died in the Lords, while the lower house retaliated by shelving all Bancroft's measures calling for the reform and speeding-up of the tithe collection system. In this fit of Commons' temper there was doubtless more than a little self-interest. An adequate system of collecting tithes might have done much to improve the quality of the clergy. But it would have borne heavily on the laity, and the merchants and country gentry were more in favor of beginning with a redistribution of episcopal wealth and cathedral endowments. So the parliamentary session ended in a deadlock, and nothing was accomplished by the Puritans.

In despair the party fell back on a final round of consulta-

[12] Historical Manuscripts Commission, *Buccleugh MSS*, III (London, 1926), 88.

tions, which resulted in the usual petitions and legal quibbles. It was denied that the bishop had authority to deprive without express warrant from the crown, and the power of the High Commission was attacked on the ground that it was only authorized to enforce conformity to the Elizabethan Prayer Book and not to the new one which was slightly revised. In any case the parson could appeal to the common law to protect him in retaining his living, on the assumption that it was a freehold. If everything else failed, it was decided that the faithful should stand together, in order to overawe the government with the prospect of creating a host of Puritan martyrs by sweeping deprivations. For a time it seemed that this device would be successful, for Bancroft, now Archbishop of Canterbury, and his fellow-prelates showed no liking for the executioner's work. They urged their adherents to answer the Puritan arguments.[13] They exhorted and admonished, but did no more.

In the end it was the will of the prince which was the decisive factor, as it had been so often under Elizabeth. In Lincolnshire, toward the middle of January, 1605, while indulging his passion for hunting, James fell in with Bishop William Chaderton and discovered how little enforcement work was being done in that area. With some heat he ordered his ministers to compel the bishops to do their duty with the Puritans. "I never changed the smallest jot of my conclusion to deprive them," wrote the veteran of many brushes with the Scotch clergy, and "if ye make not mountains of molehills .... ye need not to have troubled so far your own minds." Reluctantly and apologetically the prelates began to take action. In February, James was roused again to goad them on. Sir Edward Montagu and the Knightleys, who had sheltered the Marprelate press, presented a Puritan petition from the gentry of Northamptonshire, drawn by Sir Francis Hastings, which rashly told the King the simple truth that, if he did not grant it, some thousands of his subjects would be seriously offended with him. It was another mistake of

---

[13] William Covell, *A Just and Temperate Defence of the Five Books of Ecclesiastical Policie Written by M. Richard Hooker* (London, 1603); *A Modest and Reasonable Examination* (London, 1604). The first is an answer to the *Christian Letter of Certaine English Protestants*, the second a reply to Nichols' *Plea of the Innocent*.

the Birchet-Copinger type, a threat of effective force without the substance. James was statesman and historian enough to recognize the political theory inherent in genuine Puritanism, even if its own followers in England could not. He pointed out that the movements in Scotland and Holland had involved the use of armed force. He did not trouble himself to mention that this factor had been decisive in overthrowing in those countries the Catholicism which he professed to detest. He was content to observe that this "Puritan Devil" had cost his mother her crown, and he proceeded to protect his. The petitioners were arrested. In these circumstances the common-law judges were compelled to admit that the High Commission might legally deprive the Puritan clergy and that no procedure in their courts could block such actions. Armed with these decisions and urged on by the sovereign, the ecclesiastical authorities during 1605 admonished and suspended some three hundred of the Puritan clergy and actually deprived about fifty of them.

These figures indicate not only a measure of continued leniency from the bishops in spite of governmental pressure but also the fundamental soundness of James's estimate of Puritan behavior under stress. The machinery of the ecclesiastical courts ground slowly. There were many continuances. Some of the deprived were immediately restored to their livings, and in the long run much nonconformity must have been winked at.[14] But enough pressure was applied to divide and crush the Puritan party, and in the crisis the great majority of the forward group chose to remain within the newly restricted bounds of the established church. For five cases out of six a warning or suspension was sufficient. Only a comparatively few men were finally deprived. Some doubtless yielded out of fear and economic necessity. Dread of schismatic separatism, however, must have been the compelling factor in many cases. Twenty years of anti-Brownist conditioning, of Cartwrightian tracts, and of prison interviews were not to be overcome by a single moment of disap-

---

[14] See *The State of the Church in the Reigns of Elizabeth and James I as Illustrated by Documents Relating to the Diocese of Lincoln*, ed. C. W. Foster (Horncastle: Lincoln Record Society, 1926), pp. lxvii–lxxv, 363–71, for additional illustrations of these points.

pointment. Though the moderates writhed and protested, though they continued to grasp at legal straws and fill books with theological arguments,[15] they bowed their necks to the yoke. Indeed, some of the mildest of their number, including Sparke, who had represented the party at Hampton Court, even managed to accept the verdict of the Lord's anointed with good grace and to join in the Anglican effort to induce their recalcitrant brethren to conform.[16]

The stubborn minority found themselves driven by the hard logic of events into the ranks of the Separatist exiles. That tiny faction had also cherished fond hopes of better days under the new monarch. Rallying from the shock of their private vestiarian controversy, the Amsterdam church drew up three successive petitions to James,[17] of which at least one was actually presented. In them they repeated their professions of loyalty to the duly constituted English government, their repudiations of Anabaptist principles, and their requests to be allowed to practice in their own country the true religion as they understood it. But with the more moderate Puritan party in England getting such short shrift these optimistic Separatist advances naturally had a very chill reception. The great witch-hunter was even less anxious to entertain the Amsterdam Puritan devil than he had been the Scotch or English variety. So there was nothing for it but to hold the foreign base, continue the exile, and await reinforcements.

As already indicated, some of these were soon forthcoming from the ranks of the disappointed Puritan zealots at home. In the neighborhood of Gainsborough, Scrooby, and Bawtry,

[15] Of these, some of the most important were: *Certaine Considerations Drawne from the Canons of the Last Sinod* ([Middelburg], 1605); S. Hieron, *A Defence of the Ministers' Reasons for Refusall of Subscription* (s.l., 1607-8); W. Bradshaw, *A Treatise of the Nature and Use of Things Indifferent* ([Amsterdam?], 1605); *Twelve Generall Arguments Proving That the Ceremonies Are Unlawfull* (s.l., 1605).

[16] Thomas Sparke, *A Brotherly Perswasion to Unitie* (London, 1607); George Downame, *Two Sermons, the One Commending the Ministerie, the Other Defending the Office of Bishops* (London, 1608).

[17] They are printed with supporting documents in H. Ainsworth and F. Johnson, *An Apologie or Defence of Such True Christians as Are Commonly (But Unjustly) Called Brownists* (s.l., 1604).

where Yorkshire, Lincolnshire, and Nottinghamshire come together, Separatist groups began to organize. John Smith, who
had been a fellow of Christ's College, Cambridge, and had already lost his preaching post at Lincoln, soon became the pastor
of the Gainsborough group. Richard Clyfton headed the Scrooby congregation, which was shortly joined by John Robinson,[18]
one-time fellow of Corpus Christi College, Cambridge, who had
been forced from his lectureship at Norwich. During 1608 both
bodies succeeded in making their way to Amsterdam. There
Smith, after quarreling with Johnson—who was shortly to en-
gage also in a bitter dispute with Ainsworth on the old Frankfort issue of the powers of the congregational officers—adopted
the principle of adult baptism, baptised himself and his followers, and formed the first important one of a number of English
Baptist churches. With the disputes and schisms which troubled these bodies, and the ramifications of their doctrine, we need
not here concern ourselves beyond pointing out that one of the
Baptist factions in time came into communion with the Dutch
Mennonites, and so may fairly be said to represent a tie with
the dreaded Anabaptists, the first of the sort it is possible to discover. In 1609, Robinson became the pastor of the Scrooby
congregation, and it moved on to Leyden and ultimate fame.
But before the great "Mayflower" migration took place the
"Pilgrims'" theory of churchmanship had undergone a fundamental change by reason of contact with a less radical type of
congregationalism.

As we have seen, from the days of the first London separatists
under Grindal, there had always been some difference of opinion among the Puritan sectaries about recognizing the established church as a true one and permitting attendance upon its
services. A number of those who found themselves forced out of
the Cartwrightian position by the events of 1604–5 adopted the
moderate deutero-Brownist viewpoint on this matter, and may
therefore be labeled Non-Separatist Independents. Among their

---

[18] For the careers of John Smith and John Robinson see W. H. Burgess, *John Smith
the Se-Baptist, Thomas Helwys, and the First Baptist Church in England* (London, 1911),
and his *John Robinson, Pastor of the Pilgrim Fathers* (London, 1920).

leaders were Henry Jacob, who had once engaged in a controversy with Johnson on the theory of absolute separatism,[19] and who had been active in the preparations for the Hampton Court conference; William Ames, a fellow of Christ's College and a great theologian, who was driven from Cambridge for his opinions; and William Bradshaw, one of the prominent Puritans in the Ashby-de-la-Zouche district. In 1605, Bradshaw issued a volume[20] in which was presented at length the concept of a nation-wide system of congregational churches, each a law unto itself and administering its own discipline through its local presbytery, or session, yet all kept in harmony and free from error by the civil magistrate. As long as this all-important office was filled by an absolute monarch of the Tudor-Stuart type, the whole scheme was quite utopian; for the secular rulers who were to regulate were also subject to ecclesiastical excommunication. Speaking of this power of the churches over their civil superiors the theorist says:

> They are not to presume to convent him before them, but are themselves to go in all civil and humble manner unto him, to stand bare before him, to bow unto him, to give him all civil titles belonging unto him. And if he be a King and Supreme Ruler they are to kneel before him and in the humblest manner to censure his faults, so that he may see apparently that they are not carried with the least spice of malice against his person, but only with zeal of the health and salvation of his soul.[21]

All of which is reminiscent of W. S. Gilbert's concept of hanging a culprit most politely.

Yet this type of semi-Puritan Independency had possibilities, both at home and abroad. In England the lack of a fully developed clerical hierarchy of classes and synods was an advantage, not only because the failure of 1585–90 and the continued vigilance of the Anglican authorities made any repetition of the earlier venture inexpedient and impracticable but also because

---

[19] Henry Jacob, *A Defence of the Churches and Ministery of Englande* (Middelburg, 1599); Francis Johnson, *An Answer to Maister H. Jacob His Defence of the Churches* ([Middelburg?], 1600).

[20] *English Puritanisme, Containing the Maine Opinions of the Rigidest Sort of Those That Are Called Puritans in the Realme of England* (s.l., 1605).

[21] P. 27.

it removed from the minds of prominent laymen all fear of being made subject to clerical control. Though the semi-Separatists might in time develop a system of associations and conferences closely paralleling the dreaded Presbyterian bodies, the emphasis on the legal independence of the individual congregations made the role of these higher bodies purely consultative and so insured the comparative weakness of the clergy in this type of organization. Consequently, the Jacob-Bradshaw doctrines found much support among the country gentry and also in the lower levels of society. When, in the civil-war period it was possible to consider changing the type of magistrate and some form of Puritanism was therefore practicable, Independency came logically and rapidly to the fore under the leadership of the Cromwells, Vanes, and Iretons of that day.

Abroad, this type of ecclesiastical organization was ideally suited to the needs of scattered communities of exiles or new territories which might be settled by Englishmen who had already been converted to this point of view at home. And it was to the thought of havens overseas that the Puritan mind was now turning. As we have already seen, Puritanism flourished wherever its devotees could avoid the direct gaze of the sovereign. In semi-autonomous areas in England, in the Channel Islands, in Ireland, the Protestants tended to be much more forward than they could be in Windsor, Canterbury, or even London. The English merchants in the Low Countries had long patronized Puritan ministers, and at the end of Elizabeth's reign, as already noted, the Separatists had resumed the Marian practice, which the Geneva congregation had not perpetuated, of having overseas colonies of Protestant religious refugees. While many of the merchants had continued to support the more conservative type of Puritanism, some were for the bolder course, and by 1599 there were Brownists among the Barbary traders in Morocco, where "Mully Hammet" (Ahmed IV) tolerated both the gospel and the mass among his "infidel" visitors.[22] Now that outright Presbyterianism was discredited at home, it was not difficult to persuade many merchants to adopt the

---

[22] Peter Fairlambe, *The Recantation of a Brownist* (London, 1616), sig. E, fol. 3(v).

milder variety of Independency, and Jacob found a hospitable reception when he came to Amsterdam in 1605. In time several English churches of his persuasion were organized in the Low Countries, and in 1616 he returned to London and organized a congregation there. But, while he was still abroad, Ames and he had consultations with Robinson and brought him to the milder point of view. So it came about that the Plymouth Colony was founded by Independents of this stripe, and, when the Massachusetts Bay settlers arrived in the 1630's, direct from England, most of them were already in harmony with their southern neighbors on this point of church polity.[23] As the Puritans had opportunity in a new land to discover the dignity and purpose with which political and social responsibility endows a church, they gave it more and more of this semi-Presbyterian hue, though it never attained the full strength of the Geneva variety.

We have thus seen the Puritan grasp the all-important principle that the moral leaders of a people should have political power and that this should be established on supernational lines. We have seen the movement grow from a matter of a few university-trained reformers, backed now and then by a handful of London merchants, to a powerful force, which under Elizabeth was supported by the great majority of serious-minded Protestants, and even at the end of that queen's reign was regularly able to command a majority in the House of Commons, the nearest thing to a truly representative body which England then possessed.[24] At the same time we have seen this

[23] Perry Miller, *Orthodoxy in Massachusetts* (Cambridge, Mass., 1933).

[24] This fact, which Professor Usher grants (*op. cit.*, p. 353), is in my opinion sufficient commentary on his oft-repeated thesis that the Puritans represented only a small fraction of the clergy, a sprinkling of wealthy landlords, and their peasant adherents. Without questioning any of his figures, it may be pointed out that the number willing to suffer for their principles who were also caught by the authorities' net does not represent anything like the true number of adherents of a movement. The number of Puritans to stand trial was about equivalent to the number of Marian martyrs, yet no one supposes that the latter comprise anything like the total of the Protestant sympathizers in England at the time. On the other hand, it may reasonably be asked how many Anglicans would have adhered to their type of religion under Puritan persecution had the shoe been on the other foot in 1605? Accepting A. O. Meyer's figure of 3 per

great movement thwarted by the determination of the ruling sovereigns, who produced a great ecclesiastical rival to divide its support and so were able to drive the clergy into a sectarianism which sapped their strength, lowered their prestige, and virtually destroyed all hope of subjecting the laity to effective discipline. Even the Puritans themselves were split into factions on unimportant issues, which time and secular politicians would inevitably magnify into the tragedy of the house divided against itself a half-century later. To deal with this great royal obstacle, we have observed the baffled idealists turning over one political theory after another without finding any satisfactory solution of their problem. After glimpsing the possibilities inherent in clerical control of, or at least representation in, a government which wielded an undivided sovereignty, as at Zurich, they followed Calvin in falling back on the medieval doctrine of the two societies, with its almost incredible corollary, that the secular and temporal powers could be somehow made to respect each other's spheres of influence. We have seen the Puritans in time of stress toy with the idea of religious toleration without, however, intending it for any but themselves. We have watched them gingerly test the ideas of the social compact and democracy, but never apply them with any degree of boldness.[25] Rather

---

cent of the population for the number of Catholics in England under Elizabeth (*England und die katholische Kirche unter Elizabeth* [Rome, 1911], p. 53), I should follow Usher (p. 269) in reckoning some 75 per cent of the English to have been either religiously indifferent or without any opinions on religious questions. Of the remaining 22 per cent, I should think—at a very rough guess—at least 15 per cent were Puritan, as the term is used in this book, by the middle of Elizabeth's reign, with the proportion toward the end of the century declining somewhat but not so much as to deprive the Puritans of their clear numerical preponderance over the Anglican party. Usher's estimate that the calculation of 100,000 potential Puritan signatures to petitions means that this faction was supported by only 2 per cent of the population makes no allowance for children, people not reached by canvassers, and perhaps even persons unable to write— a category which probably still included the majority of Englishmen at the end of the century.

[25] Even among the extreme Separatist Puritans there was no agreement on the virtues of pure democracy, as evidenced by the repeated disagreements over the authority of the congregational officials. Long after the Johnson congregation removed to Amsterdam we find one of the elders denouncing a meeting of fifteen of the rank and file to work against him, as "a beginning to tread the pathway unto popular government, the very bane to all good order in church and commonweal" (Richard Clyfton, *An Advertisement concerning a Booke Published by C. Lawne* [s.l., 1612], p. 122).

the Puritans were always willing to accept the theory of divine-right monarchy if help should be forthcoming from the crown, or of divine-right nobility if the Hastingses, Russells, and Riches seemed to offer greater support.

Most vital of all was the soul-searching which we have witnessed on the question of the right of revolution. Hampered from the first by a desire to be considered more law-abiding and loyal than their Roman Catholic and Anabaptist rivals, the Puritans early adopted the theory of passive resistance. Though they occasionally ventured to overstep its bounds in practice, they were determined for the most part to adhere to this doctrine, and repeated failure and disappointment could not shake this resolve. When some of the bolder spirits momentarily went beyond this stand at Geneva, they served up their revolutionary teaching with such an unfortunate choice of sauce and trimmings as to make it unpalatable to English Protestants for nearly a century. So the Puritans spent many uneasy years restlessly exploring the possibilities within the limits of the theoretical boundaries to which they had restricted themselves. Prayers and exhortations, treatises and petitions, nonconformity and secret assemblies, conventicles and even exile—they tried them severally and collectively and then began over again. All were equally futile in the face of a government which employed stronger means. Thus ended the era of opportunity, when the modern English character was in the making. With the help of the crown the world had beaten the idealists. The monarch would pass, but the world would stay, and that is the meaning of modernity.

Yet there are degrees of defeat. While the Puritans failed to hold for the cause of idealism what their spiritual predecessors had held in the Middle Ages, they did not lose everything. Though the party was unable to secure political power, some of its ideals filtered into the national character through other channels. If discipline could not be enforced, it was possible to accomplish something by persuasion. If the chief objectives could not be obtained, some of the minor ones were yet within reach. The monarchy itself accepted the demand for an educated, preaching clergy. Bancroft's ecclesiastical program incorporated many of the moderate Puritan features of Grindal's, including some against which Whitgift had argued. Nonresidency and pluralism were reduced to a minimum, and the ecclesiastical courts reformed. The Canons of 1604 contained a Protestant explanation of the offensive sign of the cross in baptism, which was the equivalent on this topic of Knox's "Black Rubric" on the communion. The reluctant Puritans who were swept back into the official fold by the disciplinary measures of 1605–6 constituted a powerful Low Church wing of the establishment. For the voice of the nonconformist was not completely stilled, in spite of all regulations. Through such agencies Puritan theological ideas, piety, and moral attitudes could be communicated to the masses. So the movement was not without its later influence. If England could not be made into a perfect Geneva, it could be modified here and there to conform to the Swiss pattern. Accordingly, it is worth our while to examine rather more closely the details of Tudor Puritan teaching in its nonpolitical aspects.

BOOK II

Intellectual, Social, and Cultural Aspects

CHAPTER XVII

The Spirit of Puritanism[1]

THE reader who has followed the changes and variations of Puritan political theory and tactics described in the preceding chapters will realize the
difficulty of generalizing about other aspects of the
movement. In strict accuracy there were many Puritan spirits
but there was no Puritan spirit. At any given time there were
right and left wings to the party and various center factions in
between. Even if a generalization is somehow made for the
group at a given period, it is not valid at other times. As circumstances changed, so did the party attitude. The Puritanism
of 1567 differed from that of 1566; the Puritan of 1573 was one
thing and the 1574 variety was quite another person. Nor is it
possible merely to select one individual as representing the
average and describe his fluctuations as typical. Party leadership was constantly wearing out. New men took command at
intervals, while the old captains went into retirement or drifted
into the conservative ranks. This changing complexity and
variability has made possible a multiplicity of conflicting half-

[1] In the succeeding chapters the illustrations of the Puritan attitude have been
almost entirely drawn from those writers who are known to have had trouble with the
governmental authorities for nonconformity or to have been out of sympathy with the
episcopal system. The only important exception is Philip Stubbs, who supported the
system of episcopacy but never held any place of prominence in the establishment.
By thus minimizing the writings of the Anglican Puritans, the picture drawn may be
sharpened somewhat, but this procedure seemed preferable to trying to analyze the
works of such men as Grindal and attempting to determine when they were speaking
as mild Puritans and when as governmental agents. In any event, the right wing of a
party is not to be considered as typical of the whole. In cases where a Puritan made his
peace with the government and subsequently conformed to and supported the official
system, his writings after that change of attitude are not cited. The works of persons,
like Perkins, who conformed under pressure but who gave no further indication of
sympathy with the governmental policy are, however, employed if there is reason to
believe that they retained their Puritan sentiments.

truths purporting to characterize Puritan political theory. To one observer the Puritan movement was the spearhead of liberty and democracy, to another it seems the embodiment of repression and tyranny. There is a familiar story about four blind men who touched different parts of an elephant and came to widely varying conclusions as to the nature of the animal. If we keep it in mind, it may help us through the maze of interlocking and conflicting generalizations about the movement as a whole.

In their efforts to hit off the essence of Puritanism, Anglican writers have commonly stressed its factious narrow-mindedness. In their opinion, the precisionist, convinced of his theological correctness and the severity of God, refuses to compromise with worldliness and so divides the church. Not far removed from this group of critics are the bulk of literary, artistic, and journalistic observers who get only the long-nosed umbrella-carrying joy-killer within their range of vision. In their judgment Puritan doctrine debases man. The zealot calls himself a worm, and is in fact a hypocritical, opinionated bigot. Modern Nonconformists, English liberals, and Americans strongly influenced by the ideals of democracy and progress, view the Puritan as their lineal ancestor, the author of much good. Medieval historians crying up their wares, and opponents of modern industrial liberalism, such as religious and Marxian interpreters, have pointed out that characteristics of an earlier age were prominent in sixteenth-century Puritanism. They have stressed the conservative Puritan attitudes on economic problems, class relationships, and church establishment.[2]

Our affirmations are usually correct; our denials commonly mistaken. Certainly this aphorism fits the characterizations summarized above. There is much truth in all of them, but very little in the implied denials, as we shall see. Our problem in this chapter is to single out for special emphasis four or five of the most important general features of Puritanism, leaving their detailed illustration to the chapters to follow. Here we

[2] See p. 425 n. 1 and Appen. III, pp. 513–14.

shall note the Puritan's morality, his skilful combination of individualistic and collectivist elements, his zeal, his otherworld-
liness, and his clericalism. In the later chapters the bases of
Puritan theory and the means of propagating it will first be discussed. Then certain social and cultural phases of the movement will be examined more closely. The literary aspects, however, constitute a special field of study which I shall not venture to invade.

The mainspring of the Puritan's mechanism was his moral
consciousness. The beautiful and true were to him only the
handmaidens of the good. He could ride to and fro through the
Constable country and in his diary record only prophesyings.
Psalms might be sung in church, but church music which obscured the sense of the words was an abomination, and little
time should be wasted on profane tunes outside the sacred
walls. The joys of pure learning, such as the observation of croc-
odiles, smote the zealous with thoughts of sinful pride. Plato,[3]
Aristotle,[4] and the Stoics[5] may have had some influence on
Puritan thought, but no one does or can maintain that Puritanism was primarily a philosophical system. Theology it had in
quantity, but, though Erasmus had been abandoned for Luther,
this only meant that action was to replace talk, not that theology was to obscure moral ends. Even tough Calvinism was bent
backward when it met the irresistible force of the Puritan conscience. The doctrines of predestination and justification by
faith clearly remove some of the strongest incentives to Christian morality, but the Puritan coolly asserted that every nerve
must be strained in that cause nevertheless. Triumphantly he
maintained that the cardinal doctrine of Protestantism implies
that one "must not live by faith unless he be just." To expect

---

[3] Martin Schulze, *Meditatio futurae vitae, Ihr Begriff und ihre herrschende Stellung
im System Calvins* ("Studien zur Geschichte der Theologie und der Kirche," Band VI,
Heft 4 [Leipzig, 1901]).

[4] A. F. Scott Pearson, *Church and State* (Cambridge, 1928).

[5] W. F. Schirmer, *Antike, Renaissance und Puritanismus* (Munich, 1924); L. L.
Schücking, "Zum puritanischen Persönlichkeitsideal," *Neue Jahrbücher für Wissen-
schaft und Jugendbildung*, IV (1928), 179–89.

salvation without an appropriate manner of life was sheer stupidity. By the fruits we are to know the reality of faith.[6]

Was this morality predominantly rational or mainly emotional? The Puritan was quite explicit in his denials of any primacy to the intellect. Those wishing to lead the Christian life must "renounce their own reason and fight against their own judgment." The heart was above the head. The mind of a man may be deceived but the heart cannot be. "The seat of faith is not in the brain, but in the heart, and the head is not the place to keep the promises of God, but the heart is the chest to lay them up in."[7] The emotions played a great role in Puritanism, and it is quite misleading to represent the movement as one of cold rationalism.[8] But it is equally misleading to leave the impression that the Puritans were either enthusiasts or mystics. They experienced emotional outbursts and they spent time in contemplation, but their morality was of a practical sort which joined head and heart in a relationship of mutual leadership and restraint. The Puritan reasoned enough to justify the separation from Rome and so appears a rationalist from the Catholic point of view. But when convenient he abandoned reason for emotion, and so held himself and his party back from the abyss of cold intellectualism and pure subjectivism. He disciplined his emotions by the twin yokes of theological dogma and ruling elders. When he meditated, he contemplated not the Heavenly City or the Blessed Virgin but himself and his own conduct.

The Puritan moral standard was formidable in the extreme. It was all-inclusive and absolute. All acts were moral. At no moment was one exempt from ethical considerations. There would be an accounting for every idle word, and about the criterion there was no relativity or shadow of turning. As Dering once put it: "The weight of sin is not in substance of matter, but in the majesty of God that is offended, and be the thing

---

[6] *The Workes of Richard Greenham* (5th ed.; London, 1612), pp. 682 and 375.

[7] *Ibid.*, pp. 306, 291, 294.

[8] See M. M. Knappen, *Two Elizabethan Puritan Diaries* (Chicago, 1933), pp. 9–14; cf. Olive M. Griffiths, *Religion and Learning* (Cambridge, 1935), pp. 17, 54–67.

never so little, yet the breach of his Commandment deserveth death."[9] It was true that by Christ's sacrifice something like a court of equity had been substituted for the unattainable common-law standard of the Old Testament.[10] But eventually there would be a sure and searching judgment which would be to the occasional and monitory manifestations of divine justice in this life as a thorough gaol delivery to a mere quarter-sessions. In fine Shakespearian phrase the warning is given:

> Then God will take matters into his own hand. Then shall be a new quest. Then all these matters that are shuffled up and evil judged shall be judged again. . . . . In earth there are means to acquit for a season, as delusion of the judge or of the witnesses, persuasion, corruption, favor. For they be *apices juris*, points in law, they undo all justice; a cavilling justice, but *apices juris in caelo non excusant*.[11]

Then one shall find no false witnesses, no persuasion, no corruption, no reversion of sentence, no second judgment, no way to escape execution. Or, in the even sterner words of another Puritan minister, all sinners

shall one day be apprehended and arraigned before the bar of God's tribunal seat where the majesty of God shall stand above them with a naked sword of vengeance and a scepter of justice. The devil, that old Satan, shall stand on the one side to accuse them and their own conscience on the other side to condemn them and the gasping gulf of Hell underneath them, ready to swallow them up for evermore. Then shall the dreadful sentence of eternal woe and damnation proceed against them, "Go ye cursed into hell fire."[12]

God is around us like a circle, the farther on one side, the nearer on the other.[13]

In this life it was impossible to eliminate temptation and the tendency to sin. But it was possible and necessary to eradicate any inclination to enjoy or persist in wrongdoing. A current legend illustrated the Puritan attitude on this point. Scotland and Ireland, so ran the tale, once disputed the ownership of an island lying between them. A Frenchman was asked to arbitrate, and, knowing the story of St. Patrick, he directed that a

---

[9] *A Parte of a Register* ([Middelburg], 1593), p. 81.

[10] Greenham, *Workes*, p. 679.   [11] *Ibid.*, pp. 657–58.

[12] Arthur Dent, *A Sermon of Repentaunce* (London, 1583), sig. D, fol. 2(*v*).

[13] Greenham, *Workes*, p. 690.

snake should be placed on the disputed territory. If it lived, the island must be Scotch. So, said the Puritan moralist, if a sinful thought lives undisturbed in the heart, it is a sign that one belongs to the wrong group.[14] Accordingly, one must frequently examine his life and conduct, to guard against any such tendencies. So thoroughgoing was to be this examination that the believer was advised that he must "in a godly jealousy suspect himself of his unknown sins."[15] This drastic demand for a pure mind stimulated that diary-keeping type of introspection which in time helped to make the English the reserved, self-conscious race they are.

But this constant emphasis on the need of standing comparison with something outside himself had other and better fruits. For one thing it produced some remarkable examples of unselfishness and humble devotion to a cause that was bigger than any one man. There were Puritan saints in the sixteenth century, though they are often overlooked. Some of the zealous may have been blue-nosed hypocrites, but they were not typical of the adherents of the movement in its early stages. The Puritan minister did not boast of his learning or morality. He did not claim to be a "petty angel . . . . dropped out of the clouds," but preached to himself as well as to his audiences. He asked his congregation only for a living wage, not that they should "make him abound in superfluity wherewith he should be filled until he burst."[16] He opened his purse to needy prisoners, assisted struggling students through the university, and sold his crops to the poor below the market rate.

This white-hot morality also made the Puritan a prophet in his generation, one who freely rebuked both high and low alike. He preached and practiced the high doctrine that the conscientious person should feel sorrow and repent not only for his own misconduct but for that of his neighbors. We are to be humbled for the faults of others "as though we ourselves for want of instruction or prayer were in some sort guilty of their sins."[17]

[14] *Ibid.*, pp. 679 and 705.

[15] William Perkins, *Workes* (3 vols.; London, 1616–18), I, 364.

[16] Greenham, *Workes*, pp. 748 and 355.   [17] *Ibid.*, pp. 255, 259, 711.

This assumed responsibility nerved the Puritans to speak out with a directness either courageous or rash, according to the point of view. For when they spoke they were quite aware that he who would attempt to "cut consciences" and point out another's fault, however gently, must needs expect "to carry John [the] Baptist's reward for his labor and send his head for a second course."[18] Preaching at St. Clement Danes near the Temple, one of them attacked the class bias of the law-enforcement agencies, declaring that "our laws have been a long time like to spiders' webs, so that the great buzzing bees break through and the little feeble flys hang fast in them." Knowing that agents were sent to take down any remarks that could be used against him, the preacher, who was eventually silenced, denounced them and added drily, "Let [them] write that . . . . too."[19] Another offered this public prayer in reference to the greedy patrons who substituted the starveling curate for the preaching minister which the living should have supported:

O Lord, the revenger of blood, behold these men whom thou hast set over us to give us the bread of life, but they have not given it us. . . . . Let them be clothed with shame, ... and upon their gold and silver which they have falsely treasured up, let continually be written, "The price of blood, the price of blood." For it is the value of our blood. O Lord, if thou didst hear the blood of Abel, being but one man, forget not the blood of many when thou goest into judgment.[20]

Other instances of this prophetic activity, the classic case of Knox's excoriation of the Edwardian courtiers and Dering's measured denunciation of the Queen to her face, we have already described. Individual and vocal activities were not the only manifestations of a moral force which did not spend itself until it had reached the banks of the Kaw three centuries later. The details of the ideal moral life as the Puritan saw it we may postpone for consideration in later chapters. But these are general illustrations of this most important Puritan bent.

[18] Ibid., p. 750.

[19] Henry Smith, Sermons (London, 1599), p. 529 and 305; Works, ed. Thomas Smith ("Nichols Series of Standard Divines: Puritan Period" [2 vols.; Edinburgh, 1866–67]), II, 73 and 347.

[20] Greenham, Workes, p. 847.

A modern critic has condemned this one-sided emphasis on morality as failing to satisfy the ideal of a well-rounded man, the natural goal of all human striving.[21] On the theory, however, that a division of labor is an essential of any highly developed civilization it is hard to see how a well-ordered society could exist without some such specialists in the moral sphere. It is easy to belittle the Puritan practice of "thundering out the just judgments of God." It is hard to devise alternative methods of preserving that conscientious striving after higher ethical standards which is one of the finer aspects of civilized living.

Almost equally important in the Puritan's makeup was the fine balance he maintained between individualism and the needs of the social order. At first glance, it is true, he appears quite egocentric. If the system of organized morality could not keep pace with the demands of his conscience, so much the worse for the system. The Reformation was built on the foundation of not tarrying for a dilatory church. Salvation was attainable by direct dealing with God. Middlemen were expensive and unnecessary. Nominally the Puritan retained some faith in the importance and efficacy of sacraments, aside from the character of the priest administering them. But it was a badly attenuated faith, and in practice he found it much more congenial to shock his Catholic friends by maintaining that the formal Christian who lived a life of sin would meet a worse end than the Jew or Turk. He refused to accept the authority of the organized church as equal to that of the Bible, which every man might interpret for himself. He insisted that church councils could and did err. He would not even accept the pronouncements of the great Protestant reformers as final. Luther and Calvin were noteworthy in their day, but even a "mean-sighted man may see that, when the sun shineth bright and clear, which a sharp-sighted could not have espied in the dawning."[22] Or, in another favorite figure, the dwarf who stood on the giant's shoulders could see farther than the great man.

This individualism, however, did not necessarily mean the

[21] James Truslow Adams, *The Founding of New England* (Boston, 1930), pp. 82–83.

[22] Greenham to Cox, n.d., *Parte of a Register*, p. 89.

breaking-down of the current social, economic, and political fabric any more than democracy implies the anarchy with which the Renaissance mind associated it. Just as there may be liberty without license, so the Puritan could be an individualist and still oppose usury, champion sumptuary regulations, and insist on the right of the crown, clergy, and upper classes to rule the country. The point was that he insisted that the individual must be given an intelligible reason for these restrictions, rather than accept them by blind faith. "What is this but to introduce the flat ignorance of the papist?" inquired the scandalized Puritan when Elizabeth suppressed the prophesyings. But once the purpose and meaning of checks were made clear, they might be continued. Puritanism was quite compatible with collectivism, provided the union was one of free minds properly convinced.

Thus, what the modern liberal would consider the logical implications of the Reformation teachings were not carried out in the sixteenth century. The free minds of the politically influential elements, of which the Puritans were one, decided against it. Illiterate laity could not be left to interpret the Bible for themselves. The Puritan feeling of responsibility for his neighbor led him to retain the ideas of an established church and persecution for heresy. A communion of the saints without discipline was to him mere promiscuity. The example of the Anabaptists, who took a more modern line in interpreting Protestant individualistic doctrines, was regarded with pious horror. So the clergy continued to enjoy a privileged status, while Puritans, like other churchmen, drew up and accepted creeds designed to bind their adherents.

At first glance this form of individualism may not look much like individualism to the modern observer; but, when compared with the Roman Catholic attitude, it certainly appears to be such. The Protestant clergy may have enjoyed a special status, but it was a very poor role compared to that of the Catholic cleric. The office of ruling elder, held by individuals ecclesiastically ordained but actually laymen, was one to which any adult male church member might aspire; the entire congregation had a voice in choosing the minister. With the primary responsibility for his salvation and some for governing the whole church firmly loaded onto his own shoulders, the average Puritan was a bigger cog in his ecclesiastical machine than the Catholic was in his. And, when Puritanism is compared with modern collectivist systems, its individualism also appears. The sixteenth-century thinkers put no faith in the state as such. The correctness of a system would save nobody. Correctness there must be, but there must also be personal co-operation and personal responsibility. Their individualism may not have been exactly "rugged" in the modern sense, but the Puritans were equally far from the attitude of putting the main burden of maintaining a healthy society on the government.

Closely related to the moral interest and the collectivist individualism of the movement was its "zeal"—there is no better term than the Puritan's own. The explanation of this "drive" has puzzled many critics. Weber thought the answer lay in the desire for assurance of salvation and proposed a most ingenious theological-psychological solution by which the doctrine of predestination, which theoretically left nothing to man, really left everything. The proofs for his thesis seem to be stated clearly enough in the theological documents, which contain clear teaching that good works were necessary to gain the assurance of salvation. But this was only one small point in a maze of doctrines, and the facts of everyday Puritan existence strongly suggest that in reality the average Reformed churchman, like Calvin himself, worried very little about securing this assurance.[23] Troeltsch has suggested[24] that the organization and class composition of the smaller Puritan sects was the true source of this enthusiasm. Debarred from secular preferment by their social origins the members of these little groups found other out-

[23] Max Weber, *Die protestantische Ethik und der Geist des Kapitalismus* ("Gesammelte Aufsätze zur Religionssoziologie," Vol. I [Tübingen, 1920–21]); English trans., Talcott Parsons, *The Protestant Ethic and the Spirit of Capitalism* (London, 1930); cf. also Knappen, *op. cit.*, pp. 10–16.

[24] *Die Soziallehren der christlichen Kirchen und Gruppen* ("Gesammelte Schriften," Vol. I [4 vols.; Tübingen, 1912–25]); English trans., Olive Wyon, *The Social Teaching of the Christian Churches* (2 vols.; London, 1931).

lets for their energies, such as sectarian and business activity. But the Presbyterian zeal is indistinguishable from the Independent variety, and some explanation must be found for both.

Nevertheless, the community life of the Puritans is well worth considering in our search for an explanation of this phenomenon of zeal. The Puritan disciplinary organization, with its severe punishments and the importance given to lay officials, certainly offers a tempting key, though it cannot quite be fitted to the English situation, since the Presbyterian system was never fully established in the southern kingdom. But there was what might be called informal discipline—the preaching of a high standard of conduct, and the clear signs of social disapproval in case of a slip.

There was also a certain intellectual toughness and internationalism about Calvinism which cannot be disregarded in this connection. For intellectually Calvinism was thoroughly respectable in those days. Did not even the Anglicans have to sharpen many of their swords at the Genevan smithy? The Reformed creed was, like Thomism and Marxism, a well-rounded system which had an answer for all problems, both spiritual and material. Its logic, also like that of these earlier and later codes, was not always quite so universally correct and conclusive as some of its admirers maintain, but it was far better than that of Lutheranism or Anglicanism, in which the compromises thrust upon the idealist by secular rulers were so glaringly apparent. There was a natural pride in maintaining this international system which had distinguished itself by striking success in many lands. "We stand for the doctrine and discipline of the best Reformed churches," said the Puritan, and the Anglican found it hard to refute this boast.

To these two elements must be added the individualism of the Puritan. Not only was a supposedly perfect system set before his mind and conscience, with social pressure put on him to follow it, but the believer was made to feel a personal responsibility. He had his own family prayers, his own private devotions. He could himself feel the "true comfort of performing [his] duty to the uttermost of his powers." He could measure himself by this standard nightly, note his shortcomings, and resolve to improve. Of this combination of social, intellectual, and personal elements was constructed the terrible engine known as the Puritan conscience, before which crumbled many a proud Philistine wall.

It has not commonly been considered necessary for critics to point out that Puritanism was a religious system and that the theory of this religion was an otherworldly and supernatural one. To the nineteenth-century reader that was too obvious to occupy space in any treatment of the subject. We are now, however, in an age which fixes its gaze so exclusively on this side of Jordan that we sometimes forget that in sixteenth-century maps the Promised Land was given the central place. It was a very real country, and its prospect from the Nebos of this world was most inviting. Today one scholar says, "Puritanism produced modern democracy"; another, "Puritanism led to modern capitalism"; a third declares that Puritanism is the father of modern science. Perhaps the sixteenth-century Puritan did incidentally or accidentally accomplish something along those lines, but he cared nothing for these things. He was saving souls from hell. We may single out particular aspects of his activity and concentrate on them, as this volume has centered its interest on the Puritan contribution to the civilization of this world. But we must not forget that in the Puritan's opinion attention to the affairs of the next world was far more important and that, judged by his own standards, the great bulk of his interests, like that of an iceberg, lay in the realm of the invisible.

"Paradise is our native country," said the Puritan, "and we in this world be as exiles and strangers: we dwell here as in Meshech and as in the tents of Kedar, and therefore we be glad to be at home."[25] And again, "To a mind which misliketh this world, nothing can come so welcome as death, because it takes him out of the world." Or, "All is trouble and weariness and vanity to a godly mind: whether he eat, or drink, or sleep, he

[25] Greenham, *Workes*, p. 645; cf. Ps. 120:5.

counteth it a servitude unto the flesh and wisheth with David
to be rid from these necessities."[26]

In practice the Puritan does not actually seem to have meditated much on the future life. When he noted his thoughts, at
least, they were almost entirely about his conduct in his earthly
career.[27] It can be argued that for all his theology the Puritan,
like the Pietist, lived each day for the joy of religion there and
then. But it should not be forgotten that in the last analysis the
intellectual motivation—the Last Judgment and perhaps salvation itself—for this scrupulousness was otherworldly.

Certainly the Puritan was wholly supernaturalist in his outlook. Or perhaps it would be better to call him "a-naturalist" in
that pre-Newtonian age. The concept of a natural order had
scarcely dawned upon him. He thought it a matter of course for
God to give him a good thought, for that old deluder Satan to
tempt him, or for a divine judgment to be inflicted on his neighbor. God was as close to him as breathing, nearer than hands
and feet. Modern observers may lose patience with a group
which practiced passive resistance so long after its futility seems
to us apparent. But the inscrutability of God's way was part of
the Puritan theory. It was not for the subtenant to inquire why
the Almighty Overlord was so long in enforcing on evil rulers
his right of forfeiture. It was enough for them that he was the
embodiment of absolute justice, slow perhaps—for reasons best
known to himself—but in his mill eventually grinding exceeding small.

This supernaturalism had the effect of making Puritanism a
curious combination of static and progressive elements. By its
comparative emphasis on reason and on the individual the movement was undoubtedly better equipped in these respects to
keep pace with the spirit of the times than the theoretically
flexible but practically crystallized Catholic church. But its religious and theological framework was of the golden-age variety.
Taking the Bible, and the New Testament era in particular,

---

[26] Henry Smith, *Sermons* (1599), p. 254; *Works*, I, 262–63.

[27] Knappen, *op. cit.*, p. 14.

as the norm, it was constantly striving, as Firth, borrowing Blake's lines, has so well suggested, to build Jerusalem in England's green and pleasant land. The result of this conflict between the progressive and the static attitudes was disastrous in the long run, but it is hard to see how any other solution could have been found at the time. The Catholics had to be fought at first; and, when the weapon of a rival supernatural authority—a necessity in those days—was once forged and used, it could scarcely be discarded.

The curse of partisanship was another evil heritage from the early Reformation struggle. No sketch of general Puritan traits would be complete if anti-Catholicism were not included. For the Puritan never forgot or forgave the Catholic; yea, he hated him with perfect hatred. He would come out from among the superstitious and touch no unclean thing that they had polluted. This fierce prejudice blinded him to the fact that the leopard had largely changed his spots. It warped his perspective and seriously hampered his party throughout its career. He would not consider any working alliance with Rome. On the contrary, he would abhor the vestment as the enemies' uniform, and all other Catholic practices as the dregs of popery. He would even consider pulling down the churches in which the minions of Antichrist had worshiped.

Some have thought of Puritanism as a middle-class attitude, which championed the virtues of that social group and perpetuated its vices. The small-minded—as it now appears—anti-Catholic prejudice which we have been describing might seem a brick in the structure of this argument, were contentiousness the prerogative of the middle class alone in the sixteenth century. But it would be hard to find anywhere in that age a large-minded man, one who was not, according to our standards, hypersensitive about his honor. The monarchs fought one another interminably, the courtiers dueled on the slightest pretext, and the county families carried on their quarrels from Westminster to assizes, to election, and back to Westminster again with the grim persistence of mountaineer feudists. The only distinguishing thing about the Puritan-Catholic strife was that it admitted of almost no truce in political emergencies, and this was due rather to a hardness of dogma than to a class attitude.

Nevertheless, it is true that Puritanism throve best among the merchants, lawyers, and small landholders. It was too cold and intellectually complicated for the lower classes, and a creed which might set a lord on the penitent stool before an entire congregation was no religion for a gentleman. The burgher areas of Switzerland, Holland, lowland Scotland, and east counties of England were its strongholds. This does not necessarily mean that Puritanism rationalized and perpetuated middle-class ideals any more than the town-generated friars of the thirteenth century did so. That is possible, but more probably Puritanism was originally a movement of the intelligentsia which happened to find its most natural allies in the middle class. If the intelligentsia are to carry through any vigorous program, they must always have political support, and it will very likely come from a class which is rising but has not yet secured political power. In the sixteenth century this group obviously was the middle class. There is little, however, to indicate that Puritanism, with its restrictions on the profit motive and its highly technical theology, was predominantly a middle-class movement. Rather, if it must be stated in class terms, it was a Protestant clericalism, a system in which the organized intelligentsia, whoever their allies might be, played the role of the senior partner. When laymen definitely secured the upper hand, Puritanism soon ceased to be Puritanism.

CHAPTER XVIII

The Puritan Doctrine of Authority

THE one bit of Puritan theology which calls for extended examination in this work is the doctrine of authority, for it was both the strength and the weakness of the Anglo-Saxon Israel. In all social movements many things are done in a routine fashion without considering the grounds on which the actions may ultimately be justified. Many important decisions may even be made with no more than a reference to expediency or proximate party principles. But from time to time in any undertaking of importance it is necessary to take stock and recover assurance, to get orientation and authorization for a new advance. Then it is that the movement's foundation principle appears and is put to the real test. It may be "the greatest good of the greatest number," the ideal of a classless society, or the superiority of a particular race. But something of the sort there must be, some regulative principle for society as a whole, and on its validity and appeal depends the success of the party which builds upon it.

In Puritanism this ultimate principle was the doctrine of the unique and complete authority of the Bible. For the time being it was a very satisfactory guiding principle. In the destructive phase of the party's activity it was an acute-angled salient, wrecking the enemy's defenses and acting as a bulwark for the prospective Protestant empire of northern Europe. Though the Catholics accepted the authority of the scripture and disputed only its uniqueness, so effective was the Protestant employment of this tool that in the first heat of the conflict good Catholics equated a knowledge of the Bible with heresy and prided themselves on their ignorance of this element of their own faith.[1]

---

[1] *Narratives of the Reformation*, ed. J. G. Nichols ("Camden Society: First Series," Vol. LXXVII [London, 1859]), p. 185.

Constructively, this type of authoritarian doctrine was plausible enough to give determined Protestants some standing-ground against their secular allies. At the same time, like *Das Kapital*, it was sufficiently complicated to retain its efficacy for two or three generations at least. In time, however, its weaknesses became apparent, and so the Puritan structure built upon it collapsed.

At first glance the Puritan teaching on authority seemed straightforward enough. The original texts of the sixty-six books of the Old and New Testaments were the only authority to be recognized by Christians. "If any man shall add unto these things, God shall add unto him the plagues that are written in this book."[2] Popes and councils could err. They had erred. Traditions were beggarly inventions of men, full of superstitious folly corrupting the purity of the faith. The authority of the Scriptures was "divine, ... absolute, and sovereign." They were "of sufficient credit in and by themselves, needing not the testimony of any creature, not subject to the censure of either men or angels, binding the consciences of all men at all times, and being the only foundation of our faith and the rule and canon of all truth."[3]

"The rule and canon of all truth." The Bible was not only the unique authority; it was a complete one. It contained the principles of all truth and all necessary details. "The body of Scripture is a doctrine sufficient to live well," a complete guide to life. "It comprehendeth many holy sciences": Theology, "ethics . . . . economics (a doctrine of governing a family) . . . . politics (a doctrine of the right administration of a common weal) . . . . ecclesiastical discipline . . . . academie (the doctrine of governing schools well)."[4] If the Almighty prescribed the details of the tabernacle in the Old Testament, it was incredible that he had not prescribed with equal care the specifications for the church of the new dispensation. Church government is of the substance of the gospel, and discipline is an essential of faith. Christ did not die intestate, but "before his death settled

[2] Rev. 22:18.

[3] William Perkins, *Workes* (3 vols.; London, 1616–18), I, 122.   [4] *Ibid.*, pp. 10–11.

his own domestical concernments."[5] Therefore, what was not prescribed in the Bible must not be used in church. Similarly detailed regulations for education, marital relations, secular government, and all other human concerns might be found in the Good Book.

> The Scriptures are fully sufficient for all instruction and conviction, both for faith and conversation . . . . therefore all other studies, learning, and courses had in schools and universities [are] to be no further nor otherwise used or allowed than may be warranted by the word of God and be serviceable thereunto, whether for the better understanding thereof, or for convincing the adversaries, or for other good use in church and commonwealth.[6]

When the Puritan read in Proverbs the aphorism, "Spare the rod and spoil the child," he said, "My child, O Lord, will I chastise."

The reason for this absolute and universal supremacy was the divine nature of the Bible. It was not only the pure word of God but the "Scripture of God," the writing of the Most High. True, human hands held the pens, but the mortals were only amanuenses. Speaking of the Old and New Testaments, Perkins declares that "not only the matter of them but the whole disposition thereof, with the style and the phrase, was set down by the immediate inspiration of the Holy Ghost."[7] The Holy Spirit spoke the words of Bible, said another Puritan leader, adding that God "hath graven in it an express image of eternal truth."[8] Fenner declared that Luke was not only taught "the full truth of all things by the inspiration and instruction of the Holy Ghost" but "also the elegance of the grace of the order and form of speech in writing by wisdom and commission of the same spirit." And again, speaking of the writers of the biblical books, he asserted that "the Holy Ghost doth breathe both into their tongue and style so that as scribes they pen those things

---

[5] William Ames, "Preface" to W. Bradshaw's *English Puritanisme* (London, 1660). Latin original of the Preface in *Puritanismus Anglicanus* (Frankfort, 1610), sig. B, fol. 2.

[6] H. Ainsworth and F. Johnson, *An Apologie or Defence of Such True Christians as Are Commonly (But Unjustly) Called Brownists* (s.l., 1604), p. 78.

[7] Perkins, *Workes*, I, 122.

[8] Edward Dering, *Godly Letters* in *Workes* (London, 1597), sig. A, fols. 6 and 7.

which they declare by the will of God."⁹ In all but name the Tudor Puritans held the dictation theory of inspiration. Since the Bible was thus proved divine, no other authority could compare to it. Only the word of God can bind the conscience, because only he can save or destroy the souls for keeping or breaking of his laws.¹⁰

Since the Bible was nothing less than God's own writing, it was to be interpreted literally. The allegorical, anagogical, and tropological methods classified and described by Nicholas of Lyra—following Guibert de Nogent and other earlier thinkers—and adopted by medieval theologians were contemptuously abandoned as beneath the dignity of Holy Writ.

> The Scripture hath but one sense, which is the literal sense, and that literal sense is the root and ground of all, and the anchor that never faileth, whereunto if thou cleave thou canst never err or go out of the way. And if thou leave the literal sense, thou canst not but go out of the way.¹¹

No corruptible fancies of carnal reason were to be permitted in interpreting the Bible. The Christian must eschew philosophy and "vain and curious searching of God's mysteries or measuring things revealed according to our understanding."¹² All that was necessary in case of doubt was to consider the context of the difficult passage, compare it with other parts of scripture, and fit it to the general pattern of faith as set forth in the Bible. For scripture was a matter not of strife but of harmony.¹³

Since the interpretation of the sacred authority was such a simple, straightforward matter, it was possible and perhaps natural to maintain that there was only one correct exegesis. Certainly that suited the temper of an age looking for absolute certainty, with each party anxious to justify its position by appeal to a divine standard. *Hinc illae lachrymae.* Hence the fury of partisan strife that followed the general acceptance of the

---

⁹ Dudley Fenner, *Sacra theologia sive veritas qua est secundum pietatem ad unicae et verae methodi leges descripta* ([Geneva], 1589), Preface, sig. *, fol. ii.

¹⁰ Perkins, *Workes*, I, 519.

¹¹ William Tyndale, *Obedience of a Christian Man*, in *Doctrinal Treatises*, ed. Walter (Cambridge: Parker Society, 1848), p. 304.

¹² Dering, *Godly Letters* in *Workes*, sig. A, fol. 7(v).   ¹³ Perkins, *Workes*, I, 583.

principle that there is nothing but harmony in the ultimate authority for the church.

No fleshly wisdom was needed to explain or validate this system. It was self-authenticating. The right-minded man had only to look at the Bible to recognize its perfection. Echoing Augustine, the Catholics insisted that no one could see so clearly unless the organized church held the candle for him and pointed in the right direction. But the Puritan was adamant. Following Luther and Calvin, he taught that the sacred book was to be recognized intuitively as divine, without the help of reason or any human being. Let an unprejudiced man study it for himself, with the assistance of the Holy Spirit, and he will be convinced. "The Scripture is the cause why men believe the Scripture."[14] When it was asserted that only the educated were fit to judge of such matters, Hooper granted that they alone might teach but insisted that all men could understand the essential biblical doctrines without aid, just as all men can be good citizens and recognize and obey the true king without the help of professional lawyers.[15] Fifteen years later the Plumbers' Hall congregation rejected as papistical the suggestion that they should be bound by the interpretations of the Scriptures given by the learned.[16]

Such, in theory, was the Puritan doctrine of authority, but, as the modern reader can well imagine, in practice a good many weak links developed. It might easily be supposed that the canonical and textual difficulties would soon appear insuperable. If Christians can recognize the true scripture intuitively, without assistance from the church, how was it that the canon was not actually fixed for more than three centuries after the death of Christ, and then only by a church council? And since the original manuscripts have disappeared, how can we be sure of the text which is authoritative? How can we have an abso-

---

[14] Tyndale, *Answer to Sir William Thomas More's Dialogue*, ed. Walter (Cambridge: Parker Society, 1850), p. 136.

[15] *Answer to the Bishop of Winchester's Book*, in *Early Writings*, ed. Carr (Cambridge: Parker Society, 1843), pp. 214–15.

[16] Edmund Grindal, *Remains*, ed. Nicholson (Cambridge: Parker Society, 1843), p. 214.

lute authority with an uncertain text? But in fact these difficulties did not greatly perplex the men of the sixteenth century. Had they known of them, they might have replied that the cardinal doctrine of justification by faith had only been discovered in their own time. They saw nothing incongruous in the theory that centuries were needed for the truth about the canon to come to light. They had as yet no clear comprehension of the principles or difficulties of textual criticism. Only a comparatively few manuscripts were known. Scholarship saw no reason to challenge Erasmus' right to restore the spurious trinitarian verse in I John, chapter 5. If there were still a few textual uncertainties, most men of the Renaissance period felt perfectly capable of settling them when they found time. Meanwhile the text would do for all practical purposes.

It was the problem of interpretation which caused the real difficulty. Textual problems could be postponed, but the need for a satisfactory system of exegesis was pressing and immediate. From the days of the Zwickau prophets in the dawn of the German Reformation it was evident that the pure Protestant theory was impracticable, or at least in need of supplement. Left alone with their Bibles, sincere and simple-minded believers would make different senses out of the same original text. However they might eschew vain philosophy, there still remained a great deal of confusing material to grapple with. One passage commanded the chosen people to root out the Amalekites, and another instructed the faithful to love their enemy. The prophet Samuel hewed Agag in pieces before the Lord, yet the Sermon on the Mount prescribed turning the other cheek.

To meet this difficulty, the Protestants had recourse to a method of interpretation already developed in part by their Catholic predecessors. Instead of treating all parts of the Bible as equally authoritative, distinctions were drawn and some sections were regarded as the norm by which others were to be judged. The portions describing and regulating the life of the New Testament church were taken as the end of all the others, which were indorsed, neglected, or actually repudiated, according as they harmonized with the utopia of the new dispensation.

For example, the Old Testament law was divided into three categories: moral, judicial, and ceremonial. The first harmonized with the New Testament and was still binding on all Christians. The second was the particular or municipal law of the Jewish state, which might or might not be imitated by later governments, as convenient. The last prescribed the forms and rituals ordained as reminders and types of the Messiah who was to come. Now that these were fulfilled, to repeat them was an insult to the living Lord.[17]

Actually, it will be seen, this was to subject the Bible to a rudimentary historical analysis and to select for primary emphasis that portion relating to what the Christians considered the culmination of the long story. As history, the entire book remained divine and inerrant, but only a part was the infallible rule of faith and practice. Even that was subjected to further historical treatment. Luther had recognized the differences between Paul and James, and they could not be hidden. There were also discrepancies between the various descriptions of ecclesiastical officials and organization. Some further explanation was necessary. The solution adopted was to take not the biblical passages themselves but the general standard of the New Testament churches described in them as the real authoritative norm for Protestants. "That which . . . . was the use and manner of the primitive church is lawfull to be used of us."[18] It was easy to find a plausible justification for this choice as against the practice of later centuries. "For the water at the fountain's head is more wholesome and pure than when it is carried abroad in rotten pipes or stinking ditches."[19] The determination of this general standard of the New Testament period presented a nice problem in historical technique. While no final agreement was ever reached, students of the history of historical research should not overlook this important

[17] These and other facts suggest that the Puritans were not so predominantly Old Testament in their outlook as has sometimes been asserted (M. M. Knappen, *Two Elizabethan Puritan Diaries* [Chicago, 1933], pp. 13–14 n.).

[18] Perkins, *Workes*, I, 121.

[19] Hooper, *A Declaration of Christ*, in *Early Writings*, p. 26.

chapter in the development of their subject. For the number of scholars involved, the social and political importance of the results, and the interest excited make it easily the greatest of all historical undertakings.

In working over the texts, these Protestant theologians-turned-historians, as we have seen, soon demonstrated the Boyle's law of historical methodology, that the interpretation of a source varies directly as the square of the prejudice in the interpreter. "The Devil can quote scripture to his purpose," is the pious version of this truth. Anabaptists found it convenient to be strict constructionists, and the Anglicans found the loose method congenial. In between, as might be expected, were the Independents and Presbyterian Puritans. However they might denounce prelatical "sophistry" in tampering with God's ordinances, when they came to deal with the more radical sections on pacifism and communism, they also took refuge in appeals to common sense and the necessities of the Christian state. And, even when doing battle with the Anglicans, the Puritan occasionally slipped in an appeal to the "wise and reasonable man which maketh his account of likelihoods" as an authority for his opinion.[20] It was a back-door method of bringing reason and experience into the tribunal, but it let them in nonetheless. With these guides it was possible to see Genevan landscapes in Palestine, as the Hollywood producers enable us to see California mountains towering over an Alpine village. "Tell it unto the church" was clear evidence for the existence of an eldership in the apostolic age. The statement in the first chapter of Acts that "they appointed" two nominees for Judas' vacant place proved the case for popular elections.

To interpret his text, the Puritan surreptitiously brought not only reason and experience but the technique of explaining the uncertainties of an early age by the clearer outlines of its successor, a device employed by F. W. Maitland in his treatment of the Saxon period of English history. If there was any doubt that the New Testament churches did not have the

---

[20] Thomas Cartwright, *The Second Replie against Maister Whitgiftes Second Answer* (*s.l.*, 1575), p. 234; A. F. Scott Pearson, *Church and State* (Cambridge, 1928), p. 124.

clerical vestments, godfathers, or bishops who ruled their
fellow-priests, let the records of the church in the next few centuries be consulted. There no trace of them would be found.
On the contrary there were records to show when and by whom
these things were introduced. Thus one could be certain that
they had not existed in the early model organizations. So the
Puritan who professed to scorn all authority but the Bible often
found himself buried deep in the manuscripts of Cyprian,
Tertullian, and Augustine. Sometimes he professed that this
was merely for the sake of meeting the enemy on his own
ground, without implying that the faithful needed any such
traditional props for their beliefs. But in time some of these noncanonical documents came to take on a kind of secondary authority. Perkins said that the Apostles' Creed was to be vene-
rated as taught by the Apostles, embraced by the ancient
fathers, sealed by the blood of the martyrs, and used by the emperor Theodosius to end controversies.[21] It had more authority than a private Christian's writings, "because it hath been received and approved by universal consent of the Catholic
church in all ages." The meaning and doctrine in it could not be
changed, even with the authority of the Catholic church, and
the words or order only with the consent of the whole church.[22]
Also higher in authority than private compositions, though below such generally approved writings as the creeds, Perkins
placed the documents drawn up by parties or separate churches
within the universal church. Even the works of private men, if
they conformed to the Bible, could be called the word or truth
of God, though not scripture. Hence, the phrase "a preacher
of the Word." Indeed this leading Puritan even found a good
word to say for tradition at the end of the century. Tyndale
had indignantly denied[23] that there was nothing to correspond
to the written word before Moses. Perkins cheerfully granted
it. He noted that Paul must have relied on noncanonical tradition in identifying the magicians who withstood Moses as
Jannes and Jambres, since these names are not in the Old
Testament. Similarly, he declared, we accept as truth the statements that Mary died a virgin and that Isaiah was killed by a

[21] *Workes*, I, 119.   [22] *Ibid.*, p. 122.   [23] See above, p. 47.

fuller's club, though no scripture can be adduced in proof of them. So long as a tradition is not contrary to the Bible and not required for salvation, it may be accepted as a statement of what the eighteenth-century man would have called natural, if not revealed, religion.[24]

Time also brought the Puritan virtually back to another auxiliary authority abandoned in a previous generation—contemporary human judgment. The historian searching for the New Testament ideal may be pardoned for consulting the records of the apostolic age. It is difficult to see any justification but expediency for the appeal to the authority of men of their own generation when attempting to determine the New Testament standard. The fact is that the sixteenth-century English feeling of intellectual inferiority was stronger than Puritan logic. Hence the constant appeals to the example of "the best Reformed churches," and the repeated embassies to Geneva and Zurich. These requests were of course in part for political support, but there was also a real sense of intellectual dependence. As the century wore on, the tendency showed little sign of diminishing. Bownde's sabbatarian argument[25] is a heavy embroidery of Continental names and quotations on a slight fabric of borrowed reasoning. Perkins was willing to allow councils to establish religious traditions if not too numerous, absurd, superstitious, or required as essentials of worship.[26] As Hooker complained, the Puritan denounced his opponents for using human authority, but relied on it himself when convenient.

Even when the general practice of New Testament times was determined—with all these conditions—there remained two further qualifications to be made in the interests of preconceived notions, party warfare, and convenience. The Puritan thought of the primitive church as existing in somewhat special circumstances. To get the Christian movement started, God had poured out special grace and had temporarily endowed his agents with peculiar and striking gifts. Though, as we have seen, the Puritan believed in the possibility of divine intervention in his own age, he did not expect very many such notable miracles, since the necessity for them had passed. The Bible had been validated; the church established; a sufficient witness given. Let the hardhearted perish in their sins. So he discounted the New Testament institutions of apostles, evangelists, spiritual healing, and speaking with tongues as "extraordinary," not to be expected in a settled church. He also recognized a kind of judicial law for the New Testament church, regulations peculiarly adapted to life in the Levant but not necessarily binding on Christians in other climates. Foot-washing belonged in this category, and so did the institution of official widows in the church organization, persons who might be useful in performing the ablutions required in a hot country. An England which took avidly to the new invention of yellow starch because it enabled soiled ruffs to be worn longer, saw no need of being overcurious about conformity to this biblical standard.[27]

This was a considerable withdrawal from the position that the Bible was a complete authority for the church, containing detailed specifications for its organization and worship in all ages. Under pressure from his Anglican rivals the Puritan was forced, in fact, to accept their contention that only the general outlines of such a structure were to be found in the Good Book.[28] He could not find any specified time for service or warrant for the minister wearing any clothes at all. He had to admit that these matters were left to the regulation of the particular church organization concerned. The best he could do was to mutter, "Nevertheless, the surplice is superstitious," and argue that the general New Testament principles and common sense forbade wearing the enemy's uniform.

Finally, the Puritan was driven from his stand for the single sense of his authority. Allegorical interpretations were of course allowed as literary and homiletical artifices without causing any intellectual perplexity. But it is difficult to read some of the sermons and not conclude that in practice many of the Puritan preachers took the supplementary interpretation as

[27] John Whitgift, *Works*, ed. Ayre (3 vols.; Cambridge: Parker Society, 1851–53), III, 292.

[28] See above, p. 289.

seriously as they did the grammatical. In any case the tendency to think in such terms did not die out with the Reformation. In fact, Luther himself never completely abandoned the allegorical method,[29] and in explaining the passages in the Old Testament supposed to refer to the Messiah it was necessary to give this Catholic technique an official resuscitation. Calvin was honest enough to point out that the grammatical and historical meanings of such passages as the Seventy-second Psalm and the eighth and ninth chapters of Isaiah applied to events contemporary with the original writers. Nevertheless, the tradition of the prophetic witness to the coming of Christ was to be found in the New Testament, and so room had to be made for it. Only by accepting once more the despised exegetical doctrine of the multiple senses was this possible.[30] Naturally, the English disciples duly reflected this wavering on the part of their masters.

So the weapon whose apparent keenness and true temper had at first delighted the Puritan heart developed one flaw after another and soon grew dull and blunted. But unfortunately for its wielders it did not deteriorate so far as to be either utterly worthless or completely pliable. Though somewhat discredited among the most critical, there were still many attractions about it which for many years prevented this great book from losing its prestige and influence. There was the aura of sanctity which still clung to it and was rather enhanced than diminished by the difficulties of interpretation. Though the Puritan objected to the creed or paternoster being used as a charm, his well-worn Bible occupied very nearly the same position in his life. Nothing was to be laid upon it, and in a moment of trial or perplexity he might divine with it, opening it at random and following the implied advice in the first passage his eye lighted upon. The Bible's length and complexity further protected its dignity through the troublous times of intellectual criticism. If it could not be proved altogether true, under the safeguard of the exe-

[29] Frederick W. Loetscher, "Luther and the Problem of Authority in Religion," *Princeton Theological Review*, XVI (1918), 497–556, esp. p. 529.

[30] Kemper Fullerton, "The Reformation Principle of Exegesis and the Interpretation of Prophecy," *American Journal of Theology*, XII (1908), 422–42, incorporated and expanded in his *Prophecy and Authority* (New York, 1919).

getical methods employed neither could it easily be proved false in any detail. As long as believers demanded a refuge for their faith, it held much of its ground, and so molded the thought and action of the Puritans and their successors for generations to come.

Although Whitgift complained that Cartwright turned the Bible into a nose of wax, making it say what he liked,[31] this charge is surely an exaggeration. For, when all allowances have been made, the Puritans were certainly influenced by what they read in the Bible. Imagine the difficulty of constructing the Reformed system from the material in the backgrounds of its supporters, minus the sacred books. As they had influenced the Reformers, so the authoritative Testaments continued to sway their followers. Cartwright may have painted Geneva into a Palestinian setting, but, at least, the setting was dictated to him by the Bible. Because of its continuing utility, which we have described above, the book was not supplanted in its role of authoritative primacy by the Puritans when criticism had shown clearly enough that a courageous and clear-headed substitution was called for. Thus was fastened on Anglo-Saxon idealism that curse of biblicism which still warps and hampers it.

It is indeed true that even the devil can quote scripture to his purpose; but, if his arsenal were confined to that volume, it would rather hinder his operations. Idealists have been able to use the Bible to a certain extent, but it can be twisted only so far until it recoils on its handler, and most of its strength is still exerted to confine idealistic progress within the limits of other-worldly, supernatural, and Christian boundaries. In the latter part of the sixteenth century it kept the Puritans from their natural allies in the ranks of the reformed Roman organization. Even today, like the infallible and authoritative Catholic church, it renders more difficult the formation of an ultimate united front for the idealists of all the world. As we said at the beginning of the chapter, the doctrine of biblicism was both strong and weak. Time has magnified its weaknesses without adding to its strength.

[31] *Works*, III, 163.

CHAPTER XIX
Puritan Theology

THE most cursory survey of Puritan literature before 1603 will indicate clearly enough the intellectual backwardness of the movement. It is not that the bulk of this material is composed of sermons, popular tracts, and commentaries which were little more than collections of expository lectures delivered seriatim on this or that biblical book. Something of this sort is true of any religious movement. The significant thing is the character of that small fraction of their output which was devoted to theological subjects. With very few exceptions even this little was occasional and controversial rather than thorough and systematic. The Puritan felt capable of defending himself intellectually against rival religions and factions, but like his Anglican rival he fell back on Continental writers for the statement of his case against unbelievers and for a sure buttressing of the foundations of his faith. The *Short Title Catalogue* bears ample testimony to the popularity in England of the works of Bullinger and Gualter, Calvin and Beza, Zanchius and Ursinus. England also offered a good market for the works of Huguenots, though they lacked the prestige which went with an established Reformed church. Luther and Melanchthon were still read, and even Scandinavian works were not unknown. Yet there is no trace of any comparable Continental borrowing of English ideas in the Tudor period.

Of the polemical theology produced by the Puritans we have already discussed in the first part of this volume those sections directed against the Anglicans and the foes of their own household, Presbyterian or Separatist as the case might be. Plentiful and vigorous as was this literature, the anti-Catholic writings of the Puritans easily exceeded it in both respects. For every gag for the Anglican goose there were at least two arrows for the Romish wolf. In part this is to be accounted for, of course, by the greater ease in securing licenses for such literature and the governmental encouragement it received. But even aside from this consideration the greater output doubtless indicated a greater Puritan interest in this subject. The Anglican was deluded and oppressive, but the zealous thought a new sovereign would change all this. Rome was a much more serious problem, not to be solved by the mere passage of time. So the Puritans, from Tyndale on, collaborated with the Anglicans in repeating and restating the Continental arguments against the mother-church. So far as I have been able to discover there was nothing original about the product, but its bulk was enormous. Tyndale and Barnes sided with Gardiner and Edward Fox in the original attack on the power of the papacy. In the next decades Hooper, Joye, and Gilby joined with Ridley and Cranmer in answering Winchester's "devilish detection" of the mass. In the early years of Elizabeth, Jewel's comprehensive statement of the Protestant cause received vigorous support from Sampson and Humphrey. During the invasion of Seminarists and Jesuits, Puritan and Anglican stood shoulder to shoulder in the breach. Fulke and Rainolds held "painful conferences" with prisoners and laboriously published the proceedings. Cartwright as well as Fulke, who at the time of this work was reconciled to the Anglican establishment, refuted the Rhemish translation of the Bible.

Some doctrines which do not now appear to be important as partisan issues were so considered in the sixteenth century and treated accordingly. The most important of these was that of predestination. The Council of Trent had made something like semi-Pelagianism the orthodox Catholic doctrine. This seemed to most Protestants not only a detraction from the majesty of God but a shameless denial of the great truth of justification by faith. To destroy this "rotten prop" of unbelief was the chief end of the elaborate treatises on Augustinianism which came out of Continental Europe, particularly Geneva. In the early days, however, there was not complete agreement on this point among the English Puritans. In King Edward's time such a leader as Hooper, who had spent his exile at Zurich, could be attacked by Bartholomew Traheron, who had studied with Calvin, as not sufficiently orthodox in this respect.[1] Even after the Marian interlude Foxe did not take strong enough ground on this subject to please all the critics.[2] But, by the end of the century, Perkins, with the full support of his party, was stating the doctrine in practically full supralapsarian terms, and there was as yet no disposition on the part of the Anglicans to quarrel about the matter.[3] When, in 1595, the Huguenot professor Peter Baro ventured to introduce the liberal doctrines of the Dutch Arminius into his Cambridge divinity lectures, Whitgift supported the University authorities in their efforts to suppress such teaching. In November he held a small gathering of divines at Lambeth to settle the question. Resolutely, William Whitaker, Regius Professor of Divinity at Cambridge, set out for London to "stand for God against the Lutherans." Fervently his Puritan friends prayed that he might be successful.[4] But with the Archbishop on their side there was little need to worry. The result of the meeting was a set of nine highly Calvinistic articles which contained most of the doctrine later enunciated by the Synod of Dort. From eternity God had predestined some to live and reprobated others to death. Man did nothing to deserve election. The will of God was the only cause. A limited and definite number were predestined to be saved. The saints necessarily persevere, because true justifying faith can never be totally lost. With this statement of doctrine the Archbishop hoped that all would be content, and he notified Baro that it

[1] Traheron to Bullinger, September 10, 1552, and June 3, 1553, *Original Letters Relative to the English Reformation*, ed. Robinson (2 vols.; Cambridge: Parker Society, 1846–47), pp. 324–28; cf. ab Ulmis to Bullinger, April 3, August 22, December 31, 1550, *ibid.*, pp. 406, 416, 426.

[2] "Notes Appertayning to the Matter of Election," attached to John Stockwood's translation of Beza's *Treasure of Trueth* (London, 1576); *De Christo gratis justificante* (London, 1583); cf. *Acts and Monuments*, ed. Townsend (8 vols.; London, 1837–41), I, 408–9.

[3] See below, p. 375; cf. William Cunningham, *The Reformers and the Theology of the Reformation* (Edinburgh, 1866), p. 366.

[4] M. M. Knappen, *Two Elizabethan Puritan Diaries* (Chicago, 1933), p. 125.

was not fitting for an alien to be curious and stir up controversy. When the Frenchman proved recalcitrant, he was forced from his position as Lady Margaret Professor. There was some murmuring among the younger Anglicans against this effort of the Archbishop to saddle high Calvinism upon the established church. Neither Lancelot Andrewes nor Overall, who succeeded Whitaker as regius professor at Cambridge, would condemn Baro's position as heterodox. Bancroft, now Bishop of London, displayed his sympathy by ordering the clergy of the metropolis to march in the exile's funeral procession when he died, in 1599, and at the Hampton Court Conference the prelate successfully opposed the Puritan efforts to have the Lambeth articles added to the Thirty-nine as part of the official creed of the Church of England. But these protests were merely the beginning of sorrows which did not yield their bitter fruit until the next century. The articles were regularly adopted by the Irish branch of the establishment, and so it may be said that during Tudor times this doctrine was not an issue between Puritan and Anglican. During that period both Protestant rivals were treasuring and burnishing the predestinarian weapon for use against the hated papists.[5]

Somewhat similar, though of much less importance, was the interest shown in the interpretation of the article in the Apostles' Creed dealing with Christ's descent into hell. The traditional explanation was that after the crucifixion the Redeemer had made a physical tour of the underworld, first enduring its pains as part of his suffering and then, to the surprise and chagrin of Satan, departing with the announcement of his triumph over death and the adversary. This was the harrowing of hell, as portrayed in medieval picture and miniature. Calvin who preferred a spiritual interpretation of the real presence in the sacrament, also spiritualized this descent, making it a symbolic statement of Christ's suffering on the cross.[6] This interpretation had

---

[5] John Strype, *The Life and Acts of John Whitgift* (3 vols.; Oxford, 1821), II, 227–319. There had been a preliminary rumble of this Baroist controversy at Cambridge as early as 1581, when Laurence Chaderton criticized the Huguenot's views (Strype, *Annals of the Reformation under Elizabeth* [4 vols. in 7; Oxford, 1824], III, i, 68).

[6] *Institutes*, Book II, chap. 16.

the difficulty of making the phrase both repetitious and out of chronological order, since Christ's sufferings under Pilate and the burial had already been mentioned. Nevertheless, it seemed the part of anti-Catholic wisdom for Reformed thinkers to defend this gloss, and the English Puritans clung fast to it. There was controversy on this matter at Exeter as early as 1562,[7] and at Leicester about 1570.[8] The choleric Hebraist Hugh Broughton, formerly of Christ's College, Cambridge, joined the fray in 1594 with the ingenious suggestion that in this passage "hell" was to be taken to include the entire future world, and so he made the phrase refer to Christ's going to paradise. This theory received no great support, but it added to the confusion, and soon there were half-a-dozen different interpretations of these words, all commanding some support.[9] In 1595, Perkins sought to bolster up the spiritualizing theory by suggesting that the phrase merely applied to Christ's being held captive in the grave three days, lying in bondage to death for that period of time.[10] For this he was vigorously attacked by the Oxford poet and antiquarian, John Higgins, who published a defense of the traditional view in 1602.[11] Henry Jacob and Bilson, now Bishop of Winchester, also had a controversy on this subject at the end of Elizabeth's reign,[12] a fact which is a further sign of the beginnings of theological differences between the two great parties of English Protestants.

While thus belaying the minions of Antichrist on the right, the Puritan also found time to refute Anabaptist teachings on the left. To some extent the defenses of the doctrine of predestination had this additional purpose, for the Anabaptists were generally "libertarians" also, championing, in some degree, the freedom of the will. The pestiferous sectarians of Edward's

---

[7] Strype, *Annals*, I, i, 519.   [8] *DNB* art., "William Hughes."

[9] Strype, *Whitgift*, II, 220–21, 324, 359–67; cf. *Somers Tracts*, ed. Walter Scott (13 vols.; London, 1809–15), II, 1–9.

[10] William Perkins, *Workes* (3 vols.; London, 1616–18), I, 231–35.

[11] *An Answere to Master William Perkins concerning Christ's Descention into Hell.*

[12] Bilson, *The Effect of Certaine Sermons* (London, 1599); Jacob, *A Defence of a Treatise Touching the Sufferings and Victorie of Christ* ([Middelburg], 1600).

time who perplexed Hooper, and remained unreconciled even when imprisoned within the same walls in Mary's time, were of this opinion, as we have seen, and their errors had to be exposed. Another Anabaptist doctrine with which Hooper dealt[13] was the curious assertion that Christ took no flesh from his mother, that "He passed through the Blessed Virgin Mary as saffron doth through a bag." This doctrine, designed to exalt the Son and safeguard him from the taint of original sin, was the invention of Melchior Hoffman, the spiritual father of the Münster revolt, and was the belief for which Joan Bocher died. In Elizabeth's reign the Anabaptists were more important as bogeymen than as a real political or religious force, since their strength was almost entirely among the churches of the Dutch immigrants and a careful watch was kept over them. But an offshoot in the form of the Family of Love did deserve some attention. These Familists were the followers of the German mystic Henrick Niklaes, or Nicholas. In doctrine they combined Anabaptist with what were later called Quaker principles. In the middle of Elizabeth's reign the movement gained so much strength in the east counties that the Council urged the Convocation of 1581 to take action against it, and a bill to punish its adherents was introduced in Parliament. In 1579, John Knewstubs, the leader of the classis movement in Suffolk, composed a detailed refutation of their system under the title of *A Confutation of Monstrous and Horrible . . . . Heresies Taught by H.N.*, which was quite as hostile as the refutations of the more conformable William Wilkinson and the Anglican John Rogers, which appeared in 1578.[14]

Only two Puritan theologians of the period seem to have made any effort to rise above the controversial level and, like Moses "ascending the Mount Nebo," present their readers with something resembling a systematic treatment of the whole range of Christian theology. Of these, the first was the young genius

[13] *A Lesson of the Incarnation of Christe* (London, 1549); *Later Writings*, ed. Nevinson (Cambridge: Parker Society, 1852), pp. 1–18.

[14] Wilkinson, *A Confutation of Certaine Articles, Delivered unto the Familye of Love*; Rogers, *The Displaying of an Horrible Secte of . . . . Heretiques*.

Dudley Fenner, whose *Sacra theologia sive veritas qua est secundum pietatem ad unicae et verae methodi leges descripta* was published at London in 1585.[15]

So novel was systematic divinity in England that the author felt it necessary to get Cartwright to contribute a preface justifying this attempt to subject Christian truth to the bonds of logic. This the older leader did on the ground that for a jewel a small box was as good as a large one, if not better. The work begins with a definition of theology as "the knowledge of the truth which is concerning God, to the end to live well and happily." This knowledge is divided into two parts, concerning God and concerning his works or actions. God is defined as "a spirit which is, Eheje [Jahveh], I am or I will be, or the beginning and ending. That is, most simple, most holy, every-way infinite and therefore one."[16] While the finite cannot perfectly comprehend the Infinite, human beings can make out some signs of his glory, and so the traditional details of God's character— his omnipotence, omniscience, goodness, and justice—are presented in the first book, together with a short statement of the doctrine of the Trinity. Then follows a book devoted to the general nature of God's actions, such as holiness and righteousness, and the ideal reflection of them in angels and men. The third book discusses the effects of sin and the fall, the corruption of the understanding, and man's other faculties. God's covenant and the promise of Christ are discussed in the next section, which is organized about the Calvinistic analysis of Christ's office into prophetic, priestly, and royal functions. The fifth book undertakes a general survey of the Christian duties with particular reference to those of such social classes as ruler and subject, lender and borrower. Family discipline occupies the next section, and then follow three on ecclesiastical government —one on the topic in general, one on the organization of the Old Testament church, and one on New Testament government.

[15] Reprinted at Geneva, 1589 and 1604; at Amsterdam, 1632. There is a manuscript English translation in Harleian 6879. The very slight *Sacred Doctrine of Divinitie* (London, 1599; Preface dated January 1, 1589), sometimes attributed to Fenner also, is by a Kentishman, but not by Fenner, as the Preface clearly indicates.

[16] 1589 ed., fol. 1.

Sprinkled through these chapters are treatments of the sacraments, of Baptism and the Lord's Supper, and of the doctrine
and interpretation of the Scriptures themselves. The work concludes with a short section on eschatology, a description of the
last trump, the sudden coming of Christ, and the ensuing last
judgment. The method throughout is logical and dogmatic.
General classifications are subdivided and briefly described,
without any attempt at reason or persuasion. The liberal number of scriptural references after most of the statements presumably supplied the necessary proofs, and the whole work occupies only 352 small octavo pages. In spite of the indorsement of Cartwright and the intrinsic merits of this manual, it
had no great popularity or influence. It went through four editions, but remained in Latin, though English manuscript translations were made. A less penetrating type of systematization
proved more attractive to the English Puritans.

This was the work of William Perkins, fellow of Christ's College, Cambridge, to whom we have already had occasion to refer. He participated in the classis movement, but in 1587, when
he was called to account by the Cambridge authorities for
preaching against the practice of kneeling at the taking of communion, he qualified some of his remarks and retracted others.
Thereafter he was more cautious and, though always a moderate
Puritan, was not so advanced as Fenner. He was not a great
thinker, but he was a great preacher and a clever popularizer.
In Fuller's fine phrase, he "brought the schools into the pulpit,
and unshelling their controversies out of their hard school
terms, made thereof plain and wholesome meat for his people."
In 1590, five years after the appearance of Fenner's work, he
published his *Armilla aurea*, or *Golden Chaine*, which was translated into English the next year and went through at least fourteen editions as a separate volume, besides nearly as many in the
author's collected works. It is somewhat shorter than its predecessor,[17] but in all probability it is not entirely unrelated, for it

_____

[17] About 40 per cent. There are 116 folio pages in the 1616 edition of the collected
works, but in this edition a few passages have been added to the earlier version of 1591,
which occupies some 250 small octavo pages.

begins with the same definition of theology, and the same distinction between the character and works of God. There are other reminiscent touches in the earlier sections, and the order of treatment is much the same until the discussion of the office of Christ has been completed. Then, instead of dealing at length with the dangerous governmental and disciplinary problems, the more cautious Perkins gives a detailed exposition of the Ten Commandments, the sacraments, predestination, calling, justification, sanctification, and the Christian life, ending with a fairly full description of the state of souls in heaven and hell. Separate treatises on predestination, free will, and an exposition of the creed[18] helped to round out his system. Perkins was more interested than his predecessor in the problem of foreordination and free will. As a high Calvinist he took pains to defend his teachings against the Catholic doctrine and against those misguided Protestants who were flirting with Pelagianism in order to avoid making God the author of sin. He also had a somewhat smoother style than Fenner. By omitting some subdivisions and expanding others, he made his work easier to follow. But he did not possess either Calvin's forensic ability or the Genevan's grasp of the background of his subject. In later editions a few words were inserted about the arguments for the existence of God,[19] and in Perkins' *Reformed Catholike* the grounds for accepting the Scriptures as the sole religious authority are briefly stated.[20] But in spite of his great popularity, which entitles him to rank as the Puritan theologian of Tudor times, he cannot be compared with his Continental contemporaries, least of all his Genevan master.[21]

[18] *De praedestinationis modo et ordine* (Cambridge, 1598); English trans., *A Christian and Plaine Treatise of the Manner and Order of Predestination and of the Largenes of God's Grace* (London, 1606), in *Workes*, II, 603–41 (answered by Arminius in his *Examen modestum* [Leyden, 1612]); *A Treatise of God's Free Grace and Man's Free Will* (Cambridge, 1602), in *Workes*, I, 717–46; *An Exposition of the Symbole or Creed of the Apostles according to the Tenour of the Scripture and the Consent of Orthodoxe Fathers of the Church* (Cambridge, 1595), in *Workes*, I, 117–322.

[19] *Workes*, I, 11.   [20] *Ibid.*, pp. 580–83; see above, p. 357.

[21] For a more detailed presentation of Perkins' system see J. J. van Baarsel, *William Perkins: Eene bijdrage tot de Kennis der religieuse ontwikkeling in Engeland ten tijde van Koningin Elisabeth* (The Hague, 1912), esp. pp. 140–64.

In fact, Calvin cast such a deep shadow over the Puritan world that he determined the tone of its entire thinking. To this fact may be attributed the surprising lack of christological thought in this avowedly Christian movement. It is quite unfair to say that the Puritans were an Old Testament group who cared little for the teachings or attitude of the new dispensation. As we have seen, their standard of authority was a New Testament one, and they were prolific in their output of commentaries on the epistles and apocalypse. But it is true that the Four Gospels do not appear to have attracted them particularly. Possibly the Catholic treatment of the narratives of the birth and passion repelled them. Possibly their historical acumen was not such as to enable them to make much use of the otherworldly teachings themselves. Certainly the person of Christ figures very little in their literature. Before Calvin's influence became predominant, Hooper wrote a *Declaracion of Christe and His Offyce*,[22] which set the Son forth as priest and king. In the former role he taught his people, interceded and sacrificed himself for them, consecrated and sanctified believers. As king he ruled spiritually in this age, more fully in the future. But after Hooper's time nothing more than incidental treatment of the life and work of the founder of their religion can be discovered in the writings of the Tudor Puritans.

In view of the great importance of eschatology in the history of the seventeenth-century Puritan movement, we must, before leaving the subject of theology, step into the jungle of biblical theology far enough to discover, in general, how the books of Daniel and Revelation were treated in the exegetical literature of the time. There was an early and sustained interest in the dark hints of those mysterious treatises about the things to come. Diverting some of the more serviceable speculations from the medieval stream of interpretation to his own mill, Bale ventured a long commentary on the Book of Revelation[23] as early as the time of Edward VI, and throughout the century the tur-

[22] *Early Writings*, ed. Carr (Cambridge: Parker Society, 1843), pp. 15-95.

[23] *The Image of Both Churches* (London [1548]); reprinted in *Select Works*, ed. Christmas (Cambridge: Parker Society, 1849), pp. 249-640.

bulent flood rolled on in its new English channel as it also did in
the Protestant and Catholic areas on the Continent. Adhering
to the custom of their kind in all ages, the exegetes agreed that
the end of the world was imminent. They were living in the
last days, the time was short, the Lord was at hand, soon to
come, in terrible, visible form, to judge and to rule. The Protestant interpreters agreed, furthermore, that the papacy was the
Antichrist, whose approaching final ruin would herald the great
day of the second coming.

But for the rest all was disagreement and confusion as the
calculators struggled with beasts and vials, weeks and millen-
niums. Bale identified the thousand years of Satan's bondage
with that part of the Christian Era down to the time of Pope
Sylvester II, who obtained the papacy "by such necromancy as
he learned of a Saracen in Spain" and "loosened that devil
whom Christ had afore shut up, and set him again at large to
deceive afresh."[24] Foxe, the martyrologist, thought that this
millennium came between the cessation of the persecutions of
the early Christians and the resumption of executions for heresy
in the fourteenth century.[25] Many commentators devised ingenious systems for expanding the days and months of the
scripture to years and even longer periods, since Holy Writ assured them that a thousand years were as twenty-four hours in
the mind of the Absolute. If reckonings based on such systems
put the terminal date too far in the future, there was always the
compensating factor of the assurance that the last days were
to be shortened to spare the elect. So the proper feeling of an-
ticipatory tension was maintained.

For the most part, however, the sixteenth-century Puritans
avoided naming any exact date for the second coming. Along
with the mystery of why Jacob was called and Esau reprobated,
the precise time of the end was left to the inscrutable wisdom of
God. One rash soul in Tudor times did dare to be definite in his
predictions. That was Thomas Lupton, the morality writer,
who first ventured to suggest the year 1588 as the last for his

[24] *Ibid.*, in *Select Works*, p. 560.　　　[25] *Acts and Monuments*, II, 722–27.

dispensation, but lived to prefer the more discreet calculation of 1656—"from this year 1610 it appeareth not to be past forty years."[26] But most speculators followed the practice of the more cautious Arthur Dent, whose commentary on the Apocalypse, *The Ruine of Rome*, was published in 1603. He held that it was madness to think that the round numbers of the text were to be taken literally. The day of the Fifth Monarchist had not yet come.

It is thus clear that the Puritan strength did not lie in theology as understood on the Continent or in their own country in the next century. Ready-made theories from abroad were taken up by the party in England, but any variations or expansions of them almost invariably were directed toward immediate, controversial problems rather than toward digging any deeper or firmer foundations for the faith. Theory was the handmaid of circumstance. Originally, the Puritan was a doctrinaire, but he did not fit well in that milieu, leaving it as soon as possible for the more congenial fields of discursive comment and moral exhortation.

[26] *A Dream of the Devill and Dives* (London, 1583), sig. G, fols. 1–3; (2d ed.; London, 1615), sig. F, fols. 2(v)–5(v). I am indebted to Dr. Irene J. Churchill, of the Lambeth Palace Library, for kind assistance with this note.

CHAPTER XX

Puritan Propaganda

T WAS one thing for a few individuals with foreign connections to catch a moral fervor and naturalize the theological arguments to support it. To communicate this attitude to the rank and file of their less privileged countrymen was quite another matter, and the techniques employed are well worthy of our attention. We have already described the first steps: the activities of senior members of the university by which prospective clergymen and a few scions of prominent country families were reached, the composition and publication of various kinds of apologia, and the establishment of lectureships which multiplied the number of Puritan ministers. The methods employed by these ministers in dealing with ordinary laity are what concern us here.

The first thing that strikes us in observing this activity is the absence of sectarianism. True, the political leaders of the party might expend their energies in attacking Anglicanism or perhaps some rival brand of Puritanism. The theologian might write in similar terms, sharpening weapons for use on his fellow-Christians. But the subalterns out on the firing line perforce recognized that the real enemy still lay neither to the right nor to the left, but in front. Of atheism expressed in formal, philosophical terms there was little in Tudor England.[1] But of tavern unbelief there was a great deal. Scoffers, flat atheists, and "Anti-legons" (gainsayers) appear regularly in popular religious literature. In fact, the Puritan thought that the bulk of the nation had exchanged the sins of popery for neglect of religion: "before, they were altogether superstitious, now they are become

[1] George Truett Buckley, *Atheism in the English Renaissance* (Chicago, 1932).

379

wholly profane."[2] In spite of the enforced church attendance, it is doubtful whether more than quarter of the population can be said to have had any religion at all. Walking and talking in time of service was a constant problem to the zealous preacher. In that rough-and-ready age it is only to be expected that the Queen's example should be joyfully followed by most of her subjects. The average Puritan minister was too busy with the overwhelming number of these "profane" to bother much about the aberrations of his fellows among the Christian minority. Frequently he had no avowed Catholic remnants or Anabaptists in his entire parish, and these vague far-off menaces did not greatly concern him. In any case, if the indifferent could be won to the Puritan attitude, the lesser problems of the household of faith would take care of themselves.

By far the most important piece of equipment of the Puritan ministers engaged in this undertaking was their unshakable faith in the soundness of their own position. Modern writers on propaganda have sometimes defined it as the conscious and deliberate spreading of stories and opinions known by their disseminators to be false. The typical Puritan minister did nothing of this sort. He was a propagandist in the original sense of the word—one who transplanted into others convictions which were living realities in his own personality, declaring what he had himself seen and handled of the word of life. He might be troubled occasionally by the differences of opinion among the learned on matters of ecclesiastical policy,[3] but doubts about the fundamentals of the faith were, happily for him, far above his intellectual level. The village atheists were also the village drunkards and ne'er-do-wells, for the simple reason that more responsible doubters had already anticipated Shaftesbury's conclusions about a wise man's religion. In the century before Lord Herbert of Cherbury, the character of the avowed opposition to the essential Puritan message was, therefore, such

[2] Richard Greenham, *The Workes of Richard Greenham* (5th and last ed.; London, 1612), p. 303.

[3] M. M. Knappen, *Two Elizabethan Puritan Diaries* (Chicago, 1933), p. 98.

as further to strengthen the average minister's confidence in the correctness of his belief.

To the superb self-assurance which this conviction afforded, the Puritan minister added the strong selling-point of a life far superior, in the moral judgment of his contemporaries, to the normal standards of the clergy of his time. "What you are speaks so loud I can't hear what you say," runs the proverb, and some account of this practical demonstration of the merits of Puritanism must precede any description of the verbal weapons in the party arsenal. While exceptions were not unknown, the average Puritan worked at his calling far more energetically than did his conforming neighbor. Both tended to neglect the prescribed routine of morning prayer, evening prayer, and saints' days, but the time saved was not spent by the Puritan at court, at the tavern, or in the hunting field. He felt the obligation to attain to the then dizzy heights of at least a sermon a week; and, if he was frequently a pluralist, it was partly for the sake of providing more people with the opportunity of hearing regular preaching. By thus exceeding the normal demands of his profession, he also took upon himself the supererogatory task of daily study. When he added a weekday lecture to his Sunday schedule of sermon and catechizing, or a Sunday sermon to his market-day exposition, it was obvious that he was doing the Lord's work, and when he exhorted his parishioners in daily conversation, visited the sick, and started a school, it was hard to deny that he was instant in season and out of season. Permanently in opposition, he was barred from the more lucrative and influential positions in the church and so was freed from the temptations and corruptions which came with power. To his parishioners he could nearly always appear as a poor, studious man of God. When the authorities added semi-martyrdom to his other crosses by suspending or depriving him, while the ignorant idler in the next village went on quite undisturbed in his slothful way, the appeal of the Puritan message was further strengthened.

If the average Puritan minister's life made some such impression as this, an even more powerful influence was wielded by the

exceptionally gifted or unusually zealous. In every section
where Puritan influence was felt there was some local light, outstanding in character and attainments, whose saintliness attracted some of the indifferent while his example inspired his
fellow-believers to greater efforts. Of these, perhaps, the most
influential was Richard Greenham, the model minister of Cambridgeshire, whose widespread influence would entitle him to
mention even if a detailed illustration were not called for here.
A product of Lincolnshire and Pembroke Hall, of which he was
for some years a fellow, he became rector of Dry Drayton in
1570 and for two decades made it famous in Puritan circles. It
was close to Cambridge—a few miles out the Huntingdon road,
past the castle and a little to the left—so that it was not difficult
for the outside world to beat a path to his door. Indeed he frequently came in to preach at Cambridge itself, thus retaining
his influence among the students.

Greenham was a supporter of Cartwright in his Cambridge
troubles; he was involved in the classis movement; and in the
midst of the anti-Puritan drive of 1573–74 he told Cox, his
bishop, "I neither can nor will wear the apparel nor subscribe
unto it or the communion book."[4] But he was not a controversialist by nature. He thought personal religion was much more
important and told an audience of Cambridge students that to
spend time in controversy at their age was to put the roof on a
building before the foundations were laid.[5] When Cox asked him
whether the conformist or nonconformist was to blame for the
Protestant schism, he replied that it "might be either or neither. For if," he added, "they loved one another as they ought
and would do all good offices each for the other, thereby maintaining love and concord, it lay on neither side; otherwise which
party soever makes the rent, the schism it lies upon their
score."[6] When in danger of losing his living for his nonconform-

[4] *A Parte of a Register* ([Middelburg], 1593), p. 87.

[5] John Strype, *Annals of the Reformation under Elizabeth* (4 vols. in 7; Oxford, 1824),
III, i, 720.

[6] Samuel Clarke, *Lives*, bound with his *General Martyrologie to Which Is Attached
Lives of Sundry Modern English Divines* (London, 1677), p. 13.

ity, he set forth his position at length in a letter to Cox.[7] He
describes himself as a "sole poor countryman, a young scholar"
not competent to dispute with his older superior. In any case
he did not wish to reason about the matter, because he had perceived "by experience that dissension of reasons doth cause
alienation of affections." He did not judge either the bishop,
who "had conscience in many ceremonies," or his Puritan
friends whose consciences allowed them to subscribe although
they disapproved of the disputed rites. As Paul taught, they
might use them to the Lord while he refused them to the Lord.
His own conscience would allow of some ceremonies under some
circumstances, but not of subscribing to all under all circumstances. Whatever was not of faith (conscience) was sin, and he
would not "do that now for living sake [to save his living] which,
as it seemed, so in deed I erst forbare to do for conscience sake."
For that would "seem to pull down that which by contrary example I have builded." He trusted that his record of having occupied himself for three years in daily "preaching Christ crucified unto myself and country people" would entitle him to some
consideration in the present visitation, but, if not, he "would
with others give place to the peace of the church, my conscience
denying it [the use of the ceremonies] and go mourn my sins until the Lord would use me in his church or take me out of this
vale of tears." It is pleasant to record that so far as we know he
was not suspended.[8]

This moderate Puritan was a small man and usually "indifferent well in health." His affliction was a "bad concoction"
which gave him "frequent sick nights" and kept him much wak-
ing. Nevertheless, he possessed the surprising energy which appears so often to be characteristic of men of diminutive stature.
He rose each morning at four, and spoke to his people at dawn

[7] *Parte of a Register*, pp. 87–93.

[8] In his *Shepherd's Calendar in Relation to Contemporary Affairs* (New York, 1912),
pp. 188–97, J. J. Higginson has suggested that Greenham was the original of Diggon
Davie. But, since part of his argument hinges on the statement by Neal (*History of the
Puritans* [3 vols.; London, 1837], I, 229) that Greenham was suspended, the identification remains doubtful. Neal's source (James Peirce's *Vindication of the Dissenters*
[London, 1717], p. 97) says only that he was troubled, and the allusion is to this brush
with Cox.

every weekday morning except Saturday. The Thursday service was catechetical, while the rest of his talks were common-
places, or, as we should say, short topical addresses on such
themes as "Friendship," and "Affliction." On Sunday he
preached twice and catechized before the evening service. All
his sermons were characterized by the great vigor of his speaking, which commonly left him dripping with perspiration. He
visited and conferred with his people at their daily work and
gained a wide reputation as a peacemaker, arbitrating the quarrels of the contentious countryside.[9]

His deeds fitted his words. Though his living was worth one
hundred pounds a year, a very good sum for those days, he
lived moderately, and gave the rest away in a kind of impractical St. Francis fashion. At his ordination a special charge had
been given him to look after the poor, and he never forgot it.[10]
He took the lead in establishing a fund for poor students at
Cambridge, to replace the now neglected charities of the old
church. "If he saw a poor body at a distance from him as he
rode abroad he would send his man with money to him, and
when he rode by the castle at Cambridge the prisoners would
never ask him for anything, for if he had any money in his purse
they were sure to have part of it."[11] Nor did he forget that charity begins at home. He kept only two beasts himself so the poor
might have his straw. When others sold straw for two shillings
the day's thresh, he sold his for ten pence. He did not trouble
himself with reckonings and accounts, but would ask his man
what the market price was. If dear, he would say, "I pray God
bring down the price of it"; and, if it were cheap, he would heart-
ily bless God for it. During the year of scarcity (1586–87) he
worked out a very successful system of co-operative charity in
which he persuaded the twenty plow-holders of the village to
participate. They were to contribute to a common granary, each
according to his ability, some one coomb (four bushels), some a
quarter (eight bushels), and some three coombs. He himself
put in five coombs. The market price of barley had risen to ten

---

[9] Clarke, *op. cit.*, pp. 12–15.

[10] Greenham to Burghley, *Workes*, p. 864.   [11] Clarke, *op. cit.*, p. 13.

groats, or three shillings four pence a bushel, but this supply was retailed to the poor one day a week in quantities proportionate to the size of the family at one shilling four pence per bushel, until the general market price suddenly dropped.[12]

In another situation at about the same time as the general dearth, this usually moderate man approached fanaticism in his zeal for charity. The size of the bushel had been standardized by Henry VII at eight gallons, but many localities were using measures of eight and a half or even nine, which worked a hardship on visiting merchants. To remedy this, Elizabeth had the measures once more standardized by juries of London goldsmiths and in a proclamation of December 15, 1587, ordered the exclusive use of the old standard bushel. No commodities were to be sold except in measures officially sized and stamped by the clerk of the market. To Greenham, in whose vision the immediate need of the unfortunate bulked larger than general considerations of public policy, this seemed like a device further to oppress the poor. Consequently, "he objected to the public order making bushels less. He spoke publicly against it and ordered his man to refuse to carry in his bushel if the clerk of the market sent to cut it." There was trouble because of it, but "the Lord delivered him," though the standard bushel was also the struck or level one, and "he had charged his man not to strike off all the corn" when measuring for sale.[13] With the minister showing generous tendencies, it is not surprising that at times his wife had to borrow to pay the harvest help.

Greenham's success, however, was rather with people who already had some foundation in matters religious than with his own congregation, which was perhaps too rustic to make good Puritan material all at once. We read in Fuller[14] that, though

---

[12] *Ibid.* Greenham's success in this undertaking was not due entirely to his own persuasive talents. The Council had requested some such co-operation from the clergy and people of "habylytye" (Council to Whitgift, January 4, 1587, *APC* [N.S.], XIV, 277–78; cf. J. E. T. Rogers, *History of Agriculture and Prices in England* [7 vols.; Oxford 1866–1902], VI, 7).

[13] Clarke, *op. cit.*, p. 13.

[14] Thomas Fuller, *The Church History of Britain*, ed. Brewer (6 vols.; Oxford, 1845), V, 191.

Greenham lived sermons and though he watered Dry Drayton
with his tears and oftener with his prayers and preaching, neither produced a proportionate fruitfulness, and the generality of
his parish remained so ignorant and obstinate that it was a matter of general comment. "Greenham had pastures green but
sheep full lean," was the saying. When at length he removed to
London, he told his successor that he could see no fruit of all his
ministry save in one family.[15] But he was not without honor
elsewhere, and his home was commonly filled with visitors attracted by the spiritual feast he spread for them. Some, including the Separatist Robert Browne, were theological students
who at that time were thus trained by individual ministers.
Others were the "sick souls" who came to him for consolation.
"His masterpiece was in comforting wounded consciences." We
are told that "many came to him with weeping eyes and went
from him with cheerful souls," having been "restored to joy and
comfort out of unspeakable and unsupportable terrors and tor-
ments of conscience."[16] Joseph Hall, later Bishop of Norwich,
described him as knowing well how to stay a weak conscience
and how to raise a fallen.[17] Visitors with these afflictions were
entertained "friendly and familiarly" without regard to their
social status. Twice a day the little school of the prophets
and spiritually hungry gathered for devotions. After the reading of the Bible, anyone might speak his thoughts upon the subject, but Greenham's personality was of course the dominating
one. The servants would be present, but the gatherings would
not be formal. Greenham understood human nature well
enough to know the value of change in retaining the freshness
and reality of any experience, including worship, and, while he
had regular habits, he varied them sufficiently so that they did
not become mere routine.[18]

From scenes like this more of Anglia's glory would have
sprung had the Queen permitted it. For, though the fruits were

---

[15] Notes and Queries, VI, No. 7 (1883), 366.

[16] Clarke, op. cit., p. 14.

[17] "Epistles: Decade I," No. 7, in Works (12 vols.; Oxford, 1837–39), VI, 144.

[18] Clarke, op. cit., p. 12.

slow in coming or not always apparent, the living movement
was thus planted in the land. In London, Dering lectured and
bore patiently those insults which came to him in the line of
duty, even when an irate swearer, whom he had rebuked, threw
beer in his face. At Norwich, John More was preacher and
spiritual leader to the town. In Suffolk, John Knewstub cheerfully saluted the unbelievers he was trying to win. In Essex,
Richard Rogers, whose laborious diaries have come down to us,
organized congregational prayer meetings, composed treatises
on the Christian life, kept minute account of his spiritual estate,
and generally set an example to his fellows. In Kent there was
Fenner, and in Sussex Thomas Underdown; Northamptonshire
had its Hildersam, who succeeded Gilby at Ashby, and the Banbury section gloried in the ministry of Greenham's son-in-law,
John Dod, who rivaled his father-in-law's reputation, and who
added to his other virtues a somewhat mystical appreciation of
nature:

> Being at Holdonby, and invited by an honorable person to see that stately
> house built by Sir Christopher Hatton, the masterpiece of English architecture
> in that age, he desired to be excused, and to sit still looking on a flower which
> he had in his hand. "In this flower," saith he, "I can see more of God than in
> all of the beautiful buildings in the world."[19]

Space would fail to tell of Chapman and of Parker, and of Culverwel and of Newman, of Evans also and Burton and of the
rest who through faith subdued so much of the kingdom. But
many there were of this sort, quietly sowing the innocent-look-
ing dragons' teeth which in time produced Cromwell's iron harvest.

The arguments employed to win men to a religious life were
not new. Almost all of them can be found either in the writings
of that master psychologist, Augustine, or in those of St. Bernard, for they belong to religion generally, and not to Protestantism only. They range from the mildest wooings to the most
fearful threats. Much was made of the "comfortableness" of
religion here and now, the joy of a clear conscience, and the experience of "the love of God in Christ Jesus."[20] An appeal was

[19] Fuller, *op. cit.*, VI, 307.   [20] Greenham, *Workes*, p. 293.

often made to common decency and gratitude based on the sufferings of Christ for us, and, though the argument based on the
brevity of life and certainty of death was such a common one,
even then, that "use hath taken away the profit," it was sometimes used, since "with grace it works where extraordinary arguments do not." Greenham felt a little reluctant to talk of rewards and punishments. "It is good to leave sin in its own nature, but if we do it for fear of punishment or for shame of the
world rather than for conscience of sin it is not praiseworthy."
We should not "indent with God, as if he will give us riches or
health or power then we will serve him, or else not."[21] Pure love
of God is the chief mark of a righteous man. We are to be moved
by "a single care to please and glorify God in all our doings and
to approve ourselves unto him without hope of reward, though
trouble do come upon us for it."[22] But elsewhere he does occasionally use this means, noting that the Holy Ghost is content
to use this moot argument, and quoting Augustine's dictum:
From fear springs a good life, from good life a good conscience,
thence no fear, and thus God becomes sweet to the sinner.[23]
Most of his colleagues were less squeamish. The following
imaginative lamentation of the damned soul is a typical passage:

> Oh, that I might be in Hell but so many years as the greatest barn in a
> country would hold coins of wheat: nay, rather than fail, mustard seeds, for
> then at length (though it would be unreasonable long first) I should come out
> and be released: but always to be burning in the fire of Hell and never to
> come out, what a thing is it, and what a doleful case am I in?[24]

The Puritans did not stop with reason in dealing with the
"profane." There were added what used to be known in Methodist circles as "the rousements," emotional trimmings to reach
the affections as well as the mind, after the Puritan prescription
given in a previous chapter. "For the mind of man it may be
deceived, but the heart cannot."[25] Congregational psalm-sing-

[21] Ibid., p. 691.

[22] Ibid., p. 119.   [23] Ibid., p. 656.

[24] Thomas Lupton, A Dream of the Devill and Dives (London, 1615), sig. G, fol. 6.

[25] Greenham, Workes, p. 291.

ing was one means to this end. Though Elizabeth called the tunes Genevan jigs, the Puritan practice was extremely popular, at least at first, probably because it allowed more lay participation in the service than did the Catholic ritual. But the most effective implement was the hortatory sermon. In a leisurely age without newspapers or moving pictures any sermon was an interesting event, though the audience did not always give full attention. Gifted speakers could therefore command huge audiences and often secure startling results. The most famous preacher of the Elizabethan period was Henry Smith, popularly known as "Silver-tongued" Smith. Like Browne, he was distantly related to Burghley,[26] and before taking up theology he had learned something of the gentle art of poetry. He left Lincoln College, Oxford, without a degree and subsequently studied with Greenham at Dry Drayton. From 1587 to 1590 he was lecturer at St. Clement Danes, London, and there his popularity was tremendous. Whenever he preached, the church was so crowded that, as Fuller tells us, "persons of good quality brought their own pews with them. I mean their legs to stand thereon in the alleys." Printers' men took down his discourses in shorthand, and the stolen texts were rushed onto the market with an efficiency which lends some plausibility to the piracy theory of the composition of the First Folio text of Shakespeare.[27] The authentic versions ran to countless editions, and a century later the collected volume was still a family book.[28] Smith boldly scourged the corruption in church and state. Aylmer duly troubled him for nonconformity, and eventually he was forced from his position; but, when there was a prospect of a vacancy in the living, his humble parishioners petitioned Burghley that he should be given the place. "Smiths, tailors,

[26] His father's second wife was a sister of the Treasurer (John Nichols, *The History and Antiquities of the County of Leicester* [4 vols.; London, 1795–1811], II, 185; cf. *Notes and Queries*, II, No. 8 [1859], 152–53).

[27] See the Introduction to H. T. Price's edition of Smith's *Fruitfull Sermon* (Halle, 1922); cf. also Edward Arber, *Transcript of the Registers of the Company of Stationers* (5 vols.; London and Birmingham, 1875–94), II, 318, for evidence of contention between printers over the rights to Smith's sermons.

[28] Strype, *Historical Collections of the Life and Acts of John Aylmer* (Oxford, 1821), p. 100.

sadlers, hosiers, haberdashers, glaziers, cutlers and such like, most of them setting their marks," asserted that "his preaching, living, and sound doctrine had done more good among them than any other that had gone before or, which they doubted, could follow after."[29] Smith's style was rather flowery than logically vigorous, his paragraphs often consisting of striking biblical allusions and illustrations strung together with little or no supporting argument.[30]

Smith may have been rather a rhetorical artist than a consuming fire, but at least he kept the Puritan cause in the forefront of the London consciousness. Lesser literary lights had the gift of striking terror into the hearts of their audience. Perkins,[31] at Cambridge, who besides writing theology occupied the pulpit of Great St. Andrews there, smote John Cotton with the conviction of sin which led to his conversion. At Dedham, in Essex, John Rogers—a nephew of Richard Rogers of Wetherfield, but not the author of the refutation of the Family of Love—wrought trembling and sudden conversion on his hearers. In Oxfordshire, Whately earned for himself the sobriquet of "roaring Tom of Banbury," a title which suggests something of the nature of his utterances. Time was of no great consequence in Tudor England. We have records of two- and three-hour sermons. Repetition and more repetition of a single theme could work an almost hypnotic effect. When the preacher had been on one point long enough to allow the direction of the argument to be noted, the mind relaxed and the message swept on to the affections and the will. To an age which has acquired a different terminology for its idealism, the sermons may seem the dryest reading imaginable, but so now is the description of the clipper-rigged ship, which in its day and generation seemed a thing of beauty and a joy forever.

[29] *Ibid.*, pp. 102–3.

[30] E.g., *Sermons* (London, 1599), pp. 283, 309, 339; *Workes*, ed. Thomas Smith ("Nichols Series of Standard Divines: Puritan Period" [2 vols.; Edinburgh, 1866–67]), I, 306, 331, 361; cf. p. 465 below.

[31] For further details of Perkins' methods of preaching and also some references to Smith see John Brown, *Puritan Preaching in England* (New York, 1900), pp. 71–89.

CHAPTER XXI

The Puritan Ideal for the Individual: Piety

FTER persuasion came direction. When the propagandist had done his work, the prospective pilgrim needed accurate maps of the narrow path he was to follow, with all the gates and sloughs plainly marked. A century later Bunyan supplied the most famous and graphic answer to this demand. But charts quite as complete, if less picturesque, were available long before his time. Many of the Tudor Puritan ministers made a specialty of answering particular questions which were put to them on all manner of problems connected with the Christian life. These difficulties were called cases of conscience, whence the name casuistry. Greenham's answers were collected and published, and Perkins set forth five books of his answers which fill nearly all of a large folio volume.[1] From these works, supplemented by sermons and special treatises, we may extract the Puritan answers to most of the problems dealt with throughout the rest of this survey. On the subject of individual conduct, with which we are here concerned, further help may be secured from diaries which record the aspirations and spiritual struggles of their authors, and from devotional manuals and guides specially drawn up by Puritan ministers for individual instruction. While the Protestants at first lagged so far behind their Catholic rivals in this field that they were driven to adapt the literature of the mother-church to their uses,[2] this deficiency was remedied by a flood of contributions in the last fifteen years of Elizabeth's reign.[3]

[1] In the Dr. Williams' Library there is a manuscript volume (General MS I. 4. 2) entitled "Dod's Droppings" which contains John Dod's answers to such questions, but it is probably to be dated after 1610.

[2] A striking example of this is Edmund Bunny's Protestant version of the Jesuit Robert Parson's *Book of Christian Exercise: A Book of Christian Exercise Appertaining to Resolution* (s.l., 1585).

[3] Of these, some of the most important were: Arthur Dent, *The Plaine Man's Path-Way to Heaven* (London, 1601); John Downame, *The Christian Warfare* (London, 1604);

The prescribed life began with a definite Christian experience, which the prospective believer was obligated to secure. "We are all Calvinists when we pray, but all Arminians when we preach" runs the clerical proverb. The Puritan writing theology gave to God all the responsibility and, therefore, all the glory for man's salvation. But in the pulpit, as in popular writing, he was delightfully inconsistent, putting the burden on the individual. He wisely made no serious effort to explain this change of attitude. Most idealists, not excepting Karl Marx, have found it expedient to take both sides of this issue at different times. The Christian life was not a matter of attendance upon the ceremonies and worship of the church, for one might be baptized and fully confirmed without being saved thereby.[4] Infant baptism was to be performed as a sign of God's favor to his people and—it may be suspected—to spite the Anabaptists, but the Puritan saw little profit in it, or in the communion either, for that matter. Nor was salvation to be attained by simply doing better than formerly or as well as others. The best fruits of a good moral life were reprehensible if not done in faith. "The man that liveth in this world, not being a true Christian, is far more vile than the basest creature of all, even the dog or toad."[5] We must attain to a definite standard of God's appointing, not man's.[6]

Of this divine standard, correct intellectual faith was a part. The Puritan gave no clear statement of exactly how much one

Richard Rogers, *Seaven Treatises Leading and Guiding to True Happiness* (London, 1603); and *A Garden of Spiritual Flowers Planted by Ri. Ro[gers], Will. Per[kins], Ri. Green[ham], M[iles] M[osse], and Geo. Web[be]* ("The fift time imprinted"; London, 1609). Christopher Sutton's popular *Disce mori: Learn To Die* (London, 1600) and *Disce vivere: Learn To Live* (London, 1602) are harbingers of the great number of Anglican devotional works which were to come in the new century. Sutton became a favorite of James, who installed him as Canon of Westminster. On this subject see Louis B. Wright, *Middle-Class Culture in Elizabethan England* (Chapel Hill, N.C., 1935), pp. 228–96, and more particularly Helen C. White, *English Devotional Literature (Prose) 1600–1640* ("University of Wisconsin Studies in Language and Literature," No. 29 [Madison, Wis., 1931]).

[4] Richard Greenham, *The Workes of Richard Greenham* (5th ed.; London, 1612), p. 285.

[5] William Perkins, *Workes* (3 vols.; London, 1616–18), I, 378.

[6] Greenham, *Workes*, p. 284; Dent, *op. cit., passim.*

must believe, but it was assumed that the general outlines of the plan of salvation would be accepted:

They that willingly hear and joyfully embrace the doctrine that we are by law condemned for sin, by the Gospel saved through faith in Christ, and thenceforth endeavor to have this world crucified unto us, and us to be crucified unto the world and to become new creatures shall also be saved and find mercy and peace.[7]

But there was much more to finding the wicket gate than proper intellectual belief. One must next renounce and repent of every known sin. He must study God's requirements as set forth in the Bible, realize his shortcomings, and "rip up" his heart in genuine penitence. Not only the present mode of life but all the past must be dragged into the white light of conscience, dissected, and examined with a determination to overlook no slightest failing or secret desire. When the depth of his iniquity became apparent, it was to be contrasted with the height of God's standard, and one could then realize the hopelessness of his situation if no outside aid were forthcoming. Thus the penitent reached a state of "holy desperation." Convinced of his extreme sinfulness and inability to help himself, he cast himself wholly on the mercy of God. Then came the peace that passeth all understanding, the definite assurance of salvation as the Holy Spirit convinced him that by justifying faith he was numbered among the elect. This experience was extremely important and was to be carefully scrutinized, for there were false feelings of repentance and counterfeit assurances of salvation which might deceive even the subject himself. These were, of course, worse than none at all, because they lulled the unregenerate into a false sense of security, which precluded further striving.[8]

Calvin always maintained that the individual who had gone through this process could be certain of his salvation. But the test of feeling was such an uncertain one that in effect this all-important matter, like the proof for the authority of the Scrip-

[7] Greenham, *Workes*, p. 377.

[8] J. Udall, *Amendment of Life* (London, 1584); Perkins, *Workes*, I, 455–69; Greenham, *Workes*, pp. 281–94; *A Garden of Spiritual Flowers* (London, 1667), p. 156–80.

tures, was purely subjective. The way was thus opened for endless queries from anxious souls. I cannot feel any proper sense of assurance. I doubt my election. How can I be sure? While these appear to have come only from the hypersensitive and were thus not an important part of the normal Puritan life,[9] there were enough of them to give the Puritan pastors many troublesome hours. The usual solution was to go over the details of the Christian experience, minimizing its requirements in dealing with tender consciences, and finally to resort to a rather un-Protestant, but nonetheless effective, common-sense doctrine of works. Perkins reduced the ultimate requirement, the least measure of faith that could save a man, to a vague trust in God.[10] Sometimes a hatred of sin and a love of God were considered sufficient. The feeling of joy in God's promises and love for one's neighbor were other tokens suggested.[11] The ability to pray was also mentioned.[12] But good works were the most common prescription. "By the fruits we are to know the reality of faith."[13] The works did not earn merit. In theory they were done only for God's glory; they were not a meritorious cause but a sure evidence. "The Godly do good works to confirm their faith and to assure and certify their consciousness of their election."[14] In practice this brought good works back into the Protestant fold, and made it possible to preserve the original moral fervor of Puritanism from the blight of antinomianism which must logically have overtaken it had those who made the practical application of Puritan principles been doctrinaires rather than men of common sense. This teaching was also useful in dealing with sluggish Christians who showed few signs of their faith. By suggesting that this delinquency might indicate a lack of proper election, they were spurred to a higher

---

[9] M. M. Knappen, *Two Elizabethan Puritan Diaries* (Chicago, 1933), pp. 14–15.

[10] *Workes*, I, 642. [11] Greenham, *Workes*, pp. 839 and 687.

[12] "Dod's Sayings," *Memorials of the Rev. John Dod*, ed. Taylor (Northampton, 1881), p. 2.

[13] Greenham, *Workes*, p. 375.

[14] John Woolton, *Christian Manuell of the Life and Manners of True Christians* (London, 1576), sig. F, fol. viii.

plane. "Hell is full of purposes but not performance," was the Puritan quirt in such cases.[15]

It was from the rationalization of these necessities of everyday pastoral work that there developed that modification of the original high Calvinism which is known as Covenant theology. While the Puritan drew back in horror from the Arminian abyss, he approached the same depth more gradually by the roundabout method of emphasizing the limitations on God's arbitrary character which were inherent in the biblical idea of a covenant or contract between the Deity and mankind. Though God could damn everyone or elect men to be saved as his pure whim dictated, as a matter of fact he had made certain definite bargains with mankind. The terms of these could be read in black and white in the Bible, notably in the promise to Abraham and in later variations which constituted the covenant of grace under which mankind was still living. By adhering to these conditions a human being could in effect establish a kind of claim on God. In this fashion something of reasonableness could be restored to the universe, fairness to the character of the Deity, and moral responsibility to man. In the next century this theory assumed considerable importance in the teaching of Perkins' student, William Ames, and through him it was passed on to Preston and Sibbes in England, to Cocceius in Holland, and to practically all the seventeenth-century New England Puritans.[16]

Common sense was also used in dealing with the problem of sins committed after conversion. The Puritan did not take the obscurantist position of those who deny this possibility, or that of the less extreme "second-blessing" group who think that some select Christians may attain to sinlessness in this life. Nor, on the other hand, was he tolerant of complacency in such matters. The Christian was to remember that

the body of sin and wicked motions and affections shall never be out of us as long as we live but are almost continually boiling and walloping in us, foam-

[15] Greenham, *Workes*, p. 650.

[16] Perry Miller, "The Marrow of Puritan Divinity," *Publications of the Colonial Society of Massachusetts*, XXXII (1936), 247-300; cf. Ralph Bronkema, *The Essence of Puritanism* (Goes, Holland, 1929), esp. pp. 100-124.

ing out such filthy froth and stinking savor into our minds . . . . [that] it is . . . . most detestable to the mind regenerate, and that part of the mind which is renewed by the spirit of Christ.[17]

It is enough that he do his best continually to follow the ideal. God judges "by the chiefest drift, and what beareth the chiefest sway within us." Some faults might be mixed in a good character, as there might be some blemishes in a fair face, but "God judgeth according to purpose, not performance, according to affect, not effect," since there are some sins which arise not "from malice but infirmity."[18] Sin's power in the Christian was weakened and would be continuously diminished if he did his part, but it was never abolished completely, and the Almighty took this into consideration when evaluating human conduct.[19] The fatal thing was not to sin but to tolerate and enjoy such delinquency. As long as one repented of the evil and struggled against it, one was in good state. So it was not necessary to fear sin to the point of being easily overcome, as one might if one thought a single slip would be fatal. The Christian was to hate and despise sin, but neither fear nor ridicule it,[20] as the Puritan said in discussing the Marprelate tracts. Timorous Christians who feared that they had committed the unpardonable sin were given the Augustinian explanation: this sin was that of persistent indifference, and therefore to be troubled about it was sure sign of innocence.

So much for the medicine for evil. An analysis of what the Puritan considered good works will give us some notion of the positive side of his teaching, of the life on the journey as opposed to the method of shaking off the City of Destruction and its ways. The Puritan approved of both the contemplative and the active life. Fundamentally, he desired a mind so settled in a "good cause" that he could do works of each kind. Roving fantasies or light thoughts were to be zealously weeded out of his

[17] Greenham, *Workes*, p. 681.

[18] *Ibid.*, pp. 119–20, 650.

[19] Cf. Henry Smith, *Sermons* (London, 1599), pp. 288–89; *Works*, ed. Thomas Smith ("Nichols Series of Standard Divines: Puritan Period" [2 vols.; Edinburgh, 1866–67]), I, 310–11.

[20] Greenham, *Workes*, pp. 705 and 839.

mind. A good meditation was to be cherished above rubies. Mystical themes were seldom chosen, but thoughts on God, the believer's relation to him, the plan of salvation, the past conduct of the believer, and resolutions to do better were all considered a wise use of time. The ability to pray fervently, frequently, and at length; a humble, contented spirit; the power to communicate spiritual attitudes to others—all ranked high among the Puritan objectives.[21] It is thus a mistake to treat Puritanism as though it had little or no inner life. The Puritan might be somewhat less mystical than his Catholic brother, but he nevertheless possessed a fairly extensive kingdom of the mind.

On the active side the Puritan was expected to obey his superiors, love his neighbor, do works of charity, "travail in compassion towards all men, relieving the needy and such as are in distress."[22] Also he was to have a calling and "walk diligently" in it. This calling was one's particular occupation; and, though distinguished from the general vocation to the Christian life, was to be quite as zealously pursued. They that will not sweat on earth shall sweat in hell, said Smith.[23] Even the gentry who did not need to labor for daily bread must have a calling and not live as they "use to do in riding and going up and down, to spend their lives in pastimes, pleasure and doing what they list."[24] Those who were justices of the peace were to study law, help their neighbors, train their family, and keep their outer estate to posterity. If they had no office, they were to look to the poor, act as peacemakers, and patronize good ministers. How to select the proper calling was a matter of some difficulty. Greenham's general principle was that people should choose not the role that would most gratify their pride but the one most serviceable to God and profitable to their fellow-men. Once having chosen a vocation, one should live in conformity to it.

[21] Knappen, *op. cit.*, pp. 4–5; Greenham, *Workes*, p. 298.

[22] Greenham, *Workes*, pp. 120, 291, 298, 681.

[23] *Sermons* (third pagination), sig. G, fol. 1(*v*); *Works*, I, 295.

[24] Richard Rogers, *Seaven Treatises Leading and Guiding to True Happiness* (London, 1610; first published in 1603), p. 386.

Anyone dressing more elaborately than was appropriate to his particular calling was to be considered a thief.[25]

It will be noticed that this ideal is rather better rounded than some have supposed. The matter of the calling, though perhaps the chief feature which differentiates the Puritan system from the Catholic, does not dominate the others, as some have supposed. The masking of affections, the effort to suppress all traces of feeling which Schücking notes as a characteristic of the modern Englishman,[26] was not typical of the sixteenth-century Puritan. That worthy was proud of his ability to shed tears on occasion and saw nothing sickening about talk of "sweet joy" in his religion.[27] While one was to glory only in the cross of. Christ, that did not prohibit the use or enjoyment of other things. It is lawful to "eat, drink, apparel ourselves, marry or walk in some honest trade," said the Puritan casuist.[28]

The means to attaining as close as possible to this ideal were many and varied. Superstitious associations and partisan feelings led the Puritan to abandon the routine of the church year and the monastic day, the appeals to the senses such as pictures, incense, and images, and the social attractions of processions and pilgrimages. But he found passable substitutes for these things. Greenham decried absolute routine in religious observances as tending to deaden the participants,[29] but he employed a fair amount in his daily round, as we have seen, though Rogers was much more methodical. Rogers' prescribed cycle had eight points, such as thanksgiving and being humbled for our sins, none of which might be "omitted any day at all without sin, nor carelessly and wittingly without great sin."[30] A standard Puritan day was worked out, which included family prayers and a survey of one's spiritual estate. Recurring sermon days more than took the place of the festivals of the church

---

[25] Greenham, *Workes*, pp. 645, 676-77; Perkins, *Workes*, III, 136-37.

[26] See above, p. 341.

[27] Knappen, *op. cit.*, p. 9.

[28] Greenham, *Workes*, p. 366.

[29] *Ibid.*, pp. 706-7, 778.

[30] Rogers, *op. cit.*, p. 342.

year. Variations from this routine commonly had a disastrous effect on his spiritual frame of mind. "Thursday, Sabbath season me well" notes the diarist. Or on the other hand, "Omitted mine usual beginning of the day with private prayer and meditation, and the next morning rising late because of weariness I began this wretchedness."[31] Psalm-singing and sermons made a powerful appeal to Puritan senses. Fast days and conferences with fellow-believers stirred up the zealous Protestant at least as effectively as the pilgrimage roused his grandfather. In addition, the Puritan developed the powerful stimuli of Bible reading, diary-keeping, and private extempore prayer. These called for more intelligence and more concentration than any of the Catholic techniques. Doubtless, if used properly, they were capable of putting a finer edge on the spiritual life also.

Prayer was considered expecially important. It was an index of faith and sometimes was the only channel of grace. It was valuable not so much as a means of making requests known to the Omniscient but as a means by which man might feel the power of God's love which the Word proclaimed, and so confirm the statements made in preaching. It obtained the experience of the majesty, power, and goodness of God; and, while reading might get knowledge, "prayer is that which getteth feeling and experience." God infuses his truth into us through our hearing, but in prayer man actively partakes of God. It need not be audible, since "the hearty prayer pearceth heaven . . . . as the bullet out of a gun or an arrow out of a bow," though the voice might be used in private to prevent wandering and to stir up affections, and in public to attract people.[32]

In spite of the Puritans' best efforts to devise means to keep the spiritual life always at concert pitch, the "unprofitable" periods would come. The hyperconscientious self-critic of the

---

[31] Knappen, *op. cit.*, pp. 7, 76, 99.

[32] Greenham, *Workes*, p. 777.

Rogers type agonized over these. The more judicious took comfort in Greenham's words on the subject:

> As it is no small benefit, though we have not the bright sun-shining, yet to have the light of it to govern the day, the heat of it to turn away the cold, the effects of it in other works of nature: so it is no small mercy, though we have not the shining countenance of the Lord, yet to have the guiding of our affections by the light of it, the possessing of our souls in patience by some feeling of it, and the fruits thereof in the peace of our minds. Although we feel not the present beams, yet we shall see them shine hereafter. If we have not this joy of our minds as we would in the day of our vocation, the Lord will plentifully give it us in the day of our coronation.[33]

[33] *Ibid.*, p. 662.

CHAPTER XXII

Social and Economic Outlook

URITANISM was primarily a religious movement. This fact cannot be too often repeated in any discussion of its social and economic teaching. The salvation or damnation of the individual was its central theme. To think of it as being primarily concerned with the things of this world is to misrepresent it completely.[1] Starting with the election of the believer and proceeding with his justification, the Puritan did not trouble about social problems until he reached the topic of the Christian's sanctification. But this is not to say that his social policy was therefore weak or necessarily ineffective. Strong individuals properly directed should make the strongest society. If the Puritan failed to achieve this end, it was less for lack of material than for lack of opportunity to make use of it.

In Puritan theory the chief human agency of sanctification was the church. It supplied the means of grace—preaching, fasts, and sacraments—and set the standard of moral discipline. The concept of the church therefore became the determining one for social and economic policy. As we have seen, to most Puritans, even the Independents, the church meant an established, endowed institution. They were reformers, not revolutionists, and they saw no reason to destroy an existing system which with reasonable modifications appeared quite capable of satisfying their spiritual needs. But just as the Puritans felt that a state-supported church required a Christian magistrate to wield the temporal sword, so they could not imagine endowments apart from the principle of private property which would

[1] See Harold Laski, *The Rise of European Liberalism* (London, 1936), pp. 30–34.

give individuals power to convey wealth to the clergy. They were therefore insistent that each man had the right and, in fact, the obligation to maintain his economic standing in the community.

This anticommunistic attitude was strengthened by the conservative Protestant reaction to the Anabaptist movement—a reaction which took place in the dim dawn of the Reformation and was never forgotten. Anxious to dissociate themselves from such disreputable company, the Puritans used strong and unmistakable language on the necessity of preserving the traditional fabric of society. Professing to meet their rivals on their own ground, devotion to scriptural standards, they took the crucial passages in the New Testament and with the most fervid expressions of admiration proceeded to explain them away. The letter killed. The spirit gave life. The will to charity availed more than a slavish adherence to regulations originally set forth as allegorical paradoxes. After these preliminary sophistries it was not difficult to make the proletarian appear the bourgeois cause. This is Tyndale's conclusion to one such line of reasoning:

> Concerning thy goods, thou must remember that thou art a person in the temporal regiment [government]; and the king, as he is over thy body, even so is he lord of thy goods and of him thou holdest them, not for thy use only but for to maintain thy wife, children, and servants and to maintain the king, the realm, and the country and town or city where thou dwellest. Wherefore, thou mayest not suffer them to be wasted, that they were not able to do thy duty; no more than a servant may suffer his master's goods to go to wrack negligently . . . . But every man is bound to labor diligently and truly, and therewith so soberly to live that he may have enough for him and his and somewhat above for them that cannot labor, or by chance are fallen into necessity, and of that give and lend and look not for it again.[2]

In his early days as a reformer Barnes denounced the practice of Christians going to law, a sentiment which had the Anabaptist ring. But, under pressure, Barnes himself qualified this principle so fully as to make it innocuous,[3] and, with that small exception,

---

[2] William Tyndale, *Expositions and Notes*, ed. Walter (Cambridge: Parker Society, 1849), p. 66.

[3] Robert Barnes, *Supplication*, in *The Whole Works of W. Tyndall, J. Frith, and Doct. Barnes* (2 vols.; London, 1572–73), II, 207–10.

even the most radical of English reformers in a pioneer period rejected the suggestion that they should establish a pure Christianity without regard to its effect on the structure of contemporary society.

So it remained to the end of the century whenever Anabaptist ideas were discussed. The principles of private property and Christian warfare were sanctioned in the parts of the Thirty-nine Articles of which the Puritans approved, and Cartwright went out of his way to connect his ecclesiastical teaching with the doctrine of individual ownership of economic goods.[4]

But this was not to indorse anything approaching unrestricted gain-seeking. The Puritan recognized that superior ability and superior effort ought to have superior compensation, but only within reason. Like many another theorist, he had difficulty with precise details, but in an economy of scarcity he could be certain of the principle, which was stated clearly by Fenner. Replying to one of his Anglican adversaries who was defending pluralism with the suggestion that the inequality of God's gifts implied inequality of rewards, he says, "There may be a diversity of rewards given, so long as none have too little nor any too much."[5] Few would dispute this generalization. The problem, then as now, came when the definition of terms was attempted. But it is certain that the Puritan would have been horrified by the license which modern liberalism permits in the matter of fixing the upper limit for private fortunes. The otherworldly religion of the sixteenth century left little place for more than a minimum of attention to the things of this life. The Puritan preoccupation with salvation gave him an original bias against trying to better his economic or social condition. The time available here below was relatively brief and that must be spent in such a way as best to insure the prospect of a blissful eternity hereafter. As bottles and plasters about a room were signs of a sick body, so engrossment in a life of greedy gain,

[4] John Whitgift, *Works*, ed. Ayre (3 vols.; Cambridge: Parker Society, 1851–53), I, 521.

[5] Dudley Fenner, *A Counter-Poyson, Modestly Written for the Time* (London, 1584), p. 195.

which was certain to end shortly in an eternity of hellish tor-
ment, clearly indicated a sick soul, that is, insanity.

Besides being checked by this otherworldly sanction, individualistic tendencies of that day were also restricted by the
concept of the established church. For if that doctrine proved
such stony ground for communism it was equally incompatible
with an unrestricted scramble for wealth. If people were not
content with their stations in life, where was the church to secure any further financial support, or even retain what endowments it possessed? The medieval theory that any private income over and beyond normal needs should be devoted to the
church and the poor suited the reformers admirably.[6] Laymen
infected with a desire to get ahead turned jealous eyes on poorly
defended ecclesiastical property and endangered the whole
church program. How could the Word be preached if grasping
patrons appropriated most of the income of the livings in their
power, or rising merchants refused to pay tithe on their profits?
If therefore the Puritan connected salvation with the right of
private property, he also connected it with the temperate enjoyment of whatever goods God might bestow and the charitable distribution of any surplus.

Since the Puritan did not differ appreciably from the Anglican
or the Catholic in his desire for an established, endowed church,
it is not surprising that his early teaching on economic matters
is practically indistinguishable from the pronouncements of his
rival ecclesiastics. Rack rents and inclosures, hoarding and
charging what the traffic would bear, greedy lawyers and fraudulent workmen were all anathema to all clerical moralists.
"True dealing now is fled and gone," chanted the one group.
"Horn and thorn shall make England forlorn," came back the
antiphony from the other party. The complaints about social
abuses voiced by Sir Thomas More in his *Utopia* are doubtless
better phrased and better known, but certainly no more vigorous, than those of Tyndale in his *Obedience:*

---

[6] See the summary of Calvinistic teaching on this point in Ernst Troeltsch, *Die
Soziallehren der christlichen Kirchen und Gruppen* in *Gesammelte Schriften* (4 vols.;
Tübingen, 1912–25), I, 720; English trans., Olive Wyon, *The Social Teaching of the
Christian Churches* (2 vols.; London, 1931), II, 648.

Let Christian landlords be content with their rent and old customs; not raising the rent or fines and bringing up new customs to oppress their tenants; neither letting two or three tenantries unto one man. Let them not take in their commons, neither make parks nor pastures of whole parishes. For God gave the earth to man to inhabit, and not unto sheep and wild deer.[7]

These were not sectarian problems but issues on which the church in all its conservative branches stood together against the world.

There was the same similarity of outlook at the end of the reign, as may be seen from the minor Puritan writers of the time. In 1542, or soon after, there appeared a small volume entitled *The Complaynt of Roderyck Mors, Somtyme a Gray Fryre, unto the Parliament Howse of Ingland His Natural Cuntry: For the Redresse of Certen Wicked Lawes, Evel Customs, a[n]d Cruel Decreys.*[8] The author was a London mercer named Henry Brinkelow, who described himself as "banished from my native country, only by the cruelty of the forked caps of England for speaking God's truth." In his volume we find not only the typical advanced Protestant's lamentation "for that body and tail of the pope is not banished with his name" but also a large number of comments on specific social abuses. To the traditional grievances of purveyance, feudal exactions, and the dilatory, expensive legal system so common in medieval complaint literature are added protests on the newer problems of inclosures,[9] rack rents, and rising prices. There is little or nothing in the volume which cannot be paralleled with excerpts from the writings on these topics of men more conservative in their theology, notably the Catholic Starkey.[10] Another treatise by Brinkelow,

---

[7] *Doctrinal Treatises,* ed. Walter (Cambridge: Parker Society, 1848), pp. 201–2.

[8] Edited by J. M. Cowper for the Early English Text Society ("Extra Series," Vol. XXII [London, 1874]). The original title-page carried the phrase "Imprinted at Geneve in Savoye by Mighell Boys"; but, since Genevans no longer described their city as in Savoy, we must not take this statement too literally (Theodore Vetter, *Literarische Beziehungen zwischen England und der Schweiz im Reformations-Zeitalter* [Zurich, 1901], pp. 25–26).

[9] Only 500,000 acres, about a fiftieth of the country's arable land, was inclosed before 1650, so that this problem, which bulks so large in contemporary literature, should perhaps not be given so much emphasis in the future (G. E. Fussell, "Farming Methods in the Early Stuart Period. Part I," *Journal of Modern History,* VII [1935], 5).

[10] Early English Text Society ed. ("Extra Series," Vol. XXXII [London, 1878]); cf. Copwer's Introduction to *The Complaynt of Roderick Mors,* pp. x–xvi.

issued at about the same time from "Jericho in the Land of Promise," entitled *The Lamentacyon of a Christen agaynst the Cytye of London for Some Certayne Greate Vyces Used Therein*[11] contains strong words on the neglect of the poor in that city. Things were better when good father Barnes preached, observes the author.[12] Poverty and rack rents are also dealt with in a *Supplication* addressed to the King in 1546 by another Protestant zealot.[13]

In Edward's reign the Puritan continued to speak on social abuses in the language of medieval clericalism, opposing, so far as he had the power, the economic changes of the time. Throughout the reign Hooper and Knox stood shoulder to shoulder with the Anglican spokesmen on this topic. It is quite true that more Anglicans than Puritans declared themselves along this line: Cranmer, Latimer, Lever, Crowley, and Hales among the number. But the Puritan party was small at the time, and its representation in this conflict was fully proportionate to its size. Knox's rebuke of the grasping courtiers is well known, though Froude somewhat garbled the story.[14] Anthony Gilby denounced the social abuses of the time. Leasemongering was a crime; laymen who kept monastic spoils were guilty of the sin of the biblical Achan. People who resented sermons on the subject should remember that it was "not . . . . Latimer nor Lever, nor Hooper nor Becon nor Horne that speaketh to them, but the spirit of God."[15] In his exposition of the Book of Jonah before the court Hooper frequently recurred to the theme of social

[11] Reprinted by Cowper in the same volume with his other work.

[12] Pp. 90–91.

[13] Edited by J. M. Cowper for the Early English Text Society ("Extra Series," Vol. XIII). The suggestion of the editor (p. xiv) that Brinkelow was the author of the two supplications printed in this volume must be questioned in view of the strong denunciation in the second (p. 82) of the practice of usury, even when legalized. Brinkelow's *Complaynt* advocates the collection of 3 per cent interest on the half of the confiscated church property which was to be loaned to poor merchants (p. 51).

[14] John Knox, *Faithful Admonition*, in *Works*, ed. Laing (6 vols.; Edinburgh, 1895), III, 281–83; R. W. Dixon, *History of the Church of England from the Abolition of the Roman Jurisdiction* (3d rev. ed.; 6 vols.; Oxford, 1895), III, 487 n.

[15] *A Commentary upon the Prophet Mycha* (London, 1551), sig. D, fol. viii; sig. E, fol. iii(*v*); sig. H, fol. iii.

injustices and the need of enforcing the laws against them. His sympathy with what Pollard has called the "commonwealth party" of Hales and his friends may be seen in one of the illustrations employed in these lectures:

I was once in the Race of Britaine [probably the Race of Alderney] with a fore wind and contrary flood, the seas in that place going both hollow, and that by reason of a multitude of rocks in the same place. The master of the ship, to conduct her the better, sat upon the main yard to see the seas aforehand, and cried to him that steered the stern always upon which side he should steer the ship to break best the danger of the sea. The wind blowing high, whereas the master cried, "A-larboard," he that steered mistook it and steered a-starboard; and the once mistaking of the master's law had almost cast us under the water. Then thought I, it is not without cause that wise men compare a commonwealth to a ship; for one thing loseth and saveth them both. For in case the master's officer in the ship obey not his law the ship will of force drown. So shall this commonwealth and every other that when the king and his council shall make laws to help and save the poor, such as steer the hinder part of the ship behind the king's back follow not that he is bid to do but that that he listeth himself and his own private commodity to do; and thus putteth both the ship, the master, and all the mariners in danger of drowning. Amend therefore every man betime; if ye do not the Lord at length will cast ye out from all ye have, to the destruction of you and yours.[16]

Because Hooper has been attacked at some length as a tool and supporter of the exponents of the new economy,[17] two further quotations from him must be given covering these important points more explicitly. Writing to Cecil, the royal secretary, soon after his installation at Gloucester, he says:

For the love and tender mercy of God, persuade and cause some order to be taken upon the price of things, or else the ire of God will shortly punish.

[16] John Hooper, *Early Writings*, ed. Carr (Cambridge: Parker Society, 1843), pp. 497-98.

[17] C. H. Smyth, *Cranmer and the Reformation under Edward VI* (Cambridge, 1926). I have found this volume to be very useful in many ways, but the author's enthusiasm for Cranmer betrays him into making some rather rash judgments on the Puritans involved in his story. For example, Knox's salary as royal chaplain (Peter Lorimer, *John Knox and the Church of England* [London, 1875], p. 80) is referred to (p. 267) as a bribe. In connection with these sermons of Hooper's he remarks (p. 277, cf. p. 196) that "though 'intended to touch freely on the duties of individuals' [they] contained nothing that could bring a blush to the cheek of the least hardened oppressor of the poor and plunderer of the church." In so expressing himself, the writer cannot have read very carefully Hooper's remarks on false judges, the idle nobility, self-seeking gentry, grasping lawyers, superstitious and lazy clergy, and bribery and corruption in general (Hooper, *op. cit.*, pp. 451, 460, 466-67, 480-81, 496-97, 510, 555-56, *et passim*). Dixon (*op. cit.*, III, 181) considers Hooper "as unsparing as Latimer in denouncing the evils of the age" in these sermons.

All things be here so dear, that the most part of people lacketh, and yet more will lack, necessary food. . . . . All pastures and breeding of cattle is turned into sheep's-meat, and they be not kept to be brought to the market, but to bear wool, and profit only their master. Master Secretary, for the passion of Christ take the fear of God and a bold stomach to speak herein for a redress, and that the goods of every shire be not thus wrested and taken into few men's hands. If it continue, the wealth and strength of the realm must needs perish. What availeth great riches in a realm and neither the head nor the greatest part of the members to be the better for it? . . . .

So much as have more than enough buyeth when things be *good cheap* to sell afterwards dear. God amend it! It is my bounden duty, and all other true men's to persuade and teach obedience unto the people; and, thanks be to the Lord!, I can perceive none other here but love and reverence among the people to the King's Majesty, and to the laws; but Mr. Secretary, it is the magistrates, and their own doings that shall most commend them and win love of the people. Ye know what a grievous and extreme—yea, in manner unruly— evil hunger is. The prices of things be here as I tell ye; the number of people be great, their little cottages and poor livings decay daily; except God by sickness take them out of the world they must needs lack. God's mercy give you and the rest of my Lords wisdom to redress it, wherein I pray God ye may see the occasion of the evil and so destroy it.[18]

And again in the next year:

For lack of heed, corn so passeth from hence by water, that I fear much we shall have great scarcity this year. Doubtless men that be put in trust do not their duties. The Statute of Regrators is so used that in many quarters of these parts it will do little good: and in some parts, where as licence by the justices will not be granted, the people are much offended that they should not, as well as other, bag as they were wont to do.[19]

In the next reign Turner showed himself no supporter of economic innovations when he proposed the recapture of the monastic lands as part of his program for a future reformation.[20] Even after the establishment of the rudiments of the Elizabethan system of poor relief under state auspices, the Puritans found a good deal to say on this subject. One of the charges against Dering in 1573 was that he had spoken against the poor law and advocated a community of goods. His answer[21] was that he

[18] Hooper to Cecil, April 17, 1551, in P. F. Tytler, *England under the Reigns of Edward VI and Mary* (2 vols.; London, 1839), I, 365–66.

[19] Hooper to Cecil, July 6, 1552, *Later Writings*, ed. Nevinson (Cambridge: Parker Society, 1852), p. xviii.

[20] See p. 114 above.

[21] John Strype, *Annals of the Reformation under Elizabeth* (4 vols. in 7; Oxford, 1824), II, ii, 514.

had not denied the right to private property, which he shrewdly declared was asserted in the twenty-fifth chapter of Matthew, where Christ predicted his saying, "I was an hungred, and ye gave me meat," or "I was thirsty, and ye gave me drink." From the idea of giving he adduced the implication of possession, while cleverly leaving the idea of an obligation to charity strongly in the foreground. He declared that the reason that people were made rich was that they might dispense to the poor. Otherwise the riches of this world were of no use. That was the point of his complaint against the poor law. He had not objected to it as such, but to the lack of its enforcement and to its being considered a complete solution of the problem and the only means of relief. He had also advocated the allotting of the poor to the care of rich individuals in numbers proportionate to their wealth.

Ten years later another Puritan, Thomas Lupton, voiced a full-throated complaint against the times. Landlords who exacted rack rents and unmerciful fines or payments for renewal of leases, lawyers who took full fees from two parties for the same day's work, or spun out the rich man's case until the poor man was forced to abandon his claim, the impatient poor and the climbing upper classes were all duly scourged. Some bands and ruffs cost enough to clothe three or four people, and their owners were not even gentlemen. Women with expensive rings looked disdainfully on the "poor silly [simple] soul lying naked in the street, shivering with cold and almost dead with hunger" and let him die most miserably.[22]

Toward the end of the century the full-blown medieval social theory was still widely advocated by the Puritans. At Norwich, Burton held forth in a style reminiscent of Latimer and Lever.

---

[22] *Dream of the Devill and Dives* (London, 1584), esp. sig. G, fol. 1(*v*). See also John Knewstubs, *Lectures upon the Twentieth Chapter of Exodus* (London, 1577), pp. 137-50; John Wharton, *Dreame Conteyninge an Invective against Certaine Abominable Caterpillers as Usurers, Extortioners, Leasemongers and Such Others* (London, 1578). This tract in poor verse can be classed as a Puritan production since it carries the indorsement of Foxe and Crowley. Cf. S. Bateman, or Batman, *The New Arival* (London, [1580?]), for an Anglican parallel. Thomas Drant (*Two Sermons* [London, (1570?)]) represents a halfway position ecclesiastically, since he was chaplain to Grindal, but his social teaching is indistinguishable from the others.

The drones now take all the honey. The horseleeches cry for college lands. Around the court some are sick of consumption. Only a bishopric will restore them. They use church property to maintain minstrels as well as ministers. Seventy times seven lean kine are devouring seven hundred fat ones. Some can rob Peter to pay Paul, but these men can cunningly rob both Peter and Paul and pay neither. *O auri sacra fames!* What will not some do for money!

And know you of Norwich whose hearts run after covetousness, who sit and hear the preacher for a fashion, which go home and jest at him your belly's full, which censure him at your pleasure, which eat him at your feasts, which buy and sell him in your shops, which recreate yourselves with their faults, which make them your marks to shoot at and your fields to walk in . . . . know . . . . that one day . . . . they shall know that prophets have been amongst them.[23]

Greenham declared that it was best to seek first the kingdom of heaven and to lay up one's treasure there. What one possessed on earth was all given by God and so to be gratefully accepted, but like any pleasure it was liable to abuse. There was a danger that one would grow proud because of riches and not acknowledge the source, so that, if one has not material riches, he may be thankful that God keeps him from temptation.[24]

Nor was all the Puritan attitude expressed in mere verbiage either. Besides the clerical illustrations already given,[25] there are examples among the laity, from the lowest to the highest, of a recognition of a religious obligation to keep to the medieval standards. Shortly before their flight to Holland the Gainsborough Separatist congregation excommunicated a tailor because he had charged seven shillings for a doublet and hose when an-

---

[23] *Sermon Preached in the Cathedral Church of Norwich the XXI Day of December 1589* (*s.l.*, [after 1591]), sig. C, fol. 2(*v*)–sig. D, fol. 4(*v*), esp. sig. D, fol. 4(*v*).

[24] Richard Greenham, *The Workes of Richard Greenham* (5th and last ed.; London, 1612), pp. 783 and 711. John Dod and Arthur Hildersam worthily carried this medieval tradition on into the next century (cf. Samuel Clarke, *Generall Martyrologie* [London, 1651], pp. 405 and 409; "Dod's Sayings," *Memorials of the Rev. John Dod*, ed. Taylor [Northampton, 1884], p. 11; Hildersam, "On the Lord's Supper," bound with Bradshaw's *A Preparation to the Receiving of Christ's Body and Blood* [London, 1636], p. 108).

[25] See above, pp. 384–85.

other workmen said that five was a just price.[26] At the other
end of the scale were Puritan landlords like Francis Russell, the
Earl of Bedford, whom Elizabeth accused of making all the
beggars in England (encouraging idleness) by his charity,[27] and
the Earl of Huntingdon, whose virtues we find described in his
funeral ballad:

> To poor and to needie to high and to low
> Lord Hastings was friendly, all people doth know.
> His gates were still open the stranger to feed
> And comfort the succorless always in need.
>
> Then wail we then weep we, then mourn we each one
> The good Earl of Huntingdon from us is gone. . . . .
>
> His tenants that daily repaired to his house
> Was fed with his bacon, his beef and his souse;
> Their rents were not raised, their fines were but small,
> And many poor tenants paid nothing at all.
>
> Then wail we, etc.
>
> Such landlords in England we seldom shall find
> That to their poor tenants will bear the like mind
> Lord Hastings therefore is joyfully crowned
> With Angels in heaven where peace doth abound. . . . .
>
> He built up no palace, nor purchased no town,
> But gave it to scholars to get him renown,
> As Oxford and Cambridge can rightly declare
> How many poor scholars maintained are there. . . . .
>
> No groves he inclosed nor felled no wood,
> No pastures he paled to do himself good;
> To commons and countrie he lived a good friend,
> And gave to the needie what God did him send.[28]

[26] Richard Bernard, *Plaine Evidences* (London, 1610), p. 110, quoted in W. H.
Burgess, *John Smith the Se-Baptist, Thomas Helwys, and the First Baptist Church in
England* (London, 1911), p. 96.

[27] G. Scharf, *A Descriptive and Historical Catalogue of the Collection of Pictures at
Woburn Abbey* (3 vols.; London, 1877), I, 19–20.

[28] *The Crie of the Poor for the Death of the Right Honourable Earl of Huntington* (single-
sheet broadside, *s.l.*, n.d.; British Museum Press Mark: Huth 50[56]). Some stanzas
omitted. Though allowance must be made for panegyric on such occasions, there are
plenty of corroborating details. The Earl was deeply in debt at his death (Historical
Manuscripts Commission, *Hastings MSS*, II, 44–45), a circumstance which, as Lord
President of the Council of the North, he had the power to remedy had he so desired.
Not only do we have the particulars in Harleian MS 4744, fols. 135–43, of how he

Yet in the last half of Elizabeth's regin a certain chill begins to spread over Puritan social teaching. Whereas Dering and Greenham wanted Puritan charity to exceed the legal minimum, a new school developed which was content with little more than the secular standard. The poor ceased to figure as God's special charges—lovable, helpless lambs, with only an occasional hint of their impatience, to make the tale of the classes' sins complete—and appear as thriftless rogues, unwilling to work and only corrupted by charity. A hint of this change may be seen in the case of Robert Crowley, whose early work was most critical of the economic changes in the reign of Edward VI. In 1574, after his vestiarian troubles, he preached an election-day sermon in the London Guild Hall in which he shows a much more complacent attitude toward the rising merchants. While he still declared covetousness (the desire for gain) to be wrong, he pointed out that riches themselves were not evil and that God may give them easily, without strife.[29] But influential William Perkins was the chief formulator of the new teaching. His cardinal principle was that the law of nature, which establishes differences of wealth, was not abolished by the gospel.[30] "In a commonwealth all must not be equal; but some above, some under others in regard of wealth, and therefore such as have sundry farms .... may lawfully enjoy them."[31] Consequently, it becomes everyone's duty, in order to have a well-ordered commonwealth, to maintain his "own good estate and condition," and that is the first lien upon his finances.[32] When one does come to consider charity, one's family and kindred are to be preferred as

---

wasted his estate on "those greedy horse-leeches, the Puritans," who are supposed to have wrung ninety-four manors from him besides numerous advowsons, but his name is constantly cropping up in connection with odd benefactions, such as that which enabled the town of Leicester to buy coal for its poor (J. H. Thomas, *Town Government in the Sixteenth Century* [London, 1933], p. 111). His brother, Sir Francis Hastings, who presented the Puritan petition from Northampton in February, 1605, also died in straitened circumstances.

[29] *A Sermon Made in the Chappel at the Gylde Hall* (London, 1474), sig. C, fol. 4; sig. D, fol. 1.

[30] *Workes* (3 vols.; London, 1616–18), II, 128.

[31] *Ibid.*, I, 763.   [32] *Ibid.*, II, 128–35.

objects, next Christians, then people near by, and lastly strangers.[33] We are not to grieve ourselves in relieving others,[34] and, of
course, law suits to maintain our good estate and condition are
perfectly justifiable, subject only to certain mild restrictions.[35]
Much the same attitude may be found in a work published in
1597 by Henry Arthington of Copinger plot fame.[36] Nicholas
Bownde echoes the refrain. Let there be an efficient administration of the poor law with the overseers regularly visiting the
houses of the poor. But his chief concern was to prevent the
collection of assessments from interfering with religious services. On this subject he expanded at some length.

> In many places . . . . in the time of divine service you shall see men go up
> and down asking, receiving, changing, and bestowing of money: wherein
> many times you shall have them so disagree that they are louder than the
> minister, and the rest stand looking and listening unto them, leaving the
> worship of God (as though it did not concern them) and thus all is con-
> founded.

It was true that, when the collection was made at the close of a
gathering, people hurried away without giving, so that the "col-
lectors for the poor were compelled to take them there in the
midst of God's service, when for very shame by [of] starting
aside they could not refuse." But "for a man when he is de-
voutly occupied in any part of God's public worship to have
another man come and pull him by the sleeve and to whisper in
his ear and for him to draw out his purse and to change money;
whether that hinder [worship] let man judge."[37] So Bownde
leaves the subject without concerning himself to provide any
alternative method of collection. With this decline of interest in
poor relief beginning under Elizabeth it is not surprising in the
succeeding reign to find Paul Baynes, Perkins' disciple and
successor at Great St. Andrews, Cambridge, assuring his audience that "lawful prospering" and "Christian gaining" are en-

[33] *Ibid.*, p. 145.

[34] *Ibid.*, p. 128.   [35] *Ibid.*, p. 119.

[36] *Provision for the Poore Now in Penurie Out of the Storehouse of God's Plentie*
(London, 1597).

[37] *Sabbathum veteris et novi testamenti* (London, 1606), pp. 445, 363–64.

couraged by true faith, since the religious man works with a mind at peace with God and trusts him for a blessing.[38]

It is common knowledge that the Reformation meant a general decline in charitable activity throughout England. Protestant apologists were hard pressed to answer the Catholic taunt that their religion was "nothing else but plain talking and not walking." The virtual cessation of church-building in the first century of English Protestantism further confirms the general complaint of the contemporary moralists.[39] As we have seen, even the Puritans in time began to succumb to this widespread spirit of indifference. The collapse is the more noticeable since it coincided almost exactly in time with the rise of the ascetic spirit among the party of the zealous.[40] It was therefore not so much lack of vitality or energy as lack of interest which accounts for the decline in generosity.

To some extent this change is to be accounted for on theological grounds. In spite of the moral enthusiasm connected with the original introduction of the doctrine of justification by faith, and in spite of the ingenious arguments devised to explain that good works are almost necessary signs of a genuine election, the Catholic doctrine continued to be the more effective pump for alms. No doubt Greenham was correct in feeling that talk of compounding with God for rewards was offensive to spiritual Christians. But since the bulk of mankind were not spiritual Christians, selling heaven by the piece proved the more profitable business to the church. In Edward's time Crowley pointed out in a most penetrating poetical analysis of Reformation history that the doctrine of justification by faith could be more serviceable to the cause of greed than the doctrine of salvation by works. Philaute or Self-love is represented as informing the

[38] *Briefe Directions unto a Godly Life* (London, 1637; first published in 1618), p. 241.

[39] Cf. the admission by the Puritan Laurence Chaderton (*Sermon at Paules Cross* [London, 1578], sig. C, fol. v) that the Catholics' liberality exceeded the Protestant; H. Bedell, *Sermon Exhorting To Pitie the Poore* (London, 1572), sig. B, fol. iii. Philip Stubbs (*Motive to Good Workes* [London, 1593]) is most explicit and detailed on this subject. F. Trigge (*An Apologie or Defence of Our Dayes* [London, 1589]) raises a solitary voice in opposition, but the anti-Catholic purpose of his work vitiates his conclusion.

[40] See below, pp. 429–30.

gold-eating god Philargyrie, that Catholic Hypocrisie was with-holding from him some of the available profits in the social system. He offers a solution:

> I will declare
> How mad they are
>   To give him of their good
> To be made just,
> Since all men must
>   Be made just by Christ's blood.
>
> For though he ring
> Great bells and sing
>   A thousand masses and moe,
> Yet must Christ's blood
> Shed on the rood
>   Deliver all men from woe.
>
> Then you shall give
> Each man good leave
>   To withhold what he can
> From that vile slave
> That doth still crave
>   A slice of every man.[41]

Crowley's interpretation was all too correct. The zest went out of almsgiving along with the acrid odor of purgatory. In the next century the husbandman wishing to rise in the world was advised to seek one of the old-fashioned landlords who believed that their tenants' prayers could save them from purgatory and who thought it a sin to raise their grandfather's rents.[42]

Nor should the debilitating effect of the passage of time be forgotten in estimating the causes of this decline. Hooper and Gilby spoke at the height of the commotion, with the lead roofs and oak beams still on the move and the new leases still at the scriveners. By Perkins' time the statute of limitations had pretty well covered the old offenses, even in the courts of conscience, and the newer ones were not so numerous or dramatic. Social problems thus gradually drifted out of the forefront of the clerical mind. When the next great social upheaval took place in

---

[41] Robert Crowley, *The Fable of Philargyrie* (London, 1551; reprinted in facsimile, ed. W. A. Marsden [London, 1931]), sig. C, fol. viii.

[42] T. Powell, *The Art of Thriving* (first published in 1635); *Somers Tracts*, ed. Walter Scott (13 vols.; London, 1809–15), VII, 205.

England, the rise of the Quakers demonstrated that the social conscience of advanced Protestant idealists was only dormant and not dead.

But while these points are important, the political situation should also be included in any enumeration of the factors contributing to this Puritan indifference to social problems. Sectarian partisanship rubbed the bloom off the life of voluntary poverty. Protestant antipathy to Catholicism led the Puritan to denounce the practice of selling all and giving to the poor as a preparation for the monastic life.

Solomon teacheth that a man must let his water flow out of his cistern but he must keep the fountain to himself. . . . . David makes it a curse to be a beggar and he never saw the righteous man's seed begging their bread. . . . . Christ bids him that had two coats not to give both away, but one. And Paul . . . . bids every man to labor with his own hands.[43]

Even more important would seem to be the failure of the Puritan reformers to win their desired position of influence in the state. In their consequent weakness they were driven to form an alliance with country gentry and town merchants—an alliance, furthermore, in which they were in the role of dependents. To some extent they must thus have been precluded from speaking their mind freely on dangerous economic topics. Furthermore, being permanently in opposition, they never had the opportunity of putting into practice a vigorous social policy, and so in time lost interest in the subject, or at least lost their sense of perspective. It is noticeable that the most active stand on these questions was taken by the Protestant clergy in the days of their greatest power, under Edward. Why should they concern themselves with such topics in Elizabeth's time, when little hope remained of bringing about any change in the situation? There was some point in preaching on matters of individual conduct, because there was a possibility of changing individual lives. But the only effective way to reach the social problem lay through a reorganization of the established church and a change in its relations with the secular power, and Elizabeth had succeeded in making discussion of those subjects taboo.

[43] Perkins, op. cit., II, 128.

Lastly the secular government had so effectively encroached on this sphere of welfare work as to rob it of most of its interest for the zealous ecclesiastics. The Council and the justices of the peace organized and supervised the administration of the poor law. Their efforts were not wholly successful, but the system developed was doubtless much better than the hit-and-miss almsgiving of the medieval church. There remained much room for improvement, and Dering and Greenham were making a good point in trying to supplement the secular system. England and the Puritans themselves would have benefited by a studious following-up of the suggestions which were then in the air for organized easy credit for the poor.[44] But, like many modern directors of educational and other charities, the Puritan doubtless found it a discouraging business trying to compete with the power and resources of the secular state in a field where the lay authorities were increasingly successful. It was much easier to turn to such topics as those of dress and amusement, in which the record of the secular authorities was far less satisfactory from a Puritan point of view. There points against the rivals in power could be scored with great ease, and perhaps some progress made. So the Puritan, looking over his medieval heritage, largely abandoned the social gospel and took up the monastic struggle with the flesh. In no field do the evil consequences of following Calvin's doctrine of the two societies appear more clearly than in this. In a developed Zwinglian system, with a sovereignty united in practice as well as in theory, the clergy might not have yielded so easily.

It is obviously impossible to follow Puritan thought on every economic problem of the period. But one other illustration of their ultra-conservative and eventually futile attitude can be given. The teaching on usury is second only to the role of the poor as a touchstone for sixteenth- and seventeenth-century social theory. Here again we have an original antipathy which gave way to the beginnings of a rational solution of the problem in the days of Puritan strength. Then in the long opposition

[44] Cf. R. H. Tawney's Introduction to his edition of Dr. Thomas Wilson's *Discourse upon Usury* (London, 1925), pp. 120 and 159.

period under Elizabeth the party moralists lost touch with
realities. One group reverted to the original hostility to all in-
terest-taking, while another quietly accepted the secular solution of the problem, washed its hands of the whole matter, and
turned to more congenial topics. With the exception of one semi-
lucid interval no serious effort was made to develop a practical
solution for a serious moral issue, no effort to distinguish between the ethics of money-lending in an agrarian society and
those of the financing of mercantile activities. Doubtless it was
not altogether an accident that some of the strongest denuncia-
tions of the loan industry came from men such as Lupton, who
believed that half a whelp applied warm would cure the gout
and who spent much of his time collecting such valuable bits of
information.

The anonymous Puritan *Supplication* of 1546 has a strong
denunciation of the practice of usury, even when legalized.[45] But
the layman Brinkelow, writing at about the same time, advocated the taking of 3 per cent interest on the half of the value of
confiscated church property which in his scheme was to be
loaned to poor merchants.[46] In Edward's time, Hooper, writing
in Zurich in 1548, gives a somewhat oracular treatment of this
subject. He dealt with the various infractions of the Eighth
Commandment and described "usury and applying of money or
any thing else to an unreasonable gain" as "none other than
theft." He also noted that in the Bible "usury is plain forbidden." But he recognized that the civil (Roman) law permitted some taking of interest, and though he said that such
laws were "in many things scarce to be borne withal," yet he
"would they were well observed" in view of the general ignoring
of any restrictions. His wish that "men should rather refrain
from giving of money to a gain altogether than break the law
of charity" seems to indicate that, on balance, he took the Swiss
attitude of tolerating limited "charitable" usury.[47]

One of the first developments of Elizabeth's time, however,
was the publication of an English version of the opinion of

---

[45] See above, p. 406, n. 13.   [46] *Ibid.*   [47] *Early Writings*, p. 393.

Wolfgang Musculus on the usury question.[48] He discussed the suggestion that mercantile usury was less damnable than other varieties, but ended by condemning all. This became the general refrain of the impotent clerical moralists, Anglican and Puritan alike, who dealt with the subject for the remainder of the reign. An analysis of the opposition in the Commons to the usury statute passed in 1572 shows that there were no sectarian differences involved. The chief opponent, Dr. Thomas Wilson, was a prominent civilian and diplomat who later became Principal Secretary of State and Dean of Durham, but among his supporters were Lovelace, Fleetwood, and Norton, all of whom had taken an active part in pressing for ecclesiastical reform.[49] Lupton gives an extended account of the usurer's sharp practices in soliciting business and contriving to exact huge profits for technical failures of borrowers to make repayment.[50] Laurence Chaderton ranks usurers with sorcerers and murderers in his catalogue of evil men.[51] Stubbs, who believed in espiscopacy, in his well-known *Anatomy of Abuses*[52] denounces usury in spite of the statutory license it enjoyed. It was mere murder of the poor in his opinion. At Norwich, Burton listed usurers with atheists and drunkards as the object of his shafts.

But a weariness was creeping on. After delivering his soul on the subject, the Norwich zealot confessed the hopelessness of the task.

I would to God I could devise a way to make usurers turn again, but I fear me I shall not, for they which can cozen all laws will be no doubt too cunning for me.

Usury is a devil that all the disciples of Christ in England cannot cast out. No statutes, nor laws can tame usury, for he hath so many turnings and turnagains that a man cannot tell where to find him. He is in money, in wares, in buying and selling, for ready money, for time, in borrowing and lending by himself, and by his brokers, the devil's huntsmen. And this is certain; usury is grown so strong that it hath sinews and bones like a man and walked

[48] *Of the Lawful and Unlawful Usurie amongest Christians* (*s.l.*, n.d.).

[49] Sir Simonds D'Ewes (ed.), *A Compleat Journal of the Votes Speeches and Debates . . . . throughout the Whole Reign of Queen Elizabeth* (London, 1693), pp. 171–73.

[50] *Op. cit.*, sig. E, fols. 5–8.   [51] *Op. cit.*, sig. H, fol. i.

[52] Edited by F. J. Furnival for the New Shakespeare Society (London, 1879), pp. 123–29.

up and down the streets like a servingman, like a gentleman, like a merchant-man. I hope no man may justly say like an alderman. God forbid. But this I am sure of, it walketh so stoutly that it taketh the wall of all honesty and religion.[53]

Still, Burton went on talking with blind vigor against the whole practice, and most of the early seventeenth-century Puritans followed his example.[54]

There were, however, a few exceptions. Henry Smith,[55] while condemning all taking of interest, permitted the paying of it in cases of necessity. Perkins went the whole length and threw his influence on the Swiss side of the controversy. He allowed usury with Calvin's restrictions: where the borrower can earn by the bargain and where the creditor neither takes all the gain nor holds the debtor to his bargain in case of honest failure of the venture. Engrossing was denounced and the medieval doctrine of the just price retained.[56] But, lacking political power and strong ecclesiastical courts, it was impossible for the Puritans to implement these restrictions, and no effort was made to follow up the suggestions.[57]

[53] *Op. cit.*, sig. H, fols. 1–2.

[54] Richard Turnbull, "Sermons on Psalm XV" (bound with his *Exposition upon the Canonicall Epistle of St. James* [London, 1606; first ed., 1591]). M. Mosse, *Arraignment and Conviction of Usurie* (London, 1595). *The Death of Usury* (Cambridge, 1594) is largely a pirating of the above (cf. Mosse, *op. cit.*, Preface), though it permits usury in the case of orphans' estates. William Pemberton, *The Godly Merchant: A Sermon Preached at Paul's Cross* (London, 1613), pp. 116–17. H. Ainsworth, *Annotations on the Pentateuch* (2 vols.; Edinburgh, 1843 [first published in 1616–18]), I, 361; II, 318–19. Roger Turner, *The Usurer's Plea Answered* (London, 1634). Robert Bolton, *A Short and Private Discourse betweene Mr. Bolton and One M. S. concerning Usury* (London, 1637).

Mosse, writing in 1595, dedicates his book to Whitgift, though in 1584, when he preached at Norwich before the exiled Earl of Mar and the other Scotch nobles, he doubtless could be classed as a Puritan (cf. *DNB*, art. "Mosse"). On the party affiliations of Turnbull, Pemberton, and Turner, I am unable to secure any information, and they are doubtless to be numbered among the Anglicans.

[55] *Sermons* (London, 1599), pp. 91–114; *Works*, ed. Thomas Smith ("Nichols Series of Standard Divines: Puritan Period" [2 vols.; Edinburgh, 1866–67]), I, 88–108.

[56] *Op. cit.*, I, 62–63.

[57] In a cursory survey I have been unable to discover any Puritan who adopts Perkins' point of view in the early Stuart period. Gabriel Powell in his *Theologicall and Scholasticall Positions concerning Usurie* (London, 1602) allows interest to be charged if the lender sustains actual loss by the lack of the money, but he was a strong Anglican and belongs to Filmer's predecessors, not Perkins' followers. (See, however, William Ames, *Commentary on the Psalms* [Amsterdam, 1635], after Psalm 15—a reference for which I am indebted to Dr. Douglas Horton.)

With the trumpets thus giving an uncertain sound no Puritan really prepared for social battle. There is no evidence of any attempt at an intelligent compromise on the issues involved, no gesture toward working out any idealistic improvements in the secular system of regulated money-lending. Most of the Puritan leaders folded their tents and silently stole away from this difficult terrain, if they did not actually desert to the enemy.[58] Attacking papists and prelates, Arminians and actors, was a far more congenial occupation. Or perhaps a general hymn of hate against such delightfully vague opponents as the Amalekites and the Amorites was sufficient to satisfy the Puritan lust for battle.

This change of attitude, reflecting in part the current political situation, reacted in turn on the Puritan laity. As the ministers stopped cutting consciences for such delinquencies, their prominent listeners ceased to concern themselves with social problems. At the end of the century it is hard to find devout Puritan nobles of the Huntingdon-Bedford type, just as Melville had difficulty discovering any representative of the Scotch landed class who enjoyed talking religion with him after the death of Erskine of Dun. Some of the country gentry certainly retained a conscience in these matters, witness Cromwell's defense of the rights of the poor in the affair of the Huntingdon charter. But the town merchants were already beginning to acquire that reputation for cant on Sunday and extortionate, usurious greed on Monday which made them easy targets for the shafts of Ben Jonson and his fellow-dramatists in the next generation, of which the following is a preliminary sample.

> Who would imagine yonder sober man,
> That same devout meal-mouth'd precisian,
> That cries "Good Brother," "Kind sister," makes a duck
> After the antique grace, can always pluck
> A sacred book out of his civil hose,
> And at th' op'ning, and at our stomach's close
> Says with a turn'd-up eye a solemn grace
> Of half an hour; then with silken face

---

[58] James Spottiswood declared in 1616 that many of the Puritan and Anglican clergy alike were charging interest on their own loans (*The Execution of Neschech* [Edinburgh 1616], p. 41).

Smiles on the holy crew, and then doth cry,
"O manners! O times of impurity!—"
  Who thinks that this good man
  Is a vile, sober, damned politician?
  Not I, till with his bait of purity
  He bit me sore in deepest usury.
  No Jew, no Turk, would use a Christian
  So inhumanely as this Puritan.
  Dromedes' jades were not so bestial
  As this seeming saint—vile cannibal!
  Take heed, O world! take heed avisedly
  Of these same damned anthropophagi.
  I had rather been within a harpy's claws
  Than trust myself in their devouring jaws,
  Who all confusion to the world would bring
  Under the form of their new discipline.[59]

On the basis of the evidence assembled in this chapter it may
thus fairly be suggested that the contributions of Puritanism to
the rise of modern capitalism were exceedingly indirect. In
theory the zealous religious leaders were quite opposed to economic individualism. Predestinarian thinking really did very
little to encourage it; and, while ecclesiastical discipline and
books of piety developed a sturdy, self-reliant, hard-working
type of layman, the social doctrine of the party leaders was still
almost entirely medieval. What contributions Puritanism did
make were in the practical field. By dividing the clergy and opposing the secular authorities, the advanced reformers created a
situation in which it was difficult to enforce old rules. By eventually ceasing to speak about economic subjects, they removed
the pressure on their own laity to walk in the traditional paths.
Their contribution was therefore negative rather than positive,
destructive rather than constructive.

Doubtless the hyperconservatism of their economic thought
contributed to this end. For, if any adverse criticism is to be
passed on the Puritan economic and social polity during the
period when the party took an active interest in such matters, it
cannot be for willingness to accept and welcome change in these
fields, as sometimes charged, but for hostility to it. Obviously,

---

[59] W. K., *The Metamorphosis of Pygmalion's Image* (London, 1598), quoted in G. B.
Harrison, *A Second Elizabethan Journal* (New York, 1931), p. 280.

a better program would have been an intelligent acceptance of all changes likely to increase the productivity of the country, with the church's influence being employed to insure a generous division of the augmented national income. Horn and thorn did not make England forlorn but both beautiful and prosperous. Likewise the taking of interest, which filled her harbors with ships setting out for the seven seas. Few who consider the matter seriously will regret the increase in England's wealth which came about through the adoption of the new economic methods. Only the social results are questionable. By unimaginative and uncomprehending criticism of current business procedure a group which might have exercised a constructive influence on the shaping of a new world lost the confidence of businessmen and found themselves more hopelessly out of power than ever. The secular authorities, with whom the zealous clergy would not co-operate, pre-empted this large field of human life for their province. The idealists, torn by their own feuds, could not win back that full share in the responsibilities of government which would have modernized their ideas and made their contributions to the solution of social problems worth while.

CHAPTER XXIII

Asceticism

FOR all its distinguished history Puritanism has little standing in the popular mind today. If it shows signs of strength, it is bitterly denounced; if not, it is a subject of pleasant ridicule. For this situation its ascetic aspects are largely responsible. The cartoonists' hard-faced, self-righteous misanthrope arouses the hatred; the antiquated and semimythical blue laws provide the jest.

Part of this reaction comes from the legitimate rough-and-tumble of any struggle for favor and power. Rival academics have been known to employ similar tactics when budgets are limited. The moralist who censures must expect to be censured, to have his thrusts at opponents' weaknesses returned in kind, to be eaten at the adversaries' feast, as Burton put it. And, as long as the principle of division of labor obtains in the human race, these frictions will be generated. Each group, absorbed in its own undertaking, thinks of its interest as paramount. At least from the time of Wordsworth poets have been decrying the advance of railroads, machines, and other essentials of modern economic life. Even historians have been known to express indignation that all family muniment rooms are not opened to their professional pillage as a matter of course.

But part of the modern antipathy to Puritanism results merely from ignorance of its background and internal history. There is a common supposition that, after mankind had enjoyed itself reasonably well for centuries, a misanthropic French-Swiss got the idea of making everybody as miserable as possible and that English Puritanism was one of the results. Happily the progress of scholarship is making this view untenable and substituting a more balanced judgment, which in

the natural order of things should eventually correct this mis-
conception. For in a generation or two it should filter into the
textbooks, and so into the popular consciousness, in spite of the
dramatic talents of Maxwell Anderson, Hollywood, and Den-
ham, against which hares the tortoise historian must now compete.

The medievalist is reminding us that there were ample precedents for the actions of Calvin and the Puritans. The strict
ascetic tradition, begun by Tertullian and carried on by other
early Church Fathers, never lacked for representatives in the
Catholic church. Nor were these by any means confined to the
monastic orders. The regular clergy not only far outdid the
later Puritans in their rigidity, but they set the moral standard
for medieval society as a whole. Of course, the laity could not be
expected to copy them in every detail; allowance had to be made
for marriage and private property. But otherwise the moral
ideal urged in sermon and treatise was definitely monastic,[1] and
the urge to follow it was strong, as the rise of the third orders
demonstrates.

To be sure, the Reformation swept monasticism and all such
obvious survivals of the old regime into the discard, but it did not
reach to one stronghold of the old moral tradition. Whether
there had ever been a Swiss reformation or not, the medieval
ascetic ideal would have remained in the universities. The colleges were semimonastic organizations, and, furthermore, university students had long enjoyed what amounted to clerical
status. Consequently, there had been developed a large body of
disciplinary regulations, all designed to force on the student the
grave conduct befitting his position. Sober, clerkly, or "sad"
raiment was enjoined. The scholar's ears must always show—
a check on fashionable long hair—and dances in the streets were
"altogether prohibited."[2] Open shows or public plays were
barred within a five-mile radius of the university, and the

---

[1] G. R. Owst, *Literature and Pulpit in Medieval England* (Cambridge, 1933), pp.
374–470; G. C. Coulton, *Five Centuries of Religion* (3 vols.; Cambridge, 1923–36), I,
526–41; *Art and the Reformation* (Oxford, 1928).

[2] *Early Cambridge University and College Statutes*, ed. Heywood (London, 1855),
p. 94.

Cambridge authorities alleged that a royal charter of Henry III confirmed this rule.[3] Oxford had a similar statute.[4] Games were to be played only at Christmas, that is, for the twelve days following the holiday. Otherwise fellows addicted to dice or painted cards were to be expelled for the third offense.[5] Even chess was banned as unseemly for clergy.[6] Contests involving physical exercise, which today enjoy a somewhat higher repute, were also disallowed. Games with rings [*stadiis*]—whether athletic sports or quoits is uncertain—were ruled out, and one of the last acts of the Catholic authorities under Cardinal Pole was to forbid students to play football.

The Reformation had no effect on this type of regulation. The statutes forced upon the university by Elizabeth and Cecil in 1572 were no less "puritanical." Ruffs and fancy hose, dice and cards—the latter with the periodic exception noticed— loitering at fairs or in the town, playing quoits or even looking on at the game were all banned.[7] The warfare on public plays was continued, and it was solemnly ordained that the students' hair be "polled, notted, or rounded,"[8] evidence that Roundheads were not always anathema to the authorities.

It was inevitable that this standard of academic morality, being thus retained in an age which prided itself on championing the religious equality of all believers, should in time influence ideals of conduct in other domains. This process was, indeed, facilitated by the fact that some of the regulations, such as those against quoits and football, could have no theological significance whatever but were merely designed to secure dili-

[3] James Heywood and Thomas Wright, *Cambridge University Transactions during the Puritan Controversies* (2 vols.; London, 1854), I, 185; II, 33.

[4] John Rainolds, *Th' Overthrow of Stage-Plays* ([Middelburg], 1599), p. 153.

[5] *Early Cambridge Statutes*, p. 143.

[6] *Ibid.*, p. 32.   [7] *Ibid.*, Appen. 30, Arts. 46 and 47.

[8] Quoted without reference in William Pierce, *John Penry: His Life, Times and Writings* (London, 1923), p. 57. In the articles for the visitation of the Oxford halls in 1583 there occurs this question: "Whether any graduate, commoner, or scholar of your house do wear long, unseemly, ugly and disguised shaggy hair, with locks curled in most strange and monstrous manner, and who they be" (Oxford University Archives MS C. 24. 11). I am indebted to Mr. A. B. Emden, Principal of St. Edmund Hall, for kind assistance with this note also.

gence in one's calling. The Reformation Parliament passed a statute against gaming in public houses, and sumptuary legislation was not abandoned until the reign of James I. In short, many of these regulations had no more religious or sectarian significance than modern regulations against lotteries and the drug traffic.

With this medieval social and educational background it can scarcely be said that English asceticism owes its existence to Calvin. Doubtless it would have run a vigorous course without any help from abroad. It is true, however, that the treatises and example of Continental reformers gave it a strong fillip. But even there one must not put too much upon Calvin. In contrast to Luther, Zwingli had taken an ascetic line from the start, possibly because he, as a former keeper of a concubine, was reacting from precisely the opposite kind of early career. Zwingli smashed the organ in the Zurich cathedral, and the early Reformation ordinances of that canton are full of regulations against games, dances, and plays. Before Calvin ever came to Geneva similar prescriptions were adopted in that town. All that the French reformer did was to strengthen, organize, and administer a movement already well under way.

So much for the one gloomy Frenchman part of the legend. The theory that the average Puritan was opposed to pleasure as such is equally open to correction. As we have seen, he thoroughly enjoyed his religious experience, his "comfortable" Bible reading, his "sweet conferences," his "pathetic" prayers, his "pleasant" meditations, his zealous and successful activity in his calling, at times even his "cheerful" almsgiving. There was a *joie de vivre* all through his life, the perfect satisfaction of serving God to the utmost of his ability. In the enthusiastic pursuit of this kind of pleasure the Puritan often interfered with other varieties, just as his worldly contemporaries often wrought havoc with the standing corn in the hunting fields. But it was not from any antipathy to lesser pleasures as such, but only to interference with the attainment of the major objective. Even Malvolio, who tried to stop the immortal Sir Toby's revelry, did so in part, at least, to permit the household to get a night's sleep. Calvin taught that it was lawful to enjoy the good gifts of Providence—prosperity, children, food, and drink. English Puritans joined in the refrain. Christians were not to be Stoics any more than Epicureans, for Paul disputed with them both.[9] They might make use of things indifferent not only for necessity's sake but also for "honest delight," as wine to make the heart glad and oil to make the face shine. The variety of God's creatures was for man's enjoyment. Recreation and lawful sports served to refresh both body and mind and were thus not only permitted but enjoined.[10]

Where Puritan ascetic regulations did appear, therefore, they were, like the monastic ones before them, ancillary rather than primary. They were designed to clear the ground of underbrush, to permit a clear view of the objective, to keep the troops in order. Happiness itself was not under fire, but only such aspects of the lesser species as interfered with the attainment of the greater kind. It was the old story of the good being the enemy of the best. Perkins attacked the styles affected by the women of his day because they made their devotees "like an image in a frame set bolt upright: whereby it comes to pass that they cannot go well and with ease or convenience about any good business but must of necessity either sit or stand,"[11] and this utilitarian point of view was typical of Puritan asceticism in general.

To serve God effectively in church, the worship must be purged of everything—however enjoyable otherwise—that perpetuated superstition or obscured the divine message. Excessive indulgence in lawful pleasures—that is, not recreation but enjoyment as an end in itself—distracted one's mind from more important things. Spending on food and clothing sums disproportionate to one's station in life diverted funds from more deserving objects. Opinions have differed, and doubtless always will differ, as to the relative values involved. I know of no scien-

[9] Richard Greenham, *The Workes of Richard Greenham* (5th and last ed.; London, 1612), pp. 654 and 769; cf. Acts 17:18.

[10] William Perkins, *Workes* (3 vols.; London, 1616–18), I, 539; II, 142.

[11] *Ibid.*, II, 136.

tific formula by which a Shakespeare can be weighed against—
say—the Nonconformist character. Matthew Arnold was certain of the result, but it is fair to suggest that there is room for
argument.

There was also a more immediately practical justification for
Puritan asceticism. Neither sixteenth-century Geneva nor the
England of that day was existing in a vacuum. Each was beset
by potential enemies of overwhelming strength. What Savoy
and France were to the one, France and Spain were to the other.
Calvin's discipline was doubtless severe, but in the circumstances perhaps plays and banquets were superfluous. Certainly, the Genevans who recalled him from exile looked on him as a
safeguard to their independence, and the fact remains that under his direction the city-state survived a most perilous era of
invasion and unrest. Likewise, it is not altogether surprising
that the Puritan of the Armada period also thought it was time
to put the toys away.

In discussing generalizations on Puritan asceticism, it must
be once more emphasized that the party was practically unor-
ganized and almost without means of disciplining and unifying
its adherents. No national assembly could make public pronouncements or sanction literature. Accordingly, on this topic,
as on others, there were throughout its history right-wing, center, and left-wing Puritans. Opponents play up the doings of the
fanatics, while admirers stress the mild stand of the moderates.
A judicious wresting of isolated phrases from the writings of the
middle group make it possible to throw them into either side of
the scale.

Changing circumstances also present the party in different
lights. In the days of its strength its political and economic
aspects balanced its piety and rigor. When the victory over the
Spanish Armada was won, and the Puritan was hopelessly out
of power, then his asceticism appears excessive and in some
cases ridiculous. There is a difference between Olivia's steward
suppressing disorder in the normal exercise of his police powers
and Mr. Zeal-of-the-Land Busy, far off his beat, or the pious-
talking, low-acting Nicholas Saint-Tantlings. As the interest in

social and governmental problems declined, the movement got out of balance, and the restriction of secular pleasures for the sake of purely religious and pietistic enjoyment rather suggests to the modern observer the process of killing gnats with sledge hammers.

But even in this later period we should beware of being deceived by that propaganda of a successful party directed against its beaten rivals, caricature of the sort which vitiates so much of our history of fifteenth-century England. At their worst the later Puritans never went to the extremes of mortifying the flesh which were practiced by their predecessors. The scourge, the haircloth shirt, and the abhorrence of bathing were unknown among them. If some became fanatical in their activities in this field of asceticism, the last one of public social activity which was open to the Puritans, the majority of the party never lost sight of the guiding principle of destroying only the genuine obstacles in their path. Error flies around the world before truth gets its boots on. Macaulay made some sound remarks about the fundamental virtues of the Puritan character, like the contents of Bassanio's leaden casket, outweighing the superficial traits, but these pronouncements are generally forgotten. Indeed the author ignored his own warning when he described the Puritans' attitude toward pleasure in the phrase that is commonly remembered—that they objected to bearbaiting not because it gave pain to the bear but because it gave pleasure to the spectator. Little study is necessary to demonstrate the superficiality of this characterization of the seventeenth-century Puritans, and it is certainly not true of their sixteenth-century predecessors. They did object to the torture of the animal, scoring those who "make . . . . merry with the bleeding miseries of that poor harmless thing."[12]

[12] Robert Bolton, *Some General Directions* (London, 1638), pp. 155–56. The fact that Cromwell's men shot the bears that came into their power is no more evidence of delight in cruelty to animals (as T. F. Henderson's note to his edition of Macaulay's *History* [5 vols.; Oxford, 1931], I, 142, suggests) than is the practice of the Society for Prevention of Cruelty to Animals in destroying stray dogs found with tin cans tied to their tails (cf. the provision against cruelty to animals in the Connecticut Code of 1650 [*Blue Laws of Connecticut*] quoted by Percy Scholes, *The Puritans and Music* [London, 1934], p. 15, and this passage from the much-abused Stubbs: "What Christian heart

It remains to illustrate these introductory generalizations by a few details of the Puritan attitude on particular problems, reserving Sabbatarianism, learning, and domestic life for fuller treatment in succeeding chapters. We begin with music and art, partly because these topics have already been investigated in great detail, partly because they afford very clear examples of the chief principles involved in the whole problem.

All the evidence[13] goes to show that the Puritans distinguished sharply between music inside the church and music outside of it. Even within the sacred walls they did not object to music if it was an aid to what they considered proper worship. In fact, they thought that it had a perfectly proper place in that exercise, to convey and not obscure scriptural truths. Hence the popularity of psalm-singing among them, for which they soon made ample provision. The first book of nineteen metrical paraphrases was published in 1559 by Thomas Sternhold, who had been Groom of the Robes to Henry VIII. An enlarged edition of thirty-seven appeared later in the same year, with the addition of seven by a schoolmaster named John Hopkins. The exiled congregation at Geneva, as we have seen, added further touches to the work. Whittingham himself added seven, and William Kethe, later the united-front emissary to Aarau and Frankfort, did the famous "Old Hundred." By 1562 the whole book of psalms had been completed. Sternhold wrote in the common meter of the English ballad, but Hopkins and Whittingham added others. The Genevan psalter introduced the custom of a printed notation for the tunes, which were taken from the more sober of contemporary ballad music. Psalm-singing commonly preceded and followed the sermon in the Puritan system and, in the Elizabethan period, was generally popular with all sorts and conditions of Protestants. The accomplish-

---

can take pleasure to see one poor beast to rent, tear and kill another and all for his foolish pleasure? .... We are not to abuse them, for His sake who made them and whose creatures they are" [*Anatomy of Abuses*, ed. F. J. Furnivall (London, 1879), p. 178]). John Field also condemned the "cruel and loathsome exercise of baiting bears" (*A Godly Exhortation* [London, 1583], sig. B, fol. 7[v]).

[13] Collected assiduously by Percy Scholes, whose work on the *Puritan and Music* is extremely useful, though perhaps an overenthusiastic exoneration of the Puritans on this point.

ments of Drake's men in this art charmed the California native sons of that day and induced them to start the tradition of sedulous attendance on the public exercises of the Christian religion which still distinguishes that region.

What the Puritans—in common with Wyclif, the Greek church, Erasmus, and a respectable section of Roman Catholic opinion—did not like in church was music which obscured the sense of the worship. Bibliolators that they were, they could not conceive of religious sentiments being transmitted by means in which the intellectual element was lacking or by devices which overlaid rather than reinforced it. When there is no meaning, there is no edification, said Calvin. So nothing but biblical passages were sung. True, the minister might preach the Word in his own phrases, but the hymn-writer had to keep to those of the Holy Spirit. It was not exactly logical, though it could be argued that the preacher enjoyed special ordination for his work. On the same principle, whatever tended to prevent the congregation from understanding the words of their songs, or distracted their attention from a reverent appreciation of them, was to be abolished. Northbrooke gives a convenient summary of the Puritan attitude on this point:

First we must take heed that in music be not put the whole sum and effect of godliness and of the worshipping of God, which among the papists they do almost everywhere think, that they have fully worshipped God when they have long and much sung and piped. Further, we must take heed that in it be not put merit or remission of sins. Thirdly, that singing be not so much used and occupied in the church that there be no time, in a manner, left to preach the Word of God and holy doctrine; whereby it cometh to pass that the people depart out of church full of music and harmony, but yet hunger-baned [hunger-cursed] and fasting as touching heavenly food and doctrine. Fourthly, that rich and large stipends be not so appointed for musicians that either very little or, in a manner, nothing is provided for the ministers which labor in the word of God. Fifthly, neither may that broken and quavering music be used wherewith the standers-by are so letted [hindered] that they cannot understand the words, not though they would never so fain. Lastly, we must take heed that in the church nothing be sung without choice, but only those things which are contained in the holy scriptures, or which are by just reason gathered out of them, and do exactly agree with the word of God.[14]

[14] John Northbrooke, *A Treatise Wherein Dicing, Dauncing, etc. Are Reproved* (London, 1577); reprinted by the Shakespeare Society, ed. Collier (London, 1843), pp. 113–14.

Slow, thoughtful singing in unison fixed the mind on the main purpose of the exercise. Part-singing[15] and antiphonal singing played "mock holiday" with the worship of God and turned religion into gaming. Tossing the sentences to and fro was like tennis play, with each man striving to outdo his brother. The booming and rolling of the organs were open to similar objections. Complaints were made in Convocation as early as 1536. In Edward's reign the organs in St. Paul's and York cathedrals were silenced,[16] and it was planned to abolish their use in all churches throughout the land. No official action was ever taken, though the project was included in the Puritan proposals so narrowly beaten in the lower house of the 1563 Convocation. But over a hundred organs were taken down at one place or another. The Norwich prebendaries broke their own instrument in 1570,[17] and some of the Stuart bishops still retained a prejudice against them.

To music outside the church the Puritan had no particular objection. The parable of the prodigal son was quoted to justify music in the home. Robert Browne, who objected vigorously to antiphonal singing, was an expert lutanist. When it was possible to find a buyer, the Puritans were willing enough to market the discarded church organs for domestic use. But it is clear that they were comparatively indifferent to this form of recreation, as can be seen from the number of instruments that were finally melted down for the pewter in the pipes. There was a tendency to extend the use of psalms from formal worship to cover all occasions, following the biblical prescription for him that is merry. The Psalm Book of 1562 was specifically intended "to be used of all sorts of people privately for their solace and comfort: laying apart all ungodly songs and ballads which tend

[15] There are, however, some examples of part-singing and even anthem-singing in Puritan circles (Scholes, *op. cit.*, pp. 255, 260–61).

[16] T. S. Fletcher, *The Reformation in Northern England* (London, 1925), p. 149.

[17] C. H. and Thompson Cooper, *Athenae Cantabrigienses* (3 vols.; Cambridge, 1858–1913), I, 382, 452.

only to the nourishing of vice and corrupting of youth."[18]
Furthermore, many Puritans, for the reasons already indicated,
followed Becon's judgment, that "music is a more vain and
trifling science than it becometh a man, born and appointed to
matters of gravity, to spend much time about."[19] Though they
might tolerate it, they had other more absorbing interests, and
it is noteworthy that the creative musicians of the period were
mostly loyal to the old religion. The fact that an occasional
Puritan played the lute demonstrates little. The Elizabethans
were highly musical. Customers awaiting their turn in the bar-
ber's chair commonly passed the time with musical instruments
kept in the shop for the purpose, and ability to play was an
essential qualification for polite social intercourse. In the absence of any Puritan expressions of enthusiasm for the art—
such as are to be found in all other circles of the time—we must
consider the Puritans, even when outside the church doors, below the contemporary average in musical attainments and interest.[20]

Art was in the same category with music. It could be enjoyed
in moderation at home, and it had its place in church as long as
it did not perpetuate superstition or obstruct the channel for
the scriptural message. True, the churches were practically
gutted in the course of the Reformation; but this was because
nearly everything in them was connected with specifically
Catholic practices. Shrines, images, and pictures suggested
prayers to the saints, pilgrimages, and purgatory. So the mov-
able objects were taken out and burned or devoted to secular

[18] I am unable to follow Scholes' interpretation (op. cit., p. 256) of "ungodly" as
referring not to secular but to "lewd" songs. Doubtless many of the songs were lewd
enough, but the reference to the psalms as being intended for private use and the
added quotation from James seem to render this an insufficient explanation.

[19] Jewel of Joy in The Catechism .... with Other Pieces, ed. Ayre (Cambridge:
Parker Society, 1844), p. 429.

[20] Dr. Scholes' exculpation of Bunyan's attitude toward bell-ringing in the later
Puritan period (op. cit., pp. 303–8) as being due to Sabbatarianism does not seem to be
quite justified by the documents, but it should be pointed out that there was a superstitious flavor about ringing changes (cf. p. 254 above). The Commonwealth regime
and Cromwell himself represented a compromise between Puritan and secular elements,
so the fact that some musical activity persisted in their time is not necessarily proof of
what a wholly Puritan policy would have dictated.

uses. The pictures on the walls were "slubbered over" with whitewash, which the Puritans renewed from time to time when the offending murals began to show through.[21] Elizabeth approved of this destruction, and her injunctions and homilies both prescribe and indorse it. It should be remembered that after the Renaissance practically no one, whatever his religion, had any respect for Gothic art, and no sense of aesthetic loss was felt if shrines or windows built in that style were destroyed. Because no phase of this activity has excited more antipathy than the destruction of medieval stained glass, it will be well to have the Puritan feeling on the matter expressed in the original language:

It likewise appeareth what dishonor and disgrace have been offered by gross idolators which would take upon them to paint and picture out the invisible and incomprehensible majesty of the Almighty like a man whose breath is in his nostrils, whose being is not of himself, whose years are but a span long, and in his best estate is altogether vanity. Whatsoever ye do, saith the Scripture, do all to the glory of God. That is, strive to do it so, as God may get most glory by it. Are such representations of God to the advancing of his glory? What do they show and teach us that we might give him everlasting praise for? He is painted as a man, as you see in yonder story of creation in yonder window in a dozen places together [Margin: *In St. Thomas Church of Bristol*]. What may we learn by them? A man hath his being from another. If God be as he is painted forth, he hath so too, which to say is blasphemy. A man hath father and mother, but who was the Lord's father and his mother. . . . . O cursed creatures that ever first invented them, and cursed wretches that dare maintain them, if God give them not repentance. For they are such abominations as God hath flatly forbidden and condemned to the pit, yea, to the very bottomless pit of hell. Are these pictures of him that is to be praised world without end? If they be not, why are they not defaced which do so much deface the glory of our Creator? If they be not, why are they tolerated, nay if they be not why are they defended as lawful and not hurtful to any, and that even now, with shame enough in the clear light of the gospel?[22]

The Puritans did not deny that this destruction made the church service less attractive to the common people. One of their apologists refers to the

weeping and bewailing of the simple sort and especially of women, who going into the churches and seeing the bare walls and lacking their golden images, their costly copes, their pleasant organs, their sweet frankincense, their

---

[21] *The Seconde Parte of a Register*, ed. Peel (2 vols.; Cambridge, 1915), I, 239; II, 191.

[22] William Burton, *David's Evidence* (London, 1596), pp. 140–42.

gilded chalices, their goodly streamers, they lament in themselves and fetch many deep sighs and bewail this spoiling and laying waste of the church, as they think.[23]

But that was merely a manifestation of the weaknesses of the flesh, which were to be overcome by patient instruction and familiarity with better things. Like the Jews at the time of the Second Temple, Christians were to remember that the presence of the true God and the true worship were the important features of any sacred edifice:

This is the glory of the Second Temple, this is the glory of our churches. Although the walls be not painted, although their vestures be not silk, although their rood lofts be broken down, although they want their frankincense and organs, yet the Word of the Lord and his Spirit shall steadfastly in the midst of them. The gospel of Jesus Christ ringeth in them although their organs cease; that sweet savor of life to life is felt although that earthly frankincense be put out.[24]

Outside the church the Puritan remained generally indifferent to the practice of the fine arts. Country gentlemen of mixed inclinations, like Cromwell in the next century, might show signs of interest, but the average Puritan minister cared for none of those things. He did not attack the desire for beauty as such, but in his diary he never mentioned an attractive landscape or sunset.

A similar attitude may be observed in the Puritan treatment of more mundane matters. Where eating, sleeping, and drinking came into conflict with religious obligations, they were to be temporarily avoided. Carrying on the medieval tradition, the Puritans believed that abstinence which humbled the body also humbled the mind; want in the body caused one to feel the want in his soul and so turn to God. They chose to feel the Old Testament obligation as still binding on the Christian, as far as occasional fasts were concerned, and they prided themselves on being more honest and rigorous in their observance of this obligation than their Catholic rivals. Except in case of necessity

[23] F. Trigge, *An Apologie or Defence of Our Dayes* (London, 1589), p. 24 (cf. the Homilies of 1563, cited in Scholes, *op. cit.*, p. 221).

[24] *Ibid.*

nothing at all was to be eaten for twenty-four hours, and as far as possible sleep was to be omitted as well.[25]

But when these were of no immediate religious significance, there was no denunciation of food, clothing, and sleep as such. Gorgeous, even sumptuous, attire was allowed to those of exalted station as necessary means of maintaining their dignity and status. Only self-indulgence, pride, and vanity were attacked. Men of all sects and ages have thought the commonwealth endangered by lavish display which consumes goods which might be devoted to better ends. Shakespeare complained that men wore manors on their backs. Sumptuary legislation was not invented by the Puritans, and, while the social historian may linger over the details of the hated ruffs and farthingales, they need not detain the composer of a party history.

In amusements it was also the abuse and not the use that was objected to.[26] Dancing was undeniably a biblical activity. The examples of Miriam and David showed that it had both a religious and a civil use. Reason said that it helped to keep the body healthy and limber. Dancing, like music, was accordingly taught to the children of at least the better-class Puritan households as part of their education, and morris dance steps were taken to New England by the Puritan emigrants.[27] But in some circumstances it gave offense. Dances in the churchyard or in the church itself naturally scandalized the zealous, as they did in the Middle Ages. Village maypole dances were commonly preceded by a night spent by the young people of both sexes in the woods, and so drew the fire of Stubbs and his associates. There was some difference of opinion about mixed dancing, that is, dancing in which both sexes participated. Knox did not condemn it absolutely; only particular types of steps or excessive indulgence were considered objectionable. But Perkins declared

[25] N. Bownde, *Holy Exercise of Fasting* (London, 1604), pp. 26–58.

[26] Laurence Humphrey, *The Nobles*, sig. V, fol. 4(v); *Optimates* (Basel, 1559), pp. 314–15.

[27] Scholes, *op. cit.*, pp. 58–80, esp. p. 76.

that experience showed it to be generally the "fruit or follower of idolatry, fornication, or drunkenness." This bellows-of-lust argument—not unknown in Catholic writers—was the one commonly used against it. But a more general objection was that based on the believer's obligation to give an account of every idle word. How then justify "caperings" and "frisks of lightness and vanity more beseeming goats and apes, of whom they are commonly used, than men?"[28] A few extremists, of course, opposed any indulgence in the art, mixed or not, and one of their number entered a blanket indictment,[29] in which he inserted this argument to prove that dancing was no recreation:

> I have heard tell of those which have danced one half day for pleasure and have laid in bed two whole days for pain. . . . . I do omit to speak how many have been lamed with dancing, which in their youth have been such dancers that they were able to leap over logs, but in their age have scant been able to step over straws.[30]

Against the argument that participation in mixed dances was the way to get a wife the author asserted that such matters were attended to by foreordination, and that only noddies met their mates at dancing in any case.[31]

Calvin occasionally played such games as quoits. Chess was generally approved. Hunting and other bodily exercise was commonly considered proper in moderation. Perkins even went so far as to sanction bearbaiting on the ground that it was legal. The original objections to games were of the indirect sort. The losers salved their tempers with curses. These amusements commonly involved money stakes which might ruin some of the participants and certainly led to covetousness. Furthermore, they enabled the winner to get something for nothing, contrary to the medieval theory of the just price. Meeting the preachers on their own ground, conscientious Protestant gentry at first forbade their servants to play for money, but on their private games, to add interest, they put up small stakes which they

[28] Perkins, *op. cit.*, I, 539; cf. Matt. 12:36.

[29] Christopher Fetherston, *A Dialogue agaynst Light Lewde and Lascivious Dauncing* (London, 1582).

[30] *Ibid.*, sig. B, fol. i.   [31] *Ibid.*, sig. C, fols. vii–viii.

could well afford to lose.[32] This did not satisfy the moralists, however, and with the rise of the doctrine of predestination a new argument was brought forth. Since every action was fore-ordained, God personally decided all matters of so-called chance. Invoking fortune was therefore an appeal to the Almighty, whose honor was offended by making him the assistant in idle pleasures. The lot should only be used in weighty matters, and that solemnly, after the biblical fashion.[33] But it would seem that the issue which really precipitated the Elizabethan assault on these games and other amusements was the academic one of keeping students of the Inns of Court at their work.

The Judges, the Templars, and the Puritans of all professions and conditions being very sensible how the youth was alienated from religion and corrupted by cards, dice, revels, plays, and interludes, and many orders having been made against gaming in the Middle Temple either at Christmas or at any other time, in their chambers or in the Common Hall, many Puritans were engaged to write against them.[34]

Thomas Wilcox' *Glasse for Gamesters*,[35] which is listed along with Lovell's *Dialogue between Custom and Veritie* and Gosson's *Schoole of Abuse* as a result of this agitation, sums up the Puritan arguments already enumerated and clinches them with the assertion that no one in his right senses would call gaming recreation, since all the players did was to sit and worry.[36]

The Puritan attitude toward dramatic productions was also moderate at first. Bale wrote religious dramas, and he had Puritan imitators as late as the 1570's. Calvin allowed the production of a biblical play at Geneva. Dramatic dialogues were the

---

[32] Haddon to Bullinger, August, 1552, *Original Letters Relative to the English Reformation*, ed. Robinson (2 vols.; Cambridge: Parker Society, 1846–47), p. 282.

[33] Perkins, I, 539; II, 141; cf. *To the Maior* (single-sheet broadside; British Museum Press Mark: C 18 e 13[2]). There was not complete unanimity on this point. Perkins himself, though unalterably opposed to dicing which involved "chance" alone, thought that, since cards involved some skill, they might be tolerated, though dangerous (*op. cit.*, II, 142). But James Balmford protested against Peter Martyr's allowance of tables (backgammon) (*A Short and Plaine Dialogue concerning the Unlawfulness of Playing at Cards* [London, (1593)]).

[34] "Chronological Account" (Morrice, I), fol. 615(6).

[35] London, 1581.   [36] Sig. C, fol. iii(v).

Puritan controversialist's stock in trade. The Puritan Inns of Court regularly produced plays and masques, as did the Oxford and Cambridge colleges. It was to the acting profession and the theater that the Puritan objected, not to the plays themselves, just as Henry VIII's statutes had been directed at public gambling-houses but not at the games as such. The life of the professional actors and the associations of the houses where the dramas were performed revived medieval criticism of the stage. In 1575, after the failure of regulatory efforts, the London aldermen barred professional performances from the city. A heated controversy followed. John Northbrooke, a Bristol clergyman, published a treatise on the subject.[37] Stephen Gosson, a playwright whose reformation was perhaps speeded by subsidies provided by the authorities at the Inns of Court, published his *Schoole of Abuse* in 1579. This drew a sharp retort from Thomas Lodge, and the fight was on.[38] The main theme of both Northbrooke's and Gosson's objections was the nature of the particular plays produced and the social atmosphere they created, not to dramatic activity in general. When John Stockwood alluded to the subject in a sermon preached in 1579, his chief criticism was that people neglected preaching services because they wished to go early to get a good seat for the play.[39] As late as 1581, when Stubbs produced the first edition of his famous work, he could put in a preface approving of "some kind of plays, tragedies, and interludes" as "very honest and very commendable exercises." But, as feelings rose, tempers sharpened, and it would seem that on this matter the Puritans practically lost sight of their fundamental principle, that of attacking only the abuse and not the use. Stubbs eliminated his qualifying remarks from later editions of his diatribe, and, at Oxford, Rainolds, roused by an elaborate Christ Church production, developed a theoretical argument against plays in general. Re-

[37] *Op. cit.*

[38] For the details of this conflict see Elbert N. S. Thompson, *The Controversy between the Puritans and the Stage* ("Yale Studies in English," Vol. XX [New York, 1903]).

[39] *A Very Fruiteful Sermon Preched at Paules Crosse the Tenth of May Last* (London, 1579), fols. 24–27(33), esp. fol. 25(31).

viving Platonic[40] and medieval theories and adding some of his own, he put out his *Overthrow of Stage-Playes* in 1599. He maintained that the Mosaic law forbidding a man to wear women's clothes barred dramatic productions, since the idea of women actresses was then unknown.[41] Another of his cardinal principles was that "to imitate and resemble wantonness, scurrility, impudency, drunkenness or any other misbehavior is a thing unlawful."[42] The godly though anonymous printer drew from it all the stiff conclusion that "whatsoever thy flesh according to the common course of carnal men delighteth in, suspect thou there is mischief in it, though thou be able to defend it by thy reason."[43] Yet even in this sweeping presentation of Puritanism at its worst there are some brighter spots. Rainolds did not condemn the writing of plays,[44] and his last main point[45] was that dramatic performances cost money which might better be given to the poor. In those pre-Veblen days his opponents could only cry, "Judas," and claim the right to do as they pleased with their own. With analogies drawn from the economics of the world's oldest profession the Puritan made light work of demolishing such flimsy defenses. In any arguments about the distribution of the national income there can be little doubt on which side the Puritans would be today. They took no stock in the theory that the ends of society are best served by putting wealth in the hands of a few people whose spending will cause it to trickle down to the many.

[40] J. W. Mackail, "Art and Puritanism," *St. George* (Birmingham, England), VII (1904), 91–110.

[41] Pp. 8 and 82 ff.; cf. Deut. 22:5.

[42] Pp. 17 and 102–3; cf. Prov. 7:11–18.

[43] "The Printer to the Reader," sig. A, fol. 3(*v*).

[44] P. 156.

[45] Pp. 24 and 143 ff.

CHAPTER XXIV

Sabbatarianism

THE Puritan doctrine of the Sabbath deserves a chapter by itself. At first glance it might seem merely another aspect of the general ascetic attitude already described. But in fact there were several important points of difference. While all the attitudes described in the last chapter were typically Reformed, and could be duplicated in the story of earlier Continental churches of that persuasion, the Puritan doctrine of Sunday was so far advanced over that of their allies across the channel that it differs not only in degree but in kind. It represents, therefore, a bit of English originality and is the first and perhaps the only important English contribution to the development of Reformed theology in the first century of its history. As a variation from the ordinary pattern of Reformed theory it also constituted the first doctrinal difference between the contending factions in the English church[1]—the first issue on a point not related to church government or ceremony. A decade before the Arminian controversy broke out on English soil the Sabbatarian argument began to embitter party relations.

This doctrine, furthermore, instead of being merely one among many ascetic attitudes, underlay and did much to stimulate the others. Most of the early literature against dancing, games, and plays makes the profaning of the Sabbath one of the chief charges against them. In an age before weekday half-holidays or forty-hour weeks were known the religious festivals

[1] This is the usual statement, and I think it may be allowed to stand. Strictly speaking, however, the questions of vestments and ecclesiastical government were in the field of ecclesiology, or what is sometimes called practical theology. The differences of opinion on the minor point about the descent into hell (see above, p. 370) also antedate the Sabbatarian dispute.

furnished practically the only opportunities for middle- and lower-class recreation. With the development of a feeling for the sanctity of the day, organized amusement and Sabbath-breaking became almost synonymous in Puritan eyes. It is particularly necessary therefore to understand this sentiment which lent so much sting to the jeremiads of Northbrooke, Stubbs, and their successors.

Social demand plus the logic of juxtaposition combined to introduce Sabbatarianism into the Christian tradition at a comparatively early date. The church needed a regular meeting day and one which would distinguish Christians from the Jews. The Ten Commandments were generally recognized as embodying the essentials of the moral law, the Puritan whip to bring men to Christ. The code was reverenced from the beginning and was soon made one of the pillars of Christian theology.

There was, however, a very strong tradition against accepting the Fourth Commandment as equal to the others. Christ had proclaimed the principle that the Sabbath was made for man, not man for the Sabbath. Paul had denounced any superstitious observance of days as a survival of Judaism. If there were New Testament references to Sunday observance, they were extremely hazy to say the least.[2] What moral obligation remained in the Fourth Commandment was at best considered to apply only to setting aside some time for worship, not to hallowing a day in the fashion of the Pharisees. Irenaeus and Augustine gave the commandment an allegorical interpretation, making it refer primarily to the believer's rest from sin, imperfect here but to be perfected hereafter.[3]

But constant repetition of the old code inevitably developed the notion that special honor must be paid to the day of worship. By the time of Constantine the transaction of ordinary business on Sunday began to be prohibited. Amusements likewise came under the ban. By the height of the Middle Ages the application of the Fourth Commandment had been transferred

[2] Acts 20:7; I Cor. 16:2; Rev. 1:10.

[3] Irenaeus *Contra haeresios* iv. 16; Augustine *Contra Adimantum* (Migne, *Patrologia Latina*, XLII, 132); cf. Hebrews, chap. 4.

bodily to Sunday, and a long succession of council actions and theological treatises had made Sabbatarianism a minor aspect of medieval Catholicism. While Augustine's allegorical interpretation of the commandment was retained and the abandonment of Saturday thereby justified, theologicans declared that there was a moral core to the law, which required the keeping of one day out of seven. They thus transferred Sabbatarian rigors to Sunday.[4] In the opinion of the stricter churchmen the day should be occupied solely with worship and good works.[5] It is true that there was some dissent,[6] and, as with many of its other moral principles, the church did not concern itself greatly with enforcing this requirement. Violations were continuous and flagrant, witness the complaints of the preachers. But the theory was there, and from time to time efforts were made to put it into practice. Statutes were passed against working on Sunday,[7] and there were crusades against markets held on that day.[8] Casuists developed the practical details. Tostatus of Avila, a Spanish bishop of the fourteenth century, declared that any unnecessary work on Sunday was a mortal sin. In the unnecessary category he put the pursuance of one's ordinary calling, the employment of an extra cook or professional musician, washing the dishes, and even returning home from a shrine.[9]

This Catholic Sabbatarianism roused the hostility of the first reformers. The Lollards protested against it and so did Luther.[10]

[4] Aquinas *Summa* II. i. QQ 100, art. 3.

[5] G. R. Owst, *Preaching in Medieval England* (Cambridge, 1926), p. 194; "The People's Sunday Amusements in the Preaching of Medieval England," *Holborn Review* (N.S.), XVII (1926), 32–45; *Literature and Pulpit in Medieval England* (Cambridge, 1933), Index, "Holy-Days."

[6] J. A. Hessey, *Sunday: Its Origin, History and Present Obligation* (3d ed.; London, 1866), pp. 92–96.

[7] E.g., 4 Edward IV, c. 7.

[8] J. L. Cate, "The English Mission of Eustace of Flay," *Etudes d'histoire dédiées à la mémoire d'Henri Pirenne* (Brussels, 1937), pp. 67–89; "The Church and Market Reform in England during the Reign of Henry III," *Medieval and Historiographical Essays in Honor of James Westfall Thompson*, eds. Cate and Anderson (Chicago, 1938), pp. 27–65.

[9] "Commentaria in exodi," *Opera* (Venice, 1596), II, 79–87 and 169–74; cf. Richard Whitford, *A Werke for Housholders* (London, 1537), sig. D, fols. i–iii.

[10] *Auslegung der Zehen Gebot* (Wittenberg, 1528), sig. N, fols. iii(*v*)–iv; cf. Hessey, *op. cit.*, pp. 166–67.

They were unwilling to countenance anything which magnified the authority of the church. In their judgment there was no New Testament justification for sanctifying Sunday, and therefore this custom must be a papistical innovation along with prayers to the saints and pilgrimages. They were strengthened in this opinion by the Catholic practice of linking saints' days with Sunday in ecclesiastical legislation on the subject. For generations the Puritans prided themselves on working on Christmas and saints' days. At first the more zealous reformers took the same attitude toward Sunday. Tyndale maintained that no holy days were necessary at all if people could be taught without them. Christians might choose to meet on Monday, or every tenth day if they liked.[11] Barnes declared that every day is a Sabbath to the Christian, not only the seventh. "For Christ is every day born, every day risen, every day ascended up."[12] Frith said Sundays and other religious festivals were instituted that

the people should come together to hear God's word, receive the sacraments, and give God thanks. That done [he continued], they may return unto their houses, and do their business as well as any other day. He that thinketh that a man sinneth which worketh on the holy day, if he be weak or ignorant, ought to be better instructed and so to leave his hold.[13]

The Anglicans under Henry and Edward naturally took a middle ground between the Catholic and the early Puritan positions. With the Lutherans they denounced any superstitious observance of the day and granted the right to labor on it in case of necessity. But they retained the Catholic requirement of devoting the whole day, in normal circumstances, to worship, religious edification, and good works, "not because one day is more aceptable to God than another or of itself more holy than another, but because the church hath ordained that upon those

[11] William Tyndale, *Answer to Sir Thomas More's Dialogue*, ed. Walter (Cambridge: Parker Society, 1850), p. 97.

[12] "Sentenciae XV" attached to his *Vitae Romanorum pontificum* (Basel, 1555), p. 385; *Supplication* in *The Whole Works of W. Tyndall, J. Frith, and Doct. Barnes* (2 vols.; London, 1572-73), II, 205-7.

[13] John Frith, *Works*, ed. Russell (3 vols.; London, 1831), I (IV), 295. For an Anglican protest see the Book of Ceremonies prepared by the Gardiner faction (John Strype, *Ecclesiastical Memorials* [3 vols. in 6; Oxford, 1822], I, ii, 427).

days we should give ourselves wholly, without any impediment, unto such holy works as be before expressed." It was an offense against the commandment to pass the time "in idleness, in gluttony, in riot, or in plays or in other vain and idle pastime." If worst came to worst, it was better for the women to spin on that day than "to lose their time in leaping and dancing and other idle wantonness."[14] The Statute of 5 and 6 Edward VI also required the Christian to devote the day "wholly unto . . . . holy works properly pertaining unto true religion."[15]

The Marian exile contributed nothing to English Sabbatarian theory, for the Swiss reformers had followed Luther in their teaching on this matter. Calvin was emphatic that one day was as good as another. He declared that the church had the right to set some time for worship, and he insisted that servants be given occasional days of rest. But it could be every day or one less frequent than one day in seven.

> Thus vanish all the dreams of false prophets who in past ages have infected the people with a Jewish notion; affirming that nothing but the ceremonial part of this commandment, which according to them is the appointment of the seventh day, has been abrogated, but that the moral part of it, that is the observance of one day in seven, still remains.[16]

Legislation on the subject in Zurich and Geneva was directed only to securing free and quiet time for the public services of the church, and the citizen might do as he pleased at other hours of the day.[17]

Returning exiles brought no more than this attitude with them. In the Scotch Confession of Faith of 1561 the Fourth Commandment is so interpreted as to require hearing and believing the Word and reverently communicating in the sacra-

---

[14] *The Institution of a Christian Man*, the so-called Bishop's Book of 1537 (*Formularies of Faith*, ed. Lloyd [Oxford, 1825]), pp. 142–48, esp. pp. 144 and 146; repeated almost verbatim in *A Necessary Doctrine and Erudition for Any Christian Man* (The King's Book [London, 1543], *ibid.*), pp. 306-11.

[15] Cf. the Injunctions of Edward VI in Edward Cardwell, *Documentary Annals of the Reformed Church of England* (2 vols.; Oxford, 1844), I, 15–16.

[16] *Institutes*, II, 8; English trans. Allen (London, 1838), p. 315.

[17] Cf. Strype, *Historical Collection of the Life and Acts of John Aylmer* (Oxford, 1821), p. 142.

ments.[18] Knox saw nothing wrong in a Sunday evening diplomatic dinner party.[19] So far as evidence is available, the attitude of Whittingham and his friends across the border was the same, for none of them laid any emphasis on Sabbath-breaking in their works.

Modern English Sabbatarianism is therefore not Reformed or Calvinistic in its origins. So far as it had any theoretical background, it is to be found in the medieval doctrine, which survived in Anglican teaching and legislation, that the day was to be devoted wholly to religious ends. This remained the official doctrine of the church under Elizabeth, as set forth in homily, catechism, and injunction.[20] But the Queen's conduct did not conform to such standards. After morning service she commonly had council meetings, entertained ambassadors, went to shooting contests, or otherwise amused herself according to her taste. Furthermore, repeated efforts to give statutory effect to this ecclesiastical stand, by such means as changing the dates of Sunday fairs, met with nothing but failure. By permitting her churchmen to perpetuate a high doctrine on the subject and then flouting it, Elizabeth invited a reaction which eventually took the form of an even higher doctrine.

But the first urge was practical and popular rather than theoretical and theological. As in the case of the early church, the driving force came from the feeling of social need plus a reverence for the commandments as a whole. The boisterous celebration of the day with drinking and dancing did interfere with the ends of religion. The unphilosophical popular mind could not appreciate the subtle distinction between hours of service and other parts of the day, or the theological niceties

[18] London ed., sig. B, fol. iii and verso. The "strait" keeping of Sunday required by the First Book of Discipline of 1561 obviously refers only to leaving time for morning and afternoon services (Calderwood ed., p. 58).

[19] Randolph to Cecil, November 30, 1562; T. Wright, Queen Elizabeth and Her Times (2 vols.; London, 1838), I, 114.

[20] Wilkins, Concilia (4 vols.; London, 1737), IV, 184; Homilies (London, 1850), pp. 341–52; Nowell's Catechism, ed. Corrie (Cambridge: Parker Society, 1853), pp. 128–30. These and the proposed legislation on the subject are summarized in W. B. Whitaker, Sunday in Tudor and Stuart Times (London, 1933), pp. 25–32. As late as 1592, Hooker (Ecclesiastical Polity, V, § 70, 9) teaches this doctrine.

which parted Jewish from Christian elements in the two great
tables. The commandment ordered a day to be hallowed. Either it was to be obeyed or it was not. Confronted by such a
choice, the serious-minded section of the English populace did
not hesitate. From the ranks the clamor soon arose. The
humble Separatists apprehended in Plumbers' Hall in 1567 protested against the keeping of saints' days but in so doing implied that the Sunday should be more strictly observed and
bearbaiting and bowling forbidden then.[21] This strict attitude
next crept into the complaint literature of Northbrooke and
Stubbs.

Gradually it worked its way up until responsible leaders of
the Puritan party were affected. The fall of the gallery at the
Paris Garden bearbaiting pit on Sunday, January 13, 1583,
when eight people were killed, was seized upon by John Field
as a horrible warning to Sabbath-breakers, and he soon issued
a tract on the subject.[22] Though he grants that the structure
concerned was old, rotten, and overloaded, and consequently is
unable to claim a miracle, yet the fact that no piece of post,
board, or stake was left standing struck him as "an extraordinary judgment of God." He virtually equates Sunday with
the Jewish Sabbath. To him it is a day "wherein all solemn
assemblies of God's saints should be occupied in hearing his
Word, in giving themselves to prayer, in receiving his sacraments, in meditating of his wonderful works, and putting in
practice of holy duties."[23] Others took up the refrain, and the
matter was agitated at Cambridge, in the Dedham classis, and
in parliamentary petitions.[24]

Puritan magistrates took steps to insure a better observance

[21] Edmund Grindal, *Remains*, ed. Nicholson (Cambridge: Parker Society, 1843),
p. 215.

[22] *A Godly Exhortation by Occasion of the Late Judgement of God Shewed at Parris-
Garden.*

[23] Sig. B, fols. 8 and 3.

[24] Strype, *Annals of the Reformation under Elizabeth* (4 vols. in 7; Oxford, 1824), III,
i, 496; III, ii, 298; *The Seconde Parte of a Register*, ed. Peel (2 vols.; Cambridge, 1915), II,
219; *The Presbyterian Movement in the Reign of Queen Elizabeth*, ed. Usher ("Camden
Society: Third Series," Vol. VIII [London, 1905]), *passim.*

of the day. Already, in 1580, the London corporation had persuaded the Council to issue a decree against Sunday plays, a prohibition which was made effective by the end of the century.[25] About the same time the local authorities in Lancashire, Rochester, Norwich, and Ipswich began trying to repress Sunday amusement and Sunday labor. From this period on the battle was joined in full fury. Pipers and bowlers, carters and fishermen found their activities drastically curtailed if not completely forbidden by zealous justices of the peace and aldermen.[26]

Some theological rationalization of this attitude was now inevitable. It was supplied by none other than Lancelot Andrewes, in the 1580's a Puritan fellow of Pembroke Hall, Cambridge. As catechist of his institution, he delivered expository lectures on the Ten Commandments which attracted large audiences.[27] In commenting on the Fourth, he put forward virtually all the ideas which are to be found in the Puritan arguments on this topic for the next century. He asserts that the injunction to hallow the Sabbath is essentially a moral one. He supports this contention by alleging that the Sabbath existed in the Garden of Eden, before the introduction of ceremonies, and also by maintaining that the Ten Commandments as a whole are a moral code and therefore that each part is of the same character. According to him, only the day to be observed was altered in New Testament times, and he takes care to make this "in the Apostles' days" to avoid any suggestion that the church had a right to make such an important change. This alteration was made, according to Andrewes' argument, partly to commemorate such events as the Resurrection and Pentecost, partly to emphasize the fact that the Jewish dispensation had ended. But the Christian was still obligated to keep a

---

[25] E. K. Chambers, *Elizabethan Stage* (4 vols.; London, 1923), I, 287–302.

[26] Whitaker, *op. cit.*, pp. 37–47.

[27] *A Patterne of Catechisticall Doctrine* (London, 1630). For the problem of the true text of these discourses see my article, "The Early Puritanism of Lancelot Andrewes," *Church History*, II (1933), 95–104, which gives the details of this episode in Andrewes' life, and also of the relation of his teaching to the works of Greenham and Bownde.

Sabbath. When the catechist came to explain how the day was to be kept, he adopted nearly all the Old Testament regulations against buying and selling, fairs and markets, burden-bearing, journeying, and harvesting. He concludes with a description of the positive duties of the day, such as the obligations to worship God and to assist one's fellow-men by works of charity and mercy. He thus virtually made Sunday observance into a third sacrament, as one of his arguments suggests.[28]

Andrewes' work was not published until after his death, but it circulated widely in manuscript and had a great influence. Greenham, who had been a fellow of Pembroke, was a warm friend of the future bishop and paid him the compliment of incorporating most of his ideas in a treatise on the Sabbath which he composed, probably about 1590.[29] Greenham's son-in-law, Nicholas Bownde of Norton, Suffolk, took the further step of putting these arguments in the form of a separate book on the subject, which appeared in 1595.[30]

By 1599 this teaching had attracted the unfavorable notice of the authorities. Urged on by Thomas Rogers, chaplain to Bancroft and one of the Anglican apologists of the time, Archbishop Whitgift called in existing copies of Bownde's work, and Lord Chief Justice Popham forbade any further publications of the sort.[31] But, as Fuller remarked, books are most called on when called in, and the doctrine spread rapidly. In 1604, George Widley put out a restatement of Bownde's argument,[32] and, in 1606, Greenham's verbose son-in-law succeeded in issuing a much-expanded version of the original work.[33] The ensuing controversy did not wear itself out for half a century.

[28] "Days and so likewise bread and wine are not more holy of themselves, one than another, but because they be separated and set apart for holy uses" (*A Pattern of Catechistical Doctrine* ["Library of Anglo-Catholic Theology" (Oxford, 1846)], p. 153).

[29] "A Treatise of the Sabbath Day," *The Workes of Richard Greenham* (5th and last ed.; London, 1612), pp. 128–71.

[30] *The Doctrine of the Sabbath* (London, 1595).

[31] Thomas Rogers, *The Catholic Doctrine of the Church of England*, ed. Perowne (Cambridge: Parker Society, 1854), p. 20.

[32] *The Doctrine of the Sabbath* (London).

[33] *Sabbathum veteris et novi testamenti* (London).

CHAPTER XXV

Domestic Life

N THE field of domestic relations there is much to test the general thesis of this work that early Puritanism represents rather an intensification and refinement of medieval attitudes than an attack upon them. In some ways the Puritan theories of marriage and divorce are humanistic and classical rather than Catholic and medieval. They will be described as exceptions to the rule without trying to force them into the general pattern. Yet, behind and around them, there linger a good many traces of medievalism which prevent us from characterizing the entire Puritan thought on this subject as typical of the Renaissance.

The Puritan shared fully in the general Protestant assault on the Catholic doctrine of celibacy.[1] The doctrine of the priesthood of all believers meant the abolition of marital distinctions between clergy and laity. Marriage was a divine institution ordained before the Fall and open to every man. To require the clergy as a class to refrain from it was to demand more than flesh and blood could endure without sin. It meant scandalous conduct on the part of professed moral leaders. Therefore, priests might marry, and in the early days many of the advanced reformers, like Bale, signalized their conversion by doing so.

But, having stated this humane principle, the Puritan immediately began to qualify it. The logical conclusion of this

---

[1] John Ponet, *A Defence for Mariage of Priestes* (London, 1549). This was answered by Thomas Martin's *Traictise Declaryng and Plainly Provyng That the Pretensed Marriage of Priestes and Professed Persones Is No Marriage* (London, 1554). The anonymous Protestant response, *A Defence of Priestes Mariages* (British Museum Press Mark: 697 g 13 [2]) was published, with some additions, by Parker early in Elizabeth's reign.

line of reasoning apparently would have been to esteem the married state at least as highly as the celibate, as one of the good gifts of God, provided for man's aid and comfort. At times the Puritan approaches this level, with statements that marriages avoided the inconvenience of solitariness and furnished man with a pleasant helpmeet. "The wife is ordained for man; like little Zoar, a city of refuge to fly to in all his troubles, and there is no peace comparable unto her but the peace of conscience."[2] But, even if the Puritan could have completely shaken off medieval attitudes, Paul's teaching would have prevented the acceptance of any such completely humanistic attitude. "It is better to marry than to burn," said the apostle, summing up his treatment of the choice of the evils in this sphere, and so the Puritan believed.[3] Marriage was divinely ordained, it is true. Not for the pure enjoyment of mankind, however, but only as a remedy for lust, a doctrine still enshrined in the Anglican marriage service. Only *a* remedy. For there was another and a better—the gift of having no necessity, a blessing conferred by a special act of God's grace. This emancipated the blessed beneficiary from worldly cares and left him free for the service of the gospel, much after the medieval fashion. This was obviously a better remedy than marriage, for there was no marriage in heaven, and so the institution was a sign of our imperfection here.[4] This Pauline teaching was reinforced by a desire to rebut the Catholic charge that the driving force in Protestantism was the desire of monks to marry nuns. Tyndale was proud to be able to point to his continued celibacy when dealing with More's endless repetitions of this accusation. In this left-handed way, therefore, much of the Catholic attitude found its way back into Puritan circles. The standard pastoral advice was to look to marriage only as a last resort, when it became

[2] Henry Smith, *Sermons* (London, 1599), p. 12; *Works*, ed. Thomas Smith ("Nichols Series of Standard Divines: Puritan Period" [2 vols.; Edinburgh, 1866–67]), I, 8; cf. Gen. 19:20; Richard Greenham, *The Workes of Richard Greenham* (5th and last ed.; London, 1612), pp. 123–24; William Perkins, *Workes* (3 vols.; London, 1616–18), III, 671.

[3] Robert Cleaver, *A Godly Form of Householde Government* (London, 1598), p. 125.

[4] Greenham, *op. cit.*, pp. 21, 373.

clearly evident that one had not the coveted gift of celibacy.[5] Contentment in a "sole life" was revered as a mark of special grace.[6]

Corollaries to this teaching were the severe limits set upon cohabitation and the prejudice against second marriages. Even in the married state there was the possibility of fornication, said the Puritan, if the conjugal rights were used "immoderately."[7] At times this meant the Augustinian restriction to procreation alone, though at others the intent is merely to preach temperance, as in such indifferent matters as food and drink. Obviously, this is the moralist's meaning when he prescribes such abstinence during the fast periods.[8] Similarly, second marriages had fallen into ill repute because of the medieval interpretation of the Pauline prescription that the bishop should be the husband of one wife. Since the doctrine of clerical celibacy ruled out the obvious exegesis of the passage, it had been taken to mean that no one who had lost two wives one after the other and then gone into the church could become a bishop. In Puritan writings we find this medieval prejudice cropping out, though it was doubtless more honored in the breach than in the observance.[9] The whole institution of marriage was thus publicly championed in general, but privately viewed with suspicion in its particulars.

In his attitude on the position of women the Puritan was still more medieval in his outlook—with Paul once more in the background. No effort was made to restore those legal and economic rights which the Roman law had given and the church and feudalism had taken away. Man continued to be exalted as the

[5] *Ibid.*, p. 78; cf. M. M. Knappen, *Two Elizabethan Puritan Diaries* (Chicago, 1933), pp. 4 and 95.

[6] Perkins represents a somewhat more liberal point of view on this and related points. He considers marriage in itself more excellent than the single life, though the evils resulting from the Fall had rendered the latter preferable for some with the gift of continence (*op. cit.*, III, 671).

[7] *Ibid.*, I, 62; III, 689.

[8] Nicholas Bownde, *The Holy Exercise of Fasting Described* (London, 1604), p. 56.

[9] Knappen, *op. cit.*, pp. 22 and 74.

lord and master, and woman treated as the weaker vessel, made of poorer stuff and legally subject to her husband. So obvious, in fact, did these principles seem to the Puritan in this period when few women were educated that, as we have seen, much of his propaganda against Mary Tudor was based upon them. How could a woman rule the larger commonwealth when it was clearly laid down in the Bible that she was to be in subjection in the microcosm of her own home? With one accord the Puritans quoted scripture to prove that the husband was to rule the wife.[10] Greenham told a prospective bride:

> If you have the wisdom of Abigail and all other graces which are in any woman, yet if you wanted obedience to your husband I tell you true that you are nothing worth and you could have no part in Jesus Christ who denieth Himself to be governor of any that will not acknowledge their husband to be their head.[11]

The material is abundant, but there is no need to labor this point.

Yet rulership did not mean tyranny. The husband was to love and cherish the wife as his own flesh. "Doth a king trample on his crown? Solomon calleth the wife the crown of her husband." If the wife were not the head, neither was she the foot, but made from a rib that she might walk jointly with her husband "under the government of her head." She was like a judge joined in commission to help rule his household. She was not to be made into a drudge or ordered about like a servant, but the husband was to command her "as the soul doth the body."[12] The common law permitted the husband to beat his wife with a rod no bigger than his thumb, but the Puritans forbade the practice. The husband was to train and direct his wife in the right way, but he had no "office to fight" his helpmeet.

> If he cannot reform his wife without beating, he is worthy to be beaten for choosing no better; when he hath used all means that he may and yet she is like herself, he must take her for his cross and say with Jeremiah, "This is my cross and I will bear it." But if he strike her, he takes away his hand from

---

[10] Cleaver, *op. cit.*, p. 213; Perkins, *op. cit.*, III, 691; Smith, *Sermons*, p. 29; *Works*, I, 24.

[11] *Op. cit.*, p. 126.

[12] Cleaver, *op. cit.*, pp. 210, 201, 209, 197, 202.

her, which was the first part he gave her to join them together; and she may put up her complaint against him that he hath taken away part of her goods. Her cheeks are made for thy lips and not for thy fists.[13]

Perkins took the same attitude,[14] though in extreme cases he allowed the husband to appeal to the magistrates to discipline his recalcitrant spouse. But, for the most part, he must take his misfortune as his cross. "And in this case if he be impatient he may in some sort be pardoned and pitied, but he is not wholly to be excused." Many are the homely remedies for avoiding domestic strife which are sprinkled through the Puritan writings. A favorite was to allow only one party at a time to give way to wrath. Ordering the husband to love his wife's parents and "kinsfolks" was perhaps the most Spartan.[15] In a pessimistic mood Smith relied on the law, which did not grant divorces for incompatibility, to "hold their noses together till weariness make them leave struggling; like two spaniels which are coupled in a chain, at last they learn to go together because they may not go asunder."[16]

Another medieval aspect of Puritan domestic relations was the reiterated prescription that the choice of a life-partner was a matter not of individual choice but of parental decision. The Fifth Commandment was commonly interpreted to cover this subject. It is true that this authority was often reduced to a mere veto power, and on the Continent it was suggested that provisions be made for magisterial interference in case the parental attitude was unreasonable. But there is no trace of this latter concession on English soil, so far as I have been able to discover, and the fundamental obligaton to heed the parents' wishes was generally stressed.[17] Perkins says flatly that contracts made without parental consent are void.[18] Not only do they violate the Fifth Commandment but they are contrary to

---

[13] Smith, *Sermons*, p. 31; *Works*, I, 26.   [14] *Op. cit.*, III, 691–92.

[15] Cleaver, *op. cit.*, p. 173.

[16] Smith, *Sermons*, p. 44; *Works*, I, 38.

[17] Smith, *Sermons*, pp. 23–24; *Works*, I, 18–19; Greenham, *op. cit.*, p. 743.

[18] *Op. cit.*, III, 682.

natural equity, which teaches that those that have no power or right over themselves cannot bind themselves by a promise. For children in the Puritan theory were "under the government and at the disposition of their parents." But later[19] the moralist grants that widows may legally remarry without parental consent, though such conduct is still bad manners. Cleaver is somewhat milder and allows the children to take the initiative in matchmaking. He warned the parents not to sell their children for money or arrange a striking of hands before there was a knitting of hearts,[20] but he does not deny the legal right of the older generation to do such things.

There were other qualifications for a spouse besides the ability to secure the parental consent. The proposed mate must be of sound religion. The Pauline injunction of marrying "only in the Lord" was still binding. But it was not enough to be virtuous; one must also be temperamentally suitable. "For diverse women have many virtues and yet do not fit to some men."[21] Smith gives five tests for these two important characteristics, "the report, the looks, the speech, the apparel, and the companions, which are like the pulses that show whether we be well or ill."[22] One sample will suggest the general drift. By the lady's speech the greatest Puritan talker of his time explains that he means her silence. "As the echo answereth but one for many which are spoken to her, so a maid's answer should be in a word; for she which is full of talk is not likely to prove a quiet wife."[23]

The topics previously discussed in this chapter have been considered briefly because they were not matters of controversy between Protestant factions and are therefore of minor consequence in a party history. But the divorce issue must be treated at some length because it did involve such a conflict, and one, as it happens, in which the Puritan stand was modern

---

[19] *Ibid.*, p. 696.

[20] Cleaver, *op. cit.*, p. 322.　　　　[21] Smith, *Sermons*, p. 18; *Works*, I, 14–15.

[22] *Sermons*, p. 20; *Works*, I, 15. In the fashion of the time, Cleaver appropriates and paraphrases this entire passage, adding only education as a sixth test.

[23] Smith, *Sermons*, p. 21; *Works*, I, 16; cf. John Knewstubs, *Lectures upon the Twentieth Chapter of Exodus* (London, 1577), pp. 127–32.

rather than medieval.[24] It is well known that the medieval
church rejected the civil-law doctrine of regulated divorce and
allowed only separations from bed and board (*a mensa et thoro*),
which did not permit of remarriage. Annulments were, however, possible, and these largely satisfied the social demand for
divorce. These were made generally available by the ecclesiastical doctrine of prohibited degrees of relationship and the Catholic teaching that a betrothal in terms of the present tense
(*sponsalia per verba de praesenti*) constituted a valid marriage.[25]
By zealous searching of family trees for sixth cousins and forgotten godfathers, and by trumped-up testimony to precon-
tracts, it was possible to shed many a wearying tie.

The Protestants reacted against this chicanery. They reduced
the number of prohibited degrees to more reasonable proportion[26]—as did the Roman Catholics at the Council of Trent—
and they regarded all contracts as equally binding. Throughout
the sixteenth century, indeed, espousal and wedding were regarded as two essential stages in contracting a valid marriage, a
circumstance which accounts for the double vows in the Anglican marriage service. But this did not solve the problem of
providing reasonable means of escape from intolerable bonds.
It was the Protestant refusal to recognize marriage as a sacrament which left them free to doubt its indissolubility and therefore to consider the remedy of outright divorce (*a vinculo*) permitting of remarriage. Though the biblical teaching on the subject was hopelessly confused,[27] both Lutheran and Reformed

[24] It is also a phase of Puritanism on which very little has been done. There is
nothing about it in L. L. Schücking's otherwise very useful *Die Familie in Puritanismus*
(Leipzig and Berlin, 1929).

[25] For the general background see G. E. Howard, *History of Matrimonial Institutions*
(3 vols.; Chicago and London, 1904).

[26] Perkins has some calculations of reasonable and unreasonable degrees (*op. cit.*,
III, 673–78). He thought the marriage of first cousins (brothers' and sisters' children)
lawful but not expedient. The canon law as finally adopted by the Anglican church
was, of course, much stricter.

[27] Textual criticism seems to indicate that the author of the First Gospel complicated
the situation by adding the concessive clause about fornication to the original flat prohibition in Mark (10:11; cf. Matt. 5:32). But Paul sanctioned divorce in case of a
difference of faith (I Cor. 7:15).

leaders on the Continent cut the Gordian knot by adopting this drastic means. Some, including Luther, Calvin, and Beza, were moderate about the matter, allowing absolute divorce only in case of adultery and malicious desertion. Others, including Zwingli and Bucer, followed the lead of Erasmus and reverted to the civil-law doctrine of also permitting it in case of cruelty, madness, disease, etc. The scriptural arguments of both schools were fearful and wonderful, but they filled a social need.[28] Even the sober Scots, after some hesitation, decided that divorce for desertion was as scriptural as divorce for adultery, and for centuries their law was more liberal on this point than the English.

South of the Tweed those who were imitating the Continental Protestants copied this progressive teaching. Tyndale[29] echoes Luther's ideas on the subject. The remarriage of the guilty party, however, was a difficult question. Luther thought that the enforcement of the Old Testament penalty of death for adultery would solve the problem, and Joye urged the adoption of such a remedy in England.[30] But Foxe[31] thought this inconsistent with Christian charity, and, since, in any case, the secular authorities refused to sanction it, other means had to be devised. Under the circumstances, Luther had granted the possibility of such remarriage under severe restrictions, and Tyndale repeated the suggestions.

In Edward's time Hooper brought back the even more liberal civil-law–Renaissance doctrine from Zurich. His ideas created a furor not because of the number of grounds he allowed for divorce but because he denounced the double standard and permitted the wife to divorce her husband as freely as her lord might get rid of her.[32] The major outlines of the Zurich teaching

[28] Ludwig Richter, *Beitraege zur Geschichte des Ehescheidungsrechts in der evangelischen Kirche* (Berlin, 1859), pp. 6–56.

[29] *Expositions and Notes*, ed. Walter (Cambridge: Parker Society, 1849), p. 52.

[30] *A Contrarye to a Certayne Manis Consultation: That Adulterers Ought To Be Punyshed wyth Deathe* (London, 1541).

[31] *De non plectendis morte adulteris* (London, 1548).

[32] John Hooper, *Early Writings*, ed. Carr (Cambridge: Parker Society, 1843), p. 382; cf. ab Ulmis to Bullinger, August 22 and November 11, 1550, *Original Letters Relative to the English Reformation*, ed. Robinson (2 vols.; Cambridge: Parker Society, 1846–47), pp. 416 and 422.

were incorporated in the ill-fated *Reformatio legum ecclesiasticarum*, the Protestant canon-law code proposed in 1552, which granted divorce for adultery, desertion, continued absence, and extreme incompatibility. Though this was never adopted, the government did accept that part of the Lutheran-Calvinistic doctrine which taught the right of the man to divorce his wife for infidelity and then remarry. The issue was forced by the action of William Parr, Marquis of Northampton and brother-in-law of Henry VIII, in taking a second wife when his first was proved unfaithful, though no formal divorce decree had been pronounced. For a time he was sequestered from the Council, but Parliament passed an act validating his second marriage,[33] and thereafter—with the exception of the Marian interlude—it became customary, though still technically illegal in the uncertain state of the canon law, to remarry after the ecclesiastical courts had granted a separation for adultery. Cartwright attacked the "corrupt opinion of those which dream that the knot of marriage is not cut asunder by adultery," maintaining that Christ taught that, "the former yoke being broken, men were at their liberty to enter into a new contract."[34] Robert Browne was of a similar opinion.[35] Smith, preaching on the subject shortly before 1590, speaks of it as the normal procedure and the only kind of divorce permitted.[36]

Soon afterward, however, the reviving forces of conservatism within the Anglican church made a successful effort to turn back the hands of the clock, though the Puritan opposition was strong. In the early 1590's Edmund Bunny, a prebendary of York, who also held the living of Bolton Percy near that city and had a reputation as an itinerant preacher, began to oppose

[33] Repealed by 1 Mary, st. 2, c. 33; Gilbert Burnet, *History of the Reformation*, ed. Pocock (7 vols.; Oxford, 1865), II, 117–22.

[34] Thomas Cartwright, *The Second Replie against Master Whitgifts Second Answer* (s.l., 1575), p. 105.

[35] *A Booke Which Sheweth the Life and Manners of All True Christians* (Middelburg, 1582), sig. K, fol. 2(v). His permissible grounds, which included seeking the destruction of the other partner, show him to have been somewhat more advanced than the others, as might be expected.

[36] *Sermons*, p. 44; *Works*, I, 35.

the practice of remarriage after separations for infidelity. He refused to join his fellow-clergy in subscribing to an indorsement of such procedure circulated by a local gentleman anxious to remarry in those circumstances, and he later preached against the custom. Another anonymous but prominent person in the district who had so remarried was called before the Council of the North, and there Bunny, who was somehow present to champion the conservative position, pointed out to the astonished Puritan Huntingdon, the Lord President, that there was no law authorizing such unions. Rainolds of Oxford was enlisted to write on the Puritan side and composed a volume which Bunny secured and answered while it was still in manuscript, in 1595.

Whitgift agreed with Bunny; but, to keep peace in the church, he refused to permit the publication of either treatise.[37] In the canons passed by Convocation in 1597, however, a provision was inserted[38] that those receiving divorces in the ecclesiastical courts must give bond not to remarry, a requirement which enforced the Anglican opinion that these separations were only *a mensa et thoro*. In 1601 John Dove, who held one of Whitgift's London livings, supported the Archbishop's view in a sermon at Paul's Cross, which was afterward published.[39] In the following year the controversy broke out on the academic front. John Howson, the Vice-Chancellor, chaplain to the Queen and later Bishop of Durham, was engaged in an anti-Puritan crusade at Oxford, and he made this one of his points. Thomas Pie, or Pye, fellow of Merton, defended the Puritan position.[40] Alberico Gentili, Regius Professor of Civil Law, dutifully lent his support to the official view.[41] The controversy ran on into the next reign, when Rainolds' original treatise was published surrepti-

[37] Edmund Bunny, "Advertisement to the Reader," *Of Divorce for Adulterie and Marrying Again* (Oxford, 1610), sig. **, fol. 2(*v*)–sig. ***, fol. 1(*v*).

[38] Sec. 107.   [39] *Of Divorcement* (London, 1601).

[40] John Howson, *Uxore demissa propter fornicationem aliam non licet superinducere* (Oxford, 1602); Thomas Pie, *Epistola ad D. Joh. Housonum* (London, 1603).

[41] The 1606 reprint of Howson's work contains also the supporting letter of Gentili and a further anonymous answer to Pie, *In controversiam inter Johannem Howson et Thomam Pyum . . . . tractus modestus.*

tiously after his death, and Bunny's reply was allowed to appear.[42] But the tide was running strongly against the Puritans. Elizabeth had not sanctioned the 1597 canons, and their legality was accordingly doubtful, but the provision about divorces was repeated in the canons of 1604, which formally received the royal approval in due course. Furthermore, the secular courts were persuaded to recognize the new-old principle. When, in 1601–2, the remarriage question came up incidentally in a Star Chamber case concerning one Foljambe, Whitgift reported that a council of divines and civilians specially summoned to Lambeth had agreed with him, and the court ruled in the Archbishop's favor.[43] This decision was winked at, when, in 1605, Laud was allowed to marry the adulterous Penelope Devereux to her paramour the Earl of Devonshire, formerly known as Lord Mountjoy, an act which later caused the cleric much heartburning. But the decision was confirmed by the King's Bench in Porter's case in 1636,[44] and, in spite of John Milton's efforts, it was not until the end of the century that remarriage was permitted and then only by a special act of Parliament for each case—a situation which continued until the introduction of the modern procedure in 1857. Perkins advocated the Zurich doctrine of full divorce for infidelity, desertion, "malicious desertion," disease, and insanity, with equal rights for men and women,[45] but he remained a voice crying in the wilderness of conservative reaction.[46]

---

[42] John Rainolds, *A Defence of the Judgment of the Reformed Churches: That a Man May Lawfullie Not Only Put Awaie His Wife for Her Adulterie But Also Marrie Another* (*s.l.*, 1609); Bunny, *op. cit.*

[43] F. Moore, *Cases* (2d ed.; London, 1688), p. 683.

[44] G. Croke, *Reports*, ed. Leach (3 vols.; London, 1792), III, 461–63.

[45] *Op. cit.*, III, 690, 688, 683–84, though his translator gives a different impression in his Preface, sig. qqqq, fol. 6(v).

[46] A related development in Puritan teaching was the view of marriage as a civil contract. In their reaction from the sacramental theory of the rite, and in their protests against such attendant "superstitions" as the use of the wedding ring, the Puritans were disposed to minimize the importance of the clerical role in the ceremony. Their attack on the unsavory dealings in the ecclesiastical courts also led them to deny the right of the church to control such contracts. This was the sentiment which reached its climax in the Civil Marriage Act passed by the Nominated Parliament in 1653 and similar legislation in New England (John Whitgift, *Works*, ed. Ayre [3 vols.; Cambridge: Parker Society, 1851–53], III, 267, 353; cf. Howard, *op. cit.*, I, 408–35).

Though the Puritan had a keen sense of the distractions involved, once in wedlock he thought it as well to be hung for a
sheep as for a lamb. He had no idea of any such halfway covenant
as an arrangement to marry but have no children. Nor did he
ever advocate the limitation of offspring. On the contrary, the
propagation of children was one of the chief ends of marriage.[47]
Perkins did not approve of divorce for sterility, but he considered barrenness a notable affliction.[48] Children were the
pledge of a wife's love to her husband, "the right wedding-ring
that sealeth and maketh up the marriage."[49]

Assuming the arrival of numerous children, there was no
thought of allowing free play to nascent genius or an unham-
pered development of new and original traits of character. Just
as the ruler of a commonwealth constrained his subjects to attendance upon, if not belief in, the proper religious rites, so the
ruler of a household was to train up a child in the way he should
go, and no authority doubted that this way was known. "Spare
the rod and spoil the child" was not only a paraphrase of biblical
proverbs but a Puritan axiom. "Birch breaketh no bones"[50] was
another. Children were to remember the Fifth Commandment
and obey their parents, even in such matters as marriage and
the chioce of a vocation.[51] There was such a thing as too much
severity[52] but too much "cockering" of children was the real
danger. To smile or laugh at naughty words or "unhonest"
deeds of their children was a great blunder.[53]

Of the various teachings on the topic of children in the
home perhaps the most interesting, in view of recent controversy on this particular subject,[54] was the definite prescription

---

[47] Smith, *Sermons*, p. 13; *Works*, I, 9; Perkins, *op. cit.*, III, 671.

[48] Perkins, *op. cit.*, III, 690.   [49] Smith, *Sermons*, p. 41; *Works*, I, 35.

[50] Cleaver, *op. cit.*, p. 265.

[51] Perkins, *op. cit.*, III, 695; Cleaver, *op. cit.*, pp. 129–34.

[52] Perkins, *op. cit.*, III, 694.

[53] Cleaver, *op. cit.*, pp. 286–98.

[54] The last contributor to this discussion vigorously denied that the Puritan ministers
"deliberately encouraged their flocks to give these names to their children" (*Times* [Lon-
don] *Literary Supplement*, 1935, pp. 416, 432, 448, 464, 477; cf. C. W. Bardsley, *Curios-
ities of Puritan Nomenclature* [London, 1880]).

that they should be given scriptural names. This practice was enjoined by the Puritan discipline of 1586 and attacked by Bancroft in his *Dangerous Positions*.[55] Fenner named his children by such pious titles as More Fruit and Faint Not,[56] and one of the charges against the Puritan Edmund Snape, on the collapse of the classis movement, was that he had objected to a boy's being christened Richard.[57] In his treatment of this topic, Perkins merely prescribed a "fit" name,[58] but Cleaver was explicit on the subject, and his justification of the Puritan policy is worth quoting:

It is a thing worthy to be wished that all parents . . . . would give . . . . such names as are named and commended unto us in the Holy Scriptures, to the end that when they come to years of discretion they, by hearing those names, may be excited and moved to follow the virtuous life and Christian conversation of those men and women whose names they bear, which the Holy Ghost hath commended them for: and contrariwise to eschew and avoid those faults and vices which are discommended in them.[59]

It is true that this injunction was not always observed, and Cleaver takes pains to point out that faith alone saved and that there was no magical virtue about a name. But the prescription was there, and the examples show that the principle was followed, though some of the choices, such as "The Lord Is Near," "Joy Again," "More Trials," and "Sufficient" were what the Puritans considered pious phrases rather than biblical proper names.

The details of educational advice in the strict sense of the term we defer to the next chapter, but the Puritan did not think of education as consisting of book-learning alone, and much space was devoted to more general matters, such as the training in good manners, the choice of a calling, and matchmaking. The children were to be seen rather than heard, to defer to their

[55] Daniel Neal, *History of the Puritans* (3 vols.; London, 1837), III, 495; *Dangerous Positions*, pp. 104–5.

[56] A. F. Scott Pearson, *Thomas Cartwright and Elizabethan Puritanism* (London, 1925), p. 274.

[57] Bancroft, *op. cit.*, p. 105.

[58] *Op. cit.*, III, 694.   [59] *Op. cit.*, pp. 244–45.

elders, to be apprenticed to godly masters, to be married without undue regard for financial considerations, etc.[60]

Servants were considered an integral part of the Tudor household and are treated accordingly in Puritan literature on this topic. While there are some liberal touches, like the injunction to provide them with time for rest and recreation,[61] the general picture is one of low status and severe restrictions, with medieval ideas lingering on. All men were equal before God, but the Puritan, like the Catholic, made much allowance for the Fall of Man and the municipal law. Perkins justifies the holding of slaves after the Old Testament manner, with a few qualifications such as the one that there be some prospect of a jubilee,[62] and Tyndale speaks of servants being their master's property for the term of their employment.[63] Their employer is to them in place of God, and they were to obey him, even though he were evil.[64] It is assumed that the servants of both sexes will be beaten when occasion demands, the only Puritan qualification being that the master shall correct the men and the mistress the women. The servants are to be compelled to attend on the means of grace, and instructed in the proper religious life. "The master being converted must convert his servants."[65] Their conduct is to be regulated by their masters according to puritanical standards, and they are not to be permitted to amuse themselves in unseemly ways.

In short, the religious ideal was to prevail in the home. On the negative side it was to keep one on the alert against the temporal distractions of the married state, to warn a man to live in marriage as in a temptation, to guard against too much love of wife or child and too great concern about financial matters. The most profitable thing to remember, said Smith, at the close of his discourse on the subject, was Paul's statement that the

---

[60] See *ibid.*, pp. 242–344, for the full particulars.

[61] Smith, *Sermons*, pp. 38–39; *Works*, I, 32–33.

[62] *Op. cit.*, III, 697.

[63] *Doctrinal Treatises*, ed. Walter (Cambridge: Parker Society, 1848), p. 172.

[64] Hooper, *Later Writings*, ed. Nevinson (Cambridge: Parker Society, 1852), p. 81.

[65] Smith, *Sermons*, pp. 38–40; *Works*, I, 32–34.

unmarried cared for the things of the Lord, while the married cared for the things of the world. "As the corpse of Asahel made the passengers to stand, so I placed this sentence in the door of thy passage to make thee stand and consider what thou doest before thou marriest."[66] On the positive side the home was to be the smallest unit in the Puritan commonwealth, a center of secular and Christian discipline. Each household was to be kept in good order. Religious instruction and family prayer were to be carried on in each home. These, too, were pre-Reformation ideals which may be found in the Catholic writings of the first quarter of the century.[67] What the Puritan did was to make a serious effort to put them in practice, to make domestic life available to the clergy, and to permit divorce when other expedients failed.

[66] *Sermons*, p. 46; *Works*, I, 39; cf. II Sam. 2:23.

[67] Schücking, *op. cit.*, pp. 88 and 92. The author's arguments to prove Puritan household ideals to be different from those of Calvin and Luther do not appear very strong, however. Discipline by elders is not incompatible with family discipline, as we have seen, and the difference of Sabbatarian views has nothing to do with domestic attitudes. As he indicates, Luther's ideals are drawn from the medieval background common to him and the English alike.

CHAPTER XXVI
Learning and Education

IN THE scale of attitudes toward learning the Puritan is entitled to rank above his Catholic contemporary, who prided himself on his ignorance of the Scriptures; above the Queen, who deliberately strove to suppress religious instruction on the theory that an ignorant people were most easily ruled; and far above the mass of the nobility and country gentry, who were concerned only to retain their hold on the former monastic and chantry endowments, much of which had served the cause of education in the past. On the other hand, the Puritan cannot be said to have had the broad interest in pure learning, as such, which was the glory of the Erasmian humanists. His zeal for the unified control and yet wide diffusion of intellectual endeavor may be cited, however, as a compensating factor which entitles him to a not undistinguished place in intellectual history.

The Puritan idea of the relation of the individual mind to society was medieval. He regarded with horror the suggestion that every man might be allowed to teach and publish as he chose. This was not because he hated truth but because he loved it so much. In spite of the upheaval through which he had just come, he did not consider it the function of the human mind to search for new discoveries, but to expound and elucidate the system of truth, which in all its major outlines, was already known. To doubt this new-old Protestant system, to indulge in curious searchings or vain imaginations, after the Anabaptist and Arian fashion, was to hinder the true cause—in other words, the cause of truth. So, in the interests of the truth, these false teachers must be put down. The press must be censored, school-teachers licensed, Catholics and other heretics punished.

Bigoted as this attitude may appear today, it was not without some merit. When all the harsh words—and they may rightly be many—are said about the blindness and inconsistency of forbidding God to raise up any more Luthers, it must be granted that the Puritan attitude, like its Catholic predecessor, was fundamentally sound, erring only in the details of its execution. Though the limits set to scientific and cultural activity were so narrow that they irritated an undue number of the intellectuals and so provoked a fatal revolt, it may be suggested that the idea of discipline in the affairs of the mind was as sound as that of discipline in the state or in the church. Learned societies, universities, publishers, and foundations—with their weapons of payment, prestige, publicity, and promotion—exercise something of the kind even in democratic countries today. But the Puritan type of control kept the ranks of the intelligentsia much more tightly closed. Not only were they a cultural unit but they were an organized political machine which, in the ideal Puritan state, would make its power felt. And this organized intelligentsia included not only minister and schoolmaster but author and journalist, even musician and artist, as well. A mighty army which would hold up the banner of the spirit in more than empty show.

In this association of idealists and ideals the Puritan never doubted that the ethical should predominate over the intellectual and the aesthetic. Learning, like art, was the handmaiden of religion. Man was, first of all, a moral being, as the mother-church had always taught, and so development along these other lines should not be allowed to interfere with the attainment of his primary end. On the contrary, only those interests were to be encouraged which facilitated progress toward the main objective.

But where they did render such assistance they were zealously encouraged. Though they were only means to an end, the importance of the end reflected on the means. Hence the vigor with which they were pursued. It is thus that the Puritan zeal for learning is to be understood. In a religion where the Bible and preachers played such important roles it was essential that believers be literate and that the ministers be trained up to the level of being able to produce a respectable sermon.[1] The Puritan enthusiasm for learning was thus a strictly limited zeal, confined to those branches which were of direct assistance in building up the Puritan commonwealth, but it was inspired by the glory of the millennial vision to which it opened the way, and it flamed with corresponding vigor. On the Continent it made Geneva a center of intellectual as well as of religious life. North of the Tweed, and later in New England, it led to the establishment of that system of elementary education which contributed so much to the fibrous character of the inhabitants of those regions.

In England, with Elizabeth and the grasping landlords ever on the alert, no such system could be established, but the Puritans did what they could according to their abilities. To begin with, they emphatically preached the doctrine of education:

It is also the duty of parents to provide that their children may learn, at the least, to write and read, for it may be unto them a great help in the course of this life and a treasure of much greater account than money. . . . . Nevertheless the principal end thereof should not have respect to such commodity as the children may reap thereby towards the use of this present life, but rather that they may read the word of God to their comfort and instruction to salvation.[2]

The rich and noble were not to despise learning and were to have their sons instructed also. The greater the ship, the more need of a cunning shipmaster. No matter what profession one followed, experience showed that "the more skill and knowledge he hath in the liberal sciences, so much the sooner shall he learn his occupation and the more ready and handsomer shall he be about the same." Furthermore, "he that hath learning, although it be but small, shall much better understand the preachers and take endless comfort than he that hath no learning."[3] Riches, health, and beauty are unstable and fade. "Learning

[1] William Perkins, *Workes* (3 vols.; London, 1616–18), III, 95.

[2] Robert Cleaver, *A Godly Form of Householde Government* (London, 1598), p. 251.

[3] *Ibid.*, pp. 335–36; cf. Laurence Humphrey, *The Nobles*, sig. X, fols. ii–vii, sig. A, fol. iv(*v*); *Optimates* (Basel, 1559), pp. 324–34, 42–43.

and virtue never stagger, always be constant." Parents should choose their schoolmaster carefully and—noble doctrine in unflattering dress!—pay him well, just as they would a good horse trainer. To withhold endowments originally intended for educational purposes was to discourage good men from following the learned professions and so to weaken the commonwealth.

So far as they were able, they practiced what they preached and set up schools. Many ministers taught the children of the community in addition to attending to their other duties. Sir Walter Mildmay helped to found institutions at Chelmsford and at Middleton in Lancashire. He also contributed to the endowment of Christ's Hospital. At Ashby the Earl of Huntingdon founded a grammar school to be under the supervision of Anthony Gilby. At Dedham in Essex the leaders of the local classis persuaded their elders to provide that every child in town should be taught to read. A house was provided for the master, and it was arranged that half the collection taken on communion Sundays was to be devoted to paying the fees of poor children.[4] Adults were also urged to study, and Puritan ministers instructed them in their spare time. One clergyman is said to have taught forty people over forty years of age to read. At the Reformation illiteracy was widespread. Shakespeare's own father could not write his name. By the end of the century the Protestants in general and the Puritans in particular had made great inroads on this evil, though much remained to be done.

On the level of higher education the Puritans were also active. Like their Catholic forebears they thought of universities as seedbeds for the clergy, and the only new colleges founded at the universities during Elizabeth's reign were under their auspices. In 1568–69 Sir Walter Mildmay made a sizable contribu-

[4] Without studying the characters of all the founders of the hundred or more schools which were established in this period, it is impossible to get at the real motives behind the verbiage in which their purposes are set forth in the original statutes (A. M. Stowe, *English Grammar Schools in the Reign of Elizabeth* [New York, 1908], pp. 10–11, 20–23). But from the fact that the numbers of such schools doubled in the period in which the Puritans were at least one of the chief forces championing such a movement some idea may be gained of the role played by the party in the spread of the grammar-school network over the country until it could be said that every English boy had in his own neighborhood a place of education competent to fit him to enter the university (J. and J. A. Venn, *Alumni Cantabrigienses* [4 vols.; Cambridge, 1922–27], I, xv).

tion to his old college, Christ's, the Puritan stronghold, to endow a Greek lectureship, six scholarships, and a preacher. In 1582 the fellows appealed to him as a powerful patron to show them his favor in the election of a master, "to keep them from a bad and help them to a good one."[5] But when the choice fell upon the incompetent weakling, Edmund Barwell, the Chancellor of the Exchequer seems to have decided that he could get better value for his money by other means. Accordingly, at the height of the Whitgift controversy in which his kinsman Walsingham and Robert Beale were so deeply engaged, he took steps to set up a new foundation, Emmanuel College, which received the royal charter in 1584. Though he told the Queen he had no intention of countenancing anything contrary to her established laws, the whole purpose and tone of the new institution were Puritan. For this occasion, at least, Mildmay rejected the Renaissance practice, by which he had himself benefited, of changing universities into schools for statesmen, lawyers, and country gentry. Instead he reverted to the medieval notion. *Sacra theologiae studiis* ("Sacred to Theological Study") said the inscription over the gateway. In the statutes he stated his intention of founding a training school for the ministry.

> Therefore let fellows and scholars who obtrude into the college with any other design than to devote themselves to sacred theology and eventually to labor in preaching the Word, know that they are frustrating my hope and occupying the place of fellow or scholar contrary to my ordinance.

To enforce the observance of this intention, Mildmay inserted, in 1587, a provision, not found in any other college statutes of the period, prohibiting any of the fellows from lingering on at the university more than ten years after taking his M.A.[6]

The master chosen for the new foundation was a prominent Puritan, Laurence Chaderton, who had been Perkins' tutor at Christ's College. When in the course of the preliminary negotiations Chaderton was offered a more lucrative post elsewhere, Mildmay won him over to the financial sacrifice with the state-

[5] State Papers; Domestic, Elizabeth, CLII, 51 (*Calendar 1581-1590*, p. 46).

[6] E. S. Shuckburgh, *Emmanuel College* (London, 1904), pp. 6 and 23; J. B. Mullinger, *History of the University of Cambridge* (3 vols.; Cambridge, 1873–1911), II, 310–19.

ment, "If you will not be master, I certainly will not be founder." Mildmay's judgment was sound, for Chaderton was a man among ten thousand. His parents had been zealous Catholics, and he was one who came out of great tribulation. To firmness of purpose he added a muscular Christianity, an urbanity of manner, and a breadth of interest which made him acceptable in quarters where most men of his ilk were anathema. He had once saved the life of the rising Richard Bancroft in a town-and-gown riot and so was immune from episcopal attack. His father-in-law was Elizabeth's wine merchant,[7] and his favor in court circles survived the Stuart accession, for James became rather fond of him. His sturdy physique enabled him to head the college for thirty-eight years, keeping it true to its Puritan tradition. He resigned only when he was sure that his successor would be one of the same school. During his mastership the chapel, which was not oriented in Catholic fashion, remained unconsecrated. The surplice was neglected, and the members generally took communion seated, to the scandal of their Anglican brethren. As Christ's became less hospitable to Puritans, the new college rapidly took its place as a party center, until, in the early part of the next century, it ranked second in number of members only to the royal foundation of Trinity. From its doors went out many of the Puritan leaders of the next century in England and America. John Cotton, Nathanial Gilby, son of Anthony, and Thomas Hooker were fellows there. Thomas Shepherd and John Harvard were undergraduates.[8]

Inspired by Mildmay's example, Frances Sidney, dowager Countess of Sussex, who had married her daughter to the financier's nephew, spent her declining years saving money to emulate him. On her death in 1589 it was found that her will provided not only for a lectureship in Westminster Abbey on the Puritan model but also for a college at Cambridge, to be known as Sidney Sussex. In 1596 her executors succeeded in founding it. James Montagu, later Bishop of Winchester and

[7] Nicholas Culverwel, whose son Ezekiel was a prominent Essex Puritan and Richard Rogers' Jonathan.

[8] S. E. Morison, *The Founding of Harvard College* (Cambridge, Mass., 1935), pp. 92–107.

brother of the Earl of Manchester of the civil-war era, became the first master. The original statutes were largely copied from those of Emmanuel, but the executors and master did not have Mildmay's means, nor were they so faithful to his ideals.[9] The new college survived, however, and produced a number of prominent Puritans, including Oliver Cromwell.

Another fruit of the Puritan interest in education was Trinity College, Dublin. The proposal to found an Irish university had been agitated since before the Reformation. Elizabeth was not unwilling to see one established as a bulwark against the Catholics, but it was the Puritan party that furnished the requisite leadership. Luke Challoner and Henry Ussher,[10] the men chiefly responsible for the founding of the institution in 1591–92, were products of the relatively Puritan Trinity and Magdalene at Cambridge. The first provost in more than name[11] was William Travers, the author of the *Full and Plaine Declaration.* Though the Queen considered him too puritanical for the Temple, she had no objection to such a keen Protestant having a prominent post in the front line in Ireland. He served from 1596 to 1598, and, when for some unknown reason he retired to England, he was succeeded by Henry Alvey, the puritanical son of Travers' old friend and associate at the Temple, the Marian exile Richard Alvey. Trinity College was intended to be only the first of a series which should form a larger university. This hope was not fulfilled. No others were established, and for some years Trinity itself averged only ten B.A.'s a year. But the Puritan spirit did not die out. There Increase Mather took his M.A., and John Winthrop, Jr., spent two years at the Dublin institution before going to the Inner Temple.[12]

[9] In 1614 the Earl of Kent, one of the executors, annulled the original statute requiring the termination of all fellowships within seven years after D.D. standing was attained (G. M. Edwards, *Sidney Sussex College* [London, 1899], pp. 13, 24, 71).

[10] Like Andrewes, he became a prelate later, but may be considered a Puritan at this time. Furthermore, an Irish bishopric did not preclude Puritan tendencies as it did in England. The Irish church was strongly Puritan then—witness the official adoption of the Lambeth Articles there—and has remained persistently Low Church down to the present time.

[11] The Archbishop of Dublin had carried that title for a time.

[12] J. P. Mahaffy, *An Epoch in Irish History* (London, 1903); Morison, *op. cit.,* pp. 121–25.

There is no denying that the Puritans had a zeal for learning, but it was not according to knowledge. In spite of all their devotion to this cause, they never produced anything like a logical Puritan curriculum. They glorified the Bible, but they never worked out a course of study for which the one book would be the basis. The chief end of man was to glorify God, but Puritan students spent most of their time reading heathen authors. Though they represented a cause quite different from Renaissance humanism, they progressed little beyond Erasmus on the grammar-school level, and scarcely reached humanistic standards in the universities. In secondary education the best they could do was to echo the Calvinistic protest[13] against the inclusion in a schoolboy's reading of Terence and similar classical authors of doubtful propriety. Becon took a stand against them.[14] The statutes of East Retford Grammar School, in Nottinghamshire, which was founded in 1552 under foreign influence, omit this author from the prescribed list.[15] Laurence Humphrey advised that Terence be handled with caution when he discussed the education of a budding nobleman.[16] John Stockwood and Rainolds were for banning him and his like completely.[17] But even they did not propose to dispense with the ordinary run of pagan authors. In the schools where Puritan influence was strongest, Cicero and Ovid, Demosthenes and Homer continued to dominate the course of study. It is true that the learning of the catechism and attendance upon church were generally required, but definite religious instruction was largely a week-end affair, and the Bible was not commonly used as a school text. True, individual masters often used biblical passages for translation exercises and doubtless read Christian ideas into, and out of, the pagan authors. But there is nowhere

[13] The program given in *Les Ordonnances ecclésiastique de l'église de Genève* (Geneva, 1562), pp. 75–79, omits all such works.

[14] Thomas Becon, *Catechism*, in *Works*, ed. Ayre (3 vols.; Cambridge: Parker Society, 1843–44), p. 382.

[15] Nicholas Carlisle, *A Concise Description of the Endowed Grammar Schools in England and Wales* (2 vols.; London, 1818), II, 283.

[16] *The Nobles*, sig. Y, fol. iii(v); *Optimates*, pp. 340–41.

[17] Stockwood, *Very Fruiteful Sermon* (London, 1579), pp. 67–68; Rainolds, *Th' Overthrow of Stage-Plays* ([Middleburg], 1599), pp. 123–24.

to be found the genuine Christian curriculum which readers of popular expositions of Calvin's "thoroughgoing logic" might be led to expect.[18]

The closest approach was made by the left-wing separatists, some of whom, logically enough, denounced "the study of profane, heathen writers,"[19] universities,[20] and even the liberal arts.[21] At one time Robert Browne apparently endeavored to work out a genuinely Christian system of education based on the principle that "the word of God doth expressly set down all necessary and general rules of the arts and all learning." He was soon telling Burghley that he had devised a method by which "in one year scholars may well learn together those arts which scarcely in ten years they untowardly learn in the Universities." But the details of the great scheme[22] were never published, and the claims for it were so extravagant as to persuade some later scholars that the author was not quite of sound mind at the time of composition. Doubtless he thought with great penetration on this as well as some other topics, but his temperamental instability prevented his suggestions from bearing fruit.

On the university level also there was a surprising lack of innovation. Though the loose requirements for degrees left some time for belles-lettres and history, Aristotle continued to dominate the curriculum, as he had done for generations before the Reformation. More research is needed in this field, but it seems clear that his works of natural, moral, and mental philosophy, taken either straight or paraphrased in some scholastic manual,

---

[18] Foster Watson, *English Grammar Schools to 1660: Their Curriculum and Practice* (Cambridge, 1908). I have also been assisted on this topic by Professor T. W. Baldwin, of the University of Illinois.

[19] H. Ainsworth and F. Johnson, *An Apologie or Defence of Such True Christians as Are Commonly (But Unjustly) Called Brownists* (s.l., 1604), p. 78; John Strype, *The Life and Acts of Matthew Parker* (3 vols.; Oxford, 1821), II, 335.

[20] Henry Barrow, *A Brief Discoverie of the False Church* (s.l. 1590), p. 178.

[21] Richard Alison, *A Plaine Confutation of a Treatise of Brownisme* (London, 1590), p. 17.

[22] Strype, *The Life and Acts of John Whitgift* (3 vols.; Oxford, 1822), III, 229–30; cf. above, p. 309.

constituted the basic prescription for the B.A. well into the Stuart period.[23] His logic was also used, but here the Puritan movement made itself felt, for the men of the new religion made considerable effort to substitute the work of the Bartholomew martyr, Peter Ramus, for the philosopher's contributions in this field. Ramus' main purpose was to simplify the study of logic, introducing into it more of the element of natural reason and common sense. He attacked the scholastic complications of the syllogistic method and even opposed the hoary tradition of the infallibility of Aristotle himself. From the 1570's onward his doctrine was introduced in the Protestant universities on the Continent and in Scotland and, in the next century, at Trinity College, Dublin. Oxford was cool, but Puritan Cambridge was more hospitable. Gabriel Harvey was one of Ramus' earliest advocates on the Cam. By the end of the century Cambridge was generally considered a stronghold of the new system. Nevertheless, there was considerable opposition even there. An attempt to defend Ramus produced a near-riot in the Cambridge schools as late as 1595, and in the next century the work of one of his chief rivals, Keckermann, was still prescribed reading in Puritan Emmanuel, while Ramus' name does not appear on the list.[24] But, even assuming that his teaching was wholeheartedly followed by the Puritans, it was at best a modified medievalism, and its effect was confined to one subject alone. It was negative and destructive, but offered no positive basis for a Puritan Weltanschauung.

Where room was found in the curriculum for the newer learning, even in the most Puritan of colleges it remained classical and humanistic, after the grammar-school pattern. Yet, surprisingly enough, interest in Hebrew[25] and even Greek showed a falling-off during the period of greatest Puritan influence at Cambridge, and there was scant interest in history. Renais-

[23] Morison, op. cit., pp. 67–72.

[24] Mullinger, op. cit., II, 403–14; Morison, op. cit., pp. 68 and 62 n.

[25] It is worthy of notice, however, that the prominent Puritan John Udall was something of a Hebraist. He translated the Hebrew Grammar of Peter Martinius and compiled a Hebrew dictionary (The Key of the Holy Tongue [Leyden, 1593]); cf. DNB, art. "Udall."

sance science remained an occupation for men without university posts or for undergraduate amateurs in their spare time. Theological and scholastic disputations continued to dominate the intellectual world of the university in general and the Puritans in particular.[26]

The Puritan educational ideal was therefore not only lacking in depth and thoroughness but it was too narrow to make possible the perpetuation of the medieval concept of a unified intelligentsia. Even without the Roman Catholics and Anglicans to harass them from the outside, it seems inevitable that the unity of the intellectual world should have been lost under a Puritan regime. Too little room was left in its framework for experiment and the investigation of matters without direct religious importance. More statesman-like planners might have retained a loose but effective control by recognizing the indirect and ultimate value of "pure" learning, but the Puritan was not of that type. Like Calvin, he had little scientific curiosity and did not keep up with contemporary developments in this field.[27] Indifference rather than vigorous, open hostility is perhaps the best general characterization of the Puritan's attitude to secular learning which did not aid in the spread of the gospel. But when the subject was raised, he normally condemned it as a waste of time better spent in the pursuit of higher things. It was more important to know how to go to heaven than how the heavens go. As we have seen, the Holy Spirit and the Scriptures were the ultimate authorities. To glorify "carnal reason" or rely upon it for more than incidental assistance was to court disaster. When the Bible and reason conflicted, reason must give way, after the medieval precept.

At the beginning of the English Reformation, Tyndale declaimed in good Lutheran style against vain learning in general and Aristotle in particular. "Man's wisdom is plain idolatry" was the general theme.[28] At the end of the century we find the

---

[26] Mullinger, op. cit., II, 418–19.

[27] Imbart de la Tour, Calvin et l'institution chrétienne, Vol. IV of Les Origines de la Réforme, ed. Jacques Chevalier (4 vols.; Paris, 1935), pp. 177–78.

[28] William Tyndale, Doctrinal Treatises, ed. Walter (Cambridge: Parker Society, 1848), pp. 107 and 160.

conscientious Puritan student at the university, though playing with fire, bewailing his pride of knowledge and his desire for vain glory in the gathering of herbs, reading Greek, or studying chronology.[29] Indeed, there was enough of this fear of learning among the Cambridge Puritans to lend point to the *Pilgrimage to Parnassus*,[30] acted in St. John's College in 1597. In it the Puritan attitude toward learning is satirized in the person of a dullard named Stupido, who can cope with simple Ramus but not with stronger academic meat. He is represented as decrying rhetoric, poetry, and philosophy as rags and parings of learning, quite lacking in sound, edifying knowledge and no better than a pair of organs or a morris dance. Master Marprelate's tracts, a Geneva catechism, and the simple attire of a Penry or a Wigginton were good enough for him.[31] In between these chronological extremes the party representatives rang the changes on the same theme. Dering decried the false wisdom of the world.[32] Perkins thought natural wisdom a good gift of God; but unless one also had spiritual wisdom, the other became foolishness, and the common disregard of this principle he considered the "misery" of his age. "Though a man had all the wisdom of the world and by his wit could compass upon earth what his heart could wish, yet if he fail in providing for true happiness all his wisdom is but madness."[33] Greenham felt the same way. True, he condemns the extreme Puritan Stupidoes. Only the unadvised condemned all human learning, arts, science, and manual professions under a pretense of knowing nothing but Christ. But these necessary things, like the flesh, though not to be destroyed, are to be restrained and kept in proper subjection to the supreme knowledge of Christ crucified. He protests against the current tendency to rejoice more in these human attainments than in the cross. Without that, authority, learning, and knowledge are accursed. Elsewhere he tells the prospective believer that he

---

[29] M. M. Knappen, *Two Elizabethan Puritan Diaries* (Chicago, 1933), pp. 106, 108, 113.

[30] Edited by W. D. Macray (Oxford, 1886).

[31] P. 12.   [32] Edward Dering, *Workes* (London, 1597), sig. E, fols. 1–4.

[33] *Op. cit.*, III, 171.

must fight down and conquer his own reason, which will protest at the sacrifices demanded of Christians.[34] Pride in wisdom is one of the phases of the pride of life which the Christian must forsake, says Rogers.[35] "Curious heads which are ever meddling in things not pertinent to them" are the symptoms.

The suggestion, therefore, that Puritanism was particularly hospitable to pure learning or scientific inquiry can only be made in the same sense that the Weberian thesis of its relation to modern capitalism can be maintained. It made the negative contribution of furnishing a less effective barrier than Catholicism, and some of the enthusiasms it generated could be redirected to educational ends when the original objectives lost their attraction. But to make the modern ideal of intellectual liberalism the child of Puritanism is to substitute Ishmael for Isaac, the concubine's son for the true seed. For lack of any thoroughgoing educational program of his own, the Puritan paid a kind of lip service to the Erasmian teaching on the subject, but his heart was in Bible study, theological discussion, and practical religious living. Puritanism was definitely a Reformation movement; Renaissance influences on it were slight and indirect.

This should be clear from the very evidence that is used in arguments to the contrary. It is quite true that many of the seventeenth-century scientists had Puritan backgrounds, but it is equally true that many of the sixteenth-century Puritans had Roman Catholic backgrounds, and yet, no matter how much of a "medievalist" he may be, no one maintains that Roman Catholicism was exactly a congenial atmosphere for Puritanism. Puritans were Puritans because they left the Catholic church, not because they were brought up in it, and much the same thing can be said for the scientists and their relationship to Puritanism. If Sir Francis Bacon's attitude toward science is to be represented as Puritan because he had a Puritan mother, Lenin may doubtless be characterized as the personification of

[34] Richard Greenham, *The Workes of Richard Greenham* (5th and last ed.; London, 1612), pp. 365–67, 298–99.

[35] Richard Rogers, *Seaven Treatises Leading and Guiding to True Happiness* (London, 1610; first published in 1603), p. 118.

czarist ideals.[36] Indeed, the striking thing about seventeenth-century scholars and literati is that, with a few exceptions, such as Milton, nearly all of those who had any Puritan background abandoned that position before they had gone far along the scholarly road. Lancelot Andrewes is one example to which we have already alluded. The Ussher-Ward-Morton-Bedell group of young Cambridge students, whose correspondence fills so many of the volumes of the Tanner manuscripts in the Bodleian, with one accord forsook Puritanism when pressure was applied in the early years of James's reign. As Puritan sprigs at Cambridge they might, with some soul-searchings, twiddle a globe or inspect a crocodile, but, when their serious work was done, they were avowed Anglicans, and in the 1640's they sent their college plate to the King or otherwise demonstrated their royalism in equally unmistakable fashion. The men of their generation who remained true to their Puritan ideals, men such as Johnson, John Smith, and Ames had little time for studying Anglo-Saxon or comparative anatomy. The neo-Platonists came from Puritan Emmanuel, but the best and most moderate apologete for Puritanism in this field grants that they were of a different breed from the men who founded Harvard and so are not to be reckoned as Puritans.[37]

[36] Robert K. Merton, "Puritanism, Pietism, and Science," *Sociological Review*, XXVIII (1936), 4; Dorothy Stimson, "Puritanism and the New Philosophy in Seventeenth Century England," *Bulletin of the Institute of the History of Medicine* (Johns Hopkins), III (1935), 321–34.

[37] Morison, *op. cit.*, pp. 99–100. In spite of this and similar concessions (*ibid.*, pp. 44, 57–59, 157–60), it must be questioned whether the obviously fair-minded effort of the author of this important work to rise above the natural inclination to find modern liberal ideals attending at the birth of his alma mater has always been successful. It seems incredible that the St. John's men in 1597 would take the trouble to put on a play ridiculing Puritan Stupidoes if there were none at Cambridge (pp. 44–45). In similar passages the author appears unduly to minimize the moral and religious side of Puritanism while magnifying its intellectual aspects (cf. the placing of Trinity before Emmanual as an influence on the New England institution, the interpretation of Mildmay's declaration about his foundation as expressing a wish for scholars as distinct from preachers [p. 94], and the emphasis on learning as an end separate from the provision of an educated ministry at Harvard [pp. 1, 7, 247]). The fact that many Harvard alumni did not enter the ministry is obviously not a clear indication of the wishes of the founders, any more than the fact that all of Mildmay's Emmanuel fellowships eventually became susceptible of an indefinite tenure is in that case. Would it not be better to say only that the education of ministers was the predominant rather than merely the immediate purpose?

It is probable that part of the superiority of the Royalists, whether religiously Anglicans or "neuterists," in the field of science is to be explained by their political power and hence their ability to provide the necessary revenue and leisure for scholarly research. But neither in Scotland nor in Massachusetts, where at least some political power was in their hands, did the Puritans do much better than they did in England. They had the desire for a "learned" ministry but not for a general program of scholarly or scientific research.

But these criticisms must not be made without a backward glance at the splendid Puritan ideal of a unified intelligentsia and the fine work done by the party in promoting universal elementary education, however limited in scope and purpose that education might be. Indeed, the Puritan attitude toward learning may be said to be typical of Puritanism as a whole. Though it had a vague sense of the glories of the humanistic liberalism of the Renaissance, it did not come up to modern standards in these fields. But it compensated for such deficiencies by its loyalty to certain medieval values, now all too neglected, and by the new enthusiasm which it generated for spreading and perpetuating them.

APPENDIXES

APPENDIX I

Hooper's Lost Argument on the Vestments

HOOPER'S treatise on the vestments, presented to the Council on October 3, 1550, was extant at the time of the composition of Glocester Ridley's life of his illustrious ancestor. In that volume, which appeared in 1763, a short section of the original document is given.[1] It has since disappeared, and all efforts made by the Parker Society editors and others to trace it have been unavailing. Its outline can be fairly well reconstructed, however, from Ridley's "Reply,"[2] thanks to the sixteenth-century practice of answering an opponent paragraph by paragraph. The argument was in the form of the following syllogism:

Major Premise: All things to be required in the Christian church are either ordained in the Bible or are things indifferent [pp. 375–76].

Minor Premise: Vestments are neither ordained in the Bible for use in the Christian church nor are they things indifferent [p. 376].

Conclusion: Therefore they are not to be required in the Christian church.

To his major premise Hooper attached a definition of a thing indifferent as one of which "the use be not profitable or the non-use be not harmful" (p. 376). To the minor premise he attached four notes by way of proof that vestments are not things indifferent:

1. Things indifferent are to be grounded on scripture [p. 376].

2. Or, if not in scripture, they are things to be left free to be done or not done as each individual's conscience may direct [pp. 377–78], provided they are not in conflict with the Christian faith. ["Doubtful how the parties can stand together."—Ridley, *ibid.*]

[1] Glocester Ridley, *Life of Bishop Ridley* (London, 1763), p. 316.

[2] John Bradford, *Writings*, ed. Townsend (2 vols.; Cambridge: Parker Society, 1848–53), II, 375–95.

3. "They must have a manifest and open utility, known in the church" [p. 378]. ["But how agreeth this note with his saying in the first that a thing indifferently used profiteth not. . . . . How shall he agree with another that cannot agree with himself?"—Ridley, *ibid.*]

4. Things indifferent should be instituted in the church with lenity and without tyranny. "Things indifferent, degenerated, and abused are no more indifferent" [p. 378].

Then followed three political and personal arguments, the first a suggestion to the magistrates that "the matter pertaineth nothing unto them," the second "to warn them of their foes," and the third "a promise of maintenance unto death" (p. 378).

Reverting to theological reasoning, Hooper expanded his four notes. To prove that the vestments could not be ordained in the Bible for use in the Christian church, he maintained that "they show the pharisaical superstitition and priesthood of Aaron." That is, they were ceremonies foreshadowing the coming of Christ and abolished by the advent. Passages from the Church Fathers were adduced in proof of this point and of the fact that vestments were unknown in the early church (pp. 380–84). To the second note he added the argument that things cannot be indifferent which God forbids. But Paul has said that, if one builds again the things destroyed, he proves himself a transgressor (Gal. 2:18), and in the Book of Hebrews it is clearly demonstrated that the Aaronic priesthood has been abolished in the priesthood of Christ. Thus it is sinful to retain the ceremonies. Here belongs the passage cited by Glocester Ridley, ending

the Aaronic priests used vestments in their ministry because the truth of their priesthood, Christ himself, had not come: but Christ, when himself was to be sacrificed, was divested of all his vestments, showing his priesthood by this, that, because he was the truth itself, he now no longer had need of any veils or shadows.[3] ["Oh! this were a jolly argument for the sect of the Adamians, of which Ephanius saith that they assembled themselves, both men and women, naked, in the time of their divine service, to resemble the innocency of Adam and Eve in paradise."—Ridley, p. 385.]

To the third note Hooper added an argument whose outlines are not clear from Ridley's answer (pp. 385–86). On the fourth

[3] *Ibid.*, p. 373.

note, instead of expanding on the charge of tyranny, the bishop-elect emphasized the Catholic character of the vestments, asserting that he dared "as well defend the altar-stone, holy-bread, and holy-water, yea and images too, with as good authority as they defend the vestments" (p. 388).

Finally, he considers certain objections and gives his answers. Not all of this argument is clear, but he charges the bishops with considering the vestments necessary (pp. 389–90), and maintains afresh that all church ceremonies must be justified by scripture (pp. 390–91) ["This sentence . . . . taketh away the most part of all due ceremonial circumstances. . . . . For how is it possible (to) receive the holy communion but thou must either sit, stand, kneel or lay? . . . . But none of all these circumstances are commanded in scripture. . . . . Wherefore, if the said sentence were true . . . . then can we not execute Christ's institutions."—Ridley, pp. 390–91]. He denies the allegation that the change from Saturday to Sunday observance cannot be justified by scripture. His explanation of Paul's vow is that, though a Jewish ceremony, it was justified by scripture ["Here methinketh that the writer hath forgotten what he said before, that the vestments were Aaronical, which if they be granted to be, then this answer maketh all against himself."— Ridley, p. 392]. There follow charges of papistry and persecution, an explanation that the verse "to the pure all things are pure [clean]" (Titus 1:15) applies only to things accounted unclean by the Jews, and a preposterous claim that Luther was on his side (pp. 392–93). The treatise ends with the concession that the king may establish ceremonies for the church, provided they are not of the Catholic variety (pp. 394–95).

The contradictory nature of many of Hooper's remarks is evident from a casual survey of this outline. The confusion was worse confounded by the Zwinglian's claim, in answer to his third hypothetical objection, that he had proved that the "vestments appointed" were things indifferent (p. 392), apparently quite the contrary of his main thesis. It is not surprising that his adversaries accused him of holding two different opinions on this subject.[4] Apparently, what he meant by this statement can best be understood by emphasising the word "appointed." In other words, Hooper maintained that the regulation about vestments was a matter of indifference, to be observed or not, as the individual's conscience dictated.

In his reply, Ridley admitted that the vestments were the same as those used by the Catholics and in some instances by the Aaronic priesthood, and also admitted that they were not used in the early church. But he denied that the scripture must be the only guide in matters indifferent, such as he maintained the vestments to be. He cited Augustine's argument against the Donatist—who held a position similar to Hooper's—that the church must change its ceremonies to accommodate its message to changing times. The use of vestments antedated the rise of the papacy, and, even if they were once Aaronical and later put to superstitious uses, they might now be employed in a pure way, as a man might now shave his head for health's sake without implying the making of a Jewish vow (p. 385). Since to the pure all things were pure, the vestments must be things indifferent, and therefore the magistrates, who were bound to regulate Christian worship, might properly require their use.

[4] Burcher to Bullinger, December 28, 1550, *Original Letters Relative to the English Reformation*, ed. Robinson (2 vols.; Cambridge: Parker Society, 1846–47), p. 674.

APPENDIX II

Terminology

NOWHERE has party animosity left a deeper scar on Puritan historiography than in the confusion of terminology which it has introduced. Names spitefully invented or redirected—like Whig, Tory, and Methodist—have in time become respectable. But, before they achieved this general recognition, they have been understood in different senses by different people, and the situation has been further complicated by the attempt on the part of persons thus attacked to popularize less opprobrious epithets for themselves. The historian who endeavors to conduct a tour through the Puritan period consequently owes the reader some explanation of his terms.

At first glance the simplest solution might seem to be a return to sixteenth-century usage, an effort to employ only the names then in vogue. But this not only would mean some difficult rulings on points of Elizabethan speech but would result in practices strange, if not largely unintelligible, to the modern reader. To follow this rule, for example, would mean the exclusion of the word "Protestant" from the account of English affairs before the time of Mary,[1] and would clutter the pages with such archaisms as "gospeller" and "Allobrogensian" (Genevan). Since, as Hooker remarked, a thing must exist before it is named, the party historian can scarcely avoid employing certain conventional terminology when describing events in advance of its original application.

To follow what the writer might consider the most logical

[1] R. W. Dixon, *History of the Church of England from the Abolition of the Roman Jurisdiction* (3d rev. ed.; 6 vols.; Oxford, 1895), V, 262 and 338; cf. the *New English Dictionary* (hereafter cited as *NED*).

usage would only multiply confusion, since part of our trouble
has come from this practice. Loose constructionists have struggled with strict constructionists, each new writer trying to in-
validate his predecessor's use of terms, until the layman is left
in a daze.

I have therefore had recourse to the arbitrary practice of following what I consider the best current historical usage—a procedure perhaps not inappropriate when treating of those who
set such store by the example of the "best reformed." A volume
could be written on the history of these terms. I shall content
myself with suggesting their original meaning and explaining
the sense adopted in this work.

The term "Puritan" first came into use during the Elizabethan vestiarian controversy in the winter of 1567–68. It was probably used originally by the adherents of the Separatist groups
to indicate the thoroughness of their reformation. "Unspotted
lambs" and the "stainless religion" were analogous designations
in use by them at the time.[2] The term was promptly taken up
by their opponents and given a new meaning which greatly
offended at least the more moderate supporters of further reform. Interpreted as an English translation of Cathari or
Catharans, the Novatians' name for themselves,[3] it harmonized
nicely with the current practice of dubbing opponents heretics,
and adherents of old worn-out heresies at that.[4] Since Donatist
and Novatian were related sects, we occasionally meet the
phrase "Austin's [Augustine's] Puritans,"[5] and Augustine's ar-

[2] *Spanish Calendar*, II, 7; John Stow, "Memoranda," in James Gairdner (ed.), *Three Fifteenth Century Chronicles* ("Camden Society: New Series," Vol. XXVIII [London, 1880]), p. 143; cf. A. F. Scott Pearson, *Thomas Cartwright and Elizabethan Puritanism* (London, 1925), p. 18. Though it is impossible to date Stow exactly, and De Silva's statement comes through the Spanish, the latter fits Stow so exactly that I think we are justified in assuming the use of the term four years earlier than the date Pearson gives for its prominent use.

[3] John Whitgift, *Works*, ed. Ayre (3 vols.; Cambridge: Parker Society, 1851–53), I, 171.

[4] The term "Anabaptist" was thus applied to the extreme reformers on the Conti-nent by opponents anxious to bring them under the Roman law, which prohibited rebaptizing (see above, p. 16), Heylin's title for his history of the Presbyterians, *Aerius redivivus*, is a seventeenth-century example of this controversial amenity.

[5] *Puritan Manifestoes*, eds. Frere and Douglas (London, 1907), p. 6; *The Seconde Parte of a Register*, ed. Peel (2 vols.; Cambridge, 1915), I, 84, 117.

guments against the Donatists were frequently applied to the Puritans. This connection with the Donatists had the further advantage of linking the English Puritans with the Continental Anabaptists, since the Donatists were the original Anabaptists. In the mouths of their adversaries there was also about the term a holier-than-thou flavor which added to its effectiveness as a taunt. For twenty years the party champions therefore indignantly rejected the Puritan title and even tried to pin it on their Anglican opponents, as being the true schismatics.[6] Not until the time of Marprelate[7] did a Puritan voluntarily assume the title, and then not without preliminary protest. That author and the Separatists both used it then as referring to nonconformists, excluding the Brownists.[8]

In this volume I have chosen to follow good current practice as exemplified in the works of G. M. Trevelyan, who makes the term "Puritanism" signify "the religion of all those who wished either to 'purify' the usage of the established church from taint of popery or to worship separately by forms so 'purified.' "[9] As he points out, neither creed nor theory of church government was a distinguishing feature. There were Episcopalian, Presbyterian, and Congregational Puritans. Bibliolatry, a tendency to individualistic interpretation of their authority, a wariness of gaiety, and a passionate love of civic freedom and moral earnestness are other common-denominator principles, in his opinion. In dealing with the Tudor Puritans, I have perhaps varied the interpretation somewhat and have tried to bring out certain medieval features, such as their economic outlook and clericalism, but in general I am using the term in Trevelyan's sense.

"Precisian" and "Disciplinarian" were epithets used in the Elizabethan period as synonymous with "Puritan," but they

[6] Whitgift, *op. cit.*, I, 110, 172; *Seconde Parte*, I, 234; Cartwright to Hatton, n.d., in Pearson, *op. cit.*, p. 440.

[7] *The Marprelate Tracts*, ed. Pierce (London, 1911), pp. 22, 242, 245, 255, 257.

[8] Cf. J. Robinson, quoted in A. H. Drysdale's *History of the Presbyterians in England* (London, 1889), p. 5 n.; William Bradshaw, *English Puritanisme: Containing the Maine Opinions of the Rigidest Sort of Those That Are Called Puritans in the Realme of England* (*s.l.*, 1605).

[9] *England under the Stuarts* (16th ed.; London, 1933), pp. 60–71.

attained no great currency either in later party terminology or in historiographical usage.

"Dissenter" was a term which came into use in the Restoration period to take the place of "Puritan," which had been discredited in the popular mind by the events of the Cromwellian era. It was intended to apply to all those dissenting from the Anglican church. Like "recusant," it logically included both Catholic and Protestant, but in practice it was confined to one party only. It thus supplanted "Puritan" in current usage. It cannot, however, be used as the precise equivalent, since, as we have seen, there were Episcopalian Puritans who did not break away from the state church.

"Nonconformist" was the early seventeenth-century term for the Puritans who would neither subscribe nor separate. It was therefore applied to both Presbyterian and Episcopalian Puritans. By some modern historians it has also been used to designate Elizabethan Puritans who in that lax age remained within the ranks of the official organization without conforming. After 1662 the term was used as the equivalent of "Dissenter," since the "Nonconformists" were put out of the church and were forced to dissent thereafter.

The term "Presbyterian" comes from $\pi\rho\epsilon\sigma\beta\dot{\upsilon}\tau\epsilon\rho\sigma\varsigma$, the Greek word for "elder," and, as a party title, of course, refers to those who desired a system of church government on the Genevan model, with ascending hierarchical committees of elders, or $\pi\rho\epsilon\sigma\beta\dot{\upsilon}\tau\epsilon\rho\sigma\iota$, in control. In the form "presbyteriall" (replacing adjectival variants of such terms as "seignory" or "elder") it is found in English usage by 1592 and has undergone little or no change. When applied to English church parties, it designates a division within the Puritan movement. All English Presbyterians were Puritans but all Puritans were not Presbyterians.

"Independent" designates all those who desire that each congregation should be legally independent of every other, that there should be no ecclesiastical authority higher than the individual church, whether that body exercises its powers in a purely democratic fashion in congregational meeting or through a committee of officials similar to that on the first level in the

Presbyterian system. In the civil-war period "Congregational" was sometimes used as the equivalent, and after the Restoration, when the Independents were in ill repute, it was popularized by Calamy and others as a less offensive substitute. Cotton Mather in 1692 seems first to have put the form "Congregationalist" in circulation. "Independent" and "Congregational" or "Congregationalist" are therefore interchangeable terms, the duplication being due solely to party passions.[10]

"Separatist" was used as early as 1608 to designate those Independents who wished to separate from the established church. This meant freedom from the control of the secular government and the loss of its financial support; it involved, in other words, the status of a modern free church, like the status of any American church.

Conversely, those Independents who wished to retain communion with the Anglican church, and in time supplant it as a state-supported and state-regulated institution, are called "Non-Separatist." This is an awkward word and, in view of the modern Congregational trend toward associations (virtual presbyteries), conferences (synods), general (national) assemblies, and country-wide discipline, "semi-Presbyterian" would seem more logical. But "Non-Separatist" is now hallowed by usage,[11] and so is accepted here.

"Brownist" was a term applied to all Independents indiscriminately in their early days. Although there was an earlier Browne connected with the movement, the word is first heard after the rise of Robert Browne[12] and is therefore derived from his name. Since in his important early career he was a Separatist Independent, the term, if used, should be employed in that sense.

In the last century, when persecution was in even more ill repute than now, the historians of the Plymouth Colony,

[10] H. McLaghlan, *Alexander Gordon* (Manchester, 1932), p. 110; *NED.*

[11] Champlin Burrage, *The Early English Dissenters* (2 vols.; Cambridge, 1912), Perry Miller, *Orthodoxy in Massachusetts* (Cambridge, Mass., 1933).

[12] Albert Peel, *The First Congregational Churches* (Cambridge, 1920), p. 48; *NED.*

headed by John A. Goodwin,[13] turned a popular expression into
a party designation and substituted "Pilgrim" for "Puritan" in
speaking of the Old Colony, in order to dissociate their fore-
fathers from the Salem witch-hangers. "Puritan" was confined
to the Bay Colony Independents. This usage made "Pilgrim"
and "Puritan" roughly the equivalent of Separatist and Non-
Separatist. It is not to be encouraged, for several reasons. It
empties the term "Puritan" of most of its traditional content;
there was really not so much difference between the two colonies
in the matter of church-state polity; and the Bostonians made
much the same pilgrimage as their southern neighbors.

"Anabaptist" (rebaptizer) was the term applied to the extreme reformers on the Continent who rejected infant baptism.
Thus it was applied by their opponents to the seventeenth-
century English followers of John Smith and Thomas Helwys.
These sectaries, however, preferred the designation of "baptized believers," and so by the middle of the century the form
"Baptist" was applied to them. Since the English Baptists grew
directly out of Independent bodies—though not without considerable Continental influence in the case of Smith's General
Baptists—the distinction between "Anabaptist" and "Baptist"
is historically sound and can be justified on that ground. Because
the Baptists were separatist in their polity, they may be regarded as a subspecies of that larger classification.

"Arian," "Socinian," and "Unitarian" were terms for those
sectaries who denied the full divinity of Christ. Though often
used interchangeably, there should be a distinction. "Arian"
properly refers to those who believe that Christ is a secondary
deity, but one who has existed since before the creation though not
co-eternally with the Father. "Socinian" applies to the followers of Faustus Socinus, who thought of Christ as a man who became divine, and "Unitarian" to those emphasizing the unity of
the Godhead to the extent of denying any divinity to Christ
beyond a superlative degree of that sort obtainable by all
human beings. Originally "Unitarian" was an epithet applied

[13] *The Puritan Conspiracy against the Pilgrim Fathers* (Boston, 1883); *The Pilgrim
Republic* (Boston, 1886).

to the Socinians by their enemies in the effort to link them with the Mohammedans, for whom this term was sometimes used.[14]

Because of the modern assertion by the High Church Anglicans of a right to share the title "Catholic," I have frequently labeled those who accept the authority of the papacy as "Roman Catholics" to distinguish them from their Greek and Anglican rivals.

The following diagram will illustrate the distinctions discussed and put the parties in their proper relation to one another.

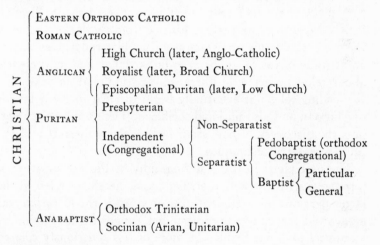

JEW, TURK, PAGAN

WORLDLY, "FLAT ATHEIST," PROFANE*

---

* Nominally these usually belong, for safety's sake, to the branch of the Christian church currently in power.

[14] A. Gordon, "The Tercentennial of a Name," *Addresses Biographical and Historical* (London, 1922), p. 51.

APPENDIX III

The Historiography of Puritanism[1]

THE historians of Puritanism constitute a microcosm. In their little world may be observed the operation of all the forces which have affected the intellectual history of western Europe from the Reformation to the present. On this tiny stage sectarian bitterness gives way to an attitude of tolerance, or even impartiality and indifference, about religious matters; liberalism and nationalism take over the leading roles but eventually begin to yield to the demands of Marxian and also national socialism. Here too we may witness the discovery of new realms of scholarly interest and improved research techniques.

The first phase in the historiography of Puritanism was coterminous with the actual struggle and therefore ended in the latter part of the seventeenth century. In it the historian was an avowed partisan and propagandist, supporting his faction by an appeal to "facts" which he more or less consciously colored to suit his purpose. Like his associates before their judges, he told the truth and nothing but the truth, but not all the truth. Though Foxe's main purpose in his great work[2] was to attack his Roman Catholic adversaries, he was naturally aware of the internecine controversy which blighted his own chances for ecclesiastical preferment and consequently devoted some space to the controversy within the Protestant ranks. He gives the details of the persecution of Tyndale, Frith, Lambert, and

[1] Because of the close connection between Tudor and Stuart Puritanism, it has been necessary to include in this sketch works relating to both periods, though no attempt is made to deal with the details of the second.

[2] *Acts and Monuments of the Christian Church* (London, 1563), ed. Cattley and Townsend (8 vols.; London, 1837–41); ed. Pratt (8 vols.; London, 1870).

Barnes by their more conservative coreligionists. With more conscious party spirit he discusses the Edwardian vestiarian controversy, ridiculing the mathematical cap with four angles dividing the whole world into four parts.[3] Because of his partisanship, Foxe has been subjected to searching criticism by Roman and Anglo-Catholic scholars, but recent research has served to rehabilitate his reputation.[4] He was prejudiced, negligent of chronology, and incorrigibly discursive, but his documents are substantially accurate; almost all the vital part of his narrative concerning the actual martyrdoms stands up under searching analysis, and he must be accepted as well up to the average of historical accuracy in his day.

A few historical arguments were adduced early in the *Admonition* controversy,[5] but the first approach to a real party history came toward its close in 1574, when the *Narrative of the Troubles at Frankfort* was published. In all probability the man chiefly responsible was William Whittingham, though the second half, which deals with the congregationalist phase of the struggle, was compiled by someone who has succeeded in concealing his identity.[6] As an active participant in the Frankfort troubles, Whittingham felt that a narrative of events before and after the Geneva secession would aid the Puritans and discredit the Anglicans. Knox's generosity, Cox's unsavory tactics, Calvin's attitude, and the subsequent squabbles of the victorious faction are clearly brought out. Whittingham knew about Hooper's vestiarian troubles, but he represents the Frankfort disturbances as the beginning of Protestant factionalism, and all too many historians have followed him in this attitude. A passage in John Knox's *History of the Reformation*,[7] written perhaps as early as 1559, but not published until 1587, supple-

[3] 1837-41 ed., VI, 640.

[4] Walter E. Bauer, "John Foxe as Historian" (Cornell University dissertation [Ithaca, N.Y., 1932]).

[5] *Puritan Manifestoes*, eds. Frere and Douglas (London, 1907), p. 112.

[6] See above, p. 119. Christina H. Garrett (*The Marian Exiles* [Cambridge, 1938], p. 122) suggests that the author of the second half was Thomas Cole.

[7] *Works*, ed. Laing (6 vols.; Edinburgh, 1895), I, 232.

ments this narrative. Knox suppressed the name of his rival and betrayer, but this magnanimity is to be explained in part by his desire to please readers at the English court, for whom the history was designed as a kind of revolutionary apologia.[8]

A much more serious effort at Puritan historical propaganda was made by John Field and his circle. John Foxe's anti-Catholic martyrology had been a great success. It occurred to the Puritans to prepare and publish a similar account of their disputations and sufferings. Elizabeth had seen to it that their work would have no such dramatic tales as their model had contained. A bishop might be worsted in an argument, but there were no brave faces peering through billows of smoke. Furthermore, her censorship made the printing problem difficult. But Field painstakingly collected and preserved his material—much of it, like Foxe's, in the form of tracts already printed. On his death some of his papers fell into the hands of the authorities, but this propaganda did not; and some years later the party, doubtless with the assistance of Lady Bacon,[9] succeeded in having some of it published by Richard Schilders at Middelburg under the breath-taking title of *A Parte of a Register, Contayninge Sundrie Memorable Matters Written by Divers Godly and Learned in Our Time Which Stande for and Desire the Reformation of Our Church in Discipline and Ceremonies Accordinge to the Pure Worde of God and the Lawe of Our Lande.* The collapse of the classis movement, however, and possibly discouragement over the loss of most of the edition of the earlier work prevented the completion of the project. The only other contribution worthy of note in this period was Josias Nichols' moderate historical apologia[10] which appeared in 1602.

Catholic and Anglican historians also dealt with the party. In 1585 Nicholas Sander's posthumous *De origine ac progressu*

---

[8] *Ibid.*, p. xxvi. The longer paper by Knox on the events at Frankfort preserved by Calderwood (*ibid.*, IV, 40–49) was not published until 1855.

[9] *The Seconde Parte of a Register*, ed. Peel (2 vols.; Cambridge, 1915), I, 13; see above, p. 301.

[10] *Plea of the Innocent* ([London], 1602); see above, p. 320.

schismatis Anglicani[11] was published at Cologne. In it he mentions the appearance of the Puritan party about 1577[12] as a judgment of God upon the heretics and an encouragement to the Catholic cause. But he does not go into detail, thinking the narrative of Roman Catholic negotiations and sufferings more important. This furnished the pattern for future Catholic writers, and from that day to this no Roman Catholic author has treated the movement at any great length

The Anglicans were by no means so indifferent. As we have seen, one of their stock arguments against Puritanism was that it was equivalent to Anabaptism. In replying to the saucy Martin in 1589, Bishop Cooper supplied this charge with a historical background. The rival movement, he said, had gone through five stages. Beginning as a private scruple about apparel, it soon became a conviction that the Anglican costume was not a thing indifferent but a matter for public protest and political opposition. Then church government was added to the grievances; a spirit of separatism developed, which was willing to divide the church; and finally a fierce war was being waged on education, class distinctions, and property rights, under the guise of an attack on the episcopal system.[13] Four years later Bancroft implemented this thesis with many more details in a small volume of one hundred and seventy pages, entitled *Dangerous Positions*. But he correctly interpreted Puritanism as part of a much broader international movement. Accordingly, he began with Calvin and traced his influence in Geneva and Scotland before coming to England. By emphasizing the political opposition to existing rulers which attended the spread of Calvinism, he tried to substantiate the charge that Puritanism meant rebellion. He had some of the Field papers in his possession, and in the course of his police activities had also secured a number of Puritan confessions. He was thus able to give a

[11] English trans., David Lewis, *Rise and Growth of the Anglican Schism* (London, 1877).

[12] Lewis ed., p. 308.

[13] Thomas Cooper, *An Admonition to the People of England*, ed. Arber ("English Scholar's Library" [Birmingham, 1882]), pp. 119–20.

detailed account of the secret activities of the party and of the classis movement in particular, portraying the latter as another illegal conspiracy. Since most of the original papers have now disappeared, his work is an exceptionally valuable source of information. Richard Hooker, in the course of the Preface to the first four books of his *Ecclesiastical Polity*, published in 1594, gives a similar though milder and much briefer sketch of the development of Puritanism.

On the other wing, the rising Independents felt moved to turn out historical apologias also. Many of their tracts are simple narratives of events, often autobiographical, since so many of their controversies hinged on matters of personal conduct. Of these, the more important were Robert Browne's *A True and Short Declaration, Both of the Gathering . . . . together of Certaine Persons and also of the Lamentable Breach . . . . Which Fell amongst Them;*[14] the *Examinations*[15] of Barrow, Greenwood, and Penry; George Johnson's *Discourse of Some Troubles in the Banished English Church at Amsterdam;*[16] and Henoch Clapham's *Chronological Discourse.*[17]

Since in theological circles historiography and propaganda were as yet almost synonymous, a lull in the struggle meant a lull in chronicling, and there was no further contribution of note until the eve of the civil-war period. Then in 1636 the Laudian Peter Heylyn published his *History of the Sabbath*. His aim was to demonstrate that Puritan Sabbatarianism was a novelty unknown to previous generations. To that end he surveyed the whole history of Seventh Day and Sunday observance from the creation to his own time. Though he drew to some extent on the results of studies made by earlier participants in the controversy,[18] the work, in spite of its bias, was a remarkable scholarly achievement which showed a wide familiarity with the sources for biblical and ecclesiastical history. For our purposes the most noteworthy feature was the concluding section, which treated the development of English Sabbatarianism after

---

[14] *S.l.*, [1583].   [16] Amsterdam, 1603.

[15] *S.l.*, 1593.   [17] London, 1609.

[18] For his relation to Bishop Prideaux see Part II, p. 262, of his work.

the Reformation. In it Bownde was pictured as the great in-
novator from whom all the later troubles sprang. Andrewes'
contributions were passed over in discreet silence.

Most later controversialists who dealt with either side of this
subject drew on Heylyn's work, but it was never properly
answered, even in the days when his opponents had free access
to the press. The Puritan version of the development of the
general strife was, however, set forth in biographical form by
Samuel Clarke. This Presbyterian divine, who was minister of
St. Benet Fink, London, from 1643 until the Ejection,[19] found
time to put out many works of popular theology and scholarship, including an English dictionary and descriptions of Germany, Holland, and the American colonies. His historial efforts, which were the most numerous, covered such diverse subjects as the career of Hannibal, the Armada episode, and a history of Hungary. Among them were several of importance for
our purposes. A set of biographies, in two parts, entitled *The
Marrow of Ecclesiastical Historie*, came out in 1649–50. In 1651
there was published a *General Martyrologie*, to which was attached the *Lives of Sundry Modern English Divines*. A collection
of the *Lives of Ten Eminent Divines* came out in 1662, and when,
in 1677, an enlarged edition of the *General Martyrologie* was
issued, with thirty-two lives attached, these ten were incorporated. Lastly, there was a posthumous publication, *The Lives
of Sundry Eminent Persons in This Later Age*, which appeared
in 1683. Clarke borrowed freely, and some of his efforts are
merely abridgments or reprints of excerpts from earlier works,
such as Foxe, Holland's *Herwologia*, funeral sermons, or small
separate lives. Indeed most of his lives are acknowledged to be
by other hands.[20] The names of many of the original authors are
attached to their works or given in the introductory epistles.
Nevertheless, Clarke implies in his prefaces that he often added
to these works from his own knowledge,[21] and some he con-

---

[19] Clarke's "Life," in *Lives of Sundry Eminent Persons in This Latter Age* (London,
1683; separate pagination), p. 11.

[20] "Baxter to the Reader," *ibid.*, sig. A, fol. 4.

[21] *Marrow*, Part I, sig. b, fol. 4(v); Part II, sig. aaa, fol. 2.

structed by his own researches.[22] He solicited information wherever available and used his prefaces and even the biographies
themselves to advertise for more. He was no stylist and often
published without alteration whatever accounts relatives and
admiring friends might choose to send in,[23] but to his efforts we
owe most of our knowledge of the personal and human side of
early Puritanism.

Between Heylyn and Clarke stood genial Thomas Fuller. For
the next generation the historiography of Puritanism was the
story of the works of these three men and their interrelations.
Fuller's inimitable style has kept his works alive to the present
day. Though the disturbances of the civil wars cost him the
income from his rich Salisbury prebend, he retained a sane and
moderate view of the ecclesiastical scene, which was a harbinger
of better things to come. In 1651 he also put out a collection of
biographies, *Abel Redivivus or the Dead yet Speaking*. Clarke's
Marrow of the year previous had contained a life of William
Perkins[24] which, except for the last paragraph, was merely an
abridgment of Fuller's sketch of that worthy, included in his
Holy State in 1642.[25] Fuller now returned the compliment with a
fulsomeness of the sincerest form of flattery, which illustrates
the free and easy literary manners of those pre-copyright days.
After detailing the authorship of some of his pieces, he adds,
"The rest the stationer got transcribed out of Mr. Holland and
other authors."[26] In his *General Martyrologie* of the same year
Clarke gives an indignant clarification:

There is lately come forth a book called *Abel Redivivus* . . . . wherein there
are three score and nine lives printed *verbatim* out of my first part of the

[22] Certainly, his own biography and those of his wife (*Lives of Sundry Eminent Persons*, pp. 152–65, second pagination) and father (*Lives* attached to *General Martyrologie*
[1677], pp. 127–31) are by Clarke.

[23] Baxter (see above, n. 20) is too strong on this point, in view of Clarke's own statements and the evidence referred to above, but he is worth quoting: "He did not make
the histories but take them made by faithful acquaintance of the dead. And he was
not to patch or paint the dead nor to add anything of his own, but to deliver naked
truth." In the same passage Baxter says, "I was going to get from old Sam Hildersam
some additions to his father Arthur's life, but his death frustrated me."

[24] Part I, pp. 414–17.

[25] Pp. 88–93.   [26] "Epistle to the Reader," sig. A, fol. 4.

Marrow of Ecclesiastical History and divers more with very little variation; which I thought fit to give the reader notice of, that so he may not be deceived in buying the same thing twice.[27]

In 1655, however, Fuller published his *Church History of Britain from the Birth of Jesus Christ until the Year MDCXL-VIII* which fully vindicated his claim to independence of mind and interpretation. While his chronology rivals Foxe's for vagueness and only the most general outline of events can be gathered from his work, it is entitled to the honor of being the first connected story of events in ecclesiastical circles to appear since the middle of Elizabeth's reign. On our subject the author made reasonably good use of what sources he had—scattered letters, the works of Foxe, Whittingham, Bancroft, and of such secular authors as Holinshed and Camden. Furthermore, too much cannot be said for the breadth of view which he, like his contemporary Clarendon, showed in describing events which had so seriously affected his own fortunes. Though his moderate Anglicanism is generally discernible, he does not come far short of the ideal he set for himself in introducing the story of the Frankfort troubles:

This I dare say: if the reader takes no more delight in perusing than I in penning so doleful a subject, he will show little mirth in his face and feel less joy in his heart. However we will be somewhat large and wholly impartial in relating this sorrowful accident; the rather, because the penknives of that age are grown into swords in ours and their writings laid the foundations of the fightings nowadays.[28]

This mildness was too much for Heylyn, now almost blind but, like Milton, still busy. He thought the wounds of the church called for vinegar as well as oil. After a preliminary blast of some two hundred and seventy pages to that effect,[29] he composed a detailed history of the Reformation,[30] and also one of Presbyterianism[31] which amplified the old Anglican thesis

[27] Sig. A, fol. 8.   [28] Ed. Brewer (6 vols.; Oxford, 1845), IV, 208–9.

[29] *Examen historicum* (London, 1659).

[30] *Ecclesia restaurata or the History of the Reformation of the Church of England* (London, 1661).

[31] *Aerius redivivus or the History of the Presbyterians* (posthumously published by his son Henry [London, 1670]).

that Puritanism and rebellion went hand in hand. Though he tells us that he used the Cottonian Library and examined many original records, he neglects the formality of footnotes, as Burnet scornfully observed, and thus makes it difficult to follow his tracks clearly. But he did succeed in constructing a somewhat more detailed narrative than Fuller's, though the acid in which he dipped his pen prevented his works from enjoying any great popularity.

As the seventeenth century waned, theological passions cooled somewhat. Though party purposes were still kept in view, the antiquarian movement was reviving, and a new emphasis on the discovery and use of original sources made its appearance among historians of Puritanism. Of this new school, the Scotch Whig and Anglican ecclesiastic Gilbert Burnet was the first great representative in our field. Persuaded to answer a translation of Sander's work on the Anglican schism which appeared at Paris in 1677, he wrote a *History of the Reformation* which came out in two parts, in 1679 and 1681, respectively. Each had an appendix of documents gleaned from the Cottonian Library, the episcopal registers, the state papers, and smaller private collections. In the second volume he alluded to the Frankfort troubles, naturally giving the Anglicans somewhat the better treatment. But for the purposes of this study his greatest service was the discovery of the Bullinger correspondence at Zurich, with its many letters relating to English affairs. Passing through the Swiss city in 1685, he saw the manuscripts in the local archives. He tried without success to borrow them, but succeeded in having copies made of some of the most important.[32] With these and other newly acquired material he was equipped to undertake a new edition of his work. But, instead of doing so, he brought out a supplementary volume containing the various additions he wished to make. This appeared in 1713, with the valuable documents in the appendix, when the author was Bishop of Salisbury. Though his original intention was to end the story with the Elizabethan settlement, in this volume he added a treatment of the vestiarian

---

[32] *History of the Reformation*, ed. Pocock (6 vols.; Oxford, 1865), III, 467–69.

controversy of the following years, composed almost exclusively of the Zurich letters.

Meanwhile other great manuscript collections were being put under contribution for similar purposes. An Essex clergyman and antiquarian named John Strype had for one of his parishioners the great grandson of Sir Michael Hicks, Burghley's secretary. The family archives contained a good part of the Cecil correspondence. Strype gained access to this, borrowed most of it, and, when his benefactor subsequently became insane, neglected the formality of returning it. From it and other less important material which he assembled he fashioned an awesome series of Tudor histories and biographies, almost exclusively ecclesiastical.[33] Like Burnet, Strype was mildly Anglican in his point of view, but his lack of style and his devotion to the sources kept his personal opinion from obtruding itself to any great extent. He used the annalistic method, but within the yearly limits he neglected chronology and arranged matters in very rough topical fashion, so that in his topsy-turvy world cause often follows effect. Confusion is worse confounded in his story of the Reformation before 1558 by his practice of putting in his *Memorials* only supplementary matters not to be found in Burnet's work. Furthermore, he had little critical sense and was frequently inaccurate in the transcription of sources. But for all his faults he must be loved because, after his fashion, he put in print materials which otherwise must have been virtually inaccessible, though in time many of them found their way into the Harleian and Lansdowne collections and so into the British Museum. His text contains long extracts from sources, and for nearly every page of text there is a page of appendix reproducing

---

[33] *Memorials of Thomas Cranmer* (2 vols. in 1; London, 1694); *Life of the Learned Sir Thomas Smith* (London, 1698); *Historical Collections of the Life and Acts of John Aylmer* (London, 1701); *The Life of the Learned Sir John Cheke* (London, 1705); *Annals of the Reformation in England under Elizabeth* (2 vols. in 1; London, 1708–9; continued in 4-vol. eds., 1725–31, 1731–37); *The History of the Life and Acts of Edmund Grindal* (2 vols. in 1; London, 1710); *The Life and Acts of Matthew Parker* (2 vols. in 1; London, 1711); *The Life and Acts of John Whitgift* (2 vols. in 1; London, 1717–18); *Ecclesiastical Memorials Relating Chiefly to Religion . . . . under King Henry VIII, King Edward VI, and Queen Mary I* (3 vols.; London, 1721). These works were reprinted in a nineteen-volume set in the early part of the last century (Oxford, 1812–24) and supplemented by a two-volume *General Index* compiled by R. F. Laurence (Oxford, 1828).

letters, speeches, and draft proposals of all sorts, a rich and as yet unexhausted mine of information, however much caution must be used in working it.

Before Strype had quite finished his task, his materials were used by Jeremy Collier, who composed the first full-length history of the English church to appear since the time of Fuller.[34] Like Fuller, Collier wrote under great provocation, for he was a Non-juror and had suffered much for his cause. But he too managed to control his feelings, and, though his point of view is made clear throughout, he tells a sober, orderly tale. He prints a few additional documents, but he was not particularly interested in the Puritan side of his story and so need not detain us further.

On the Dissenter side there was a parallel historical movement. A little group of Baxter's Nonconformist associates and successors in London carried on the work which his older friend Clarke had begun.[35] While Calamy was qualifying as the martyrologist of the Ejection with his biographical studies,[36] plans were under way for a more comprehensive history of Puritanism. Roger Morrice, Vicar of Duffield in Derbyshire and chaplain to Denzil Lord Holles, was one of the ejected in 1662. Settling in London as a merchant, he prospered to such an extent that he could afford the luxury of amanuenses. With such assistance he undertook to collect materials and produce the desired work. From the son of a Norwich Nonconformist

[34] *Ecclesiastical History of Great Britain*, Vols. I and II (London, 1708 and 1714); edited, with a life of the author, by Thomas Lathbury (9 vols.; London, 1852).

[35] See Albert Peel's Introduction to *Seconde Parte of a Register*, I, 1–27, esp. p. 19; and his "Richard Baxter, Roger Morrice and Matthew Sylvester," *Transactions of the Congregational Historical Society*, V (1911–12), 298–300.

[36] *Reliquiae Baxterianae* (London, 1696). Matthew Sylvester's name appears as the editor, but most of the work was done by Calamy (see Alexander Gordon's careful account of him in the *DNB* and his "Calamy as a Biographer," *Transactions of the Congregational Historical Society*, VI [1913–15], 233–47). *The Abridgment of Mr. Baxter's History* (London, 1702; 2d ed., London, 1714); *Account of the Ministers . . . . Ejected* (London, 1713); *Continuation of the Account* (2 vols.; London, 1727). The latter three (4 vols.) were edited and condensed into two volumes with additions by Samuel Palmer in 1775 under the title of *The Nonconformists' Memorial* (2d and improved ed.; 3 vols.; London, 1802–3); re-edited and amplified by Arnold G. Matthews as *Calamy Revised* (Oxford, 1934).

minister, who had in turn obtained them from Sir John Higham, a Puritan M.P. of Elizabeth's time, he secured the manuscripts prepared in the 1590's for the conclusion of the *Register*[37] and filled numerous folios with notes and preliminary drafts. The amelioration of party feeling at this time is illustrated by the fact that he was on friendly terms with Strype, and he seems to have made use of the Anglican's papers. He also secured copies of additional Zurich letters and used the manuscripts of William Petyt of the Middle Temple, keeper of the records in the Tower. But most of his notes are taken from Fuller, Heylyn, Burnet, and other secondary works. If we may judge by the false starts he made, the task was rather beyond him. Yet, when he died, the project was not dropped. His manuscripts were preserved, apparently by his friend Dr. Williams, in whose library, so generously endowed and made accessible to the public, they are now housed. Morrice's fellow-antiquary, John Quick, made further collections, and Quick's son-in-law, John Evans, arranged with his friend Daniel Neal, a Congregationalist minister in London, to complete the work. Evans was to do the portion down to 1640 and Neal the remainder to 1689. Evans died in 1730 with his task uncompleted, but Neal carried out the whole plan without seeing Evans' draft.[38] His four volumes appeared one after another during the period from 1732 to 1738, under the title of *The History of the Puritans*. Each was greeted with a full-length critical review of several hundred pages from the other side, mostly the work of the Cambridge antiquary, Zachary Grey.[39] Neal came off rather well in these

---

[37] "Chronological Account," II (Morrice MS I), 617 (8). This is a discovery made by Miss Edna Bibby, who reports it in detail on page 155 of her Manchester University dissertation (1929), "The Puritan Classical Movement of Elizabeth's Reign."

[38] Preface to Vol. I (p. x; 1837 ed.).

[39] Isaac Maddox, *A Vindication of the Government, Doctrine and Worship of the Church of England* (London, 1733). Grey supplied most of the material for this volume (see *DNB* art., "Maddox," by A. Gordon). Z. Grey, *An Impartial Examination of the Second Volume* (London, 1736); *Impartial Examination of the Third Volume* (London, 1737); *Impartial Examination of the Fourth Volume* (London, 1739.)

Neal replied to Maddox in *A Review of the Principal Facts Objected to the First Volume* (London, 1734), which Grey answered in *A Review of Mr. Daniel Neal's History of the Puritans* (Cambridge, 1744). The later criticisms were handled in part by Joshua Toulmin in his edition of Neal's work in 1797.

encounters. He easily disproved the more sweeping partisan charges, of which perhaps the most interesting was that of disturbing the peace by resurrecting old controversies. He did not claim to be infallible, and he cheerfully accepted correction in matters of fact, citing Wharton's wholesome observations to Strype, that

the commission of errors in writing any history of times past being altogether unavoidable ought not to detract from the credit of the history or the merits of the historian, unless it be accompanied with immoderate ostentation or unhandsome reflections on the errors of others.[40]

Neal's work is a landmark in Puritan history for several reasons. He was a man of his century and wholeheartedly accepted the theory of religious toleration. He therefore made no effort to excuse or justify the persecuting tendencies of his party in its earlier stages. Furthermore, though a clergyman himself, he was an anticlerical, believing in the separation of church and state and preaching the doctrine that ecclesiastics should confine their efforts to the spiritual realm. Through him these points of view entered the stream of Puritan historiography in which they have long been predominant. Neal also made great use of Morrice's transcript of the Field manuscripts, some of which had so long been awaiting publication to complete the ill-fated *Register*. Though he was not always accurate and critical in his use of this material,[41] he gave the world the flavor of it and many illustrative samples. Lastly, his narrative was well organized, coherent, and readable if not brilliant—a structure which has stood the test of time. Revised, edited, and re-edited,[42] it remained the standard work on the subject until the

[40] Neal, *Review*, p. 60.

[41] Peel, *Seconde Parte*, I, 20–22.

[42] Corrected edition (2 vols.; London, 1754); edited, revised, corrected, and enlarged by J. Toulmin (5 vols.; Bath, 1793–97); reprinted (London, 1822); abridged by E. Parsons (2 vols.; London and Leeds, 1811); Toulmin's edition revised (3 vols; London, 1837), etc. The last mentioned is the edition cited in this work.

Neal practically ignored the existence of the Baptists in his work. To remedy this defect, Thomas Crosby, using materials collected by Benjamin Stinton, wrote their story in four volumes (*A History of the English Baptists from the Reformation to the Beginning of the Reign of George* [London, 1738–40]). He accepted the Continental Anabaptists as belonging to his group, though he minimized their social views. There were several other historians of this denomination in the succeeding years, but, since it and

advent of more critical writers fifty years ago, and even yet no satisfactory comprehensive substitute has appeared.

After Neal's time the study of Puritan history went into the doldrums which becalmed most ecclesiastical history for the next century. In this time the only notable event was the publication in 1813 of a biographical supplement to Neal's work, in the form of a three-volume work called *The Lives of the Puritans*. The author was Benjamin Brook, a Staffordshire Independent clergyman. His work ran the gauntlet of severe criticism from the men of the establishment, in which the charge of rousing sleeping dogs is repeated.[43] He was, indeed, not up to Neal's standard, either for accuracy or for fairness to the Anglicans who came within his range.[44] But he did for the earlier Puritans what Calamy had done for the later, and supplied us with at least some details of nearly five hundred lives. He also worked through the Morrice "Transcript" which Neal had used and gives many more extracts, though often in an abridged and garbled form.

With the coming of the Victorian era religion once more became respectable, and the contentions of Anglo-Catholics and Evangelicals sent scholars—now lay as well as clerical—scurrying to the sources again. As might be expected, the Reformation phase of Puritan history attracted the most attention. A new edition of Foxe's epic was prepared, and the works of Puritan divines like Smith and Sibbes were reprinted.[45] The Parker Society, organized in the interests of the Low Church party, published fifty-six volumes of the writings of the English

---

the Society of Friends were not important in our period, we shall not treat the historiography of these groups in any detail. For a full discussion of Baptist and Congregational historiography see Champlin Burrage, *The Early English Dissenters* (2 vols.; Cambridge, 1912), I, 1–21.

[43] Brook, *The Reviewer Reviewed* (London, 1815).

[44] Peel, *Seconde Parte*, I, 20–24.

[45] *Sermons of Mr. Henry Smith* edited by the author of "Our Heavenly Home" (2 vols.; London, 1866). A separate and different edition is that in "Nichols Series of Standard Divines: Puritan Series," *The Works of Henry Smith* (2 vols.; Edinburgh, 1866–67), which is the edition cited in this work. *The Complete Works of Richard Sibbes*, ed. Grosart ("Nichols Series of Standard Divines: Puritan Series" [6 vols.; Edinburgh, 1862]).

reformers, a collection to which all later scholarship is greatly indebted. In it many of the works of Tyndale, Coverdale, Hooper, Bale, and Cartwright were made easily available.[46] The society also financed further researches in Switzerland and skimmed at least the cream from the foreign archives.[47] With these and similar material Anderson and Demaus expanded our knowledge of the advanced reformers, expecially the translators.[48] A certain number of rather inferior works, however, carried the story farther and reflected a growing interest in the later phases of Puritan activity.[49]

One fruit of Victorianism was a revival of denominational pride on both sides of the Atlantic, and to this we owe the next great development in Puritan historiography—the rise of a school of historians who were at the same time genuinely liberal and thoroughly scholarly. The Congregationalists led the way here. In England a London banker, Benjamin Hanbury, and a Southwark minister, John Waddington, had made a start.[50] But the real impetus came from New England, whence a clergyman of means, H. M. Dexter, set out to gather systematically the available sources for the early history of his denomination, and to present the results in fearless fashion, let the chips fall where they might. When he finished, he had suggested that the founder of his own denomination was insane and that John

[46] In this period also the Hanserd Knollys Society reprinted ten volumes of source material relating to the history of the English Baptist movement.

[47] C. H. Smyth (*Cranmer and the Reformation under Elizabeth* [Cambridge, 1926] reports further researches made without great success. An exploration of the Frankfort archives has also been made with disappointing results (Rudolf Jung, *Die englische Flüchtlingsgemeinde in Frankfurt-am-Main 1554–9* [Frankfort, 1910]). Christina H. Garrett's recent *Marian Exiles* (Cambridge, 1938) would seem to exhaust the possibilities of further important discoveries in these repositories.

[48] See my "William Tindale—First English Puritan," *Church History*, VI (1936), 201–15, for a somewhat fuller treatment of the historiography of this subject.

[49] Benjamin Hanbury, "A Sketch of the Life of Thomas Cartwright," in Vol. I of his edition of Hooker's *Ecclesiastical Polity* (3 vols.; London, 1830); Benjamin Brook, *Memoir of the Life and Writings of Thomas Cartwright B.D.* (London, 1845); J. B. Marsden, *History of the Early Puritans .... to 1642* (London, 1850); *History of the Later Puritans .... to the Ejection* (London, 1852).

[50] Hanbury, *Historical Memorials Relating to the Independents* (3 vols.; London, 1839–44); Waddington, *John Penry, the Pilgrim Martyr* (London, 1854); *Congregational History* (5 vols.; London, 1869–80).

Robinson never held the liberal ideas of progressive revelation commonly attributed to him. He based his conclusions on his reading of the sources, and in the appendix of his book[51] was a census list of 7,250 titles, making up "Collections toward a Bibliography of Congregationalism." In America, Dexter's work was continued by Williston Walker, of the Yale Divinity School,[52] but his mantle really fell on Alexander Gordon.[53] Gordon was a Scotch Unitarian who ultimately became principal of his denominational Home Missionary College, Manchester. His real flair, however, was for accurate scholarship, especially of the biographical and local historical type. Fortunately, his active career coincided with the period of the compilation of the *Dictionary of National Biography*, and he contributed to every volume of it, to and including the 1901–11 supplement. In all he wrote 720 articles containing 778 biographies. In other words, he was the Brook—much improved—of his generation.[54] His scattered contributions on local Puritan history and other related subjects were also stimulating. And he was ever willing to go out of his way to assist a beginner, as the grateful writer can testify.

The effects of this new attitude were not long to seek. In 1889 A. H. Drysdale, a Presbyterian minister, produced a workmanlike history of his denomination,[55] using most of the available materials. But the real bloomtime came at the turn of the century. Denominational historical societies were founded in rapid succession. The secretaries and the editors of their various *Transactions* came forward with solid works of their own. The growing interest in historical research at the universities

[51] *Congregationalism of the Last Three Hundred Years as Seen in Its Literature* (New York, 1880); Dexter's *England and Holland of the Pilgrims* (published posthumously [New York, 1905]) is also important.

[52] *The Creeds and Platforms of Congregationalism* (New York, 1893); *A History of the Congregational Churches in the United States* (with chapters on the European background ["American Church History Series" Vol. III (New York, 1893)]).

[53] See the biography by H. McLachlan (Manchester, 1932).

[54] Others who wrote biographies of Puritans for the *DNB* were Thompson Cooper, A. B. Grosart, Augustus Jessopp, J. B. Mullinger, G. G. Perry, and C. Fell Smith. Miss Smith ranks with Gordon as a conscientious and able biographer.

[55] *History of the Presbyterians in England* (London, 1889).

sent young men into the field. Denominational lines were often forgotten in the friendly rivalry while each group helped to discover and tell anew the story of the other as well as its own. Among these workers there was no finer spirit than F. J. Powicke, whose writings[56] breathed a spirit of earnestness combined with tolerance and worldly wisdom. William Pierce was rather more militant, but did useful work on the Marprelate Tracts and Penry.[57] W. T. Whitley, the mainspring of the Baptist Historical Society, duplicated Dexter's work for his denomination,[58] and among his many other valuable works are a general *History of British Baptists*[59] and a thorough edition of the works of John Smith.[60] Whitley rejects Crosby's theory of a relationship between his group and the Continental Anabaptists. A Plymouth Unitarian pastor, W. H. Burgess, did much of the pioneer work on Smith, as well as a life of Robinson.[61] An American scholar, Champlin Burrage, discovered many new documents dealing with the early history of the Independent Puritans, and in his interpretation rightly recalled Neal's dictum that not all the early Independents were complete separatists. His zeal sometimes outstripped his judgment, but in his later work he set right some of his earlier slips, and his discoveries of new material[62] are the most important made in our time. Albert Peel, of Leeds and Oxford, and now editor of the *Congregational Quarterly*, finally completed the work of making

[56] *Henry Barrow . . . . and the Exiled Church of Amsterdam* (London, 1900); *John Robinson* (London, 1920); *Life of the Reverend Richard Baxter* (London, 1924), and many of less importance.

[57] *An Historical Introduction to the Marprelate Tracts* (London, 1908); *The Marprelate Tracts*, edited with notes (London, 1911); *John Penry* (London, 1923).

[58] *A Baptist Bibliography*, Vol. I: *1526–1776* (London, 1916); Vol. II: *1777–1837 and Addenda from 1613* (London, 1922).

[59] London, 1923.

[60] 2 vols.; London: Baptist Historical Society, 1915.

[61] *John Smith, the Se-Baptist, Thomas Helwys, and the First Baptist Church in England* (London, 1911); *John Robinson* (London, 1920).

[62] Robert Browne, *A New Years Guift*, edited with an Introduction (London, 1904); *True Story of Robert Browne* (Oxford, 1906); *The Retractation of Robert Browne* (Oxford, 1907); *New Facts concerning John Robinson* (London, 1910); *The Early English Dissenters* (2 vols.; Cambridge, 1912); *John Penry . . . . as Revealed in the Original Record of His Trial* (Oxford, 1913).

available the unprinted portion of the Field manuscripts.[63] His careful work has put all who are interested in the subject in his debt. He has also made other contributions,[64] and there is the promise of more to come. To the Presbyterian side of the story W. A. Shaw has contributed two stout volumes on the 1640–60 period,[65] while the Scotch minister, A. F. Scott Pearson, has scoured all available repositories for his studies of Cartwright and his times.[66]

Last but not least, Anglican scholars have graciously co-operated. W. H. Frere, the late Bishop of Truro, though far from Puritan in his own sympathies, led the way. Besides making available important sets of sources, the episcopal visitation articles of the Elizabethan period and the documents for the *Admonition* controversy,[67] he contributed a very useful and fair-minded survey[68] of developments under Elizabeth and James. C. E. Whiting has given us a detailed study of Puritan literature of the Restoration period,[69] while W. P. M. Kennedy,[70] C. H. Smyth,[71] and J. A. Muller[72] have also made contributions from the Anglican side.

Space does not permit of reference to the many serviceable

[63] *Seconde Parte of a Register* (2 vols.; Cambridge, 1915).

[64] *The Brownists in Norwich and Norfolk* (Cambridge, 1920); *The First Congregational Churches* (Cambridge, 1920); "From the Elizabethan Settlement to the Emergence of Separatism," *Essays Congregational and Catholic*, ed. Peel (London, 1931).

[65] *A History of the English Church during the Civil Wars and under the Commonwealth* (2 vols.; London, 1900).

[66] *Thomas Cartwright and Elizabethan Puritanism* (Cambridge, 1925); *Church and State: Political Aspects of Sixteenth Century Puritanism* (Cambridge, 1928).

[67] *Visitation Articles and Injunctions of the Period of the Reformation*, ed. Frere and Kennedy ("Alcuin Club" [3 vols.; London, 1910]); *Puritan Manifestoes*, ed. Frere and Douglas ("Church Historical Society" [London, 1907]).

[68] *The English Church in the Reigns of Elizabeth and James I*, Vol. V of *The History of the English Church*, ed. Hunt and Stephens (London, 1904). The companion volumes by J. Gairdner and W. H. Hutton in this same series are also useful.

[69] *Studies in English Puritanism from the Restoration to the Revolution* (London, 1931).

[70] *Elizabethan Episcopal Administration* ("Alcuin Club" [3 vols.; London, 1925]).

[71] *Cranmer and the Reformation under Edward VI* (Cambridge, 1926).

[72] *Stephen Gardiner and the Tudor Reaction* (New York, 1926); *The Letters of Stephen Gardiner* (New York, 1933).

works of Puritan local history, but some outstanding examples
may be listed.[73]

In the midst of this activity three men published surveys of
the Puritan movement. In 1908 James Heron, "Professor of
Ecclesiastical History, Belfast," produced a *Short History of
Puritanism*. It only professed to be a handbook for study
classes, but it showed knowledge of the sources and contained
a good outline of the facts. Two years later the Bunyan scholar,
John Brown, put out a similar work.[74] Henry W. Clark's *History of English Nonconformity*[75] was more pretentious. The second volume, however, dealt with the period since the Restoration, and in the first so much space was taken up with interpretation that the factual outline presented was by no means
complete. All these authors were clergymen, but they emphasized the modern individualistic and liberal side of Puritanism.

Hitherto we have confined our attention to those writers who
treated Puritanism from a religious point of view. But there are
others to be considered. Among the political historians are, of
course, many who have touched on Puritanism. We mention
only a few of the most important. Carlyle's resuscitation of
Cromwell is too well known to require comment. Macaulay,
following the liberal tradition in a somewhat more conventional
way, did more than any other writer to fix the popular notion of
a Puritan as a stern ascetic. Yet, politically he thought of the
Puritan as his spiritual ancestor, and on balance he was warmly
commendatory, though most people have forgotten it.[76] Gardiner, Firth, A. F. Pollard, and G. M. Trevelyan have reflected
much the same Liberal party outlook.

[73] T. W. Davids, *Annals of Evangelical Nonconformity in Essex* (London, 1863); John
Browne, *History of Congregationalism in Norfolk and Suffolk*; John Waddington, *Surrey
Congregational History* (London, 1866); William Urwick, *Nonconformity in Herts* (London, 1884); Robert Halley, *Lancashire: Its Puritanism and Nonconformity* (2 vols.;
London, 1869); W. H. Mildon, "Puritanism in Hampshire and the Isle of Wight from
the Reign of Elizabeth to the Restoration" (University of London dissertation [1934];
summary in *Bulletin of the Institute of Historical Research*, XII (1935), 36.

[74] *The English Puritans* (Cambridge, 1910).

[75] 2 vols.; London, 1911.   [76] See above, p. 430.

The last-named four were all university teachers, and, generally speaking, this Liberal—with a capital *L*—attitude has been predominant in academic circles where Puritanism has been made the object of "pure" scholarship. The works of T. C. Pease,[77] Louise Fargo Brown,[78] W. K. Jordan,[79] and G. L. Turner[80] may, I believe, be fairly classified under this heading. But there are variations, both on the left and on the right. S. E. Morison and his Harvard group endeavor not only to reconcile Puritanism with modern political liberalism but with modern academic liberalism as well.[81] Percy Scholes belongs in the same category, though he is a product of Oxford University.[82] On the other hand, R. G. Usher's attitude[83] is rather more Anglican than that of some of the professional exponents of that position. He believes that Elizabethan Puritanism was never more than a very small clerical movement with almost no popular support. While his views have not won wide support, his stimulating critique of the traditional liberal attitude has at least served to check undue optimism among the majority writers and to supply some balance to the field.

Among the social and economic historians the relationship of Puritanism to the rise of modern capitalism has attracted great attention. The thesis first put forward by Max Weber,[84] ostensibly to disprove the Marxian theory of economic determinism, has been corrected and improved by another German liberal, Ernst Troeltsch.[85] But the revisionist socialistic historians, who

[77] *The Leveller Movement* (Washington and Oxford, 1916).

[78] *The Political Activities of the Baptists and Fifth Monarchy Men* (Washington, 1912).

[79] *Development of Religious Toleration in England*, Vol. I: *From the Beginning of the English Reformation to the Death of Queen Elizabeth* (London, 1932); Vol. II: *From the Accession of James I to the Convention of the Long Parliament* (London, 1936); Vol. III: *From the Convention of the Long Parliament to the Restoration* (London, 1938).

[80] *Original Records of Early Nonconformity* (London, 1911).

[81] See above, p. 479, n. 37.

[82] *The Puritans and Music* (London, 1934).

[83] *The Reconstruction of the English Church* (2 vols.; New York, 1910); *The Presbyterian Movement* (London, 1905).

[84] See above, p. 348. [85] *Ibid.*

are not squeamish about Marxian orthodoxy, have not hesitated to take it over, as Tawney[86] and his school have demonstrated. The Webbs,[87] Berens,[88] Georg Lenz,[89] and Edouard Bernstein[90] are others who have given a socialist interpretation to different phases of the Puritan movement. Possibly Heinrich Bauer's recent life of Cromwell[91] is the first of a similar line of Fascist treatments.

Lastly, the work of literary historians deserves attention. They too have not been uninfluenced by old party passions, whose slow cooling may be traced in their works. As might be expected, most of the early surveys of Puritanism from the artistic or aesthetic point of view belong to the school of Ben Jonson, Butler, and Hawthorne. Puritanism to these writers is a harsh, unlovely thing which hampered the free, well-rounded expression of the English spirit. Matthew Arnold[92] preached this doctrine with great vigor in the mid-Victorian era. He saw in the doctrines of predestination and imputed righteousness the essentials of the Puritan outlook and regarded them as a most inadequate basis for moral development. Furthermore, genuine culture, in his opinion, involved an interest in the beautiful and the true—sweetness and light—as well as in the good. To concentrate on the ethical alone to the practical exclusion of the others was Hebraism. Changing the figure somewhat, he dubbed the middle-class Nonconformists who took this attitude "Philistines," the enemies of the children of light. Arnold was not so one-sided as is often supposed. He was not opposed to morality as such. In fact, he was a great moralist

[86] *Religion and the Rise of Capitalism* (London, 1926).

[87] *English Poor Law History*, Vol. VII of *English Local Government* (London, 1927).

[88] *The Digger Movement in the Days of the Commonwealth* (London, 1906).

[89] *Demokratie und Diktatur in der englische Revolution* (Munich and Berlin, 1933).

[90] *Kommunistische und demokratisch-sozialistische Strömungen während der englischen Revolution des 17. Jahrhunderts* ("Die Geschichte des Sozialismus," Band I [Stuttgart, 1895]); English trans., Stenning, *Cromwell and Communism* (London, 1930).

[91] *Oliver Cromwell* (Munich, 1934).

[92] "Barbarians, Philistines, Populace"; "Hebraism and Hellenism"; "Porro unum est necessarium"; "St. Paul and Protestantism"; "Puritanism and the Church of England," *Works* (15 vols.; London, 1903-4), Vols. VI and IX.

himself and insisted on a proper ethic as an essential of culture. He was not even opposed to Presbyterianism, which he recognized in his historical survey as part of the national tradition. What he objected to was the Nonconformists' withdrawal from public life and their concentration on what he regarded as a narrow and outworn creed. His temperament and the circumstances in which he wrote, however, led him to emphasize the anti-Puritan side of his position. Paul and Calvin fare rather badly at his hands. Shakespeare is praised and Watts damned.

Arnold's interpretation of Puritanism was somewhat modified by a critic of the next generation, Edward Dowden,[93] Professor of English Literature at Trinity College, Dublin. While similarly unfavorable to the Puritan attitude as a cultural milieu, he points out that the doctrines which Arnold took for the essence of Puritanism were really common to almost all Protestants. He stressed the immediacy of the Puritan relationship to God as contrasted with the Anglican indirectness of priest and ceremony, which he thought left more room for the appreciation of humanity, nature, form, and color. This point of view—which is too obvious to be fathered on Dowden alone—has been widely followed, and something of it may be seen in the works of such writers outside the literary field as Usher and R. H. Tawney. Recent critical expositions of this negative attitude toward Puritanism may be found in the works of Sir Herbert Grierson[94] and Margaret Storm Jameson.[95]

But there is also a minority report. E. N. S. Thompson in his survey of the relations of the Puritans to the stage[96] was surprisingly sympathetic to the arguments of the Elizabethan moralists. Stuart Sherman followed this with a wholesale effort to rehabilitate Puritanism and restore its good repute.[97] He minimized the moral and repressive features and emphasized the human traits of individual Puritans. But the progressive

[93] *Puritan and Anglican* (London, 1900).

[94] *Cross Currents in English Literature of the Seventeenth Century* (London, 1929).

[95] *The Decline of Merry England* (London, 1930).

[96] *The Controversy between the Puritans and the Stage* (New York, 1903).

[97] *The Genius of America* (New York, 1923).

features of the movement interested him most, and it was as the champion of improvement and reform that he pictured the typical Puritan. This bold hypothesis did not receive much support—indeed, it was little more than a passing phase in the mind of its author—but later critics have been somewhat more cautious in their generalizations since he wrote. The comparable though much more serious attempt of Percy Scholes, already mentioned, to remove the artistic and musical stigma from Puritan hands will doubtless have a similar effect.

In addition to these general treatments of the literary aspects of Puritanism, there have also been, of course, numerous studies of the Puritan features of particular authors. Spenser and Milton are naturally the chief themes, but Shakespeare, Donne, and many others have been handled in this way. Masson's great life of Milton must be mentioned as a real contribution to the field of Puritan studies, but a detailed study of the interpretations of particular authors must be left to the experts. An attempt to follow the arguments for the various explanations of Spenser's allegories has had a chastening effect. Such things are too wonderful for the historian. He cannot attain unto these mysteries.

The writers in the literary field mentioned thus far have been those who have treated literature or, at most, culture as their central theme and have considered Puritanism only as it has affected their major interest. There are others, however, who interpret their commission much more broadly. Though technically in the field of literature, they are actually historians, composing accounts of past developments with only a secondary attention to their literary aspects. Freed from the sense of obligation to master and present the details of the historical background, they may show a philosophical breadth of interpretation which is most stimulating. But, for lack of such a topographical map, they may also miss a good many of the turns and twists which must be made in any thorough exploration. This school is well represented in Germany. W. F. Schirmer's *Antike, Renaissance, und Puritanismus* shows it at its best. The author sees clearly that Puritanism is not an isolated phenomenon but that the same attitude can be traced throughout the history of the church. L. L. Schücking's *Die Familie in Puritanismus* and Levy's *Das Sabbath in England*[98] are other fruits of this same school, though in more limited fields. In America, where a similar development is under way, Louis Wright's *Middle Class Culture in Elizabethan England*[99] is the most comprehensive study of this sort which touches on our field. It is valuable for the many rare works to which it gives references. Helen White's *English Devotional Literature*, Caroline Richardson's *English Preachers and Preaching, 1640–1660*,[100] and G. T. Buckley's *Atheism in the English Renaissance* are other works of this sort, though of more restricted range. W. F. Mitchell's *English Pulpit Oratory from Andrewes to Tillotson*[101] is a similar treatise from an English university.

Despite all these studies, much remains to be done in the field of Puritanism. To speak only of the Tudor phase, there are doubtless many valuable manuscripts yet to be discovered, and certainly a great number of sources to be edited. The records of ecclesiastical courts are as yet largely unworked. Guarded by prohibitive fees and scattered about in every conceivable place, from the basement of Somerset House to the attic of the provincial lawyer who acts as diocesan chancellor, they rouse unprintable thoughts of envy and despair. Short of the long-delayed governmental action no satisfactory solution of the problem can be seen, though here and there some progress can be reported. The other type of unexplored manuscript repository with great possibilities is the country-house muniment room. From one of these came the minute-book of the Dedham classis. There will be many disappointments here. For the *Reports* of the Historical Manuscripts Comission and examination of such sample sets as the Huntingdon and Barrington papers show that many of the prominent Puritan patrons left few written traces of their interest. But in the vast quantities of material as yet unsifted there must be much new information. Among printed sources the best field would seem to be the works of the Puritans themselves. Some beginning of this work has been attempted in this volume, but the writings are voluminous, varied, and com-

[98] Leipzig, 1933.
[99] Chapel Hill, 1935.
[100] New York, 1928.
[101] London, 1932.

plex. They will repay much closer examination, and some will bear editing. Barnes, Turner, Bale (whose writings have been badly cut by the Parker Society's Victorian editors), Humphrey, and Perkins certainly deserve modern editions, and Dering, Greenham, Laurence Chaderton, Richard Rogers, and Arthur Dent might also be considered. In fact, scholarship would benefit greatly by a Cartwright or a Baxter society to supplement the work of the Parker group by dealing with the later period.

There are also great gaps in the secondary field. There are no satisfactory biographies of Hooper and Grindal, or, for that matter—with one or two exceptions—of any of the other figures mentioned above.[102] Among the lay patrons Beale, Morice, Knollys, Mildmay, Wroth, Rich, Huntingdon, and even Leicester have yet to be properly treated. A careful examination of their political ambitions, influence, and interrelations should be of great assistance. There is enough material for a monograph on the struggle with Whitgift in the 1580's and more than enough for one dealing with the Puritan political maneuvering before and after the Hampton Court conference. The Puritan lecture system, Puritan casuistry, and Puritanism in the universities are among the many other unworked topics. Lastly, further attention to Puritan local history is essential if any sound conclusions are to be reached on the vexed question of the actual strength of the party at any given period. On such a quasi-illegal undertaking as Tudor-Stuart Puritanism it is, of course, difficult to obtain sufficient evidence for statistical purposes. But lists of signers of petitions, of ministers suspended or "troubled about the surplice," of private patrons and members of corporations appointing Puritan lecturers will furnish some clues. By careful analysis and a plotting on maps it should be possible to get some clearer notion of the process by which Puritanism spread over England and of how strong its hold was on a given community at a given time.

[102] E. S. Shuckburgh's translation of William Dillingham's life of Laurence Chaderton (Cambridge, 1884) supplied that need. The forthcoming work on Bale by Jesse W. Harris should fill that gap. The works by van Baarsel on Perkins (see above, p. 375) and by Pearson on Cartwright have already been mentioned.

APPENDIX IV

Facilities for the Study of English Puritanism in American Libraries

THERE are many institutions with good general collections of sixteenth- and seventeenth-century English works. Of these, the best is the Huntington Library at San Marino, California, which possesses over 40 per cent of all the items listed in the *Short Title Catalogue*, and also some manuscript material. A short analysis of the contents of the manuscripts of this period in this library has been made by Professor Conyers Read and may be consulted at the library. The Ellesmere papers are the most important single collection for the subject of Puritanism in the possession of this institution. These are the family documents of Thomas Egerton, the Lord Chancellor, and include among other items the notebook of John Penry (No. 483; cf. p. 294 n.), papers relating to his case (Nos. 2146–56), and the originals of the records of the trials of the Separatists in 1593 (Nos. 2101–17) which Champlin Burrage (*Early English Dissenters*, II, 45–61) copied from Harleian 6848–49. The Hastings papers, which include many letters of the Puritan patron, Henry Hastings, the third Earl of Huntingdon, are disappointing, since most of the Earl's correspondence was of a purely business nature.

Among the university libraries which contain good working collections of printed source material are those of Harvard, Yale, Cornell, and Chicago. The Boston Public Library, the Folger Library in Washington, D.C., and the Newberry Library, Chicago, are also well equipped in this field. At other places efforts are being made to accumulate books printed in this period, notably at the University of Illinois and at Washington State College, Pullman, Washington.

Of special collections on the subject of English Puritanism by far the best is the McAlpin in the library of Union Theological Seminary, New York City. This was made possible by the generosity of the late D. H. McAlpin and his family, and brought together largely by the efforts of Dr. Ezra H. Gillett and Professor Charles A. Briggs. It contains over fifteen thousand volumes, and the number is being steadily increased. A very useful printed catalogue[1] was recently published. Yale University has the library of the great historian and bibliographer, H. M. Dexter, which numbers nearly two thousand items. Princeton Theological Seminary also has a collection of some two thousand volumes, formerly the property of the British scholar, A. B. Grosart, purchased in 1885. The best collection in the Middle West is located at William Jewell College, Liberty, Missouri. In 1902 this institution acquired the library of the celebrated London preacher, Charles Spurgeon, who had spent a lifetime collecting works on this subject, especially biblical commentaries and Puritan sermons. In this library of some seven thousand volumes are over one thousand published before 1700. It is probable that there are similar accumulations elsewhere which ought to be better known and more thoroughly exploited by neighboring scholars. In any case, the American student interested in this field may expect to find source material within a reasonable distance.

[1] Charles R. Gillett, *Catalogue of the McAlpin Collection of British History and Theology* (New York, 1928–30).

SELECT BIBLIOGRAPHY

SELECT BIBLIOGRAPHY

I. MANUSCRIPTS

LONDON
    British Museum
        Harleian, Sloane, Egerton, and Additional
    Public Record Office
        State Papers, Domestic Series
    Lambeth Palace
        Lambeth, Bacon, and Miscellaneous
    Dr. Williams' Library
        Morrice and General

OXFORD
    Bodleian
        General Bodleian
    University Archives

CAMBRIDGE
    University Library
        University and Baker
    Gonville and Caius College
    Moore

SAN MARINO, CALIFORNIA
    Huntington Library
        Ellesmere and Hastings

II. PRINTED PRIMARY SOURCES

[For works referred to in the text, but not listed here, consult the Index.]

Acts of the Privy Council. Ed. J. R. DASENT. 32 vols. London, 1890–1907.

[AINSWORTH, HENRY.] *A True Confession of the Faith and Humble Acknowledgment of the Allegeance Which Wee Hir Majesties Subjects Falsely Called Brownists Doo Hould.* [Amsterdam?], 1596. Reprinted in WILLISTON WALKER (ed.), *Creeds and Platforms of Congregationalism.* New York, 1893.

ANDREWES, LANCELOT. *The Patterne of Catechisticall Doctrine.* London, 1630. Also in "Library of Anglo-Catholic Theology." Oxford, 1846.

AYLMER, JOHN. *An Harborowe for Faithfull and Trewe Subjectes.* Strassburg, 1559.

BALE, JOHN. *Illustrium Maioris Brittaniae scriptorum . . . . summarium.* [Wesel], 1548.

———. *Yet a Course at the Romyshe Foxe.* Zurich, 1543.

BANCROFT, RICHARD. *Dangerous Positions.* London, 1593. Largely reprinted in *The Presbyterian Movement.* Ed. R. G. USHER. London, 1905.

———. *A Survay of the Pretended Holy Discipline.* London, 1593.

BARNES, ROBERT. *The Whole Works of W. Tyndall, J. Frith, and Doct. Barnes.* 2 vols. London, 1572–73.

BECON, THOMAS. *Works.* Ed. JOHN AYRE. 3 vols. Cambridge: Parker Society, 1843–44.

BOWNDE, NICHOLAS. The Doctrine of the Sabbath. London, 1595. Enlarged ed., *Sabbathum veteris et novi testamenti.* London, 1606.

———. *The Holy Exercise of Fasting Described.* London, 1604.

BRADFORD, JOHN. *Writings.* Ed. AUBREY TOWNSEND. 2 vols. Cambridge: Parker Society, 1848–53.

BRADSHAW, WILLIAM. *English Puritanisme: Containing the Maine Opinions of the Rigidest Sort of Those That Are Called Puritans in the Realme of England. S.l.,* 1605.

A Briefe Examination for the Tyme of a Certaine Declaration Lately Put in Print. London, 1566.

BRIDGES, JOHN. *A Defence of the Government Established.* London, 1587.

BRINKELOW, HENRY. *The Complaynt of Roderyck Mors.* Ed. J. M. COWPER. "Early English Text Society: Extra Series," Vol. XXII. London, 1874.

BROWNE, ROBERT. *A Booke Which Sheweth the Life and Manners of All True Christians.* Middelburg, 1582.

———. *A Treatise of Reformation without Tarying for Anie.* Middelburg, 1582. Reprinted by T. G. CRIPPEN. London, 1903. Also in "Old South Leaflets: General Series." Vol. IV, No. 100. Boston, n.d.

———. *A True and Short Declaration. S.l.,* [1583?]. Reprinted in the *Congregationalist.* London, 1888.

BUNNY, EDMUND. *Of Divorce and Adulterie and Marrying Again: That There Is No Sufficient Warrant So To Do.* Oxford, 1610.

BURTON, WILLIAM. *Davids Evidence.* London, 1596.

———. *A Sermon Preached in the Cathedral Church of Norwich, 1589.* London, n.d. [after 1591].

Calendar of State Papers, Domestic, Elizabeth. Ed. ROBERT LEMON, M. A. E. GREEN, *et al.* London, 1856, etc.

Calendar of State Papers, Spanish. Ed. G. A. BERGENROTH *et al.* London, 1862, etc.

CARDWELL, EDWARD (ed.). *Documentary Annals of the Reformed Church of England.* 2 vols. Oxford, 1844.

CARTWRIGHT, THOMAS, *A Replye to an Answere Made of M. Doctor Whitegift.* [*S.l.,* 1574.] Reprinted in Whitgift's *Works.* Ed. JOHN AYRE. 3 vols. Cambridge: Parker Society, 1851–53.

———. *The Second Replie against Master Whitgiftes Second Answer. S.l.,* 1575.

———. *The Rest of the Second Replie. S.l.,* 1577.

CLAPHAM, HENOCH. *A Chronological Discourse.* London, 1609.

CLARKE, SAMUEL. *General Martyrologie to Which Is Attached Lives of Sundry Modern English Divines.* London, 1651. Enlarged ed., London, 1677.

———. *The Lives of Sundry Eminent Persons in the Later Age.* London, 1683.

———. *The Marrow of Ecclesiastical History.* London, 1650.

CLEAVER, ROBERT. *A Godly Form of Household Government.* London, 1598.

COOPER, THOMAS. *An Admonition to the People of England.* London, 1589. Reprinted by EDWARD ARBER, "English Scholar's Library." Birmingham, 1882.

Corpus reformatorum. Halle, 1834, etc.

COSIN, RICHARD. *Conspiracie for Pretended Reformation.* London, 1592.

COVERDALE, MILES. *Writings and Translations.* Ed. GEORGE PEARSON. Cambridge: Parker Society, 1844.

[CROWLEY, ROBERT.] *A Briefe Discourse against the Outwarde Apparell and Ministering Garments of the Popishe Church.* [*S.l.*, 1566.]

DENT, ARTHUR. *The Plaine Man's Path-Way to Heaven.* London, 1601.

——. *A Sermon of Repentaunce.* London, 1583.

DERING, EDWARD. *Workes.* London, 1597.

D'EWES, SIR SIMONDS (ed.). *A Compleat Journal of the Votes Speeches and Debates . . . . throughout the Whole Reign of Queen Elizabeth.* London, 1693 [first published in 1682].

EGLI, EMIL (ed.). *Achtensammlung zur Geschichte der zürcher Reformation in den Jahren 1519–1533.* Zurich, 1879.

FENNER, DUDLEY. *Sacra theologia sive veritas qua est secundum pietatem ad unicae et verae methodi leges descripta.* London, 1585.

FOXE, JOHN. *Acts and Monuments.* Ed. GEORGE TOWNSEND. 8 vols. London, 1837–41.

FRERE, W. H. (ed.). *Visitation Articles and Injunctions of the Period of the Reformation.* "Alcuin Club Collections," Vols. XIV–XVI. London, 1910. (Vol. II with W. P. M. KENNEDY.)

FRERE, W. H., and DOUGLAS, C. E. (eds.). *Puritan Manifestoes.* London 1907.

FRITH, JOHN. *Works.* Ed. THOMAS RUSSELL. 3 vols. "Works of the English Reformers." London, 1831.

FULKE, WILLIAM. *A Briefe and Plain Declaration.* London, 1584.

FULLER, THOMAS. *Abel redivivus, or the Dead Yet Speaking.* London, 1651.

GAIRDNER, JAMES (ed.). *Three Fifteenth Century Chronicles.* "Camden Society: New Series," Vol. XXVIII. London, 1880.

GILBY, ANTHONY. *A Pleasaunt Dialogue betweene a Souldior of Barwicke and an English Chaplaine.* [London], 1581.

GOODMAN, CHRISTOPHER. *How Superior Powers Oght To Be Obeyed of Their Subjects.* Geneva, 1558. Reprinted in facsimile. New York: Facsimile Text Society, 1931.

GORHAM, GEORGE C. *Gleanings of a Few Scattered Ears during the Period of the Reformation in England.* London, 1857.

GREENHAM, RICHARD. *The Workes of Richard Greenham.* 5th and last ed. London, 1612.

GRINDAL, EDMUND. *Remains.* Ed. WILLIAM NICHOLSON. Cambridge: Parker Society, 1843.

HOOPER, JOHN. *Early Writings.* SAMUEL CARR. Cambridge: Parker Society, 1843.

——. *Later Writings.* Ed. CHARLES NEVINSON. Cambridge: Parker Society, 1852.

HUMPHREY, LAURENCE. *De religionis conservatione et reformatione vera.* Basel, 1559.

———. *Optimates.* Basel, 1559.

JEWEL, JOHN. *Works.* Ed. JOHN AYRE. 4 vols. Cambridge: Parker Society, 1845–50.

JOHNSON, GEORGE. *Discourse of Some Troubles in the Banished English Church at Amsterdam.* Amsterdam, 1603.

JOYE, GEORGE. *An Apologye To Satisfye W. Tindale.* S.l., 1535. Reprinted by Edward Arber. Birmingham, 1882.

———. *The Letters Which John Ashwell . . . . Sente Secretly* [Strassburg? 1531?]

KENNEDY, W. P. M. (ed.). *Elizabethan Episcopal Administration.* 3 vols. "Alcuin Club Collections." London, 1924.

KNAPPEN, M. M. (ed.). *Two Elizabethan Puritan Diaries.* Chicago, 1933.

KNOX, JOHN. *Works.* Ed. DAVID LAING. 6 vols. Edinburgh, 1895.

LASCO, JOHN À. *Opera.* Ed. ABRAHAM KUYPER. 2 vols. Amsterdam, 1866.

Letters and Papers . . . . of the Reign of Henry VIII. Ed. J. S. BREWER, JAMES GAIRDNER, *et al.* London, 1862, etc.

Livre des Anglois. Ed. J. SOUTHERDEN BURN. London, 1831. Reprinted in his *History of Parish Registers in England,* pp. 271–88. London, 1862. Also reprinted, with notes, by A. FERRIER MITCHELL. S.l., n.d.

LUPTON, THOMAS. *A Dream of the Devill and Dives.* London, 1615 [first published, 1584].

The Marprelate Tracts. Ed. WILLIAM PIERCE. London, 1911.

MORE, THOMAS. *Workes.* London, 1557.

———. *Works.* Ed. W. E. CAMPBELL. London, 1927, etc.

———. *Apologye.* Ed. A. I. TAFT. "Early English Text Society: Original Series," No. 180. London, 1930.

MOSSE, MILES. *The Arraignment and Conviction of Usurie.* London, 1595.

NICHOLS, JOSIAS. *The Plea of the Innocent.* [London?], 1602.

NICHOLS, JOHN G. (ed.). *Narratives of the Days of the Reformation.* "Camden Society: First Series," Vol. XXXVII. London, 1859.

NORTHBROOKE, JOHN. *A Treatise Wherein Dicing, Dauncing, etc. Are Reproved.* London, 1577. Reprinted by J. P. COLLIER. London: Shakespeare Society, 1843.

Original Letters Relative to the English Reformation. Ed. HASTINGS ROBINSON. 2 vols. Cambridge: Parker Society, 1846–47.

PARKER, MATTHEW. *Correspondence.* Ed. JOHN BRUCE and T. T. PERROWNE. Cambridge: Parker Society. 1853.

A Parte of a Register. [Middelburg], 1593.

PERKINS, WILLIAM. *Workes.* 3 vols. London, 1616–18.

PHILPOT, JOHN. *Examination and Writings.* Ed. ROBERT EDEN. Cambridge: Parker Society, 1842.

PONET, JOHN. *A Short Treatise of Politike Power.* S.l., 1556. Reprinted in 1639 and 1642.

RAINOLDS, JOHN. *A Defence of the Judgment of the Reformed Churches. That a Man May Lawfullie Not Only Put Awaie His Wife for Her Adulterie But Also Marrie Another.* S.l., 1609.

————. *Th' Overthrow of Stage-Playes*. [Middelburg], 1599.

ROGERS, RICHARD. *Seaven Treatises Leading and Guiding to True Happiness*. London, 1603.

————. *A Garden of Spiritual Flowers Planted by Ri. Ro[gers], Will. Per[kins], Ri. Green[ham], M[iles] M[osse], and Geo. Web[be]*. London, 1609.

The Seconde Parte of a Register. Ed. ALBERT PEEL. 2 vols. Cambridge, 1915.

SMITH, HENRY. *Sermons*, London, 1599.

————. *Works*. Ed. THOMAS SMITH. 2 vols. "Nichols Series of Standard Divines: Puritan Period." Edinburgh, 1866–67.

STUBBS, PHILIP. *The Anatomy of Abuses*. London, 1583. Reprinted by F. J. FURNIVAL. London: New Shakespeare Society, 1879.

TRAVERS, WALTER. *A Directory of Church Government Anciently Contended For*. London, 1644.

————. *Ecclesiasticae disciplinae et Anglicanae Ecclesiae ab illa aberrationis plena e verbo Dei et dilucida explicatio*. [La Rochelle?], 1574.

TURNER, WILLIAM. *The Huntyng and Fynding Out of the Romishe Fox*. Basel, 1543.

————. *The Huntyng of the Romyshe Wolfe*. London, 1554.

————. *The Seconde Course of the Hunter at the Romish Fox and Hys Advocate* [*The Rescuynge of the Romishe Fox*]. [Zurich?], 1545.

TYNDALE, WILLIAM. *Answer to Sir Thomas More's Dialogue*. Ed. HENRY WALTER. Cambridge: Parker Society, 1850.

————. *Doctrinal Treatises*. Ed. HENRY WALTER. Cambridge: Parker Society, 1848.

————. *Expositions and Notes*. Ed. HENRY WALTER. Cambridge: Parker Society, 1849.

TYTLER, P. F. (ed.). *England under the Reigns of Edward VI and Mary*. 2 vols. London, 1839.

UDALL, JOHN. *The State of the Church of Englande Laide Open in a Conference betweene Diotrephes, a Byshop, Tertullus, a Papist, etc. S.l.*, 1588.

USHER, R. G. (ed.). *The Presbyterian Movement in the Reign of Queen Elizabeth*. "Camden Society: Third Series," Vol. VIII. London, 1905.

WALKER, WILLISTON (ed.). *The Creeds and Platforms of Congregationalism*. New York, 1893.

WHITGIFT, JOHN. *Works*. Ed. JOHN AYRE. 3 vols. Cambridge: Parker Society, 1851–53.

[WHITTINGHAM, WILLIAM.] *A Brieff Discours of the Troubles Begonne at Franckford. S.l.*, 1574. Reprinted by EDWARD ARBER. London, 1908.

WILKINS, DAVID (ed.). *Concilia Magnae Britanniae et Hiberniae*. 4 vols. London, 1737.

Zurich Letters. Ed. HASTINGS ROBINSON. 2 vols. Cambridge: Parker Society, 1842–45.

III. PRINTED SECONDARY SOURCES

ALLEN, J. W. *A History of Political Thought in the Sixteenth Century*. London, 1928.

ARBER, EDWARD. *The First Printed English New Testament*. London, 1871.

BAARSEL, J. J. VAN. *William Perkins: Eene bijdrage tot de Kennis der religieuse ontwikkeling in Engeland ten tijde van Koningen Elisabeth.* The Hague, 1912.

BROOK, BENJAMIN. *Lives of the Puritans.* 3 vols. London, 1813.

BROWN, P. HUME. *John Knox.* 2 vols. London, 1895.

BUCKLEY, GEORGE T. *Atheism in the English Renaissance.* Chicago, 1932.

BURGESS, W. H. *John Robinson, Pastor of the Pilgrim Fathers.* London, 1920.

———. *John Smith, the Se-Baptist, Thomas Helwys, and the First Baptist Church in England.* London, 1911.

BURNET, GILBERT. *History of the Reformation.* Ed. NICHOLAS POCOCK. 7 vols. Oxford, 1865.

BURRAGE, CHAMPLIN. *The Covenant Idea.* Philadelphia, 1904.

———. *The Early English Dissenters.* 2 vols. Cambridge, 1912.

———. *The True Story of Robert Browne.* Oxford, 1906.

CHESTER, J. L. *John Rogers.* London, 1861.

COLLIER, JEREMY. *Ecclesiastical History of Great Britain.* Ed. THOMAS LATHBURY. 9 vols. London, 1852.

COOPER, C. H. and THOMPSON. *Athenae Cantabrigienses.* 3 vols. Cambridge, 1858–1913.

COULTON, G. C. *Art and the Reformation.* Oxford, 1928.

———. *Five Centuries of Religion.* 3 vols. Cambridge, 1923–36.

DEMAUS, R. *Hugh Latimer.* London, 1869.

———. *William Tindale.* Ed. RICHARD LOVETT. London, 1904.

DEXTER, H. M. *Congregationalism of the Last Three Hundred Years as Seen in Its Literature.* New York, 1880.

The Dictionary of National Biography. Ed. SIDNEY LEE and LESLIE STEPHEN. London, 1885, etc.

DIXON, R. W. *History of the Church of England from the Abolition of the Roman Jurisdiction.* 3d rev. ed. 6 vols. Oxford, 1895.

DOLFUSS-ZODEL, ELSA. *Bullingers Einflusz auf das zürcherische Staatswesen von 1531–1575.* Zurich, 1931.

DOWDEN, EDWARD. *Puritan and Anglican.* London, 1900.

DRYSDALE, A. H. *A History of the Presbyterians in England.* London, 1889.

FARNER, ALFRED. *Die Lehre von Kirche und Staat bei Zwingli.* Tübingen, 1930.

FRERE, W. H. *The English Church in the Reigns of Elizabeth and James I.* London, 1904.

———. *The Marian Reaction.* London, 1896.

FULLER, THOMAS. *The Church History of Britain.* Ed. J. S. BREWER. 6 vols. Oxford, 1845.

GAIRDNER, JAMES. *The English Church in the Sixteenth Century from the Accession of Henry VIII to the Death of Mary.* London, 1902.

GARRETT, CHRISTINA H. *The Marian Exiles.* Cambridge, 1938.

GRISAR, HARTMAN. *Luther.* English trans. E. M. LAMOND. 6 vols. London, 1913–17.

HESSEY, J. A. *Sunday: Its Origin, History and Present Obligation.* 3d ed. "Bampton Lectures . . . . in . . . . 1860." London, 1866.

HEYLYN, PETER. *Aerius redivivus or the History of the Presbyterians.* Ed. HENRY HEYLYN. London, 1670.

————. *Ecclesia restaurata* or the *History of the Reformation of the Church of England*. London, 1661.

————. *The History of the Sabbath*. London, 1636.

JACKSON, S. M., *Huldreich Zwingli*. New York, 1900.

JACOBS, H. E. *A Study in Comparative Symbolics: The Lutheran Movement in England during the Reigns of Henry VIII and Edward VI and Its Literary Monuments*. Philadelphia, 1908.

JORDAN, W. K. *Development of Religious Toleration in England*. 3 vols. London, 1932–38.

JUNG, RUDOLF. *Die englische Flüchtlingsgemeinde in Frankfurt-am-Main, 1554–59*. Frankfort, 1910.

KENNEDY, W. P. M. *Studies in Tudor History*. London, 1916.

KRONENBERG, M. E. "Notes on English Printing in the Low Countries (Early Sixteenth Century)," *Library*, IX (4th ser., 1929), 139–63.

LASKI, HAROLD. *The Rise of European Liberalism*. London, 1936.

LORIMER, PETER. *John Knox and the Church of England*. London, 1875.

MAITLAND, S. R. *Essays on Subjects Connected with the Reformation in England*. London, 1849.

MARTIN, CHARLES. *Les Protestants anglais réfugiés à Genève au temps de Calvin*. Geneva, 1915.

Mélanges d'histoire offerts à M. Charles Bémont. Paris, 1913.

MERRIMAN, R. B. *The Life and Letters of Thomas Cromwell*. 2 vols. Oxford, 1902.

MILLER, PERRY. *Orthodoxy in Massachusetts*. Cambridge, Mass., 1933.

MORISON, SAMUEL E. *The Founding of Harvard College*. Cambridge, Mass., 1935.

MOZLEY, J. F. *William Tyndale*. New York, 1937.

MULLER, J. A. *Stephen Gardiner and the Tudor Reaction*. New York, 1926.

MULLINGER, J. B. *History of the University of Cambridge*. 3 vols. Cambridge, 1873–1911.

NEAL, DANIEL. *History of the Puritans*. 3 vols. London, 1937.

OWST, G. R. *Literature and Pulpit in Medieval England*. Cambridge, 1933.

————. *Preaching in Medieval England*. Cambridge, 1926.

PEARSON, A. F. SCOTT. *Church and State*. Cambridge, 1928.

————. *Thomas Cartwright and Elizabethan Puritanism*. London, 1925.

PEEL, ALBERT. *The Brownists in Norwich and Norfolk about 1580*. Cambridge, 1920.

————. *The First Congregational Churches*. Cambridge, 1920.

PEEL, ALBERT, *et al. Essays Congregational and Catholic*. London, 1931.

PEILE, JOHN. *Biographical Dictionary of Christ's College, Cambridge*. 2 vols. Cambridge, 1910–13.

PIERCE, WILLIAM. *An Historical Introduction to the Marprelate Tracts*. London, 1908.

————. *John Penry: His Life, Times and Writings*. London, 1923.

PLOMER, HENRY R. "The Protestant Press in the Reign of Mary," *Library*, I (3d ser., 1910), 54–72.

POLLARD, A. F. *Thomas Cranmer and the English Reformation*. London, 1904.

POWICKE, F. J. *Henry Barrow . . . . and the Exiled Church of Amsterdam.* London, 1900.

RICHTER, LUDWIG. *Beiträge zur Geschichte des Ehescheidungsrechts in der evangelischen Kirche.* Berlin, 1859.

RIDLEY, GLOCESTER. *Life of Bishop Ridley.* London, 1763.

SCHICKLER, BARON FERDINAND DE. *Les Eglises du refuge en Angleterre.* 3 vols. Paris, 1892.

SCHIRMER, W. F. *Antike, Renaissance und Puritanismus.* Munich, 1925.

SCHÜCKING, L. L. *Die Familie in Puritanismus.* Leipzig and Berlin, 1929.

SCHOLES, PERCY. *The Puritans and Music.* London, 1934.

SMITH, PRESERVED. *Erasmus.* New York, 1923.

SMYTH, C. H. *Cranmer and the Reformation under Edward VI.* Cambridge, 1926.

STEELE, ROBERT. "Notes on English Books Printed Abroad, 1525–48," *Transactions of the Bibliographical Society*, XI (1909–11), 189–236. Also printed separately. London, 1912.

STRYPE, JOHN. *Annals of the Reformation under Elizabeth.* 4 vols. in 7. Oxford, 1824.

———. *Ecclesiastical Memorials.* 3 vols. in 6. Oxford 1822.

———. *Historical Collections of the Life and Acts of John Aylmer.* Oxford, 1821.

———. *History of the Life and Acts of Edmund Grindal.* Oxford, 1821.

———. *Memorials of . . . . Thomas Cranmer.* 2 vols. Oxford, 1812.

———. *The Life and Acts of Matthew Parker.* 3 vols. Oxford, 1821.

———. *The Life and Acts of John Whitgift.* 3 vols. Oxford, 1822.

TAWNEY, R. H. *Religion and the Rise of Capitalism.* London, 1926.

THOMPSON, ELBERT N. S. *The Controversy between the Puritans and the Stage.* "Yale Studies in English," Vol. XX. New York, 1903.

DE LA TOUR, IMBART. *Calvin et l'institution chrétienne.* Vol. IV of *Les Origines de la Réforme.* Ed. JACQUES CHEVALIER. 4 vols. Paris, 1935.

TROELTSCH, ERNST. *Die Soziallehren der christlichen Kirchen und Gruppen.* Vol. I of *Gesammelte Schriften.* 4 vols. Tübingen, 1912–25. English trans. OLIVE WYON. *The Social Teaching of the Christian Churches.* 2 vols. London, 1931.

USHER, R. G. *The Reconstruction of the English Church.* 2 vols. New York, 1910.

VENN, J. and J. A. *Alumni Cantabrigienses.* 4 vols. Cambridge, 1922–27.

VETTER, THEODOR. *Relations between England and Zurich during the Reformation.* London, 1904.

WEBER, MAX. *Die protestantische Ethik und der Geist des Kapitalismus.* Vol. I of *Gesammelte Aufsätze zur Religionssoziologie.* 3 vols. Tübingen, 1920–21. English trans. TALCOTT PARSONS. *The Protestant Ethic and the Spirit of Capitalism.* London, 1930.

WHITAKER, W. B. *Sunday in Tudor and Stuart Times.* London, 1933.

WHITE, HELEN C. *English Devotional Literature (Prose) 1600–1640.* "University of Wisconsin Studies in Language and Literature," No. 29. Madison, Wis., 1931.

WILSON, J. DOVER. "Richard Schilders and the English Puritans," *Transactions of the Bibliographical Society of London*, XI (1909–11), 65–134.
WRIGHT, LOUIS B. *Middle-Class Culture in Elizabethan England*. Chapel Hill, N.C., 1935.

IV. UNPUBLISHED THESES

ANDREWS, GEORGE A. "History of the Puritan Discipline, 1554–1593." Washington University dissertation. St. Louis, 1932.
BAUER, WALTER E. "John Foxe as Historian." Cornell University dissertation. Ithaca, 1932.
BIBBY, EDNA. "The Puritan Classical Movement of Elizabeth's Reign." Manchester University dissertation. Manchester, 1929.
CHERRY, ALTHEA. "The Life and Political Theories of Christopher Goodman." University of Chicago dissertation. Chicago, 1935.
DONALDSON, GORDON. "The Relations between the English and Scottish Presbyterian Movements to 1604." London University dissertation. London, 1938.
HARRIS, JESSE W. "The Life and Works of John Bale." University of Illinois dissertation. Urbana, 1935.
HUME (MAGUIRE), MARY. "The History of the *Ex Officio* Oath in England." Radcliffe College dissertation. Cambridge, Mass., 1923.
KNAPPEN, M. M. "Richard Greenham and the Practical Puritans under Elizabeth." Cornell University dissertation. Ithaca, 1927.
MILDON, W. H. "Puritanism in Hampshire and the Isle of Wight from the Reign of Elizabeth to the Restoration." London University dissertation. London, 1934.

INDEX

INDEX

33906